MW00341576

THE RESTAURANTS

OF

NEW YORK

1990 Edition

Seymour Britchky

A FIRESIDE BOOK
PUBLISHED BY SIMON & SCHUSTER INC.
New York
London
Toronto
Sydney
Tokyo

F

Fireside
Simon & Schuster Building
Rockefeller Center
1230 Avenue of the Americas
New York, New York 10020

COPYRIGHT © 1978, 1982, 1983, 1984, 1985, 1986, 1987, 1988, 1989
BY SEYMOUR BRITCHKY

ALL RIGHTS RESERVED
INCLUDING THE RIGHT OF REPRODUCTION
IN WHOLE OR IN PART IN ANY FORM.
FIRESIDE AND COLOPHON ARE REGISTERED TRADEMARKS
OF SIMON & SCHUSTER INC.
DESIGNED BY EVE METZ
MANUFACTURED IN THE UNITED STATES OF AMERICA

10 9 8 7 6 5 4 3 2 1

LC 83-641140

ISBN 0-671-65824-7

The following reviews appeared, in somewhat different form, in *Seymour Britchky's Restaurant Letter*: Al Bacio, Albero d'Oro, Alo Alo, Ambassador Grill, An American Place, Andiamo, Aquavit, Arcadia, Arizona 206, Arquà, Audrone's, Aureole, Au Tunnel, Azzurro, Ballato, Ballroom, Barocco, Bernard, Le Bernardin, Bice, Le Bilboquet, Bistro Bamboche, Bistro du Nord, Blue Nile, La Bohême, La Boîte en Bois, La Bonne Bouffe, Bouley, Brazilian Pavilion, Brive, Bukhara, Cabana Carioca, Café Crocodile, Café de Bruxelles, Café de la Gare, Café des Artistes, Café Greco, Café Luxembourg, Café San Martin, Cameos, Canal Bar, Canastel's, Canton, La Caravelle, Cave Canem, Cedars of Lebanon, Cellar in the Sky, Cent Anni, Chanterelle, Chelsea Central, Chez Jacqueline, Chez Josephine, Chez Louis, Chez Pierre, Chin Chin, Cinco de Mayo, Le Cirque, La Colombe d'Or, Contrapunto, La Côte Basque, Le Cygne, Da Nanni, Da Silvano, Da Umberto, Dawat, Duane Park Café, Due, Ecco, Elio's, Erminia, L'Escale, Espace, Eze, El Faro, Felidia, Flamand, Florent, Four Seasons, Fu's, Gaylord, Gotham, La Goulue, La Grenouille, Grove Street Café, Gulf Coast, Hasaki, Hatsuhana, Huberts, Hulot's, Indochine, Jacqueline's, Jane Street Seafood Café, Jean Lafitte, Jockey Club, John Clancy's East, Lafayette, Lattanzi, Lola, La Luncheonette, Lusardi's, Lutèce, Le Madeleine, Malaga, Manhattan Ocean Club, Man Ray, Marie-Michelle, La Métairie, Metro, Mike's, Miss Ruby's Café, Mondrian, Montrachet, Il Mulino, Nicola Paone, Il Nido, Nippon, Omen, Onini, Orsini's, Orso, Palio, Palm and Palm Too, Parioli Romanissimo, Park Bistro, Le Périgord, Periyali, Pesca, Petaluma, La Petite Ferme, Petrossian, Pietro's, Poiret, Polo, Il Ponte Vecchio, Positano, Post House, Primavera, Primola, Provence, Prunelle, Quatorze, Rakel, Raoul's, Le Régence, Remi, La Réserve, Restaurant Raphaël, La Ripaille, Ronasi, Rosa Mexicano, Rosolio, Russian Tea Room, Sabor, Sala Thai, Salta in Bocca, Sam's, San Domenico, Sandro's, Santa Fe, Scarlatti, Sea Grill, Seryna, Sfuzzi, Shinwa, Sichuan Pavilion, Sign of the Dove, Sistina, Smith & Wollensky, Sofi, Stephanie's, Sukhothai, Sushizen, Table d'Hôte, Tango, Tempo, Thai Royale, Time & Again, Trattoria dell'Arte, Troika, La Tulipe, Union Square Café, Vico, Village Atelier, Voulez-Vous, Water Club, Wilkinson's Seafood Café, Le Zinc.

The following reviews appeared, in somewhat different form, in *New York* magazine: Akaihana, Bangkok Cuisine, Barbetta, Carolina, Chalet Suisse, Christ Cella, Claire, Coach House, Csarda, Darbár, Gibbon, Nanni, Oyster Bar & Restaurant, Pinocchio, Raga, Le Relais, René Pujol, Trastevere and Trastevere 84, Vašata, Windows on the World.

CONTENTS

INTRODUCTION

Unfortunately it is no longer possible for the author to answer individually the thousands of letters that arrive each year. The form letter sent in reply to such mail after the suspended sentence of 1988 (when the authorities found in favor of the Postal Service in its suit charging that the author's admittedly passionate rejoinders to certain hypersensitive pen pals constituted obscene defilement of the United States mails) was met with disapproval from correspondents who took issue with the preprinted suggestion that their fan letters were intended solely to provoke a reply and, willy-nilly, a priceless autograph.

Since direct forms of dealing with the epistolary deluge have been met with calumny and apoplexy, the author has chosen to go public, to answer in this space, instead of in the mails, those questions he is asked most frequently and those he deems to be of the greatest general interest. The reader will judge for himself how apposite are the replies.

Herewith a selection from the past year's mail (the names of the letter writers have been changed for their own good), together with the author's answers. These answers, though approved by the author, are written by his Administrative Assistant for Out-of-House Correspondence. Accordingly, depending on AA's fluctuant moods, the author is sometimes referred to in the third person masculine, sometimes in the third person neuter, and sometimes by pet or other informal names.

Q. *How large a role does influence play in your profession? May an inferior restaurant enjoy a favorable review in return for baksheesh? Is there a one-time payment, or are collections made regularly?* —Arthur Flegenheimer, Bronx

A. How inferior?

Q. *I hear you wear flowing robes when you go out to eat in restaurants to hide how fat you are so people in the restaurant won't know right away you are a restaurant critic because all restaurant critics are fat. True or false?*
—G. Ross, Great Neck

A. True. But over his flowing robes Fat Boy wears a suit of chain mail, because restaurant critics have sick-making taste in flowing robes.

Q. *Do you and the other people in New York who write about restaurants get together all the time to cut up touches and exchange humorous stories and anecdotes about the funny things that happen to you all the time?*

—Tamara Kosmos, Hicksville

A. All the time.

Q. *Do you cook?* —A. Black, New York

A. It smokes, but it never cooks.

Q. *Why is it that in your books we never read anything about our favorite restaurant, the Quilted Giraffe?* —Mr. and Mrs. Barold Whine, New Paltz

A. The Quilted *What?*

Q. *Last week I went to a restaurant where a waiter said he knew who you were and he said you were eating in the restaurant right then and he pointed to a guy and he said that was you. I went over to say hello and you stood up but you fell and broke your chair and landed flat on the floor. When you reached up I thought you were trying to shake hands but you were just trying to get your drink. OK. But how come you had on such an ugly necktie? Do all restaurant critics wear ugly neckties?* —S. Lopata, Manhattan

A. Huggums wears *beautiful* neckties. That was Bryan Miller.

Q. *How many times do you go to a restaurant before you write about it?*

—Lulu Waldorf, Manhattan

A. As often as twenty-five times. Piggy says if you cannot figure the place out in, say, ten visits, you make an eleventh, then a twelfth, and so on until you can.

Q. *Who do you think you are, calling yourself a restaurant critic? What makes you so smart?* —N. T. Gatza, New York

A. Smart Boy is one of the few holders of the Certificate in Home Economics granted by the executive trainee program of General Foods. And before embarking on his present career he spent ten years writing recipes for the backs of cookie, cold cereal, and frozen taco packages. Many restaurant critics equal— but none surpass—these qualifications.

Q. *What is your favorite restaurant?*   —B. Meuniere, Manhattan

A. Buddha always smiles indulgently when challenged with this poser face to face. "Favorite restaurant *for what?*" he always answers, and you should see his eyes shine with anticipation when he is about to broaden the outlook of yet another awestruck follower. Then he brings out the Two Hats. He puts slips of paper, each with the names of a different dish, in one hat, and another set of slips, each with the name of a different restaurant, in the other. Next he picks a dish from the first hat, a restaurant from the second. That restaurant is the best restaurant for that dish, get it? He keeps that up until he has used up all the dishes and all the restaurants. This Zen strategy for dining out is one of Buddha's least appreciated aspects.

So if you want to know Buddha's favorite restaurant, you have to know "*for what.*" Please resubmit your question together with a check for $12.95, and you will receive Buddha's complete list of dish-restaurant matches, together with a Dishlocator Map, which will tell you where to go—with compass points.

Q. *The other night my mother-in-law saw me in a fancy restaurant with a close friend who is not my wife. Now my mother-in-law wants to know how come I never take <u>her</u> to fancy restaurants—and how much longer I expect her to keep her mouth shut. What would you suggest?*   —Donald John, Central Islip

A. Ask Gael.

Q. *I have researched the subject, and I find, to my astonishment, that you have been writing about restaurants for almost twenty years! Is time not passing? Is the hour not late? Should you not embark on an adult career now?*
                                            —Adele Shepherd, Providence

A. Please submit a job description for the position you offer, together with information about salary, experience required, hours of work and annual vacations, as well as health, retirement, and stock option plans. Babypuss will Federal Express a résumé soonest.

Ten Sensible Rules About Going to, Eating in, Paying at, and Departing from New York Restaurants

1. RESERVATIONS. Before going to a New York restaurant, telephone to make a reservation. True, reservations are often not accepted, but this is sometimes because the restaurant no longer exists. By telephoning you determine whether the place is still in business, and, if so, whether you can get a table when you want one.

2. NO RESERVATIONS. If a restaurant does not accept reservations, it is probably because it is so busy that it can get away without offering the convenience. Ask if the place is likely to be crowded when you want to go. Sometimes you will get a helpful answer, sometimes an honest one, sometimes both.

3. COMPLAINTS. It's no fun to complain throughout your meal. After all, you go to a restaurant to enjoy yourself, your food, and your companions. But it's a good idea to complain about *something* early on. People who complain are people who seem to know what they want and what they are about, and they get better treatment than the timid or unsure. If you are shy or diffident, or don't know what you want, that's too bad, but it need not be a guarantee that you will not enjoy eating in New York restaurants.

4. SENDING BACK. If you don't like something you ordered, tell the waiter it tastes terrible and send it back. Do the same thing if what should be hot food is cold or if there is anything else clearly wrong with what is brought to you.

5. WINE. If you like wine but don't know much about it, order an inexpensive bottle. Modestly priced wines are the most reliable ones in restaurants. They are what they are. Restaurants are not the place to give yourself a wine education; it is much too expensive and unreliable. Expensive wines in restaurants may be too young or too old, or damaged from poor storage, and if you're unsure of yourself, you may not know why you don't like what you get and whether you really ought to return it. If there is a sommelier (the man with the chain around his neck), his business is to sell you wine (after suitable discussion), pour your first glass, and generally convert the purchase and consumption of a bottle of mild booze into an important event. Few New York restaurants have sommeliers anymore, but those that do generally have pretty good wine stocks. If the sommelier seems like a decent sort and if you want to spring for a fancy bottle, tell him how much you are willing to spend, and he will recommend a bottle at the price, and probably a good one.

6. EMERGENCIES. If you need service at once and are unable to catch your waiter's or captain's eye, the best system is to rise from your chair and approach

the nearest responsible member of the staff. The late English conductor Sir Thomas Beecham used to brush dishes to the floor to get attention, but since most dining room floors in New York restaurants are carpeted, this ploy might go unnoticed. Flinging dishes against walls or ceilings, however, is a surefire way to bring the help.

7. YOUR CHECK. Review it. It's wrong about one time in ten; in your favor about one time in a hundred. Ask for a menu to check the prices if you think you have been overcharged or charged for a more expensive item than the one you ordered. Check the addition. Of course, you may have had a few drinks and a bottle of wine, while the waiter is probably sober, so he may be right and you may be wrong.

8. TIPPING—HOW. Don't leave your tip under a plate. It simply is not done. If you want to give someone a tip, hand it to him. If you don't spot him, leave the money out in the open where it is easy to see. If you're tipping on a credit-card voucher, write in the tip *and write in the grand total*. If you do not, an emendation may be made favoring the waiter and penalizing you. This is so common that the credit-card companies have a name for it; they call it an "override."

9. TIPPING—HOW MUCH. Par is 15 percent of the before-tax food total, plus some lesser percentage of the liquor and wine. If you are served by both a waiter and a captain, 20 percent is fair, most of it to the waiter, the exact proportion depending on whether the captain did no more than cursorily take your order or if, at the other extreme, he thoroughly explained the menu, prepared sauces and desserts, and helped with the selection of wine.

Reasons for tipping more: You ate the least expensive items on the menu and occupied the table for three hours; the service was terrific; you are feeling expansive.

Reasons for tipping less: The reverse of the above, except that waiters should not be penalized for your depression unless it is their fault.

Sommeliers should be tipped $2 per bottle, but no less than $3 in total if they have been really helpful.

10. DEPARTURE. Leave when you are good and ready. It is your right to eat at your own pace, including lingering over a second cup of coffee. Enjoy possession of a table that others are waiting in line for. Later they will.

A Note on Using This Book

The restaurants in this book have been classified as "inexpensive," "medium priced," "expensive," or "very expensive."

When the book went to press, these categorizations were roughly defined as follows—for a three-course dinner for one, with coffee, not including wine, tax, or tip:

Inexpensive:	Under $25
Medium priced:	$25 to $35
Expensive:	$35 to $45
Very expensive:	Over $45

By the time the book is printed, bound, distributed, and purchased by you, these definitions, in many instances, will no longer be accurate. First, prices in all restaurants seem to go up steadily—that is inflation. Second, if an inexpensive or medium-priced restaurant is doing very well, it may shift from one category to the next—that is the profit motive. A press-time $30 dinner may run to $40 by the time you eat it.

In some few instances specific prices of dishes or drinks or wines are referred to in the text. They are meant to give an impression of the restaurant's pricing policy. The information was correct when written, and the impression is probably still correct, even if the exact price has changed.

The Ratings

★★★★	Excellent
★★★	Very good
★★	Good
★	Good (but not *as* good)
●	Acceptable
○	Unacceptable

Restaurant Listings

BY TYPE OF FOOD

ETHIOPIAN

FRENCH

GREEK

HUNGARIAN

INDIAN/PAKISTANI

ITALIAN

JAPANESE

Akaihana **29**

Gibbon **177**

Hasaki **188**

Hatsuhana **189**

Nippon **239**

Omen **240**

Seryna **317**

Shinwa **320**

Sushizen **335**

Tango **337**

LATIN AMERICAN

Brazilian Pavilion **79**

Cabana Carioca **85**

Cinco de Mayo **128**

Mike's **225**

Rosa Mexicano **300**

Sabor **306**

Santa Fe **313**

MIDDLE EASTERN

Café Crocodile **86**

Cedars of Lebanon **110**

RUSSIAN

Petrossian **262**

Russian Tea Room **303**

Troika **347**

SANDWICHES/LIGHT FOOD

Arizona 206 **45**

Due **155**

Orso **243**

Petaluma **259**

Sfuzzi **319**

Trattoria dell'Arte **345**

SCANDINAVIAN

Aquavit **41**

SEAFOOD

Le Bernardin **63**

Claire **132**

Jane Street Seafood Café **198**

John Clancy's East **202**

Manhattan Ocean Club **218**

Oyster Bar & Restaurant **245**

Pesca **257**

Petrossian **262**

Sea Grill **316**

Wilkinson's Seafood Café **360**

SPANISH

STEAKHOUSES

SWISS

THAI

VIETNAMESE

BY RATING
★★★★Excellent

★★★Very Good

Al Bacio **30**
Albero d'Oro **32**
Alo Alo **33**
Ambassador Grill **35**
Arcadia **43**
Audrone's **49**
Au Tunnel **52**
Bangkok Cuisine **58**
Barocco **60**
Bernard **61**
Bice **66**
Bistro du Nord **70**
Blue Nile **72**
La Bohême **73**
La Boîte en Bois **74**
Brazilian Pavilion **79**
Café de Bruxelles **88**
Café de la Gare **89**
Café Greco **92**
Café San Martin **95**
Canal Bar **98**
Il Cantinori **101**
Cave Canem **108**
Cellar in the Sky **111**
Chelsea Central **118**
Chez Jacqueline **120**
Chez Josephine **121**
Chez Louis **122**
Chez Pierre **124**
Le Cirque **130**
Contrapunto **138**
Due **155**
L'Escale **162**
Florent **170**
Gaylord **176**
Gibbon **177**
Gulf Coast **186**
Hulot's **193**
Indochine **195**

Jacqueline's **197**
Jean Lafitte **199**
Jockey Club **201**
Lola **208**
La Luncheonette **209**
Le Madeleine **215**
Malaga **217**
Manhattan Ocean Club **218**
Man Ray **219**
Marie-Michelle **221**
Mike's **225**
Il Nido **237**
Onini **242**
Orso **243**
Park Bistro **253**
Pesca **257**
Petaluma **259**
Poiret **268**
Primavera **275**
Provence **279**
Prunelle **280**
Remi **291**
Ronasi **298**
Sea Grill **316**
Sfuzzi **319**
Sistina **325**
Smith & Wollensky **327**
Stephanie's **332**
Sukhothai **333**
Table d'Hôte **336**
Tempo **339**
Trattoria dell'Arte **345**
Troika **347**
Vico **354**
Village Atelier **355**
Water Club **358**
Windows on the World **362**
Le Zinc **364**

19

BY NEIGHBORHOOD
DOWNTOWN, INCLUDING CHINATOWN AND LITTLE ITALY

TRIBECA

SOHO

GREENWICH VILLAGE

20

Sabor **306**   Village Atelier **355**
La Tulipe **348**

EAST VILLAGE

Bernard **61**   Hasaki **188**
Cave Canem **108**   Indochine **195**
Gaylord **176**   Sukhothai **333**

EAST SIDE, 14TH STREET TO 33RD STREET

American Place **37**   Park Bistro **253**
Canastel's **99**   Pesca **257**
Cedars of Lebanon **110**   Positano **272**
La Colombe d'Or **136**   Tempo **339**
L'Escale **162**   Union Square Café **350**
Espace **163**   Water Club **358**

EAST SIDE, 34TH STREET TO 41ST STREET

La Bonne Bouffe **76**
Nicola Paone **236**   Time & Again **342**

EAST SIDE 42ND STREET TO 50TH STREET

Ambassador Grill **35**   Nanni **234**
Bukhara **83**   Oyster Bar & Restaurant **245**
Chalet Suisse **114**   Palm and Palm Too **249**
Chin Chin **125**   Pietro's **264**
Christ Cella **126**   Sichuan Pavilion **322**
Hatsuhana **189**   Smith & Wollensky **327**
Lutèce **212**

EAST SIDE, 51ST STREET TO 59TH STREET

Bice **66**   Lafayette **203**
Brazilian Pavilion **79**   Mondrian **227**
Brive **80**   Il Nido **237**
Chez Louis **122**   Nippon **239**
La Côte Basque **140**   Le Périgord **254**
Le Cygne **143**   Prunelle **280**
Dawat **152**   Rosa Mexicano **300**
Felidia **167**   Scarlatti **314**
Four Seasons **172**   Seryna **317**
La Grenouille **183**   Stephanie's **332**

WEST SIDE, 51ST STREET TO 59TH STREET

WEST SIDE, 60TH STREET TO 72ND STREET

WEST SIDE, ABOVE 72ND STREET

OPEN ON SUNDAY

Open Late (Until Midnight or Later, Each Night the Restaurant Is Open for Business)

Arizona 206 **45**
Ballroom **56**
Café Luxembourg **94**
Café San Martin **95**
Canal Bar **98**
Carolina **107**
Cave Canem **108**
Chez Pierre **124**
Claire **132**
Contrapunto **138**
Due **155**
Elio's **159**
El Faro **166**
Felidia **167**
Florent **170**

Gaylord **176**
Hasaki **188**
Indochine **195**
Jean Lafitte **199**
La Luncheonette **209**
Le Madeleine **215**
La Métairie **222**
Metro **224**
Petrossian **262**
Primavera **275**
Santa Fe **313**
Seryna **317**
Union Square Café **350**
Le Zinc **364**

Suitable (By Reason of Economy or Menu or Accommodations) for Large Family Groups

Albero d'Oro **32**
Blue Nile **72**
Canton **103**
Cedars of Lebanon **110**
Christ Cella **126**
Csarda **142**
Grove Street Café **185**
Indochine **195**

Malaga **217**
Oyster Bar & Restaurant **245**
Petaluma **259**
Raga **283**
Sala Thai **307**
Sukhothai **333**
Thai Royale **341**

Outdoor Dining and Enclosed Gardens

Aquavit **41**
Aureole **50**
Barbetta **59**
Bistro du Nord **70**
Chez Jacqueline **120**
Chez Pierre **124**
Da Silvano **149**
La Goulue **181**
Hasaki **188**

Lutèce **212**
Le Madeleine **215**
Provence **279**
Raoul's **286**
Le Relais **290**
Restaurant Raphaël **295**
Sea Grill **316**
Smith & Wollensky **327**
Le Zinc **364**

Bring Your Own Wine (or Whatever)

Bernard **61**
Café de la Gare **89**
Canton **103**
Grove Street Café **185**

Table d'Hôte **336**
Thai Royale **341**
Trattoria dell'Arte **345**

THE
RESTAURANTS
OF
NEW YORK

★★AKAIHANA

2164 Broadway (near 76th Street)
LUNCH, MONDAY TO FRIDAY; DINNER, DAILY.
Reservations: 724-8666.
Credit cards: AE, DC, MC, V.
Inexpensive.

Except for "Health Food" places themselves, only Japanese restaurants are really acceptable to the physical-fitness set. And except for certain Japanese customers (those groups of businessmen who seem to smoke and drink as if bent on calling up Prohibition days), the crowd in Japanese restaurants will sometimes seem as trim, erect, and scrubbed as the corps de ballet just out of the shower. Of course, this is especially noticeable here on the youthful and wanton Upper West Side, where nourishment in eating places is at best a secondary agenda. And you cannot miss it in Akaihana, a bright and shiny box of a place that lures the sound-body types not only with its bean curd, seaweed, and raw fish but also with a setting, of playfully angulate lines and nursery colors, that is notably neat and clean—though it manages to skirt the antiseptic with artful whimsy.

If you want to look like you belong, you will use chopsticks, and you will sit up straight. Leaning forward to shorten the haul is not done. Under the circumstances, you may find sashimi easier to handle than the sometimes fragile sushi bundles. The fluke sashimi is of vivid brightness, the raw fillets intertwined with slivers of lemon; the pungency of mackerel is easy to take when the fish itself is fresh; and the likes of yellowtail and sea bass, though these are not especially flavorful fish, are brought to life by the leaves of fresh ginger with which they are served. Among the sushi items, the octopus is of exceptional silkiness—a shaft of it is served belted to a block of rice with a band of deep-green seaweed. But if you come here when the three principal kinds of tuna are on hand, it is well to concentrate on those, for they set one another off smartly. The regular tuna is dark red and beefy, the toro (fatty tuna) mild and of an almost fluffy texture, the bonito fibrous and a little high. All of them make good sushi.

From among the two dozen dishes listed as appetizers (some of which are also listed as main courses, or can be converted to same by ordering a double portion): kaibashira furai, three plump, rich, deep-fried sea scallops, their flavor clear, their surfaces browned and crisp; hijiki, cool sea-gamy seaweed mixed with strands of root vegetable and flavored, strikingly, with ginger; agedōfu, blocks of soft bean curd, deep-fried until their surfaces are firmed, served in a dark and salty soy sauce that is dotted with button mushrooms; kara-age, chunks of boned chicken that reach you steaming hot, as if just out of the deep fryer, served with mustard and oranges—the citrus makes the dish seem a bit Chinese; shumai, little steamed noodle dumplings stuffed with a spicy pork forcemeat—you eat them with a fiery mustard; and negimayaki, sheets of beef wrapped around shafts of scallion—the meat is rare, and the gently cooked scallions retain some of their bite.

Shio is a method of broiling fish in its skin, with much salt, that causes the fat under the skin to permeate the meat—to excellent effect when things work out right. Akaihana prepares salmon this way (salmon shioyaki) and removes the salty skin before serving it—sure enough, the meat is not itself very salty, but its flavor is notably enriched. And the place frequently offers a deep-fried sea bass, the big slices of it reassembled into the entire beast minus its bones—it comes off as an especially buttery fish, the crusty surface moist with oil and lightly soured with vinegar.

Fresh fruit is usually available for dessert, as well as those peculiar Japanese ice creams.

★ AL BACIO

245 East 84th Street
DINNER.
Reservations: 744-9343.
Credit cards: AE, DC, MC, V.
Expensive.

It is easy to make money. Find out how others are doing it, and do exactly the same thing. People interested in making money, and interested in nothing else, have been at that game for 300,000 years (a recent estimate of the age of the human race). When, however, you contaminate the imitation, put, you should pardon the expression, your "personal stamp" on it, you are guilty of the Artistic Heresy (the sin in which the entrepreneur ranks himself—that is to say, his taste—above that of the market), and you usually sacrifice profit in return for nothing at all—or, often, for disaster. With scores of clubby Italian joints packing them in all over the Upper East Side, comes one Roberto Cazzaniga, proprietor here. He could have visited, say, Elio's, Sistina, and Primola, added them up, divided by three, and had a sure thing. But no, he wants to do it *his* way. If he had in mind something on the order of, say, the *Rite of Spring*, or *Ulysses*, or even Maxwell's Plum, his egoism would be glorified by the immensity of his vision. But Cazzaniga does not want to shock anybody. All he wants is to break a few rules and get away with it. Under the circumstances it is easy not to deplore the two-thirds emptiness his place enjoys almost nightly. Who, after all, does not prefer, anytime, a big winner to a petty original?

Your disdain would be tempered by sympathy were it not for the satisfaction and length with which Cazzaniga describes to you his singular concept. His restaurant, he explains, is a Roman garden under a Roman sky. It abjures the clangor and clutter (conviviality) of his competitors, aims for a relaxed comfort (sedateness) that will appeal to the mature (infirm) of all ages. (You take it that the purpose of the background music is to demonstrate how near to inaudibility both Antonio Vivaldi and Billie Holiday can be played.) He even states—in this, and in this alone, he is unique—that his food is merely decent, every bit as good as it has to be, but no better. (He does not, you understand, want to stress you with gustatory sensations that rouse.) With such objectives it is no surprise that the place is better than he intends. The Roman garden, for example, is, happily, instead, a comfortable oblong dining room, the banquette down each side upholstered in a blue cloth that simulates those intricately patterned Italian papers—like nineteenth-century endpapers—in one of which Al Bacio's small menu is bound. The tables are in two long rows at the banquettes, the facing armchairs in dark blue slipcovers down to the pale wood floor. A great vase of flowers stands on the floor at each end of the room, and there is art here and there on the cosmetic-pink walls, most of it so harmless that the one or two truly dreadful pieces stand out. That sky overhead (it must be midnight) is midnight blue, but it is lowered just like a ceiling—by broad stripes of white cloth, on the diagonal, that are stretched across white tracks from which tiny spots cast soft light about the room. And sure enough, the Third Avenue crowd has been avoiding this place as if it were the New Jersey living room they left behind with their first spouse.

And why not? For this polenta with cheese, though the four rectangles of browned cornmeal are covered over with hot melted fontina of strong flavor, is no better than at a dozen other places, and here you cannot see the bar from your table—and even if you could, nary a model is seated at it. So you concentrate on your food, on this grilled eggplant, the thin slices shaped like broad tongue depressers, drenched in oil, and strewn with capers; on this pasta e ceci, the dense soup of noodles and chick-peas that, in this version, lacks the tangy or bitter edge of greens that in certain renditions of this dish offsets its weight, though the sprig of rosemary floated on top adds a good fragrance and the cheese that is grated on a bit of sharpness. Pretty good pasta dishes: the linguine and shrimp, in their herbed and buttery broth, would be perfect if not for the iodine in some of the crunchy crustaceans; the spaghetti carbonara is the real thing, salty and rich, thick with egg yolks, chunky of its strong and abundant Italian bacon; and, the winner, penne ai carciofi, in which minute slivers of artichoke, deep fried, browned, crisped, are mingled with the hefty pasta in a sauce that is little more than velvety oil and seasoning— add cheese, and the simple dish becomes complex.

Presumably a regional dish from an extremely small region, one in which the citizens have both pea-patch backyards and oceanfront front yards, onto the latter of which squid are washed up, so that on moneyless days the locals can make do with this item—such must be the source of the combination of squid and peas, the pinkish, quite tender, and iridescent meat of the seafood in striking contrast to the emerald green orbs that nestle in its concavities—good food that would taste even better if you had grown up with it. Big browned scallops and thin spears of green asparagus approximately repeat that color scheme in their winy and parsleyed broth. The swordfish is firm and moist, but a bit less than fresh, which is too bad, for the steak is slicked with a rousing tomato sauce that is dotted with capers and strong black olives. But then you go over to the "carne" department, and almost everything goes wrong. The osso buco has taken on almost none of the flavor of the spicy density of vegetables that is the good sauce in which it was cooked— the meat is white and pallid, served long before it is ready. The fritto misto—chunks of calf brain, artichoke, zucchini—suffers for the hard-fibered inedibility of the artichoke leaves, though otherwise this is nicely fried food that is roused by the lemon you squeeze on. You order your filet mignon rare, and even the outside is rare—pale gray, actually —as if the knack of charring, or browning the surface of beef while barely cooking it is beyond this kitchen.

The Parmesan cheese is ok, if not the headiest, most aged in town—you may have yours with a tart, crisp apple. The sweet desserts, displayed on the rolling cart, include a sharp and citric lemon tart on a dark pastry; an uncompromisingly rich chestnut mousse cake encased in chocolate; and a zabaglione torte described also as a tirami sù cake— black cake, a rich tan cream that, by its flavor, seems to put it more in the zabaglione than the tirami sù family.

★ ALBERO D'ORO

1580 Second Avenue (near 82nd Street)
DINNER
Reservations: 517-4448.
Credit cards: AE.
Inexpensive.

Back when the Lattanzis, mother and sons, ran a mere four Manhattan eating places (Erminia, Lattanzi, and the two named Trastevere), no one quarreled with the proposition that the family knew what it was about—after all, all the restaurants thrived. Then they opened Albero d'Oro, and close observers, casual observers, and passing halfwits were compelled to conclude that said evaluation of the family's prowess had been hasty. It was plain to see that the new place was hilariously, hysterically misguided, some kind of joke, an unintentional but acute satire of parvenu design, a restaurant that (one fellow tells another when he can stop laughing long enough to catch his breath) you must see to believe. Thereupon it was all clear. The Lattanzis are not restaurant geniuses at all. The earlier essays owed their success to a chanced upon formula: the corniest of rustic Italian settings, low light, and dramatic Italian food. That the food was good may well have been neither here nor there. (To find out, you would have to open a like place, serve inferior food, compare your results to the Lattanzis'.) Albero d'Oro occurred, of course, because members of the family had come to believe what people were saying about them. To a hardheaded business type the financial disaster that was the original Albero d'Oro would have been all the corrective needed to put him back on the Italian rustic straight and narrow. But no, like the investor who clings to a plummeting stock in the hope that eventually it will return to the inflated price he paid for it, the Lattanzis clung to this bleeder. Refusing to concede that their misjudgment was total, they attempted to fine-tune the enterprise by making minor alterations to the room, which is the restaurant business equivalent of medicine for a dead patient. As countless rodent experiments have established, repeated failure eventually induces quixotic, desperate, even irrational responses—accordingly, the Albero d'Oro of today.

If you (can bear to) recall the ox-blood lacquer interior that was the original place (a wise man described it, when it was new, as an outside-in purple limousine), be informed that even now it has not been entirely discarded. The walls up front, the ceiling throughout, and the little room at the back are as was, as is the deep-garnet carpeting. But the main central area of the restaurant has been painted subtropical stucco flat white, has been hung with a handful of dreary paintings, meant to look sunny, in genuine frames. It is as if an in-progress renovation has been interrupted, and only by prior knowledge can you tell which look is coming, which going. (Maybe the work continues in the middle of the night.) Either way, it is as if the restaurant, short of working capital, were hastily opened in hopes of generating the cash with which to finish the job, a state of affairs seemingly confirmed by the distress prices: pasta as low as $8, veal $12, shrimp or snapper $13, dessert $3.50. There are those who, for such economies, are willing to overlook the unfinished condition of the place; others reason that to be reminded—throughout dinner, by screwball surroundings—that one is here for reasons of thrift is too high a price to pay for a bargain.

You may be aware that in the Lattanzis' West 46th Street store, the one called by the family name, "Lattanzi," an Italian-Jewish menu is offered, in addition to the regular menu, each night from 8 P.M. on. Some of that menu's dishes are available here, including the artichokes that are the best-known dish of that cookery. They reach you as nuggets, trimmed of the inedible portion of the leaves, tender, firm, handsomely golden brown, saturated with the garlicked oil in which they were boiled—the pool of oil that remains in your plate when you have dispatched the vegetable is easily sopped up with the restaurant's good chewy bread. What is given as "grigliata" is a vegetarian mixed grill of mushrooms, endives, and radicchio, the three enriched with oil, vibrant of garlic, well seasoned, the slight bitterness of the endives and radicchio in nice contrast to the woodsy mushrooms. The carpaccio is just-cut beef, the thin slices adorned with sprigs of fresh basil, tart capers, leaves of parmesan cheese—a squeezing on of the supplied lemon livens the dish. In this, the age of futuristic pizza, here is pizza primeval. It is not even exactly round. The thin, crackling, amorphously shaped bread does, however, just about cover your circular plate, and, in unrelentingly primitive fashion, it is covered over with melted mozzarella, a dense tomato sauce, and dried herbs—the stout-flavored thing glistens with the olive oil with which it is polished just before you get it. The sauce of the fettuccine stracotto is described as "beef tomato sauce." You expect meat sauce, but what you get is spaghetti with beef stew—winter food, and not bad for that. Rotolo is a roulade formed by rolling a sheet of green pasta with a filling of ricotta and spinach— you get two immense slices cut from the log, the pasta is firm, the filling is soft and steamy, everything very pretty in the stout tomato sauce.

You do well to avoid the most expensive item on the menu, zuppa di pesche, for the seafood stew suffers from rank mussels and iodized shrimp. And you are no better off with the red snapper with raisins and vinegar—another item borrowed from that Italian-Jewish menu, but on 46th Street the dish is dramatic, while here it is pallid. You will prefer the house calamari, in which an abundance of squid is mingled with mushrooms, slivers of garlic, and emerald green peas that, in this briny red sauce, are sweet relief to the sturdier side of the dish. Have your chicken roasted with rosemary and garlic, and it is obvious that this is a tasteless bird. Have instead the pollo e salsiccia, and the chunks of chicken are merely relief to the mushrooms and the nuggets of vigorous sausage with which the bits of bird are mingled. As you will guess from the prices, the veal is sliced *very* thin, with the result that in the scalloppine dishes the meat is often *very* dry.

The ricotta cheesecake is light and the tirami sù is a child's sweet, but the napoleon is good, a custardy richness between flaky layers of pastry.

★ ALO ALO

1030 Third Avenue (at 61st Street)
LUNCH AND DINNER.
Reservations: 838-4343.
Credit cards: AE, DC, MC, V.
Medium priced.

By whim of the interests behind this place, small platforms have been installed high up on the walls, and on them have been placed large figures of misshapen waiters and waitresses standing in grotesque poses, bearing demented expressions. Delighted with the comic effect, the house has hired a live staff that, unable to match the physical appeal of the models overhead, does duplicate their mental state. The random quality of their exertions notwithstanding, the particular crowd that has found this place goes on grazing here. At Alo Alo, only by their raiment can you tell the keepers from the animals.

Actually the two-story-high corner-site installation is as much greenhouse as zoo—not by virtue of any growing things for the livestock to nibble on, rather by way of the massive glass walls almost all around, through which tourists who come to this part of town may pause to watch the specimens feed. Because the barrier between the interior of the restaurant and its surrounding city streets is transparent, the place has something about it of a sidewalk café, what with its clear view of the vehicular and pedestrian traffic through this busy intersection and the dense and casual spread of its unlinened marble-topped tables. Your introduction to the place is the bar, at which you usually spend a waiting period even if you have arrived at the very hour of your reservation. Here you find pairs of salesmen exchanging big talk for the benefit of the young lady nearby who temporarily rebuffed them with the explanation, "I think I'm waiting for somebody." You ask the barmaid to list the available beers, and her pained response makes clear that she has heard the stupid question many times before. She brightens, however, as she returns her attention to an admirer on the other side of the bar, a gentleman suffering from temperature confusion—his collar is turned up, but his shirt is unbuttoned to the belt. Eventually you are led to a table. Like all of them, yours is right beside another, and when your waiter tries to take orders from both tables at once, you refuse to play. You point out that your opponents, having been presented with menus, enjoy an unfair advantage.

But the worst, for which everything that has gone before prepared you, is not yet to come. What you get to eat is not only better than anything else about the place, it is mostly commendable: grilled vegetables, long, thin slices of zucchini, big sheets of egg-plant, crescents of red pepper and yellow pepper, quarters of endive, and a single huge mushroom, all of them blackened a little and dressed—and enriched—with good olive oil; fried eggplant, the thin slices wrapped around a bit of goat cheese and leaves of fresh basil; warm carpaccio, the leaves of raw meat apparently brought up to tepid solely by the heat of the plate on which they are served—they taste like rare roast beef, but they are served with a mound of chopped tomatoes in a tart dressing, a garnish that, very nicely, takes over the dish; veal soup, a hot, clear broth of strong meat-and-vegetable flavor—you find lengths of crisp root vegetable and tender veal at the bottom of the bowl.

You ask for an order of pasta con piselli (pasta with peas), which, the menu states, is "to be eaten with a spoon." Of course it arrives without the spoon. It may also be eaten with a fork. Happily, it consists of firm but tender little pasta shells, big sweet green peas, and slivers of ham, all slicked with butter—you add ground cheese, which fortifies the dish. You order spaghetti alla rugula, which the menu describes as "spaghetti with aru-gula, Parmesan cheese..." Your waiter asks if you would like yours with Parmesan cheese. This is a primitive kind of dish, little more than buttered and seasoned noodles, the arugula more a color than a flavor—the Parmesan makes the stuff sturdy without altering its satisfying plainness. You get small green gnocchi in a smooth and creamy tomato sauce that is fragrant, a little, of fresh basil. And you get tarocchi, lengths of curled pasta mingled with chunks of tomato, capers, and slices of rather tasteless black olive—an obvious dish, but a vigorous one, the olives notwithstanding. Each day there is a risotto of the day, sometimes a simple and creamy preparation in which the grains of firm rice are combined with Parmesan cheese—a mother's milk kind of dish.

The steamed salmon is fresh but slightly overdone, so that it has lost some of its oil and some of its flavor—the "sauce" of warm, chopped, dressed tomatoes redeems the dish. The handsomely browned chicken has considerable chicken flavor for such a tiny bird, and its mustard sauce is subtle, does not overpower it. The "veal chop with garlic," you figure, is garlic flavored—it is a nice enough little chop, browned and moist, but the garlic is present only as a garnish of whole browned cloves.

You look around and note that almost everyone goes for the monumental chocolate dessert, a layered affair of black cake at the bottom, three inches of rich mousse at the center, curls of pure black chocolate gilded with confectioner's sugar on top. The fruit tarts and the crème caramel are not bad.

Wine is as little as $11, but you may need two bottles, the second for that long dry spell while you wait for your check. The pasta dishes and risotto are available in half orders, but they go for at least 75 percent of the full-order-price—which you learn only when you get your check.

★ AMBASSADOR GRILL

1 United Nations Plaza (at 44th Street)
LUNCH AND DINNER.
Reservations: 702-5014.
Credit cards: AE, DC, MC, V.
Medium priced.

Restaurants in hotels have always been suspect. They fail many ways, but what they lack when they do is a human being behind them, someone with an idea of the restaurant he wants, the rules of the place to follow from the idea. Committees and compromise, inputs from staff men and guidelines from manuals, of such are restaurants in chain hotels, for instance in this corporate place, and you first figure out that you are at the mercy of disembodied regulations when the lady who leads you to your table grabs a couple of menus and a wine list before she does so, and then, instead of leaving the documents with you, walks off with them because, as your waiter subsequently explains, "If you don't ask for them, she can't put them down." (Here in the perfect world, human discretion has been eliminated.) Soon enough it is your waiter's own turn to go through idiotic paces, so when he sets upon your table a perfectly legible printout of the day's special dishes, he then proceeds to recite its contents complete.

You will recall that when the Grill opened in the late seventies, its spiffy interior (the dining room is a design descendant of the velvet-upholstered limousine) was received with approval, its intercontinental menu (the place is hard by the UN) with reservations, its gimmicks (in each multinational basket of breads there stood, like a great sail, a matzo the size of a road map) with slaps upon the thigh. It has since been several things, none of which has caught on with its guests (of an evening you see but a sprinkling of transients from upstairs), with its neighbors (UN delegates prefer a dozen other places nearby, though lower-level functionaries sometimes crowd the bar), or with the city as a whole (few "go out" here). Today, the restaurant serves better food than ever, but the food of Gascony in a setting that is at once cushy and high-tech is only one of the anomalies with which the place is stuck at this point in its erratic search for identity. The dining room is all dark plush and glitter, recessed banquettes around the sides in which you can almost hide, deep armchairs that embrace you, and a level of light that just about undoes the intended intimacy. The light source is the famous ceiling, an installation of clear and mirrored glass that reflects itself upward in an endless inverted crystalline cascade—very nice, but you do wish it did not illuminate the place like a bathroom. In further argument with the posh appointments is the open grill, all its unbeautiful works exposed, the wall behind it the color of aluminum siding. Get yourself a table along the side, and out of sight of the works, and you will be comfortable, though no matter where you sit, the nursery-pink linen is another off note, as are most of the notes that trickle in from the 88-key doodler in the cocktail lounge.

Actually, the regular menu is in two parts, Gascony on the right, mostly French food of no particular province on the left. From the left: a tartare of two salmons that is not exactly that, rather a coarse-chopped raw-salmon patty, sticky and well seasoned, surrounded by supple and deep-pink leaves of smoked salmon that contrast with it strikingly despite the near relationship; and warm poached shrimp, three big ones and very crunchy, of sweet, clear flavor in their smooth, fragrantly herbed, and buttery sauternes sauce. From Gascony: a warm salad, a great mound of crisp greens that, moistened with a vinegar dressing that is at once sweet and sour, has buried in it chunks of rich foie gras, nuggets of fresh salmon, and little slivers of garlic; and a skewer of lobster and wild mushrooms in a pool of butter, the morsels of lobster meat very much themselves, even though they have taken on much flavor in the grilling, the woodsiness of the mushrooms a good foil to the seafood.

John Dory (on the left), an estimable European swimmer, is brought here, filleted, and wrapped around an herbed, strongly seasoned, and vegetable-dotted shellfish stuffing to form a kind of seafood sausage—it is grilled, reaches you a little dry, its listed mustard sauce like a lemony hollandaise, the ambitious dish amusing but no more. From Gascony there is this poached hen, the juicy, tender parts, under a thick and deep-green herb sauce, served with a cup of the fatted broth in which the bird was done—you are served also a chunk of judiciously seasoned sausage and an array of whole vegetables, little carrots, a zucchini, a potato in its skin among them. Firm white beans are the bulk of the Gascony cassoulet, the thick sauce in which they are bound redolent of bacon fat, the top of the dish breaded and browned, in it chunks of that bacon, much strong duck, the giblets too, and disks of very sweet-spiced sausage. The sole Gascony finfish listed is salmon yet again, a dull slab of it, with it a candied garlic sauce that seems to be with it but not for it—a pretty arrangement of many vegetables adorns the plate.

The crème brûlée is little more than a rather heavy hot-and-cold custard. You do better with any of the three Gascony desserts: a hot apple pastry, touched with brandy, that is a mingling of the slivered apple with pastry flakes—the vividly fruity sweet is garnished with an intense vanilla ice cream; a poached pear that is of Gascony by virtue of its being done in Gascony wine—the sweet-spiced fruit is purple of its red-wine treatment, is served in a pool of its syrupy poaching liquid, is garnished with a winy pear sherbet; and a prune ice cream, dotted with black patches, that is saturated with Armagnac—alcohol does not freeze readily, so the ice cream, though of high flavor, has the texture of mousse.

★★AMERICAN PLACE

2 Park Avenue (enter on 32nd Street)
LUNCH, MONDAY TO FRIDAY; DINNER, MONDAY TO SATURDAY. CLOSED SUNDAY.
Reservations: 684-2122.
Credit cards: AE, DC, MC, V.
Expensive.

You will recall the hoopla that, some years ago, attended the opening of the New York edition of La Coupole, venerable café-brasserie-restaurant of Paris. The local version lacked a certain something—everything—and folded. Next at these premises a visitor from Los Angeles, the Ritz Café, which had more to recommend it but too little to survive—it, too, crept off. Comes now, from a point no more remote than Lexington and 70th, the restaurant of one Lawrence P. Forgione, and this time the original was not left behind to fall back on. "This is the place!" quoth Forgione, in effect, "for An American Place," never mind those who failed here, and here has he put his entire uptown operation, indefinite article and all. It may have been the spaciousness of these quarters that lured him, for the store he abandoned was a contorted little room made even knottier by half again as many tables as it practicably could hold. But, though his new address is Park Avenue, he knows that he has departed the city's most moneyed precincts. Accordingly, he has dropped the stiff prix fixe he exacted on upper Lex in favor of a menu that is not only lower priced but à la carte. Think on it: What you spend is up to you.

Restaurant designers who, when confronted with the challenge of a large installation, automatically set their minds to the task of "breaking up the space" would do well to consider what has been done—and undone—here. The previous occupant divided the space and subdivided it, installed partitions, enclosed booths, as if eating were a private act best shielded from onlookers, as if public spaces were meant to replicate private ones. Many patrons chose to wait for one of those enclosed booths rather than accept a table in the dining room proper, but they were attracted by the uniqueness of such accommodations in New York, for, as they learned, actually to eat in one was a trial in vague frustration. Within those cells the visual diversion, vocal accompaniment, and sense of community that the crowd in a restaurant provides—which restaurant goers, often unawares, come to seek and depend on—were lost. The citizen who pursues privacy when out to eat with company is confused (in modern parlance, conflicted). So is the restaurateur who converts a large space that begs to be a convivial eating house into a dozen intimate hideaways. Now, happily, except for a short partition between the bar and the dining room, everything at this site that is not structural has been knocked down. The clutter is gone. The space above and around does not exactly ennoble those within it—it must be more than just big to do that—but it is flattering, and it can impart a sense of expansive good feeling to those capable of such heights.

Which is not to say the installation is beauteous, for in turning the Café into the Place a penny or two were pinched, as much of the old as rationalization could justify was retained, and though there is nothing automatically wrong with such light renovation, when the new elements fail to take into account the old, chaos results. For some insane reason it was decided to do the upper walls in the mottled yellow ochre that, for all but the most formal Italian restaurants, is these days the in skin, complete with sunny overtones of the Mediterranean and old-gold resonances to the Renaissance. These qualities need not disqualify it for other settings, but here it has been juxtaposed with the leftover wood paneling, clubby and weighty, with which the lower walls and massive columns are faced, and the leftover wood is a bulky, clumsy intruder in the otherwise gilded and airy setting. The large white-linened tables are distributed with much space around them. Also around them are chairs of an austere species more to look upon than sit. They are uncushioned, stained to match the wood walls, and their slotted wood backs are anchored only at the base, so when you lean back they give a little; but the flat arms slope downward from the elbow, and the wood seats leave an inch or so more than usual of thigh overhanging, so that during dinner you slide forward until you are on your spine, hands on your knees, ape recumbent.

You may, of course, strike the monkey pose right at the start if what you want are "peanut barbecued gulf shrimp," half a dozen of them, charred, crunchy, juicy, of untainted seafood flavor, their peanut sauce a reminder for a moment of spicy Thai food. What are given as "Chesapeake Bay" deviled crab and oyster fritters, a compacture mounded up over three oyster half-shells, could be from much farther away, what with the remoteness of their seafood flavor, for this is a case of high-class ingredients reduced to boardwalk food, the mustard sauce you apply its sole appeal. But then there are these lobster and wild mushroom croquettes, and though once again you find less flavor than the ingredients began with, much of it remains, and, moreover, the croquettes are steamy and light, very handsome in their perfectly formed red-brown crusts—a smooth and spicy red-pepper sauce and a garnish of crisp asparagus spears are their well chosen foils. "Slow roasted adobo-style duck" reaches you as a hot meat filling wrapped in a couple of cornmeal pancakes, the two adorned with grilled rings of red onion and served in a sauce dotted with kernels of corn—good food, albeit weighty for a first course.

Food in the indigenous American manner is the stock in trade here but, what with the influence of Japan on things American, it is no departure to serve domestic sea scallops in an Oriental setting, specifically green-topped radish sprouts (like other sprouts, they taste like string), shredded daikon radish, and a radish-and-orange-rind sauce—the juiciness of the browned scallops is just about bursting through their browned surfaces, and the sauce and garnishes dramatize their ocean flavor. Nothing imported about the salmon, the big fillet surfaced with a crackling coat of cracked wheat, a nifty textural note, but you wish the fish were fresher and rarer. A garnish given as "pheasant and forest mushroom ragoût" does this super impression of pork and beans, but the pheasant itself is fine, this least tasty of the game birds revealing about as much flavor as it can. You order your "charred New York black angus steak" medium rare, only to learn that "charred" is the operative word, that if at medium rare the beef is not yet black, it gets more fire till it is, so that it loses much of its blood-juiciness and is dominated by the flavor of carbon—which at this intensity is not a flavor for food at all. The steak comes with a well-seasoned and cheese-enriched layering of potatoes and sweet potatoes, and with a good sauce of caramelized onions that would be swell on beef more judiciously done.

Among mostly good desserts there is a dull angel food chiffon, a white slice of something glutinous, chunks of angel food embedded therein—but there is no denying the liveliness of its fruit sauce and of the berries with which it is garnished. The bread pudding is adorned with stewed cherries and moistened with a cool, pecan-dotted bourbon sauce. The banana betty is in a deep ramekin, the sweet fruit, ripe and hot in its custardy sauce, under a quarter inch of graham crackers reduced to a powder—the dessert reaches you with about a pint of rich, thick whipped cream. That cream comes with the apple pandowdy as well, the sweet and sweet-spiced fruit under a disk of crusted bread.

In the business many years, Forgione is still not entirely on his own, still carries on his menu the silly crutch of a quote from James Beard (identified as "Friend and Mentor"): "The truth is," Beard solemnizes from beyond, "one must be inspired to cook. For you know, we always learn from others and end up teaching ourselves." The poor man, groping for paradox, found only incoherence.

★★ANDIAMO

1991 Broadway (near 67th Street)
LUNCH, MONDAY TO FRIDAY; DINNER, DAILY.
Reservations: 362-3315.
Credit cards: AE, MC, V.
Expensive.

Integration of the classes—anyway, town house-by-tenement propinquity—was once intrinsic to the Upper West Side: swells on Central Park West, Riverside Drive, and West End Avenue (which never quite made it as Park Avenue West); the polloi on Columbus, Amsterdam, and Broadway (which made it quite nicely as Main Street to the millions); and fraternization along the numbered side streets. Today, of course, the young live high on Daddy's credit cards, what a pleb wears for the morning shape-up is high style by cocktail time, and the smiling census taker is greeted at the Dakota penthouse door by a gent in gray underwear and a three-day growth (who offers her a snort). The bemused sociologist squints a little and wings it. Your West Side, he says, is in transition.

In transition, children, everything is a sign of the times, though Andiamo is surely the only restaurant in town that services a built-in shelter for the homeless. You enter not to Andiamo at all, but to Café Bel Canto—a public place (as minuscule lettering on the glace façade informs you), which is not the same as a place of public accommodation—wherein you may, though few do, sit at a table and purchase and consume nothing, or picnic on what you brought with you or what someone left behind (if you get to it before the busboy), and stare out the glass front at Broadway's perpetual parade. Bel Canto is the technical equivalent of one of those promenades or malls or pocket parks or plazas by way of which real (and other) estaters make zoning trades with the city—an amenity for the masses, more rentable space for the estater. In this instance, however, the public space works out to a sidewalk café, the table service concession for which, by remarkable coincidence, is held by the restaurateur at this very address; the amenity, being the very picture of a commercial establishment, gets but a trickle of nonpaying guests with no place else to go, the very occasional loner who comes in out of the climate. The clincher is the no-smoking policy, discouraging as it is to those for whom a handout cigarette may be the day's high point. Anyway, by 1 A.M. everyone must vacate—some shelter! that closes when you need it most.

You turn your back on the implications of all that, bypass the Café via a tree-lined path along its southern edge (segueing from background Franz Schubert to background Louis Armstrong in the act, though sometimes it is the other way around), and enter to

39

Andiamo itself, three stories, easy, of lofty, dramatically architected space, tables at the bottom, more of them on a level up that abuts the space like a theater balcony. Works of certified art are all about, some two-dimensionals that extend from the lower to the upper story fit panels of the big walls as if tailored to them. There is a bronze sculpture at this turning, decorative artifacts in the comfort stations and, on a raised platform, an ancient upright piano, the player at which and the nude upon which are given as "Piano Player" and "Nude" (with artist's name and medium) on the printed handout that identifies the items as part of the collection of the restaurateur and, it develops, art collector in charge, a Lewis Futterman. The art does nothing for the space, just asserts itself for its owner the way a Mercedes Benz does the job for someone else. While Futterman is working the public sector out front, he works the private one in ways that would get less imaginative restaurateurs shaking their heads. A disclaimer reads, "All pieces are from the private collection of Lewis Futterman. Work by the artists is neither directly or (sic) indirectly on sale through this organization. However further information about the artists, including catalogues, is available as a convenience to ANDIAMO's patrons." All things considered, it is not preposterous to figure that Futterman is building demand for the artists he already owns.

You are seated in handsome chairs of steel and black leather—they comfortably give a little in response to your shifting weight. The tables are white-linened, the light is soft, there is no smoking *anywhere*. After a while you figure that, since Futterman believes so consistently in all the right things, there must be a consultant who provides him with correct Upper West Side attitudes. Even the help have been sold on him. A waiter tells you how respectful Mr. Futterman is of his chef's "creativity." A waitress, in re the smoking prohibition, drops to an awed whisper to tell you that Mr. Futterman feels *very* strongly about it. Which would be all right in Andiamo if the poor sucker in Café Bel Canto could at least bum a cigarette and smoke it where he got it.

Andiamo, its name and Italian-accented menu notwithstanding, is not an Italian restaurant. That creative chef (really, Futterman, should he not, consistent with humanistic employee relations practices, be credited by name on the printed menu?), however, makes more of his carpaccio than many an Italian competitor, the thin slices of just-cut red meat, in a pool of herbed olive oil, adorned with flakes of flinty parmesan cheese and, at the center, a mound of vibrant, chunky, many-textured caponata, the flavors of its elements—among them olives, celery, red peppers, tiny florets of cauliflower—all vivid. The sautéed shrimp are prettily presented, a mound of salad at the center of the dish encircled by a chain of shrimp, those, in turn, within a perimeter of cucumber salad—the shrimp, though salted past reason, are of abundant ocean flavor, and the salad's lemon dressing adds a nifty note of fruit to the good dish. A half dozen pasta dishes are $9 to $13 as first courses, more as main courses, among them capellini in a pesto sauce that is dominated by basil, reveals little of the cheese or garlic you expect in sauces that go by this name; and angel hair with seafood, the thread-thin noodles—in an herbed, enriched, saffron-flavored, and tomato-studded sauce—mingled with much fresh squid, scallops, and chunks of firm fish, the pasta surmounted by a sweet mussel and one tiny, tender clam, each in its shell.

You order snapper, and you are given a great browned slab of the fish in a lemoned butter of such richness as to be just shy of excess—but the fish is fresh and moist, and of clear, sweet flavor. You ask your waiter if the listed squab is not actually a pigeon. He allows as how it is and confesses that the staff is discouraged from using the more familiar term because it suggests the residents of local sidewalks. You yourself are willing to assume they are from out of town, and you order one. The meat of the bird, though not rare, is of a pink glow, its flavor is clear, fennel and browned potatoes are its good foils.

The veal chop is plump, its juiciness sealed within browned surfaces, the meat served on a sweet-spiced mash of lively, almost bitter swiss chard, and the two are set in a sauce that is livened by black raisins. You ask that your rack and loin of lamb be prepared medium rare, they reach you distinctly rarer than that, the two thick chops and half dozen slices of loin of a glistening red glow, the meat tender, its lamb flavor strong, its balsamic vinegar sauce sticky and fruity, a mound of polenta a nice offset to the rich food.

You choose a flavor of ice cream, and you choose what to have poured over it from among four additives: grappa and raisins, amaretti and Scotch, espresso, nougatine. Your waiter, who says he has tried them all every which way, suggests chocolate with grappa and raisins, and it is true, the fruit, marinated in the sturdy liquor, nicely accentuates the rich cream. Hot sections of pear in brandy are wrapped in flaky pastry that is whited with confectioner's sugar and garnished with that chocolate ice cream again—a good sweet. The honey saffron custard looks like a crème brûlée, is notably fluffy, the honey works fine—about as well as sugar—but that saffron flavor is incomprehensible in this dish.

★★★ AQUAVIT

13 West 54th Street
LUNCH, MONDAY TO FRIDAY; DINNER, MONDAY TO SATURDAY. CLOSED SUNDAY.
Reservations: 307-7311.
Credit cards: AE, DC, MC, V.
Very expensive.

A pair of townhouses seven stories high, one behind the other, surround an atrium through which, halfway up, the buildings are bridged. Between dawn and dusk, daylight floods the glass-domed space, and at certain times of year rays of actual sunlight pierce through to ground level, but at night a moon and a sky full of stars do nothing to relieve the darkness of the hidden vault. This, however, is midtown space, vastly valuable, and now some Swedes, having noted that the base of the atrium would make a singular restaurant setting, have taken possession of it—along with adjacent portions of the two lower stories of the front building—and installed the first serious Scandinavian restaurant to open in New York in decades. It appears that, happily, Swedish restaurant design is not characterized by the desperation for effect with which that pursuit is beset in New York. No element of this place is unconventional, nothing is designed to overwhelm, the restaurant is plainly commodious in a way that is its own stunning effect.

You enter, by descent of a few steps, to the upper floor of this two-tiered place. Here is the informal half of Aquavit, a long stand-up bar, unlinened tables, the comparatively simple Swedish menu supplemented by a short list of the Danish open-faced sandwiches called smorrebrod—they have names (e.g., H.C. Andersen, Tivoli, Havsstrykare), and they have unlikely seeming sets of components (e.g., smoked eel with scrambled egg and chives) that are the evolved culmination of centuries of intrepid Danish sandwich eating. Bypass that café by descending further, and you come to the inner room of Aquavit proper, pale walls, soft light, a banquette under a row of small framed paintings, and a couple of tables right beside the large windows at the back of the room, which look out to the lofty backyard, these sheltered inside accommodations presumably for the convenience of those who are afraid of heights even from the bottom. A few more steps down, and you are in the atrium itself, to your left the sloping west wall of gray ceramic tiles down which a sheet of water endlessly flows; to your right a vertical cliff of polished opal-gray marble; across the way, under four large paintings, another banquette, of gun-metal leather. Within these bounds has been created, by a balance of appointments, an installation that manages to be a cushy interior in the out-of-doors: a random arrangement of creamy-linened tables, little steel lanterns that burn like candles thereon, capacious armchairs of leather and tubular steel around them; dark blue carpeting of a small geometric pattern, that in this low light seems softly mottled; white birch trees that reach a couple of stories up; and, above the tops of those, and extending almost to the top of the atrium, great two-dimensional kitelike mobiles, of colored cloth mounted on wood slats, that tame but do not quite undo the dark void overhead—a sharp clap of your hands, and the whole place echoes.

Mention Scandinavian food, and the American reflexively thinks of a smorgasbord. No such buffet is presented here, but if your problem is that without one you will not feel you have eaten Swedish, the house lists a smorgasbord plate. It is composed of more elements than can possibly register on a single mind, among them herrings and fish roes, a hard cheese and a livery pâté, cured salmons, salads, more, but though they are fine, you are more likely to come away with a clear idea of what you have eaten if you begin with something unassorted: a thick slice of deep-orange gravlax, firm, supple, and tender, the marinated salmon infused with dill and served with a sparkling dill-and-mustard sauce; a tartare of salmon and oysters, the fresh raw fish and shellfish chopped, seasoned, herbed, and bound together into a light and sticky mass that is at once oceanic and sweet; a salad of dark wild mushrooms that become wondrously earthy in the oil with which they are dressed—fresh greens, walnuts, and hard-cooked quail eggs add, respectively, crispiness, crunchiness, a bit of eggshell; arctic venison pâté, a rectangle of reddish-brown forcemeat, studded with pistachios, in a pastry frame, adorned with lingonberries, and garnished with strands of celery root in a thick dressing—you do wish the pâté were not cool, but still the flavor of the strong meat is clear; a salmon soufflé, about the size of a large egg, on a layer of spinach within a browned puffy-pastry dome—this is not a soufflé as you know it, its weight and texture are those of a quenelle, but the salmon flavor is clear, dramatized by the dilled red sauce in which the construct is set.

You have by now noted that salmon is much of this menu. There are in fact three salmon dishes among the main courses, and of those the juniper-smoked salmon is commended to your attention. The fish is only barely smoked, so that it is not cooked through, yet it takes on a heady smokiness. Then it is cooked, once again lightly, so that when it is served, its center is a deep rosy pink, it is juicy, and it is of almost dazzlingly complex flavor—the somewhat tart sauce of trout roe is in striking contrast. In Scandinavia, fancy food is often French food in Nordic variations. Thus this Dover sole, the fish halved, skinned, boned, reassembled, done through but not overcooked, and served in a white wine sauce that is lightly browned on the plate—the three fish roes with which it is adorned add gamy zest to the perfectly prepared dish. And thus the turbot, a massive nugget cut from a huge fish, the bones at the center like spikes, the dark skin you peel away almost like leather, the meat firm and of a delicate flavor made nutty by the browned butter your waiter spoons on—a horseradish garnish northernizes the dish. The snow grouse must be a tiny creature, for your serving of its meat is but a few thin leaves—still much is made of the bird, it is in a tart and creamy sauce that is dotted with lingonberries, and it is garnished with a sharp puree of celery root, with a browned and crusted slice of potato tart that is vigorously salted and of strong potato flavor, and with a kind of meatball, presumably of the grouse itself, that is solid, powerfully seasoned, satisfying. Arctic venison again, the thin slices of loin blood-juicy in their spicy, fruity,

42

and much enriched apple and juniper berry sauce. But for red meat that is both closer to home and far from the usual thing, consider the poached tenderloin of beef, the thick disks much like slices cut from a broiled loin, for the rims are browned and the centers rare, but these reach you in a clear and stocky broth in which you find also leeks and little carrots, slightly bitter baby turnips and halves of potato with their skins on, and a marrow bone—you may season the meat with sharp mustard and/or coarse salt.

The rich, dark chocolate cake is notable for the nutty flavor of its almond crust and the intensity of the bright-red raspberry puree in which it is set; the crème caramel for its lightness and for the black raisins in its sauce; the clafoutie for the warm hominess of the cooked Swedish blueberries, the dark and crumbly pastry, the extraordinarily thick and tart crème fraîche served with it; the brambleberry sorbet for the depth of its berry flavor; the so-called smalandsk cheesecake for the nuttiness, grittiness, distinctiveness of the mixed cloudberries, lingonberries, slivered almonds, and for the deep vanilla flavor of the ice cream served with the odd mixture.

You may prefer to drink beer and aquavit with dinner—très, très Scandinavian. There is superb Carlsberg beer on tap and several flavors of aquavit—in Scandinavia caraway is the usual flavor.

★ ARCADIA

21 East 62nd Street
LUNCH, MONDAY TO FRIDAY; DINNER, MONDAY TO SATURDAY. CLOSED SUNDAY.
Reservations: 223-2900.
Credit cards: AE, DC, MC, V.
Very expensive.

Whether by calculation or chance, Anne Rosenzweig, chef here, has built her reputation in part by culinary flattery. She incorporates in her fancy food elements of home cooking that are rarely so honored. The attachment of certain authorities to the humble dishes on which they were reared is thus redeemed. Dress the quail with kasha, make pasta taste like borscht, use crème fraîche like sour cream, construct a dessert of macadamia nuts (the caviar of junk food, a jar was always produced for special occasions), and you are close to uncovering a food critic's most carefully clothed secret: nine times out of ten she would rather have a pastrami on rye. It is not, of course, that those foods are out of place in new contexts, rather that Arcadia does not deserve extra points simply for incorporating, say, smoked whitefish in its seafood salad.

This is a small place. The seating is tight, the booking is tight. You arrive at the hour of your reservation, maybe get seated half an hour later. You are not dealt with in a take-it-or-leave-it manner, you understand, the house fervently does wish that those nursing brandies and coffee refills would vacate, but there you are. That, however, is the lesser of the tightness problems. The greater is the one with which you may well be stuck throughout dinner, for Arcadia, installed in a storefront that would do comfortably as an eight-chair barbershop, strains to seat 50 at dinner. You enter to a small room occupied by a bar and, often, a crowd around it, the two of which it accommodates more or less readily. But someone had the wishful notion, back when this place was laid out, that the room could hold four tables as well, and has since overlooked the visible fact that to eat at any of them is to be stuck between a throng and a hard place. When you reserve a table at Arcadia, you understand, you specify the back room—which is only a little better. Webster defines Arcadia as "a region or scene of simple pleasure and quiet," which surely describes the swath of sylvan mural that segues from spring through winter in its perimetric four-season sweep around the dining room. Having perhaps been mindful that there would be population enough on the banquettes below his painting, the muralist excluded from his quiet region all fauna, sapiens and otherwise.

The peaceful fantasy, however, does not offset the real congestion, for the seating at the straight banquettes along the sides is cheek to cheek to cheek, though if there are two of you, you are better off side by side than face to face, for the smaller tables for two would barely accommodate a game of solitaire. (If you do not smoke, the waiters and waitresses automatically remove the ashtrays, to free up square inches. You may wish to have the obtrusive flowers removed as well.) Still, those tables are not as bad as the two in the narrow center aisle. Seated at one of these, and without Zen training, the incessant pedestrian traffic to your left and right will have you convinced by coffee time that you are caught in a stampede. Happily there is a large table in each of this room's four corners, the only entirely comfortable accommodations in the place. If you are four, arrange in advance for a corner table.

Rosenzweig's inclination to the down home extends to her nomenclature. Consider, for example, this so-called crabmeat cocktail, which does not explain itself until it shows up in a big martini glass, the fresh seafood, all its sweet flavor intact, a mass bound in a saffroned and lemony mayonnaise and set on crisp greens. And it extends to her corn cakes, one of the three ever present dishes on her regularly revised menu. You are served four of these golden disks, they are delicately browned, light, of vivid cornmeal flavor, sweetened a bit by the whole kernels of corn with which they are dotted, and served with a great dollop of crème fraîche—thick and creamy, but you wish it had more tartness and character—that is adorned with minced chives and what are given as "caviars," a gram or two of a black one, two or three of a pale-golden one, the roes dim in the context of this well-made but self-consciously fancified dish. But some of her good ideas are sans cutes, among them this grilled leek, the white stalk—delicately charred and moistened with herbed butter—protruding from a block of flaky puff pastry that is stuffed with a sweet, sharp onion marmalade. But the pasta with salmon, beets, and dill, though eminently edible, is coy theater. That it looks as if it would glow shocking fuchsia in the dark is the least of it. That everyone in the place who gets a copy giggles, then announces that it tastes like borscht, is the point. You do wonder why there is pasta that tastes like borscht when there exists already borscht that tastes like borscht. Culinary humor, maybe. For those who might otherwise miss the joke, there is a dollop of cool thick cream at the center of the dish. (The chunks of good salmon in among the noodles establish that when you add salmon to borscht—or its farinaceous counterpart—you still have borscht.)

The chimney-smoked lobster is another perennial dish, and if you get here just once, it is the main course to have. This is a tiny lobster, done over a fire, an exacting business—too much fire, and the lobster will be dry and stringy. But these crustaceans seem always to arrive moist and supple and juicy in their tarragon butter, and the smokiness they pick up in the making dramatizes but does not obscure the meat's sweet flavor. The dish is served with celery root cakes—they are like potato tarts, buttery within their crusty surfaces, the good root flavor almost subsumed in their vigorous seasoning. What is listed as "Arcadian fish stew" sports two great wings that protrude from the sides of its soup plate, crusts of bread spread with a vibrant garlic sauce, and you may find them the high point of this bouillabaisse variant, for though the soup is saffroned, brandied, touched with citrus, threaded with leeks and tomato, it is of a certain thinness, and though the mussels in their shiny black shells are sweet, the mound of seafood at the center of your plate is overcooked, the scallops have lost their richness, the fish its identity. You are asked how you want your duck steak, and it arrives accurately medium rare in its polished and somewhat fruity port wine sauce—the duck is tender, juicy, of clear flavor, there are slices of earthy wild mushrooms in the sauce, the wild-rice pancakes are crusty, the kale that adds a note of green to the dish is otherwise a dull presence in the lively company. The roast veal shanks are another variant, this one on osso buco, the meat—well cooked, firm, moist, and just falling off the bone, but of little flavor— served with the ricelike pasta grain called orzo, everything in a stocky sauce the acidity of which does not undo the somewhat leaden solidity of this winter food.

Of Rosenzweig's variations on familiar themes, her reinterpretation of cheese and fruit is, it is hoped, the most disastrous: dabs of three cheeses, one of them sweating, two of them drying out, with three crusts of toasted brioche on which slivers of grilled pear have settled into a shriveled and dejected state. The stiff-textured chestnut flan has nothing on plain flan. But the pear and cranberry crisp is light and fruity, accented with bits of crisped sweet pastry, enriched with cinnamon-flavored whipped cream. And, as ever, the chocolate bread pudding—the third perennial—is of a comforting warmth and solid chocolate depth in its lightly brandied sauce.

Talk to the floor staff and they will tell you that since her connection with "21" Rosenzweig works here an average of three nights a week. Some think the food is better when she is on hand. Whatever the reason, few kitchens in New York produce food so superb and also so dreary, the best dishes those that have always been on the menu. The East Side crowd that once filled this place has been in part supplanted by a new set, and though it has been reported that Arcadia requires jackets and ties, guys in pullover sweaters now eat here unmolested.

★★ARIZONA 206

206 East 60th Street
LUNCH, MONDAY TO SATURDAY; DINNER, DAILY.
Reservations: 838-0440.
Credit cards: AE, DC, MC, V.
Expensive.

Odds and ends—including heart-shaped wreaths of red peppers on the walls and a single tomahawk—are all it took to transform a stucco alpine ski lodge (this was briefly Stamperl 206) into a clay hovel of the American Southwest. Cement, adobe, whatever the building material is or is meant to resemble, the stuff was spread with a rubber trowel, for 206 looks like a plastered low-ceilinged cave, complete with fireplace just inside the entrance, built-in rough-hewn wooden benches along the walls, loose cushions on them, and a wide-plank floor that, presumably, is laid over bare earth. The companionably shoulder-to-shoulder seating is at virtually adjacent tables, their wood tops the size of chessboards. Occupied, as it is, by recent seniors, the place throbs a little with the jollity of a sloppy college bar. Look through the front window, and you would guess that most in the crowd are working on burgers, and that the youthful staff, in unisex pink shirts and khaki work pants, hang out here on their nights off, when some of these customers are themselves working the floor. Either way, your waitperson has to get within four inches of your ear to make audible its recitation of the special dishes of the night, for the mating sounds in these hard-surfaced surroundings, taken together with the piped-in Top 10 (which occasionally share their air with Willie Nelson, who settles an old score with Hoagy Carmichael by singing "Stardust"), get first call on your tympana.

But it is not burgers the crowd is on; instead, a Californiated version of Mexican and American-southwestern food, with not-so-faint traces of everywhere else on earth. Among the offerings are these bicontinental ravioli, the pasta packages, filled with a hot paste of pungent goat cheese, set in a spicy and brick-red pepper sauce that is strewn with sprigs of fresh coriander, all the elements fine, though this particular new-world sauce with this old-world pasta is an instance of culture shock unresolved; a flour tortilla filled with a creamy and mildly spiced filling that is mostly sweet crabmeat, with it a tart green salsa and well-garlicked cubes of cold tomato; a lamb salad that is several slices of cool, rare meat with crunchy halves of baby artichoke and marinated tomatoes, all in a tangy vinaigrette; and pan-fried sweetbreads, the slivers of organ meat, rich within their crisped surfaces, mingled with sautéed wild mushrooms and bits of bacon and strewn over half a black-skinned, sweet, earthy squash.

Though the tabletops are wee, the dinner plates are the size of ashcan covers, so with two plates on one table, the air space over the occupants' laps is inevitably violated. Making it a point not to knee your dinner when you cross your legs, you edge up to the rim of your plate and insert your fork into a transatlantic mound of "seafood risotto with saffron & roast poblano chili," the big grains of wet rice—the dish is soupy—dotted with rich scallops, crisp sweet-tasting shrimp, chunks of lobster, the liquid green and spicy hot of the chiles ground into it. Hot peppers again, this time rubbed into the surface of a chicken that is breaded, crisped, and served on a layer of kale—the moist meat of the bird is suffused with the flavor of the hot pepper. Because the rib-eye steak is about as thick as it is wide, the fibrous meat is tender and blood-juicy despite the heavy black crust it picked up in the grilling—the good meat is garnished with whole onions. In what is given as "venison black bean chili," morsels of the game meat are mingled with a nubbly mix of beans, corn kernels, whole shallots, all in a fiery black liquid that is enriched by the blood of the venison—the dish is adorned at the center with a dollop of sour cream, and you soak up the last of the hot liquid with the toasted corn bread that accompanies it.

Appended to the restaurant is the Café, a so-called grazing establishment in which you select small plates of food from among those that are listed by price category ($6, $8, $10, $12) on blackboards posted here and there. The room is open and airy, especially by comparison to the restaurant proper, and determinedly casual—the seating is on white-painted metal folding chairs with padded seats, the floor is of big red tiles that look like they have been walked on for centuries, and the cooking facilities are right in the room with you, so the help is never out of sight. You wave, and a giddy young man comes by, laughs sympathetically as he takes your order, as if your recitation were really a humorous recounting of minor problems, is beside himself when, presently, he is able to deliver your fried onions, the huge pile of tender, delicately crisped rings, of sweet and clear onion flavor, set beside a pool of hot-spiced chocolate-brown molé sauce. His hebephrenic tittering accompanies also the barbecued oysters, the crisped mollusk meats in a folded tortilla, roused by their green-pepper sauce; and the fried calamari, in which the circles of somewhat toughened but clear-flavored squid are set in a sauce of tomato and cumin over which another sauce, of black beans and garlic, has been dribbled; and the smoked quail, the grill-marked bird stuffed with peppercorn-dotted wild rice and garnished with a tangy fruit chutney.

Café desserts: a nutted persimmon pudding pie, adorned with whipped cream, that is

46

dull despite its sweet spices; and a layered affair of ice creams and sherbet—the flavors are, respectively, fig, walnut, and cranberry-tangerine—in which the three parts seem to cancel one another out, leaving something that is little more than cold and wet. Restaurant desserts: a sweet-potato empanada that is a hot, sweet-spiced yam mash wrapped in a light pastry and garnished with maple ice cream; an apple pear crisp that is like kids' food, the soup plate of cooked fruit, under a crisped sugary topping, moistened with cool cream; something given as "natillas with anise crème anglaise," which turns out to be a fluffy floating island, the big white meringue strewn with pine nuts and fennel seeds in its licorice-flavored sauce.

Lone Star beer *on tap*—and though light, the creamy stuff has body and sparkle, comes up through clean pipes, is served in clean glasses, holds its head and texture, is good with this food.

★★★ ARQUÀ

281 Church Street (at White Street)
LUNCH, MONDAY TO FRIDAY; DINNER, MONDAY TO SATURDAY. CLOSED SUNDAY.
Reservations: 334-1888.
Credit cards: AE.
Medium priced.

Come here on foot, and your evening is made, for to enter this place after a walk through its gray environs is a change of scene from the coal mines to the seashore. Arquà is your basic urban hideaway (a largely imaginary genre, there never were many examples), a first-class eating place, comfortable and festive, hidden away in an otherwise grim neighborhood. Of course in today's New York, the restaurant is a beachhead rather than an outpost—purveyors of high-tech housewares, secondhand lace, and poster art will inevitably follow.

As if to emphasize the drama of this store in this setting, its interior has been given a paint job of mottled amber that glows warm in the room's abundant light. The furnishings are simple, around twenty white-linened tables in three rows, a plain wood floor, tall windows on the Church Street and White Street sides (the windows on White provide excellent views of the male traffic into and out of the Baby Doll Lounge—"Go-Go Girls" and "Topless Dancers"—across the street), Deco light fixtures on the walls, and great handsome paper lanterns, three of them, hanging from the high ceiling. A barmaid wearing hoop earrings you could toss a basketball through tends the little bar up front, its top of polished brass framed in pale wood; desserts and wines are displayed on a table nearby, next to it a pot of flowers stands on a carved-wood pedestal. Your waiter is in a white shirt, white apron, suspenders, a more-or-less garish four-in-hand—he answers your questions willingly, usually correctly. Early in the evening he waits on folks from the Street who have chosen to eat well before crossing the river—in that crowd, both genders wear suits, carry attaché cases. Things get colorful later on, e.g., this gent in a nose ring, nightmare shirt, and leopard-spotted hair. "*How* did he do that?" whispers an uptown lady, cringing.

Sgombretti are little mackerel, and if you require rousing, begin with these, the fillets of tiny fish, cold and a little sour, piled high with sweet slivers of oiled onion, all in a pool of marinade that has in it thin disks of crunchy, bright-orange carrot. The marinated squid is almost as vivifying, the many rings reach you mingled with chips of crisp celery, the two in a garlicky oil that intensifies the flavor of the tender, vividly fresh seafood. For a bit of satiation along with your stimulation, you will do well with the radicchio alla griglia, for when the red lettuce has been oiled and grilled and charred a little, taleggio is melted over it, the rich stuff seeps in among the hot, crunchy leaves—their slight bitterness is in stunning contrast to the creamy cheese. Solider still is the stuffed artichoke, the heart in four quarters, the quartered stem attached, each part packed with a meaty filling that is overlaid with a glinting strip of good bacon. For utter solidity, as for a hunger unbound, you will opt to begin your dinner with polenta pasticciata, a mound of cornmeal the size of a cake, soft and moist and of a high, grainy cornmeal flavor, upon it chunks of sausage, much fennel in their flavoring, and sautéed onions, the two in a bright red sauce, thin slices of hard Parmesan on top—hot, homey food that you eat your way through in a sweat.

Half orders of pasta are iffy; sometimes you get them, sometimes not. If you are refused half an order of the gnocchi alle quatro erbe, be glad, settle for a full order, for these white nuggets have both lightness and solidity; though firm, they are soft enough to be reduced between your tongue and palate; and they are adorned with a dollop of tangy tomato sauce and with strands of fresh herbs—the wondrous dish takes on a good edge when you add ground cheese. Pappardelle del dogi are wide, weighty noodles served here with little leaves of radicchio that are in striking textural contrast to the substantial pasta—the good sauce is light, creamy, nubbly with ground sausage. Each day there is a risotto of the day, and you are in luck if you come when the rice is served with cuttlefish and its ink, the glinting black-stained grains, threaded with lengths of the seafood, of an elemental ocean pungency that is deep and sea-gamy. A serving of that rice is a mammoth dune in which a gentleman's fedora could be buried, and though no prizes are given, people do stand around and watch when anyone undertakes to begin his dinner with the aforementioned polenta and continue it with an order of this.

Your grilled swordfish is the size of your dinner plate and half an inch thick, grill-marked outside and juicy inside, sweet and tenderly fibrous, nicely garnished with cool tomatoes adorned with fresh basil. A fish soup appears on the menu, but sometimes a more elaborate one, which your waiter identifies as "Italian bouillabaisse," is offered; this is a collection of sweet little clams in their shells and a couple of crunchy shrimp in theirs, lots of squid and sections of fresh fish, all in a spicy and tomato-redded oil—hefty, vibrant food. The grilled chicken is handsomely browned, moist, takes on some of the flavor of the rosemary with which it is done, is surrounded by chunks of roasted potato that are crusty outside, soft inside. You get those same potatoes with this special-of-the-day veal chop, the bronzed and glistening eye of meat bifurcated longitudinally and packed with taleggio and spinach—unlike most cheese-stuffed veal chops, this one is light, and its tender meat is pink and glistening within its seared surfaces.

The house makes a good version of the rather obvious sweet called tirami sù; unlike most it is not puddinglike, its chocolate, rich cheese, and coffee-flavored ladyfingers all distinct elements in the lively layered affair. The millefoglie is a couple of pale and flaky pastries, a polished custard between them, confectioner's sugar on top. The ricotta cheesecake is cool and moist and light, the flavor of its browned top a zest to it, and it is served with good sauces, one pale and lemony, the other red of fresh raspberries. The firm, grainy-textured pear, purple of the red wine in which it was poached, is heady with the flavor of cloves.

★ AUDRONE'S

342 West 46th Street
LUNCH AND DINNER. CLOSED SUNDAY.
Reservations: 246-1960.
Credit cards: AE, DC, MC, V.
Medium priced.

When, a few years ago, the restaurant Dimitri disappeared from its Columbus Avenue site near Lincoln Center, that short-changed part of town lost one of its few honest eating-and-drinking establishments. The straightforward place served both its neighborhood and the thousands of patrons of the performing arts who came for a visit every evening. The interests behind Dimitri did not, however, take their money and run very far—only as far as the Theater District's so-called Restaurant Row, where, under a new name, they continue to serve patrons of the performing arts, but where there is not much in the way of neighborhood to provide commerce once the eight o'clock curtains have risen. So, as at almost all the restaurants on this block, Audrone's hums for early dinner; at five minutes before eight, the exiting crowd wears out John's right hand (John, ex Dimitri, is your host) with handshakes, and, in exiting, is a danger to passersby on the sidewalk; by five minutes after eight, the help outnumbers the customers. The physical place is a small bar up front, a dining room beyond it that is all white and black and pale gray, with watercolors on the walls, flowers and white linen on the tables, and mirroring here and there that gives the room a silvery glint. This is a cool setting, and it does take a crowd to warm it up.

From a menu that is diverse even by today's standards: gravlax, a great sheet of the supple cured fish, less oily than most, served with a dollop of strong mustard sauce that is greened with fresh dill; a thoroughly oiled terrine of eggplant, a slice cut from a loaf, the layering of spinach the principal secondary ingredient, a chunky mash of stewed tomatoes its good garnish; a duck salad that is an abundance of warm meat and mushrooms strewn over a great mound of arugula, radicchio, endive; that salad again, minus the duck and mushrooms and in a lively dressing, a nugget of creamy goat cheese hidden among the leaves; sautéed sweetbreads and mushrooms, the organ meat crisped, the mushrooms earthy, the two served over a thick slice of bread, which soaks up their well seasoned sauce; linguine in a green seafood sauce—the scallops, shrimp, squid, and mussels are all fresh and of good flavor, but you do wish the herbed sauce were not soupy.

When not cured, the Norwegian salmon that goes as gravlax goes instead as poached salmon, of which you are served an utterly fresh and juicy fillet—the fish is moistened with a buttery sauce that is thick with parsley. But if you are here on a day when monkfish provençale is offered, you may prefer that comparatively bland swimmer, for its garlicked sauce, thick with olives and tomato, is dark, deep, and complex, as of flavors hidden in flavors. Seafood again, shrimp and scallops broiled on a skewer—the lime-honey-horseradish glaze with which the seafood is treated has little impact, shows up on your plate as a somewhat irrelevant puddle, but there is no faulting the freshness and judicious grilling of the shellfish. The roast chicken is nicely browned, is served well by

49

the garlic and tarragon with which it is done, but it started out as a bird of little flavor, for which a cure has not here been found. The peppered sirloin steak is good beef, but its coating of coarse-ground pepper almost overpowers it. Sometimes cassoulet is offered, which is not, of course, pretheater food (unless you have cultivated the sensible practice of leaving during the first intermission), for this is weighty stuff, the beans firm but cooked through, the sauce in which the elements are bound dark and earthy and sticky, the chunks of lamb, duck, and sausage abundant and distinct—the casserole dish in which the cassoulet is served is stuck under the broiler at the last minute, so the top is browned and crusted when it reaches you.

Come once, and crème brûlée is the dessert to have, the custard cool and light and fluffy, its caramelized surface warm and crackling. When the tart of the day is of cranberries, the thick, rich whipped cream cannot offset the straight sourness of the raw-seeming fruit. When it is of pecans, it is what you would call pecan pie—this one is of spicy nut flavor on its flaky pastry. You wish the cold raspberry soufflé were frozen—its consistency is that of a pudding—but it is fruity and rich, the caramelized sugar top a nifty note. The orange cheesecake is New York cheesecake flavored with orange, but that touch of citrus is less than it takes to leaven the weighty, creamy richness; for those to whom this kind of cheesecake *is* cheesecake, this is the real thing.

★★AUREOLE

34 East 61st Street
LUNCH AND DINNER. CLOSED SUNDAY.
Reservations: 319-1660.
Credit cards: AE, MC, V.
Very expensive.

Heralded in the press as a showcase for the talents of Charles Palmer, erstwhile chef at Brooklyn's River Café, Aureole is by no means Palmer's own. It is, in fact, only the most recent of the enterprises in which the team of Nicolette Kotsoni and Steve Tzolis are factors. Perhaps you know Kotsoni and Tzolis, at least by sight. One or both are often on hand at Il Cantinori, on East 10th Street, or at Periyali, on West 20th, the other restaurants in their little chain. Actually, Tzolis you are not likely to recall, for his behavior is simply that of an entrepreneurially concerned party adding his effort to the common cause. His partner, however, while for all you know she may make an even greater contribution than he, betrays a different order of concern. Kotsoni is of the furrow-browed hand-wringers, the quiveringly attuned disaster dreaders. She is enough to make you hand over an eleemosynary contribution without even sitting down and head elsewhere for a dinner that will not be interrupted any minute by the end of the world. Anyway, that is how she *did* come across. Success, it seems, is a specific for anxiety, and with the easing of her symptoms, with the new confidence concomitant thereto, Kotsoni has asserted her proprietorial rights, has stuck this place with one of her dreams. In a confession to the press she has allowed as how she has "had this design in...mind for some years now." It is easy to believe she has had it in mind since infancy.

Through its outsize plate glass front window, you see from the street that Aureole's public rooms are installed in the first and second floors of its townhouse, and that the second floor is set back like a mezzanine, so that the area just inside the front door, around the bar, is two stories high. You note also that the whole place—anyway, as far as you can see—has been painted a sweet, buttery tone of pale ivory. And, still from your street vantage, you get your first look at the design by which, for all those years, Kotsoni's imagination was never deserted. The lofty wall opposite the bar has been adorned with applied molded forms, in shallow relief, of members of the playpen animal kingdom. This is Kotsoni's "design idea," and it turns up throughout the restaurant, with, here and there, similarly applied representations of the plant and vegetable life among which Bambi et al traipse and frolic. The fauna and flora, you understand, are subsumed in the same vanilla-ice-cream paint as everything else in the place. To whom is this diverting? Does *your* dining room look like the nursery? Even in their fantasies adults are no longer children (unless of course they are). Aureole is otherwise a straightforward installation, wood floors, white-linened tables, tweedy tan upholstery on the downstairs banquette. Huge bursts of flowers are mounted here and there on the walls, smaller ones, in mock birds' nests, are on every table, but instead of livening the restaurant, they only emphasize by contrast its sugar-coated insipidity. With a few simple deletions, Aureole would be a perfect blank waiting to be designed.

Modern American menus read like manifestoes. The most extreme of them list hardly a dish with even a trace of antecedence. Among declarators of that independence Palmer is a wild-eyed leader. Even with daily revisions to the printed bill of fare he manages almost unerringly to avoid any connection between dishes of his own and dishes in the public domain. Prod your memory as you may, you will not call up an ancestor of "sea scallop sandwiches in crisp potato crusts." You approach a dish of this kind the way you approach a new appliance. Careful, these are sandwiches you do not pick up, for they are of the open-faced variety and upside-down, potato pancakes on top, scallops below, the pancakes handsomely browned and vigorously salted, much like Swiss rösti potatoes, crusted, moist, of vivid potato flavor, while the good scallops are juicy and rich in their buttery, mildly citrused sauce—withal, the dish fails as an entity, consists of delicious parts thrown together by bewildering fate. Further aleatory adventures: a "warm skate salad" in which the fillet of fresh fish, moistened by a cream dressing dotted with black caviar, is served with potato dumplings that contrast with the delicate fish more by way of their temperature (hot) than their flavor; another "salad," one in which spears of peeled asparagus, cool and crunchy, confront an almost sugar-sweet mound of richly oiled eggplant across a plate—perfect partners, but not for each other. The carpaccio of yellowfin tuna almost qualifies as an everyday dish, thin slices of the raw, utterly fresh fish draped over a mound of salad, the greens livened by the onions and mushrooms with which they are mingled. Order the "ginger-cured salmon," and you are presented with a plate filmed with red fish that has been dotted with coarse-ground pepper, moistened with olive oil, adorned with leaves of the sharp green called mâche— this is fish made assertive, and it is served with a sweet Vidalia onion topped with rich cream.

With respect to certain of the main courses, too, you will ask why. Why, for example, sautéed halibut surmounted by "oak-smoked" shrimp. The thick fillet of fish is fresh, seasoned and browned, but cooked almost to the point of dryness, with some sacrifice of flavor, and the big shrimp on top, never mind that they are mushy, seem stranded at a way station where they have no business. As the grilled Maine lobster is mostly itself, it has no explaining to do. Its juicy, tender, crisped meat is out of the shell, its sweet flavor rather vigorously potentiated by the wood smoke of its grilling—a layer of buttery chard is under the lobster, a tangle of paper-thin slivers of sweet ginger over it. Slices of the meat of a mallard duck, dark, glistening, a little rare, their fatted edges crisped, are arranged on a platform of the misshapen little noodles called spaetzle—meaty morels are the black nuggets that adorn the meat. What distinguishes the tea-smoked squab from some other squab is, you guessed it, tea-smokiness, the intensity of which does not diminish the strong flavor of the bird's dark, almost gamy meat. You are lured to the veal medallions by the artichokes, onions, and Niçoise olives listed as components of the dish—the veal is artfully sautéed, is browned and juicy, the chunks of artichoke are fresh, firm, of unmistakable taste and texture, and the deep-fried onion strands are crisp and sweet, but the slivers of black olive do this all too convincing impression of black olives that come in a can and taste like plastic. Tradition does inform one dish: The grilled beef tenderloin is prepared with mushrooms (chanterelles) and is served in a red-wine (Barolo) sauce, neither of which quite make up for the rather bloodless pallidness of the overdone meat.

Lively desserts, among them a terrine of apple and cinnamon, of wonderfully clear apple flavor, that is garnished with slices of glazed apple and caramel ice cream; a warm cheese-and-pear tart in which the whipped cream cheese is fluffy, the pear sauce cool, the chunks of pear firm, pleasantly gritty, of ripe pear flavor; a lemon curd tart that is a good version of the familiar thing, its garnish of grapefruit ice striking for the bits of candied rind with which it is studded; a hot raspberry financière that is a muffin of dark and nutty cake dotted with ripe berries and garnished with dollops of good whipped cream that are topped with slivers of almond; a lively pecan spice cake served with pumpkin ice cream and garnished with rousing brandied dates.

★ AU TUNNEL

250 West 47th Street
LUNCH AND DINNER. CLOSED SUNDAY.
Reservations: 582-2166.
Credit cards: AE, MC, V.
Medium priced.

Imagine a fellow moving this decades-old establishment (used to be called *Pierre* au Tunnel) from one site to another, and, in taking advantage of the opportunity, putting together a new installation that would have looked old-fashioned when the old place first opened. People with an unclear recollection of where this place used to be and what it looked like (it was a block to the north and looked vaguely like a tunnel) walk in here and think this is the original place with a new paint job. Presumably you have to admire a respect for the past so devotional that it not only preserves the old days, but recreates them faithfully. The only thing this new incarnation of Au Tunnel lacks is age. It comes off as a brand-new relic. The red carpeting glows, and the stucco walls appear to have been just troweled on. The decorative pottery and the copper pots and pans gleam. Of course there are beams on the ceiling, framed maps and prints on the walls, a deer's head over the fireplace (with a rifle nearby). The half-timbered front room houses the bar, as well as a couple of tables at a red banquette. There is a small mural up here, a whimsical café scene—someone probably had to be unearthed, so convincingly does it replicate this lighthearted, between-the-wars style of illustration, a combination of five-cent magazine covers and the funnies. The bar is often busy before curtain time, as is the dining room. On weekends the place even gets some after-theater action. Come what may, the waitresses—most of them French—run the place with brusque, somewhat motherly efficiency.

In the course of a day, they probably deliver several dozen orders of this coarse, powerfully seasoned, well-fatted pâté—you eat it with the good, chewy bread, and with strong mustard. If you have that pâté as part of the hors d'oeuvres variés, you get a heavily garlicked, almost purple salami and a cool headcheese as well, the latter bits of meat and organ meat embedded in a firm and fragrantly herbed jelly. You get a big plate of smoked salmon—it is garnished with onions and capers, but is best taken with oil and a little lemon. The cool mussels are sweet tasting, with not a bad one in the lot—a rarity these days—but they are claylike, almost hard under their tangy sauce ravigote. The snails here are above average for the West Side—these are not the little leathery ones, they are big and plump, but their green and garlicky sauce is almost painfully salty.

Have the trout meunière on your first visit here, and it may be your last, for the fish is prepared in nut oil—or a bad imitation thereof—rather than butter, which gives it a dull, lifeless quality. In a place like this you go for the coq au vin, a great abundance of the stew in a strong, dark, and winy sauce that is studded with nicely sautéed mushrooms and whole onions; or you go for the tripe, served here in long, chewy lengths, in a fatted broth that is powerfully seasoned and redolent of root vegetables and herbs; or for the rabbit in its thick white-wine sauce, again with mushrooms and onions, and garnished with a big mound of eggy noodles, or for the tête de veau, great slabs of tongue, rich slices of brain, not to mention a complex cross-sectional slab of meats and cartilaginous meats of various textures and colors, all of which you moisten with a hot, thick vinaigrette that is studded with capers. With many of these dishes, when you have dispatched what you took to be your serving, you discover that, in the iron pot on the edge of your table, more is waiting.

On the marble board, two or three cheeses at room temperature and in good condition: Very good Brie has been had here, though on occasion neither pears nor apples nor any other fruit suitable for cheese and wine is available—the orange you are offered is all wrong. Perfectly nice raspberry tarts and blueberry tarts have been served with whipped cream that is fortified with Grand Marnier. The chocolate cake is given sparkle by the thin shelves of fruit preserves between the layers. The mocha cake, with mocha sauce, is a good standard sweet.

• AZZURRO

1625 Second Avenue (near 84th Street)
DINNER.
Reservations: 517-7068.
Credit cards: AE, DC.
Beer and wine.
Medium priced.

Italian restaurants half-a-building-lot wide are inserting themselves, all over the Upper East Side, into real estate slivers that heretofore mainly accommodated over-the-counter sidewalk-service head shops. The layout of these restaurants is inevitable: a row of tables down each side, an aisle between, a counter at the back, and, beyond that, a kitchen (usually out of sight) the cramped dimensions of which you infer from the brevity of the printed menu. Azzurro, however, differs in a couple of respects from its competitors. The others are dim, candlelit places, all rusticity, and they are hidden away on side streets, while this is a garishly lighted long box of a store right on Second Avenue; and, far from being rustic, it is assertively urban. Its waiters, for example, a collection of swaggering young gents recruited, obviously, on some street corner, are dressed in boldly patterned shirts, bow ties the size of mustaches, and baggy pleated pants that hang, from low on their hips, to the very floor (concealing from view the occasional absence, in their shoes, of anything resembling socks). The room they work looks like the sample living room in a renovated tenement going condo. The ceiling here is a vivid shade of post-card-sky blue, complete with recessed lights that, organized in stray clusters, are meant to look like constellations of stars. The long north wall is brick, the one opposite of white plaster, and the place is hung with framed astronomic and geographic engravings, complete with Latin lettering, you should know Azzurro has class. On rainy days a rubber runner is laid on the floor in the aisle between the rows of tables. It is laid there also on dry days.

A couple of blue sheets (they match the ceiling) are the printed menus, historic documents that bear traces of the olive-oiled fingers by which they have been handled apparently since the days of the first printing. They list the likes of this spiedino di mozzarella, a melted-cheese sandwich, actually, the hot mozzarella oozing out from between the well-oiled slices of fried bread, the two triangular sandwich halves dressed with a sharp and salty sauce of pulverized capers and anchovies. Equally rich but quite another matter, is this cool caponatina, a mellifluous eggplant stew that has an intensity of eggplant flavor you encounter only when the vegetable has absorbed every drop of olive oil it can possibly hold, and when, moreover, it is aggressively seasoned and gar-licked.

Do not, however, let your happy selection of appetizers mislead you into thinking that your first judgments of this establishment were ill considered. In fact, it is a rare dinner here that is without at least one gross flaw. Consider for example this capellini con caposanti e gamberi, a dish of thin spaghetti with scallops and shrimp in tomato sauce, in which the shrimp are not merely tainted with iodine, but, apparently, marinated in it. So on your next visit you go for a red sauce without seafood, rigatoni con pomidoro e basilico, and the hefty tubes of noodle arrive in a chunky, oil-rich red sauce that is heady with fresh basil.

The menu lists no specific varieties of finfish, mentions only "fish of the day." Any-way, the fish is grilled (as are all the main courses). And sometimes the grilled item is a slab of grouper that, if it has not been long frozen (to account for its tastelessness and pulpiness), does a terrific impression of having so suffered. But another night you get an eminently decent swordfish steak, its own flavor clear and sweet, the imparted flavor of the grill present but not overwhelming, a garnish of cool roasted red peppers very good with the hot seafood. Then again there is this grilled chicken—which could actually pass for that grouper. And then there is this herbed veal chop, which would be yummy had it been separated from the fire as soon as it was done. But it is all a matter of luck, and another time you find the so-called porterhouse steak (it is really a sirloin) eminently well grilled, the pink, silken meat tender and blood-juicy within its charred surfaces. At Azzurro it is well to know the ropes. One of the ropes to know is that potatoes and a green vegetable come with the main courses. Your waiter will not mention this when he tries to sell you, say, some spinach. Turn him down, you get some anyway. Order some, and you will get spinach and green beans as well—with a charge for the spinach, which otherwise would have been part of your dinner at no cost. It is probably just chance that when the spinach carries no charge it is fine, but that when you pay for it, it is loaded with sand.

Most nights only two desserts are offered: zuccota, a mass of chocolate ice cream beside a mass of strawberry ice cream, the two embraced by a crescent of sponge cake soaked in rum, nuts and candied fruits all about—a rousing excess; and tirami sù, among the more restrained versions, a layered affair of cream cheese, chocolate, white cake, liquor, cinnamon on top. These are large servings, and when you ask to split a dessert you get an extra plate and two spoons.

★★BALLATO

55 East Houston Street (near Mott Street)
LUNCH AND DINNER. CLOSED SUNDAY AND MONDAY.
Reservations required for dinner: 226-9683.
No credit cards.
Beer and wine.
Medium priced.

Mrs. Ballato now presides over the late Mr. Ballato's famous hideaway. The old gentleman was something of a professional character; his survivor is anything but. She is slight, blue haired, courteous, sweet. She helps you off with your coat, apologizes for the weather. If she fails to embrace you on your arrival because she does not know you very well, she will at least place a hand on your shoulder when you leave, now that you are old pals. Except that the restaurant is a little more relaxed than it was under the governance of its occasionally bristling founder, the change in proprietary style has changed it very little.

You enter to a small anteroom, wherein a shelf of books and magazines has been installed for the diversion of customers waiting for tables. Your coat is put in a closet, the portal of which is hung with amber beads. There is a glass icebox stocked with wine, cheese, fruit. Farther back the oblong dining room holds two rows of square tables, eleven all told, four chairs at each. The walls are surfaced with broad panels of plain cloth, and they are hung with scores of photos and pictures of John Ballato, framed articles about the restaurant, a Sinatra poster, a good number of Warhol prints, and other assorted contemporary graphics (when SoHo decided to come into existence, it chose a site not far from this place). The rear wall of the dining room hardly exists, for it is wide open to the brightly lit and immaculate kitchen (into which you must enter for the facilities and the pay phone).

The uptown set that used to crowd the curb outside with waiting limousines has deserted Ballato in favor of the slumming that has in recent years been provided for them on their own Third Avenue. But Ballato is still busy. Many of the gentlemen who come regularly look as if they ought to be the mayor of Brooklyn. You would swear that others are off-duty policemen, except that their ladies wear more jewels than a cop's salary can account for. Large families come here (a couple of tables are pushed together), and Greenwich Villagers in search of a better bargain than their own pricey neighborhood offers. It is a comfort-loving rather than a luxury-loving crowd, and they are here for the familiarity of the surroundings, the reliability of the food, the straightforward service.

The baked clams and the mussels reganate are browned and crisped, their breading easy on the dried oregano—they come in pools of parsleyed and buttered broth. Roasted green peppers are stuffed with a pungent meat-and-cheese filling, and they are dressed with a spicy tomato sauce—satisfying food.

Good pasta: lovely green noodles in a sauce that is little more than cream and cheese, the dish ornamented with a sprinkling of sharp red pepper; very good linguine with fresh clams, cloves of browned garlic and much parsley in the briny butter; excellent manicotti, the pillows of pasta stuffed with pully cheese and covered with an honest red sauce that is still bubbling when the casserole reaches your table.

If you can bring yourself to do it, order the octopus. It is served, be warned, in rather undisguised long shafts, but the slightly rubbery meat has a sharp gaminess that is worth learning to like, and the strong red sauce, thick with garlic and onions, will help. On occasion this establishment has served bass that would have pleased much more a couple of days earlier, in a sauce livornese devoid of the olives and capers that title leads you to expect. But the scampi are good—big and crunchy shrimp in a creamy tomato sauce that is thick with rice.

You get a giant portion of brains, and the rich meat arrives sizzling, crusted with seasoned breading. A small spoon protrudes from the dark marrow of the osso buco, the tender meat barely clings to the bone, a thick and gravylike mushroom sauce moistens the meat and its garnish of rice. But better than almost anything in the place is the rolatine of veal, the browned cylindrical packages filled with a spiced stuffing of strong cheese, sausage, herbs, the meat moistened with a sturdy brown sauce.

The menu lists "assorted cheeses," but a decent fontina is all you can usually get. The zabaglione is the usual hot and winy froth, but it comes with a bonus of tissue-wrapped macaroons. When the restaurant is busy your waiter may discourage the zabaglione on the ground that it takes twenty minutes. It takes five. The cheesecake is distinctly Italian —wet, light, and sugary.

★★BALLROOM

253 West 28th Street
LUNCH, TUESDAY TO FRIDAY; DINNER, TUESDAY TO SATURDAY. CLOSED SUNDAY AND MONDAY.
Reservations: 244-3005.
Credit cards: AE, DC, MC, V.
Expensive.

Tapas, Spanish snacks or hors d'oeuvres, are the main attraction here, cold ones and hot ones, the selection varied from day to day. The cold ones, around fifteen little dishes of this or that, are held before you, all on one tray, by your waiter, while he describes them one at a time. Those you want are put before you there and then. Hot ones—they are fewer in number—you learn about only from his recitation. Many who dinner here regularly limit themselves to these small plates, but the printed menu does list a handful of main courses, cheese and fruit may be selected from the rolling cart, and you choose sweet desserts from those displayed on butcher blocks just inside the entrance. In Spain, eating tapas is an informal business usually undertaken together with the consumption of spirits, especially sherry. Accordingly, the upper level of the restaurant portion of the Ballroom (there is also an attached nightclub) is given over in large measure to a tapas-and-liquor bar (over which hang hams and sides of dried fish, huge ropes of dried red peppers and strings of garlic, sometimes game birds complete with plumage), behind which the usual array of whiskeys and such is augmented by a big selection of sherries. Along the length of the bar, platters of this cold item or that are placed, each flagged with the price of a serving. Locals sometimes stop by for a drink, have a second, sample the tapas, and, what with one thing or another, do not head home until they have done the equivalent of dinner. The dining room is otherwise a somewhat rambling affair illuminated by the soft light of white globes, with palms here and there, pots and pans elsewhere, backlighted stained-glass windows opposite the bar, white tiles on the floors, sheets of white butcher paper on the white-linened tables. The original Ballroom was one of the earliest eating places in SoHo, back when art galleries were most of what was there, and as a gesture of respect to the source of its commerce, that place commissioned a mural in which the then trendy artists and dealers were portrayed sitting around the old Ballroom itself. The work has no appropriateness in this store other than a nostalgic one, but if you want a reminder of those days, here it is, dominating the lower level. A diagram identifying the characters in the scene may be consulted.

Cold tapas: morsels of octopus, tender, not rubbery, of clear pulpo flavor, in a some-what spicy redded oil that clings to their surfaces; bay scallops in a rather obvious curry sauce that suggests a canned spice mix—a couple of brussels sprouts bulk up the little plate of food; one big squid packed with a fruited and sweet-spiced filling of pork and nuts, served in a tart and chunky tomato sauce; two thick slices of eggplant in a green, fiery Moroccan paste; chorizos in a rare setting, the strong Spanish sausage chopped into little dice and dressed with a spicy vinaigrette that is thick with minced red peppers.

Hot tapas: grilled gambas, the barely cooked-through shrimp of immaculate flavor in their peppery oil, very nice with the strong onions you find on the same plate; a stew of crayfish and morels, very little seafood in those carapaces, of course, but the mushrooms are fine, as are the red peppers with which they are mingled; sautéed shiitake mushrooms in a sweet, well-oiled sauce that is dense with bits of tomato, strands of onion, fresh sweet peas; a couple of quite substantial baby lamb chops moistened with spicy oil, strewn with sprigs of fresh, fragrant rosemary, and garnished with fluffy rice; in season, a single soft-shell crab, judiciously done in olive oil, served with an avocado sauce of which it has no need; fried plantains and yucca, the hefty strips of fruit and root in a napkin-lined basket, bread substitutes more or less, the kinds of pallid starch you must grow up with to love, the bits of garlic with which they are touched not enough to excite them—or, probably, you.

Among the few listed and unlisted main courses, there is a vigorous chicken stew, its dark and lemony sauce laden with fresh, heady cilantro greens, the big chunks of chicken intermingled with onions, potatoes, morels; and an especially rich veal dish, the lean tenderloin roasted within a fattier meat wrapper, the entire construct blackened on the outside, the meat at the core pale and juicy—you are served a thick slice in a sauce that is herbed, winy, dotted with black peppercorns.

The standard, very rich chocolate desserts of the day are available, and they are fresh. The excellent sponge cake, firm but not heavy, is moistened with orange liqueur. The pecan pie is notable for the strong coffee flavor of its filler. Your waiter will probably garnish your dessert with the good house whipped cream, maybe with a strawberry or two as well.

In the adjoining club, cold tapas and drinks may be ordered before the show. For a couple of seasons of the year, this is the place (anyway, on this side of the Atlantic) where Blossom Dearie is witty and musical at 6:30 P.M.

★ BANGKOK CUISINE

885 Eighth Avenue (near 53rd Street)
LUNCH, MONDAY TO SATURDAY; DINNER, DAILY.
Reservations: 581-6370.
Credit cards: AE, DC, MC, V.
Inexpensive.

In the dim clutter that is this little place, one fixture stands out especially—an illuminated fish tank, complete with bubbles and swimming fish. Sometimes, during a lull, you will espy a member of the staff staring into the tank, wide-eyed, as if he were getting a preview of paradise itself. Innocence, it appears, is not dead. But to find any in a New York restaurant, you must choose a place that is in the hands of a national group relatively new to the big city. Among the—to us—childlike qualities of the people who run this place are courtesy (the service is invariably sweet), patriotism (portraits of Thai royalty adorn the walls), and piety (small figurines of Buddha and other divines are on display). Even the prices are innocent—that is, low. And the strongest drink you can get is wine. The food itself, however, is far from innocuous. Some of it, in fact, borders on the violent. So as you skip about among the items on the menu, beware of those marked with stars—they look as guileless as anything else you get to eat here, but they are armed.

Some, of course, are more lethal than others. Tod mun pla, for example, carries but a small stiletto. This, the menu informs you, is, of all Thai dishes, the most famous (which may tempt you to repeat certain generalizations about the unfathomability of the East). It consists of deep-fried fish patties that, though they are steamy and fresh, are of almost no identifiable flavor—however, they take on a little life when they are dipped in their tart, sweet, somewhat spicy sauce. What this restaurant calls egg rolls may also elude you. They carry no weapon at all, are like pastry sausages stuffed with clear noodles and bits of meat and vegetables, are disappointing unless you think of them as street food—they would make fine snacks from a vendor. But the satés are good. If you order the beef saté, you are served six short wooden skewers, each of them bearing many thin slices of dark, shiny beef, warm and tender—you dip the meat in a brown, mildly spicy sauce that is thick with chopped peanuts.

There is a printed menu, and there is a blackboard on which are listed a half-dozen additional items. The latter listing is every bit as permanent as the former, and happily so, for it includes the LARGE FLOUNDER TOPPED WITH SHRIMP CURRY. The fish is indeed large, and it is whole, fresh, prettily browned, and covered over with lots of crisp shrimp that are mingled with strands of sweet red pepper and green peppers—little hot ones—in an oil that is at once creamy, fiery, subtly fruited. You get a good chicken dish here, called kai yang—many sections of bird, deep fried and crusty, which you dip into a cool, spicy fruit sauce. The only duck dish is the one listed on the blackboard as ROAST DUCK TOPPED WITH CHEF'S SPECIAL SAUCE $9, but not otherwise described. The item seems inspired—if that is the correct word—by Chinese cookery, consisting as it does of great chunks of the duck, with peppers and pineapple, in a hot brown sauce dotted with green peas. It is well made—the flavor of the duck is vivid despite the competition—but takes getting to know.

If you come here only once—and if you tolerate intense spice—do not pass up the nam sod. This is minced pork served at room temperature (and that condition in itself deters some). But the pale ground meat is studded with whole peanuts and strands of sharp onion, it is moistened with lime juice, and it is made fragrant with a heady admixture of cilantro and bits of fresh ginger—a stunning dish. A couple of good beef dishes: pra neua, a kind of beef salad, the slices of meat mixed with onion and scallions, all in a dark, sour, spicy sauce; and neua pad king, slices of charred beef with onion and mushrooms and strands of scallion greens in a sauce that is flavored with ginger. The noodle dish to have is the one marked with a star—pad Thai. These are fried noodles, a little dry and crackling, slightly sweet, mingled with chopped peanuts, bits of white scallion and green, shrimp, and chopped egg, the whole fiery hot.

The desserts are puddinglike and dull.

★★BARBETTA

321 West 46th Street
LUNCH AND DINNER. CLOSED SUNDAY.
Reservations: 246-9171.
Credit cards: AE, DC, MC, V.
Expensive.

Outdoor cafés and dining gardens are showing up around town in record numbers. But for eating out of doors, nothing has so far touched the wooded court that is this establishment's tranquil oasis out back. The peaked white umbrellas, linened tables, and gurgling fountain that fill the clearing are a setting for a classy picnic indeed, with not only moonlight but many of the comforts of indoors to boot, including the occasional cat—they explore in the bushes and walk along the tops of the low garden walls just as if they were sentries on guard.

Its outdoors has always been Barbetta's main lure, but these days the food—which was never less than very decent—is a little better than ever, some of it even first-rate. If you are interested in trying a lot of it, begin with what the menu refers to as the "Grande Antipasto Piemontese" (Piedmont food is this restaurant's specialty). It includes a creamy, emerald green paste of robiola (rich Italian cream cheese) and fresh basil; a brandied mousse of buttered, well-seasoned liver; slivers of cold eggplant imbued with oil, rimmed with blackened skin, dotted with tomato sauce and cooled melted cheese; fresh squid in a spanking vinaigrette.

If you liked that basil mixed with cheese, you will like it again in pesto on hot pasta, for the sauce is powerfully fragrant with fresh basil, and the narrow, flat noodles called trenette are cooked to the proper point—tender but firm. Barbetta's primavera sauce, also served on flat noodles, is of a tart tomato brightness that manages to dominate the dish without obscuring the flavors of the fresh green vegetables that are its bulk. Some days lots of rice dishes are offered, but the house pushes risotto Piemontese: The dark, nubbly grain, oiled and moist, is mingled with mushrooms and small slices of liver—an earthy and satisfying dish that is at once primitive and subtle.

The cold whole trout is cooked until its skin is crisped, then marinated until it is tart—an utterly refreshing summer dish. The cold bass is fresh and firm, but its thick mayonnaise is rather heavily salted. Happily, the tuna sauce in this restaurant's vitello tonnato is not recognizably of canned fish—the weighty puree, polished with oil and studded with capers, is spread across broad slices of cold veal that are fibrous but tender, a little crusty at the edges. You may have your veal hot: The paillard is very delicate, barely browned, its blood-pinkness just cooked away, super when you squeeze on a bit of lemon; but the brandied scaloppine with wild porcini mushrooms, though otherwise well prepared, is dominated by an excess of the booze. Good birds: a charred duck, the rich meat strikingly cut by its fruity—not sugary—lemon sauce, and a pot-roasted squab buried in a tomato-and-vegetable sauce that is artfully soured with lemon. Hot slivers of sautéed sweetbread are mingled with wild mushrooms and a dark, winy marsala sauce— the rich meat is very nicely browned.

Sharp Parmesan cheese is usually on hand, as well as strong, biting Gorgonzola. For an Italian restaurant, this place turns out a mean chocolate mousse—thick, dark, bitter-sweet, adorned with whipped cream that is rich yet light. The St-Honoré is mostly a light puff pastry, its syrup glaze caramelized, its custard filling smooth and cool and sweet. Some of the desserts are even Italian, including a zuppa inglese of good sponge cake, a judicious amount of rum, and the house's splendid whipped cream.

When it rains, you eat inside—crystal chandeliers, brocade-upholstered chairs, silken drapes, the works.

★ BAROCCO

301 Church Street (at Walker Street)
DINNER
Reservations: 431-1445.
Credit cards: AE, DC, MC, V.
Medium priced.

A noisy, convivial, thriving place in which the highly conversational customers at the tiny, closely assembled white-linened tables are quite upon one another, to their apparent indifference. The square room is low ceilinged, dimly lit by soft-glowing Deco light fixtures mounted on the walls, and in it you are surrounded by glass—big vene-tian-blinded windows that look out on the intersection of Walker and Church, a mir-rored wall above the black banquette that runs along the room's east side, panels here and there of those glass bricks that look like big ice cubes, all to a slick, slightly glitzy effect. The illumination is not so dim that you fail to discern the exposed pipes and ducts that crisscross the ceiling, the valves and wheels connected thereto. The background music is distinctly audible above the talk. Neckties spotted here, if any, are the whimsical accessories of certain ladies' blouses. This is TriBeCa, Manhattan's frontier, and every-one is up to something, or is young enough still to think so.

The waiters and waitresses pick their way through the furniture and guests, turn to the next blank page of their order pads as they fly, give and receive information and instruc-tions with dispatch, inform that the special sardines of the day (they do not explain why there are unlisted dishes "of the day" when the menu is printed and revised daily) are hardly prepared at all (decapitation aside), being as they are marinated raw and served in the herbed and well-seasoned oil in which they were steeped, skin and bones in place and quite edible, the flavor of the oiled little swimmers at once oceanic and gentle. What is given as "verdure al forno" will seem like caponata to you (the name it goes by another night), but whatever you call it, it comes as a substantial mound of baked and cooled vegetables slicked with olive oil, the chunks of eggplant and tomato, the sliced peppers, the onions and celery and slivers of olive all mingled with sour capers, and quite rousing with the house garlic bread ("fettunta," $2 the hefty slice, crusty outside, soft but chewy inside, the garlic pungent but not overpowering). You are advised that "the chef will not" (as if it is a matter beyond house control) *divide* an order of pasta (much less prepare a half order), so your spaghettini con pomodori freschi, when it arrives in its deep plate, is accompanied by a bare plate onto which the more adroit member of your party transfers approximately 50 percent. This is a perfectly good and simple pasta dish—firm noodles, a tangy and chunky tomato sauce, sprigs of fresh basil—but it is undone by its admixture of hot pepper, an alien presence that has no business (and performs no function) among those straightforward ingredients. You will be more content with the ravioli, their emerald-green hue (unaided, spinach does not create this effect) merely a distraction, for the pasta envelopes are supple, their spinach-and-ricotta filling smooth and rich, their red sauce tangy. But charcoal-gray is today's hot pasta color (squid ink its pigment), against which the rings and lengths of squid with which the long strands of spaghetti are mingled gleam iridescently. The broth of the dish, however, is too thin to be called a sauce, and though the liquid is briny and impressively dusky, it is without the inky sea-gaminess of this stuff at its best.

On a good day Barocco grills a whole fresh snapper, delivers it to you very handsomely packaged in its crisped, metallic-pink skin—the fish is firm, cooked through, juicy, all its snapper flavor intact. On a lesser day, the four giant shrimp that, in their shells, have been peppered, parsleyed, and grilled on a wood skewer are, with respect to three of them, sweet and crunchy, and with respect to one of them, distinctly off. A nicely grilled chicken, its skin crisp, the moist meat done to the bone, has all the flavor of a Cornish hen (none), though the rosemary with which it is prepared helps. Rosemary again—this time it clings to the surface of a judiciously grilled veal chop, suffusing the browned meat with its heady flavor. Your medium-rare lamb chops arrive blood-rare, but they are good anyway, handsomely striped by the grill and redolent of garlic. The steak, though decent, has been fired and nothing else, and in a restaurant of this type, you expect the influence of oil, garlic, an herb, something.

The ricotta cheesecake does this imitation of a cream-cheese cheesecake—it is sugary and heavy on its doughy pastry. The peach tart is many substantial chunks of ripe, fruity fruit on a much better pastry.

★ BERNARD

145 Avenue C (at 9th Street)
LUNCH, SUNDAY; DINNER, DAILY.
Reservations: 529-3800.
No credit cards.
No liquor.
Medium priced.

Presumably one ought to consider Bernard in disregard of its surroundings. A restaurant, after all, is a restaurant, and what with the availability of New York's for-hire door-to-door vehicular transportation, no spot of civilization buried anywhere in the city's urban jungle is farther away than curbside chez vous. But just as there are those who insist you cannot know the art unless you know the artist, that the work itself is not all, others hold that the restaurant Bernard is not all of Bernard, that it is defined by the environment in which it maintains life—that, in other words, geography is destiny. Unfortunately, it all, how you say, depends. The Upper East Side, for example, does not define Tavern on the Green—that circus could be anywhere. But this is Avenue C at 9th Street, a setting nothing can ignore. Taxi here, sit down for dinner, and your thoughts immediately run to images of contrast, Hilton Hotels in Calcutta, country clubs in the Siberian tundra. Not that Bernard is any kind of posh, rather that it is the best of the restaurants that have opened in any of the experimental neighborhoods the government established to evaluate the long-term benefits of benign neglect. If you wish to prepare a study of your own, show up while there is still light in the sky, wander around these environs. You will see buildings that are not only abandoned, but in a seemingly permanent state of semidemolition, boarded-over storefronts that have been vacated for reasons other than rising rents, small city parks—or are they vacant building lots?—that serve also as encampments, complete with tentlike housing. In fine weather the streets are thick with people, as they are also in bad weather. If Bernard is a sign of impending gentrification, you cannot tell it from its external appearance, for the restaurant in no way calls attention to itself—there is neither a sign to identify the establishment nor a house number for those who have only the address. Happily, you will know the place at once by its situation relative to the beacon diagonally across the intersection from it, a spiffy video emporium that, all bright lights, heralds the new age.

Bernard, on the other hand, even on the inside, has chosen to harmonize with, if not to mirror, its backdrop. Which is to say this renovation of an ancient storefront is not of the gut-it-and-start-over variety, is, rather, a fresh coat of paint and lots of plants. Still, there is white linen, air conditioning, sweet service, and at around 8:30, an amped accordionist who, after his set, goes from table to table passing the plate. From certain parts of the L-shaped room you get a good view of the open kitchen and of the cook, who is in a white athletic shirt, tight pants to just below the knee, and a baseball cap worn backwards. Sometimes folks wander in the front door, a gent selling roses wrapped in clear plastic, children on a dare, occasionally someone in need of directions to Avenue C. But the crowd at the tables (each of them seated on one of thirty different kinds of secondhand side chair) is well washed and ironed, pioneers of respectability, citizens who are in this neighborhood because they would rather die than leave Manhattan Island, and would rather die than drop $700 a month, per room, on rent. Occasionally a carload of uptowners comes by, throws itself a condescensive slumming party at one of the big tables, leaves in the waiting car in which it arrived. The house is French, and transatlantic visitors sometimes show up, kiss their charming hostess on both cheeks, sit down to what is given as "Organic French Food."

It is more organic than French, for most of the hot food, from a menu that changes daily, is grilled, a cooking method that, theoretically, may be entrusted safely to trained orangutans, which is to say cheap help. Grilling is easier to master than, say, sautéing, but even the best-intended biped gets distracted now and then, looks away from the grill for a few crucial minutes, and that probably accounts for the done-to-death condition of some of these grilled (then chilled) marinated vegetables, which you wish were more aggressively seasoned and/or garlicked, for unaided they are dominated by the flavor of their blackening, though the freshness of the good ingredients is clear—the thick eggplant mayonnaise served with the dish is fine but does nothing for the vegetables. Happily, the griller was attentive when doing the shark, and these nuggets of hot fish are firm and juicy, fibrous but tender, set in a good sauce, dark and winy, that is flavored with sesame seeds. Sautéing is undertaken, however, and these sautéed shiitake mushrooms are of exceptionally concentrated flavor—they are mingled with mustard greens and Swiss chard, and they are powerfully garlicked. Garlic again, this time chips of the raw and pungent article strewn over the beef carpaccio, which is tender meat, oiled and black-peppered, garnished with slices of lemon.

Once again you put yourself at the mercy of that griller, and you are served fillets of sturgeon that have been reduced to fibrous mats. You grow cautious, go for the blackfish because it is baked, not grilled, and sure enough this usually mild-tasting swimmer has more flavor than the sturgeon, is thoroughly imbued with the taste of the oregano with which it is baked. Grilling a chicken is less exacting than grilling a fish, and this bird is juicy within its charred skin, strongly garlicked, overlaid with sweet dark-sautéed onions. The grilled lamb is sliced meat cut from a joint, is tender and of good lamb flavor, is notable for the array of fresh (and, of course, organic) vegetables with which it is served. Good vegetables garnish most of the main courses here.

The lemon mousse is fresh and bright, arrives in a champagne glass, is thick with fresh strawberries. Eschew the strawberry custard, for the berries have grown tired after their long immersion in the custard. You cannot complain about the crème caramel— after all, you have uncomplainingly consumed hundreds just like it. But the chocolate mousse, if not a thing apart, is at least of a rare high order, the dollops of chocolate glistening, almost black, and of deep chocolate flavor—they reach you in a pool of coffee sauce that is not quite strong enough to keep you awake.

Do not forget to bring your own wine, for the nearest liquor store, a couple of blocks north, is one of those places in which all the bottles and all the help are behind clear bulletproof plastic, and the shop specializes in the likes of Riunite and the wines of Barton & Guestier.

★★★★ LE BERNARDIN

155 West 51st Street
LUNCH AND DINNER. CLOSED SUNDAY.
Reservations: 489-1515.
Credit cards: AE, DC, MC, V.
Very expensive.

Never before has fact become legend as fast as the fact of Le Bernardin. Nothing more need be done. Let the restaurant fall into dysfunction and disrepair, reverence would be the payoff, never mind never an empty table. You half expect, what with the future assured, evidence of the sins of old age here in the establishment's youth, maybe a bit of overbooking, perhaps a dash of scorn for unfamiliar patrons, conceivably a more casual approach to the cooking than obtained during the first years. You will have to look elsewhere for reinforcement of your cynical side. Le Bernardin is not flawless, and it is not exactly as it was when it was new—if nothing else, the nervous excitement is gone —but if you remain capable of being thrilled, the thrill is not gone. And if Le Bernardin seems now to have found a natural slot for itself on the local scene, that has been accomplished by an adjustment of the scene, not of Le Bernardin, for this is that great rarity, a restaurant that redefines, even if only a little, the very notion of a restaurant.

But though this is an imposing physical place, with respect to its looks it redefines nothing at all. It is in fact part of the minor miracle of Le Bernardin that its culinary individuality is not subsumed in the intended monumentality of its architecture, albeit for many who would otherwise fail to grasp what the fuss is about, the grand space serves as a satisfactory explanation. If you see this dining room plain, however, its message is plainly deceptive, for it bespeaks—reverently—the traditional, while within it are served seafood dishes (and almost nothing but seafood dishes) the like of which, a decade ago, would have gone back to the kitchen, after one bite, for more fire.

Here you are, store level of the headquarters building of nothing less than the Equitable Life Assurance Society of the United States (landlords to and backers of Le Bernardin), a corporate entity whose balance sheet tilts with every fourth fatality in the northern half of the western hemisphere, so how come, you wonder, not health food?—instead of, that is, the almost cooked, barely cooked, and uncooked seafood that here obtains, which any life insurance executive of only yesterday readily could have identified as sources of grievous viral, bacterial, and parasitic disorders. Anyway, at Le Bernardin you scorn these hazards in a setting that would persuade even the exec that here he is safe, for it encapsulates (if that is what so spacious a capsule does) all that is most board-chairmanly in executive suite design. Le Bernardin is a great rectangle of a room, high ceilinged and softly lit, all dark blue and stained wood, its front window, which runs the long length of the place, hung with pale curtains of pleated gauze, the well-spaced tables clothed in white linen (a few of them aglow in the light of overhead spots) and surrounded by capacious armchairs and side chairs upholstered in blue cloth of a soft water-lily pattern, the total effect massive and commodious, like the lofty common room of an ancient club. As in all ancient clubs, paintings hang on the walls—these of the sea and seafood, boats and watersides—and they are part of the redemption of these otherwise stolid quarters, for though none of this art is immortal, it is handsome, is part of what humanizes the businesslike interior. No closer to immortality, but an even greater part of what warms this room, is one Maguy Le Coze, mistress of Le Bernardin (and sister of its chef), a smashingly attired presence whose looks and charm quite take your mind off the frumpiness that, by unavoidable comparison, she imposes on those around her at tables other than your own.

Your attention to Maguy is distracted only by the works of the Le Coze in the kitchen, Gilbert, who turns the trick with the likes of this pounded (raw) tuna, a great rosy pink circle within the rim of your large plate, the fresh, sweet fish, battered almost to a paste, but with its fiber intact, glistening with the oil that enriches it, and strewn with minced chives, which give it tang and sparkle. Raw fish again, this time black bass, a species that has swum in the Atlantic presumably since pre-Columbian times, but which became a common New York restaurant item only after it appeared on this restaurant's first menu. Le Coze fashions it into a tartare to which black caviar has been added, and of which you receive three egg-shaped masses arranged like the points of an asterisk, with them dark-toasted crusts of bread that are soft at the center—you eat the stuff straight or on the bread, and it is notable for its tender stickiness, and for the keen zest of the caviar to the delicate fish. Le Bernardin is not without an occasional comedown, as for example this truffled salad of sea scallops, in which fresh greens in a vibrant vinaigrette are surmounted by thin scallop slivers under a couple of disks of black, nutty truffle—all is well but for those scallops, which are at best of fugitive flavor. But there is no shortage of flavor in the fricassee of shellfish, tiny clams, tiny mussels, oysters, all in their shells, and all bathed in a sauce that, tasted alone, is an herbed and buttery brine, but which does different things to the different mollusks: merges with the oysters, gentles the tender clams without at all undoing them, enriches and heightens the mussels in their shiny black shells. The house obtains Louisiana shrimp that are, of course, devoid of iodine, broils them in their shells, serves them split in a buttery sauce, sweetened by shallots, that is greened by the parsley that makes it fragrant—this is an elemental dish, a clear expression of shrimp flavor underscored by a sauce that is at once rich and light. The house lists clam chowder, and just as this French enterprise on American shores makes do with American seafood solely, so it makes do with chowder as an American dish, does not Gallicize it, tries merely to perfect it, and though the bits of clam in this bowl have been toughened in the making, the nubbly soup is otherwise a model blend of unthickened creaminess, peppery seasoning, tiny nuggets of firm potato, and briny clam flavor.

What is listed as "Lobster and Mashed Potato Pie" would better be given as "Lobster-and-Mashed-Potato Pie," in which case you might well pass it up in favor of a preparation in which the crustacean is less alloyed. But there is nothing wrong with the rather country dish in this urban setting, a casserole of mashed potatoes, browned and crisped on top and thick with chunks of lobster that are moist, supple, and of vivid lobster flavor in their sturdy tuberous setting. Finfish are most of the main course menu: poached halibut in a vigorous and herbed-green vinaigrette—you may find the snowy white meat obscured by the powerful sauce when you take but a little of the former in much of the latter, but as you go through the dish you note a dazzling, constantly shifting interchange between the components; browned fillets of pompano in a pool of butter that is dappled with green splashes of Italian parsley of heady flavor; that black bass again, a fillet, its attached skin crisped, set in a pool of brick-red lobster sauce of powerful lobster shell flavor, and garnished, stunningly, with a ball of potato-and-fennel puree, the three elements in wondrous contrast to one another; the pavé of codfish, a thick block of the sturdy white fish, its glistening interior rare, almost pink, its top coated with a dense layer of black caviar, the whole set in a pool of briny cream and garnished with a sprig of dill—which, if you consume a bit of it with each bite, leavens and livens the stout seafood; and these thin-cut scallops of salmon in a preparation credited to Troisgros, their barely cooked surfaces whited a little, the rare interiors a glistening coral, the strands of sorrel in their buttery sauce sour and metallic, striking foils to the pink meat.

Fifteen dollars will get you a glass of port and a slice of Roquefort, the blue-veined cheese strong and deep and creamy, and not a bad transition from those seafoods to these sweets: an almost weightless millefeuille of flaky pastry interleaved with thin slices of tart apple and sweet white raisins, set in a pool of sour-apple sauce, and garnished with a ball of icy apple sherbet; another millefeuille, sheets of pastry again, between them an airy pistachio cream, the whole in a chocolate sauce that is black, polished, intense; a dessert that seems at first like something children make in a refrigerator of store-bought crackers and whipped cream, which, when you set aside that impression, is a delicate interplay of crisp, cool chocolate wafers and fluffy banana mousse; the house chocolate cake, light for its richness, thick layers of sticky mousse between thin ones of black cake, their chocolate flavors of liquorlike clarity and strength; a couple of irregularly shaped sheets of crisp coconut meringue, between them browned, acid-sweet chunks of pineapple and a rich pastry cream—a dish of many taste and texture contrasts; and what is given as "a variation of caramel desserts," a fluffy caramel mousse, light floating islands onto which melted caramel has been dribbled, an exceptional flan that is cool and smooth, a caramel ice cream that argues in favor of the proposition that not every flavor is suitable for ice cream—all four arranged in a tangy (you guessed it) caramel sauce.

★ BICE

7 East 54th Street
LUNCH AND DINNER.
Reservations: 688-1999.
Credit cards: AE, MC, V.
Expensive.

Designed the way it is, Bice (bee-chay) would best be left untouched. But, big but, it is a restaurant, the interests behind it insist on letting people in, they add captains, waiters, busboys, everyone makes noise and moves around, which converts the lively-looking place into an aural and visual circus. It is like the effect you get if, for laughs, while watching an old-time Technicolor production number, you turn way up the volume and brightness on your TV. All of which is too bad, for this is a space niftily fitted out, albeit with so many points of visual focus, and so little provision for the absorption of sound, that the installation succeeds in inverse proportion to the number of people present to enjoy it. Bice's façade is of doors that fold away, so that the softly lit barroom —polished wood, a handsome curved bar, cocktail tables of pink marble, tall wine cabinets, and colorful modern art—is a quasi outdoor café if the weather is balmy, and if you are having your drink at the very front, hard by the zephyrs of East 54th. The dining room farther in is more brightly lit. Its overhead is a modernistic version of a beamed ceiling—it rises to four peaks, each of them rimmed and strutted with metal beams, some pewter colored, some painted white. Glowing light fixtures of polished brass and parchment are mounted on the walls, tasteful prints hang between them in thin black frames. The banquette that encircles the place is upholstered in a striped fabric of muted colors—olive, dull gold, raspberry. And the column that rises through the center of the room is flanked by similar banquettes that extend out from it like wings, and face both to the front and rear—on the shelf that is the top of each wing stands a huge white urn holding a great burst of flowers. The tables are covered with beige linen, the commodious armchairs are of honey-colored wood, the carpeting—the room's one false note—is a blue-and-ivory tartan that looks like a cheerleader's skirt. Like all fashionable spots, Bice is frequented by two crowds, the real crowd, and the crowd that comes to see them. Mostly the two miss each other, for the gawkers are here on weekends, when they encounter mostly one another rather than the midweek set. The latter is made up, in part, of chichi ladies in Miro dresses and wrist clocks, others pleased to be built like snowpeas and to wear their hair pulled back so tight it looks painted on; gents in unpadded double-breasted suits over polo shirts, and others who are more tailored—these latter sport cuff links, handkerchiefs in the breast pockets of their trim-fitting jackets, silken cravats, even the occasional cigarette holder complete with cigarette. This set visits from table to table, they relentlessly agree with one another and smile a lot, then move on.

Whatever you wear, you do well with the swordfish carpaccio, the thin-sliced, translucent, and vaguely pink raw fish applied like a film to the big round plate, moistened with good olive oil, and strewn with strands of carrot and celery, dice of tomato. You do equally well with the lobster-and-arugula salad, the morsels of shellfish, tepid, moist, and of good flavor, garnished with hearts of palm and slices of ripe avocado, and set on a platform of the strong wild greens—a dressing that clings enriches the dish. Have either of those rather than the grilled eggplant, the thin sheets of the vegetable fibrous and of no eggplant character, the bread stuffing mealy, the tomatoed topping of melted cheese not enough to make the dish. One night your waiter assures you that the house does not make half orders of pasta, the next night another fellow winks at you, says that *for you* he will arrange half orders not only of pasta, but of risotto. Anyway, half orders are two-thirds the price of full ones, and the gnocchetti sardi al Gorgonzola, though in a good, parsleyed, and powerfully salty cheese sauce, is of little curls of pasta that insist on reverting to shape; the taglioline primavera are thin strands of noodle in a soupy mush-room-and-vegetable sauce that comes to life only when thickened with an abundance of cheese; and the risotto nero is a watered version of the black squid-and-rice dish that is devoid of sea-gaminess.

Italians do not find halibut in their own waters, but they manage well with the ones they find in New York—this fillet, fluffy and white within its grill-marked surfaces, is of sweet flavor, and it is cleverly garnished with warm chopped tomatoes in warm vinaigrette. A little garlic and much salt and pepper have been applied to the surface of the baby chicken, so when it is grilled, the browned skin becomes a sharp zest to the pale meat. The sometimes available osso buco is undercooked in its sour sauce, so if it is veal you want, have what is listed as rack of veal, the supple meat pale, tender, and of a clear, homey roast veal flavor. The battuta di manzo is pounded-thin beef, oiled and blood-juicy, its vivid flavor emphasized by the garlic, rosemary, and black pepper that have been applied to its surface.

Bice makes much of its gelato, but it is eggy, almost custardy, cloying to the American taste for American-style ice cream. You may have yours with warm apple pie, which is applesauce on a pastry, which reaches you at once and cold (the house is in a hurry, wants to turn you over promptly, means to recover its investment by Labor Day). The cheesecake is of cream cheese on something that, while it looks like a graham cracker crust, tastes like nothing at all—the thing is rich, is served with spooned-on strawberries in syrup. The chocolate cake is a thickness of sweet chocolate under a darker, craggy chocolate top.

• LE BILBOQUET

25 East 63rd Street
LUNCH, DAILY; DINNER, MONDAY TO SATURDAY.
Reservations: 751-3036.
No credit cards.
Medium priced.

This is the one that, when it first appeared, operated without a published phone number. It was assumed the place was about the business of being, how you say, exclusive. But no, that is not this establishment's bag. Rather, it was determining just how much it could get away with, and in the early experimental days it tried to get away without a listed telephone, imagining that spouses, administrative assistants, messengers, et al, would be dispatched in all weathers for purposes of making reservations, cancellations, deposits—who knows, maybe even donations, for no one could tell what sacrifices these Americans would make if the establishment inflicted upon them sufficient contempt. Well, the no-telephone ploy did not produce (when his telephonic cord is severed, an Upper East Sider is not cowed, he is addled), but much else did.

First there is your waitress (French) who feels that it is required of her to define for you, item by familiar item, the entire menu, including such puzzlers as le pâté, le steak tartare, and la salade de poulet, which, her beguilingly accented English being what it is, takes her as long as it will take you to eat—your enchantment is such that you do not explain to her that the ordeal is unnecessary, not to say inefficient (inasmuch as the entire floor appears to be under her care), that others are expressing by dramatic gesture their need for her assistance. Then, another time, there is your waiter (French) of the other persuasion, who tells you nothing until it is too late: that at least two (the two you ask for) of the nine still wines on the list are unavailable, that at least two (the two you ask for) of the six listed appetizers are "out." (You may have been plain lucky in choosing two main courses of the seven listed that, in fact, you may have.) All this in a room that could comfortably accommodate a ping-pong table and a couple of close-up players, which instead has been fitted out with a scant score of tables for two (for groups of three or more tables are pushed together), a zinc bar at the back, and art on the yellow walls, the effect of which density, when the place is, as normally, packed, being a concentration of noise heretofore known only to the eating places of the generation just behind the one that eats here. The accompanying background music is ordinarily inaudible, but even when the din is full blast the periodic dumping of dirty dishes into a tub concealed in a corner is punctuation that gets through. In the midst of all of which festivity there suddenly appears a managerial type in a red flannel shirt. He is sleepy, he crawls behind the bar, runs one hand through his tousled hair, lifts the phone with the other, pecks out a number, fails to make a connection, all the while regarding, with somnolent proprietary satisfaction, the scene, forty Americans shouting at one another inaudibly, all of them content.

They are eating the likes of that pâté, a dark, mousselike, livery thing speckled with bits of truffle and framed in dark jelly, moist and powerfully seasoned, and served with a great mound of harshly salty and acidic little pickles and with triangles of, for some reason, toasted whole wheat sandwich bread; or they are at a salade d'haricots verts, the thin green beans at once soggy and tough; or at les endives au Roquefort, the blades of endive arranged like points of an asterisk on the plate, at the center a ball of good Roquefort surmounted by walnuts, the decent ingredients in a distinctly sour pink dressing; or, when it is the soup of the day, at the onion soup, the hot stuff in a little ceramic pot, melted cheese and soaked-in-soup bread at the top, lots of onions at the bottom, the broth between dark and vigorous if utterly without distinction.

Mostly cold main courses, among them a caper-dotted steak tartare, a single anchovy across its top, that, though of fresh-ground beef, is little more than (timidly) seasoned meat, a raw hamburger rather than a steak tartare, much in need of the enrichment of oil or egg yolk or both. The chicken salad, happily, sports real chicken flavor, the walnuts are crunchy, the red and yellow peppers are fresh, and the mayo dressing is the right enrichment. When the poisson du jour is Dover sole, you are served the four imperfectly boned quarters of a fish, floured, browned in butter, firm, moist, and of clear sole flavor. And when lamb chops are the plat du jour, you suffer only for their being overdone—otherwise the three chops are tender and of pungent lamb flavor in their powerfully garlicked sauce.

Your waitress offers, in her puzzling but enchanting English, a plume pie, and you are served a plum tart that is of dull purple fruit on a pastry that tastes like marzipan. The tarte tatin is hot, but the chunks of apple, though dark, are only vaguely caramelized, and the whipped cream is loose. The lemon tart is best, thin disks of lemon over the tangy custard, and a decent pastry.

★★BISTRO BAMBOCHE

1582 York Avenue (near 83rd Street)
DINNER. CLOSED SUNDAY.
Reservations: 249-4002.
Credit cards: AE.
Medium priced.

That ten small tables have been inserted here tightly, where seven or eight larger ones could have been arranged comfortably, you are willing to overlook. A living, after all, must be made, and what with the rents in this neighborhood, etc. An excuse for the paraphernalia, however, you will not find, even if you look under the boldly patterned tablecloths, or within the folds of the napkins that sprout like fans from the large wineglasses, or between the glazed bricks of this one wall, or between the chocolate-brown-painted stones of this other, or tucked under the mattes of these dainty engravings, or behind the tall strips of glass that, wide enough to reflect a child standing sideways, look like salvaged mirror leavings. Nor will you have any luck looking under the red tiles that make up this floor, or over the ceiling's acoustic tiles, which are held in place by black bands that form a bold windowpane pattern—you can't miss them. And if, while looking, you find that you need more light, turn up the lights—they are housed in tulip sconces fastened to the walls. While you are at it, turn up the background music too.

But the price is right, most of the food is good, and this is a cheerful little family operation. So put on your dark glasses, come here, and begin your dinner with, say, a bowl of hot and buttery sorrel soup—it has the good sour edge of that green, and it is served with crusty croutons. Or begin it with this mousse of scallops, a two-tone semicircular slice cut from a loaf, the pale D-shaped portion the firm and peppery seafood mousse itself, the green base a contrasting stripe of spinach—the third color is pale pink, the tomatoed sauce in which the mousse is set. If you attempt to do caviar in a low-price prix fixe, something has to give—here it is the caviar, which is served, one little black dollop and two little red ones, on three silver-dollar-size blinis, with crème fraîche. To paraphrase the wise man, a little bit of caviar is like a little bit of love. Unless, of course, it is mediocre caviar. Avoid that in favor of the profiterole Bamboche, a nugget of chou pastry under a mixture of chicken and mushrooms in a creamy sauce that is fragrant of fresh dill.

The salmon is steamed in paper, with vegetables and dill, and if the process goes on too long, as it sometimes does here, the fish loses its oil, and thereby its character—but this is fresh salmon, and fine when fine tuned. The Bistro's menu is a brief one, but its range of ingredients is even briefer. That first-course combination of scallops and spinach repeats itself, but much more impressively, here among the main courses. These are sea scallops, six huge ones that have been sautéed until they are browned and crusted, and they arrive on a mound of strong spinach that is dotted with pine nuts and black raisins. Just before the dish is served to you, your waiter pours over it a pitcher of black butter that sizzles and pops when it hits the food—a good dish, in which each of the disparate elements is vivid. The Bistro stuffs chicken with chicken, makes a roulade of white meat around a greened chicken mousse, and serves the big knob of hot stuff in a creamy sauce of assorted wild mushrooms—including a few black, crinkly morels. There are sweet green peas and crisp carrots in among the eggy noodles on which the sweetbreads are served. The thin slices of organ meat are crisp, and the noodles are peppery and creamy —simple, striking food. The entrecôte is a good steak accurately prepared—it comes with a couple of crusty little potato pancakes.

For an extra dollar you may have a well-made little soufflé for dessert—the house flavor is apricot, and the soufflé has a clear fruit taste that is emphasized by a slight acid edge. The chocolate soufflé cake is weighty, moist, and intense—it comes with whipped cream. You may have some almond-studded vanilla ice cream—the hot chocolate sauce is poured on just as it is handed to you.

★ BISTRO DU NORD

1312 Madison Avenue (at 93rd Street)
LUNCH AND DINNER.
Reservations: 289-0997.
Credit cards: AE.
Medium priced.

You do well to come when the weather is fine, to arrange for one of the handful of tables out front on Madison Avenue—for the placement of Bistro du Nord at the corner of East 93rd is something of a leap, an encampment in Maine when no one has even pitched a tepee in Vermont or New Hampshire, and the establishment's lock on the spiffy-bistro market in this remote region has got the tiny, thickly-tabled interior of the place stuffed with humankind from one fringe of the dinner hour to the other. But while inside diners hastily drop their shoulders to avoid the glancing blows of waiterly hips, share ashtrays willingly and conversation unavoidably with their inches-away neighbors, the privileged few in the open air are free to stretch out, flick butts to the curb, and exchange flirtatious indecencies with the passing parade. Still, many months are cold, sometimes it rains, and even in good weather the tables outside are few, so chances are your Bistro du Nord experience will be an interior one, full of torment and despair, as you repeatedly ask yourself what you are doing here, and at intervals ask your charming hostess when your table will be ready for the doing of it—she smiles reassuringly, jollies you along expertly, and you willingly give her more time.

The site of all this clamor is a small one-and-a-half story store that has been divided into a small two-story restaurant. You are looked over on arrival, and if it is estimated you will have trouble standing tall in the mezzanine, you get a ground floor assignment. Those who apply to work here are similarly appraised, which is why the waiters, who at first appear to have been chosen for their youth, turn out to have won their assignments because they are not yet full grown. You enter to the lower level dining room, the floor of red tiles, the wood-framed zinc bar the size of a road map, behind it the stack of miniature stereophonic components that drive the pint-size but loud-mouthed speakers mounted on the wall above. Opposite the bar is the mattress-ticking banquette, beside it a row of tables for two that only appear to have been shoved together for a large group. This room is the full one-and-a-half stories high, so there is space for an airy chandelier overhead and, on the upper walls, for the large mirrors that lean forward and reflect back down any stray sound caught trying to escape. It is in this room that but a dozen waiting make up the throng passage through which is the particular occupational hazard of working in this place. The room is hung with photos, handsomely framed, of high life in black and white, and a stepwise series of them accompanies you on your walk up the narrow stairs to the crawl space that is the upper level, where you find more photos, these artsier (among them a few sepia-colored Paris scenes of Eugène Atget), another banquette, its tables as intimately arranged as the ones downstairs, and a handful of additional tables, a few of them at the railing over which you may look down at the crowd below. Throughout, the place is much pale ivory, a bit of wood trim, white linen, those photos, and little else—quite handsome, and about as tidy as the cramped space permits.

You figure the kitchen is no larger than what the public rooms lead you to expect, for the menu is of a brevity, albeit of a variety: two salmons formed into a squat cylinder, the deep-orange wall of strong smoked salmon, the contents a sticky salmon tartare overlaid with crème fraîche that is adorned with sprigs of dill; a striking, light, and lively dish given as "scrambled eggs," which, at most, should be given in the singular, for your egg, mingled with cheese and chives, fits easily into a decapitated eggshell, wears a substitute cap of good black caviar; caviar again, this time eggplant caviar, the rather too blender-ized puree, fresh-made and dominated by eastern spices, garnished with well-oiled sau-téed peppers mingled with slivers of garlic and green olive; an assortment of charcuterie, a purple, peppercorn-studded hard salami, a pale garlic sausage, and a slice of fat-rimmed pâté that is ripe, moist, pink at the center, judiciously seasoned.

Whoever ordered the tables held no discussions with whoever chose the dinner plates, for even when two of the latter are touching at table center, they violate the air space over the laps of you and your companion. Taking care not to put weight on the protruding edge, you undertake the pasta of the night, sometimes thick spaghetti in an almond pesto that is buttery, nutty, fragrant of basil, adorned with hefty strands of browned chicken. For a greater amount of chicken and no noodles, you order a half bird—its skin is browned, its meat has chicken flavor, the bone of its leg has been removed, a breading that is green with fresh herbs inserted in its place, with more breading packed between the skin of the breast and the white meat. A big winner is the salmon, the substantial fillet cooked through but rare, almost beefy at the center, served in a warm vinaigrette that sets it off dramatically—the fish is strewn with sprigs of fennel greens, a nifty note. A big loser is "le steak d'agneau haché au poivre," a lamb ham-burger from which the blood and flavor have drained away in the cooking.

The Bistro's crème brûlée is touched with sweet spice, livened by the thin strands of grapefruit rind across the top. What is called "le pavé (paving stone) au chocolat" is a block of thick, dark, rich chocolate mousse, slightly orange flavored, in a black chocolate sauce. There is much hard cider in the sauce sabayon you get with the decent apple tart.

★ BLUE NILE

103 West 77th Street
LUNCH, SATURDAY AND SUNDAY; DINNER, DAILY.
Reservations: 580-3232.
Credit cards: AE.
Inexpensive.

You descend half a dozen steps to a rambling room, clean and well lighted, its sanded pale-wood floor sealed and glistening, the walls surfaced with grass cloth and with Ethiopian art and paraphernalia—musical instruments, household instruments, instruments of unfathomable function: so far, your standard ethnic restaurant. But then you notice that something is missing. Where, you wonder, are the tables and chairs? And what, you wonder, are all these *things*? The "things," as well as you can make out, are elephantine egg cups made of straw, with removable straw lids, and when your hostess/waitress (she is in what you take to be native Ethiopian costume) invites you to sit, you notice that the straw construct (it is your "table") to which you are assigned is surrounded by foot-high, 12-inches-across, three-legged stools with concave seats—a curled-up cat would fit in one precisely. You, however, do not fit quite so well. Lower yourself onto one of these, and then lean a little, so as to move your center of gravity (you will find it at, roughly, the midpoint between your breastbone and your spine) outside the stool's airspace, and off you topple. It happens here two or three times a night. No one laughs. (Laugh, and you mock a whole culture—and the crowd here is largely academic, both faculty and student.) The victim rights himself with the solemnity of the forcefully evicted temperance ranter picking himself up off the sidewalk outside the saloon door—he is ruffled, but his seriousness of purpose is undiminished. (It is for fear of falling that regulars choose stools that enable them to lean their backs against a wall.) Mere fallers off, however, are the least of the sufferers. Many writhe throughout dinner, for to fold one ample abdomen and two abundant thighs into this low-down geometry effects a compression that pushes dinner back where it came from. Cruelty is it to lure here a certified stout.

The lid is removed from the top of your egg cup, a cloth is spread, and your food is brought on a tray that is lined with the crêpelike Ethiopian bread called injera. In addition, folded sheets of injera, looking much like linen napkins, are provided to each eater. If you and your company have ordered, say, four dishes, each of them—appetizers, salads, main courses, whatever—occupies a space on the single tray, and everyone eats from whichever of the dishes he fancies—but (big but) without benefit of silverware. You tear off a patch of injera, pick up a quantity of food with it, consume the two together. Since almost all the dishes are stews or mushes, after two or three sorties, your fingers are, inevitably, a mess. Dress appropriately. When you have run out of your own injera, you use some of that with which the tray is lined, or you obtain more from your waitress. Many of the dishes are flavored with berberé, a fragrant spice that is much of the character of Ethiopian food. And, happily, the food—some of it spicy-hot—is mostly good.

Among the foods you may have on your tray, there is azefa, a cold and lemon-sour paste, mustardy too, of lentils and onions—very rousing; shuro wot, a hot chick-pea mash, touched with ginger and basil, but too lightly—the dish is solid but pallid; yegomen wot, in which the sharp taste and fibrous texture of kale is offset by the plainer taste and texture of the chunks of potato buried in it—the slightly spicy dish is flavored with onions and peppers; doro wot, a very hot chicken item (the house chooses to call it "New York's spiciest dish") in which the chunks of bird, along with a single hard-cooked egg, are buried in a dark, sweet, strong sauce—the chicken is suffused with its flavor; yasa wot, supposedly a fish dish, but one in which the bits of seafood are simply a carrier for a mild berberé-flavored tomato sauce; ye'beg tibs, a dismayingly bony lamb dish in which too little of the pungent meat benefits from a very vibrant sauce that is sharp with black pepper and heady with rosemary; and tibs wot, another red-meat dish, this one much more satisfying, for there are chunks of sturdy beef in the hot, glistening, and garlic-flavored stew.

The desserts are Western, commercial, decent, the likes of carrot cake and pecan pie. Some of them have embarrassing names: "darkest Africa chocolate chip cake"; "the emperor's pumpkin-chiffon cheesecake." With dessert you get a fork.

Beer is best with this food, and Carlsberg, Dos Equis, and many other good brands are available, even Guinness Stout.

★ LA BOHÊME

24 Minetta Lane (near Sixth Avenue)
LUNCH, SUNDAY; DINNER, TUESDAY TO SUNDAY. CLOSED MONDAY.
Reservations: 473-6447.
Credit cards: AE.
Medium priced.

Note that the restaurant is named for Bohemia (La Bohême), not for the opera about an impoverished girl with a bad cough (La Bohème). Note, too, that by its menu, prices, appointments, and situation, it aims itself at that legendary Bohemia, composed of the more-or-less literate more-or-less poor—starving but happy artists, threadbare but secure academics, doing-not-too-badly-thank-you writers temporarily in the advertising business—that once was Greenwich Village. You may have thought, what with all that is new in New York, that that old crowd no longer existed, certainly not here in the Village, which got itself gentrified even before that concept was a dirty word. But no sooner did La Bohême turn up, than the earnest old set dug out its berets, tweed jackets, and baggy pants, its sensible shoes, burlap skirts, and heavy sweaters, and headed here as if this were Stewart's Cafeteria reincarnate. The NYU cells, it seems, have been dormant, not dead, and this is the rallying place they have been waiting for. (The sober gentlemen in suits and ties—with counterparts in matching jackets and skirts—that you see at tables here and there about the dining room, their watchfulness constant but unobserved, are here on duty.)

Blue-collar appointments, of course. A plank floor, walls of rough wood or plain stucco, butcher paper on the densely arranged tables. The wide-open kitchen at the rear is a people's theater in which honest work, complete with sweat, is put on daily except Monday. Particularly moist is he who, at arm's length, tends the pizza oven, the flames of which warm not only him but also the back half of this deep store, which is about ten degrees hotter than the front, an area that, in subtemperate seasons, gets an opposite treatment each time the front door is swung. The thick, shiny wires, red or blue or yellow, that emanate from gray colanders nailed high on the walls and hang in loops from the ceiling, are a designer's joke that the client lacked the self-confidence to laugh at and take down.

Bistro food plus pizza plus pasta, including a perfectly nice artichoke that suffers for being icebox-cold; a gamy and pistachio-studded pâté; slices of saucisson chaud that, though dotted with peppercorns, are a little flat, in need of their hot mustard—they are garnished with disks of new potato in a warm, oily dressing; snails that are plump and tender in their sizzling butter—you wish they were more assertively seasoned. The pizzas are of thin bread (one time crisp, another time mealy), the one known as Minetta a vigorous thing of black olives (beware the pits), strong anchovies, and sour capers on the herbed cheese; the one called Gitane a waste of decent snails, for they are nothing but six textural notes here among the red peppers, garlic, and black olives again—the pies are moistened with olive oil just as they are served. The spaghetti with fresh basil, though the green leaves are in evidence, lacks the herb's fragrance, and the cheese that you permit to be added to the coarse red sauce does little to liven it. The fusilli aux fleurs du jardin is two colors of the corkscrew pasta, several colors of vegetables, and a garlicked tomato sauce in which those elements fail to coalesce.

But then you order a fish of the day, grilled tuna, and the thin crosshatched steak of fresh fish is moist and of vivid tuna flavor in its pale, buttery sauce. Much flavor, too, in the slices and parts of the browned and crusty confit of duck, though the bird is a little dry. Of course there is a steak pommes frites, and the charred beef is tender and accurately done, the big mound of thin French fries crisp and light.

The browned apple tart is of fruit that retains a bit of its tartness on a flaky pastry. The frozen lemon soufflé is icy, acidic, and sweet in its crimson pool of berry puree. Have either of those rather than the marquise, a square of mousselike chocolate cake in a spongecake frame that is low on chocolate strength—its sauce, a Frangelico sabayon, seems only to wet it.

★ LA BOÎTE EN BOIS

75 West 68th Street
DINNER.
Reservations: 874-2705.
No credit cards.
Medium priced.

The particular accomplishment of this place is that in it are combined innumerable clichés (ilk: French country inn) to an effect almost wholly lacking in hilarity. Also combined in it are an abundance of small tables in a room almost wholly lacking in space, which may be why no one is laughing. So to eat here is to endure thy neighbor and his wife. (When, for example, neighbor forestalls his host from pouring the Côtes du Rhône because, as he puts it, he wants "to breathe it for a while," and when host thereupon nods with accordant solemnity and departs, wife grabs the bottle and pours herself some right off. Explains she, "I don't think they breathe anyway.") La Boîte is a semisubterranean little store that you approach by descent of a couple of steps to a glass-enclosed, lace-curtained alcove. Through that, then down a few more steps, and you are in the low-ceilinged wee cave itself. That ceiling, of course, is of rough plaster, and, as surely, it is beamed, as surely as the floor beneath it is of old wood. The walls all around are surfaced with burlap, except where they are of bare brick or rough timbers. And it hardly needs saying that there are wildflowers on the white-linened tables. What gives rooms of this kind their especial poignance is the lovingly assembled collection of mock mementoes on the walls and shelves. At La Boîte, however, you get not only the common framed prints and mirrors, copper pots and pans, painted pottery, basket, pitchfork, and scythe; but also the quite rare hand iron and wooden shoes; and the virtually unheard-of hatchet, brass bugle, blue-glass syphon, and—the winner—a little loom with a two-inch woof.

Your host is a nervous man within a calm one. He is slight, wears tinted glasses. You can actually see him not wringing his hands. His politesse is so without warmth that you pity him for his felt need to affect it. When he asks you if everything is all right, it is kindness to cut the whole thing short with a smile and a one-word answer. Now and again he escapes to an alcove behind the dining room, where he tranquilizes himself with a cigarette.

If only because it could not possibly be, the food is not as dated as the setting. The little menu even lists a stylish rillettes de saumon, which reaches you as a couple of cool eggs formed of ground salmon, their intense fresh-fish flavor sweet and breezy—the salmon comes with chopped onion, capers, a scallion, lemon. Order poached leeks, and you get three or four big ones at room temperature. They are fibrous, robust in fact, but tender, moist of a vinaigrette that is mostly good oil—the big stalks are strewn with chopped egg and garnished with glistening slices of cool ripe tomato. Saucisson chaud is a virtual inevitability on menus of this sort, and here the three great slices of fatted ground meat are redolent of sweet spice and garnished with a mash of parsleyed lentils —your waiter spoons a dollop of fiery mustard onto your plate. The place even puts forth a good fish soup that it styles "Marseillaise." The dark, saffron-flavored stuff is earthy and has a briny marine edge—it comes with hard crusts of bread and with a mild red-peppered rouille, but not with the pungent garlic sauce often used to fortify this dish.

The salmon is prepared in paper, and it is brought to you in paper, and your waiter tears the paper open for you (thanks), but leaves it on the plate as a kind of shell that you must hold aside with one implement while eating with the other—only to find that though the mustard sauce is not very mustardy, the fish itself is distinctly fishy. So you will prefer to take your chances with the fricassée de poussin à l'ancienne, coq au vin to you, and this is a good stew in which the chicken tastes like chicken, in which the mushrooms and onions and chunks of bacon add a good coarseness, and in which the sauce is smooth and thick and winy. You cannot fault these perfectly nice lamb chops, though the rosemary the menu leads you to expect is not in evidence. For abundance you opt for the kidneys, and you get a huge circle of them, clean and crunchy in their dark, stout sauce, arranged around a mound of buttery rice that is studded with sweet green peas.

A clafouti is a dessert of cherries (usually) baked in a pancake dough, and though it is intended to be a homey, heavy thing, when it is served cool, it can be almost gummy, as this one is—serving it in crème anglaise, as La Boîte does, adds a note of misplaced fanciness. But the sherbet is cleverly served, six spheres of three flavors, orange, pear, and an intense cassis, set in a pale-green pool of pureed honeydew. The so-called salade d'oranges is of cold orange sections, strands of tangy orange rind over them, and a couple of little balls of that orange sherbet, all set in cherry liqueur—sprigs of fresh mint are strewn over the fruit. The place turns out particularly light and firm oeufs à la neige, the great knobs of sweetened egg white—in crème anglaise—adorned with a dark butterscotch sauce that is thick with chopped nuts.

★★LA BONNE BOUFFE

127 East 34th Street
LUNCH, TUESDAY TO FRIDAY; DINNER, MONDAY TO SATURDAY. CLOSED SUNDAY.
Reservations: 679-9309.
Credit cards: AE.
Medium priced.

A shallow, narrow, low-ceilinged little rectangle of a place, noisy and sometimes hectic, with all the comforts of a crosstown bus plus food. At the controls, an animated French pixie. Her safe station is behind the short bar at the front, whereat the press of those waiting for tables, those leaving (they are trying to penetrate the dense little crowd to get their coats), and those entering through the front door combine to form a human gridlock standoff. Madame is calm throughout, exchanging pleasantries in her first language with countrymen of hers who obtained places at the bar early on. But her eye is always on the works, and when a place is free and ready, she plucks from the crowd those up next and hustles them to their table (which is of bare, dark-stained wood, a paper place mat at each place). All tables are along the circumference of the room. The floor is of wood. The ceiling is low. The plaster walls are casually hung with framed art. The place is worked by a couple of ladies who thump through their paces with energy and goodwill. They are French, and they thrive on this occupation, which seems to cheer as it wearies. Many of those who crowd La Bonne Bouffe work or live in the neighborhood. (The others shop there.) They include editorial types from Crown Publishers, medical types from University Hospital. Watch for the inevitable *Gastrointestinal Cookbook*.

The skeletal menu is fleshed out with numerous dishes of the day, among them, often, a splendid endive salad, an abundance of the crisp, yellow-tipped leaves surrounded by mâche, sprinkled with chopped hard-cooked egg and fresh parsley, dressed with good oil. You wish the asparagus had been cooked more briefly, for it is a little limp, but it is fresh, of vivid flavor, and it is livened by a pungent vinaigrette. Something given as "salade de primeurs" is a cold mingling of various marinated vegetables, much like a ratatouille, but crunchy, including such elements as cauliflower and green beans—the rousing concoction is tart, a little sweet, crisp, oily, strongly seasoned. The house pâté is salty, well fatted, strong. The snails surpass the New York bistro norm—they are plump and tender, in an abundantly parsleyed butter that, for all its salt and garlic, is not obvious. Even the onion soup is good—stout, thick with slivered onions, weighted with a chunk of bread, covered over with pully browned cheese.

A great length of snapper, fresh, moist, handsomely browned, is served strewn with sautéed mushrooms, capers, bits of lemon. Chunks of lotte, the French swimmer that calls itself anglerfish at this end of the Atlantic, is served the same way sans the lemon— you squeeze on the citrus yourself. Both these grenobloise preparations have the sparkle of fresh food, alertly prepared, brought to the table at its peak. There is always duck with orange sauce, sometimes duck with honey sauce—the good-tasting birds are well roasted, moist, a little crisp—and the sweetness of the sauces is tamed with vinegar. What the house proudly lists as "Escalope de Veau Bonne Bouffe" is an inelegantly weighty dish of veal, mushrooms, browned cheese—it is heavy but satisfying, perfect if plain hunger is your problem. Sometimes sweetbreads are offered, and the thin slices of organ meat are steamy, hot, fluffy within their crisped exteriors. Two great crescents of liver, sliced thin and then sautéed hot, are at once crusted and rare—the sweet, delicate meat is in a red-wine sauce that is thick with slivered shallots.

The fruit tarts are fresh, and there is a fluffy custard between the fruit and the flaky pastry, but the productions are somewhat unfortunately protected from the environment by a heavy glaze of clear syrup. The crème caramel and ice cream items—peach melba, poire belle hélène—are fine. Sometimes there is offered an almond chocolate torte— this dark and intense sweet is doused with almond liqueur.

The principal irritant is a policy of charging higher prices for daily specials than you are likely to anticipate from the prices of the menu items—that sweetbread special of the day, for example, is about as expensive as a filet mignon; a duck off the menu is higher than the listed one; etc.

★★BOULEY

165 Duane Street (near Hudson Street)
LUNCH, MONDAY TO FRIDAY; DINNER, MONDAY TO SATURDAY. CLOSED SUNDAY.
Reservations: 608-3852.
Credit cards: AE, DC, MC, V.
Very expensive.

Nestled among the TriBeCa warehouses, and hardly a taxi meter click from the Odeon itself, here is a French manor house built to full scale. Thirty gently sloping hectares of cabernet sauvignon around it (the area bounded by Canal Street, West Broadway, Vesey Street, and West Street would do), and an engraving of Château Bouley could go on a wine label. The great front doors could easily serve as the frontispiece for a modest south-of-France cathedral, and once within the anteroom onto which they give, you are surrounded by the massive walls, these the color of pale sandstone, behind which subtropicals keep their cool. In the spacious oblong dining room itself, three great columns are a row down the long axis, their heads the foci around which eight lofty ceiling vaults, four to each side of the room, rise to their peaks. The intended look is Provençale, there are antiques of the region here and there, the doorways and interior windows are in arched frames of dark wood, as are the big front windows—their sills thick with greenery—which are hung with pleated curtains of white gauze. The large linened tables—surrounded by capacious armchairs upholstered with elaborate tapestry cloth—are set with wildflowers in pottery vases, with Limoges china of a gay and fantas-tical botanic pattern, with little shaded lamps. The room has its false notes—the sophis-ticated harmless art, the slick swath of mint green that is the banquette along one wall, the functional dull-colored carpeting, all of which suggest that perceived necessity dic-tated compromises—or that a backer's taste did. It must be concluded that Bouley was installed in this remote corner of the city for reasons of real estate economy, for no one eating here is doing so for having failed to get a table in one of the places on West Broadway—these folks mostly come from uptown in cabs, or from across the waters in sedans, though sprinkled among them are a few who have converted nearby lofts into basketball courts for living. They are attended to by a formal staff in black and white, gents who know the menu and explain it patiently to their moneyed customers.

In its first days Bouley offered certain dishes that, you figured, were on the menu in artistic defiance of popular taste, since the eponymous chef, being also the proprietor, could choose not to pander. Surely no one expected to sell many sea urchin soufflés, or much eel, or even this lobster, being as it was embedded in cold jelly? Anyway, the items were delisted soon enough. The artist discovered that there is little satisfaction of self-expression alone. He found that he wanted also to be loved—and too few loved, for example, that clammy lobster. It was a dish more interesting than winning, experimental work in which chunks of good lobster meat were interred in a cold, brown aspic spread with a thin layer of white sauce, a dollop of black caviar at the center—chilling food at first encounter, also rousing, a poetic dish that yielded pleasure only in repayment of close attention. The smoked-eel millefeuille, on the other hand, was easy to like but, for most, hard to order, the named ingredient not a favorite in these parts, which is too bad, for the dish, a kind of napoleon, had immediate appeal, the shelves of flaky pastry interleaved with the smoky seafood and slivers of firm potato, all in a sauce that was dark and powerfully herbed. The fresh sea urchin and blue crab soufflé attracted little interest because, as food, sea urchins have charms solely for those creatures that are its natural predators—withal the little soufflés tasted like crabmeat, cheese, and not much else. But a word of pasta ensures the acceptance of any dish, and it may well account for the survival of the cherrystone clam ravioli, for though these noodle packages are in a light and creamy sauce that is thick with vegetables and minced clams, the whole clams that fill the ravioli have been rubberized in the preparation. Shrimp, wild mushrooms, and foie gras are the star ingredients in the panaché of three salads, the sautéed mushrooms woodsy on their spiky greens, the charred and crunchy shrimp of clear, sweet flavor in the eggplant wrappers, the blackened slivers of hot liver in striking contrast to the enriched spinach on which they are set. But thicker slabs of that same foie gras, served on their own, will sometimes reach you blood raw, and the so-called "corn blinis" with which they are served materialize not as blinis at all, but as a mound of cornmeal studded with whole kernels—nice, but not what you were sold.

Lobster, to which you responded so coolly when it was cold in jelly, is available warm, au sancerre rouge, that is to say in a red-wine sauce that is smooth and sticky, fruity and faintly sweet, very striking with the firm, moist meat of the crustacean. Plump and succulent sea scallops, lightly browned in the sautéing, are served with a pile of black-olive pasta, the gray strands mingled with slivers of vegetable, everything set in a fragrantly herbed red sauce and strewn with leaves of fresh marjoram. You wish these skin-on fillets of baby snapper were not a bit dried out in the grilling, for their spicy sauce of yellow tomatoes, fragrant of sage, suits the delicate, nutty fish. Ask for pigeon, and you get the whole bird: half of it roasted, browned, glistening, a little rare, and of vivid pigeon flavor—it reaches you on a slice of grilled foie gras; the other half, rolled up in a leaf of cabbage and braised, sports just as much flavor, is juicy and just as rare, its tenderness in nice contrast to the leaf wrapper. Morsels of sweetbread and kidney, the former oleaginous and rich within their crusted surfaces, the latter clean-tasting and crunchy, are arranged on your plate, with sautéed chunks of wild mushroom, in the form of a cutlet, little onions, lengths of green bean, and baby carrots all around, the whole in a sauce of cider vinegar that is herbed, smoky, and a little tart. The lamb, arranged over mashed potatoes, is rare and strong, and the good meat, moist of its juice, is garnished with a nifty zucchini tart: dime-size slivers of zucchini and yellow squash, under a good tomato sauce, on a flaky pastry.

Babas are eggy cakes that are usually moistened with liquor. Here three little ones, very light, form a circle with three eggs of intense, icy tangerine sherbet, all in a pool of light sauce that is tangy of Grand Marnier—a vivifying sweet. The chocolate entry is a trio: rich mousse in a spongecake frame; a fresh, moist, and dark layer cake, pistachio flavored, under a slick black icing; and an almost black sherbet. The soufflés are a mere duet, one of raspberry (whole berries in it), the other a nutted one of chocolate and pear, the two garnished with creamy ice cream, minuscule slivers of blueberry, tiny red grapes. The apple crêpe soufflé is a browned pancake folded around a rich and almost chewy apple sauce—it is garnished with a kind of fruit fantasy of raspberries, blueberries, dice of peach, quartered strawberries, all the fruit ripe and firm. The millefeuille of fig, though well made—layers of flaky pastry, between them a creamy filling dotted with bits of fig—lacks fig flavor, but there is compensation in the acidic citrus ice with which it is garnished.

★ BRAZILIAN PAVILION

316 East 53rd Street
LUNCH AND DINNER.
Reservations: 758-8129.
Credit cards: AE, DC.
Medium priced.

South America, to North Americans whose education about the physical world came from the *National Geographic*, means the tropics, lands where civilization and its amenities are but temporary clearings in a timeless jungle. This civilized clearing, in the jungle that is New York, is itself formed of those disparate elements, for though it is a tidy place, the greenery, broad wood beams, exposed brick, and native art hung through-out are assertive primitive elements among which the white-linened tables, smooth white-plaster walls, and the service of the cordial dark-haired waiters suggest a way of life stubbornly competing with nature. Like all Brazilian restaurants in New York, this is a comparatively inexpensive place, so it is frequented not only by members of the local Brazilian community but by neighborhood people on their lesser nights out, and also by members of those UN delegations (here in UN country), sent by nations for which a UN mission is a government budget item second in magnitude only to maintenance of a standing army.

Mindful of the limitations of their expense accounts, the diplomats begin their din-ners with one of the several low-cost soups, among them the vigorous caldo verde, an herbed and pungently salted chicken broth that is thick with collard greens, disks of crisp potato, morsels of strong sausage; or cream of black bean soup, a slightly thin and certainly not creamy substance that is, nevertheless, of vivid bean flavor—you add to the soup, according to your taste, the chopped raw onions served with it. For delegates from oil-producing states, there is the pricier aperitivos brasileiros, a couple of giant hot shrimp, sweet and crunchy, covered with bits of browned garlic, served upon a salad of no distinction that features lengths of canned hearts of palm. Similarly the abacate recheado, in which two other perfectly nice shrimp, these cold, surmount a fresh-made seafood salad, bound in a mayonnaise dressing, that is packed, too bad, into an overripe avocado.

As all the world knows, and as is printed on the menu, and as your waiter tells you anyway, feijoada is the national dish of Brazil. It is perhaps best described by what, more than anything else, it is not. It is not Japanese. It consists of individual plates of many things, among them a deep dish of beans in which are buried slices of fat sausage, lengths of thin sausage, little boulders of stewed beef; another plate of beans, and a gravy thick with onions, either of which you may spoon over the contents of yet another plate, this one laden with buttery rice, all of which you season with the powdery zest—a ground root native to Latin America—called manioc; raw oranges and steamy leaves of metallic-tasting kale complete the array and provide relief. This is a somewhat attenuated version of the genuine article, but it is solid food that will hold you until the holidays. The Pavilion, unfortunately, does not offer the peasanty codfish dishes you find in most local Brazilian places, so for sturdy seafood you opt for the vatapá, a thick and spicy-hot seafood puree that is dotted with nuggets of finfish and shellfish, onions and peppers, and served with the inevitable white rice. In such items as the moqueca de peixas, fish and clams in a sauce of palm oil and coconut milk, you detect a failed effort of fanciness. The big lobster dish goes as logosto catalão, chunks of lobster, removed from and returned to their big shell, in a nutty and creamy mushroom sauce that is browned a little just before it is served. Frango bossa nova is lots of dark-fried chicken, quite crisp and yet a little—pleasantly—greasy, strewn with bits of browned garlic, and served with redded rice that is studded with fresh vegetables. Lots of steak dishes, among them churrasco gaucho, a good slab of beef, tender, fibrous, salty, served with a pitcher of so-called gaucho sauce, a sour and hot-spiced relish of tomatoes, onions, peppers.

What the house calls "marmalade" is a compacture of pureed fruit, sweet, tangy, and dark. The guava shells are like preserves, the chunks of sweet fruit in a dense syrup— they are served with an inelegant Brazilian cheese. The banana cake is layered with ripe fruit. The winner is a dark brown milk pudding, thick and sweet, very nice with the good house coffee.

From the low-priced Brazilian and Spanish list, you order a half bottle of white wine, and it is maderized, must be sent back. Anyway, beer is the right drink with this food— pass up the more familiar Brahma for the brand called Tijuca, which has body, depth, and a touch of fruitiness.

★★★ BRIVE

405 East 58th Street
DINNER. CLOSED MONDAY.
Reservations: 838-9393.
Credit cards: AE, DC, MC, V.
Very expensive.

In every generation of restaurant owners, there are a few who think it warmhearted and humanistic and terribly cozy to have come up with the idea of a restaurant that will be not like a restaurant at all, but, rather, like someone's own (as it is egregiously put) home, when only a moment's consideration would reveal what they have always known but never thought, that there is as much sense in a restaurant like, say, an apartment as there is in an apartment that resembles a restaurant. Surely no one wants a living room that looks like the Oyster Bar? More to the point, no one heads out to dinner in search of the looks he just left (very likely a three-room simplex with six-foot kitchen, seven-foot ceilings, and plumbing that constantly clears its throat.)

You counterpose that, in New York anyway, certain living rooms could indeed make it as restaurants. Quite. But holders of titles thereto are not those who entertain the dream of restaurant as domicile. Consider for example Robert Pritsker, proprietor here. Brive's look suggests he is sharing with you the carefree days he spends in his narrow-gauge railroad flat. The linked cells are furnished in a style usually associated not with grander spaces, but with retail furniture outlets, in which almost every square foot of floor is given over to wares. Similarly Brive, in which there is nary a table to every seat at which one may march up and sit down. It is more a matter of pulling in your waist, of clutching your jacket tight (so the tails do not sweep someone else's table linen as you wriggle into position), of hoping it will not be necessary to leave your seat and return before dinner's end.

You enter to the most comfortable room of the restaurant's four in a row, commodious because there are no tables in it, only a small service bar, the reservation book on a stand, and, your first intimation that this is restaurant as dwelling unit, a sofa, upon which you would sit to wait for a table if ever this place were that busy. You proceed to the first of three dining rooms: at the banquette along one side (its cubist fabric matches the one on that sofa) the tables are as tightly assembled as theater seats, while the tables and antique chairs across the way are occupied by folks who wait with their hands in their laps, eat as if handcuffed, look behind them to judge the clearance before inching their chairs back to stand. Except for the Oriental rug on the floor the next room looks like a nursery in which each stroke of the Rorschach pattern on the walls (Plate 10) was created by an angry child who knew how to reject his food. Room three is a skylit appendage that is humanized by a bit of yellow-painted brick, a few paintings (which, in this close setting, you view through your reading glasses), and a padded panel that, though it obscures a view of the backyard, damps what would be intolerable noise if even a couple of those who fill this room's ten chairs got boisterous.

Like many households, Brive has its eccentrics, specifically the weird captains for which it has some renown. Not all of them, you understand, but there is this obsequious mouther you wish to be rid of as urgently as you want to be out of a net of clinging cobwebs. He hands you the menu and mentions a listed dish that is not available: "I'm soooo sorry. I'm terribly, terribly sorry." (The end of the world.) Of this night's substitution of sea scallops for bay scallops: "But they are the tiniest and most delicate available, and the preparation, I assure you, is *absolutely* unchanged." (A miracle.) To your request for water: "I'll see to it *immediately*." (You must ask for it again.) To your one-word utterance, Thanks: "Oh, my pleasure indeed." (You should have kept your mouth shut.) Women are addressed in the third person possessed, as in, "Would m'lady desire her coffee now?" You are not so foolish, but an unfortunate at the next table asks him if he recommends the liver. "*Wholeheartedly,*" he, eyes closed, hand over heart, intones, and the group of four cringes as one.

Pritsker's "humor." He invents dishes, gives them names that, meant to be funny, fall flat. (He does not know it, but as to what is funny, he is tone deaf.) He juxtaposes foods of disparate cultures, or what could be called fancy food with what may be called earthy food. Thus, from this elaborate kitchen, you are served lobster and Chinese meatballs, or

81

salmon "en sauerbraten," or chicken wings in paella. This is the kind of brandished salt-of-the-earthiness in which the American traveling in France says he likes French food as much as anybody as long as it's a hamburger ha ha. Most people outgrow it. Not Pritsker. But he cooks well, the dishes that are meant to shock are also eminently edible, and since this weakness may be his only flaw, you, as you would any harmless tic, ignore it.

It is like him, for example, to serve oysters on what appear to be potato chips, but which are listed as "celery root wafers," and which, being tasteless, have no bearing on the dish anyway. But there is no denying the fresh, plump, warmed-through oysters and the celery-root fragrance of a white sauce that, though rich, is almost airy—deep-fried threads of the root overlay the oysters, their crispness a good foil to them. The afore-mentioned sea scallops have nothing to apologize for, the handsomely browned and glistening meats of a silken texture and vivid flavor, the listed "star anise sauce" very much in the background, what with the vigor of the scallops and of the heady dill that adorns them. Until now you thought of the white bean as a bean that is, well, white and of a certain texture and flavor. Here the white bean is red, but you overlook that minor matter in the context of this multi-element salad and three-way polenta garnish: the beans in among vibrant greens and crunchy shrimp of bright and sweet flavor; chunks of artichoke hearts that, though soft, have lost none of their taste; and three dented circles of toasted polenta, the concavities occupied by, respectively, another shrimp, a salty anchovy, a sprig of rosemary—a diverting plate of food. You still find tongue in many New York restaurants, but all of them are kosher or kosher-style delis. Accordingly Pritsker cannot resist offering veal tongue as part of a fifty-dollar-plus prix fixe, the tongue-shaped slices of tender meat, coated with browned horseradish that has lost most of its potency, in a pool of redded oil that is studded with bits of vegetable, at the center of the plate a clump of strong spinach mingled with more horseradish, this time white and strong—the dish is fine but forgettable.

The title "Surf as Turf" is one of the poor man's more hollow-clanking jokes. (Were he to audition at one of the clubs in which aspiring comedians sacrifice themselves before an audience, a silent reception, punctuated by cries of "The hook, the hook," might well exorcise his delusion of wit.) The dish, however, is fine: the tail of the lobster in a vigorous shellfish sauce fortified with lobster coral, the unlikely garnishes porky meatballs, crisp water chestnuts. That salmon en sauerbraten is good enough to make you forget its self-conscious title, the substantial fillet juicy and of almost blatant salmon flavor in its dark vinegar sauce, with it a mash of sweet, crunchy cabbage wrapped in a deep-red cabbage leaf, florets of broccoli, crisp ginger. Duck breast two ways: rings of the pink meat packed with a salty olive stuffing; and slices of the meat, crisp skin attached, under sprinkled bits of marinated scallion—too bad a portion of the duck is too tough for teeth. Come here once, and lamb is the thing to have. Some Pritsker quirk must account for calling the thin-sliced meat "tournedos," but that does not detract from the succu-lence and lamb-pungency of the piled-up layers of juicy meat in their so-called rata-touille sauce—which, whatever it may be, at once sweetens, strengthens, and enriches it.

A "date tulip" is made by pounding part of a date into a sheet and forming the sheet into a small cup to which the remainder of the date is attached like an appendix. The cups are filled with a tangy lime mousse, they are set in a pool of tequila, and they are surrounded by three towers of pound cake that soak up the booze, thus becoming "babas au tequila"—a lively, bracing sweet. Most of the desserts are compendia, among them: a chocolate plate in which the crisp-topped muffin of chocolate cake is notable for its runny center; an assortment of nut cakes—almond, hazelnut, pine nut—in a liquored cream dotted with bits of candied fruit; and a wondrous lemon-and-poppyseed tart, the fluffy lemon curd much livened by the seeds, the tart just right in its coffee-flavored sauce—a dollop of bound, black, sticky-sweet poppyseeds is a bonus.

On Sunday casual dress is encouraged.

★★BUKHARA

148 East 48th Street
LUNCH AND DINNER.
Reservations: 838-1811.
Credit cards: AE, DC, MC, V.
Medium priced.

Consider, if you will, an otherwise dignified Indian restaurant somehow persuaded to identify its perfectly respectable subcontinental dishes by such titles as "Skewered Salad," "Mellow Cream Chicken," and "Fish du Jour," not to mention "Frontier Dal," and, for dessert, "Crème de la Crème" (the last described as "A classic recipe"). The restaurant's main courses, moreover, occupy a section of the menu headed "Bukhara Sapors*," and, sure enough, follow the asterisk, and you will come to a footnote, to wit, "*'Sapors': A quality perceptible to the sense of taste; flavour. From Latin sapor, taste, from sapere, to taste." The interests behind the place have apparently been sold the idea that, in New York, such gimmickry is what it takes to make a restaurant go (and that, incidentally, local consultants are masters of the technique of pandering to the barbarians who are the local market). It is both good news and bad that Bukhara will survive its own hype: On one hand, the place is of merit; on the other, some of its success will probably be attributed to the thinkers who vulgarized the place in the supposed service of public relations. The approach was surely conceived and committed at an all-night "creative" meeting, everybody grooving, for the boys even came up with a lofty slogan. Dig it: "Savor the flavor from a place in time." In its favor, it may be said that it will always seem new because it will never be remembered. Lardner! thou should'st be living at this hour. In his absence: "Capture the rapture in a spot real hot." "Down your din din in a manner Indian." "Taste of the best of East of the West of." Readers are dared to do worse. A contest will not be held.

Bukhara is situated in a midtown New York hotel, sees fit to give over part of its space to a "cocktail lounge." Accordingly, you enter between two worlds. The walls to your right are hung with groups of Indian copper trays, elaborately engraved and intricately painted, stunning art in the everyday. But to your left is the bar, presided over by a barman who derides orders for nonalcoholic drinks, and sat at by traveling business guys who exchange ribaldries with him, sedate themselves, manage to make it upstairs before passing out. Most frightening is the baby grand, which, from five to eight too many evenings of the week, is tinkled behind singing that is loud enough to be heard in the dining room. But you have faith, and you keep walking—to a dining room that is relief, both from what this place publicly says about itself and from that first encounter with it. The beamed ceiling is low, the light is soft, and the sound is muted. By way of four thick stucco columns (you could put a sofa along each of their four sides) positioned at the theoretical corners of a smaller square within this square room, the place is subdivided into sections, parts, niches—within them are situated well-spaced, massive unlinened

83

tables of deep-dark wood, most of them at banquettes, the seats and backs of which are plump cushions covered with patterned cloth of earth-red colors. Huge trays and urns of hammered copper—glinting red-gold—are here and there around the room, and clusters of copper lanterns hang from the ceiling. But mostly you are aware of the glorious rugs—of course, Bukhara rugs—that are aglow on the walls. Protruding into the dining room from its west side is the glassed-in enclosure that is the restaurant's kitchen—watch its operation, and you learn nothing of Indian cooking, but the installation does give off a friendly glow.

Much is made of the silverware you do not find at your place, for it is intended that you eat with your fingers (moist hot towels are supplied before and after you eat). If you prefer to use implements, ask for a knife and fork—*not* chopsticks. Before making that request, however, consider that, though the species has come far in fifty millennia, its antecedents include a smiling, ever-present monkey on everybody's back. Like other first experiences, after two minutes of eating with your fingers, it all seems atavistically natural, not to say habitual. Idiotically, the place provides large napkins with strings attached —you are meant to make the napkin into a bib by tying the strings around your neck, as if holding food with your fingers were less secure than using silverware. Of course the reverse is true, so if you wear your prettiest necktie, you may show it off throughout dinner. Just avoid fondling it.

Finger instead the roasted fish of the day, often pomfret (bream), a swimmer of vivid taste, the whole fish, in its skin, spiced, lemoned, and carefully roasted—the flavorings permeate the light, fresh meat. Prawns are roasted in the same oven, from which they emerge crunchy and sweet, their marine flavor potentiated by the citrus, garlic, and spices in which they are done. Lots of chicken on the menu, and though your instincts may steer you off the one encumbered with the name Mellow Cream Chicken, in this instance the dopey title does convey something of the dish, for the morsels of bird are marinated in cheese and cream (with spices) before they are skewered and grilled, and the browned finished product is at once succulent and light. What goes as "Khyber Chicken" is more like what you usually get in Indian restaurants, the lightly floured surfaces of the parts blackened a little, the meat fibrous and tender. Though veal is not a fundament of Indian cookery, it does not follow that veal may not be prepared by Indian methods. Accordingly, "Royal Veal" (it was midnight before they all jubilantly agreed on that one), a couple of chops that, having been soaked in a seasoned mixture of rum and yogurt before grilling, retain more moisture and exhibit more life and flavor than much of the veal you get in local French or Italian places. The "Lamb-è-Chasma" is a kebob item, the chunks of garlicked meat tender, blackened, of clear lamb pungency. Ground beef potently seasoned, then formed into sausagelike cylinders around skewers, then broiled, is given as "Bolan Rolled Beef"—the meat is made pale by the ingredients with which it is combined, but the glistening cylinders are of colorful flavor, tangy, sharp, heady of their spices. Beef of yet another color, "Escalopes Bukhara," consists of very thin sheets of the meat, interleaved with cottage cheese and dried fruits, and baked— each clump you sample differs from the last, now a creamy one, now one that is perfumed of some Indian spice, now one that conceals an exhausted chunk of pineapple.

With those main courses you may select from a brief list of vegetables, among them cauliflower, the crunchy and glistening marinated florets encased in the browned and spicy batter in which they were baked; and stuffed roasted potatoes, the giant tubers skinned, hollowed, blackened, and packed with a fragrant filling dotted with sweet green peas. Many breads, among them "Roomali Roti," which the poets on the account describe as "light as a handkerchief"—presumably much was lost in translation, for this bread has the texture of steamed matzo, though its wheat flavor is not bad. The mint paratha is livened by its sprinkling of the herb, the bharvan kulcha may be had with a thin layer of herbs and vegetables between the two of bread, and the khurmi naan is a bit like a pizza, the circle of bread spread with a light tomato sauce within its raised edges. The cool fruited yogurt is a nice foil to the hot food, and the place produces an exceptionally buttery dal, the thick souplike mash of lentils supplied, happily, with a spoon—theoretically you eat the dal by scooping it up with bread, but hours would be required to dispose of a bowl that way. Much is made of the supposed nonspiciness of this restaurant's food—in fact, much of it is hot, though never searingly. The heady, grassy green sauce on your table, however, is incendiary, and seems only vaguely appropriate to most of the dishes.

"L'Orange Crème" (it was getting toward sunup when the boys got around to naming the desserts) is two-thirds of an orange peel packed with grainy ice cream. Rasmalai, not on the menu, is a good dessert of sweetened cottage cheese in a pool of milk.

Beer is the best drink with this food.

★★CABANA CARIOCA

123 West 45th Street
LUNCH AND DINNER.
Reservations: 581-8088.
Credit cards: AE, DC, MC, V.
Inexpensive.

Life in Brazil is ever gay, or so you may conclude from depictions of it in the brilliantly colored murals that adorn the walls of the stairway leading to this primitive second- and third-story eating place. One flight up, through the parti-colored door, and you are at the pea-green plastic lunch (and dinner) counter and bar, which is lined with stools upholstered in plastic the color of Sunkist oranges. The ancient coffee urn looks like a public triumphal sculpture in stainless steel. The nailed-up wooden shelves suggest the carpentry in a general store in a jungle clearing. Here at the counter New York's Brazilian bachelors eat with dispatch and drink Brazilian beer from the bottle. And nearby, at most times, one or both of this restaurant's bosses—gentlemen in white shirts (sleeves rolled up), neckties, and aprons—are to be found. Either of them is a candidate for mayor of New York's Brazilian community. They know half the customers who walk in (the other half are not Brazilian), but are sweet and hospitable to everyone. The dining room proper has varnished wood walls, garishly colored paintings, a density of tables (most of them occupied most of the time) covered with blue cloths, and steel chairs upholstered with red, white, and green plastic. The front windows are overgrown with greenery, which filters somewhat the overhead view of 45th Street continuing downhill. The third-floor dining room is more of the same, but no counter. Cabana Carioca is not a quiet restaurant. But, happily, much of the noise is the sibilant and singsong sound of the Portuguese language spoken with polite passion. New York's seekers after ethnic curiosity come here too, to broaden themselves by contact with another culture and to fatten up on the immense servings purveyed here at low prices.

Two of you can share a single order of ameijoa à bulhao pato, twelve giant cherry-stone clams (almost as big as full-size quahogs), served in a huge iron pot that holds also three inches of oiled, parsleyed, and briny broth. Clams this big can be chewy, if not tough, and these are such that you may want to have at them with a knife and fork, to eat them in two or three bites. What the Cabana calls a special appetizer of shrimp, you will, on inspection, identify as a lunch and a half. The many shrimp are mingled with black olives, and the dish is singular for the strength of the olive and olive-oil flavors that the hot shrimp have absorbed. The fried sausages are spicy, crusted, and pleasantly greasy, and the lettuce on which they are served is, in effect, dressed—and wilted—by the fat that drains out of the sausages onto the leaves. The caldo verde (green soup) is thick with potato, studded with chunks of strong sausage, laced with sharp kale.

About a quart of black beans and a platter of rice in which you could bury a small mammal are delivered to every table. As an accompaniment to those try the bacalhau à braz, a primitive dish, at once vigorous and homey, of salt cod mingled with black olives, sautéed onions, eggs, and plenty of potatoes. The paella here is not a standout. It is, of course, copious, half a lobster tail and plenty of shrimp, scallops and squid, sections of chicken, sausages, and green peas buried in the rice, but the seasoning does not bring out the individuality of these ingredients, though the chicken, which has absorbed the seafood flavors, is thereby converted into an interesting item. There is an odd lobster dish here—listed as lagosta à cheff—that probably has more allure to those with Brazilian memories than to the rest of you. The decent crustacean is covered over with a seasoned and browned bread paste, giving it an undetectable charm. A menu entry of "carne porco alentejana" is described as "pork bits with clams." Actually the chunks of meat are the size of paving stones, which is to say almost as large as the clams. Both are delivered to you in a pot of sufficient girth to hold a dozen of each, as well as more of those sausages, all in a buttered broth—the meat is tender, the clams fresh, the broth powerful, the entire production adorned with the coarse but good fried potatoes that garnish many of the main courses here. The fried chicken carioca style is a good, moist bird, well crusted, saturated with the flavor of garlic. Of course there is feijoada, which, as all the world knows, is the national dish of Brazil—buried in the black beans are joints of meat, chunks of meat, ribs of meat, sausages. The dish is garnished with slices of raw orange, buttered kale, and manioc, the tangy zest always served with feijoada.

The flan differs from those you get in Spanish restaurants in that it is the color of salmon. The desserts of guava, guava paste, caramelized milk, and hard cheese may well be skipped. The Brazilian coffee, of course, is strong and good.

★★CAFÉ CROCODILE

354 East 74th Street
DINNER CLOSED SUNDAY.
Reservations: 249-6619.
Credit cards: AE.
Medium priced.

It seems like only yesterday, this little place was called Andrée's Mediterranean Cuisine, it was a homelike, family-owned restaurant to which you brought your own wine, in which you were greeted at the door by Father, in which you ate Mother's cooking, and in which you were waited on by two teenage daughters. Eventually Andrée's got a license to sell wine and beer, but Andrée, during her tours of the dining room, could be overheard to say that she did not want to sell hard liquor because she did not want that kind of crowd, did not wish to deal with those who, past a certain drinking point, turn fractious. Now the teenage daughters are no longer in evidence, and a full liquor license is. The knowing put the facts together, point out that the costs of college schooling are at a high.

Whatever the motivation, Andrée & Co. have now put the parlor of their brownstone to the best use yet. Gone are the prints and rugs on the walls, the bureau, the big bare Spanish table. The room has been slicked and smoothed of its idiosyncrasies, painted a pale yellow, adorned simply with tinted mirrors, pots of flowers, a couple of painted Mediterranean views seen through mock windows in the back wall. You still enter to what is clearly the downstairs hall of what is clearly a residence, but once you have made a left into the dining room, with its rows of white-linened tables and cane-and-bentwood chairs, you are out of domesticity and into a public place that, especially when it is well populated, is convivial, even a bit noisy, though Andrée's followers are hardly a boisterous set.

Andrée cooks the way she always cooked, makes many of the dishes she always made, but, by way of a menu that is now handwritten and strictly à la carte, dinner at her place is today a casual—café—affair. It is now clear that the household aspect of the former establishment served to stiffen, rather than unbend, dinner chez Andrée. Leaving home, you will recall, was a search for release from constraints. At home, moreover, you were never served the like of this brandade de haddock fumé, the hot mash of fish browned on top in its shallow casserole, the hearty, pungently seasoned stuff of stout and smoky fish flavor. Andrée's tarte à l'oignon is almost a delicacy, the sweet strands of onion in a parsleyed custard that is light and fluffy, the two on a flaky pastry. Merguez are lamb sausages, here they are sweet, charred, a little hard, of clear lamb flavor, the sausages flanking a rectangle of pully fried cheese, both elements in a dense and lively red sauce. Pasta shows up on the menu now this way, now that, sometimes pasta puttanesca, the vigorous tomato-and-anchovy sauce thick with black olives and capers.

Andrée is not impervious to modern influences. Consider, for example, the seared tuna, in which the fish is actually rare, though apparently marinated to a point at which it is in no way raw—the tuna is spicy and tart, the strips of ginger and leek with which it is adorned in nice contrast to the fresh, meaty fish. Order squab and you get the whole bird, most of its bones out, a chestnut-and-apricot stuffing in—this is a small bird, of less flavor than an older one, but the meat is moist, its character is far from remote, and the dressing is good, fruity without being sweet. Each day there is a couscous of the day, sometimes couscous of beef and lamb and chicken, on one end of the plate a mound of the little couscous granules surrounded by stewed vegetables and fruits, the other end weighted with substantial chunks of the meats, all of pungent flavor, the whole served with a pitcher of the complex broth in which the food was cooked, and with a fiery paste with which you may fortify the broth and/or the meats and/or the vegetables and/or the couscous. The rack of lamb reaches you as a great knob of meat from which four ribs protrude, the meat coated with an herbed breading that has become a fragrant crust in the roasting—the lamb, when you cut into it, is bursting with blood juiciness.

What is given as "choc au chocolat" is a cake of remarkable chocolate intensity, the chocolate livened by subtle admixtures of supporting flavors, vanilla, orange, brandy among them; the cake reaches you garnished with ripe strawberries and rich whipped cream. The crème caramel is fine, the cherry clafoutie seems more like fruited rice pudding than the cake of that name (albeit this is a pleasant sweet), and the frozen mocha crème royale is creamy and cold, of deep coffee flavor.

★ CAFÉ DE BRUXELLES

118 Greenwich Avenue (at 13th Street)
LUNCH, TUESDAY TO SUNDAY; DINNER, DAILY.
Reservations: 206-1830.
Credit cards: AE, MC, V.
Medium priced.

Again in new hands, these French, the Café retains a Belgian menu and, of course, its original deviantly configured three-room layout within a Greenwich Village hairpin corner formed by the intersection of skewed Greenwich Avenue with resolutely east-west 13th Street. The skinniest part of the place, at the bend in the pin, is given over to a zinc bar and some bare-topped tables at which those who prefer to remain within sight of the bottles may snack. The restaurant then widens into a center room, to which you enter, this the Café's so called café, which, giving, as it does, on the kitchen, and the entrance from out of doors, and the stairway to the facilities, and both other rooms, and the unregulated traffic attendant thereto, is to be avoided for dinner, though you cannot avoid it when you show up, for it is in the café that you stand—properly awed by the framed photo of the king and queen of Belgium and by the array of good Belgian beers displayed on a high shelf—waiting to be noticed, while staff members float by, each slowing down long enough to promise to be with you in a minute. You do wonder as to the whereabouts of one Patricia, listed on the menu as "your host," but never seen. At its third and widest part the restaurant is a conventional, comfortable dining room, mottled-umber walls, a deep-green banquette along one side, white-topped tables surrounded by black-enameled side chairs, lace curtains on the windows. The place has a sleepy quality to which the sometimes bemused staff seems appropriate (though on occasion you are waited on by individuals who do seem determined to do what they set out to do before they permit themselves to be deflected to something else), and their insouciance, though not contagious, is not infuriating, for they inhabit the world of the twenty-minute hour, which is to say, if you are able to prolong consumption of, say, your pâté over the course of an hour, waiting twenty minutes for the beaujolais you want with it is not so bad. When, however, you ask to have your Beaujolais chilled, and the not cold wine is brought in one of those insulating sleeves in which wine that is already cold is *kept* cold (instead of in an ice bucket, in which wine that is not cold is *made* cold), you realize that suspension of senses other than just your sense of time may be essential if you are fully to appreciate this place.

Very good with your eventually cooled wine is the warm salade Liègeoise, chunks of chewy bacon, sweet sautéed onions, tender green beans, and thin slivers of firm new potato, all in a warm, herbed dressing that is tart of sherry vinegar. An oddity given as gâteau bressan is a block of chicken liver custard, the fluffy and powerfully seasoned meat pureé in a dark mushroom sauce that is sweet of port wine. You get snails here like snails you get nowhere else in town, anyway their setting, for these big, black, plump nuggets are in a pool of melted Roquefort cheese, strong, powerfully salty, enriched with butter and cream, and greened with parsley—you use up a foot of bread mopping up the rich cheese sauce. As a cat washes, so does a Belgian eat mussels. Accordingly the house obtains the good ones devoid of the rank taste you encounter in most New York mussels, serves a dozen of them, in their half shells, under a browned, buttery, and vigorously garlicked breading the aroma of which warms the neighborhood of your table from the moment the dish arrives.

As a Belgian eats mussels, so does a Belgian eat French fries, and during main course time your table is graced with a metal tumbler in which stands a paper-wrapped sheaf of them. They are served with good mayonnaise, but one time in three the fries are greasy, and they are never the crisp, light, vividly potato-flavored article you encounter on Belgian soil. The place makes much of the pallid swimmer called lotte, the fillets of fresh, snowy fish browned, moist, and enriched by a thick and buttery sauce of leeks. Waterzooi is a Belgian national dish. Made in the more usual way, with fish, it is available here on Wednesday, but the chicken version is on the daily menu. For all the complexity of its ingredients, the result is mother's-milk food, a creamy white soup dense with morsels of pallid chicken breast and with strands of vegetable—just the thing, it seems, if you are not well. For those who are up and about, however, there is chou-croute (on Sunday), a hillock of astringent sauerkraut overlaid with a slab of ham, slices of gamy sausage, a good frankfurter, and lengths of hefty bacon—you will want also strong mustard and Belgian beer. The house turns out a good carbonnade, the Belgian beef-and-beer stew, this one very dark, thick with chunks of fibrous and tender meat, fragrant of garlic. The steak pommes frites is a not bad sirloin, accurately done, cross-hatched and charred by the grill, of decent beef flavor.

Avoid both the café Liègeois, a watery, coffee-doused, vanilla ice cream thing, and the poached pear, also watery in its insipid white-wine syrup. The chocolate cake is intense (Belgians eat chocolate the way they eat mussels and French fries), and the Belgian waffle is light, just a carrier for the good strawberry sauce and fluffy whipped cream.

You will find bottles of suitable wine, but Belgian beer is the better drink with many of these dishes. The remarkable, light-seeming, exceptionally strong beer called Duvel is $4.25 a bottle.

★ CAFÉ DE LA GARE

143 Perry Street (near Washington Street)
DINNER. CLOSED MONDAY.
Reservations: 242-3553.
Credit cards: DC, MC, V.
No liquor.
Medium priced.

A white, rough-plastered cube of a little store, with a stamped-tin ceiling and tables for 30 chairs, to which you bring your own wine—your basic amateur restaurant, but professional enough, which is to say most of the tables do not rock, the linen is linen, not paper, and the food is not only unexperimental, but seems so. With respect to those who wait on you, doing so is their only agenda—their courtesy is such that you are not given to understand that befriending them is part of your responsibility as a customer. And when the place turns unexpectedly busy, as it sometimes does, though a certain slowness may set in, chaos and panic do not. The light is low, there are tiny candles on the tables, and the posters on the walls, including two of Cartier-Bresson photos, undo the starkness of the room. If you find the background music—aimed at the Benny Goodman, Ella Fitzgerald crowd—too loud, the house willingly turns it down.

From a very brief menu that changes every two weeks, and to which a couple of specials are added each night: a hot cream of watercress soup on a potato base, its leafy flavor in nice contrast to the little dollop of curry-flavored crème fraîche with which it is adorned; rillettes of fresh and smoked salmon, the latter adding a good saltiness to the vivid salmon flavor of the cool pink stuff; a sparkling cold salad of rich sea scallops and short lengths of sharp scallion in a tangy dressing made with balsamic vinegar; and a walnut-studded pâté that, because it reaches you cold, conceals the complexity of flavors within it, which are of chicken liver, pork, bacon, brandy.

Perhaps because the restaurant won a lawsuit (though no damages were awarded) having to do with its cassoulet, when the menu otherwise changes every other week, the cassoulet remains. You get something like a half-gallon pot of the stuff—happily, not filled to the top—sizzling around the edges, in which are buried chunks of pork, strong sausage, and preserved, peppery duck, altogether a good cassoulet, for the liveliness of its garlic-flavored sauce, as against the dead-weight white-bean leadenness of many versions. You get good rabbit, the chunks of meat, on the bone, in a tangy apple cider sauce that is thick with black raisins, and with crescents of apple, added late, that are crisp and a little acidic. The poulet chasseur is of a bird that actually tastes like chicken, and its Madeira sauce, with mushrooms and strands of fresh tarragon, is earthy and smoky. Pass up the baked sole with oranges and grapefruit, roulades of the fresh fish stuffed with the fruit and adorned with it, but the dish needs some kind of sauce to make sense of the disparate ingredients.

The problem with the desserts is that they come out of the icebox, under which circumstances this banana coconut tart tastes like a diner item, and the chocolate truffle cake like intense chocolate but like nothing more. The Paris-Brest suffers the treatment better, a rich cream between the two big chou pastries, slivered hazelnuts and much confectioners' sugar across the top. You wish the fruit flavor of the peach bavarian were more vivid, and that it did not need to borrow richness from the whipped cream that adorns it.

No spirits, bring your own wine.

★★CAFÉ DES ARTISTES

1 West 67th Street
LUNCH AND DINNER.
Reservations: 877-3500.
Credit cards: AE, DC, MC, V.
Expensive.

One may eat well here, also not well, but no matter, for the Café is a restaurant that is better than its food, has functions that are quite apart from ingestion. Consider, for example, these three ladies seated at the bar of an evening. None of them is having anything stronger than coffee, the counter before them is spread with linen napkins, each has before her a plate and fork, and they are working their way through the Great Dessert Plate, a compendium of the Café's innumerable sweets arranged, slice by slice, on a giant platter at the center of which stands a silver champagne glass filled with whipped cream, big ripe strawberries on top. The desserts need not be uniformly of merit when their communal consumption this way transforms a just-us-girls evening at the movies into a celebration of life. Calories go unmentioned throughout the rite, and at its end one player announces that "we should do this more often," and the three trisect the bill.

Though the Café attracts the well known, it is a celebrity place in reverse, one in which the famous are their unpublic selves; correlatively, there is not much gaping, as it is the custom of the restaurant's plebes coolly to ignore the elite (though visitors from across the waters may fail to pick up on the code). For both the celebs and the merely prosperous are here (almost no one else is here) for lower-case café comforts that have to do with conversation, down-home cooking (of European dishes usually available at more stylish prices), and surroundings that, for all their spiffy charms, seem well worn. The habitués are happy, too, with the civilized and competent staff, some of whom seem to be habitués of working here, have been at it for many times the normal tenure of a waiter or waitress in any New York restaurant to which he is not indentured.

You enter, from the building lobby, to the principal room, at the center of which stands a great table on an iron base, displayed upon it most of the desserts you saw consumed at the bar in the previous scene. One long side of this room is a windowed wall on 67th Street, and just within it there thrives a jungle of greenery that echoes the plant life aspect of the Café's best known appointments, the murals—of animal life in sylvan settings, most of the animals young and healthy examples of the unclothed human female—that were painted for the café decades ago by Howard Chandler Christy. Where the paintings are not, the walls are mirrored, notes of glinting crystallinity in the otherwise lush room. You go up a few steps to more tables and chairs, more of those Christies, and, a little further along, the three-sided bar, the booths and tables around it under drawings and small paintings that relate to the larger murals, on the bar itself, under low-hanging, soft-glowing halophane lamps, racks of hard-cooked eggs, shelled nuts in cocktail glasses, baskets of salted crackling things—the facility is busy with those waiting for tables, post-Lincoln Center tipplers, even people with no agenda other than maybe one more. Whatever your business, the Café humanizes it, for this is, before anything, a civilized place.

You cannot, however, civilize a herring, which is nevertheless attempted in this tripartite serving of marinated herring, one part the untamed article, sweet and sour and supple, salty and strong, next to which the two variations thereon—the same herring in mustard sauce, and the same mingled with beets—are minor desecrations. But then there is an item that seems always present on the Café's ever-changing menu, salmon four ways (the serving "for one" is first course enough for two), in which neither the cool poached salmon, nor the delicately dill-flavored gravlax, nor the firm and well-salted smoked salmon, nor the herbed and rather obvious salmon tartare need apologize to any of the others. Another collection of which a single order will hold two, the assorted planked cochonnailles (delicatessen to you), on this occasion including jambon persillé, nuggets of dark and chewy ham bound in a firm jelly that is green with fresh parsley; an almost loud sausage lyonnaise, fatty, salty, a little gamy, and very good with the strong mustard that is supplied; a rich, cool, gelatinous sweetbread headcheese; a pâté that was denatured in its overcooking, though it is well seasoned, its chopped walnuts a nice note; slices of decent ham; and a wad of rillettes that lacks the strong seasoning essential to this fatty pounded meat. The sautéed wild mushrooms are fresh, their flavor vivid even in strongly garlicked butter. With respect to pasta, you will never go wrong never going near it here, this fettuccine with bacon, sausage, and broccoli, for example, in which each element is surprised, but not delighted, to meet the others.

Salmon again, smoked again, but this time just enough to flavor it, not to cure or fully cook it, the final cooking a separate step, so the substantial fillet of fresh, pink fish reaches you browned and juicy, its sauce choron (béarnaise pinked with tomato) watery but, happily, dispensable. The scallops are billed as sautéed, but they reach you uncolored and wet, as if stewed tepid in their own juice, and the coriander with which they are done has lost its flavor in the slow preparation. The veal chop is coarse, of veal that is red rather than pink, near beef. The idea of lamb chops in a Parmesan crust reads so bad you figure it must be good. It is bad. Anyway, as all the world knows, selecting meat at the Café des Artistes involves reading the menu thoroughly, considering carefully the possibilities, and then ordering the pot au feu, a kettle of fibrous and tender potted beef that has taken on a deep, complex flavor from the stock and vegetables with which it was done—the good, clear broth, with slabs of turnip and cabbage and potato, plus leeks and whole onions, are part of the act, as is a fat-filled marrow bone, with all of which you are served sharp mustard and a feeble horseradish sauce, though the wondrous dish needs no help.

Order Stilton and fruit, and you are served enough strong cheese for a solid lunch, with walnuts and with half a Granny Smith apple sliced thin. The sweet desserts include a pasty sweet-potato-pecan pie on sallow crust; a so-called joy of bonaparte, a light napoleon of lemon custard, rich whipped cream, and ripe strawberries; a layered mocha dacquoise of good, chewy meringues, mocha cream, and rich whipped cream; and the ilona torte, which has been listed since the beginning, the current version a rich coffee-flavored chocolate cake coated with walnuts—a sumptuous sweet.

The selection changes, but each night there are sixteen wines that you may have brought to your table in baskets, and the waiters and waitresses usually know the best bottles. The proprietor here is George Lang. Sometimes he appears on the premises. Happily, he leaves at home his violin.

★ CAFÉ GRECO

1390 Second Avenue (near 72nd Street)
DINNER.
Reservations: 737-4300.
Credit cards: AE, DC, MC, V.
Medium priced.

Maybe it has something to do with the amplified bouzouki music by way of which, in tavernas that have come and gone from the New York scene, so many unaccustomed local eardrums were reduced to powder; or else it is the Greek habit of doing lamb until the inside looks like the outside; or could it be that the Greek restaurant chromosome is imprinted solely with the coffee shop gene? Anyway, though one or two places thrive, the Greek restaurant is barely a category on Manhattan Island. Comes this place, mindful apparently of that lore, and of the contrasting record of the Italians, with a solution: Make it Greek, but make it also Italian, call it, if necessary, *Mediterranean*, a bit of near-Eastern food will not hurt, and if the mostly French and California wine list abjures entirely the hated word "retsina," then you may take a chance and give the place a name that reveals its Grecian identity.

Tall glass doors framed in honey-colored wood are the foldaway façade before which, when the weather is fine, are placed cocktail tables with tops of false marble (in New York you cannot be too careful, cocktail tables have been known to walk). The marble of the tables just inside is real, and there is a little mural above the bar of goddesses, gods, and multi-species creatures cavorting in, you figure, god's country. The restaurant begins as a narrow place that grows wide as it proceeds down ever lower levels, spreading at the back to a couple of good-size rooms. The interior is all buff colored and putty colored, with brass rails along the descending path and tiny overhead spots that cast soft pools of light here and there. There are prints on the walls, there are flowers on the tables, and the statuary just outside the windowed back wall makes reference to the Greek classical past—cement cherubs doing cherubic things. The tables are covered with white cloths over blue ones, the help wear blue-and-white-striped shirts, the blue-and-white Greek flag is not otherwise on display.

In this setting the strong pink of the salmon carpaccio is very pretty, and the slices of fresh raw fish are sweet, moist, glistening of the good oil that has been poured over them—the fresh basil and chopped pinenuts are nice notes of fragrance and texture. The seafood salad is not exactly what dishes of that name turn out to be in Italian restaurants, for in this the scallops, strands of shrimp, and circles of squid are mingled with lettuce —the bulk of the salad—in a creamy and lemony dressing. The hot spinach pie is the usual thing of spinach, redolent of strong cheese, between layers of flaky pastry—the homey solidity of the dish is in no way undone by the unexpected cucumber salad served with it. A sweet mash of onions, hot and thick, on a pizza pastry is the base of a tart that is topped with thin slices of grilled eggplant, zucchini, tomato, and melted cheese—satisfying, inelegant food.

If you liked that salmon raw, know that Café Greco has more than one way with a salmon. Grilled, the red fish reaches you under an herbed sauce of roasted red peppers and salty black olives—the fish is judiciously done, is moist but cooked through. As is this grilled chicken, a nicely crisped bird that reveals much of its own good flavor and much of the flavor of the grill, though its winy sauce, the pile of nameless couscous served with it, and the garnish of seemingly wood-fibered leeks somewhat undo the effect. A block of ground lamb under pastry that is blackened in spots is served in a pool of tomato sauce that is threaded with onions, herbed, powerfully seasoned—this is the house moussaka, lamb-gamy, weighty, winter food. You figure that maybe the roast lamb is at least autumn food, but this *is* a Greek restaurant, the meat has been rendered bloodless and harsh, and it is garnished with "white beans" like the baked beans you get out of an American can, and with a strong, almost sparkling black-olive tapenade that cannot save the situation.

The raspberry napoleon is assembled long before it is served, so the berries have become limp in their pastry cream. The hazelnut chocolate cake, a layer of praline under the chocolate icing, is intense, but that is all. Happily the baklava is served with a scoop of cold and creamy vanilla, for the thing itself, a sweet-spiced and honey-flavored density of ground walnuts wrapped in pastry, is stiff and dry by evening.

★★CAFÉ LUXEMBOURG

200 West 70th Street
LUNCH, SUNDAY; DINNER, DAILY.
Reservations: 873-7411.
Credit cards: AE, DC, MC, V.
Medium priced.

When executive chef Patrick Clark separated himself from the powers behind
TriBeCa's Odeon (their flagship store) and Café Luxembourg (its West Side offshoot),
more was lost downtown than up—understandably, for Odeon, the better place, was the
tougher act to perpetuate. Not to worry, the loss of Clark resulted in a loss of business to
neither establishment. Reputations outlive. And here on the West Side, where most of
the Café's competitors are tuned to those whose standard of comparison is the college
cafeteria, Luxembourg's share of the grownup market remains safe.

You will recall that, upon a time, American economists discovered that they could
get famous only after making inaccurate predictions from high government places. Similarly, today, restaurant architects know that they achieve celebrity status only when—like
Sam Lopata and Adam Tihany, for two—their interiors have been home to spectacular
bankruptcies. Which calls to mind Café Luxembourg, a whimmy assemblage of parts
that do well by one another, it seems, solely by chance, a dining room apparently
designed around someone's happenstantial overstock of yellow paint and yellow tiles—
the place fills nightly, if not despite the absence of creative visuals, then because of it.
The buttery, softly lit room is thick with tables (a carafe of water and a shot glass of
toothpicks on each), and you are comfortably seated—albeit, often, hard beside a
stranger—on café chairs or on the dark-red banquettes that rim the room here, cut
through it there. The aisles are dense with help, waiters in white, waitresses in black, and
though their recitation of the day's specials requires a surreptitious glance at a crib sheet,
and though one course sometimes arrives before the previous one has been cleared, the
staff is available, civil, even cheerful. The crowd they serve cannot be defined by age or
income or occupation, for it is made up of those who know that this part of town has
little better to offer. In part by way of their multiplicity Café Luxembourg is a convivial
neighborhood place.

Since the beginning, the Café has listed this country salad, and it still reaches you in
sparkling condition, the greens crisp, the crumbled Roquefort firm and creamy and
sharp, the chunks of bacon strong and a little resilient, the whole, overlaid with buttered
crusts of bread, in a tangy, mustard-thickened dressing. Bread on the pea soup as well,
this time floating croutons on a polished purée that is hot, of earthy flavor, and surprisingly smooth, and lacking the slightly rough texture you may expect in pea soup. Shrimp
that reach you right are always noteworthy, and these sautéed crustaceans are sweet,
crunchy, devoid of iodine in their shiny pink shells—their lemony sauce, threaded with
bits of artichoke, is fragrant of fresh dill. What the house calls chicken liver pâté, you
call a rich, almost fluffy mousse—it arrives in a little ramekin, crisp and vividly flavored
slivers of almond on top, with slices of toasted rye bread onto which you spread the
smooth stuff. Have that any time rather than the carpaccio—you cannot resist the

thought that in Clark's day the raw meat would not have been sliced in advance, to reach you discolored and bloodless under its mustard mayonnaise.

Each night there is a pasta of the night, sometimes firm and eggy noodles mingled with substantial chunks of fresh salmon and smoked salmon, moistened with butter, and fragrant of the fresh dill that livens the well seasoned dish. You order a grilled brook trout, and you are dismayed by the infantility of the specimen served—still, the boned fish is fresh and sweet in its crisped skin, and its creole sauce, thick with little shrimp and sweet peppers, is hot and tangy. Order roast chicken, and instead of half a little bird, you get some smaller fraction of a big one—big birds have more flavor than little ones, and this chicken is crisped and juicy as well, is served in a dark, vigorous, and heavily herbed sauce of the roasting juices, which you spoon onto the mashed potatoes that are part of the dish. Cassoulet is another item that has never been dropped from this menu, and, as ever, the density of beans, studded with duck, pork, and chunks of sausage under its handsomely browned bread-crumb crust, is sturdy in its tomato-redded sauce, though the meats have lost some of their distinctiveness in the making. You can get a good steak here, but when you are not so lucky, the beef is chewy, its flavor subsumed in the excess of charcoal on its surface.

Pass up the calvados and apple terrine, a slice of something pale, cold, and wet, cut from a loaf and set in a bit of liquored sauce. Better is the crème brûlée, though you wish the cool custard under the crackling caramel top were fluffier. Under a storm of confectioner's sugar is not quite concealed the apple and prune dartois, a paleness of stewed apples dappled with crushed prunes and wrapped, like the filling of a strudel, in pastry —the item is garnished with rich whipped cream. The big winners are the lemon tart, the citric custard more sour than sweet on its grainy pastry; and the chocolate meringue cake—a chewy meringue and fluffy whipped cream among layers of rich black cake, an abundance of chocolate shavings on top.

★ CAFÉ SAN MARTIN

1458 First Avenue (near 76th Street)
LUNCH, SUNDAY; DINNER, DAILY.
Reservations: 288-0470.
Credit cards: AE, MC, V.
Medium priced.

Almost nothing about this restaurant, except the help and half the food, is Spanish —anyway, not Spanish in the New York manner. There is nary a bullfighter poster on the walls. Black wrought iron is nowhere in evidence. The rooms do not simulate a stone-walled wine cellar in a medieval Castilian castle. The restaurant is, in fact, airy, all white, with greenery standing in the front windows (right next to the piano—which is harmlessly tinkled—and not far from the glittery little bar, and the handful of tables that are arranged in an L around it). There is more greenery hanging from the skylight that is centered over the two-steps-down main dining room at the back. Colorful, ornately framed oils adorn the walls, and handsome cane-and-bentwood chairs surround white-linened tables that are set with painted plates and pale-blue napkins. When the place fills up—with a prosperous but not flashy uptown crowd—it hums and bustles. The hard-working waiters (in white shirts and vests and long, striped aprons) and the captains (in dark suits) are all courtesy, and they keep the place running smoothly.

Café San Martin is not an especially expensive restaurant, but for $14.50 you may discover for yourself that a small plate of baby eels—these are virtually embryonic eels—looks like a small plate of short spaghetti. And with the sizzling oil, browned garlic, and blackened and fiery red peppers in which the creatures are served, they as well could be, for the forthright flavors of the sauce conceal whatever subtle merit this rarity might have to disclose. More of that garlic in the garlic shrimp—but it fails to obscure the iodine that ruins these poorly chosen crustaceans. Opt instead for xangurro, which arrives in the little dish in which it was cooked. The food consists of crabmeat, sherry, and a powerful dose of clove—a substantial patty of the flavored seafood is baked under a breading until the crust is browned. It must be told that this establishment does no better shopping for mussels than it does buying shrimp. The green sauce is good—smooth, creamy, loaded with fresh parsley—but there are, among these mostly lovely mussels, a few that are considerably louder than that piano. Disks of Spanish sausage, with slivers of red and green peppers, are sealed—with seasoned red wine and oil—in a little pillow fashioned of aluminum foil, and then heated. The shiny balloon is placed before you and cut open. Steam pours forth. The morsels of spiced meat are good with the salty wine and vegetables. Of course, there is black bean soup—it may not be as thick as you like it, but it has a deep flavor, and the onions that come with it are recently chopped, so they are strong.

The Café serves one of the best paellas in town—barring the occasional mischance of encountering those less-than-perfect shrimp or mussels. The rice is oiled and red and spicy, studded with chunks of exceptionally sweet and peppery sausage, plump scallops, mussels and shrimp, clams that are sometimes a bit tough for having been cooked too long, red pimentos, green peppers, and glistening sweet green peas. The paella is prepared only for two. If you want lobster in yours, there is a surcharge. All those items of shellfish, as well as a substantial slab of fresh striped bass, make up the zarzuela de mariscos, which—in its broad pottery dish—is immersed in a creamy sauce. Parillada is that same collection again, this time broiled, all the elements of vivid flavor, served with a pitcher of spicy tomato sauce. Hake, a cousin to cod, is a big item in Spanish cookery. Here it is served in a manner given as "à la Vasca," in which the hefty, flaky fish is buried in a thick, green sauce that is both lemony and spicy. The pale meat is garnished with clams and mussels and halves of hard-cooked eggs, all of which are usually fine. But the entire production is served over a few shafts of canned white asparagus, which, perhaps at the sacrifice of some authenticity, could be omitted to excellent effect. A so-called grain-fed chicken is roasted artfully on a spit when you order it (you must allow time). The skin is crisp, the meat is moist, but the flavor of the bird, though a little better than most contemporary chickens, is still shy of the real thing. Much of the rest of the menu is given over to French and Italian dishes—entrecôte au poivre, fettuccine Alfredo, and the like—but that is not what this restaurant is about.

Happily, the deviations from Spanish restraints extend to the dessert menu: a tart of slivers of ripe banana, creamy custard, crumbly crust; a kiwi tart much like it, the green fruit glistening and sweet; a raisin-studded bread pudding that is made tangy by strands of lemon rind; clafoutis of cherries or blueberries, in which the stewed fruits are buried in, and stain, the dark cake; an intense and airy chocolate mousse cake; a whole orange, peeled and sliced, served under strands of orange rind that have been marinated in Grand Marnier. None of the sweets is extraordinary, but all of them are more than decent.

★★CAMEOS

169 Columbus Avenue (near 68th Street)
LUNCH AND DINNER.
Reservations: 874-2280.
Credit cards: AE, DC, MC, V.
Medium priced.

The shortage of praiseworthy eating places on the Upper West Side is symptomatic of certain conditions: in this part of town lesser places do just as well, and every neighborhood gets the restaurants it deserves. You point out that in the vicinity of Lincoln Center, at least, merit may well make a difference, for this subsection of the neighborhood draws folks from all over town—a condition that surely contributes to the success of Café Luxembourg, Café des Artistes, and one or two other spots for which a case could be made. To the short list you may now add Cameos.

Up the stairs, enter, and you suspect at once that Cameos is no ordinary matter, for not only are there no peanuts in the bowls of nuts on the U-shaped bar, but you are not even admonished when you poke around for walnuts and pecans. You do pause, if not recoil, at the sight of the white baby grand, but be advised that the gent who has at it, starting well into the dinner hour, treats with respect the tunes he plays. The restaurant proper is one room and then another in a line, the windows of both, stocked with greenery, overlooking from a safe distance the vehicular and pedestrian traffic on Columbus Avenue. At about the time the music starts, the light is dimmed, which softens the slick, hard-edged lines of this vaguely Deco installation. The white-linened tables are well spaced, what noise there is is muted by the cushy carpeting, and the staff, in their blue shirts, buttoned at the cuff, and their four-in-hands, are as cool as the place itself.

At first you reject out of hand, because of the name, what are listed as "close to heaven crab cakes." You reconsider, however, when you find that for no other dish does the menu descend to the cutes. Turns out the cakes may at least be closer to heaven than anything else on the menu, the patties handsomely browned, almost fluffy, a little moist, their vivid fresh-crab flavor potentiated by judicious seasoning, their tangy citrus sauce, livened with minced chives, in vibrant contrast to the sweet seafood. Back down to earth, but at little sacrifice, for grilled leeks and Irish bacon, the lean meat strong and smoky, the vegetable touched with the flavor of the grill, the two in a tart beurre blanc that is light, smooth, fragrant of fresh thyme. The first course given as "warm duck breast salad" is really a light lunch, an abundance of spiky greens, dense with walnuts and utterly fresh in their lively dressing, overlaid with slice upon slice of tender, rare duck. An experimental item listed as "fast-seared American foie gras" is seared too fast, is not, properly speaking, seared, is tepid liver that is not at all redeemed by its madeira sauce.

A couple of pasta dishes are listed, and as your memory is fresh of the good crabmeat in those crab cakes, you opt for the linguine with crabmeat and peppers. Sure enough, in this setting the chunky seafood is even more clearly itself, and there is nothing wrong with the pasta or with the red, green, or yellow peppers, either, but the dish is like a salad without dressing, all solids, with little of the moisture needed as a medium in which the parts can become a dish. Luscious salmon, the great slab of meat fresh and juicy, its pale poaching-liquid sauce touched with fennel and herbs. The medallions of venison are many slices of the rather livery meat in a port wine sauce that is at once peppery and fruity. Not that there is anything wrong with the house steak itself, but the thin French fries served with it are hot, light, devoid of grease, soft within their delicately crisped surfaces, and the "maple glazed" steak, though it reveals little effect of the glaze, is huge, accurately done, tender, beefy.

The lemon cheesecake is heavy, if not quite leaden, in its pool of raspberry sauce, and the lemon and raspberry charlotte is hardly more than opaque Jell-O. But no fault is to be found with the intense chocolate tart, its crackling crust, or the rich whipped cream served with it; or with the plum clafoutie, the browned and eggy cake studded with and stained by the stewed red fruit—with it, more of that whipped cream.

★ CANAL BAR

511 Greenwich Street (at Spring Street)
DINNER.
Reservations: 334-5150.
Credit cards: AE, DC, MC, V.
Medium priced.

The food here is better than it has to be, for the place has nothing to do with eats. You determine what it does have to do with by way of a single well-timed drink, say midnight, Saturday. The store is a dull red glow on bleakest Greenwich Street, that glow the light seeping through the red venetian blinds that, inside, cover the store windows. You enter—through a door marked only with a house number—to a point near the elbow of an L-shaped room, the broad top of the L off to your left as most of the main dining room. The base of the L is to your right, is in part the balance of the dining room, in part, at its far end, a barroom, complete with long black-topped bar, stools anchored to the floor as at a diner, much nudity in the framed pictures on the wall. During late-night hours, that base of the L—part of the dining room, then the barroom —is Canal Bar: tables within booths, tables surrounded by chairs, seated at all of them a density of sitters thigh by thigh, as tightly arranged as matches in a matchbook; at the bar a crush of standees shoulder to shoulder, fronts to backs, intimate as bristles on a brush. Those at the tables, of course, are the winners in this crowd, certified artists garnished with this week's mate, dealer, and patron-in-training, among them guys with long hair and collarless shirts open to the belt, ladies with heavily glittered left cheeks and brilliantly rouged right ones, adolescent girls, in 18-inch (hem to cleavage) dresses, so ecstatic to be in this company in public that if you did not know better you would attribute their glow to substances. And, of course, those at the bar are the losers: the usual pairs and trios of young women talking animatedly to one another while their eyes sweep the crowd; gents in jeans, leather jackets, and fedoras; others in jeans, studded jackets, and one earring; others in jeans, dinner jackets, and illustrated T-shirts. Men come here and speak French loudly—they think American women find it sexy, and though it does get a lot of attention, so does anything. Sorriest are the males in business suits and white shirts, ties removed and stuffed in pockets, who gape about and wonder how, *how*, to become part of this hot scene. With respect to the remainder of the dining room, and a second room situated within the crook of the L (royal-blue-and-vanilla-striped walls and amoeba-shaped mirrors), visitors could as well be eating back home on the Upper East Side for all the thrills this place affords—you do see outlanders of wry expression who clearly wonder what the fuss that brought them here is about.

They need not go home entirely frustrated, decent food is the sop Canal Bar throws to those who come and get only dinner, like this 8-inch niçoise pizza, the crisp and wheaty crust surfaced with pully cheese, oiled thin-sliced tomatoes, a salty black olive at the center of each of the four slices; crackling leek tarts and tomato tarts topped with strong browned cheese and strewn with fragrant Italian parsley; black and white linguine, the two shades of narrow noodle mingled with lengths of squid, chunks of tomato, and black olives; and this marginal white bean salad, which is hot, mingled with shreds of duck and chunks of garlic sausage, and very unlike what you think of when you think of white bean salad, more like what you think of when you think of pork and beans.

Roast lobster, reads the menu, and the not large crustacean does indeed seem to have been done dry and done carefully, so that it retains its moisture and flavor—the halves of the split tail, side by side, are surmounted by a mingling of the claw meat and spinach. Vivid grill marks adorn the swordfish, as do sautéed tomatoes, flavored with basil, and florets of broccoli—the warm, seeded tomatoes seem to gentle the medium-rare fish. The grilled duck is done rare, sliced thin, and arranged over mounds of spinach and sautéed potatoes, the whole in a dark, peppercorn-studded red-wine sauce—not a lot of duck flavor, but fortifying food. The big winner is the rack of lamb, four thick chops, legs up, under them enriched mashed potatoes of real potato flavor, beside them lengths of grilled eggplant and a dollop of pesto sauce.

You do better with the light, almost fluffy crème brûlée under its dark, crackling crust, and with the powerfully nut-flavored hazelnut mousse, dotted with nuts and dribbled with black chocolate, than with the undistinguished chocolate mousse cake, which is served with one of those chocolate-mint ice creams that taste like toothpaste.

• CANASTEL'S

229 Park Avenue South (at 19th Street)
LUNCH, MONDAY TO FRIDAY; DINNER, DAILY.
Reservations: 677-9622.
Credit cards: AE, DC, MC, V.
Expensive.

You wonder where they found him, this perfect host. He has the manner that, even when the restaurant is half empty, lets you know the place is hot. You call ahead because you will be fifteen minutes early, and a sweet voice on the phone assures you, no problem. Host, however, though thirty tables are in disuse, looks at you, then at his watch, then back at you, clearly unable to reconcile your behavior and his imperishable moral standards. Arrive alone, in advance of your other (again there are dozens of places where you could be seated), and he tells you—with obvious distaste for the distasteful demands of his work—that "Your table is not ready. When your guest arrives, your table will be ready." He suggests you make yourself one of the horde at the bar. The fellow is, of course, the complete coin, obverse and tail, and when he deals with those he must please, he is the complete sniveler. The rest of the staff, however, are fine.

Canastel's contributes much toward the goal of providing table space for all of New York all at one time. Where otherwise a mere score of one-bedroom apartments could be installed—to sleep, say, 100 companionable inmates—there is instead this place, with tables, chairs, and bar to accommodate twice that many. This approach to the housing problem comes, moreover, complete with Italian country cooking and uniformed attendants. This commons is high, wide, and long, its pale walls pink in the room's pink light, pink linen on its innumerable tables, each table surrounded by comfortable bentwood armchairs with cushioned seats. Tall foldaway glass doors look out on 19th Street and on Park Avenue South. The easternmost wall is illustrated, and through its painted portals you "see" painted views of old Italy and the Italian sky—the effect manages to be at once undecorative, unrealistic, and untrompe l'oeil. The downtown side of the place is given over to an open kitchen; and, near it, a long table with thirty platters or so of about a dozen appetizers; and, under an awning, within an arc of cocktail tables, wicker chairs, and wicker sofas, the bar, perched on one end of which there is a young lady in summer casuals and shades—she sits there in the lotus position, never smiling, apparently immovable, and though she is attractive, she is clearly jaded and bitter. Someone has taken her temperature and ascertained that she is a mannequin, and now the crowd ignores her.

If you are in luck, the waiter or waitress assigned to your care will be familiar with the relative merits of the items on the antipasto table, and will assemble for you a good collection. More likely, you will get both the bad and the good, including deep-red sun-dried tomatoes that are enriched with, and glistening with, oil; rolled-up browned leaves of sautéed zucchini that retain a bit of crispness, and others of sautéed eggplant that are soft and of strong flavor; crisp and lightly dressed slices of artichoke heart; a seafood salad of mostly shrimp and lobster in a creamy white dressing—the shellfish is a bit mushy; a sweet and crunchy roasted red pepper stuffed with a chopped, pungently seasoned mixture of anchovies and olives; a negligible amount of good smoked salmon; sweet-spiced little clams in their shells; tasteless mussels in theirs. Of course, if you think your eye is keener than your waiter's judgment, you may march up to the display and make your own mistakes.

Like many of the city's new Italian arenas, this one, mindful of the eating habits of its recently undergraduate clientele, has a pizza department. The pies are an extra-large hand-span across, and this one, given as alla napoletana, is of nicely risen, slightly chewy dough, a scant layer of mozzarella, slivers of tomato, anchovies arranged like the spokes of a wheel, and a sprinkling of oregano—it is at once light and satisfying, and though it is also strong (of those anchovies), it comes, like all pizzas here, with a little dish of red-pepper flakes, which you add for incinerative purposes. Add too many, and you may find it necessary to snuff out the inferno under a foothill of pappardelle del pastore, which is composed of broad, thick bands of pasta lightly bound in a sauce of cream and ricotta cheese, with, at the peak, a dollop of tart tomato sauce that is flecked with basil—comforting food, for which the red sauce does little more than set off its pleasant blandness. For pasta that is meant to more than soothe you, there are these orecchiette, dented noodle nickels, the firm disks in a slightly creamy tomato sauce that is thick with ground sausage, crunchy with tiny florets of broccoli, and fragrant of garlic.

The deep-fried squid is not greasy, but it is not light either, and the coarse—and cold—tomato sauce with which it is served helps not at all. The snapper is fresh, the big fillet in an herbed and briny tomato sauce that is slick with good oil—the fish comes with a couple of good clams and several of this establishment's tasteless mussels. What goes as pollo agliato comes off as chunks of tolerable sautéed chicken that are not improved by the wine and garlic with which they were prepared. Similarly the veal chop

Milanese, to the listing of which has been added the name, complete with quotation marks, "Canastel's." This is simply a chop that has been pounded beyond the borders of its plate, breaded as if to protect if from the environment, fried as if to dehydrate it, and buried under chopped tomatoes as if to conceal it—the tomatoes are allegedly marinated, but they are dry, and fail to provide the dressing that could partially redeem the meat. The paillard of beef is tan rather than browned—the oil and rosemary help, the promised garlic is absent, and the chopped tomatoes that disappointed you on the veal chop repeat themselves here. With any of these main courses you are advised to avoid the leaden fried zucchini.

The napoleon is of flaky pastry, much rich whipped cream, and an even richer custard. Have that any time instead of the tirami sù, the dessert of ladyfingers, cream cheese, coffee, and booze that, in this rendition, is a very sweet goo.

Stick to the first courses, pizzas, and pastas, and you can do well here. After that you are on your own.

★ IL CANTINORI

32 East 10th Street
LUNCH, MONDAY TO FRIDAY; DINNER, DAILY.
Reservations: 673-6044.
Credit cards: AE, DC.
Expensive.

Prosperity has made an honest place of Il Cantinori. It is now possible to dinner here and not find it necessary to put your eyes back in their sockets after a look at the check. Today almost everything offered is listed on the photocopied menu, revised each day, and even the handful of unlisted dishes your waiter describes do not turn out to be notably more expensive than the menu prices lead you to expect. Beware, however, of imported fish—go so far, if you care, as to ask the price before you order it.

Il Cantinori is the air-conditioned farmhouse, rusticity without the bugs, white linen on the tables and straw seats on the chairs. There is a front room, a back room, a bar in the corridor between them. Under the striped canopy, when the weather is fine, three tables are set out on the little porch that becomes an extension of the front dining room when the restaurant's façade—tall glass doors framed in honey-colored wood—is folded back. Inside, the walls are mostly of pebbly stucco, partly of exposed brick, with farm implements (nonmotorized) mounted on them here and there. The unconvincing ceiling beams, of blacked and roughened wood, are massive enough to support this place and everything else on the block. The view through the big back-room skylight is a swatch of sky and the unprepossessing back of the surrounding buildings. The white-shuttered windows on the brick back wall are the one off note of American Federal among the many of Italian Bucolic. Throughout, the handsome floor is of great, square, faded terra-cotta tiles, probably recovered from a demolition, for they look like they have been walked on for centuries. In all, the place is comfortable, part of the reason the good-size tables—even the tables for two are ample.

In the aisles between them rolls the cart, on it a row of white porcelain plates—in each a vegetable—from which you make a selection: broad strands of red and yellow peppers, skinned and roasted, oiled and crunchy; big gray beans, firm and pleasantly gummy, strewn with parsley, well salted, saturated with the flavor of oil; chunks of rich eggplant; blackened mushroom caps filled with chopped red peppers that are pungently seasoned and fragrantly herbed; tomatoes stuffed with rice, the grains firm, polished with oil, the tops of the tomatoes blackened a little. It is likely that if you come here the day the chanterelles come here, the wild mushrooms will be fine, but come a day or two later, and they have lost their earthy flavor—serving them hot over cold bresaola does not help.

Spaghetti in a sauce given as "pirata" is the noodle in a red paste dotted with bits of squid, shrimp, mussel, garlic—you wish the sauce were spicy rather than harsh, that the seafood had as much to do with its impact as the garlic. But then there is this *gray* spaghetti, the strands dyed, in the making, with the ink of squid, and that jet-black ink, thick with slivers and circles of squid meat, is the sauce itself—pungent food, oceanic and rousing. Each day a risotto is listed, sometimes rich with seafood—this is a brusque and briny dish, nubbly and spicy, devoid of finesse and completely satisfying.

The word "dentice" is often used on local Italian menus to represent "snapper." The two are not related, and perhaps to demonstrate the difference, this place sometimes obtains the genuine articles, fish that have swum in the Mediterranean, and serves them—grilled, skinned, and filleted—in this kitchen's version of livornese sauce, a smooth, pale-pink tomato sauce, slightly sour, with a couple of cracked black olives in it. Though carefully done—the fish is firm and moist—this swimmer, anyway this example of it, is of a flavor that is more than subtle, a condition due, perhaps, to meticulous preservation carelessly extended. You get an artfully grilled chicken here, moist meat cooked to the bone within a crusty and well-seasoned skin—the bird itself is not of exceptional flavor, but this is good food, which you liven by squeezing on the lemon that is provided. But if it is a bird you are after, and if it is on the menu, have quail instead. Quail is all dark meat, it is of powerful flavor, and at Il Cantinori it is served cut into small parts (a bone conveniently protruding from each) that are set in soft polenta—the scent of the bay leaves with which the parts are mingled permeates the meat. The rabbit stew is many huge chunks of the pale, tender game in a peppery sauce. The veal chop, oiled and broiled, is done to the perfect point—it is charred, cooked through but pink and juicy, livened a little by the sprigs of sage that adorn it. The lamb stew, with artichokes, is deep and gamy, its mahogany sauce winy and redolent of lamb fat—you either like that kind of thing or you do not.

The salads are not notable for the crispness of their greens. Your waiter suggests "champagne" grapes. You question him. He goes off and returns. Yes, he assures you, they are Pinot Noir. They are tiny, red, firm, sweet, and juicy, but you do wonder what Pinot Noir would not be reserved for wine. Another time the house tries to rescue some dreadful apricots by serving them in white wine—they remain dreadful apricots, green, dry, sour. Good cheeses are on hand, and the Parmesan is fine with fresh figs. The raspberries are ripe under their cool, frothy, well-balanced zabaglione.

★★CANTON

45 Division Street (near Market Street)
LUNCH AND DINNER. CLOSED MONDAY AND TUESDAY.
Reservations: 226-4441.
No credit cards.
Beer.
Medium priced.

Legendary belletrists, architects of international repute, prize-winning playwrights, world-class photographers, literary critics with hyphenated names, potent behind-the-scenes editors, byline journalists, and, even, headliners from the world of sport—all these types get themselves to Canton and, if necessary, wait, along with everybody else, on the street, or in the little alcove just inside the front door, for a turn at a table. Once within, they are at the next table to clusters of gents in jeans and plaid flannel shirts—their leather jackets are draped over the backs of their chairs, and their noses are three inches from their plates when they eat. Pop-eyed, purple-complected fat men come here, sweating and breathing hard, raving eaters, apparently let loose on one-night passes for an oral binge. You see silver-haired academics in rimless spectacles, Hispanics in sunglasses. And when the invading hordes from Queens hit Chinatown on weekend nights, discriminating defectors slip away from the squads of Szechuan addicts for something more subtle here. But what is unique about Canton's clientele is that, invariably, at least a few of the tables are occupied by mixed groups—of Chinese and Occidentals. And thereby depends some lowdown: Though this restaurant has had a menu printed up—complete with such categories as "Soup for One," "Soup for Two," "Chop Suey," "Chow Mein," "Egg Foo Young"—production of this document was clearly just a gesture to the suchness of the situation, for the composition of almost every meal consumed here is determined not by consulting a list but by conversation with the proprietor—a woman whose youthful appearance fails to signal the mature calm and good cheer with which she efficiently governs this place. Her English is as good as yours. But without a satisfactory written summary of the kitchen's real repertoire, white folks and other non-Asians often feel the need for some almond-eyed support during their encounters with the lady of the house. Unless you are unusually persistent, or have been here often and are known, singsong inquiries in native Chinese will yield more information than tuneless, grunting queries in New York English. Still, splendid dinners have been had on first visits by blonds. And if you feel that you must command—rather than ask questions—there are some swell orders in the paragraphs ahead.

Canton is a big, brightly lit, high-ceilinged, boxlike store, a cash register at the front, a stainless-steel coffee urn and some steel shelves at the back, and enough Formica-topped tables—some of them the huge round kind suitable for banquet dinners—to seat around sixty. This place has a Chinatown bare-necessities elementality about it, but it is in no way tattered or ramshackle or improvised. The walls are faced with a cheerful yellow quasicloth covering; the tables do not rock; the waiters are in crisp jackets; everything looks clean; and a lovely stained-glass fish adorns the front window—seafood is Canton's specialty.

But first, the first courses, a number of which your hostess and the regulars refer to, in English, by code names. "The lettuce," for example: one of those dishes consisting of flavored ground meat, which you make into a bundle by rolling a spoonful of it in a lettuce leaf, which package you then hold in your fingers and eat. What particularly distinguishes this version from that available in other restaurants is that the leaves of lettuce are large and unperforated, so the operation can be carried out without spillage. What further distinguishes it is that the meat is mingled with fresh green peas for sweetness, water chestnuts for crispness, strong garlic for flavor. The mixture is light, with a hint of charring in its flavor. Something called "buns" consists of three small slices of meat—lean pork, sweet ham, and tender white chicken, all lightly oiled and a little blackened—impaled on a wooden skewer, the meats accompanied by a two-part muffin of barely baked dough. You make a light, tasty sandwich of the "bun" and the succulent meats. The fried dumplings are fine, but they are much the standard thing, not notably superior to what you get in many places.

Seafood. Pan-fried butterfish: two whole fish, impeccably fresh, each the size of a gentleman's hand, strewn with scallion greens; the skin of the fish—which is crisped to a light, brittle flakiness—is a zest to the light meat within it. This is an easy fish to eat, for the side bones are delicate enough to swallow. The steamed flounder is big; it arrives spread out on a great platter in a pool of oily broth that is so hot the fish continues to cook on the table—you must eat it quickly, while it is fluffy and retains its subtly fibrous texture. The flounder is strewn with scallions and ginger, which are striking against the gentle white meat.

Sturdier seafood. Conch: slightly cartilaginous slices and morsels of the oceanic meat, mingled with ginger and scallions and bits of pepper that you encounter as a surprise every third bite or so, all vibrant in their peppery oil. Squid: the tubular shafts of the fresh, tender meat scored, as if by strokes of a sharp-pointed fork, darkened by a black-bean sauce, made tangy with little disks of scallion and bits of fresh, loud ginger, the whole a dish that is powerful but never weighty.

The roast duck is simple: a half bird cut into slabs that an expert can hold in chopsticks while chewing the crisp skin and moist meat from the bones—an occasional peppercorn adds a touch of fire to the rich meat. The herbed chicken is more complex, the skin coated with herbs that have been blackened in the cooking, the meat moistened with a black sauce that is salty, sweet, a little hard, but hardly too much for this chicken —for Canton obtains chickens that are as flavorful as the chickens of your memory.

Lotus root, that crisp, vaguely perfumed and prettily perforated legume, is mixed with meats here: pork and lotus root, the pork juicy and sweet, with crunchy snow peas, whole cloves of garlic, and ginger in the oily but not heavy dish; beef and lotus root, the slivers of beef medium rare, microcosmic steaks, water chestnuts and snow peas and mushrooms the bulk of the multitextured dish. Canton is capable of turning out such things as roast pork with wide noodles, one of those complicated assemblages the components of which are identifiable only by sight. But one of the simpler noodle dishes is superb, the thin strands of rice noodle moistened with dark oil and dotted here and there with bits of scallion and bits of ginger—as elegant as the most refined Italian pasta. You get terrific string beans: the vegetable barely cooked, crisp and hot and oiled, tossed with slices of red pepper, ground pork, and garlic, all in a gravylike and pungently seasoned dark-brown sauce. Many dishes are not always available. Skip dessert, unless you want some cool canned fruit.

Booze of all nations—Scotch whiskey, Wild Turkey, California rosé, cognac— adorns the tables, for you bring your own.

★★★ LA CARAVELLE

33 West 55th Street
LUNCH, MONDAY TO FRIDAY; DINNER, MONDAY TO SATURDAY. CLOSED SUNDAY.
Reservations: 586-4252.
Credit cards: AE, DC, MC, V.
Very expensive.

Each year fewer remain and, on the evidence of the scant attendance here, they seem to be shuffling off even more rapidly than actuarial tables would project. "They" are the conservators of old money who, in the days when La Caravelle *was* La Caravelle, peopled in genteel throngs its glittering rooms. Now, at dinner, this venerable (but still pretty) former bright star of the New York night is almost all alone with her memories. The legendary celebrity aisle that leads into the dining room proper, for example, tables-for-two before the cushy banquettes down the length of each side, are now MPT—*empty!* Nothing can be made, after all, of a celebrity aisle without celebrities. Or, more to the point, with celebrities who show up in double-breasted suits that threaten to slip off the shoulder, their pouting companions in silks that hang from outspread shoulder pads like drop curtains. You would understand, if not necessarily agree, if La Caravelle preferred to discourage that kind and just reminisce about the past.

With the retirement from this institution of Roger Fessaguet, its first chef and recent maître d'/partner, the establishment loses its last connection with the early days. With the simultaneous departure of Michael Romano, the unlikely Italian-American but French-trained chef who had taken this place a small step forward from its haute cuisine origins, and his replacement by another local boy, a very young David Ruggerio, Romano's former second in command, the house makes it clear that it will not cling desperately to what remains of the shrinking clientele from its bejeweled beginnings. The new menu, notwithstanding the presence on it of a few dishes served here when Ruggerio was born, is a longer step toward the near present than the one taken by the previous administration. The dining room, however, remains what it has ever been, a fantasy, sedate and aglitter, of crimson velvet, snowy linen, fresh flowers, and pretty, painterly murals of France—street scenes and park scenes and scenes of open squares, the Tricolors in all of them frozen where they have fluttered for three decades. Will the newish cooking thrive in, even revitalize, this reliquary of a fair but fading style? No reason why not, for the only logic of what works in New York is that the folks go where go the folks—the well, of course, must be primed.

If you bypass snail dishes on French menus on the ground that they are all minor variants on the familiar escargots bourgignonne, know that, with respect to snails at today's La Caravelle, the past is past. Not only are these morsels plump and meaty and tender, but they reach you in an herbed pernod sauce, dotted with bits of tomato and fennel, that is hot, heady, polished. Six of the snails are placed around the perimeter of your plate, at the center of which a circle of couscous holds within it more snails, mounded up—that couscous, of vivid wheat flavor, is in almost startling contrast to the escargots. Order grilled shrimp, and you are delivered of three giants, in their shells and split, their powerful sea taste potentiated but to no degree obscured by the flavor of their grilling—the crustaceans are garnished with a salad of many greens of many wild flavors in a lively dressing. The house smokes its own salmon and, sure enough, it is unlike other smoked salmon, much of the unsmoked flavor of the fish intact, the smoking flavor distinctly woody, the meat itself supple, tender, velvety when polished with oil. Unsmoked salmon is formed into a roulade with a mousse of paler fish that has been threaded with spinach, and you are served a couple of spiral-patterned slices cut from the loaf—this is light, almost fluffy stuff, its marine flavor delicate but clear, and it is at once enriched and livened by its pale sauce, which is dense with minced chives.

You are distressed to note that your lobster, though juicy and of full flavor, is more than a little resilient, which suggests that the beast met its end in an unrelaxed state of body—lobsters, like you, become tense when shocked, and they need a period of R&R before being shocked for the final time. Withal, this is good food, the fairly luscious meat out of its shell, set in a sauce that is enriched with foie gras, and garnished with a great swirl of fettuccine that is studded with small, sweet, wild morels. Striped bass has become a rarity on local menus—it seems the innocent swimmer can concentrate substances not yet officially classified as nutrients. The fillet you are served reveals by its flavor nothing to suggest it is less than good for you, and as its surface is handsomely browned, its interior firm and juicy, and its buttery, tomato-dotted sauce thick with flakes of artichoke, you dispatch the production in a trice, confident that you will thereby lengthen your days. Sweetbreads, as everyone knows, are yukky. Pinguid and all that. They are almost never prepared at home, for it is a rare family of more than one in which every member will eat them. But every slaughtered animal yields them up, low demand keeps their cost down, and offering them—especially as part of a $55 prix fixe dinner—makes financial sense. As it happens, it makes all kinds of sense, because an acquired taste for sweetbreads is never given up, since possession of it marks you a connoisseur. You glance at the Caravelle menu, you announce to your companions that whenever sweetbreads are listed you look no further, you order them—and find that every known method has been employed to counterbalance the oleaginous quality that, to so many, is off-putting: The sweetbreads are themselves browned and crusted; they are overlaid with a crisp potato pancake that cuts their richness; and they are set in a sauce that is spanking rather than rich—all of which makes for a striking dish. Two little quails seem like not much to eat, but these roasted, split birds are packed with a stuffing that consists in part of whole, large, meaty wild mushrooms, and the strong meat and extravagant dressing make a robust plate of food.

The dessert cart is wheeled to your table, and there is no problem, if you are so disposed, about having a little of this and a little of that—a tart and fluffy lemon layer cake, much of it whipped cream that is rich and airy; a nifty apricot tart that is set on a flaky pastry and strewn with browned almonds; a blueberry tart of plump ripe berries and more of those almonds; a raspberry mousse of liquorlike intensity. There are soufflés, which may be ordered for one person, and the one of chocolate and coconut works, the flavors are fine together, and the production is handsomely risen, browned, light.

★★CAROLINA

355 West 46th Street
LUNCH, MONDAY TO FRIDAY; DINNER, DAILY.
Reservations: 245-0058.
Credit cards: AE, MC, V.
Medium priced.

Here in America, American food is a novelty. Without half trying, you can go through life without eating any. But even if that is, in fact, what you have so far done, you will recognize the stuff at first bite. Knowing what you know about America, when you encounter American food, you are immediately convinced that, yes, this is what Americans would have eaten in those precosmopolitan times when this country's cookery—like every cookery—derived willy-nilly from what ran, swam, and grew nearby. Of course, you can die not only happy but virtuous never having touched the stuff. There is no moral side to the resurrection of a neglected style of cooking. You do not become a patriot by eating crab cakes instead of quenelles de brochets. But, these days anyway, do it, and you are at least fashionable. For there is, it seems, this little trend: not to so-called nouvelle American cuisine, which is precisely as American as François Mitterrand; but to the very cooking with which, for example, Mary Todd failed to cheer up Abraham Lincoln.

The installers of this place at this address moved into freshly abandoned quarters, and they kept what they found—that certain combination of the rough-hewn and the posh that, for a while there, was the favored look of new New York spots. The front room's soft light illuminates slick, glossy walls of pale gray, within which the tables are set with pale-pink linen. But overhead the beams that stripe the ceiling are coarse and splintery, and you walk on a plain wood floor. The curved bar comes from Paris and sports a well-burnished zinc top. But it is the back dining room that the public has come to prefer, and to reach it you proceed through a narrow, tiled passageway, a windowed wall of which reveals the kitchen—and its staff at their labors. Surely the word "glitz" was in mind when this room was executed. It is small, and the tables form a tight square before the taupe-colored suede banquette with which it is rimmed. The four walls are solidly mirrored up to the skylight ceiling. At the center of the room, under the skylight, a single potted palm stands on the carpeted floor. The mirrors all around reflect and re-reflect the scene, which recedes from you to infinity. The candles become a thousand glittering lights. The couple of dozen diners become a throng. Even the sounds of the room are reflected by the glass, so the cheerful crowd makes a din.

What cheers them is a cup (or bowl) of the house chili, an earthy, spiced stew, thick with little chunks of beef and, in the Texas manner, devoid of beans. The barbecue on lettuce is a big mound of firm but tender sliced meat, mildly spiced by the thick barbecue sauce with which it is coated, served on cool leaves of iceberg, and garnished with a single great circle cut from a red pepper. Carolina offers what it calls "hot smoked sweet sausage," and this is a pleasantly vulgar-tasting, coarsely peppered and abundantly fatted forcemeat, garnished with sautéed green and red peppers and onions, and served with barbecue sauce.

Though much of the food here has a convincingly American character—that is to say, if no backwoodsman ever ate it, he should have—some of the dishes are merely influenced by the influence, which, of course, is not to say they are not yummy. The cool fillet of beef, for example—thin slices of rosy roasted beef, their edges crisp—is very nice, with its sprinkling of capers and strands of red onion and strong, tart mustard-and-caper sauce. The green-chili soufflé, for another example, is a well-risen, handsomely brown-topped production; the mousse that is its insides is light, glistening with butter, and spicy; and the ramekin in which it is baked and served is lined with hot little green peppers. And then there is the Carolina pizza (named, one supposes, for the restaurant rather than the bi-state region), in which the base of hot, pully, fairly loud cheese is spread with peppers and onions.

In the kitchen there is a wood fire, over which are cooked regular menu items as well as daily specials: a salmon steak, utterly fresh, juicy, and flaky, gloriously charred, and served with a sparkling tartar sauce—but somehow, good as this fish is, you are disappointed that it has picked up so little flavor from the fire; what are called "red pepper shrimp," crunchy seafood, deeply flavored by the spice but marred by a touch of iodine; your basic shell steak—it takes well to this fire, which imparts a delicately crackling blackened surface to the beef while drying it not at all. Another section of the menu is headed "Hot Smoke," which a footnote more or less explains as, to paraphrase, meat cooked in a pit by scented wood smoke, the temperature never allowed to rise above 200 degrees, for as long as twenty hours. Ribs get this treatment, and they are tender, very meaty, and come with a red sauce the pungency of which is of flavor, not just strength. And breast of chicken gets the treatment, yielding white meat that is powerfully smoky, moist, livened by its charred surface. Sometimes the house hot-smokes pork—the resulting meat is rich and delicate, only slightly smoky, exhibiting mainly the sweet taste of the pork itself.

Here you get genuine strawberry shortcake, a hillock of biscuits, ripe berries, an abundance of whipped cream, and a sweet and tangy berry syrup. Something given as vanilla cream with black-currant sauce is a great, craggy mound of vanilla mousse in a pool of the intense sauce. The apple crisp is a cinnamoned, sugar-crumbed thing of crisp cooked fruit, much like a pie without a crust, and the mud cake is a chocolate cake of a nice coarseness—both are served with good whipped cream.

All the still table wines are American.

★ CAVE CANEM

24 First Avenue (near 2nd Street)
DINNER. CLOSED SUNDAY.
Reservations: 529-9665.
Credit cards: AE, DC, MC, V.
Medium priced.

No storefront betrays the presence of the restaurant-cum-disco housed in this refurbished old tenement, and it is in fact an entirely domestic scene that greets you when you open the street-level door: a mommy, a daddy, and a baby, all Doberman pinschers, pets of the proprietor on their way out for the nightly stroll, at the other end of their taut leashes a lady who gets back in protection more than she gives in comfort, for this is a defiantly ungentrified corner of the so-called East Village, where the restaurant's Latin title in translation ("Beware of the Dog") suggests an urgent subtitle ("And of Everything Else, Too"). You wish it were raining, for your inclination to sprint, not walk, the few steps from cab to front door could use the meteorological cover. Here near the intersection of First and 2nd everyone is suspect until proven dead, the streets being thick with folks who, no matter how they get by, are leading lives far more tempered than what their circumstances easily could explain.

Up a few stairs, then across a tiled floor in which the figure of a snarling canem (doggy) has been worked, then into the restaurant proper, an evocation of the grandeur that was Rome after the electricity was turned off. In the dim light you see, along one wall, what at first appears to be a row of four-sided tents, bifurcated and thereby made two-sided, which on closer inspection turns out to be a row of four-sided tents, bifurcated and thereby made two-sided. Each of them is furnished with an iron bench for two (complete with free-floating bolsters), a table before it. Within these semiprivate accommodations, couples of various (well, three) possible gender configurations dine, wine, and, presumably imagining two more walls to their tent, entwine. Across the room another seeming mirage, a wall of bedsheets, each sheet draped to resemble a toga worn by a stick figure, the togas stiffened in place by application of wet plaster that eventually dried. If you recall SoHo when it was new, you know the artsy and not-so-artsy crowd here—asymetric hair, basic black and straw hat, short shifts over long tights, mixed couples in identical clothes, unmixed couples in hardly any clothes, and, especially on weekends, anthropologists from across the waters here on field trips.

The waiters, what with their white turtlenecks and long white aprons, appear to be not so much dressed in white as swathed in it (more or less in the manner of Roman senators). Among them you encounter the inaudible, the pontifical, and, most trying of all, the uninflected garrulous, he who tells you that such and such is in a sauce made with red wine and shallots, and who adds, in the identical tone of voice, that it is also sumptuous and exquisite. To which you presumably answer, "Not what I had in mind. Haven't you anything that's luscious and sublime?" No, but the battered little circles of fried calamari are crisp and devoid of grease, and though their herbed and lemony mayonnaise has a nice tartness, the mustard-garlic-horseradish sauce, which, happily, reaches you in a separate dish, is caustic. What goes as heliogabalus—you know, silly, heliogabalus?—consists of three wee disks cut from a seafood sausage (less to eat than what you expect is often an issue here) that is rather sweet, as is their rich shellfish sauce, so the bitter greens tangled among the disks are a nice note. The nutted pâté is cold, cloying, much in need of the fiery mustard served with it. But the boar pancake—you know, silly, boar pancake?—is hot, the morsels of tender meat, with raisins and vegetables, wrapped in a thin pancake and set in a dark and winy sauce, though with all that is going on, it hardly matters that the meat is boar, rather than, for example, bear. The "salad of edible flowers" is a green salad that incorporates two or three flowers. The salad of "wild and gathered greens" is a green salad that does not. In both, the greens are fresh, the dressing made with good oil.

You are not asked how you want your broiled tuna, it arrives rare, barely warm, and therefore the lump of herbed anchovy butter with which it is surmounted declines to melt—still, this is fresh fish, firm and tender and meaty within its crosshatched surfaces. Have your soft-shell crabs straight, and you get two of them, nicely crisped in their garlicky sauce of herbs and minced scallions. Or you may have a single crab astride a fillet of monkfish, the shellfish and finfish good foils to each other, the two in a sauce that is smoky of tarragon. It is true, the listing, "salad of grilled quail and artichoke," refers to the bird in the singular. Still, a solitary quail is a lonesome dinner, even when accompanied by a great pyramid of salad greens adorned with lengths of red pepper, a crescent of ripe papaya, and chunks of artichoke—good food, but starvation for the protein habituated. The lamb chops, at considerable loss of their character, are crisped in an herbed and eggy Parmesan cheese batter. Why?, you may well ask. The black-currant sauce served with them does not provide the answer. So if it is red meat you want, it is the sirloin of beef you will have, the very decent steak adorned with whole shallots and chunks of bone marrow in its dark and winy sauce.

Mostly good desserts, among them a pie of many fruits that tingles with sweet spices; an array of melons, fruits, and berries; a layer cake of raspberry mousse and chocolate mousse set in an intense raspberry sauce; a good chocolate mousse cake that is little more than a concentration of chocolate touched with orange. With any of those you may have the liquored whipped cream of the house. The cashew ice cream is one of those flavors that gets you concentrating real hard—yes, you *can* discern the cashew flavor.

The downstairs disco offers an empty swimming pool, made-up cots, murk, alcohol, music.

★★CEDARS OF LEBANON

39 East 30th Street
LUNCH AND DINNER.
Reservations: 725-9251.
Credit cards: AE, DC, MC, V.
Inexpensive.

The history of the Cedars of Lebanon (on East 30th Street, not in the Levant) is one of repeated redecoration in pursuit of anonymity. Originally a seedy place and then a garish one, in both those incarnations the Cedars threatened to become camp-fashionable. Now the place is Motel Byzantine, with a Cocktail Lounge barroom, red carpeting, shimmering wallpaper of golden branches on a soft gray ground, paneling of dark, grainy wood, and beige-linened tables softly illuminated by lights recessed in the deep-maroon ceiling. You note also, at one end of the long dining room, a platform, the appliances on which suggest that on occasion players of amplified instruments perform there. Story is that though the $5 lunch is quite an attraction by day, by night this establishment's neighborhood is deserted. To attract the folks it has been necessary to make of the mere restaurant a social scene—anyway on Friday and Saturday nights.

On those evenings rows of tables are shoved together to accommodate great gatherings of clans. Swarthy, black-haired Easterns in three-piece suits bring blond girlfriends here—to show off their culture to their ladies, and to display their conquests to their compatriots. When the ouzo on the rocks has been flowing for a while, the gents remove their neckties. If things are going swimmingly, the giggling ladies put them on. Flashbulbs pop. The waiters move really fast. And promptly at 10:15 the 10 o'clock music starts. The thumping, modal wailing and loud singing get them clapping their hands. One waiter half closes his eyes and sways a little to the music as he delivers a dozen skewers of shish kebab, and the ladies in the party shriek in delirium at the wanton departure from role. The real frenzy begins later, when the belly dancing starts.

Between passions the crowd eats kibbee nayeh, chopped raw lamb, lightly oiled and seasoned, mixed with cracked wheat. They eat thick hommus and a smoky and well-oiled baba ghannoush, tabbouleh that is lemoned and fragrant with greens, hot spinach pies, cold grape leaves that are oily and lemony and filled with sweet-spiced rice. They drink a yogurt soup that is minted, soured with lemon, hot. That shish kebab is abundant, two big skewers of broiled marinated lamb, chunks of tomato, onion, pepper. The kaftah kebab is two great logs of ground lamb, spiced and juicy and steamy. The baked kibbee is like a nutted and grainy ground-lamb sandwich, black and crusty, served with warm stuffed grape leaves—a homey and satisfying dish. The place makes a coarse couscous, a hefty lamb stew that is here served in a red sauce with chick-peas, big chunks of root vegetable, and a mound of hot, moist grain. Steaks, chicken dishes, even a couple of seafood dishes, fill out the menu, but lamb is the basis of this food.

The honeyed and nutted pastries are served here in good versions—the baklava, with its brandylike sweetness and thickness of ground walnuts, is much above average. The bird's nest is a flaky little circle of pastry, like a doughnut without a hole, its center filled with honeyed pistachios.

★ CELLAR IN THE SKY

1 World Trade Center
DINNER, ONE SITTING. CLOSED SUNDAY.
Reservations: 938-1111 (deposit required).
Credit cards: AE, DC, MC, V.
Very expensive.

The Cellar lures neurotics and other mildly disturbeds. It offers, after all, what the emotionally unfinished long for—"return" to that perfect childhood that never was, when everything was taken care of. The long, varied menus that ordinary restaurants offer are probably full of promise to you. But to the chronically undecided they are a threat. You see these types everywhere—they read the bill of fare as if it holds an indecipherable secret, look desperately at dishes on nearby tables, ask questions not only of the help, but of one another, want urgently to order the right thing, invariably end up fearing they have not. To them, losing the right to choose is like a reprieve from final exams. All at once, they cannot fail.

Naturally, Cellar in the Sky does not promote itself as respite from the wearies of decision making. Though the menu and the five wines served with it are fixed of an evening (every two weeks, everything changes), this format is ostensibly aimed at perfection—the flawless marriage of foods and boozes—not at escape. And of course those who come here do not admit that they are symbolically seeking the cared-for condition of ideal infancies. Rather, they persuade themselves that a visit to the Cellar is an expression of their connoisseurship (not to mention a conspicuous display of their position in life). You actually see people here closing their eyes and wrinkling their foreheads as they ecstatically inhale the bouquets of wines that are surely embarrassed over all the attention. Which is regrettable, for the Cellar is best used for what it is, an eating place that, given half a chance, is an excellent background for your private purposes, with the succession of foods and wines a series of mild diversions that only occasionally command your attention. Moreover the duration of the dinner and the nature of the setting may be exactly suitable when your goals are interpersonal (persuasion) rather than gastronomic. For you can easily pass three or more hours here over dinner; and the room, a dim aerie set within Windows on the World—away downtown and away up in the sky and with no view of any worldly thing outside its walled confines—seems as remote from New York as the cabin in the sky itself.

You must ride up 107 stories in the elevator with the honeymooners and farm equipment conventioneers and members of the East Cupcake Gourmet Society on their annual field trip—all of them bound for Windows. But once inside the Cellar, you are effectively alone. The physical place is muted, and its frequenters observe library decorum in apparent honor of some of the appointments—racks of esteemed wines on the walls, wine cases with the names of legendary châteaux burned into the wood. The wine-cellar theme is expressed as well in the bare tables—around a dozen of them—and the low archways that straddle the massive pillars. You sit in chairs of wood and leather that are much like director's chairs, except that they do not fold. The place is illuminated by pinpoint spotlights—they cast gentle beams here and there, which are reflected by, among other things, those wine bottles, casting bits and spots of soft light on the polished tables and marble floor. A guitarist strums.

A uniformed gentleman (title: wine steward; function: wine pourer) asks if you would like champagne or kir royale. The kir royale, you understand, is the same champagne (in this instance the Piper Brut of 1980), to which has been added a bit of crème de cassis, an effective method of making wine into soda pop. So much for high oenological seriosity. That particular champagne—like almost all Cellar wine—is nothing special, actually somewhat hard, but worthy of better than dilution with alcoholic syrup.

Champagne is really appropriate to almost no food, but here it lasts through the quasi cocktail hour that is built into the extended dinner, when it is served to you with whole grain crackers and then with individual little leek tarts, two-inch quiches, really, that are just made, quite fluffy, sport a vivid flavor of the vegetable; and through the first course, cool sections cut from a roulade of sliced chicken wrapped around spiced mussels, those garnished with tender asparagus spears that are moistened with a good vinaigrette. The 1981 Puligy-Montrachet Clavoillon of Leflaive is a wine that is perfectly polished, but with more of the maker's finesse in it than fruit. It accompanies a creamy frogs' leg soup that is much like a billi-bi—briny and stout. The same wine is poured with ridiculously oversalted ravioli of snapper and celery—they are otherwise of good flavor and texture in their cream sauce. No amount of exposure to air by pouring and by twirling in the glass can overcome the prematurity of this Freemark Abbey Cabernet Bosché of 1975, which clearly will not be ready for at least three years. To serve it with this venison makes verbal sense (big wine with game) but no other, for this meat is tender and sweet next to its fruit-and-pumpkin garnish, and the next wine, a Léoville Lascases of 1970, all elegance, suits it more than the good cheeses with which it is actually served.

The Cellar of course serves sweet wine with dessert. This is a fine Niersteiner Oelberg Beerenauslese of 1976, fruity but not obvious, heady and fairly intense. It would be great with nothing at all, or with foie gras. But no wine—not sweet wine, not fortified wine, not champagne—makes much sense with sugared food. (Brandy makes some sense, coffee makes more.) To serve this wine with an atrocity called "coffee and chocolate charlotte"—a layer of chocolate pudding over a layer of coffee pudding on a chocolate-snap crust—is a really super boo-boo.

The wines of the evening are listed, with the food menu, on a little sign on each table. You may, if you wish, limit yourself to the best wines of those offered, or have your wines in an order other than the suggested one.

The prix fixe dinner is $77 per person, including wine, plus tax and tip.

★★CENT'ANNI

50 Carmine Street (near Bedford Street)
LUNCH, MONDAY TO FRIDAY; DINNER, DAILY.
Reservations: 989-9494.
Credit cards: AE.
Medium priced.

Much has been written (even more has not been written) about the multiplication
of Italian restaurants in New York. Many attribute the phenomenon to the introduction
of a lighter style of Italian cooking than obtained in the old days (when the standard
Italian restaurant sported red-and-white checked cloths on the tables, empty chianti
bottles in baskets hanging from the ceiling, and sauces on which it was possible to float
meatballs). All of which is, of course, nonsense. Italian cooking took hold when Italian
spaghetti manufacturers conspired among themselves to adulterate all pasta packaged for
export with small quantities of an addictive drug known only to Italian spaghetti manufacturers, the result being that today the catch-phrase, "I feel like a plate of spaghetti" has
become even more familiar than the erstwhile frontrunner, "I feel like a beer." You know
the result: French restaurants, American restaurants, all kinds of restaurants are now
compelled to peddle the noodle just to survive. Unfortunately, in all this culinary tur-
moil the city has begun to forget about pasta *qua pasta*. Children, just because you
cannot get enough of the stuff, it does not follow that you hve to accept any stuff at all.
As a helpless drunk still prefers Anchor Steam to Budweiser, one pasta fix is better than
another. None of which is meant to suggest that Cent'Anni is just a spaghetti joint,
rather that when you choose to indulge your lust at this place, a number of interesting
variations are available: very thin spaghetti, for example, capellini, in a vigorous lobster
sauce that is winy, briny, sea-gamy, rousing; short hefty spaghetti, penne, for another, in
a dark sauce that is nubbly of ground veal and vibrant of fresh sage; even heftier pasta,
rigatoni, in a bright tomato sauce that is thick with chunks of sautéed zucchini, a dish
that quite transcends its simplicity; rigatoni again, this time "alla medici," in a rich
cream sauce in which vegetables and wild mushrooms are important elements—no
surprise there, but so is this white meat of chicken, its flavor an unexpectedly vivid
element among the others; and pappardelle, the broad thick noodles in a stewlike rabbit
sauce that is redded with tomato—the thing acquires particular depth when cheese is
grated on. Half orders of pasta are served, so there is no problem hving yours as a first
course. Still, you may prefer to start with a seafood salad in which scallops, shrimp, bits
of celery, and lengths of red onion are roused by a lemony dressing; or, when they are
offered, with stuffed eggplant or sautéed pleurotte mushrooms, the former cold and tart
and salty in their tomato sauce, the latter, though powerfully garlicked and seasoned, of
clear mushroom flavor.

Come here once, and the main course to have is the whole snapper. You are shown
the grilled fish, its coppery scales glinting; it is taken away, returned to you as four filleted
quadrant lengths—the fish is fresh, light, moist, its flavor potentiated by the olive oil
and seasonings in which it is done. You will be delighted to learn that tripe is always
available. If you have not yet mastered getting this particular offal behind your teeth,
Cent'Anni is a good place to try again, for tripe, if it is well handled, has no taste of its

113

own, and its texture does not seem quite so gummy when it is one item among many, as in this stew, with its strong black olives, tomatoes, onions, carrots, the entirety made especially hearty when strong cheese is added. The rabbit that was fine with those pappardelle is unfortunately cooked to death in what is given as coniglio alla fiorentina. The baby rack of lamb, served as four small grilled chops, is fine.

It is well to know that, though not listed, several good cheeses and fresh fruit are available. The zabaglione is obvious, sweet rather than winy. Sometimes there is a strawberry layer cake that is so sugary it hurts real teeth.

Oh, yes, the physical restaurant itself—a clean, well-lighted, white-painted place, rows of tables and chairs, a little bar at the back, and pictures on the walls that disagree among themselves as to plumb. Cent'Anni has a new ceiling, is less noisy than it once was, you can even hear the variously Italian-accented waiters as they courteously and intelligently deliver the word.

★★★ CHALET SUISSE

6 East 48th Street
LUNCH AND DINNER. CLOSED SATURDAY AND SUNDAY.
Reservations: 355-0855.
Credit cards: AE, DC, MC, V.
Expensive.

Chalet Suisse has been in New York for around a half century. A few decades ago it changed hands, and fifteen years ago it moved from its original 52nd Street site to the present one on East 48th. Restaurant guidebooks from the 1930s reveal that some of the dishes served now were served then. But during its long and consistent history, Chalet Suisse has never been the rage. It is, and for years has been, simply a marvelous restaurant, characterized by the most fundamental restaurant virtues. Enough people know about the place to keep it quite humming, but they do not make a lot of noise about their knowledge. Chalet Suisse is not mentioned in the gossip columns. Faces seen on television are not seen here. And the city's culinary avant-garde have never discovered the restaurant's merits (though the hot new places they tout every year cannot, ten times in eleven, warm this one up).

Chalet Suisse has the look of an old-fashioned European country inn. Its comfort derives from its simplicity. Rough plaster walls, the color of aged ivory, are hung here and there with oil paintings and pottery. The ceiling beams are of dark wood. Ironwork and suggestions of arches and pillars divide the room into snug areas, and the banquettes along the sides are fitted into niches. The tables are surrounded by slat-back chairs that have loose cushions on the seats. The restaurant is softly lighted by sconces that give off an amber glow.

Much of the pleasure of eating at Chalet Suisse traces to its civilized service. The standard is set by your host, a gentleman who seems to take pleasure in touring his restaurant floor to fill a glass here, provide a fresh plate there, answer questions, whatever. Happily, the waitresses follow his example. They are dressed in what are, presumably, native Swiss costumes, brightly colored, trimmed with lace, protected by gaily striped aprons. And they attend to their tasks with alertness, intelligence, and goodwill. It is enough to make you cry.

At lunchtime, the most tasteful executives of the least frivolous industries decorously crowd the place to the rafters, filling it with the soft, cheery tinkle of ample coin. At night, vintage New Yorkers, sometimes whole families of them, relax here in a manner most at-home. The Chalet is also well known to visiting European businessmen, Stockholmers and Amsterdammers and Düsseldorfers, who have found here the little plot of Manhattan Island that is echt home away from Frau.

Swiss food, as all the world knows, derives in large part from German, Italian, and French cooking. It is, however, less ponderous than German, less emotional than Italian, more forthright than haute cuisine, more dramatic than cuisine bourgeoise. So much for eminently destructible generalizations. Whatever its provenance, much of what the Swiss eat is sui generis—like bündnerschinken and bündnerfleisch, the salted-and-dried ham and beef of Switzerland. The ham is pink, smoky, and high, with fiber in its texture, fat around its rim; the beef is a stronger red but a paler flavor, rather gentle for a cured raw meat. Each is served in abundant portions, the rosy slices spread across broad plates. The so-called cervelat salad is humbler stuff, disks of porky sausage adorned with marinated onions and moistened with a light vinaigrette. The meats and the sausage are especially good with the strong, salty breads and the splendid sweet butter served here, and they may be nicely supplemented with an order of mushrooms Ascona, in which the chunks of fresh mushroom are served in an herby and slightly sour sauce that is thick with morsels of tomato.

Among the hot appetizers, the sleeper is the ravioli milanese. It is not like what you get in your neighborhood spaghetti joint. These tender pasta envelopes are filled with fluffy ground meat, greens, and grain; they are bathed in buttery consommé; and they are strewn with just-ground strong cheese and fresh parsley. The dish is airy, it seems to sing a little, and it disappears weightlessly, miraculously. There are wondrous snails, deeply flavored by the stock they were poached in, served in an herbed and well-salted butter; a cheese-and-onion pie that is actually a hefty quiche larded with sautéed onions; and délice d'Emmenthal, crescents of strong Swiss cheese that have been breaded and deep-fried until the cheese is hot, soft, and pully, the crust brown and crisp.

When your enchanting waitress spoons some médaillons de veau aux morilles onto your hot plate, she always asks, "May I keep the rest of this warm for you?" And when she delivers the balance (having observed that you vanished the first helping in a twinkling), she brings a fresh hot plate as well. This second delivery, if you forget to expect it, can render you deliriously happy, for this delicate veal, in its polished brandy sauce, studded with woodsy wild mushrooms, is at once easy, earthy, and rich. Then there is the veal chop sauté au marc du Valais—a large eye of meat on a long bone that is dressed in a little paper pant, the meat white, flecked with glistening brown, and moistened with a dark sauce and dozens of hot, sweet white grapes. There is a crusty rack of lamb, touched with garlic, utterly tender, juicy, and slightly high—racks of lamb are not roasted better within a day's drive of this restaurant. Liver and kidney à la Suisse is composed of bite-size chunks of the meats in a stout, herbed, gravylike sauce. Another dark sauce, this one winier and more polished, is served with slices of tender beef as filet de boeuf à la mode du chef. Whatever you do, do not pass up the rösti, the remarkable Swiss potato dish in which partially cooked potatoes are formed into broad pancakes that are then fried until golden. At Chalet Suisse the pancakes are crusty and tender, and if you are not yet in love with your waitress, you will capitulate completely when she comes around with a second plate.

The outstanding, low-priced main course is a cheese fondue called Neuchâteloise. It is perhaps a bit more work than eating in a restaurant ought to be, but this dish, brought to you bubbling over a flame in an enamel pot, dispels quibbles. The soft, slightly pully, nutmeg-flavored mixture of Emmenthal and Gruyère cheeses, mingled with wine and kirsch and a little garlic, is solid and heady, and it thickens and becomes stronger as it simmers. A basket of bread cubes is supplied, and you eat the dish by dunking the bread in the hot and fragrant stuff.

If you wish to continue dunking, the chocolate fondue (for two) is yet another bubbling pot, this one filled with chocolate that is at once creamy and sharp and sweet, slightly liquored, into which you dip slices of fruit—pineapple, banana, apple—thereby creating your own hot little candies. Chocolate is prominent throughout the dessert list. The chocolate mousse has an emphatic, almost naked chocolate intensity; the coupe chocolat is little more than a perfect sundae: vanilla ice cream and the kind of rich and fluffy, unsugared whipped cream that is just about unobtainable in restaurants these days—you pour a strong, hot, nutted chocolate over the two white creams and eat. The apple tart, a simple pastry filled with crisp fruit, is a good vehicle for more of that whipped cream—as is Aargauer rüblitorte, a lightly liquored carrot-and-almond cake—as is the surprise Valaisanne, a crisp meringue that is mounded over with fresh strawberries that have been cured with Grand Marnier. The dessert menu is long, and all the sweets are pure and fresh.

★★★ CHANTERELLE

2 Harrison Street (at Hudson Street)
DINNER. CLOSED SUNDAY AND MONDAY.
Reservations: 966-6960.
Credit cards: AE, MC, V.
Very expensive.

When Chanterelle appeared at its first home on the corner of Grand and Greene, it was one of many SoHo restaurants the looks of which were determined in part by what was found on site. In these places the gutting, smoothing, and furnishing were minimal, dictated by tight budgets, and much imaginative appreciation was focused on anything found that could be used. Often mongrelism resulted. But from time to time, as when a hybrid or mutant better suits its environment than existing species, a combination of the abandoned and what was brought in made a new whole of startling "originality"—in quotes because such results were often accidental.

Such was Chanterelle I, wherein the spare lines, a triptych of a stamped-tin ceiling (from which three chandeliers begged to be hung), tall windows on two sides through which street lights shone, simple but handsome furnishings—a desk and armoire in addition to the tables and high-backed chairs—made a room of a dignity, restraint, even spaciousness (though the space was not large) that were peculiarly Early American. Anyway, something like that, for its character was singular and elusive—in describing it you lost it.

That room is gone forever, after ten years as a rented store. The new Chanterelle, being in premises owned by the restaurateurs, may well last through the summer of the next century. Yet in putting the new place together an attempt has been made to perpetuate the old one in larger quarters. You are told that Chanterelle II actually devolves from the new site, that nothing was carried over from the old place that did not suit the new one. Maybe. But to innocent eyes this looks like Chanterelle I multiplied by around

1.75, in the process of which transfer and enlargement the fugitive magic of the original has been lost. More to the point, what the new place would have been if its design had not been hobbled by the old one is also lost.

None of which is to suggest that today's Chanterelle is grotesque. In fact it gives no offense, you may well be flattered by its size and openness. But whereas the character of the old place could be lost in the telling, there is nothing so fragile in the cool luxe, fabricated of almost the same elements, that is the new one. The dining room is a broad, high-ceilinged oblong, suggesting in its proportions, if not its dimensions, a great hall, an effect reinforced by three brass chandeliers that, in a row down the room's long axis, hang from the tailored-to-fit, white-painted, stamped-tin ceiling. Like the original, the new Chanterelle is a corner store, this one with six outsize windows notched into its pale-apricot walls, four on Harrison Street, two on Hudson—low curtains on each of them shield diners from the eyes of passersby. A single large white-linened table stands under each window, with ten more distributed, much space around them, across the gray carpeting. A giant burst of flowers is illuminated by overhead spots at one end of the room. Only one element relates not at all, or only by stretched imagining, to the old place: stained-wood pilasters, complete with finials just below the ceiling, that are affixed at intervals to the room's walls. Columns that hold up nothing always look silly, and in these no way was found around that difficulty. If there were ever some chance that the grace of the original Chanterelle could have been transplanted to this site, the grandiose columns queered it.

Fear not, this is still Chanterelle. Civilization spoken here. Occupiers even of tables other than your own appear to pass the tests of sanity and taste, albeit here, south of Canal, you note more Wall Street dress than you did up in SoHo. And you are still waited on by a cordial staff in white shirts and white aprons, they still know the menu inside and out despite its bi-weekly revision, and they are, blessedly, neither too much with you nor out to lunch.

Yes, this is still Chanterelle, which means, among other things, that though the menu is rewritten every two weeks, the grilled seafood sausage is always a first course. But, as if to suggest that the more things remain the same, the more they change for the worse, you get one that is touched with the iodine of some poorly chosen shrimp, and only your reflexive distaste for reflexive moralizing keeps you from conclusions about success and overconfidence. Anyway, you do not hit that bottom again, surely not in these oysters with cabbage and caviar, in which the bluepoint meats are warmed through but not really cooked—their "raw" flavor is intact—are returned to their half-shells in their own sweet, briny, slightly enriched juice, where they are joined by a bit of fine-slivered cabbage for texture, and a dollop of black caviar that, for all its intensity, does not obscure the oyster itself. In the "salad of salmon" you find as many kinds of greens, almost, as leaves, some of their wild flavors like those of fragrant herbs, to which have been added edible flowers and slivers of salmon—and also bits of salmon skin, fat attached, that have been crisped until they are almost hard, like the nuggets of bacon in a salade frisée. What goes as an oxtail terrine is a cold, dark jelly, of deep broth flavor, in which are embedded a many-textured assortment of chunks and shreds of meat and disks of carrot, the bright orange very pretty on the murky ground. Another terrine, this one cool, a compacture of foie gras from which you are served a pale-pink, buttery-seeming slice that you can just about spread onto the warm toast served with it—the rich meat is garnished with shredded radish in a red wine vinaigrette that is tart, bracing. When foie gras is not offered that way, it may be offered another, sautéed and hot, the organ meat pink and rich and juicy within its browned surfaces, its striking sauce dotted with cracked black peppercorns and strands of sweet, gentle onion. Withal, your luck is at its best

117

when you and the vegetable ragout are here the same night, for the harmless-seeming dish (it looks like vegetable soup) startles you with the potent taste of its vegetables, sweet carrots and fragrant fennel and celery among them, in the dark and earthy broth—flakes of black truffle account in part for the intensity of the flavors.

What is innocently listed as "lobster and sauternes" is, too bad, an unexceptional lobster, but the word "sauternes" understates the rich sauce, which is of heady shellfish flavor potentiated by the red lobster coral with which the sauce is dotted. The swordfish is utterly fresh, the three chunks you are served—they are about the size of children's blocks—are handsomely browned, rare but warmed through, and their buttery lemon sauce is almost frothy in its lightness. But if you must choose between that and salmon, the pink one is the fish that takes better to being "undercooked," for when it is rare and right, as it is here, salmon has a lusciousness like that of ripe melon—the salmon is roused by its lemoned and caper-dotted sauce. When there is squab, the bird is juicy in its crackling skin, its winy sauce is livened by small chunks of bacon, and some sweet and buttery cabbage is the nifty foil to the strong meat. But then there is the rack of lamb, its rosemary sauce a marvelous concentration of the herb, the tender, rare meat pink and glistening—and of almost no lamb character. And then there is this saddle of venison, which is garnished with a mound of woodsy wild mushrooms flanked by sharp, almost bitter kale that is in striking contrast to them, everything in a sauce that is dark, strong, edgy—but this venison is indeterminate meat, could be any meat.

Better cheese trays than Chanterelle's are not found in New York—the selection changes constantly but is always broad; the cheeses are at their peak, the fruit is firm and ripe, the walnut bread is fresh and light. In rhubarb season Chanterelle does rhubarb things, makes a millefeuille or a tart, in each of which the fruit has been judiciously tamed, so that it is sour but not overpoweringly so within the good pastries. A homey apple tart is warm, sweet spiced, is garnished with "spice" ice cream—a cold complexity of warm spice flavors. Prunes and dried black figs are served in red wine—the chewy but tender fruit is at once gentled and livened by the wine, and it is garnished with good whipped cream strewn with chopped walnuts. Ice creams and sherbets, lively ones and delicate ones, are always available.

★ CHELSEA CENTRAL

227 Tenth Avenue (near 23rd Street)
LUNCH, SUNDAY TO FRIDAY; DINNER, DAILY.
Reservations: 620-0230.
Credit cards: AE, MC, V.
Medium priced.

Your basic converted saloon, long bar up front, barbershop-tile floor, 4-bladed fans under the stamped-tin ceiling, jukebox. A joined pair of vintage telephone booths—complete with working phones, folding doors, and little fans that spin—forms the hint of a partition between the barroom and the dining room in the back, which houses rows of white-linened tables, dark bentwood side chairs around them. The standing coat racks are all right, the exposed brick here and there is surely to be expected in a place of this kind, and the posters contribute to the slightly cluttered comfort of the softly lighted place. But even if it were to be established that the construct of mirrors and stained glass that dominates the back wall is the only surviving example of a long lost folk form, no right-thinking landmarks commissioner with any kind of eye could possibly be restrained from smashing the hideous thing if allowed near it.

Styled "An American Bistro," the Café undertakes to ennoble such Americana as the shrimp cocktail. There is no denying the fiery sparkle of this cocktail sauce, nor the excellence of the oil with which the salad at the center of your plate is dressed, and it is always a pleasure not to find the shrimp hanging on as if in a struggle for life to the edge of a glass cup of cracked ice, but the crustaceans themselves, their good texture notwithstanding, are only of the remotest seafood flavor. Each of the five fried oysters is surmounted by a strand of roasted red pepper, and they are all set in a lemony mayonnaise that sparkles a bit, but the oysters are in a batter that outweighs them, overwhelms them, they have been fried too long, at considerable sacrifice of flavor, and the shoestring potatoes with which they are garnished only add to the impression that this is boardwalk food with airs. Happily, this American Bistro is of the melting-pot school, makes immigrant dishes its own, wraps great sheets of grilled eggplant around warm slabs of mozzarella and chunks of roasted red pepper, serves the packages in an herbed and seasoned oil. Nor do difficulties arise if the foreigners are of impure lineage, as is this duck salad, the slices of warm, dark, tender meat of exceptionally vivid flavor against the well-dressed lettuce and tomatoes over which they are strewn—the other side of this item is a couple of crusts of bread, the slices of goat cheese on each surfaced with fresh herbs.

The excess of salt on this salmon suggests it was seasoned by someone, then seasoned by someone else, but that is not enough to undo the fresh, carefully grilled fillet—the fish, and the fresh spinach pasta served with it, are in a thick and creamy sauce that is fragrant of dill and dotted with bits of tomato. Another creamy sauce, this one spicy and threaded with long strands of chive, moistens the thin, thin angel hair pasta, which is tossed with sautéed shrimp that, this time, are full of flavor. The grilled chicken benefits from its charring, for the bird itself is bland, and it is spread with the minced scallions and tomatoes that were stranded on it when the dull sauce of which they were a component was poured over—the muffin of wild leek risotto at the center of your plate has the dried surface of a thing that has been waiting to be called. You get a more than decent grilled sirloin, though its degree of doneness is not exactly what you specified.

The hazelnut mousse tart is just a sticky richness of little hazelnut quality—it is garnished with loose whipped cream. So is the chocolate amaretto cake, which is almost black under its deep-brown icing, of sharp chocolate strength, the amaretto a good note of heady clarity in the rich setting. The deep dish sour cream apple pie is a great thickness of apple slices overlaid with a great thickness of sweet-spiced pecans—a vigorous if obvious dessert. The lemon curd tart is notable for the sourness and smoothness of the custard on the rather dull pastry.

★ CHEZ JACQUELINE

72 MacDougal Street (near Houston Street)
DINNER.
Reservations: 505-0727.
Credit cards: AE.
Medium priced.

The picture side of an old French monochrome postcard has been blown up, framed, and mounted on the wall right next to the short bar that occupies one end of this small restaurant. The fuzzy picture depicts a section of the beach at Nice, circa 1910. In it you see ladies and gentlemen of the era, some with parasols, strolling under the palm trees. Nearby, rowboats have been pulled up onto the sand. Like all old photographs, it reminds you of your mortality. And, like many, it may make you nostalgic for a past you never knew—and, in so doing, cause you to appreciate this place for the little it does preserve. For Chez Jacqueline manages (happily, without the assistance of embarrassing trappings) to recall a bit of subtropical France in the era before it was invaded by the second half of the twentieth century—a function without which the restaurant might be no more than marginally noteworthy. It is the combination of more-or-less down-home French cooking and modest, mildly evocative surroundings that makes this place more than what it is.

What it is is a plain, low-ceilinged rectangle of a store, its length parallel to Mac-Dougal Street. And what it is when the weather is fine is a parallel place, out on the sidewalk, under the long awning that runs from the northern to the southern end of the establishment. For, just as in many eating places along the Riviera, when it is hot outside, it is cooler inside; but when it is at all temperate outside, it is hotter inside. Jacqueline's dining room sports air-conditioning vents, but they do little to stand in your way if what you wish to do is have a good time and sweat. Outside, you get this really terrific view of the little park that extends from MacDougal to Sixth Avenue just above Houston Street—and the gay carousings therein of the neighborhood's aspiring young goons-to-be. Inside, the white-linened tables are in neat rows. The floor is tiled. The walls are vaguely patterned in a way that suggests the very thick walls of houses in hot parts of the world. A palm here and a philodendron there add marginally to the semi-equatorial effect.

To the gruff gentlemen who serve you, learning restaurant ways was not second nature. One chap breathes hard and stares at the ceiling as he itemizes the daily specials. And the boss appears much more at ease when he is pouring himself a glass of wine at a table of his pals than when forcing himself through the motions of proprietorial politesse.

If nothing about the physical restaurant and its style put you in mind of its region of origin, the brandade de morue may. This is a provençale dish of salted codfish, oiled and pounded into a paste, fortified with garlic and flavored with parsley until (in this version) the mash is a brilliant green—the dish is served here in a shallow casserole dish, hot from the oven, and it is very good with cold wine of any color. Jacqueline serves, sometimes, a good octopus salad—cool morsels of the resilient but tender meat, with bits of shallot and much parsley, in a dressing that is little more than good oil. That is much to be preferred to her mussels—their powerfully garlicked tomato broth is fine,

120

but the mussels themselves are rank. The snails here are leathery little morsels, their red sauce at once strong and tasteless. But the cool mixture of potatoes and chunks of garlic sausage in a thick mustard dressing—an occasional dish of the day—is rousing and satisfying. Another daily special is a stuffed suckling pig. The beast is displayed to you— reclining on its side—its rear portion already partially sold off by the slice. His innards and meat have been made into a well-fatted and abundantly sweet-spiced forcemeat, with pistachio nuts, with which its tegument is packed. You are served a round slice, rimmed with pigskin—to the inside of which clings a thin layer of rich meat. This is a good—but pinguid—dish, and strong mustard and bread may be essential to you for its consumption.

When soft-shell crabs are around, this place has been known to get little ones, and to sauté them with lots of garlic and parsley—you wish they were crisper, but that hardly matters when the crabs are this small and delicate. The poulet basquaise consists of substantial sections of chicken in a rather coarse tomato sauce that is thick with onions and green peppers. Once in a while the house offers rabbit—this is a good stew, of well-browned meat simmered in white wine, in which sharp green olives and strong black peppercorns are striking notes. Of the lamb dishes: the herbed and crisped rack— served intact—is simple and unimpeachable; the gigot—served in quarter-inch-thick slices—is a little chewy, its white beans a little soft. Of the beef dishes: the steak is tough in its rather harsh pepper sauce; the daube niçoise, though not of first-rate stew meat— the chunks are tender from long cooking, but have little beef character—is hearty, notable for its strong black olives.

Not a dessert house. An otherwise well-made dacquoise—of layers of meringue and two colors of pastry cream—is robbed of its delicacy by its thick chocolate icing. Something variously given as champagne mousse or champagne cheesecake is a tasteless fluff. The black currant mousse pie is light, cool, pallid.

★ CHEZ JOSEPHINE

414 West 42nd Street
DINNER. CLOSED SUNDAY.
Reservations: 594-1925.
Credit cards: AE, MC, V.
Medium priced.

Josephine Baker was an American singer and dancer who made a big hit in Paris in the twenties and remained in France, most of the rest of her life, as a music-hall entertainer. Though talented, she knew that talent was no surety of success, so she often performed with most of her clothes off, was reportedly sensational when wearing nothing but a G-string and bananas. The elfin Frenchman who runs this place tells you that her hobby was adopting people, not necessarily de jure, and that he was one of her unofficial wards. In this place, his tribute to her, he has theatricalized a long and narrow room with yards of red velvet, much cerulean-blue paint, mirrors, zebra carpeting in the little back room, a piano complete with pianist in a mirrored alcove, and scores of posters, paintings, caricatures, and sepia photos of Josephine herself, wearing very little, or in a fedora and dancing with a guy in a tux, or dancing on a piano, the look in her eye, when you can see it, mischievous and gay. You figure she might have found this place small of scale, but that she rarely found things beneath her; and that she would have been indulgent of, even amused by, a restaurant host who, like her boy here, presses himself on you with more fervor than you wish to share about this, his enterprise. To get away with that, his fervor would have to be like Josephine's itself.

Bistro food and dishes that are its contemporary equivalent: gently warmed, crisped oysters, fresh and plump in their half-shells, touched with lime juice and a bit of fresh fennel; judiciously poached leeks, firm and crunchy, in a warm vinaigrette made with pungent olive oil; a robust salad of assorted fresh greens with crusts of garlicked bread; thin pasta in a buttery sauce, fragrant with basil, that is thick with wild mushrooms and both fresh and sun-dried tomatoes. The main dishes include the oddly named lobster cassoulet, oddly because it is made with scallops and shrimp as well, not to mention a disk of seafood sausage, all those elements, with black beans and chunks of tomato, in a buttered and briny soup; the oddly named chicken Alvara, oddly because fried chicken would describe it better, the parts of moist bird, in a sweet batter that peels away like a tender shell, garnished with dry corn bread (butter helps) and French-fried sweet potatoes (nothing helps); boudin noir, the rich pudding of seasoned blood and fat in charred, crackling casings, with French fries that, on occasion, are limp; a crusted, accurately grilled steak that is a little dry within its almost harsh coating of pink peppercorns, with French fries that, on occasion, are crisp.

The otherwise fine raspberry tart is ice cold. The chocolate cake, though given as "Le Délice Josephine," is an ordinary commercial chocolate item, anyway its equivalent.

★ CHEZ LOUIS

1016 Second Avenue (near 54th Street)
LUNCH, MONDAY TO FRIDAY; DINNER, DAILY.
Reservations: 752-1400.
Credit cards: AE, DC, MC, V.
Expensive.

A mini-bandwagon is heading back to bistros, and the dying Manhattan Market, to save itself, has, with several buckets of saucy red paint, yards of crimson cloth, a carload of garlic, and the new name, hopped on. It is a case, however, of imitation without understanding, the fashionable clothes without the style, the retold joke with the punch line at the beginning. Not that you cannot eat well here, or that to run a bistro you must have grown up in the tradition, rather that a bistro, by its nature, is a community place—though good ones attract folks from all over—one that draws its identity from the harmonious interaction of he who runs it with those he understands how to serve. Chez Louis is an exploitation of the mode without the calling, which is to say, getting in on a good thing. The only vision behind Chez Louis is a vision of a simpler, more profitable, more merchandisable operation than Manhattan Market. There is of course nothing reprehensible in turning an additional dollar, but peddling the imitation as the article, it is hoped, will always be vulgar. The proprietor has been quoted as saying that he is going to keep working at this place until he "gets this perfect," as if running a bistro were a trick that can be mastered by application, like wriggling your ears. His method is to lay on thick certain superficialities (much crimson, much garlic, and himself in a white jacket awkwardly carving roasts in the dining room), while pandering to local taste—an evening's main courses may consist almost exclusively of chicken, lamb, beef, swordfish, salmon. Pig's feet, you understand, are not here. While flattered that this is down-to-earth dinnering, the folks are getting what they always eat anyway.

You still enter to the lofty barroom, the long counter of polished gray stone, behind it a triptych of mirrors framed in carved wood, the floor of white barbershop tiles, the monumental hanging lanterns apparently relics from some torn-down cathedral space—the parts are handsome, but this is a cavernous room, in desperate but usually unsatisfied need of a crowd at the bar to warm it up. The dining room is up a few steps at the back, and looks like a movie set. That is to say, the long walls on each side are of suitably Toulouse-Lautrec scarlet, and the aperitif posters on them are unmistakably French, but the rear wall (gray glass looking out on a gray backyard cityscape), and the floor (dark-gray carpeting), and the ceiling (a sound-baffling mid-tech geometric arrangement of painted boards) look like the unmade-up parts of a room on which the camera will not focus anyway. The effect is, how you say, transient, unpersuasive. You think of La Goulue on East 70th Street, or, in a completely different bistro vein, of Le Relais on Madison Avenue, and you know how shoestring is this version of the genre.

Still, the cost of converting the gray box that was Manhattan Market into the red one that is Chez Louis must be picked up, and so even the prices here scorn bistro preconceptions. You are exacted, for example, $5.95 for this admittedly well-made little bowl of customary onion soup, its broth, based on a deep stock, thick with onions that have been sweetened and darkened by slow cooking—and though the melted cheese that seals the contents in their vessel is not of notable flavor, its pulliness is a nice textural note in the steamy context. But the snails (in shells, in dents, in a snail plate), though plump and tender, have not enough flavor of their own to get away with this greened but timidly seasoned butter. You get a giant sheaf of warm, fresh asparagus, the stalks peeled to their tender white cores, with a pitcher of warm chervil vinaigrette that lacks nothing except sparkle. The terrine of foie gras is a couple of cool slices cut from a loaf, a thickness of duck fat along an edge, the tight-packed morsels of rich liver sweet, pinguid, and in good contrast to the toasted slices of warm, eggy brioche with which they are served. What are given as "roast wild mushrooms" are about a dozen fresh shiitakes, whole cloves of garlic among them, the two blackened, hot, and knee-deep in their herbed butter.

You order it (the seafood salad) because you are surprised to find it on this menu, and you regret it, because (a) the cool ingredients—plump sea scallops, sweet mussels, shrimp, the tail of a tiny lobster—though in no way off, have lost their liveliness during the time between their preparation and their consumption, and because (b) their herbed dressing, of good oil, lacks the tanginess that could bring the elements to life. But the grilled salmon is fine, the great side of pink meat, moist under its black-striped top, spread with a piquant sauce of pommery mustard. You order the roast chicken for two, and the two of you are brought a bird that is so fetching in its browned, glistening skin, that is so fragrant of the garlic with which it has been roasted, and that is so small, that each of you (just for a brief, instinctual moment, you understand) resents the presence of the other—moreover, the scrawniness presages a certain thinness of chicken flavor, though the bird is carefully prepared, juicy but cooked through. Much is made of showing you what you are presently to eat, and your waiter, as he holds your veal chop in its pan under your nose (before it is taken away and magically transferred to a plate), confides, clearly feeling stupid, "We're supposed to show it to you first." When it returns, unchanged in its new surroundings, you find that the eye of meat, browned and herbed and very handsome at the end of its long bone, is not exactly the plump thing, bursting with moisture, that is a veal chop done to the moment. The chop, garnished with a clump of warm, garlicked watercress, comes also with some of the roasted vegetables that are otherwise available à la carte—a crunchy beet that is metallic and sweet within the blackened skin you peel away, an earthy turnip, cloves of garlic, a single tender carrot (unfortunately cold); comes also with a small version of the potato pie that is served in a double portion with that chicken: The crusty exterior is strewn with chopped raw garlic, and though the interior of the small pie is an abundance of firm little slices of vivid potato flavor, the big one is just mush within its skin. The roast lamb is listed as being served only for two, but your waiter allows as how late at night there is sometimes a rack available for one, and asks how you want it. You want it medium rare. Waiter returns with the nonsense he has been fed, that racks of baby lamb must be cooked to medium if they are to be cooked through at all, when, clearly, the facts are that the lamb has already been roasted, that the house is accepting small orders to facilitate selling off the roast before the end of the night. You get lots of these tender, strong flavored but bloodless little chops, and they are in a slick, blackened coat (which could have been achieved only by long exposure to heat)—the good roasting juices are salty and blood-strong.

Some decent Roquefort may be had with the excellent house bread—it is sour and chewy within its crunchy crust. Cherries, berries, gooseberries, grapes, and other fruits, depending on the season, may be had singly or mixed, with rich whipped cream. The unfortunately titled "chocolate sweetness cake" is a holdover from the Market—it is flourless and of a chocolate intensity exceeded only by that of the black, sticky icing with which it is surfaced.

★ CHEZ PIERRE

170 Waverly Place (at Grove Street)
LUNCH, FRIDAY TO SUNDAY; DINNER, TUESDAY TO SUNDAY. CLOSED MONDAY.
Reservations: 929-7194.
No credit cards.
Medium priced.

A two-small-room corner store with, when the weather is fine, sidewalk tables outside under the red awnings. The eight back-room tables are in a space you would find ample for a sink, WC and stall shower. Of course the tables are small—eating at one is like eating off an upended orange crate—and in certain parts of the room, what with the jigsaw-puzzle furniture arrangement, the cooperation of your neighbors is essential when you must leave your place. In the comparatively wide-open space of the front room, there is actually an ample round table beside the Waverly Place window, with an excellent view of the Northern Dispensary (founded 1827). In the Grove Street window there are flowerpots and bottles of wine, and in the room itself, between an ancient wood floor and a stamped-tin ceiling, the walls are hung with old mirrors, an antique thermometer, and posters—Paris, the Statue of Liberty—including one that obscures all but a thin opening at the bottom of the interior window through which food is passed from the closet-size kitchen to the dining room. There is a rack in one corner, with hangers for coats—it will not hold many in goosedown season. Plain wood chairs surround the white-linened tables, and the place is frequented by types to whom eating in restaurants is not a diversion, but a practical matter—foreign accents and languages are often heard here. The help is never far away, and the absence of pretension yields more comfort than the rather functional appointments take away, against which you must weigh the danger that, when you visit, you will be beset by Edith Piaf, in the background, enumerating her difficulties.

More than in most places, here it is good to know what the house does well, for the lesser dishes—the cold and coarse pâté and, when it is offered, a flat fish mousse—are no clue at all to what the better ones are like: big tender snails in the mild but well-seasoned and heavily parsleyed butter; an abundant salad of crunchy walnuts and crisp endive in a tart and thickened vinaigrette; another salad, this one of fresh romaine, red cabbage, and tomatoes in a brisk red-vinegar dressing—it is served with crusts of bread that have been spread with strong goat cheese. Pass up the roast pork (its tangy mustard sauce fails to rouse it), and do not expect much from the rump steak, a knob of red meat, short on blood-juiciness, that is only as exciting as the black pepper with which it is coated. Opt instead for the poulet chasseur, much good chicken, with mushrooms, in a spicy red sauce; or, when it is offered, the osso buco, the tender and steamy veal moist and lean and peppery—the thing is surrounded by white rice that is dotted with onions and red peppers, and you get the marrow out of the bone by using the other end of your fork; or for one of the fish dishes of the day—one time snapper in a white sauce thick with capers, another time blackfish of such sweet flavor that, happily, it is moistened with nothing but the butter in which it was done.

The desserts are what you expect—eggy crème caramel, rich chocolate cake, and a tarte Tatin notable for apples that, though caramelized, reveal much of their tartness.

• CHIN CHIN

216 East 49th Street
LUNCH, MONDAY TO FRIDAY; DINNER, DAILY.
Reservations: 888-4555.
Credit cards: AE, DC, MC, V.
Inexpensive.

Someone started to build a steakhouse, maybe an across-the-street branch of Smith & Wollensky lacking only a footbridge to that many-chambered beef pavilion, then switched culinary gears—for with its straight lines, wood lower walls, benchlike oxblood banquettes, this is for guys, right down to the waiters, in their black vests over long-sleeved white shirts, white aprons to the ankle. There is even a clubby little room off the bar, like rooms that, in beef-and-potato establishments of yore (and not so yore), used to be set aside for what were coyly referred to as private family gatherings. There is even a row, all around the room, of framed photos that, in a steakhouse, would be glossy black-and-whites of ballplayers and/or movie stars and/or pols, and/or pugs and/or Frank Sinatra. Here they are faded sepia-tinted Chinese family pictures of, at a guess, 60 years ago, none of them taken on these premises, none of them signed, Your pal, with best wishes to the proprietor. Only the few-steps-down rearmost dining room—rows of tables and chairs, Chinese vases in wall niches—suggests unambiguously Chin Chin's Orientality.

As you are served pickles in certain steakhouses, you are served picklings here, a bowl of bean sprouts that, as in any context, taste like string, and a bowl of vegetables, sometimes mostly cauliflower livened with sprigs of coriander, sometimes green beans with strands of red onion, both in rousing hot-spiced sesame marinades. Thereafter you are at the mercy of the menu, though it is no one's responsibility but your own if, despite the description, you go for the thousand-year-old (give or take) eggs. Shelled, quartered, and dusky moss green, they have the flavor of egg yolks mixed with flour and ammonia and a texture you have avoided since you grew teeth—you reward yourself for every unbelieving mouthful with either a pickled shallot or a leaf of fresh ginger, the bright garnishes that redeem a little this familiar Chinese prison staple. The shredded roast duck salad is one of those dishes in which the Chinese reveal their talent for assembling ingredients that neutralize one another—the huge mound of duck and tomatoes and shredded leaves has the flavor of nothing but its cool, vaguely sour dressing. But there is real food here. Whatever the snails were done in, they emerge tasting like salted potted meat, which is not to say they are bad, and they reach you in a garlicky broth that is thick with coriander. But the so-called crispy fried squid tastes like boardwalk food, and the cold chicken soong—packed into pockets carved out of sides of wet iceberg lettuce —is a lot of noodles and a little chicken in a nutted and sugary sauce that is of an insipidity. The first course winner is the vegetable duck pie, mock Peking duck, a vegetable composition that, if it does not taste like duck, is a lively, crackling imitation—your waiter wraps it in pancakes, with a length of cucumber, another of scallion, and a thick, dark plum sauce. As at most contemporary steakhouses, one section of the menu is headed "pasta," albeit even at Smith & Wollensky you cannot always get your very favorite noodle dish. So when you are across the street and get a certain craving, phone Chin Chin for prompt delivery of some crispy pan-fried egg noodles, a garlicky dish in which the great farinaceous tangles are part crispy, part straight al dente, in among them slices of mushroom and slivers of pork, crunchy shrimp that are heady of iodine, emerald-green snowpeas, and more, all the elements of this complexity of clear, if not always good, flavor.

Encouraged by the salmon in black bean sauce—the large fillet of fresh, juicy fish under strands of red and green pepper, and in a broth that is thick with the strong, pleasantly gritty beans—you try the clams in black bean sauce, and the mollusks, leathery in their shells, arrive in a sauce that is little more than thickened, darkened, salted water. The country style chicken is treacly, the red peppers that are in evidence add little fire, though you find no fault with the spinach on which the chunks of fried bird are set. Of the sautéed leg of lamb with leeks it may be said that the lamb flavor is clear, of the crisped orange beef that the marmalade flavor is clear.

Chin Chin offers for dessert ice cream, fruit, a Mandarin rarity called sorbet. You need a beverage that will, how you say, cut this food—sake or whiskey will do.

★★CHRIST CELLA

160 East 46th Street
LUNCH, MONDAY TO FRIDAY; DINNER, MONDAY TO SATURDAY. CLOSED SUNDAY.
Reservations: 697-2479.
Credit cards: AE, DC, MC, V.
Very expensive.

Considering the kind of gross feeding that goes on in this place, its properness is at least odd. Guys wash behind the ears, comb their hair wet, and put on a dark-blue suit to come here and sit themselves down to a lobster the size of a Bedlington terrier. While eating with, at the very best, both hands, they are being tended to by well-trained gentlemen who by their administration of very serious intensive care seem to transform this well-organized gluttony into a solemn pursuit. When you are first seated, one of these white-aproned officials arrives at tableside to recite, with admirable if not perfect completeness, the menu (there is no printed one). He returns later wheeling a serving stand laden with food and paraphernalia. The more senior of the Christ Cella waiters are at ease, their once carefully learned politeness now second nature. The younger members of the staff are less than at home with their schooled demeanor, and sometimes they seethe a little as they respond to your inquiries—with answers that might be taken for short if they were not complete. However, when asked "What's good?" the old and young alike preface their responses with the same aperçu: "This is the best steakhouse in New York," it goes, uttered, always, with a gravity that would be entirely appropriate for the divulgence of a medical diagnosis.

The formalities begin when you arrive and are greeted by an accountant type in one of those dark suits, white shirt, necktie, and 1940 haircut. Though he flashes a bit of camaraderie with people he knows—a thin smile, a clutched shoulder—with most he is very much the church usher, first peering through his Franklin glasses at the book, and then indicating the way with a nod of the head and a half gesture of the hand. If he does not know you, and if you have not made specific arrangements to the contrary, he will probably point you upstairs to the second floor, where are housed the two bleakest of this restaurant's solid, comfortable, but far-from-lovely dining rooms. The upper deck has been gussied up in recent years with grass-paper walls and pale, pleated drapes on the big front window—still, the gloomy seascapes that look out over the spread of well-spaced tables on the old wood floor seem to reflect rather than offset the spartanness of the surroundings.

The five rooms downstairs are smaller, cozier, clubbier. One is the barroom, in which two of the wood-paneled walls are adorned with the front end of one antelope each. One of them is mounted sideways (he is in position to peer *along* his wall), with one shoulder intact—a triumph of the stuffer's art. To the stand-up bar, baskets of hot, crisp-fried matchstick potatoes are delivered from time to time, to help the lined-up gents wash down their drinks. The three barroom tables are choice ones, but they are usually not used on slow nights. The ivory-colored walls of the other downstairs rooms have had a pattern of blue-green squiggles applied by means of an embossed paint roller—the kind of beautification usually found only in apartment-house hallways. The brightly lighted and somewhat turbulent wide-open kitchen abuts on one of these dining rooms—just inside it is that famous single, large table that is available to customers who, perhaps nostalgic for simpler times, enjoy eating in the kitchen. Wherever you sit, you are surrounded by at least 80 percent guys (the spectrum is from successful used-car dealer to successful non-corporate-law lawyer) and 20 percent dolls (the spectrum is from girl-friend to wife). Once in a while you will see a female executive here, in among a gang of male managers of equal rank. The lady's two-piece suit seems designed to get her lost in this crowd, and in fact she does seem lost—somewhere between the genders. Almost all the time everybody in the place is not a feminist.

And *almost* everybody in the place, at one time or another, gets the Caesar salad, a copious mound of crunchy romaine lettuce and crusty croutons in a clinging, egg-thick-ened dressing that is sharpened with anchovy, made fragrant with garlic. A lighter thing is the spinach salad: broad, deep-green leaves of the fresh raw vegetable dotted with chunks of bacon and moistened with a good, tart—almost sour—vinaigrette. The shrimp in the shrimp cocktail are sometimes tasteless, but they are not tainted with iodine. If you must start with shellfish, the crabmeat and lobster cocktails are the only way to go: abundant amounts of cool, fresh, and sweet meat, served with a standard—but very strong and sparkling—cocktail sauce.

Several varieties of finfish are usually on hand, and you get big sides of such as snapper and striped bass. They are almost always moist, fresh, of clear flavor within their darkened surfaces—sometimes, alas, they are a little overcooked. An order of scallops is several score of the plump, rich little morsels, lightly floured and browned. Of course, all this time you have just been doing lobster avoidance. Christ Cella sells large lobsters, very large lobsters, and lobsters that will serve for two or three of you—though you see fellows here dispatching these giants solo. The lobsters are usually perfectly broiled—now and again one is overdone. While you are extracting the big, supple length of ocean-sweet meat from the red carapace, your waiter—at his serving stand beside your table—is extracting the meat from the claws and arranging it for you on a second plate.

As all the world knows, New York steakhouse beef is now only sometimes what it once was. But Christ Cella seems to serve what once was more often than does any of its rivals. You get sirloins that are fibrous, tender, and with that distinctive beef flavor in which succulence and mineral sharpness are combined. At their best, the filets mignons are firm, tender, and velvety—never mushy, as this cut of beef elsewhere often is. The roast beef is good too, the big rib at least an inch thick and tasty. It is a sign of the intelligence that informs this place that though you are asked how you would like your red meat cooked you are not asked that if you are having veal chops, for there is only one right degree of doneness for veal chops, and you usually get your two big ones done that way here—they are bloodless but still juicy, pink but not red. The batter-fried onions are an immense pile of thin strips, crinkly and sweet. The hashed browns are a giant pancake about the dimensions of a professional Frisbee—it is deeply browned, blackened in places, the chunks of good potato firm under the crusty top.

Now the dessert cart is wheeled by, on it three monuments: a slab of cheesecake, a slab of rum cake, a slab of napoleon. The last two are inelegant sweets—and so is the cheesecake, but it is a perfect example of a certain kind of rich, creamy, sugary, lightly lemoned combination of airiness and weight that is integral to a place like this.

★★CINCO DE MAYO

349 West Broadway (near Broome Street)
LUNCH AND DINNER.
Reservations: 226-5255.
Credit cards: AE, DC, MC, V.
Inexpensive.

You enter to a mildly raucous bar, a row of tables across the aisle. If you do not get seated here, you are conducted through the kitchen to the big dining room beyond, which consists of an orchestra and a balcony—there is even a kind of stage, where, when he is not performing in the front room, the Mexican harpist positions himself, passionately plinks, and, sometimes, wails. (It sounds very native, but attention reveals that some of his tunes—though not his style—are contemporary gringo.) When the harpist is performing out front, the jukebox thumps in the back, and when he is working the back, etc. Depending on where you are, your surroundings may consist of rough plaster painted pink, bare brick, whitewashed brick. There may be pipes and conduits crisscrossing the ceiling. You will be within loud shouting distance of lots of tropical plants. The place is lighted by factory lights, track lights, candles. The constant din is dense enough to render harmless the sound of a load of dishes being dropped into a waiting tub. The tables are packed with young people, the aisles with young waiters and waitresses. Sometimes, unpredictably, everyone applauds the harpist. Naturally, he seems surprised, and a brilliant smile radiates from his dark, flat Indian face.

No sooner are you seated than you are brought a basket of chips and a dish of exceptional green sauce—it is not especially hot, as these things go, but hot enough, and it is fresh, polished, heady with cilantro. (Refills cheerfully provided.) Your ceviche comes in a glass, chunks of lime-cured fish buried in a cold, thick, and citrus-sour red sauce. The guacamole is served as "guacamole treat," and many regulars here start their dinners by sharing one of these big bowls (formed of fried tortilla) of about a pint of the avocado mash—its texture is distressingly sticky, but that is offset by its good avocado flavor and by the bits of moist tomato and strong onion with which the paste is dotted. Taquitos de moronga are tortilla tubes filled with bits of blood pudding, leaves of cilantro, raw onions—you pick up the warm bundles with your fingers, and like much of the food here, they are good with beer. The tortilla soup is a nice enough tomato-reddened broth, many slivers of tortilla in it—you add mild grated cheese, and that makes the simple stuff substantial, though not fascinating.

The menu lists two specials for each day of the week. Come on Wednesday, and you may have mejilliones à la Mexicana, a huge glass bowl of fresh mussels—sweet, tender, not claylike—in their shells, mounded up over the hot broth they were steamed in, garnished with redded rice, and served with a short stack of hot tortillas that come wrapped in tinfoil. Any day of the week you may have the alambres à la Mexicana, crisp marinated shrimp that have been grilled with onions, tomatoes, and violently hot green peppers—the dish is served with seasoned rice, of which you will need all, at once, if you bite into one of those jalapeños as if it were an apple. The budin de tortilla is weighty, utterly satisfying, a triangle cut from a great pie of alternating layers of chicken, cornmeal pancakes, and a top layer of melted cheese—you get a pitcher of hot green sauce which is a good foil to the solid dish. The tripe stew (menudo norteno) is a million slivers of the pale, tender, gummy innard and an equal number of white beans, all in a salty and red-peppery broth—you may add chopped onions and/or dried oregano and/or lime juice (three slices of lime are supplied) to modify the hot stuff according to your temperament.

What is called Kahlúa mousse is a fluffy and obvious thing of whipped cream and the liqueur under chocolate shavings. There is flan and little else.

All the familiar Mexican beers are here, and also Negra Modelo, an especially well-balanced dark beer that is at once malty, creamy, and refreshing.

★ LE CIRQUE

58 East 65th Street
LUNCH AND DINNER. CLOSED SUNDAY.
Reservations: 794-9292.
Credit cards: AE, DC.
Very expensive.

Mindful that the privilege of dinner at Le Cirque is not easily earned, you telephone some weeks in advance to reserve a table at 8, or, if that more suits the house, 8:30—even 7:30—some hour that, in the pattern of New York life, is feasible and comfortable. You have identified yourself by a homely name, have mentioned no affiliation, are informed that, on the dates you propose, you may dine either at 6 or at 9:45. You suggest dates weeks later. On those dates, presumably by remarkable coincidence, only 6 is available or, if that is not suitable, 9:45. You begin to mention dates later still, but are interrupted. Though the gentleman with whom you are dealing quite democratically expresses no opinion as to what you should do with your time, he clearly abhors wasting his own. "The date," he carefully explains, "does not matter. You may have a table at 6 or at 9:45." The problem is solved, of course, when, a day later, another voice identifies itself as that of an executive of a major outlet of news and opinion, which voice readily arranges for tables on the very dates and at the very hours you originally proposed. The respect with which you are treated when you, instead, show up is clearly bemused, for, in the event, you look like an ordinary shlub. Sirio Maccioni (proprietor here) smiles at you, sure enough, but in the manner of one who longs for—even, self pityingly, regrets the loss of—a society in which class distinctions are clear and binding. Poor Sirio—with his slicked-down hair and accidental face, in his surely hand-tailored but too tight suit—is not aware that, though the moneyed and powerful are his clientele today, in any reverse revolution, he and they will be separated at the first cut.

It is always somewhat dismaying to enter this fabled place, for no sooner are you in the door than you are upon a table (nary a square inch of Le Cirque's real estate is nonproductive) seated at which, and well within the territory of the front-door traffic, are three or four of the most monumentally downcast faces anywhere above the level of the starving. They came for grandeur, dreamed of seeing a show of pols and party givers, maybe even folks up on felony counts, and, instead, here they are in the theater lobby. They will, in effect, eat, leave, and not have been to Le Cirque. They are unaware that theirs is among the most commodious accommodations in the house, for with respect to the dining room proper, no other in New York, at any price, is more densely tabled and chaired. There are sites at which four tables can share an ice bucket, and each table's wine is within easy reach. The waiters and captains quite by reflex stretch their bodies thin to move about, and regular customers have learned routes to the facilities that, though circuitous, bypass the most thickly obstacled terrain. With respect to the appointments, the framed panels of latticework wallpaper are occupied, as ever, by monkeys engaged in human pursuits, the square columns are mirrored, the deep-rose banquettes match both the chemises on the backs of the chairs and the short skirts on the seats, from under each of which protrude four skinny white fluted period legs. There are flowers on the white-linened tables, and the sconces on the walls, you judge by Sirio's tie, must have been chosen by himself—they are made up of clusters of thin black arms that thrust into the room glowing lights that amount to frowning gargoyles of floral configuration. Half the ladies are in pearl chokers, many a long-sleeved black dress is adorned by mink at the cuffs. Gentlemen are close-tonsured and (by meal's end) flushed over their tight white collars—you see among them liver-spotted sybarites, their noses inches from their plates, shoveling north the fettuccine. Le Cirque's best dressers are in black and white and work the floor, and these days the service is positively human. A captain compliments you on your French; you counter by pointing out that his English is better than Sirio's; he shrugs, so much as to say, "Whose isn't?" With time, it seems, the staff has learned to laugh off Maccioni's way of snapping his fingers and grandly pointing (as a conqueror to distant lands), to underscore a peremptory command.

Why is Sirio not instead pointing out that this marinated tuna ought to be left in its marinade long enough to flavor it and maybe make it tender, for the thick-cut sheet of fish is resilient and lacks seafood—or any other—character, though it is cleverly served over a crunchy mash of tart sorrel. Much more itself is this peasanty terrine of beef shanks and leeks, the thick square, cut from a loaf, a mosaic of the dark, tender, deep-flavored, fibrous meat, which is studded with short lengths of pale-green leek—you moisten the sturdy stuff with a sharp and creamy horseradish sauce. A place like this would not be a place like this without foie gras, and it is usually listed among the daily specials, the pan-sautéed oleaginous meat served, oddly, with a salad of young greens, and, sometimes, with sections of citrus fruit—the garnishes are nifty foils to the extraordinarily rich, browned liver. Never mind that Le Cirque is a French restaurant, Sirio is Italian, and these days he consoles himself for the loss of his former French chef, Alain Sailhac, by listing more than just a token number of Italian dishes—presumably the current Frenchman in the kitchen, Daniel Boulud, has fewer veto rights than his predecessor. Anyway, in black and white are listed fettuccine with truffles—even the truffles are black and (or) white, according to the season—and these are wondrous, eggy noodles, their sauce creamy and cheesy, and when the truffles are black, your captain scrapes the big, dark flakes until you yawn—they flatter, but add only a dim note of nuttiness to the good dish.

Of course you should laugh off simply by virtue of its name the "Homard de Maine au Curry," which may be not so loosely translated as "lobster in college sauce," the sort of thing you made in your school days with any suitable or unsuitable solid protein, curry powder, and any suitable or unsuitable liquid, for example milk—the mound of lobster meat at the center of your plate, every ounce of sustenance to be found in, at a guess, a six-ounce crustacean, tough despite its youth, encircled by little balls of fruit, and seated in a sauce the color of sulfur. Less depressing is the Dover sole, the nicely floured and sautéed fillets browned and moist, overlaid with skinned sections of orange, grapefruit, lime—the fruit is in nice contrast to the heavily salted fish. The lamb stew would be better were the meat better butchered, for instead of the great nuggets of tender, fibrous lamb you hope for, you get misshapen chunks threaded with cartilage—still, the sauce is complex and fragrantly herbed, and the vegetables and elbow macaroni with which the meat is garnished make of the item a lively dish. Italian food to the rescue, the osso buco that, from time to time, appears on this menu, M. Boulud reduced to, but apparently stimulated by, alien responsibilities, the great knuckle of spicy veal tender and juicy on its hefty bone, in which, when you poke about, you find much rich marrow— the veal is in a deep, meaty, onion-sweet sauce that, though livened with tomato, is far from a mere tomato sauce, and it is garnished with fresh noodles and root vegetables.

From among the pastries you do well to select, when it is on hand, the pithiviers, the tart of puff pastry and ground almonds that, when well made, as here, is a dessert that, by its airiness and sweetness ends a weighty dinner lightly. The crème brûlée is good, the fluffy custard under a crackling caramel top. The circular apple tart—skinlike leaves of apple on a skinlike pastry, a ping pong ball of vanilla ice cream at the center—may be admired for its subtlety. The chocolate soufflé (for two) reaches you dry, devoid of chocolate character, in much need of the sugared whipped cream served with it.

★★CLAIRE

156 Seventh Avenue (near 19th Street)
LUNCH AND DINNER.
Reservations: 255-1955.
Credit cards: AE, DC, MC, V.
Medium priced.

There is an eating place in Key West called Claire, and this one derives from that one. The Floridian isle's remote situation—it is the southernmost point of the continental United States, connected only by a causeway to the rest of the world—probably accounts for the community's independent style of culinary development. If Claire's menu fairly represents Key cooking, it may be concluded that the islanders subsist largely on what may be fished from the waters around them. The look of this restaurant suggests that they like to take their catch out of the tropical heat into a cool, dark place to eat it.

This cool, dark place is a couple of stories high, big, two-roomed. Up front is the bar (with an armrest of glossy python skin), under an overhang on which rests a collection of pottery perhaps meant to suggest the fruits of undersea salvage operations in the once pirate-infested waters around the keys. A big trelliswork panel—with built-in, slowly spinning four-bladed fans—lowers the ceiling in this part of the place. More trelliswork separates the front from the back room, in which—in season—three tall palm trees reach to three skylights overhead. Throughout, beams from track lights pierce the dusky atmosphere. The tabletops are covered with gleaming pastel oilcloth and broad crisscrossed bands of white butcher paper. At them are seated, mostly, gentlemen of exceptional neatness, trimness, cleanliness, and posture. The self-conscious among you are invited to come here and feel like a frump. Actually, there are always on hand enough lumpy nuclear-family types for anyone not to feel out of place.

The regulars keep their figures eating the like of these Chincoteague Bay oysters. They are opened to order, are fresh and sparkling. The seviche of tuna is fresh, raw red fish, "cooked" by the acidic lime-juice marinade in which it is served with dill and capers. Claire turns out a good gravlax, the supple cured salmon heady of its dill flavor, served with a rich mustard sauce. And it produces an exceptional squid salad, the slivers and circles of pale, tender seafood in a cool but fiery olive-oil dressing. You get well-chosen mussels here, a rarity these days in New York. They are in their shells, mingled with strands of sharp red onion, and mounded up over the hot broth—of white wine flavored with garlic, herbs, lemon—in which they were steamed. For some reason there is Thai beef salad on this menu, and though some purist somewhere can probably prove that it is no good because it varies from the Oriental recipe, it is nevertheless one of the best in town. But you have to be able to take it, for the warm ground meat and the chopped onions and scallions with which it is mixed are in a spiced lemon dressing that can be numbing if eaten greedily. The Bahamian conch chowder is thick soup, peppery, with a nutlike flavor, laden with conch meat.

Claire is yet another restaurant that essays the New Orleans dish called blackened fish. In this version the panfried fillets reach you with an especially spicy crust—the fish within is said to be redfish, is utterly fresh, falls into tender flakes. One kind of shark or another is usually on the menu, sometimes black-tip shark. This is not the world's tastiest swimmer, but its preparation—it is sautéed with dill, sherry, and mushrooms—turns it into a plate of more than decent food. River catfish is presumably not found in the ocean around the keys, but Claire manages to obtain some anyway—the skinned and boned fish is breaded and fried in a pan, and its delicacy and moistness are startling when you encounter them within the hot, brittle, and greaseless crust. Norwegian salmon is also foreign to the Gulf of Mexico, but this place has figured the species out. The hefty slab of pink fish is broiled to the perfect point, dressed with a light cucumber-and-dill sauce —a superb dish. Tiny bay scallops are served here, lightly floured and sautéed until the surfaces of the plump little morsels are delicately browned and crisp—the scallops reach you in a gentle sauce of butter, white wine, a bit of lemon. Claire often combines meat and fish. It sautés shrimp and chunks of beef with hot peppers and sweet peppers, onions and fresh basil, and creates a dish in which the complexity of flavors is as vivid as its color scheme. With less success, it serves broiled tilefish under crisped strands of ham, with chopped scallions and walnuts—this is well made, but tilefish can be pallid, and the other ingredients do not rescue it.

Though mainly a seafood house, Claire consistently turns out some of the best filets mignons around. As thousands of cookbooks say, but as few restaurants do, these little steaks are rimmed with bacon before they are broiled, which imparts all the flavor the tender meat needs—the beef reaches you with the bacon in place, under a big mushroom cap.

As you surely guessed, there is key lime pie. The citrus flavor of its pale chiffon is vivid, lovely against the graham cracker crust. You wish that the whipped cream with which it is served did not on occasion do this excellent imitation of cream "whipped" by a blowing machine. Something called chocolate chambord is a splendid black layer cake soaked in raspberry liqueur. Chocolate and booze come together yet again in the Mississippi mud cake, in which the cake—of strong chocolate flavor and genuinely mudlike weight and texture—is served in a pool of approximately 60-proof buttered whiskey. The pecan pie is dark, spicy, and rich, topped with crunchy pecans—good with whipped cream when the whipped cream is good. The chocolate walnut pie is sticky, its pastry doughy. The cheesecake is of cream cheese, but it is light.

This is a busy place, but arrive even when there are a dozen empty tables and you may well be asked—quite officiously—to have a drink at the bar before you are seated. The menu informs you that what it refers to as "waitwomen" and "waitmen" are in shirts by J. G. Hook, Inc.

• COACH HOUSE

110 Waverly Place (near Sixth Avenue)
DINNER. CLOSED MONDAY.
Reservations: 777-0303.
Credit cards: AE, DC, MC, V.
Expensive.

Nothing about this restaurant is as remarkable as its reputation. To find something similar, you must go to the great books, the ones nobody reads. Wander through the place of an evening, consider those present, and you will understand at once why this reliquary of Institutional Cuisine, though open to the public, remains almost exempt from any threat of ordinary human assessment. The restaurant is attended principally by the very folks who, in the ritualistic course of their lives, sit through Philharmonic concerts, church sermons, political eulogies, and commencement addresses in states of blank, contented reverence. They do not attend for the message, of course, but for the occasion. And they come to the Coach House for the occasion. They would no more judge this place than they would their own goodness, for the Coach House is truly loved. But it is not loved in the way that, say, a lover is loved. Rather, it is loved forever and unquestioningly, like money.

You arrive to a sign outside, RESERVATIONS ONLY, JACKET AND TIE REQUIRED. This is presumably meant to keep the riffraff out, for Mr. Leon Lianides himself, the proprietor, has been seen seated with the bare necked. As to the reservation "requirement," if you look like you can pay your way, and there is a table, it is yours. You enter to Lianides, a grim presence, who receives you more or less the way the warden receives the recidivist. He looks you up in his book, waves you on your way. Next step is a large lady whose job it is to decide the kind of table you deserve—she transfers you to an escort, to whom she has whispered instructions. He leads you to a table for two that would be fine for sandwiches and coffee but that seems skimpy when you are about to drop $100. You ask for something large, point out a larger, untenanted table that is just like those occupied by other couples. No dice. You settle for something upstairs, in the so-called Hayloft (Siberia), where a table for two is of human proportions. Later, you walk downstairs to see what has become of the table you wanted. It is occupied by two gentlemen only, fellows of more apparent substance than yourself, while what you rejected remains in disuse.

Actually, the upstairs is the more commodious of this restaurant's two dining rooms. The tables have space between them, and the traffic is light. The brown walls are hung with painterly paintings, the ceiling is beamed, and the great, airy, long-limbed chandeliers hang low, within reach of a tall man's antennae. Similar ceiling fixtures illuminate the lower level, a considerably larger high-ceilinged room that glows with the Colonial *Gemütlichkeit* that, to the enduring contentment of Coach House partisans, sets the place apart from the trendy and/or funky and/or foreign restaurants that are 99 percent of this ostensibly American one's local competition. This room glitters with a kind of year-round holiday festiveness, which is the sum of its wood paneling and exposed bricks, beamed ceiling and red carpeting, hunting scenes and still lifes all about in handsome

134

frames. The table linen is pink, and it is set with fresh flowers and cherry-colored napkins.

If you are given a table upstairs, you may very well get seated and nothing else. After a while you must seek out the help—you find them around the corner, arms folded, chatting. Sometimes the house offers one or two special dishes of the day—if you do not ask about them, you may not find out about them. Order a bottle of California Chardonnay (from among the many on the list), and your captain upstairs does not listen to your order, but returns with three or four Chardonnays and word that "these are the ones we have." Downstairs the courtesies are better observed, but in either location the waiters tend to be bizarrely matched to their responsibilities. There are a couple who understand English no better than they speak it, and one who chews gum (or something) throughout dinner, demands your order in the manner of a district attorney, and carries his hands in the position of the forepaws of a dog walking on his hind legs.

Which is not to say that you cannot eat well here. There are the raw oysters, for example, which are opened to order, are cool, sweet, and briny, and come with a standard cocktail sauce. But the smoked turkey seems to have been frozen (or close to it) and thawed, for the pink slices are not so much moist as wet, their smoky flavor is vague, their garnish of horseradish and cream the only life of the dish. Of the hot appetizers the shrimp are the clear winner. You get five big ones in a pool of dark, rich sauce, the former crunchy and of vivid—albeit iodine-tinged—flavor, the latter dominated by good mustard. For years the Coach House has offered its special baked-clam appetizer for two, and during all that time it has never mastered the knack of heating clams without toughening them. Moreover, though these are good, fresh littlenecks, their buttery, heavily seasoned herb sauce is too indelicate for their gentle flavor. Among edible snails there are big, plump, tender ones, and there are little leathery ones. Here you get both kinds in a very green so-called garlic butter that would not sully a baby's breath. These days the famous black bean soup is the best it has ever been—thick, winy, sharply seasoned, dotted with chopped egg, a slice of parsleyed lemon on top.

You are shown the whole roasted bass (for two), and then it is boned and served to you not in its promised dill sauce but in butter and lemon, with chopped dill and parsley strewn over the fish—this is perfectly good food, fresh and not overcooked, but not what the menu leads you to expect. The house sautés big lumps of crabmeat with strands of ham and serves them in lemon and butter—the seafood is first-rate stuff, fresh and sweet, but these days the ham is coarse and salty, so the subtle interplay of the two principal ingredients is lost. The presence of chicken pie on this establishment's menu accounts in part for its reputation for being American. This dish is precisely the chicken in glue you remember from your high school cafeteria, here served over a shingle of tasteless baked dough. The mignonnettes of veal have the dead flavor of something warmed over; they are served with mushrooms that also seem reheated, and with meaty chestnuts. Sometimes the rack of lamb is fine—simple, tender, juicy, accurately prepared, of good flavor. But not infrequently it reaches you incinerated, its exterior like the surface of a marshmallow left too long in the fire. The roast beef gets a place of honor in a box near the center of the menu—the slab of meat is thick, pink, picturesque, has everything but beefiness. The sirloin steak, because it is not well seared, loses much of its blood-juiciness even when cooked only to medium rare. With these treats the restaurant serves good potatoes (baked, sautéed), or carrots so overcooked that a sharp glance turns them to puree, or spinach so plain it seems naked—eating it is much like eating grass.

The Coach House has served Stilton that is not only ripe but senile, having deteriorated into a loud, brown paste. But the chocolate cake—a rich mousse between crusts

135

that are almost black—has a good, intense chocolate flavor. The hot-fudge ice-cream cake is lightly lemoned sponge cake, deeply flavored vanilla ice cream, and warm, thick chocolate fudge—a good adult sundae, which is not to carp. What is called the chef's custard is a kind of bread pudding with a bright raspberry sauce. The apple tart is prettily golden brown and conventionally sweet-spiced—the apples, however, are mushy. The dacquoise—nutted layers of meringue and mocha cream—is good when you get it fresh. But if you come just once, the dessert to have is the pecan pie, the only distinctively American dish the house turns out in an exceptional version: lots of nuts, and the brown-sugar filler has the wonderful complexity of aged, fruity mincemeat. The pie is served with superb whipped cream.

You have to look out for yourself at the Coach House. Order, say, oysters, roast beef with a baked potato, and—at the end of your dinner—chocolate cake, and you may pay $37. You could have paid $29, but when the waiter asks if you would like spinach or carrots with your roast beef, you are being lured over to the more expensive, dinner side of the menu, and you drop $8 for a dreary vegetable. Restaurants with both à la carte and prix fixe menus will usually try to find the cheapest way to charge you, but the Coach House has not perfected this nicety.

A few wines are $12, some are around $15, most are around $20 or higher—up to three figures—despite which you never know what you are getting until it arrives, for the list states no vintage years, and some of the red wines are far from ready.

★★LA COLOMBE D'OR

134 East 26th Street
LUNCH, MONDAY TO FRIDAY; DINNER, MONDAY TO SATURDAY. CLOSED SUNDAY.
Reservations: 689-0666.
Credit cards: AE, DC, MC, V.
Medium priced.

From its modest start as a one-room restaurant in this indeterminate neighborhood (neither Gramercy Park nor Murray Hill calls this dim block its own), La Colombe d'Or has kept to its rustic look—until now. You inquire of your waiter about the single change that, you fear, may be the harbinger of others: the white chemises that now clothe the backs of the restaurant's stick-and-straw farmhouse chairs—which, through the years, have given in charm what they withheld in capacious comfort. The man tells you the slipcovers have been added to make the room seem more formal, and you cannot deny the good business judgment that informs the change, for ever since the New York *Times* went halfway overboard about the merits of this establishment in the hands of its most recent chef, the place has been the repair of those who take their leads from the press, which is to say, those who do not want to be told what a restaurant is like, only whether or not to like it. With respect to such folk it is well if the physical place reinforces their received views, and posh does that job best. It is, of course, useful to feed them well, but far more important, if they are to be kept coming, to tell them by signs they recognize that they are in the right place. You hesitate to guess what will follow the chair shirts.

Meanwhile, but for the new clothes, The Golden Dove remains what it has been, two softly lit rooms with a country look of exposed brick, rough masonry, dried flowers, fireplaces (in disuse), and chair cushions and banquettes that are upholstered in pat-

136

terned cottons of the kind you think of as French country prints. The floors are of red tiles, lace curtains hang over the front windows, and the wood paneling here and there looks like the kind of thing lifted from old cabinetwork, stripped, and retired to walls and panels where all it has to do is look old. The wood-topped tables are bare—except for beige napkins spread over their centers. The rooms are hung with reproductions of twentieth-century art (much Léger), their presence a reference to a preexisting restaurant of this name in the south of France—the original, however, hangs originals.

As the province is Provence, you begin your dinner with soupe de poissons, a saffroned and well-oiled density of sharp, edgy seafood flavor, the slice of toasted French bread at the center spread with a garlicky paste. But as the time is the present, the definition of Provençale is stretched to include this cucumber soup, a cool, creamy, tart, and pale-green thickness, nubbly and strewn with minced chives, in which you find small pink slices of smoked salmon—a nifty note. The tuna carpaccio adjusts itself to the Mediterranean context by the elements with which it is served, the sweet and velvety raw fish covered over with basil, slivers of strong, hard fennel, pungent Parmesan, and much good oil. What distinguishes the house ratatouille are the nuggets of artichoke and strands of red pepper with which the more usual ingredients—eggplant and tomato among them—are supplemented, everything in a tart and pungently seasoned oil. Withal, the big winners are this salad of shrimp, in which the crunchy and utterly sweet crustaceans, with celery and white beans, are roused by a dressing that is startling for the saffron that reddens it; and the grilled quail, the small bird exceptionally meaty, its juiciness and strong flavor set off by the crisp grill-marked skin.

One pasta dish is listed, and you do well to take its singularity as a sign that it is but an unenthusiastic nod to those who expect pasta on any menu offered later in the day than breakfast, for the fettuccine are in a sauce so rich, and so little else, that it obscures by its dull pinguidity the flavor of the wild mushrooms that are presumably the main attraction. The cod is not exactly a heady expression of Provençale flavors either, but the fillet, lightly browned and moist, is very much the coarse species in plain, and the rough, herbed mash of lima beans and tomatoes on which it reaches you is the quintessence of what has come to be called comfort food. On the seasonally changing menu salmon is served sometimes this way, sometimes that, on occasion the grill-marked fillet set on lentils that have been livened with bits of other vegetables, the fish itself roused by the mustard glaze with which it is polished. From time to time, folks who are otherwise good company debate the subject of where in New York to find the best bouillabaisse. You could as well argue about where in Mexico City to find the real moo shu pork. But while the issue persists, it cannot now be aired in disregard of the one served here, what with its dark red broth, fenneled and saffroned, the firm finfish and delicate littlenecks, the sweet mussels and tender lobster, all the ingredients except the last more or less suffused with the flavor of the soup, arranged over them two crusts of bread, one spread with a garlicky aioli sauce, the other with a fiery pink rouille. Maybe it has to do with what rabbit is obtainable in New York but, as in many places, the meat in the Dove's rabbit fricassee is nameless, could be any meat, so though the sauce is salty, spicy, thick with wild mushrooms, more is asked of it than it can do. With respect to the duck the menu reads "braised and sautéed," which your waiter translates as a grilled breast and a braised thigh, two dishes in one, and sure enough, the sliced breast, tender, rare, and glistening, is of exceptional duck flavor, while the thigh, crusted with sweet spices, though decent enough, seems an answer by sweet-spice disguise to the question of what to do with the lesser part of the bird—still, if only for that breast, a first-class dish.

It is difficult to determine the apple tart's virtues, if any, what with a filling that, no matter how you strain to set aside childhood memories, tastes like apple sauce. In cranberry season there is a cranberry tart, and it is as if little or nothing has been done with the fruit other than to put it in proximity to its pastry. But then there is this lemon sabayon, the fluffy and citric froth on a dark and crumbly pastry, the garnish of grapefruit sections in bright contrast despite the citrus family resemblance. The big winner is the walnut tart, a compacture of crunchy nuts and caramel on a thin pastry, garnished with a ball of rich vanilla.

★ CONTRAPUNTO

200 East 60th Street
LUNCH AND DINNER.
No reservations (751-8616).
Credit cards: AE, DC, MC, V.
Medium priced.

Of itself Contrapunto says that it serves "unusual pasta dishes not generally found elsewhere," which is so. This fact, together with the fact of some lively first courses, is the only, albeit not inconsiderable, excuse for undergoing the place, for Contrapunto is crowded, noisy, and, in its harsh light, none too lovely to look at either. Here you are in the Yellowfingers/Arizona 206/Arizona 206 Café/Contrapunto complex, and when you pass through the East 60th Street portal at the base of the stairway, your options are open to all four possibilities—until you commit yourself to Contrapunto by embarking on the one-flight climb. At the top of the stairs you find a six-foot-by-six-inch bench on which you must wait your turn (no reservations), but at least this site affords an excellent view of patrons (not only from Contrapunto, but from the lower level as well) on their way to and from the facilities. You may if you wish wait for your table downstairs at the Yellow-fingers bar—around comes your turn, down goes the Contrapunto host, back up with him drags he you. If you are lucky he has for you a windowside table overlooking Bloomie's or, not quite so diverting, a windowside table overlooking East 60th. Other tables have little to offer except yet other tables terribly hard by, and if you note the occupants, you note, too, that some of them, minks tossed over the backs of their chairs, are accompanied by gents in three-piece navy blues, for in addition to the young, the place gets adults who, of an evening, have not available to them any money but their own. The light fixtures on the walls look like inverted World War I helmets attached by wires to dialless telephone torsos. The linen on your table is protected from your indiscretions by a sheet of glass. The shiny, sealed-in-plastic white menus are blinding when they reflect onto your retina beams from the overhead spots that hang from the oppressively low ceiling. This is waiters and waitresses kindergarten (presumably employees who perform well here are graduated to Arizona 206), the staff is young, are cute in their party costumes of long white aprons, white shirts, bowties, and a pair of Daddy's suspenders.

The phrases "virgin olive oil," "extra virgin olive oil," and "Tuscan olive oil" appear in the descriptions of all but two of the first courses, and, as it happens, the substance, albeit uncredited, is present even in the two: roasted red and yellow peppers of strong, sweet flavor arranged among leaves of endive, strewn with fresh herbs and with slivers of raw, strong garlic, and set in a pool of the ubiquitous oil; big caps of wild mushrooms, each adorned with coarse-chopped Italian parsley and with bits of garlic (this time not quite raw), the earthy fungi in more of the famous oil, this time strongly peppered; braised hearts of radicchio, warm and chewy and pleasantly bitter, garnished with a salad of diced tomato, limp arugula, and little morsels of mozzarella, the ever present oil this time supplemented by balsamic vinegar; and what is given as pinzimonio caprese, a couple of ounces of the famous Tuscan juice, fortified with coarse-ground black pepper, in a ramekin that is surrounded by sliced peppers and tomatoes, smoked and unsmoked mozzarella, hard slices of good fennel, each of which you moisten with the oil.

Pasta. The recipes are fine, the renditions occasionally less so, as this plate of malfatti aragosta, in which the pasta packages, though filled with lobster, scallops, fresh fennel, and leeks, suffer from a flatness of flavor, as if they have been cooked and waiting, and in which the buttery sauce reveals little of the excitement that the listed lemon and chervil promise. But a good version of the capelli marina piccola is worth gambling on, for when the dish is right, the mound of noodles at the center of your plate, threaded with strands of sundried tomato and leeks, is heady of its abundant fresh basil, and it is surrounded by a dozen littlenecks in their shells, warm and fresh and tender—a stunning dish. The fettuccine uccelletti is a great tangle of the wide noodles with strands of leeks and chicken, strong and salty ham, and chunks of mushroom, all the flavors clear in the white-wine-and-tomato sauce, particularly that of the fresh oregano that gives the dish its fragrance. You order the tagliarini forte because the title and the jalapeno listed as an ingredient suggest a hot dish on this cold night. You are disappointed as to the heat, detect but a hint of the infamous Mexican pepper, though the garlic is clear enough, the Italian bacon pungent, the arugula with which the noodles are threaded revealing much of its sharp green flavor—the child in suspenders grates on the Parmesan until you tell her to stop, or until her Mouli grater runs dry.

The raspberry tart has become a little dry by late in the evening, the apricot tart is a heavy dried-apricot paste on a leaden dough, the raspberry-mascarpone ice cream is a mistake—especially its icy raspberries and nuggets of unadulterated cream cheese—and the burnt chocolate ice cream is not especially burnt, though it is rich, intense, velvety. With your ice cream you are served one of those nutted, rusklike biscotti that are flavored with amaretto—it is the best end-of-meal item in the house.

If you want beer with your pasta, be warned, nothing is available but Amstel Light or a thin, flat Italian substance called Raffo. If you want to *share* a pasta, the menu announces "Our dishes are balanced in form and size so that splitting is inadvisable, and we prefer not to do so. However, split orders will be charged $10.00 *extra.*" (Emphasis theirs.) You may, however, pass things around at the halfway point—to confirm that the "balance as to form and size" is bushwa. A few non-noodle main courses are offered.

★★★ LA CÔTE BASQUE

5 East 55th Street
LUNCH AND DINNER. CLOSED SUNDAY.
Reservations: 688-6525.
Credit cards: AE, DC, MC, V.
Very expensive.

Though Henry Soulé intended La Côte Basque as casual relief from the solemnity of his legendary Pavillon, New Yorkers have persistently treated the place as a ranking star, complete with all the formality attendant thereto, in the haute cuisine firmament. That is, a distinction is not made between going out to dinner (at, say, La Caravelle) and simply grabbing a bite to eat here. And yet Soulé has had his way, for he seems to have built lightheartedness right into the place. Only under the grim duress of Henriette Spalter—Soulé's close friend, and the establishment's long-term interim proprietor after his demise—was the restaurant in the grip of the kind of ceremonial lockjaw for which New York's most expensive French restaurants are (often unjustly) known. Today, under the seemingly casual care of its present owner, Jean-Jacques Rachou, one gets the impression not so much of a restaurant made cheerful by how it is run, rather that an attitude of benign sanction fosters the conviviality intrinsic to it. La Côte Basque is, of course, the prettiest restaurant in New York, and in its current happy state, it is easy to imagine that the good cheer in which one is here immersed is of its rooms' very textures and palette. The lofty plaster walls are the color of old ivory, the chairs and banquettes are of cherry-red leather, the beams and timbers are the near-black of espresso coffee, and among those there are the foggy or sunlit blues and tans and subtropical greens of Bernard Lamotte's murals, affectionate depictions of seaside towns, their harbors and beaches—and the countryside around them—on the Côte Basque itself.

The present management has enlarged the original place—it is now almost a full circle of rooms, with the bar and the hidden kitchen at the center—but the expansion has been so artfully carried out that it is impossible to fix, without the aid of memory, the borderline between the old part and the big new room just west of the bar. Some of the artwork has been moved, and mirrors have been installed, but the feeling of the place has been preserved—except that the large rear room, with its panoramic view of the harbor of St. Jean de Luz and the views of the town through trompe l'oeil "windows" in three other directions, has now become the closest thing in the place to an intimate corner (it seats around seventy). When Rachou first took over, word got out to the city's well informed that good things were happening here, and during the early years of his regime, the restaurant was frequented by an engaging crowd. Today the place is popular, so you may spot too much makeup on your right, cringe at too much noise on your left, and catch, from across the room on a Saturday night, the judgments of intrepid weekend restaurant samplers. As one such puts it, "This place has it all over La Groonawee" (though he would surely agree that there will always be those for whom nothing will ever match those wonderful days at summer camp).

Generalize, and, promptly, you must list your exceptions. Still, it appears that you do a little better here with special dishes of the day than with menu items. The listed salad of crabmeat and lobster, for example, is perfectly nice seafood and a good thick sauce that is almost emerald green of its fresh herbs, but the shellfish lacks a certain sparkle—it is fresh, but you will not for a moment suspect that it was in the briny this very morning. And the listed gratin de homard aux morilles, for another, is that nice lobster again, this time combined with sweet black morels in a hot sauce of almost liquorlike headiness— and yet you can get a copy of this dish in which the overdose of salt is almost its undoing. The printed menu is not, of course, barren. Consider the quenelle de brocheton, a great sausage-shaped log of fish mousse, solid but not heavy, its brusque pike flavor vivid against a Nantua sauce that is at once honey-sweet and tangy of the flavor of lobster shells. The menu lists a good snail dish as well, the plump morsels mingled with sautéed wild mushrooms, and bound in a red-wine sauce that is concentrated, sticky, and silken. But when your captain informs you that quail is available, you will do well to set aside the printed menu in favor of that little bird, for it is served here filled with a fluffy and well-seasoned dressing that is enriched with sweetbreads, and it reaches you, in the form-fitting pastry in which it was baked, at the center of a pool of concentrated red-wine sauce, surrounded by hot white grapes—the elaborate treatment does nothing to diminish the clarity of the pungent natural flavor of the quail itself. At other times there is fresh duck liver, and the slices of unctuous meat, very rapidly browned, cooked through but retaining much blood-rare flavor, are laid over a mound of chestnut purée, are adorned with a few raspberries, and are moistened with a dark sauce that is touched with fruit— the sauce is fine with the meat, but it is particularly dramatic with the sautéed wild mushrooms that are yet another element on the wide-ranging plate.

You will pass up the bass—fresh fish, nicely prepared, but revealing little or none of its natural flavor—in favor of the grilled Dover sole with mustard sauce. The English swimmer reaches you filleted, the four quarters returned to their original positions, and though the exteriors are done to a glinting copper highlighted by flecks of black, the meat under the surfaces is unsullied milk white, moist, shining, and firm, its delicate flavor intact—the smooth, weighty mustard sauce, sharp but subtle, sets the fish off without obscuring it. Order a roasted chicken, and you are shown the whole big bird (poularde), its skin taut and glazed. It is taken away, and you are brought great slices of the white meat—they are cooked through but have lost none of their moisture, and they have chicken flavor that, by today's standards, is pungent—the bird's earthy sauce is fragrant of tarragon without being obvious. The noisettes of veau may be the most remarkable dish on the menu, for the nutty flavor of the pale, lightly browned and juicy little steaks is of a strength almost never successfully imparted to veal—do not, however, become so engrossed in the meat that you neglect its truffle sauce, the slightly "burnt" flavor of which is its stunning seasoning. When there is venison, sautéed scallops of it are served with matching slices of that duck liver you had as a first course. This is mild venison, but its light, clear, slightly sour sauce poivrade, dense with peppercorns, rouses it smartly. You do not expect cassoulet on the menu of a restaurant of this particular class, but the current management has always offered one. For the clarity of the different meats and sausages, and for the perfect texture of the beans, firm but not hard, this is a flawless version—but it is a bit refined, lacks the coarse edge that you may well think of as an essential element, if not the essence, of cassoulet.

Scores of soufflés stream from this kitchen of an evening, all of them handsomely browned and proudly risen. It is not unusual for a table of, say, eight, to be dealt eight of them. The waiters circle the party, puncture the tops, spoon in the sauce—mostly raspberry sauce into soufflés lightly flavored with Grand Marnier. Other sweets: a tart of thin-sliced apples on parchmentlike pastry, very nice for its austerity, for the bite of its slightly sour fruit; apples again in the tarte Normande, the minced fruit between layers of a light and creamy cake; a flat rice pudding cake not improved by the bits of fruit with which it is studded—it is set in an apricot sauce that helps not enough; a Grand Marnier mousse that is creamy but light, the liquor clear but discreet; a rich, polished chocolate mousse in which, happily, there is intensity but not chocolate overkill.

★★CSARDA

1477 Second Avenue (at 77th Street)
LUNCH, SATURDAY AND SUNDAY; DINNER, DAILY.
Reservations: 472-2892.
Credit cards: AE.
Inexpensive.

In the old days it would have required all your fingers and toes to count the Hungarian restaurants on the Upper East Side. Today only a handful cater to the neighborhood's small but apparently vigorous Hungarian community. Of the scant half dozen, this is the one that, by virtue of its uncompromising Hungarian flavor—of food, of the surroundings in which it is served, of the staff that serves it—and its consistently decent cooking, is the best. Accordingly the place gets a largely Hungarian crowd and a contented one. Of an evening you will spot Second Avenue shopkeepers—gentlemen alone with their newspapers next to couples who sometimes eat just as silently. But there are gayer gatherings, too, in which dramatically made-up ladies with cigarette holders and Gabor hair—or the mahogany-colored hair that one thinks of as gypsy—laugh the evening away in the company of mustachioed Magyars. Sunday is family day, and the place is packed with multigenerational gatherings, over which an elder presides from the head of a row of pushed-together tables.

The site of all this mitteleuropaisch happiness is a foursquare, brightly lighted little cube of a place, with walls of white plaster, a floor of red tiles, a density of tables. The restaurant is hung with old-country pottery, native costumes, boldly patterned little rugs, and framed art, much of it of equine subjects—Hungarians are great horsemen. You are served by waiters in white shirts or by strawberry-blond soubrettes in red blouses—they look sexy, and very likely are, but their ministrations are motherly. Your wants are heard by them with a concerned attentiveness that will, at least a little, intoxicate.

Whatever you order, your dinner begins with the little dish of cool, crisp, sweet-and-sour cucumber salad that is a given in these places. That is the lightest thing you will eat. The marinated herring is more like it—a slab of briny, soured fish under crisp onions in thick cream. The chopped liver is eggy, thick as paste, onioned, polished with fat. A firm lump of seasoned ground meat is the core of the stuffed cabbage, which is buried in mild sauerkraut, moistened with a creamy sauce that is pink with paprika, and garnished with stewed green pepper and disks of strong sausage. Stouter still is the lecsos kolbász, that same good sausage in a spicy, stewlike setting that is thick with onion and peppers. But the first-course big winner is brains and eggs—a peppery hot mush, prettily parsleyed and strewn with hot paprika; it is light and steamy, but rich.

If you come only once, the dish to have is the stuffed roast chicken. You get half a big bird, and its vivid chicken flavor is emphasized by the dark, aggressively seasoned liver dressing that is stuffed between the white meat and the glazed, crisp skin. The roast duck is even crisper, its dark meat even juicier, of stronger flavor. The garlic medallions of veal are of good meat, but the sauce they are served in these days is a pale version of what used to be little more than straight pureed garlic. The roasted veal shank looks like an instrument of violence: a big bone, a great knob of dark meat at one end—you wish it were tastier. Four thick slices of meat make up an order of roast pork—the meat can be a little dry, but this peasanty food is satisfying. Four slabs more are an order of boiled beef, succulent meat, with the sharpness common to this dish—you will notice it not at all if you apply the strong horseradish. The beef goulash is a powerful stew, hefty chunks of fibrous, tender red meat, their surfaces dark, in a thick brown sauce, garnished with the tiny, eggy dumplings called nockerl. More nockerl with the calf's liver paprikash, a giant mound of pleasantly greasy morsels of liver, threaded with strands of onion and green pepper, all moistened with a reddened, peppery oil—weighty food.

Palacsintas may be had filled with chocolate or (the genuine article) with apricot preserves. These are tender pancakes, good when filled with the sweet jam and sprinkled with confectioner's sugar and chopped nuts. The strudels—apple or cherry or cheese—are hot, light, flaky.

Pilsner Urquell from Czechoslovakia is carried, but often a slight residue of detergent in the glasses flattens the good beer.

★★★ LE CYGNE

55 East 54th Street
LUNCH, MONDAY TO FRIDAY; DINNER, MONDAY TO SATURDAY. CLOSED SUNDAY.
Reservations: 759-5941.
Credit cards: AE, DC, MC, V.
Very expensive.

In the more than fifteen years since the opening of its first store, Le Cygne has done business at three sites, while its kitchen has been in charge of that many chefs and more. Its reputation, too, has not always been what it was the last time you looked. There was the occasion when no less than the New York *Times* mistakenly declared it the purveyor of "the best haute cuisine French fare in the city," and a time more recent when it seemed to almost everyone that the place had grown complacently dull, that though you could find little or no fault with it, even much to praise, you were content never to return. Its latest and prettiest quarters seemed to have lost their charm. Though every stick was in its original place, the rooms that were almost universally praised when Le Cygne III was new had apparently not worn well. But drop in on The Swan today, and though all the original pieces continue in place, the restaurant is revivified, a condition that traces not indirectly to yet again a new man in the kitchen, one Jean-Michel Bergougnoux, his provenance Lutèce, before that Le Régence. Though only the food has changed, everything has changed. The stodgily traditional haute cuisine of Le Cygne's recent years has been supplanted by cooking bound to no tradition at all, the menu an array of dishes that aim only for flavor, excitement, pleasure. Accordingly the restaurant's stuffy clientele has been augmented, albeit not entirely replaced, by citizens of a wider world—engaging folks with whom you yourself might be content to dinner—and it is the magic of their quickening presence that accounts for the restaurant's lively new life.

Le Cygne is two townhouse floors connected at the front by stairways that, from the anteroom to which you enter, curve upward to the left and right, to converge on the second floor. The place is all pastels, much gray, soft blue, off white, with vague murals —of flowers on the street floor, landscapes one flight up—that soften somewhat the trim, almost geometric layouts. What has not changed is the cordiality of the restaurant's service. Le Cygne years ago did away with the tiresome business of addressing you by honorific and name at every encounter. These days the policy is to give you gladly what you want when you want it. It makes almost everybody happy.

Almost everybody would be happy with the "Petits pannequets d'huîtres en gelée de poulette au vinaigre de balsam," no less, six uncooked oysters arranged on your plate at the odd-numbered clock points, the three that are wrapped in spinach alternating with three that are not, all of them set on a circle of stock that was jellied on the plate with a rich white sauce trapped under it. The oysters are impeccably fresh, briny and sweet, and they are variously set off, livened, enriched by the spinach and the jelly and the rich sauce. You order what is listed as "lobster salad," so you are surprised, albeit not disappointed, that it reaches you warm, for the meat of the crustacean—out of its shell, and arranged on your plate in the form of a lobster—is perfectly done, warm, juicy, of sweet ocean flavor, and it is set in a tart, fruity, and buttery orange sauce that rouses it nicely. Order snails, and the plump morsels reach you embedded in a red disk that is a strong herbed hash of tomato and red peppers, a tasty setting in which the snails tend to get lost, so they serve principally as a textural note. Even modern menus have their inevitabilities, of which foie gras is the most certain. Here the oleaginous meat is served in thin slices that are pink and moist within the crisped surfaces, the rich liver set over an apple puree that is creamy white, the dish strewn with parsley and adorned with sour red berries.

Three fillets of salmon are set in a light, almost brothlike sauce that is dotted with lentils, parsley, and bits of vegetable of many colors. The pink fish, cooked through but a little rare, is warm and juicy, and it is garnished with disks of crisped salmon skin, their resilient texture and vigorous flavor nice foils to the fish and its sauce. It is a minor matter that the chicken is of only remote chicken flavor, for what you are served are slices cut from a construct formed by wrapping the white meat around woodsy wild mushrooms, the slices in turn set in a dark and sticky sauce that is fortified with foie gras. Of the roasted rabbit you are served lengths of white meat, with it you receive a sauce that is heady of the rosemary with which the game was done—the meat is garnished with a pouch, formed of flaky pastry, that is stuffed with an earthy compacture of mushrooms and watercress. That rabbit is good, but an even greater production is made of the venison, the tender, vaguely livery meat in a slightly tart sauce that is dotted with cranberries and blueberries, garnished with halves of small roasted pears that are hot and fruity, and with a muffin of rich chestnut cake.

Among the items held over from Le Cygne's more traditional days are, happily, its impeccable soufflés. Consider, for example, the lemon soufflé—devoid of the candylike lollipop sweetness that is the ruination of most lemon soufflés, it is loftily risen, fluffy, almost weightless, lemony but not sour, strikingly sauced with hot raspberries. The plate of black currant desserts includes an almost violently intense sherbet, a sweet pear that is deep purple of the currant liquid in which it has been poached, a currant mousse, and a small circular tart of dark pastry on which whole currants are piled high. The so-called apple fritters are slices of battered and sautéed apple, the tart, crisp fruit set in an enriched apple puree and garnished with ripe raspberries.

★★DA NANNI

151 East 82nd Street
DINNER. CLOSED SUNDAY.
Reservations: 772-6690.
Credit cards: AE, DC, MC, V.
Very expensive.

It is around twenty years since Nanni opened his first New York restaurant, a clubby and convivial joint on East 46th Street that remains in place, is still popular and of merit. For a number of years Nanni ran a second restaurant in the East 60s, where the food was fancier and pricier. That one he has now given up, presumably in favor of this. It may be assumed that, what with the rewards of success, this time he was in a position to create the restaurant of his dreams. Nanni is short, gruff, energetic, you imagine he does not mind mixing it up, so it is something of a surprise that his dream betrays a yearning to regress: The new restaurant is small, womblike, the kind of place that used to be called intimate, and to which you did not bring your wife. Except for the white table linen, Da Nanni is surfaced, almost throughout, with solemnly dark, elaborately patterned red cloth—the padded walls, the banquette that runs the length of the room, the seats of the chairs, the circular tops of the bar stools, all dark sanguineous red. The mirrors and the art are in ornate frames. A tiny lamp stands on every table, fringes hang from the brass lampshade. The carpeting is dark, the room softly lit. By instinct, you talk quietly. You are expected also to wear a jacket and tie—after all, Nanni himself does (except when he is in kitchen whites), but he does not press the point, for many of his customers in this place got to know him in the midtown restaurant, to which they went in any old thing. To his staff, however, Nanni makes no concessions, so the gentlemen in black and white are unfailingly courteous, some of them to the point of deference.

You compose your antipasto from the items displayed on a cart that, at your request, is rolled to your table. If you come here when cold whiting is on the cart, you are in luck, for the fish has been carefully cooked—is browned, moist, firm—and it has been dressed and enriched with good olive oil—excellent food with bread and white wine. You are doubly in luck if asparagus is on the cart, for these are thin shoots, carefully peeled and judiciously poached, so they are crunchy, and they are served with a cold and glistening emerald-green sauce that is well oiled, tart, heady of herbs and garlic. Your captain pushes the white beans (which he likes to refer to as Abruzzi caviar because it always gets a laugh), and they are not bad, though you wish they were firmer; and he speaks up for the marinated mushrooms, which are polished with the good house oil. Order carpaccio, and you are served not so much a dish as the makings of one. The raw beef is sliced, but that is all that has been done to it. At the center of your plate you find a section of lemon and a mound of minced parsley. You are provided with mustard sauce, you are offered ground cheese, olive oil is available. You make of your beef what you wish, too bad that what you wish for is beefier, blood-juicy beef, though what you are given will serve if you dress it well. The house is willing to prepare half orders of pasta, so even these somewhat weighty gnocchi (they require that you put your teeth in play) may be a first course, their tomato sauce, at once tart and creamy, a good foil to the firm dumplings. Quite another tomato sauce is involved in what is called "penne alla

145

rugola," the short tubes of hefty pasta in a vigorous red sauce that is studded with chunks of garlic, the entire dish overlaid with leaves of arugula that, warmed only by their proximity to hot food, retain all their uncooked flavor. On occasion the house serves fettuccine—the wide noodles in a creamy sauce that is earthy of porcini mushrooms. Cheese works wonders on those three pasta dishes, but you do well to omit it from the seafood risotto, in which the mound of herbed rice, moistened with a pinked and stocky broth, is studded abundantly with morsels of shellfish and tomato—deep, complex, satisfying food.

Order calamari, and you get an abundance of the fresh and tender squid, the circles and the sheafs of small tentacles in a hot, herbed, and redded broth. Order red snapper, and you get a great slab of the snowy fish—it is lightly browned, set in yet another pink broth, this one enriched, and it is garnished by a handful of small clams that, though warmed through, are delicate and tender. You order chicken scarpariello, and you are asked if you want it on or off the bone. You opt for "on," and even so, the nuggets of chicken are of less than vivid chicken flavor—still, the dish is well made, the bird moist, cooked through, handsomely browned, heady of rosemary and garlic. In New York restaurants, about one veal chop in ten is everything a veal chop can be, and even where they are done right, they are sometimes done wrong. At Da Nanni they are sometimes done right, and on your lucky day, you get a chop the pink juiciness of which is trapped between seared surfaces, so that the chop is plump, seems almost to be bursting. On Thursdays, and occasionally on other days, the house makes osso buco, and if the meat is not quite falling off the bone, it is moist and tender, and its sauce is strongly seasoned, dark, thick with vegetables.

The peaches in wine are sweet and tangy, the acidity of the plum tart is leavened by its good shortbread pastry, the creamy cheesecake is moist and smooth, and the tirami sù is rich, spongy of its ladyfingers, of strong chocolate and coffee flavor. When there are berries, they are ripe.

★★DARBÁR

44 West 56th Street
LUNCH AND DINNER.
Reservations: 432-7227.
Credit cards: AE, DC, MC, V.
Medium priced.

You will recall that back in the seventies New York had a brief fling with Indian food. Those were the days when Raga, Shezan, the now-defunct Gaylord, and several other restaurants arrived on the scene and revised local notions about eating habits on the Subcontinent. (Until then, Indian restaurants had been perceived as sources of cheap, suspect, stewlike dishes called curries, in which exotic and fiery spices concealed, rather than emphasized, the characteristics of the foods they flavored.)

The fling is over, but it has left its mark. To this day, meritorious Indian restaurants are commonplace in New York, are even well attended, but they are no longer talked about. It is the misfortune of this one, Darbár, that it came to town years after its predecessors, in the early eighties, when a new Indian restaurant could get a favorable reception in the press, as this one did, and yet generate no excitement in the community.

Had Darbár been part of the wave—well, ripple—of the seventies, it would today have a past, a history of glory days, a reputation. Instead, though it is among the city's preeminent Indian eating places, arguably the best of them, it is known mainly to the midtowners who work nearby and sometimes fill it for lunch, and to those rare diners-out who do not mind places that have never made it as a scene—their numbers are too few ever to crowd Darbár for dinner, so you may walk in here any evening, without a reservation, and get yourself a choice table at once.

Native artifacts are as inevitable in Indian restaurants as native waiters. Usually these adornments amount to a stringed instrument on one wall, a cooking implement on another, and, somewhere, a carved screen. In a few places, the appointments are in fact diverting. But Darbár, alone among New York Indian restaurants, is more an Indian environment than just a decorated store. Step through the front door, and you are in a small vestibule that, from floor to ceiling, is of burnished hammered copper, glinting red-gold, in a pattern of row upon row of perfectly rounded, tipped hemispheres that closely resemble, visitors always note, ripe examples of the female breast. Through another door, and you are in the two-story anteroom of the restaurant proper, from which a curved stairway ascends to the upper level. On the wall to the left of the stairway hangs a majestic and elaborately patterned rug—all ivory and gold, accented with a deep, vibrant blue, it bridges the two floors, and gleams in the soft light of the overhead spots that play upon it. Just under the rug, at the foot of the stairs, stands a dome-topped ceremonial vessel of polished brass—it is taller than a fire hydrant, and its slender, curved spout, which reaches from the base almost to the top, is balanced by a threadlike handle, almost as tall, that describes in outline a great ear. The walls throughout are of a glowing cocoa-colored velvet, and upstairs and down, the place is hung with wood carvings, paintings on silk, tapestries, elaborately framed mirrors, panels of brilliantly colored cloth or carpeting, and, downstairs at the back, more of that hammered copper, an entire wall of it, this time in a pattern that no stretch of mind will perceive as suggestively representational.

These appointments, you understand, are not merely decorative—they are, to a certain extent, the place itself. They seem to shape and define it—in one instance, quite literally, for the best tables in the house are the handful of semi-private ones along one wall of the lower level, each of them shielded on two sides by tall screens of carved wood that are framed with rods of glinting brass. Withal, you are dismayed to note that in this handsome and exotic place the background silence is mutilated by the same domestic music you endure while holding the phone for the next available service representative.

At Darbár, the service representatives are emissaries from the homeland, and they reveal, through their colorfully accented English, a good familiarity with the menu, and a willingness to discuss it with you cordially. Conversation out of the way, they deliver, from a regularly available selection of three, some of the most stimulating soups in town (this even though soups appear almost not at all in India's cookery, and were developed there, it is said, to accommodate the peculiar preferences—and poor teeth—of the English). Among them is a mulligatawny, in this version a thick, lentil-based puree, touched with tomato, that, despite the complexity of its herb-and-spice flavoring, makes an impact of direct, primitive earthiness. Another is called palak shorba, also a thick soup, but headier and sharper—of the spinach with which it is threaded, and of sweet spices and strong pepper.

Deep-fried vegetable fritters and turnovers are much of the standard Indian first-course menu, and among those available here, there is an exceptional onion bhajia, in which a packed and tangled mass of herbed onion strands is dipped in a flour batter and then fried until crisp. Like all of Darbár's deep-fried dishes, this one is light, crusty, and

147

retains just enough greasiness not to be dry—at its center you find a nugget of onions that is sweet and tender. The anguri samosa is a big pyramidal turnover filled with a great assortment of herbed and seasoned vegetables, much like a hot vegetable salad within a flaky shell. Those are first courses for hunger. There are also some designed for the lack of it, stimulating ones like channe ki chaat, a mound of cold chick-peas mingled with chunks of potato and lengths of onion, all of them made rousing by a tamarind sauce that is at once fruity and spicy. The cold dish called crab Bombay is also meant to waken the palate, but, though this is perfectly good crabmeat, as modified by its sweet and sweet-spiced sauce, it is at best only interesting to the Western palate. There are shrimp pakoras and chicken pakoras, each dish a dozen or so very lightly battered and deep-fried morsels, the shrimp crisp and of notably clear shrimp flavor, the chicken just as beauti- fully browned, but mushy, and devoid of chicken taste. All the deep-fried appetizers take well to any of the three condiments served with dinner: a cold herbed yogurt, a tamarind sauce, and little chunks of root vegetable that have been marinated and, thereby, made violently spicy.

Indian attitudes toward the preservation and preparation of seafood differ from your own. In Indian restaurants, finfish, especially, may be impeccable one time, inedible the next, and in this respect Darbár has nothing on the competition. Consider the pomfret tandoori, on occasion a perfect dish, on occasion what seems like an oven-baked frozen fish—handsomely reddened and blackened on its scored exterior, but pasty, mealy, and almost raw at the bone, devoid of fish flavor throughout. The lobster tikka, also done in the oven, is the tail meat of a substantial crustacean, out of the shell, carefully baked so that it is moist, tender, and cooked through—still, its lobster flavor, though sweet, is slight, and the impact of the lemon, garlic, and pepper with which it was treated before baking is at best subtle. But the most familiar tandoor dish—chicken tandoori—is always in good form here, the tender, moist young bird dramatically charred and suf- fused with the pungent spices of its marinade.

Red meat in many forms, among them saag gosht, massive chunks of lamb (or, if you wish, beef) immersed in a hot, black, and buttery mash of spicy spinach—the meat is firm, fibrous, of strong lamb flavor; shahjehani biryani, which is billed as a rice dish, though predominant among the items you find buried in the huge mound of glistening pale-brown grain are chunks of good lamb yet again, plus raisins and nuts, as well as spice seeds that you experience as unexpected bursts of flavor—the food is wondrous for the interplay of diverse elements, and when you add its warm yogurt sauce, you enrich the dish without disguising it; and goat rogan josh, another complex production, this one of almost sugar-sweet goat meat in a yogurt sauce that is textured with bits of ginger and almond—fresh coriander is the heady note in the sturdy stuff.

Vegetarians will find here sustenance requiring no compromise of ingestive proscrip- tions, for elaborate dinners may be built solely of Darbár's vegetables (offered both à la carte and in an assortment called vegetarian thali) and breads. Among the vegetables: dhal, a thick and creamy mash of lentils, their solidity leavened by their spiciness; bayngan bhurta, an oily and rich eggplant paste perfumed with coriander; a mixture of sliced mushrooms and plump fresh peas called mushroom matar, in which the two main elements are bound in a thick sauce that is fragrant of sweet spices; buttery spinach, dark and pungently seasoned, the lumps of mild cheese buried within it mainly a textural contrast to the fibrous green. Among the breads: poori, the balloonlike wheat bread that is made here in a version of particularly vivid grain flavor; naan, a soft, lightly browned leavened bread with a flavor much like that of matzo; and onion kulcha, a big winner, another unleavened bread, this one filled with—and moistened by—buttery onions.

The appeal of Indian desserts is elusive. The ones that resemble Western desserts usually come off as inferior by comparison. The others resemble candy. Burfi, for instance, described as "almond milk fudge," is, unfortunately, that. And the kulfi (ice cream), as the menu warns you, is "made from thickened milk cooked for several hours." Kheer, a creamy, grainy, cardamom-flavored rice pudding strewn with ground nuts, is the best sweet in the house.

★★★ DA SILVANO

260 Sixth Avenue (near Bleecker Street)
LUNCH, MONDAY TO FRIDAY; DINNER, DAILY.
Reservations: 982-2343.
Credit cards: AE.
Expensive.

After a decade of fighting off the credit card infection, Silvano Marchetto counted his empty chairs one night and (with a scornful aversion of eyes, you may be sure) let American Express in. For the first time, you may now eat at his place and find yourself among folks who, because they declare income, care to document deductions. There are better reasons for coming here, however, than curiosity about such strange types. Marchetto was, after all, among the most talented of the pioneers who, in the seventies, brought to New York undrenched Italian food, and the decline in his restaurant's popularity in recent years did not reflect any slippage in his kitchen's performance, devolved, rather, from a plethora of new competitors cooking in similar style, and from their willingness to do what he would not: pay for the convenience credit of others. It got to the point where you could, on occasion, walk in here and regret it—that is, if half-deserted eating places depress you. Happily, word of Silvano's concession to the bankers has got around, and on occasion the place now bustles again.

The author of that one-man passive resistance movement does not look unlike the part, and if you came here when the place was new (back when Rockefeller was vice-president), you will readily recognize the proud bearing of the short, compact fellow. His stance is unchanged, as is his compactness, though of the latter there is these days half again as much. But his recent willingness to go financially modern is no surprise if you judge him by his forward-looking attire of an evening—tasseled tan loafers, slightly harem trousers of delicately wrinkled muted-gray plaid, a striped shirt open at the neck to the beads, and a black painter's smock to mid-thigh, its collar partly concealed by long hair that, combed back, reveals the jewel in one earlobe. You can't miss him.

His place is a couple of well-lighted, vaguely rustic rooms, the white-linened tables, flowers in tiny copper pots thereon, surrounded by pale-wood chairs with straw seats. You walk on a floor of small quarry tiles. Where the walls are of brick, they are hung with wood-framed mirrors here, coat hooks there; and where they are of ivory-painted plaster, with those dim reproductions of Renaissance art that, in certain Italian restaurants, appear to be stuck up instinctively, as if for purposes talismanic, presumably in the expectation that this devoir to the cultural heritage will provide protections elsewhere secured by a mezuzah on the doorpost, a crucifix over the bed. An espresso machine stands on the service bar in the smaller room (to which you enter), in front of it a display of appetizers, desserts, wine. In both rooms there are hanging and standing flora in the front windows. When the weather is fine you may eat at the marble-topped tables out front, under the blue canopy.

A printed menu exists, and you are handed a copy, but the document is just a gesture to the situation. You glance at it, but at the same time you switch on your tape recorder, for the arrival of the menu signals the beginning of your waiter's spiel, a recitation of the fifteen or so special dishes offered each day—it is from among these that most dinners are assembled here, for your announcer does his best to make them sound yummy. A couple of menu items: panzanella, a bread salad, chunks of wheat bread moistened with vinaigrette and mingled with morsels of tomato and strands of pepper—sometimes with other vegetables as well—the fragrantly herbed and well-seasoned salad cool and stimulating; and scampi in graticola, shrimps that are lightly breaded, judiciously grilled, moist and crunchy, and, too bad, more than a bit touched with iodine. From off the menu: fresh fennel, the almost hard white slices of a sweet and pungent licorice flavor, mingled with bits of tomato and gentled with balsamic vinegar; equally fresh asparagus, the great green shoots peeled down to their tender cores and, though served hot, moistened with a *cool* dressing of velvety olive oil and lemon—the vegetable is garnished with glistening white knobs of almost fluffy buffalo mozzarella.

A handful of well-made pasta dishes are listed on the printed menu, but they are mostly familiar items, and the man standing beside your table suggests you have your spaghetti today's way. You agree, and the firm, supple strands reach you in a creamy and nubbly tomato sauce that is thick with sweet-spiced, fennel-flavored ground sausage— green peas are a pure, green note in the otherwise strong and fragrant dish. Much is made here of spinach: come when rotolo is offered, and you are served slices cut from a log that is formed of a sheet of pasta and a vigorously seasoned filling of spinach and ricotta—strong Parmesan cheese is grated on at the table, and it adds a pungent edge to the hot, rich stuff; but you are in especial luck if you come when the spinach (again with ricotta) has been formed into gnocchi, for the dumplings are at once well bound but light, pleasantly sticky, and their vivid spinach flavor is potentiated by a mild admixture of sweet spice—moistened with hot, clear black butter, the gnocchi too may be advantageously fortified with grated-on cheese.

Orata, a distant relative of the snapper, is flown to Silvano from the Mediterranean, so that he may marinate it in herbs and olive oil, grill it whole, and serve it as four great-flaked filleted quarters—the marinade enriches the fish and invigorates its remarkably vivid ocean flavor. He also gets local seafood, prepares it a local way—the sautéed shad roe is grainy but moist, its nutlike taste potentiated by the butter in which it is done, by fresh parsley, by the lemon you squeeze on. Your waiter informs you that the squab is spicy and well done, meaning that it is coated with mildly hot red pepper and cooked through—this bird is all dark meat, of powerful flavor, and though its fat has largely been lost in the roasting, it is moist of the olive oil with which it is slicked. You get an abundance of rabbit, on the bone, in a winy sauce that is fragrant of herbs, the firm chunks of pale meat peppered and darkened on the surface, their sauce thick with bits of organ meat. You depart from the off-the-menu specials in favor of the listed veal chop, and you are a bit disappointed that, though not dry, the big chop is not bursting with moisture either—it is just about redeemed by a tomatoed sauce that is fortified with bits of chicken liver, livened by sweet peas. Back to the specials, a steak styled "Robespierre," marinated in olive oil, rosemary, black pepper, grilled, served sliced, the blood of the meat and the marinade forming a "sauce" of heady strength—this dish takes especially well to the handsomely browned roasted potatoes and sautéed zucchini that are the usual vegetable garnishes here.

The good Parmesan you had grated onto this dish or that may also be had straight, if

150

you wish, with one of the brightly dressed house salads. Ricotta ice cream, you will be fascinated to note, is vanilla ice cream with a slight ricotta flavor. Torta de la nonna (Gramma's cake) is a fluffy white cake, lightly lemoned. The grape pie is an abundance of plump, white, seedless grapes in a nicely browned pastry with a latticework top.

★★★ DA UMBERTO

107 West 17th Street
LUNCH, MONDAY TO FRIDAY; DINNER, MONDAY TO SATURDAY. CLOSED SUNDAY.
Reservations: 989-0303.
Credit cards: AE.
Medium priced.

You may recall Umberto Assante from the restaurant Cent'Anni. It was he who, in that restaurant's first years, kissed hands at the door, sat down at your table but kept his eye ferociously on the visible and, probably, invisible staff's every gesture, presided over the establishment's then ascendancy to a rarefied position among the city's Italian eating places. Recall him or not, others do. No sooner were his name and this address announced than the obscure site became a hot repair. Da Umberto is that familiar myth but real rarity, the warm, lighted place on a block that otherwise goes to sleep when the sun goes down, a destination to which the knowing alone are privy. This, however, is burgeoning Chelsea, Da Umberto is after all but one avenue block from Barney's, another from Lower Fifth, is thus ideally situated to become the fulcrum around which the Joyce Theater to the west, the Union Square Green Market and Zeckendorf Towers to the east, the Flatiron District to the north, seething Fourteenth Street to the south, and all within their orbit, merge, spin, and take off together in a riotous new birth of freewheeling cultural and commercial urban efflorescence! Barring that, it will have to settle for being the primary source of a hot meal north of the Village and south of the Shuttle. And, yes, food tastes better where you least expect it.

Da Umberto is a deep high-ceilinged room that, by partitions extending into it a little from each side, has been divided into a suggestion of three rooms, one behind another. You enter to the barroom, on your right the green-marble bar, behind it the bottles before a mirrored wall, across from it a display of foodstuffs and wines, next to that a large white-linened table, black bentwood side chairs around it. In the second room the tables and chairs are well spaced, and beside a glistening white-tiled wall, on a high marble counter, under overhanging hams, salamis, strings of garlic, and copper pots and pans, are displayed the salads, grilled vegetables, and meats that comprise Umberto's cold first courses and slightly less than encyclopedic antipasto. In room three your diversion is the kitchen at the back, visible through glass, and spiffy. Throughout the restaurant the walls are of the mottled umber that Italian places have recently taken to, the floor is of hardwood up front, big red tiles at the back, the light is ample, and if the treatment is a bit stark, the crowd that crowds the place adds color.

From that marble counter: a garlicky seafood salad, squid and scallops and little shrimp, their character distinct, moistened with velvety olive oil; firm chunks of artichoke accented with the flavor of the grill; Genoa salami strong enough to bring you to attention; grilled red lettuce, crunchy and a little bitter; dark-skinned baby eggplants that are soured and rousing; gamy cured beef; pale and tender veal in a thick, caper-dotted tuna purée; a salty and thoroughly oiled caponata, eggplant and olives and more in a thick tomato sauce; disks of sautéed zucchini, oiled and charred: all these things are fresher, more vivid, more alive than their counterparts almost anywhere else in town.

Pasta et al: rigatoni fagiolata, hefty tubes in a vigorous red sauce that is crunchy with white beans—a stout, peasanty dish; another tomato sauce, this one frankly and fragrantly garlicked, on soft but firm little gnocchi; red again, the remarkable capellini con aragosta, filament-thin strands of pasta in a lobster sauce that is briny, stout, thick with moist chunks of the sweet white meat; panzoti, a white entry among the reds, pasta envelopes stuffed with spinach and served in a buttery sauce, at once rich and light, that is nubbly of walnuts and strong Parmesan; a rice dish, risotto con porcini, the brown and stocky meal earthy of the wild mushrooms with which it is studded.

It is perhaps not exactly what you expect, but when there is salmon on hand, you get an impeccably fresh fillet, browned a little, that is as rare and rosy as the latest French article in its piquant mustard sauce. Da Umberto styles itself a Florentine restaurant, so you opt for the tripe because it is listed as trippe Fiorentina. Were it not named for a city, you would call it a country stew, the lengths of innard resilient but tender in their well-seasoned red sauce, which is thick with strong black olives and strands of root vegetable. Order quails, and you get four halves, their dark meat of intense flavor, their stuffing vigorously seasoned, nicely garnished with blocks of browned polenta. One dish bears your host's own name, scaloppine all'Umberto, the browned veal, pale and juicy, mingled with slices of artichoke in an herbed and winy sauce that is tinctured with a bit of tomato—the thin slices of delicate meat take on the flavor of the bay leaves that cling to their surfaces. Sometimes the house offers suckling pig, boned, packed with a garlicky stuffing that is redolent of rosemary, formed into a roulade, and roasted—you get a couple of thick slices cut from the great log, the tender, abundantly rich meat glistening of fat within the rims of crisped skin.

Though the Parmesan is hard, flinty, vivifying, the Gorgonzola both creamy and gamy, if you limit yourself to but a single cheese, you will do well with the Sardinian ricotta—it tastes like earthy butter, you have it moistened with olive oil, seasoned with fresh-ground pepper, and you eat it with a salad of arugula in a tart red-vinegar dressing. You wish there were less sugar in the well poached and sweet-spiced pear in red wine, and that the almond cake were livelier, but you have no quarrel with the cheesecake, which is cool, wet, weighty, touched with orange under its browned and white-sugared top.

★★DAWAT

210 East 58th Street
LUNCH, MONDAY TO SATURDAY; DINNER, DAILY.
Reservations: 355-7555.
Credit cards: AE, DC, MC, V.
Medium priced.

The subcontinental mind, alas, judges Western courtesy quantitatively. The more, it judges, the better, The New Yorker, on the other hand, when up to his ears in salaams, takes it that he is the victim of rudeness; or, if he is of psychoanalytic bent, of hostility; or, at least, that he is the victim of a bore. It is decades now since the imperial yoke was lifted from the Indian back. Are not Indians now taught in school that it is unnecessary —never mind risible—to fawn on Occidentals? On anyone? Does your host really imagine that if he doubles over, clasps his hands, and inquires after your well-being maybe thirty times during dinner, you will ever return? You figure that "the treatment" (as the treatment may well be called) is intended to elicit an expression of your hostility to the foreigner, thus confirming the foreigner's suspicion of your prejudice, thus justifying his administration of the treatment in the first place. You figure, too, that if you tell the smiling groveler to go away please, he will go away mad; that if you do not tell him to go away please, he will not go away; that, ergo, you cannot win; that, as you cannot win, you may as well tell him to go away please.

At the front door a turbaned giant in ceremonial dress bows you in, as a warm, fragrant breeze of Indian spices enwraps you on its way out. The rooms, however, do not deliver on the exoticism of that promise, for Dawat avoids the trappings of New York Indian restaurants as you usually know them. It is open and sunny, all pink and pale green, modern Western chairs around pink-linened tables that are set with copper service plates, nothing notably Indian about the pink-and-turquoise plaid cloth on the banquettes that rim the room, or about the few tropical trees. There are, however, these carved wooden heads, clusters of them here and there on the walls, their left sides painted one way, their rights another, giving them a queer one-eyed look. Their significance is lost on locals, which is not to say they are not decorative, but take them down, hang a curtain over the interior window that, at the back of the restaurant, provides a view of the spiffy kitchen, and this could be a place of any nationality or none. Conceivably as a corrective to the thinness of visual flavor, Dawat is patrolled by a handful of ladies in saris, hostesses, it seems, without portfolio. Signal one of them, and perhaps she will come by and ask if everything is satisfactory.

If, however, you have mastered, and are comfortable with, snapping your fingers for attention and flicking them to be let alone, you will do well at Dawat, for the food, unlike some of the help, is self-respectingly assertive: four shrimp that go as "Madhur Jaffrey's Baghari Jhinga" (her name is all over this menu), the little crustaceans in a heady and wondrously complex sauce dominated by garlic and mustard; MJ's "Bhaja," deep-fried leaves of spicy spinach in a nubbly batter garnished with slices of potato that, though of clear flavor, are mealy; keema samosa, triangular turnovers of light, flaky pastry filled with warm and gently seasoned ground lamb and garnished with strong redded onions; and dahi aloo poori, which is served from what is given as MJ's "Snack Cart," a vehicle adorned with more of those wooden heads, from which you are served bread crisps the size of half-dollars, those strewn with chick-peas and nuggets of potato, those dribbled with yogurt and with a fruity tamarind sauce, everything then sprinkled (from shakers) with spices—judiciously, so that none of the many flavors is obscured.

A principal appeal of Dawat is in the dishes it offers that you do not find elsewhere, notable among them the Parsi-style patra-ni-machhi, in which a fillet of fish, sometimes salmon, in a coriander chutney is wrapped in a banana leaf and steamed—the seafood is fresh, firm, moist, and the spiced density of green coriander in which it is buried imparts to it a wild herb flavor. Of course there is tandoori chicken, and this one is red, blackened, suffused with the moisture and spices of its marinade, nicely garnished with onions that are oiled and hot. Many other chicken dishes, among them chicken sag, the lengths of white meat in a pungent, sweet-spiced .pinach puree. Though tiny, the lamb chops masala have an almost muttony meat strength, and though the lamb is cooked through, it is utterly tender in its tart, spicy, gravylike yogurt sauce. The meat in the goat biryani is milder and sweeter than that lamb, the nuggets of fibrous goat buried in fluffy saffroned rice that is studded with nuts and raisins. Mostly good vegetables: thin, darkened slices of

153

eggplant that lose none of their powerful eggplant flavor to the fruity tamarind sauce in which they are done; mustard greens, the hot mash a little spicy, a little bitter; crunchy chickpeas in a hot-spiced sauce that has been made fragrant with coarse-chopped coriander. The somewhat heavy wheat bread called paratha is prepared here in a version flavored with mint—the lively herb leavens the bread's weightiness.

Carrot halva is a hot carrot mash studded with pistachios and white raisins and topped with a bit of whipped cream—good, though perhaps not what you think of when you think of dessert. The sweet-spiced rice pudding, though thick, is rousing. Ice creams and sherbets are available.

Beer is good with some of this food, wine with none of it.

★★DUANE PARK CAFÉ

157 Duane Street (near Hudson Street)
LUNCH, MONDAY TO FRIDAY; DINNER, MONDAY TO SATURDAY. CLOSED SUNDAY.
Reservations: 732-5555.
Credit cards: AE, DC, MC, V.
Medium priced.

As there are restaurants in which the food is secondary, so are there restaurants in which it is all. This enterprise, obviously constrained by monetary limits, has taken over the premises from which Tapis Rouge departed little mourned. The newcomers have made only surface changes, and though the result looks nothing like the predecessor, in part that is because it looks like nothing at all. Past the short bar, and you are in a small room in which dark-brown pilasters divide into squares the side walls of pale-wood veneer, and in which the front and rear are surfaced with an intricately woven cloth of neutral colors and geometric pattern. Overhead, papillar lights form a square, as they did under the previous administration. Underfoot the once black-painted floor has been scraped down to grainy wood. And in the aisle, where once there was a red carpet, there is now a green runner that looks like what is rolled out in apartment house lobbies on rainy days. Still, if the room is not prepossessing, it is inoffensive, can even turn cheerful when it is filled and you have been toasting absent friends.

Here a mostly Italian menu is in Japanese hands. No reason why wonderful food cannot be bred by the mating of these two, but in certain dishes Japanese delicacy is overwhelmed by Italian indelicacy. Part of the problem is mindset, for if you are prepared for Italian food and are served, let us say, this grilled marinated duck breast with arugula, you find that the arugula blares while the tender duck barely whispers to you of its Japanese wine marinade. No ambiguity about the seared tenderloin of beef, however; five thin slices of tender, bright-red beef (carpaccio with crusted edges) arranged like the points of an asterisk, a mound of strong, slivered Parmesan at the center, fresh, fragrant thyme strewn over all. The house smokes wild mushrooms, but restrainedly, so their flavor is heightened, not obscured, and serves them over a lemony salad of endive and red peppers—a wonderful balance of the diverse ingredients. The marinated eggplant is probably another Japanese article the subtleties of which require a certain attunement—surely it does here, for this strikes you as simply excellent eggplant, well oiled, arranged on crusts of bread with slivers of tomato and mozzarella and fresh herbs. The pappardelle (broad, weighty noodles) are fine in their nubbly, rather primitively meaty and lightly enriched meat sauce. Even finer is this risotto with porcini, the hot meal earthy, buttery, and deep.

Come once, and the thing to have is the casserole of northeastern seafood, which you may prefer to call seafood-in-the-pot, for it reaches you in a fluted, straight-sided china bowl in which a variety of finfish and shellfish, each apparently tended separately, each done to its own precise finishing point, are mounded up over a complex broth that reveals a great breadth of earth and ocean flavors. You are warned that the blackened salmon is rare—it is, and it is also fresh and done through, and the charred herbs and spices with which it is surfaced are a vivifying zest to the gentle pink meat. When you begin with not a great chicken, it hardly matters that its skin is browned, crusty, and alive with herbs, or that the bird is set over flavorful strands of orange rind, zucchini, red peppers—you still end with not a great chicken. Good osso buco, a slight variation on the usual thing, the massive knob of juicy meat surfaced with ground Parmesan and set in an especially intense but elemental tomato puree, the rice served with it stained deep yellow by the saffron that flavors it. Somehow a "pan fried Cajun ribeye" has sneaked onto this menu.

The pear hazelnut tart is a clear and lively expression of the cool fruit and crunchy nuts within a light, crumbly pastry—the tart takes well to the raspberry coulis in which it is set. The apple linzer tart is warm, so the whipped cream on it is falling apart when it reaches you—still this is good fruit, spicy and tart. The poached fruits are dark, spicy, many textured in their lemony syrup. The biscotti pudding, two slices cut from a loaf, sweet of licorice liquor, reaches you in a custardy sauce that is heady of its coffee flavor.

★ DUE

1396 Third Avenue (near 79th Street)
LUNCH AND DINNER.
Reservations: 772-3331.
No credit cards.
Medium priced.

Presumably architect Charles Gwathmey did this place free, for the interior is not so much a job of design as a portfolio of architectural materials, tricks, devices, which is to say, an advertisement for himself. A report in the press, however, to the effect that a million dollars was spent here suggests either that the handsome young Lusardi brothers (who made their money at the more straightforwardly appointed Lusardi's on Second Avenue) are just a couple of innocent old-country hicks who have been had by slicker Gwathmey; or that the announced big ticket is a false lure, aimed at those who will come just to see what that kind of money buys. For if this installation was not assembled from the leftover materials of a few dozen others, it must now be clear, even to the interests behind it, that that aleatory route could have achieved an equally shanty effect. From the portholes in the facade to the asphalt-tile floor (of diagonal stripes bold enough to trip over), to the rear ceiling of faux acoustic tiles, to the front ceiling of smoked glass, to the checkerboard wall of genuine (fuzzy wuzzy) acoustic panels and mirrored panels and terra-cotta panels, to the table tops of dark-gray mock terrazzo framed in light-gray mock terrazzo, to the dinky black folding chairs, to background music that seems the very expression of those parts, this place is designed—if that is the right word—to get you in and out by keeping you awake, alert, active, ready for your next stop before you have quite made this one. Maybe it was a failure of nerve, or of imagination, or maybe it was an inability to shake off safe old habits, but the house did not go all the way, for the food is mostly good, the service mostly sweet, aspects of Due that argue with its physical and aural appointments, creating a disharmony that may leave you confused as to how, as the movie critics put it, you are expected to respond.

Respond in advance. Hold with yourself a tranquility session of your preferred mystic persuasion, don a pair of your darkest shades, show up imperturbable, ready to smile back coolly at every attention-seeking element of your gaga surroundings, and commence your dinner with, say, a selection from the carpaccio list, maybe salmon carpaccio, which the menu identifies as "seared," but which reaches you utterly raw from the edges in, the thin sheet of pale-pink meat, which covers your plate, sweet, utterly fresh, garnished with sprigs of dill, and adorned with curls of a thick white sauce that is of intense olive oil flavor; or perhaps venison carpaccio, a meat that, from the evidence of this dish, benefits from treatment by fire, for this nearly raw red game reveals little venison character, gains much from the tart sauce of crushed capers with which it is spread. What goes as tagliata di manzo is a rather formidable item to be listed at the top of a menu, a minor sirloin steak, sliced, tender, beefy, albeit two hues rarer than what you ordered, garnished with a sautéed mingling of wild mushrooms and onions, herbed and well seasoned.

Due presents you with a separate menu headed "focaccia," which are small, circular flat breads that, when bifurcated the hard way, are readily converted into sandwiches. Good bread, but, what with the paucity of filler between the slices, you may find yourself mentally comparison shopping this place versus the sandwich counter at your neighborhood drugstore, especially with respect to the focaccio gorgonzola e tonno, which does this really sensational impression of your basic tuna melt. The focaccio al prosciutto d'oca is unquestionably more distinctive, for even a doctor's prescription will not elicit from your pharmacist the likes of goose prosciutto and asparagus—good flavors, albeit not especially with each other, and, what with the restraint with which the goose is inserted, Due's meat sandwiches are no threat to the ascendancy in this borough, in that department, of the kosher deli. To make of your sandwich enough, you may supplement it with an item from the salad list, the tomato salad, for example, which deviates in several particulars from the items mentioned on the menu, but which is an abundance of tomatoes, their ripe flavor nicely overpowered by fresh, fragrant basil, black olives, strong olive oil; or the insalata di cappone, greens, radishes, mushrooms, hard-cooked eggs, and, the star, strands of chicken of vigorous chicken flavor, all in a thick mayonnaise. Main courses, as such, are not listed, but a few are offered each night, among them on occasion grilled salmon, the giant fillet fresh and juicy in its buttered but watery sauce of white wine and lemon.

Pasta (of which you may order half portions): rigatoni al piccantino, which is made with anchovies, which is to say seafood, to which, therefore, cheese is traditionally not added, so when your waiter offers you cheese, he wants you to know he knows his traditions, so he offers also an unfinished sentence, "We don't usually offer cheese with this dish . . . ," which gets you wondering how he decides when to offer and when not to offer, albeit you promptly decline, and, sure enough, the hefty ribbed tubes of firm pasta in this olive-studded thickness of anchovies and tomato make a dish that needs no reinforcement—the sprigs of basil on top are in striking, fresh contrast; spaghetti al rosso di gambero, the basic noodle in a slightly bitter sauce that is a dark and oily radicchio paste studded with morsels of crunchy shrimp; canestrelli alla peperonata, in which your basic tomato sauce is thick with strips of pepper and chunks of eggplant; and conchiglie ai broccoli, the shell-shaped pasta in a cheese-thickened sauce of tasteless broccoli florets and, happily, nuggets of pungent Italian bacon that quite rescue the dish.

The exceptional raspberry tart is a big thin cookie, on it a light, lemony custard, on that a scattering of small ripe berries. The chocolate crêpe is tepid and a little clammy. The chocolate cake is fudgelike, and its whipped cream seems composed principally of air. The rich and creamy hazelnut ice cream is notable for the vivid clarity and strength of its nut flavor.

★★ECCO

124 Chambers Street (near West Broadway)
LUNCH, MONDAY TO FRIDAY; DINNER, DAILY.
Reservations: 227-7074.
Credit cards: AE.
Expensive.

Every once in a while a restaurant comes along that, maybe right away, maybe after a misstep or two, finds itself exactly in the swing of its place and time. Such is Ecco. It has been here on this street, where TriBeCa merges with the Financial District, since 1984, and it has become a clubhouse in which the two sets, one of which loosens its tie, the other of which does not own one, commingle in perfect peace—not only with each other, but with the Ecco staff, men in aprons who are both a reflection and a source of the good feeling that pervades this place. (Notwithstanding, you have to be a regular before Roberto, the waiter at the next table, will get himself a glass, pour himself a finger of your wine, and by way of either a smile or grimace announce his verdict.) All of which camaraderie is possible, in part, because the physical place itself defers to neither the financial nor the artistic side, in fact retains the baronial look these premises sported during the decades when a German beer hall held the lease; and, in part, because the place purveys the Italian cooking of this time, the appeal of which quite transcends New York's classes and subcultures.

You enter to a deep space two stories high, a long bar on your right, behind it mirrors and glass-fronted cabinets, framed in dark wood, that reach most of the way to the ceiling, the silhouette of their monumental finials making a mahogany skyline. Facing the bar across the aisle is a red banquette, a row of white-linened tables before it, this the not bad seating that goes to walk-ins when all the tables in back are booked, its good view of the bar, which can be jammed at cocktail time, often diverting. The path between the bar and banquette is of ancient barbershop tiles, as is the floor of the big dining room beyond it, a great spread of mostly large tables and a row of big booths, beveled mirrors built into the wood paneling that encircles the room halfway to the ceiling, higher up on the walls old posters, framed, most of them theatrical, a theme that is picked up on the rearmost wall, on which has been painted the image of tied-back, to-the-ceiling red curtains, as in a theater. The day Ecco opened, nothing about it seemed new. Today it seems not a day older. And while it would be premature by a number of centuries to call the restaurant timeless, the straightforward character of this honest (albeit imperfect) place will surely preserve it past the demise of all but a handful of its competitors.

At the juncture of the barroom and the dining room are displayed, on a dozen or so big platters, the many elements of Ecco's antipasto, and you are free to repair there in the company of your waiter to choose, from the extensive selection, what pleases your eye: roasted halves of red pepper, sweet and crunchy, rich with oil, stuffed with chunks of skinned tomato in a tangy vinaigrette and with pitted black olives that are strong and salty; short lengths of zucchini, stuffed, undistinguished; thin leaves of the same article, grilled, the taste of the charring a zest to the oil-enriched vegetable; eggplant done the same way, and of a flavor far more intense; a lemony and well-garlicked seafood salad that is notable for the abundance of fresh octopus (the morsels tender, not rubbery) among the shrimp, circles of squid, crunchy bits of celery, short lengths of red onion; a rousing caponata that is dominated by the morsels of celery and eggplant in the cool, oily, and well-garlicked dressing.

You may well have the habit of reading right past the familiar words prosciutto and melon. Here, however, you do well to pause and consider, for the dish is made up of huge chunks of juicy melon, utterly ripe, over which are spread great sheets of the good, gamy, pungently salted ham. What goes as "gamberi fantasia" reaches you as several sweet, judiciously sautéed shrimp, firm and crunchy in their shells, mingled with mushrooms and chunks of artichoke that, on unfortunate occasion, are soft, as if done in advance. You may therefore be happier with the clams oreganate, the meat of the bivalves tender, the breading nicely browned, herbed, well seasoned, albeit lacking the garlic you expect in this dish. The house will not serve half orders of pasta. So bring a friend who, with respect to the noodle, shares your taste, and order the spaghetti puttanesca, a vigorous interpretation of the familiar dish, its red sauce pungently fortified with anchovies, and dotted with chunks of green and black olive, plump and sour capers, cloves of garlic; or capellini primavera, the thinnest of thin spaghetti in a delicate sauce, hardly more than moisture, in which the mushrooms, peas, carrots, and florets of broccoli are mingled with slices of garlic yet again—your waiter grates on the good cheese until you tell him to stop.

No finfish on the menu, but a couple usually appear on the blackboard of daily specials your waiter brings to your table. The salmon "Luigi" is a thick steak, fresh and full of moisture, in an herbed, buttery, and mildly garlicked white-wine sauce. You get tiny soft-shell crabs here, delicate and crisp in their lemony butter. Sometimes there are lamb chops, their lamb flavor is strong, and they are garnished with dressed chunks of tomato, tart and salty. You do well to order the grilled sirloin rather than what is given as "bistecca alla Ecco," a pounded sheet of meat that is short on beefiness, long on gristle.

If you are in search of an intense chocolate cake, look nowhere else. This one is of almost miraculous chocolate concentration, and it is served with real whipped cream that is thick, unsweetened, rich. The cheesecake is the real Italian article, a little fruity, solid but not heavy. The strawberries are big and ripe, very good with that whipped cream.

★★ELIO'S

1621 Second Avenue (near 84th Street)
DINNER.
Reservations: 772-2242.
Credit cards: AE, DC, MC, V.
Medium priced.

The craze for clubby restaurant-saloons has subsided, which is to say knockoffs of this place now materialize on New York's Upper East Side with less frequency than ethnic parades. Now more than five years old, Elio's has survived both its initial hot popularity and the hasty competition of its imitators, is today a sturdy—not yet a stodgy—landmark in the flux that is this neighborhood's restaurant scene. Elio's derives from its scruffy neighbor, Elaine's, a media hangout with which this restaurant's eponymous godfather was associated before he went straight. Faces seen in one place are sometimes seen in the other, but at Elio's it is not required of these stars that they show up with a three-day beard and a despondent air, or with a drunken strut, or with a lubriciously chattelistic posture, brazenly brandished, toward their biped of the evening. Here you find quite another scene.

Echt Elio's is Sunday night, when gangs of *Times* guys, trim-tonsured and in suits and glasses, having spent the day at home with their own paper, re-bond—for best results with pasta and cheese—in preparation for the solemn work of the week ahead. Today's *Times*man is responsible to a competitive degree, and it is not till most of the wine has been drunk that anyone is bold enough to switch the talk from local, national, and international affairs to office politics. Mondays to Thursdays are professionals' nights, and the at-home ease with which these doctors, lawyers, and Wall Street bankers take their $50 dinners—the way others grab a sandwich and coffee between the subway stop and the fourth-floor walk-up—will put your social conscience in mind of the sharp economic stratification of American society today. Or else it will not. Friday and then Saturday are, well, Saturday right after Friday. The point most carefully demonstrated by certain of the guests these evenings is that the ladies, being supported by the gentlemen, no longer type for a living. This to establish, fingernails are permitted to grow until, at a point an inch or so from fingertip, they take right turns, as if lost, go off in a new direction in search of home base. (So adorned, a lady must grip her steak knife like a golf club.) All this in a handsome, well-lit, wood-paneled room, a bar up front on the left, a handful of linened tables on the right, most of the tables in the back, under six great white hanging globes. Elio's is noisy, but not painfully. The floor is worked by white-shirted, white-aproned gents who have confidence and aplomb, but do not violate the no-nonsense tenor of this place with any excess, in carriage or speech, of finesse. They do, however, all they have to do.

Ask one of them, and he will bring you an order of raw mushrooms, a great pile of the almond-colored slivers, crunchy and earthy, slices of crisp fennel mixed in, sheets of Parmesan, hard and sharp, on top—the salad is good straight, is better when your waiter pours over it, from a tall spouted bottle, the strong-flavored olive oil served here. Suggest to your companion the clams oreganate, an exceptional version of the familiar dish, the tiny littlenecks, in their shells, fresh and tender and sweet, their lightly oiled breading, judiciously seasoned and delicately browned, just touched with oregano. The spaghetti in its nubbly meat sauce has possibilities that are not apparent when you sample it as is, for though honest, the dish is of a plainness—but add an amplitude of Elio's good ground cheese, and it is transformed, becomes at once sharp and deep. There is spaghetti also with seafood, a good dish that would be even better if the iodine were subtracted from the shrimp (or the shrimp from the dish), for the simple red sauce is thick with scallops (their rich pink roes attached), sweet little clams, and chunks of firm clear-tasting fish—the added parsley is chopped coarse, and little sprigs of it you encounter in this bite or that are sudden, unexpected bursts of fresh green flavor. A couple of rice dishes are listed, including risotto with porcini, the buttery grain (it is almost, but not quite, hard), black dotted with chunks of the wild mushroom—the very sturdy stuff is marred one time by sand imperfectly washed from the parsley.

Each day there is a fish of the day, and when it is salmon, you get a thick slab of it, sometimes with green peppercorns, the dark dots of pepper, in their creamy sauce, very pretty on the surface of the moist and sweet pink meat. Elio's zuppa di pesce is distinguished by the great chunk of lobster, supple and tender, among the tender scallops, morsels of firm fish, and fresh clams and mussels in their shells—the briny, saffron-flavored broth is thick with chunks of tomato. The chicken ortolana is a boned, sautéed breast, often not a good beginning, but this one is in a light tincture-of-tomato sauce, and it is overlaid with good mushrooms and, striking notes, with red peppers and black olives, which make for a vibrant, vigorous dish. There are places around town that, in recent years, have demonstrated that hot meat and cold salad may be artfully combined. Elio's attempts it in what they give as "milanese capricciosa," a pounded veal chop, lightly breaded and sautéed, that is covered over with a dressed salad of tomatoes and red onions, but the drama of such dishes is barely in evidence here, for the dressing is mild and the veal, of course, has little flavor of its own. The lamb chops are apparently sautéed rather than grilled, so they are of a succulence rather than of a browned strength —their slightly redded sauce is thick with slivers of garlic.

A loud and creamy Gorgonzola and that strong Parmesan you had with your raw mushrooms are fine with the house salads, which are of crisp greens—the salad and cheese benefit from Elio's terrific bread, which is fresh, grainy, chewy, crusty. You wish that, under its glassy surface of caramelized sugar, the crème brûlée's cool and creamy custard were lighter. The black and white layers of the hazelnut cake are subtly nutted— the cake is surfaced with a slick black icing. You may have fresh strawberries or raspberries with a rich zabaglione that is cold and winy.

★★ERMINIA

250 East 83rd Street
DINNER. CLOSED SUNDAY.
Reservations: 879-4284.
Credit cards: AE.
Beer and wine.
Expensive.

A dozen white-linened tables, a flickering taper on each of them (they poke feebly into the dimness, painfully onto your retina), and about a carload of rusticity are the principal ingredients of this place. The recipe is a familiar one, for this is yet another enterprise of the family that brought you, first, Trastevere, and then, Trastevere 84. With a couple of winners already to their credit, and, one assumes, more confidence than ever, they have risked in this enterprise a deviation from the menu that worked so well the first two times around. But it is really a cooking method, more than the character of the food, that distinguishes this place not only from its predecessors but from most restaurants on earth, for at Erminia, as the menu has it, "All entrées are grilled in Wooden Fire."

Unfinished, splintery beams cross the ceiling. The walls—of brick, or of dark, knotty planks—are hung with primitive pottery and with street lanterns that glow dully. The dried flora all about are, of course, wildflowers and grasses. The two little windows at the front are bedecked with potted greenery. At the back of the room, bottles of wine are displayed on an upended old barrel. These snug quarters accommodate you fairly well —you can actually get comfortable once you have wriggled into the chair that is wedged into the space between the wall and your table. But if you arrive a few minutes early for your reservation, or if the people you are scheduled to succeed have no further plans and are lingering, the only place for you to wait is out on the street.

So come here when the weather is clement. And if your host comes outside to commiserate for your delay, tell him to go back and arrange for some vongole alla Erminia to be served as soon as you are seated. You get eight fresh, hot, tiny, and tender littlenecks, in their shells, moistened with a winy sauce that is fragrant with wild mushrooms and shallots. You get an artichoke dish here unlike any other in town. It is described as "artichokes completely cooked in olive oil, garlic, in earthenware pan," and the strands of crunchy heart, though strongly salted and weighty with the garlic-flavored oil in which they were cooked, have a vividness of artichoke flavor that is not obscured at all, but only potentiated, by this preparation. What is given as bruschetta alla Erminia is a slab of toasted bread—brushed with oil, herbs, and slivers of onion—baked under mozzarella cheese until the cheese is hot, browned, pully, and loud. The dish is garnished with dressed tomatoes, and when their vinaigrette drifts across the plate, it adds a striking tartness to the weighty open-face sandwich.

Pasta. Pappardelle alla ricotta, a mound of long strips of broad noodle, quite firm, in a sauce of herbed, creamy cheese, served with a dollop of pungent tomato sauce on top—the dish is homey, elemental. Bucatini alla pescatora, very thick spaghetti, surrounded by shrimps and baked clams and mussels in their shells, the pasta in a well-oiled, fragrantly herbed and almost excessively salted thick red sauce. Orecchiette alla Erminia, little pasta morsels shaped like ears, moistened with oil, flavored with garlic, mingled with bits of broccoli and sausage, and adorned with a few spoons of light tomato sauce—a rare dish, in which all the elements work and none dominates. Gnocchi di patate, a simple item of firm little potato dumplings—their slight gumminess is the right texture with this deep, thick, and spicy tomato sauce.

Though some of the help here worked at the Trastevere restaurants, a member or two of the staff are apparently new to this territory and have not yet cracked their English texts. One of these informs you that the fish of the day is "malibu fish," which he describes as "like sole fish." Rather than never know what he is talking about, you order it, and receive a great long steak of—halibut! The firm fish does well in the low temperature of a wood fire, and the flavor of its charred surface is a good zest to the juicy white meat. The fish is garnished with baked clams and oysters in their shells. That fire also does well by chicken—the bird is oiled and herbed (much rosemary), lightly lemoned and abundantly garlicked, and it is garnished with sweet roasted peppers and hefty shafts of roasted potato. Even the steak is well served by that fire—with low temperature

161

cooking, the good beef retains all its tenderness. The sirloin is garnished with a skewer of good grilled mushrooms.

The deep-fried apples are three disks of crisped hot fruit, much like sweet fritters, sprinkled with confectioner's sugar. There are ice cream items of intense Italian ice cream sweetness.

No hard liquor. What the menu refers to as "caraffa wine" is available by the caraffa.

★ L'ESCALE

43 East 20th Street
LUNCH, MONDAY TO FRIDAY; DINNER, MONDAY TO SATURDAY. CLOSED SUNDAY.
Reservations: 477-1180.
Credit cards: AE, DC, MC, V.
Medium priced.

A true bistro, but you enter to a dimly lit bar, on this stool or that a hunched-over figure with a drink, a cigarette, and, you imagine, a single, bitter, unending thought. The bar is tended, however, at least on occasion, by a willowy young woman in a squat, brimmed, coal-black hat (one of those hats Dickensians were when singing carols), and she serves also a convivial clientele you think of as her own, younger types for whom a few drinks can still cleanse the mind of reality. Past a wine rack that serves as a half-hearted room divider, and you are in the dining room proper, a rough wood floor, exposed brick, posters on the walls, rows of tables and chairs, a candle in a little tumbler on each table, the light of which, in certain parts of this spottily illuminated space, is essential to reading your menu. The background music is soft, is only occasionally Edith Piaf pitying herself, is more often French café music, the kind that, no matter what it is played on, sounds like accordion squeezings. "L'Escale" is "port of call," an unlikely name for this place, for no one voyages here. The restaurant is part of its arrondissement, serves the same folks time and again. Those who use it presumably appreciate the brisk cheer of the mostly French staff, have learned the highs and lows of the menu. But even to outlanders L'Escale has its uses: Since it is known almost solely to locals, an assignation between a citizen of, say, Morningside Heights and one of, say, TriBeCa, would here be utterly anonymous.

You are of sound mind if you assume that "mousse de brocolis au beurre citroné" is baby food. And yet the out-of-a-mold, lightly bound dome has broccoli flavor of such intensity and vigor as to transfer it from the green vegetable department into the world of actual food—the thing is warm, but it reaches you in a pool of lemon butter cool enough to defeat the intended enrichment. You are surprised not at all, however, at the pungent taste of the eggplant terrine, a hot layered thing of eggplant and bell peppers, well seasoned, thoroughly oiled, topped with a disk of browned goat cheese of equally strong but totally contrasting character—good food, though you wish it were not of a mushiness. Naturally there is a garlicked pâté, and it is fatted and chunky, dotted with pistachio nuts, served with fiery mustard—add bread and cold wine, and even those persistent thoughts at the bar could be, at least for a time, dispelled. Just as naturally there is saucisson chaud, a rather coarse garlic sausage gentled by the warm potato salad served with it.

Weekends bouillabaisse is on the menu, and groups of guys come here, order it for each and all, cool themselves with beer as they work through the substantial servings. This is not great bouillabaisse, the broth is strong but blunt, the lobster—by its visible red-shelled presence the star of the show—is of scant lobster flavor, but the mussels are sweet, the clams are tender, the shrimp and scallops retain their character, and though the same cannot be said for the finfish, at least it is firm—but it is the guys' jolly communal consumption of the production that makes it more than itself. On New York menus the steak of tuna, if it is not supplanting, is taking an equal place beside the steak of beef. If you are choosing between the one and the other, at L'Escale you do well to go with the one, for this is fresh tuna, rare but cooked through, and its red-wine sauce, thick with minced scallions, sets it off stunningly. The other steak, though accurately done, is a little tough, its black-peppered surface is coarser and hotter—whole peppercorns among the cracked ones—than you had in mind, and you do wish the French fries, which are thin and of clear potato flavor, were crisp as well. The braised veal shank is a thick cross-sectional disk of meat, bone at the center, topped with cheese that is browned before you get it—the meat is juicy in its dense gravy, sports much of the stocky flavor of the liquid in which it was done, falls in tender shreds from the bone, is garnished with a potato stew that is heady of fresh herbs.

No cheese is listed, but since cheese is an ingredient of a menu item, you ask for and are served a slab of firm, sharp, creamy Roquefort. The tarte tatin is fine, great chunks of hot dark apple on the flaky pastry, crème fraîche on the side. With the tangy lemon tart you get both raspberry and lemon sauces. When there are berries they are ripe.

• ESPACE

9 East 16th Street
LUNCH AND DINNER.
Reservations: 463-7101.
Credit cards: AE, DC, MC, V.
Medium priced.

You are familiar with the syndrome: A million dollars, maybe two, is spent to turn a space the size of the Sheep Meadow into an acid-trip restaurant fantasy. Instantly, the place packs them in. Eventually, however, just as instantly, it goes out of style, night after night the restaurant looks like the floor of the stock exchange on Sunday afternoon. Comes along whoever is behind this place, with the interesting idea that perhaps you can do it without the million dollars, maybe two. Admittedly this is no Sheep Meadow, is hardly more than a couple of tennis courts. It does not, however, have the one million, maybe two, look. It has the plaster-it, paint-it, install-a-monumental-bar-and-hope-for-the-best look. Accordingly, when you are seated at certain tables across the aisle from said monumental bar, you discover, as you lean your elbows on your table, that, when your left elbow has made firm contact, your right has six inches to go; that your martini, when it is filled to the lip with respect to the right side of your glass, is half an inch shy with respect to the left. The several altitudes of the distant ceiling have not been triangulated, but who cares, the ancient thing, of stamped tin, has been made almost to disappear by application of black paint. And in place of the million, maybe two, in architectural conceits, Espace has installed paintings by one Milo Reice, small ones, large ones, even a triptych. Each of them speaks eloquently to their common theme, that Reice is no one you would care to have dinner with.

Another departure from the run of these restaurants, this one sells French bistro food, you cannot get spaghetti here. You can get pretty good grilled squid in a thick tomato sauce that is nubbly with capers; snails that, the menu states, have been simmered in Burgundy with herbs—the treatment yields fragrant, almost perfumed snails—garlic, too, an unlisted surprise; a more-than-decent salad of fresh asparagus and wild mushrooms. The rabbit pâté is nutted, is of clear rabbit flavor, is served with grainy mustard and with a sweet-spiced mash of red cabbage. Brandade de morue is a dish of pounded and seasoned codfish. For some reason, or none, it is here packed into cold tomatoes and garnished with a bit of salad, exactly as if the instructions on the back of the box had been misplaced.

What is given in French as "ragoût de coquilles Saint Jacques" is given in English as "scallops with pernod." The scallops seem to have been warmed and nothing more, the pernod was probably lost in translation. The grilled paillard of chicken is tough and dry. In favor of the grilled salmon it may be said that the fish is utterly fresh, it is only a little overdone, and the sorrel on which it is served brings real life to the dish. Limp French fries accompany the not bad steak, and the cold lump of Roquefort butter with which it is surmounted refuses to melt, no matter how intently you stare at it. The sautéed liver is fine in its livery sauce, its good garnish of caramelized leeks the making of the plate. Come here once, however, and you will look no further than the boudin blanc, the veal sausages spicy and lively, not at all heavy, the accompanying potato tart crusty, well-seasoned, of real potato flavor.

In this day of intense chocolate desserts Espace offers a layered thing of pallid mousse and pallid cake. The lemon curd tart would be a perfect one but for the layer of chocolate between the lemon and the pastry—the thing is served, happily, with threads of lemon rind, whipped cream, ripe raspberries. The crème brûlée, under its burnt top, has the texture of a sauce, when you were hoping for custard. You can do worse than the fruity plum tart on almond pastry—it is served in a crimson pool of raspberry sauce.

★★EZE

254 West 23rd Street
DINNER. CLOSED SUNDAY AND MONDAY.
Reservations: 691-1140.
Credit cards: AE, DC, MC, V.
Expensive.

Rhymes with fez. Is a town on the Riviera between Nice and Cannes. Makes an odd name for this place, the menu of which is only fractionally Provençale, the physical appointments suggesting the south of France not at all (though whoever put them together may think otherwise).

A flashing neon arrow would help, for the signs out front have you heading downstairs in search of the entrance when the right direction is up the stoop to the parlor floor of this old house, within which the high ceiling provides just the note of emptiness needed to cap the austere installation. Simplicity was sought, nakedness was found, and it will take a boisterous crowd to liven this place, a full house anyway. Blindfolded, however, you are entirely comfortable here, for the straightforward layout of the L-shaped place—15 tables or so, chairs around them, plenty of room between them, a small bar with a handful of stools—is noncontroversial. But you do wish something could be done to warm the pallor of the upper walls (which are separated from the lower walls by a chair rail of cream-of-split-pea green), to liven the gray industrial carpeting, to simplify and dignify the patterned and pleated and busy lace curtains in the windows. With respect to the chairs, it would be best to start over, for they are upholstered in a fabric that means to be bold and manages to be murky, even lugubrious in the deathly-white frames. For some reason a khaki-colored ceiling was chosen, and from it hang chandeliers of real or simulated green-oxidized copper, which are matched by sconces mounted on the walls. Eze has managed just to catch the new manic-depressive chic at the very nadir of its swing.

So dry your eyes, smile bravely, and address the carpaccio of sea scallops, the thin-sliced mollusk meats formed into a sheet across your plate, delicately dressed, and adorned with splashes of heady, fresh coriander, dabs of crushed black olive, and lengths of strong-flavored roasted red pepper—a wonderful array of tastes, which is a bonus, for in this room the colors alone are worth the price. The herbed salmon, though listed as a salad, turns out warm, four substantial nuggets of the browned and well-seasoned fresh fish set, surprisingly, among cold beets and arugula. On the weekly changing menu there is always pasta among the appetizers, on occasion this fettuccine in an herbed sauce of anchovies and garlic, a dish that, though obvious, fails as an expression of its listed ingredients; and on occasion these ravioli, in which the tender packets, filled with a green mash of Swiss chard, are in a creamy and nubbly anchovy sauce, the lively, satisfying dish redolent of Eastern spices.

The blue prawns, shrimp to you, are crunchy, free of iodine, and of vivid shrimp flavor in their creamy and well-herbed leek-and-tomato sauce—the crustaceans are nicely garnished with a new potato and a mound of strong spinach. Order swordfish, and you are delivered a thick slab, impeccably fresh, charred a little under its heady sauce of lemon and rosemary. Order the rack of lamb, and, perhaps intentionally, you are not asked how you want it. Turns out you want it the way the kitchen wants to turn it out, the three little chops blood pink, and garnished with a dollop of sweet onion-garlic jam that is set in the meat's dark, slightly acidic, rich sauce. You will recognize that the cassoulet is cassoulet by way of the meats buried among the beans, but this is a leaden version, all the parts subsumed in the heaviness.

For a boutique restaurant, one in which it is meant that a few unusual things will be done well, and in which very little else is meant to be done, you do wonder how it goes unnoticed that the grapes served with the perfectly nice Stilton are wilted. The crème brûlée is cool and fluffy under its crackling paper-thin caramel crust. The profiterole is notable for the intensity of its espresso ice cream flavor, the strength of its chocolate sauce. A ball of rousing grapefruit sherbet garnishes the grapefruit tart, which is a simple thing of peeled grapefruit sections (a bit of their sourness gone), thick cream, a crumbly pastry. The praline ice cream cake, a slice cut from a roulade, is cold and sweet and densely nutted in its pool of chocolate.

The menu changes weekly.

★★EL FARO

823 Greenwich Street (at Horatio Street)
LUNCH AND DINNER.
No reservations (929-8210).
Credit cards: AE, DC, MC, V.
Medium priced.

Some years ago new plastic-topped tables were substituted for the old ones, which were retired after a generation of loyal, wobbly service. And the prices do creep up, but no faster than the rising cost of, say, newspapers. The place is even painted from time to time, though of course nothing is ever applied to the surfaces of the murals and bullfight posters with which the restaurant is, as they say, adorned. In fact, it will not be long now before the ladies with fans and the gentlemen with red capes—the subjects of said art—will be discernible only to veterans of the place, those who will be able to flesh out the murky outlines with the aid of memory. Nobody alive remembers when this four-square establishment first materialized on this remote corner, but the policy has always been the same: Place a large number of customers in the bar, where they will happily drink, make noise, and patiently wait for tables; when their turns come up, seat them at tables at the back of the barroom, or in the dining room at the rear, where they will happily drink, make noise, incidentally eat like pigs, and wobble out euphoric. Any Greenwich Villager who does not go through this bacchanalia once or twice a year is just one of those fellows who will go to the grave never having crossed against the light blindfolded. The lure of the place is in its low prices and in the solidity and abundance of its food. But cheap Spanish eats of commendable quality are not rare, while a popularity like El Faro's is. The secret, of course, is the popularity itself, which is self-perpetuating—lots of people come here to be where lots of people come.

As in all Spanish restaurants of this ilk, you are provided with a dog bowl of salad with which to divert yourself while waiting for what you ordered. This item, of chopped iceberg in a thick, red-peppered dressing, though edible, is not so much one of the courses of your dinner as it is a tradition, part of the ritual of eating at a Spanish restaurant in New York—like standing up for the Hallelujah Chorus. That "salad" out of the way, you proceed to an order of salpicon, a cool and lemony seafood salad, mingled with herbs and chopped egg whites. Or to a bowl of gazpacho, the cold red vegetable soup frankly sour, deeply oiled, garlicked, but lacking the croutons and chopped vegetables that can make the dish striking. The shrimp ajillo consists of lots of little shrimp, garlicked and spicy, covered over with hot oil and bread crumbs, which form a crackling topping when browned. The fried calamari are circles of resilient but tender squid, artfully deep fried, so that the good batter is crisp and not greasy—you squeeze on lemon to make the dish sparkle.

The minuscularity of a number of this restaurant's tables becomes especially evident when main-course time comes around, for you are provided not only with a large dinner plate from which to eat but also, in most instances, with a great iron pot from which you fill and replenish it. If you have ordered the lobster in green sauce, the pot is filled with a thick, emerald-green broth in which the parts of your lobster are immersed. The green

166

soup is winy, briny, pungently seasoned, fragrant with parsley, and the chunks of lobster meat in their red shell, though perhaps a little overcooked and chewy, seem particularly sweet in this setting. El Faro makes good paellas, the one called Valenciana of disks of sharp and fatty sausage, big sections of moist chicken, shrimp and mussels, fresh (though toughened) clams, sweet green peas, all buried in moist, sweet-spiced rice. This place has always put out an exceptional chicken villaroy, that odd dish that, though it seems like an anomaly on Spanish menus, turns up on almost all of them in New York. The unlikely item consists of chicken white meat coated with béchamel sauce, battered, and deep fried. In the version made here, the chicken is moist, the sauce airy, the outer crust crisp and light. What El Faro unashamedly calls "Duckling Bar B.Q." of course easily transcends its title. The big slabs of bird are formed by cutting right through the ribs, as if the duck were a loaf of bread—the mahogany-colored slices are moist of their fat without being fatty; the skin is almost black without being burnt or dried out; and the whole is sprinkled with crisp almonds. If you squeeze on juice from the quarters of orange with which the bird is garnished, the meat becomes tangy without losing any of its richness. But enough of all this fancy food. No dish on the menu is so much at one with this place as the Spanish omelet, a great pancake of lightly browned egg almost as big as the dinner plate itself, thick with chunks of potato, with strands of pale and sweet sautéed onion, and with little nuggets of smoky Spanish ham, the whole vigorously peppered. This tortilla, as it is called, with some of this establishment's fried potatoes—much like fresh, hot potato chips — will put you in mind of Western omelets and fries raised to a high order. A Spanish omelet is very good with cold red wine.

The desserts—flan, natilla, guava with cream cheese—replicate precisely the versions of those things that have been served for decades in Spanish restaurants all over Manhattan.

★★FELIDIA

243 East 58th Street
LUNCH, MONDAY TO FRIDAY; DINNER, MONDAY TO SATURDAY. CLOSED SUNDAY.
Reservations: 758-1479.
Credit cards: AE, DC, MC, V.
Very expensive.

You enter to a display, on a sturdy old sideboard, of weighty Italian red wines in bottles the size of fire hydrants. Nearby, in tall cabinets with glass doors, innumerable brandies, liqueurs, eaux de vie, in bottles adorned with labels of every pretension. The furnishings are old and weighty, and though Felidia dates from this decade, its appointments are dictated by an ancient restaurant formula: more or less equal parts of rusticity and posh. You proceed, in the dimness, under the low ceiling, past a massive brass-topped bar to yet another display, this one on tiers of green marble: plates and platters of cold shellfish, meats, vegetables, ripe fruits, at the top a great burst of flowers. At this point you are at the dining room proper, all chalky stucco, wood paneling, and fancy brickwork, a floor of red tiles, the white-linened tables surrounded by high-backed chairs, their padded seats of elaborately woven tapestry cloth. A brass-railed stairway (a potted plant at the end of each step) leads to the upstairs dining room: white walls, skylights, much greenery—a bit of crowdedness too, this the slightly less commodious of the two floors. The staff is in formals, but the clothing on the prosperous crowd varies: wizened tycoons in loose-fitting size 36 suits accompanied by pinched ladies in silks and pearls; big fellows who, though in the required jackets, wear their shirts open at the collar (the upper alimentary canal thus stripped for the action of feeding the massive frames); bejeweled visitors from across the East River (the owners of Felidia once ran a restaurant in Queens, and some of the friends they made there visit them here); and many a uniformed East Sider—the gents in suits, the ladies in impeccable little numbers out of Bendel's or Bonwit's, for this is one of the city's most revered Italian restaurants. It *is* good, and when it was new, it seemed likely to become superb—it did not, but it would be idiotic to fault the place for the failure of that eventuality.

You unavoidably pass that fetching display of food on the way to your table, and so you are tempted to sample the cold appetizers, of which your waiter will prepare an extensive assortment. Though the dishes have clarity and freshness, some of them lack the vigor their lively appearance leads you to expect. But, happily, while you are waiting to learn that from experience, you may be brought a plate of the house garlic bread, of which, says the Texan at the next table, to his awed guests, "You can't get this stuff anywhere else on earth." It is good garlic bread, crusty, buttery, laden with powerful, vibrant garlic, and it becomes the foreground, when you eat it with the (background of) cold appetizers: long, delicately sautéed tongues of eggplant rolled into roulades; roasted yellow peppers, skinned, succulent, very sweet, suffused with the oil in which they were done; firm white beans mingled with strands of red onion; slices of fennel that are fresh, crunchy, almost hard; crisp, nicely cooked shrimp that are, unfortunately, of only vague seafood flavor; circles of tender squid; and strands of rather cartilaginous tripe—these last especially, but some of the other items as well, in need of a dressing more vigorous than the velvety oil with which they are polished. Hot appetizers too, sometimes sautéed porcini mushrooms, the flavor of the slices earthy and also rooty, vigorously but judiciously salted, strewn with fresh parsley.

An occasional oddity among the specials of the day is risotto nero con seppia, rice with squid and its ink, the mound of firm grains glinting, pitchy, threaded with slivers of squid, the flavor of the dish oceanic and sea-gamy, and yet, like much of the food here, a bit timid about itself—still, good food, the like of which you do not encounter daily. Capital pasta: occhio (heavy pasta tubes) in a pink and creamy tomato sauce that is thickened with cheese, weighted with ground peppery sausage, sweetened and brightened with green peas and strands of red pepper; firm, hot, light gnocchi, the little morsels in a well-oiled pesto sauce that is of almost winy basil fragrance—strong cheese grated on at the table adds sharpness to the heady dish; fuzi alla fortuna del cacciatore, which is to say, two-inch tubelike lengths of pasta with one kind of game or another—when the game is quail, the sauce of the bird's meat is a dark and rich one, touched with tomato, and you get chunks of the bird as well, the meat pungent of the distinctive, almost chocolate flavor of quail.

You may, if you wish, eat simply here, by way, for example, of this grilled snapper, the utterly fresh fish nicely browned, moist, just beginning to flake, all its nutlike flavor intact. Not much fancier and just as carefully timed is the chicken roasted with rosemary and brandy—the moist sections of bird reach you encased in their lightly crisped skin, and they have real chicken flavor that has been made woodsy by the herb, stout by the brandy. New York is no city in which to serve a less-than-first-class osso buco, for folks hereabouts have been at the dish since the days when Little Italy was one block of tenements and half a dozen restaurants. Here the big knuckle of meat is tender but dry, and lacks both the succulence and the spiciness of the dish at its best, though its rather tart red sauce helps. An order of roast baby lamb is a couple of tiny chops, the eyes of pink meat of almost fluffy tenderness, and a few slices of loin, these distinctly resilient—the sauce that moistens the strong-flavored meat is redolent of fresh rosemary. You do not often run into elk, but in season here they are—anyway, medallions thereof, the tender, blood-dark, and somewhat livery meat handsomely charred in its heavily seasoned red-wine sauce.

It is likely that at this point you will want, rather than a weighty dessert, something lively, and the Felidia salads are crisp and sparkling in their smooth, subtly seasoned oil. With them you may have Parmesan cheese that makes you sit up straight—it is hard, flinty, rousing. The zuccotto, a roulade of sponge cake, chocolate, and whipped cream, is astonishingly light for its richness. The chocolate mousse cake is not.

Good service, though the upstairs crew seems to be a distinctly second team, including a captain who is always around when you want him least. He just about butters your bread. Order a bottle of rather young and perfectly clear sfurzàt, and you have to stop him from demonstrating the art of decanting.

★★FLAMAND

349 East 86th Street
DINNER.
Reservations: 722-4610.
Credit cards: AE, DC, MC, V.
Medium priced.

This could have been a neat, clean, harmless, nondescript room. You could have found yourself judging the place by its good food and whimsical service alone. But, no, someone had to go and improve it in a manner that misses utterly the intended bistro mark. You really cannot find much fault with the tweedy brown rug, and you would never notice the ceiling of acoustic tiles were there not hanging from it mammate chandeliers that glow the color of sallow Caucasian skin. Even the walls, dark pink with brown columns, the colors, more or less, of rare meat and milk chocolate, will probably fade well with time, though for the present much attention is called to them by the prints and travel posters stuck up, apparently, wherever there was a helpless empty space. Still, the winners are the stained glass scenic (you know—trees, rocks, water, sky, each its own color of glass) installed in the rear wall, and backlighted by the kitchen behind it; and, in the front window, the flowers that, in a foot-high scallop shell of black enamel, stand on a knee-high pedestal of mock marble, the unique composition framed in tied-back curtains of snowy gauze. Almost, but not quite, is this taste redeemed by its innocence. Meanwhile, in the background, there is Edith Piaf, failing yet again to ennoble self-pity.

You know from the title this place purveys, as the house puts it, "cuisine belge," which is to say, weighty food. It is therefore perhaps wise to begin with the like of this salade d'endives au jambon, scores of strands of the yellow-tipped leaves arranged on your plate like the spokes of a wheel, at the hub a dollop of good mayonnaise that is laced with little slivers of pungent ham—a lively salad, but you do wish the ratio were reconsidered, for you run out of dressing long before you are out of endives. You suffer from no such ham deprivation when you have the meat served to you in large rolled slices with ripe pear. What is given as "gratin Ostendais" benefits particularly from the clear sweet seafood flavor of its shrimp and scallops, which reach you buried in a small soup bowl of thick, herbed cheese sauce that has been browned before serving. The solidity of that stuff has nothing on the sweetbread-filled pannequet aux ris de veau, a thin, nicely browned, vaguely sweet pancake wrapped around great chunks of sweetbread, the rich organ meat in a spicy white sauce that is parsleyed just before it is served.

No restaurant is Belgian, of course, unless it lists waterzooi, and of the versions offered in the few Belgian restaurants that have come and gone on the local scene, Flamand's seafood waterzooi is the first to give any idea of why it is any nation's national dish. This is a briny white broth, creamy but not thick, peppery but in no way harsh, in which you find strands of fresh vegetables and seafood that, though part of a stew, have been judiciously done, so that these morsels of salmon are firm and of clear flavor, and these scallops, while they take on the creaminess, retain all their own richness of taste. Order quails, and you get three of the little birds, browned and moist and strong, set in a sauce that is thick with bits of endive. Flamand's blanquette de veau is in a thick sauce of Duvel beer (one of the world's most remarkable liquids), the big chunks of tender meat mingled with fresh mushrooms in the tart gravy—you do well to drink Duvel with the dish, but be aware that its polished and creamy texture conceals an almost violent level of alcohol. For some reason Belgians cannot leave well-enough alone, they produce such things as cherry-flavored beer, and though it is not suggested you drink the stuff, it is the basis here of an excellent sauce (thick, spicy, tangy, and with just a touch of fruit), in which Flamand serves huge logs of tender rabbit.

Belgium is chocolate country, and sure enough, its chocolate cake is wonderfully intense—too bad it reaches you cool. The marjolaine is a layer cake of chocolate, nuts, good chewy meringue. It seems that the dearth of hazelnut flavor in the hazelnut cake is a function of a day-old state. Anyway, come to Flamand once, and the croustillant aux pommes is the dessert to have, a great construct of pastry leaves, like the petals of some grandiose flower, under them a mound of sweet and sour and tangy stewed apples—on occasion, the thing takes forever to make, but you get it in sparkling, just-made condition.

★ FLORENT

69 Gansevoort Street (near Washington Street)
LUNCH AND DINNER.
Reservations: 989-5779.
No credit cards.
Inexpensive.

Though once an old diner that catered to the meat-packing and warehousing industries in this grim waterfront neighborhood, Florent gets its lunch-counter looks as much by design as inheritance. The plastic and stainless steel are where they always were, but look closely by the room's bright light, and you see that they are largely new plastic, new steel. There is a coffee maker behind the counter, display cases—with sliding glass doors—for desserts, a slicing machine. The floors are of (probably the original) terrazzo, fluorescent-light fixtures are on the ceiling, chrome pipe chairs surround the tables. The working-class crowd that once frequented the old place is not, however, fooled. They do not constitute even a discernible fraction of the current clientele. Perhaps they have come in but gone elsewhere after reading what they thought was the posted menu, for high up over the counter are mounted three panels of black signboard with white lettering stuck on, the kind of fixtures that usually carry such advice as "bacon w egg .75 w 2 eGg $.95¢." Here, however, the signs offer only the day's weather report, the latest pollen count and reservoir levels, and the fares of various airlines to major American and European cities. Imagine, if you will, a longshoreman with too many drinks in him coming here for a bite to eat, looking at the sign, and finding that nothing is under $49. He leaves, of course, vowing to go a little easier, hereafter, on the juice.

Jet-set whimsy in a proletarian environment is aimed, of course, at the intercontinental youth crowd, chaps who talk four languages, shave three times a month, dress like automobile mechanics—the occasional beret does show up—and have with them willowy, lofty-cheekboned models who are sheathed in black rubber and wear doughnut-shaped earrings, of silver or gold, that hang to their photogenic shoulders. But that crowd has not managed to keep Florent to itself. Word has got around. You find here, mixed in with the world travelers, recently baccalaureated New Yorkers who, though they are going places in quite another world, wish to keep up with this one. Answers one of these to her suited-and-tied escort: "I *happen* to know you're wrong. Le Zinc is *definitely* Eurotrash. I'm surprised at *you*, David." David is crushed.

David attempts to pump himself back up with some invigorating fish soup Provençale—a dark, saffrony, but slightly thin broth that is dense with strands of vegetable and bits of seafood, while his overseer gives 100 percent of her attention to an appetizer portion of "Alex's Mussels Provençales"—a score or more of the local mollusks (some of them, unfortunately, a little loud) mounded up, in a great glass bowl, over several inches of the redded, spicy, and oceanic broth in which they were done. Meanwhile, their companions pretend nothing has happened, attend to a rather scant portion of leeks, the cool strands in an herbed and mustard-thickened vinaigrette; and a plentiful salad of strong arugula that is mingled with walnut halves and dressed with walnut oil. The smoked chicken is good—you get many thick slices of the white meat, they are tender, mildly smoky, of clear chicken flavor, and they are garnished with small black olives that are oily and strong. The red-meat first courses disappoint; the pâté is cold and rather grossly liverish; the rillettes, the fatted dish of pounded, seasoned pork, also suffers from the cold—it is clammy at this temperature; only the hard slices of purple garlic sausage survive the chilling.

The fish are of the day, sometimes a misnomered tuna "steak" allegedly marinated in wasabi, which arrives as half a dozen little shafts of the fish, nicely grilled, touched with citrus, but not, detectably, with the listed Japanese radish; and sometimes grilled bluefish with rosemary and garlic, the fresh fillet artfully browned and crisped, the oil-rich meat moist within its crusty exterior, the promised flavorings only subtly present. You no longer find tête de veau on many local French menus, but Florent sometimes offers it. "Tête de veau," you understand, is "head of calf." But not to worry, you are served only a cross-sectional slice—sans staring eyes—its rim a ribbon of leathery but tender skin, within it a mosaic of glutinous sections, cartilaginous ones, meaty ones, the gummy and gamy stuff in a hot, creamy, thick, and fragrantly herbed vinaigrette. The plump blood sausages are deep brown and rich—but not particularly tasty—in their crackling wrappers, and they are served over sautéed onions and apples that are moist, sweet, and powerfully flavored of thyme. The medallions of veal are hefty charred slices of grilled meat, but this is coarse veal of little flavor, and it needs a sauce—you are offered a choice of them, and you pass up the pallid mustard sauce for the sharper and deeper one of shallots and wine. The same wine sauce helps but does not cure the tough and sinewy sirloin steak. Most of the main courses are served with French fries that, often, are thin, crisp, and of real potato flavor.

The crème caramel is eggy and light in its lively syrup of browned sugar. The zuppa inglese is many chunks of liquored cake and candied fruit under good whipped cream. And the lemon tart is a thin layer of tangy citrus custard on shortbread pastry. Plums that have been cooked in sugared, gingered vinegar are served under whipped cream—lively food. There are ripe berries, but sometimes they have been ripe since at least the other day.

You can arrive at 8 o'clock and find yourself alone in the place—the planes are late. But when you leave a couple of hours later, there may be a horde waiting for tables.

• FOUR SEASONS

99 East 52nd Street
LUNCH AND DINNER. CLOSED SUNDAY.
Reservations: 754-9494.
Credit cards: AE, DC, MC, V.
Very expensive.

Cocktail time, and it is easier to order another drink than to get off your stool and push through the four-deep crowd of middle-level businessmen who press around the famous square bar. Above your head, the larger part of the two-part Richard Lippold sculpture threatens, as it has for more than a quarter century, each of its innumerable thin brass rods—they form a kind of futuristic cloud—vertically suspended by two almost invisible threadlike wires. That is, most hang by two, a few by one, their second wires having snapped, these rods of course askew. Yes, the Four Seasons is coming apart. And though, as the bartender assures you (with a nervous upward glance), repairs on the Lippold will be made soon, millions of jokes over the decades about the imminence of cranial perforation are, all at once, less funny even than they used to be.

The big bar, under its overhead hardware, occupies acreage in a corner of the Bar Room, one of the restaurant's two spacious, blocklike, three-story-high dining rooms, this the one you attain when you have climbed the grand stairway from the street-level lobby. Lippold's smaller cloud is diagonally across from its mate, and it is here in the Bar Room, under these works of elevated art, that, at lunchtime, higher-ups in New York's publishing industry negotiate affairs. Many have "their own" tables, at which, by appointment, they receive, as on visiting day. The inner walls are of broad, to-the-ceiling matching panels of dark, black-grained wood, the outer ones of lofty windows, innumerable thin chains of brass and copper looped across each of them, each chain just above another—the chains ripple and flow, collectively, with the currents of air just inside the tall sheets of tinted glass. In this cavernous setting, even these large tables—they are covered with pale linen—seem drawn to half scale. You are seated on banquettes of deep-brown leather, or on wide leather chairs with steel frames, and though you are vaguely segregated from the celebrants at the bar by low partitions of dark glass, the noise of the tipplers makes its way to the dining room proper, and during dinner the calm otherwise imposed by this room's grand spaciousness is undone by the boys' bibulous jubilations. The Bar Room is presumably that half of the Four Seasons set aside for real New Yorkers (as distinguished, presumably, from the tourists attracted to the more pretentious Pool Room), and its brief menu flatters a local's no-nonsense image of himself by accentuating the kind of cooking—grilled meats, grilled fish, crab cakes, pasta—that is fancied by those who refuse to make the switch to filter tips or zippered flies. Actually, frequenters of this room are just squares with local addresses, folks who are as tickled to eat in the legendary Four Seasons as anyone, but like to be cool about it. "Grabbed one of the girls from the office last night, and went over to the Four Seasons for drinks and a couple of steaks—not a bad spot, and you don't have to wait for a table like at the Palm." Etc. In the Bar Room you may also order from the more extensive Pool Room menu, excluding only those dishes that, in the Pool Room, are finished on serving stands equipped with Sterno burners—that fancy stuff just don't go here in the Bar Room. In shape and size, the Pool Room (which you reach by way of a long corridor) is almost the Bar Room's twin—except that instead of a bar in the corner, there is a gurgling white-marble pool, brightly illuminated, at the center, bottom-lighted rubber trees in tortured postures at each of its corners. The trees, taken together with the pots of greenery that, along the windowed walls, hang from the ceiling on long wires, do much to queer the room's grandeur—in this respect the trees take second place only to the overfeds who, in outfits that transform them into pictures from the Sears catalog, come to this place in order, solely, to have been in it.

The Seasons is pushing so-called Spa Cuisine (low calorie) these days, very American, you can tell how good for you it must be by how little you want it. Consider, for example, the squid salad with black beans, a pile of squid, a pile of beans, cold. Were it known widely that such exotic ingredients could be this flat, they would be staples, all across the contiguous forty-eight, at boarding schools and prisons. You desert the Spa section of the menu for the breast of pigeon with figs, only to learn that in addition to Spa Cuisine, there is also the *influence* of Spa Cuisine, for the dish is made up of four small slices of not bad squab arranged like the quarter-hour points on a clock around a not yet ripe fig at the center of the plate, the two upon a film of cranberry puree. The merits of this fruit with this meat are difficult to gauge when the fig is favorless, but the sauce is lively with the squab. Nor will you bloat up on an order of what is given as "crisped shrimp filled with mustard fruits," nicely battered deep-fried shrimp that are filled with nothing, least of all shrimp flavor, garnished with a single morsel of nameless fruit in the mustard sauce. Grilled gravlax sounds like a promising idea, but it involves cooking the salmon twice, by marination and then by fire, which accounts for its denatured quality—that is somewhat offset by the fresh dill that adorns the grill-marked slab, but finally its harsh saltiness, simply too much sodium chloride, renders the article almost inedible. Relative safety in pasta: lobster ravioli, the firm sheets of noodle mingled with sweet peas in a lobster sauce that is vibrant of concentrated lobster flavor, though the chunks of lobster, apparently added at the end, are cold at their centers; and pappardelle with chanterelles, the broad, hefty ribbons of eggy noodle mingled with wild mushrooms that are fresh, crunchy, earthy.

Apparently when the crabmeat that goes into the crab cocktail is getting on, it goes into the crab cakes, for these have the unmistakable air of decomposition, and you are tempted to leave them where they are and move yourself to a table across the room. Well bred, you instead exchange them for blackened redfish, two lengths of firm, fresh white meat, their surfaces a rough skin of charred spices, the fish garnished with fiery black beans that are overlaid with strips of red pepper—a nice plate of food. What started out as fresh, sweet snapper is grilled until dry—it is served with a sauce choron (béarnaise pinked with tomato) that is cold. It is not, however, your now diminished level of expectation that accounts for the seeming excellence of this duck, for the crisped bird's succulent meat is in fact of strong, clear duck flavor, and its peach sauce, which is dark

173

and sticky, is of brandylike intensity—the bird is garnished with a great half of poached peach, firm, glistening pink, of vivid fruit flavor. Around town, what goes as beef paillard is something pounded thin, rapidly grilled, at once browned and juicy. Here it is thicker than the usual thing, of necessity done more slowly, yielding but little of the dramatic contrast between a crusty surface and a blood-pink interior—its diablo sauce duplicates bottled steak sauce. You are better served by the skillet steak, for though its smothered onions seem sugar sweetened, the thick slab of fibrous, tender meat has real beef flavor.

When you select from the good cheese tray offered in the Bar Room, you are offered also a variety of fresh fruit—the cheese is served with a chewy, nutty walnut bread. The chocolate soufflé is a well-made example of the standard thing, fluffy and of a strong chocolate flavor, in this instance enriched by the milk-chocolate sauce your waiter spoons on. The chocolate velvet cake is, no doubt, technically a cake, but seems more like solid chocolate. Blackened edges are a zest to the slightly sour Italian prune tart. The baba is a firm sweet cake soaked in rum—the inserted layer of cooked peaches is a nice note. An abundance of sweet spice accounts for the distinctly American cast of the crisp and nutty blackberry-pine-nut pie.

Four American states and five other nations are represented on the long wine list.

○ **FU'S**

1395 Second Avenue (near 72nd Street)
LUNCH AND DINNER.
Reservations: 517-9670.
Credit cards: AE, DC, MC, V.
Medium priced.

It is your lucky night, so you get seated at a table right beside (almost all the tables are right beside) a table at which the lady who is mistress of this place is visiting. She is explaining to her honored customers the special lengths to which she goes to train her staff—or, as she calls them, her boys. "You know what I call them?" she asks. "I call them *my boys!*" She laughs. "You know, every Friday I hold a special class for them. You know what I teach them? I teach them to say madame, sir, good evening, thank you. You know where I take my chef, my captain? I take them to Lutèce, to the Four Seasons, to Le Bernardin. I want them to know there is something else." It is more as if she wants them to know that something else is all there is, for Fu's is denatured Chinese, the enterprise of one who wishes, at once, to capitalize on her background and get as far from it as possible. The restaurant is built on the notion that the trappings of successful Western restaurants are what those places are about, and that those devices will work the wonders for Fu's that they did for, say, Lutèce, the Four Seasons, Le Bernardin. Of course she is right. This place hops—with customers who, like her, judge restaurants by whether there are captains in tuxedos, never mind that the civilities they murmur have been memorized phonetically.

You enter to what the house surely thinks of as its cocktail lounge, though it is tiny for the classification, a slick little black-topped bar, a gleaming steel rail for your elbows, another for your shoe. Behind the bar, wine is stored in a diamond pattern of racks to which your attention is called by the rods of glowing light that are the edges of each bin. The floor is of marble, the wall is a black mirror, potted palms stand in the corners. The bar is tended by, presumably, one of the lady's boys, this one, somehow, a girl. She must handle not only the bar before her but also, through a window in the wall behind her, the dining room. With the dining room she has only the trouble that results from there being more to do than she can handle. With the bar her problem is that she and her customers speak different languages, and she has no time for slow talk or slow listening. You ask what beers are on hand. She answers, but the only brand she can pronounce clearly is Tsingtao. (As it happens, the menu deals with this subject: "Our subtly and artfully blended drinks and the personable responsiveness of our staff are the ingredients with which we hope to transport you into the spirit of Fu's welcome.") Your wait for a table is rarely long (Fu's, though in certain other respects modeled after fancy midtown places, does not encourage those seated ahead of you—or anyone else—to hang around once the check and fortune cookies are delivered), and presently you make it to the nightclubby dining room, much charcoal-gray, pink, black mirrors, all softly lighted, at the center of the room a massive rectangular column—black glass yet again—hung with glowing strands of light. The banquettes are red velvet and cushy, but the chairs do not fit the tables—the legs of the former collide with the bases of the latter, so you can get only so close to dinner.

Your hostess has observed that non-Chinese restaurants offer special dishes of the day. Accordingly, she offers them too. But she has failed to note that such dishes are, often, either seasonal foods that cannot be listed on printed menus all year round, or dishes chosen for the variety they add to an otherwise limited menu. At Fu's, the menu includes more than forty main courses, and the ingredients of the specials simply duplicate those of the listed items. But you figure out the thinking behind the practice quickly enough when the captain tells you that today's featured dish is shrimp in Grand Marnier sauce.

In search of safety, you repair to the printed menu, send for tangy spicy shrimp, not bad, the cool morsels in a nutty and slightly spicy sauce that is threaded with citrus rind. But the hacked chicken and sesame noodles are dreary versions of those familiarities, their usual drama lost because they are premixed and waiting for you—you even find a few strands of chicken among the noodles, as if the two items occupy adjacent tubs and visit each other. The fried dumplings are of normal flavor but of abnormal greasiness. The shu mei—little noodle dumplings filled with pork—are, for some reason, fishy, and are apparently glued together (your captain must pull them apart to divide an order). An order of steamed stuffed mushrooms consists of two mushroom caps, a shrimp on each.

You give the house the benefit of your now considerable doubt, choose your main courses from among the "chef's specialties," fail to regret it with respect only to the home-style chicken (though it is marked with the "hot & spicy" asterisk, it is not especially), nicely battered and crisped morsels of chicken in among a ginger-flavored assortment of sautéed vegetables. The jumbo shrimp Fu's style are utterly without shrimp flavor, though it is probably a decent dish—the shrimp are mingled with water chestnuts and snow peas in a clear and sticky sauce—when the seafood element is itself. The crispy sea bass Hunan style tastes like candy. Fu's (sliced) steak is finished, on a side stand beside your table, by pouring over it a vegetable stew—a way of giving the customers the steak they want while permitting them to think they are eating Chinese. Of dishes not among the so-called specialties, the "banana chicken" (that is the concoction's title) is exactly what you think it is. In the crispy beef Hunan style, the shreds of meat are suitably crisped and chewy but utterly devoid of beefiness—bean sprouts, scallion greens, carrots, and a lot of salt complete the dish.

For dessert, pineapple is recommended. That the place does not offer cherries jubilee or crepes suzette is a function, surely, of the time it takes to prepare them, for Fu's likes to turn you over in forty-five minutes flat.

★ GAYLORD

87 First Avenue (near 5th Street)
LUNCH AND DINNER
Reservations: 529-7990.
Credit cards: AE, DC, MC, V.
Inexpensive.

Though East Village residents will tell you they like it down here, would live nowhere else even if they could afford to, the interests behind this establishment hold to the view that bohemians, given the wherewithal, fancy the trappings of the good life. Consider, for example, Friday and Saturday nights at Gaylord, when the house stations a giant in a turban outside its front door, his function being to open the door for you and, as you pass through, to wish you a pleasant dinner. You enter, are greeted by yet another anomaly, musicians, their shoes off, seated cross-legged on a small platform, plucking and thumping on, respectively, a sitar and tabla. These amenities, though there are dozens of Indian and/or Pakistani and/or Bangladesh restaurants east of Fourth Avenue, north of Houston Street, and south of 14th, may be peculiar, in these parts, to Gaylord. Gaylord is one of the few subcontinental restaurants in the vicinity that, by its looks, would not seem out of place in more moneyed parts of town, and it is very much a destination for special occasions here in the land of dropouts.

What additionally distinguishes Gaylord from most of its neighborhood competition is the smoothness of its walls, the thickness of its carpeting, the engraved brass service plates at your place when you are seated, the handsome art, some of it behind glass doors that are elaborately framed in carved wood, and, maybe most of all, the waiters in dark suits and dark four-in-hands and the women in saris (they seem to be added to the staff on busy nights), by all of whom you are favored with courtesy that never flags. Truly, it is as if these were the days of British dominion, when the Indian drove the interloper mad with his persistently cooperative, utterly mechanical, quite opaque politesse, by way of which the inquisitors were left in the dark, the real questions unanswered.

Withal, though this may be, with respect to East Village Indian restaurants, the most visually presentable to the middle class, it is well to know its idiosyncrasies, for you may eat splendidly here one night, drearily the next. Chicken chat will at least assure you of a positive start, the cold chicken in a creamy, powerfully hot-spiced, and fruity sauce, through all of which the flavor of the chicken is actually clear. You even do well if, out of a wish to sample the several vegetable fritters and turnovers, you opt for the platter of assorted appetizers, for the items, filled variously with sweet banana, spicy green pepper, potato, are carefully deep fried, crisp, virtually devoid of grease, all of them very good when inflamed with the rather violent relishes served here. But you must conscientiously avoid the tandoori mixed grill, which quite persuades you that it is composed of bits and pieces stolen from tandoori dishes prepared during the past week. And the shami kabab, lamb patties, are dry, powdery, devoid of lamb, or any other, character.

Turn the page of your menu, but cover with your hand the lower left corner, "vegetarian specialties," among which are the likes of this begun bhorta, a baked eggplant item that reaches you as a nameless mash, and shag ponir, in which the spinach is of decent sweet-spiced flavor, while the cheese with which it is studded is rubbery. Orthodox Hindus will not eat beef dhansak, and neither should you. The chunks of meat are no worse than the normal run of stewed beef, but the lentil gravy out of which you fish them is thin, as if it has not yet attained its intended state. A better stewlike dish goes as shrimp sabji, the shrimp with any of three vegetables, your choice cauliflower, the florets as crunchy as the sweet shrimp themselves, the sauce in which they are joined heady of fresh cilantro. The familiar rice dish called lamb biryani is served here in a good version, the rice studded with chunks of tender lamb and sweet black raisins. Though the tandoori appetizer was dreadful, main courses cooked in the clay oven reach you in impeccable condition—the tandoori chicken and tandoori fish (on occasion fresh swordfish) are redded, hot, moist, suffused with the flavors of their spices. Good breads, poori, for one, those great balloons of unleavened wheat; aloo nan, for another, hot bread stuffed with spicy potatoes.

At Gaylord inexplicable Indian desserts remain inexplicable Indian desserts.

★ GIBBON

24 East 80th Street
LUNCH, MONDAY TO FRIDAY; DINNER, MONDAY TO SATURDAY. CLOSED SUNDAY.
Reservations: 861-4001.
Credit cards: AE, DC, MC, V.
Very expensive.

Not far from the Whitney, hard by the Met, and on the very flank of Madison Avenue's gallery row, Gibbon caters to a world of curators and donors, dealers and collectors, even artists. That set eats elsewhere, too, of course, but of all its uptown hangouts, only this one provides a setting that is sufficiently reliquary for the conduct of affairs that involve both high culture and high finance. The restaurant occupies the ground floor and second story of a venerable townhouse, and though the appointments are mostly Japanese, the rooms in which they have been installed suggest the insular mansion of some old New York family—the kind of place occupied by the dowager, the butler, and the matched pair of snarling mastiffs.

Down a couple of steps to the lower, more commodious of the two levels—softly lit and brick-walled, at the front a bar and a fireplace, at the back a number of tables formed into groups by partitions of elaborately woven and tied bamboo. Up a flight of stairs to the stark parlor floor, high-ceilinged and harshly lit, the walls covered with raw silk of an indeterminate color, the tieback curtains on the huge windows a somewhat more straightforward dirty beige. The four-panel painted screen hung high on one side of the room is probably a masterpiece, but to the untutored eye it is an essay in faded gray on faded silk. But none of that matters. Those who frequent the Gibbon are past caring about superficialities. There is well-bred old money here, in old clothes: well-worn tweeds and flannels, button-down shirts and club ties, calf-length dresses and sensible shoes—and yards of pearls. When high-level salesmanship is going on, you see mixed groups consisting of the moneyed, the middlemen, and the artist—the last distinguished from his companions by his taciturnity and open collar.

One of Gibbon's more successful ecumenical creations is a shrimp appetizer in which four crunchy, sweet crustaceans and a couple of disks of crisp lotus root are served in a crimson sauce the house calls strawberry vinaigrette—it is more like a fortified puree of the ripe fruit, but that brilliantly chosen dressing is the making of the dramatic dish. Most of the food here is strikingly presented, including an item in which two chimneys formed of peeled and seeded lengths of cucumber stand side by side on a handsome square blue plate. The columns are filled with and surrounded by chunks of good, cool lobster meat, which are coated with a thick mayonnaise.

The Gibbon has one flaw that, particularly in Japanese restaurants, is deadly—its fish sometimes tastes less than fresh. The knowing therefore eschew the first course of assorted sashimi, for that defect is utterly off-putting in fish served raw. But there is another sashimi item on the menu—it is called usuzukuri—that, for some reason, never seems off. The dish consists of innumerable slices of white fish, each of them paper thin and translucent, arranged on a plate like the filmy, smoky-white petals of a huge white flower, a mound of shredded scallion at the center, on that a smaller mound of strong grated radish. You add the radish, according to your tolerance for fire, to a little dish of citrus-flavored soy sauce, dip the fish in the sauce, and eat—the flavor of the fish is clear despite the pungency of the sauce. There are hot first courses as well, among them minced cherrystone clams mingled with chopped mushrooms and served, in three big clam shells, on buttery spinach and under a browned breading—spicy, earthy, bracing food. A dish called tataki is billed as "charred filet mignon delicately raw inside." It turns out, to your surprise, to be cold, the strands of meat not charred at all, in fact barely browned. Still, this is good food, the thin red strips of rare and tender beef strewn with curls of shredded scallion and garnished with caviar and grated radish—you dip the meat in what the house calls "sauce Gibbon," a salty soy sauce dotted with sesame seeds.

The meat of a lobster is taken from its shell, sautéed, piled back into the shell, and served in a soy sauce made nutty by sesame—the carefully prepared lobster is firm and sweet, that sauce a fine foil to it. But the steamed pompano sometimes suffers for being a little over the hill. So if you wish to take no chances when you try this place, opt for the main courses of meat: sautéed scallops of pale, juicy veal, nicely browned, in a complex soy-based sauce that is sweet, salty, thick with leaves of watercress; or the six-rib rack of lamb, brought to you intact, its surface handsomely browned, the meat pink and of strong lamb flavor, the sauce of roasting juices given a slight Japanese accent with a bit of soy sauce.

All the desserts are Western ones, among them an intense, black-frosted chocolate cake that seems to call for a glass of milk; a lemony, lemon-rindy, creamy, and polished lemon mousse—fluffy whipped cream comes with it; and a rich banana ice cream of vivid flavor.

★★★ GOTHAM

12 East 12th Street
LUNCH, MONDAY TO FRIDAY; DINNER, DAILY.
Reservations: 620-4020.
Credit cards: AE, DC, MC, V.
Expensive.

A silvery replica of the Statue of Liberty, about a fifteenth the height of the original, is the sole icon among the otherwise nonvenerative impedimenta with which this vast space is cumbered. The Lady is allotted, moreover, only a peripheral position in the huge room. And yet for years now hordes of devotees have made the Gotham Bar & Grill (to give it for the last time its full name) their most revered destination for prandial devotions. During much of that time, wags have suggested, the crowds consisted of less-than-intrepid tourists who, the big Liberty being off on an otherwise void island, visited this one rather than none at all, for the restaurant's wares, qua restaurant wares, though of merit, could not reasonably account for Gotham's mad popularity. Others, however, better informed, suggested that its success was traceable to the influence of Jerome Kretchmer, principal owner, former functionary in the Lindsay administration, sometime man about town, whose connections, political and otherwise, accounted not only for the restaurant's success, but for the persistent and quite gaga comments in the press that in large measure engendered it. Could be, but the media, whose business is factuality, have no better than an average batting average in prognostication, while Gotham has now caught up with its best notices.

That is to say, the food has. The physical place remains as was, a collection of hideous parts amounting only to their sum. Informed by a whimsy that, having lost its way, took itself seriously, Gotham is a nightmare of Levantine conceits, parapets, squat towers weighted down by concrete finials—orbs, urns, pyramids—carefully splattered columns reminiscent of the pattern on a housepainter's hat, and, hanging like laundry from the ceiling, ballooning light fixtures, of what looks like pale tricot, that a wise man once described as "underpants for some species of legless behemoth." A long banquette, upholstered in dark tapestry cloth, is an unhealed diagonal wound down the center of the room. On entering you climb up a few stairs only to climb down a few others into the dining room, and throughout there are equally pointless changes of level "to break up the space," you can hear some dim designer mindlessly explain. Those who frequent Gotham, and they are many, are by now presumably inured to its visual affronts. In this setting Miss Liberty is a phoenix rising.

So you eat with your eyes fixed rigidly on your companion's—or on your plate, and if what you find there is Gotham's "seafood salad," you may well not look up till you have vanished it. Of dishes that go by this name, no other reveals the lightness, liveliness, tender freshness of ingredients, clarity of seafood flavors, and textural concordances of this one. Even visually the thing is prepossessing, for it reaches you as a tall cone, partially wrapped in the thin, splayed slices of a firm, ripe avocado, spiky greens sprouting gaily from its apex, the whole glistening of the silken olive oil with which it is dressed. Among its parts there are tiny sweet mussels, chunks of juicy Japanese octopus,

179

rich scallops, morsels of lobster, more, all roused by the lemon in their dressing and by the herbs with which they are mingled. The skate, a fish admired in France, is usually scorned here. To put it across to Americans, this place serves it in an anything-but-naked form, as the principal element in a warm salad in a warm vinaigrette, thick with herbs and dotted with capers, that excites the otherwise pallid swimmer—the fish is garnished with rings of grilled red onion, cool and sweet. Exceptional veal carpaccio, the pale, thin-sliced meat filmed with oil, strewn with strands of bresaola, adorned with curled tongues of pungent Parmesan, and garnished with a lively, leafy salad—a stunning dish. This place will make of anything, even a quail, a salad. It is a lovely little bird, flattened, browned, crisped, its strong meat juicy, set on a disk of minced greens and slivered mushrooms in an almost sour dressing, and garnished with a bit of well-oiled potato salad. Gotham does its own smoking of ducks, serves up a dozen slices of the supple, fat-rimmed meat formed into an arc around a towering construct of lettuces, at its base a mound of greened and gingered rice and a spicy, vividly fruity apricot-and-pear chutney —sparkling food.

Steak au poivre is nowadays often of tuna, and the new dish has more to recommend it than its supposed beneficence, vis-à-vis beef, in re your blood vessels. Raw or rare, tuna apes beef, and, as they say, blindfolded (and tight) you cannot tell a steak of one from the other—anyway, a heavily peppered one. Moreover, tuna is not tough, clings less tenaciously than beef to the spaces between your teeth, can be chopped up and made into tuna fish salad—a use to which beef has never successfully been put. (Send no recipes.) All that in mind, you opt for Gotham's tuna version rather than its beef, and once again you are presented with the arc of little slices that is this establishment's signature layout, the fish supple, red and rare but warmed through, its peppered edges crisped, its sauce a so-called shellfish bordelaise that is at once sharp and enriching. A simpler fish is the black bass, it is only itself. Here its fillets are browned, the attached skin is crisped, the pale meat reveals more of this species' subtle flavor than is usually preserved, and it is nicely set off by the mushrooms and baby vegetables with which it is garnished, and by the dark, somewhat tart sauce in which it is set. You order roast chicken, but what you notice first is a tangle of thin, crisp, golden strands of deep-fried potato, greaseless and of vivid potato flavor, with which you mindlessly distract yourself until you recall your original purpose, the bird, which has chicken flavor that brings back memories of chicken flavor—you can taste the grain on which it was fed. The rack of lamb arrives as two thick double chops, the meat glowing pink within edges that are dark and crusty of the herbs-and-mustard paste with which they are coated. Persist, however, and you will hit a loser, loin of rabbit that is formed into a half-dozen columns, each of them bound in smoky bacon that imparts a foreign, porky taste to meat that, as far as you can tell, has no flavor of its own.

Your taste for the peanut butter coupe will depend on your tolerance for peanut butter ice cream—the whipped cream, chocolate, and caramel sauce, and the cookie that sprouts from the top, are unimpeachable. The warm chocolate cake, being neither very intense nor particularly mild, is thereby a homey, comforting sweet—its garnish of rum raisin ice cream is fine, but has no special business with it. In that same spirit is the pear and bitter-chocolate turnover, the gentle fruit moderates the strong chocolate, the two are wrapped in flaky pastry, are garnished with vanilla ice cream—hospital food at its best. The poached fruits are fine, the pear, prunes, apricots, and figs retain their flavor and texture in the winy, sweet-spiced syrup. Yes, yes, you are right, hospital food at its best again—but at its best it is no longer hospital food.

★★LA GOULUE

28 East 70th Street
LUNCH AND DINNER. CLOSED SUNDAY.
Reservations: 988-8169.
Credit cards: AE, DC, MC, V.
Medium priced.

To survive, this establishment had to be transformed, for it began (in the early seventies) as one of the principal destinations in New York of what was then called the jet set; and it became, less than a decade later, just a neighborhood place, one at which the habitués usually arrive on foot. The change was effected, however, without the alteration of so much as a physical—or conceptual—stick of the place. So if you have not been here in some time, prepare yourself for a double déjà vu: the restaurant is still what it was in the beginning; and it is still a startlingly clear memory of Paris.

You will recall that La Goulue is an entrance room and two vaguely separated dining rooms; that up front there is a tiny zinc bar and a few cocktail tables with brass-framed marble tops; that, under a deep-brown stamped-tin ceiling, the walls are of dark wood, except where they are inset with the big plate-glass mirrors that, even when this place was new, looked as if they were losing their silver in random streaks and patches; that the floors are of broad wooden planks, the curtains of lace; that the dining rooms are rimmed with high-backed banquettes of caramel-colored leather; that the rooms are lighted by sinuous Art Nouveau wall sconces; and that the tables are set with white linen, glinting crystal and china and flatware, and flowers in slender vases. If you are still having difficulty dispelling the notion that, this setting notwithstanding, you are in the same old Big Apple, consider the serving staff in their black-and-whites and long white aprons. Most of them are those businesslike French professionals for whom discussions between consenting adults on the subject of food are serious matters but never solemn ones. Even the few non-Gallic members of the staff have picked up the habit of straight talk, if not yet easy conversance with their subject. And now that La Goulue no longer gets the crowd that used to come here only because the place was fashionable, you find yourself surrounded by folk with whom even you yourself might consider having dinner. They are here for the restaurant's comfort, for its more than decent traditional food, for the pleasure of being among others whose minds are as sound as their own. And in summer, some of them are here for the breezes. For when the weather is fine, tables are set out on the sidewalk under the awning, a stand of greenery at each end of the row. Some even come with their dogs, tie them to a nearby tree, blow them kisses during dinner, deliver snacks. The view is only of East 70th, but when you consider the places into which much of New York is clamoring to get, you realize that a two-hour dinner on this quiet street is actually a month in the country.

You do not expect, in these times, the bistro food of forty years ago (though you would not complain if it were offered). You are content, even happy, to settle for the traditional New York bistro menu in contemporary terms, for actually, with respect to many dishes, that is simply the old item upgraded. This smoked salmon, for example, is far from the salted and oily red meat that was once a staple in New York French restau-

181

rants a rung or more below the caliber of haute cuisine. It is, in fact, a great sheet of rosy, velvety seafood, of light texture and of a sweet, only vaguely smoky flavor, served to you with good olive oil, lemon, capers, and sharp and crunchy chopped onions. You are disappointed to find that the so-called haricots verts are not at all the tiny, almost thread-like green beans the name suggests, but, rather, everyday green beans, albeit young and tender ones—still, this is nice light food, the cool green shafts mingled with slices of fresh mushroom in their tangy, mustard-flavored dressing. The duck pâté is distressingly dark and dry, a function of an overextended stay in the oven, but the peppercorns with which it is studded and the pungent mustard with which it is served help. Why tomatoes and mozzarella are on this French menu is a mystery, more of one when you find that the cheese is crumbly, a little loud, not at all like the smooth and milky Italian article. The plump snails are a decent version of the standard item in their parsleyed, garlicked, and strongly seasoned hot butter. And the onion soup, under browned cheese that has a crust of bread concealed beneath it, is dark and sweet, thick with onions.

If it seems to you that outdoor eating calls for picnic food, consider this cool (but not cold) lobster, which arrives with the meat of the tail still encased in the split carapace, that of the claws out of its shells, all of it firm and of a fresh ocean flavor, garnished with cool vegetables, and served with a big dollop of rich mayonnaise—very nice with cold white wine. But in the right season you may gladly forgo the illusion of a picnic for the reality of soft-shell crabs, for La Goulue obtains little ones, flours them, sautés them rapidly in hot butter, and delivers them in tender, delicately crackling condition. Sword-fish is often the finfish of the day, the big steak fresh and fibrous and juicy, served under a strongly tarragon-flavored sauce béarnaise that seems actually to combine with and enrich the juicy fish. That swordfish is quite sound, but this salmon is striking, the side of fresh fish firm and flaky under a sorrel sauce that is a slightly sour, distinctly earthy, and vaguely metallic deep-green puree, which contrasts dramatically with the pink meat. The suprême de volaille is a boned and nicely browned breast of chicken in a tart vinegar sauce that is hot and smooth, as if the sauce was finished just a moment before it was served. Only a few red-meat dishes on the menu, among them a tournedos à l'estragon, in which the two-inch thick filet mignon—its silken meat tender, but not especially tasty—is provided with plenty of flavor by the winy tarragon sauce in which it is served. Light, crisp French fries and grilled tomatoes come with the steak.

You inquire of your waiter the condition of the Brie. He is frank with you. But come on a night when it is in good condition, and you get lovely cheese, its chalk-white shell a nice bit of texture against the soft, buttery center. Ripe berries are served with whipped cream that is very sugary but otherwise fine. The raspberry mousse cake consists of the mousse, a jellylike icing on top, chocolate at the base—a fun sweet. What the house gives as "orange napoleon" is nothing like what you think of as a napoleon. It consists of sections of orange and strips of rind that have been steeped, with whole cloves, in cognac—a cold, rousing dessert.

★★LA GRENOUILLE

3 East 52nd Street
LUNCH AND DINNER. CLOSED SUNDAY AND MONDAY.
Reservations: 752-1495.
Credit cards: AE, DC, MC, V.
Very expensive.

Surely no one any longer takes The Frog as an exponent of French cookery. But in its time, it was a seriously intended restaurant—and, at the same time, a club for the rich and chic (with, of course, accommodations for plebes who wished to come and gawk). Though some are persuaded that it continues as one or both, all that really remains of the restaurant's heyday is its special look, albeit that alone may well justify adding to that list of experiences—those you plan to have only in order not to have lived without them—one dinner at La Grenouille.

From the start, the restaurant distinguished itself by an audacious stroke of interior adornment. Its space is nothing special, a high-ceilinged oblong, narrower at the front to allow for stairs up to the second floor, but instead of an architect to make something of it, the house called in a florist. He made what is surely the flower sale of the century, for during the twenty-five years and more of its existence La Grenouille has been stuffed with flowers, bursts and sprays and bouquets of them on the tables and in every corner —at some points flowering branches extend to the high ceiling—so that the air seems textured, and you see about you as if through an atmosphere quickened by botanical energy. At first the place was otherwise of a simplicity—pale-green walls, mirrored panels, a crimson banquette that rimmed the smaller front room (for the inner circle) and the larger space behind it (for everyone else), shaded lamps on the white-linened tables, a handful of painterly paintings in ornate frames, and that was about all. Little has been altered, but enough to change everything, for the walls are now faced with padded cloth, and though, happily, the once noisy restaurant is now quieter, that single element of stuffed posh has undone the directness that was the room's visual foundation. The other changes have been more gradual. The Frog's clientele is in the natural course shuffling off. Of an evening the back of the place is filled (with new money), the front only half filled (with older gold that is almost uniformly silver haired). And while the restaurant continues to thrive on its reputation, its kitchen gets by with a brief menu (and virtually no special dishes of the day) that, after a training period, could be entrusted to high-IQ orangutans. Contemporary good cooking has passed La Grenouille by.

You will recall that after checking your coat you entered to an anteroom in which an assortment of hors d'oeuvres are displayed, these formerly an element of La Grenouille's culinary repute. The number of items is fewer these days, and though the celery root is as crunchy and tangy as ever in its lively dressing, the cucumber salad as sweet and delicate and rousing, the well-oiled ratatouille a compendium in which the several elements retain and reveal their individual flavors, not all is well. You are served mushrooms à la grecque, a dish that, in this era of fabulous mushrooms tame and wild, is simply too good an imitation of canned mushrooms to be anything but a joke; poached salmon that is just loud; asparagus spears that have been carefully peeled—then cooked

183

until limp. Where once the house served an assortment of pâtés and terrines, a single terrine of pheasant is listed, and though the thing itself is buttery and of delicate but clear flavor, you are dismayed that its cranberry garnish is arranged over shreds of whitish lettuce that would be discarded in any but the most cost-conscious diner. And yet, as ever, there are the clams corsini, and if one night they are not quite the delicate balance of seafood sweetness and brine, of garlic and herbs and wine that once obtained, even a practitioner of the highest IQ will, over the decades, vary from the standard to this minor degree now and then. But the house surprises you completely with what is given as "le gâteau de choux au foie gras," literally cabbage cake with foie gras, a layering of steamy leaves of the humble vegetable interleaved with thin slices of the distinguished liver, the cabbage enriched by the tender, gentle meat, the two in a sticky sauce that is hot, winy, sweet.

There cannot be a Frog without frogs' legs, and the Frog, which has always risen to the occasion of its name, sautés fresh ones until they are handsomely browned and suffused with the butter and garlic in which they are done, serves them to you with all their own good flavor intact. Nothing, happily, has ever caused the house to delete from its menu "les quenelles de brochet," dumplings of pike filmed with a winy white sauce and garnished with fluffy, nubbly white rice—the dumplings are of clear pike flavor, are judiciously seasoned, are firm but light, and the all white, rather austere presentation belies the vigor of the food. But then there is this so-called bass stuffed with herbs, fillets of fresh fish done to a point of sacrifice of much of their moisture and flavor, a mass of buttery herbs on and between and around them, but nothing about the dish suggests that the elements have any special business with each other. As for the duck in red wine, though the sauce—of pommard—is a wonderful concentration of good burgundy, the bird is tough and tasteless.

A couple of the listed desserts (in addition to the soufflés) should be ordered in advance, one of them a hot, fluffy individual chocolate cake set in and filled with a rich and intense chocolate sauce; the other a hot individual apple tart that is of an airy pastry, the layering of thin-sliced apples at the center adorned with an egg of honey-and-ginger-flavored ice cream. The homey and sturdy French apple cake called pithivier is made here in a particularly sugary version that nevertheless avoids excessive sweetness. The lemon tart is vibrant, the raspberry tart dull—flat pastry, a bit of custard, albeit berries that are fresh and ripe.

The service is always sweet, but there is at least one young captain who fills your wineglass almost to the top so that he will not have to bother with it again soon; who does not mention to you, when he takes your order, that certain desserts should be ordered ahead; who, when he later tells you about the other, ready-made, desserts neglects to mention maybe half of them, and never shows you any of them—he is cordial, you understand, knows his job, knows even better how to make it easier.

● GROVE STREET CAFÉ

53 Grove Street (near Sheridan Square)
DINNER. CLOSED SUNDAY AND MONDAY.
Reservations: 924-9501.
No credit cards.
No liquor.
Expensive.

Supposedly there are, around town, cozy neighborhood restaurants in which more-than-decent food is prepared and served, by amateur but dedicated crews, in unpretentious surroundings. The discomforts that necessarily obtain in such places, it is thought, are trade-offs for economy—maybe you bring your own wine, obtained at liquor-store cost, and presumably the menu prices are low. Of course no such places exist. Any establishment taken to fit the description is really a cooperative fantasy—between a clientele that likes to believe it is in on a good, private thing, and a management that, in fact, is.

What distinguishes this Village example of the genre from most of the others is that the collection of recipes from which the kitchen works includes some real winners. The house, however, knows not which those are, alternates the good with the dreary. And though you do bring your own wine, you may find a disaccord between the food prices and, say, a tiny table hard by the radiator. The cubical store is wee, the brown fabric on the walls is adorned with a tiny floral print, the four-bladed fan hangs from a dark-red ceiling, and you walk on a dark-red rug. The bentwood side chairs that surround the white-linened tables are, in some places, back to back. The waiters are eccentric, but, of course, each in his own way. Your host is short—not in stature. You arrive, spot an emptying table by the window, ask if you may have it. Goes he, "Do you *mind* if we set it up first?" Oh, the disturbances.

Have: the grilled seafood sausage (the milky-white forcemeat is firm and well seasoned within its handsomely browned casing—you do wish the pinked beurre blanc were warm) and the smoked quail (the cool halves of the little bird are tender and of strong flavor—you do wish that the chutney garnish were at something higher than icebox temperature). Eschew: the "jumbo lump crabmeat gratinée" (crab fibers under a darkened topping, a shellfish imitation of macaroni and cheese) and the sautéed garlic lamb (a meat gruel that would constitute an accomplishment if made from leftovers). Have: the fillet of Norwegian salmon (handsomely browned, medium rare, and of perfect freshness, firm texture, and clear flavor in its smooth beurre blanc) and the roast duck (a decently roasted bird with a tart red-cabbage garnish that is its excellent foil) and the roast pork (supple meat in a thick and fruity sauce of apricots and prunes). Eschew: the fusilli in three-meat bolognese (bland and wet, like something made from the contents of two poorly drained cans). Have: the walnut ice cream (gritty of ground nuts and of deep walnut flavor under its strong chocolate sauce) and the chocolate roulade (intense but light chocolate cake and rich whipped cream). Eschew: the raspberry mousse (the pallid stuff is rescued neither by the whipped cream on top nor by the few berries under the cream nor by the brownie on the side) and the lemon curd tart (the custard is harshly acidic on its burnt pastry).

You bring your own wine.

185

★ GULF COAST

489 West Street (at 12th Street)
LUNCH, SATURDAY AND SUNDAY; DINNER, DAILY.
No reservations (206-8790).
No credit cards.
Inexpensive.

It is Saturday night, and the chap at the door—he is in jeans and plaid shirt—informs all comers that there will be a two-hour wait to eat. Nobody pays him any mind. It is not that no one believes him, rather that no one cares. You give him your name, affix yourself to the back edge of the crowd along the bar, and eventually get a drink from one of two bartenders—their perpetual motion is interrupted only to light cigarettes (their own). Called Gulf Coast, this place is in fact Fort Lauderdale-on-Hudson (you can see the river from the West Street window), and it constitutes the eternal spring vacation that, by its frequenters' lights, is the natural consequence and reward of their recently earned bachelor degrees.

Gulf Coast is a brightly lighted two-room saloon with an ancient bar in the front room and with a corrugated-aluminum ceiling and an old wooden floor throughout. The plastic-top tables are stocked with sugar in sugar pourers, bottles of hot sauce, stacks of paper napkins. Most of everything else about Gulf Coast has been chosen to satisfy its clientele's addictive nostalgia for the present. The tape deck, for example—it is ever on, and only at full volume—produces the very sounds with which, ever since their parents learned to sedate them with electronic audio and/or visual devices, these children have obliterated their inherited cultural past. Many who come here do not disconnect their Walkmans until they are safely inside the door. (Look around, and you see a suspicious abundance of a kind of bliss that owes nothing to controlled substances.) The back bar is festooned with snapshots and picture postcards, lots of them from Florida. The inside neon signs include one that advertises Ford trucks, another that welcomes tourists, yet another that advises of the availability of hot plates and sandwiches. The principal difference between the help and the customers is that the former, as they suddenly, impulsively, jiggle and shuffle to the irresistible background beat, are likely to do so while in the very act of handing you your dinner. Meanwhile, at the next table, a young lady in jeans and sweatshirt, her left ear bejeweled, rises slowly, like a cobra, from her chair, writhes to the music as she does so, gyrates for a while, and gradually subsides back into her place. Her friends seem not to notice. The central figure here, most nights, is the gallant young lady whose job it is to extract from the crowd the customers scheduled to occupy the next table. Her straightforward method is to shout out names while wandering among the multitude. Occasionally she hollers from behind the bar. Other times she bellows while standing on a chair. Mostly she goes unheard and gets no response—still, she remains cheerful. About every ten minutes, the competition she gets from the tape deck is augmented by the roar of the 60-horsepower cement mixer in which half-gallon batches of blue margaritas are whipped up. The blue margarita is the big drink here. Order one and you get a glass of pale-turquoise foam adorned with a slice of lime and a

186

plastic fish. After a while the drink separates out into its component parts: Windex on the bottom, suds on top.

The "two-hour" wait for a table rarely exceeds sixty minutes, but if even that seems long, and if you have worked your way to the physical bar itself—have the use of a square foot of its actual surface—you will do well to get yourself some tamales (three for $1.95, six for $3.50) while you wait. The steamed, string-tied cornhusk packages are filled with ground meat that is coated with cornmeal. You untie, unwrap, and, with gingerly care, lift out the thumb-size contents with your fingers—the fragile, sausagelike constructs are mildly spiced, very light, and their clarity of flavor suggests that the force-meat was made fresh not long before you ordered it. Nibble slowly, and you may be seated by the time you dispatch your last tamale, in which case you may proceed to a plate of chilled shrimp, a couple dozen small crustaceans (a half pound, according to the menu) in their shells, distributed over a plate at the center of which stands a double-shot glass of red sauce—the shrimp have been cooked with celery salt, which heightens their sweet flavor, and that cold sauce is nubbly and spicy-hot. You get the same cold sauce with hot food too, including the lightly battered and deep-fried crab claws, yet another two dozen lengths of good seafood, these crisped in a fryer that, evidently, is regularly replenished with good fresh oil. Considerably more batter encases the fried and stuffed jalapeños, which reach you looking like three harmless fritters—their contents, however, are searingly hot green peppers filled with mild and pully cheese that can only begin to mitigate their impact.

Blackened redfish (here called "peppered redfish"), though not on the printed menu, is usually among the specials listed on the blackboard. The big fillet is fresh, cooked through but moist, and its gleaming mahogany-colored coat of herbs and spices is of a strikingly complex flavor that does nothing to hide the sweetness of the fish itself. Order catfish and you get the entire beast, battered and fried, the delicate meat fresh and steamy within its crust. The grilled chicken, though well made—handsomely browned and crisped, cooked through but not dried out—suffers from the tastelessness of the bird itself. A bigger and tastier chicken supplies the meat for the chicken and dumplings, a homey and utterly satisfying item that is just a bowl of a weighty, well-seasoned chicken gravy that is thick with slices of dumpling and hefty chunks of meat. What is listed as "red beans, rice, and sausage" is many of the first, much of the second, and a big, strong and somewhat fatty example of the third—inelegance in abundance, the red beans in a gravy that is thick with shreds of meat.

The desserts include treacly bread pudding, a buttermilk pie that is much like the kind of custard pie that used to be sold in glassine envelopes, a lime cream pie that is sticky and sweet (albeit of tangy lime flavor).

★★HASAKI

210 East 9th Street
DINNER.
Reservations: 473-3327.
Credit cards: AE, MC, V.
Medium priced.

The East Village suffers from cancer in reverse, here and there a few healthy cells multiplying in, and slowly taking charge of, a malignant environment. The regeneration is most visible along the broad avenues, but new life may be found also on the side streets, even, as in the instance of Hasaki, at their extremities. The change of scene is abrupt. Down a few steps from the grimness that is this stretch of East 9th Street, past a bit of greenery and a tiny stone wall, and through the door to a little vestibule in which, when this place is busy, the patient locals, mostly young, wait, in faded well-washed cottons, or in jeans and oversize sweaters, in sandals or in sneakers, much of their attire by way of disguise, for the current cost of living in this part of town is such that many of its citizens spend the better part of their days away from it, in straight clothes, earning the rent. When there is a little something left over, the more discerning of them repair here, for Hasaki is one of very few eating places in this arrondissement in which the food equals food of the same kind in other neighborhoods. Similarly the physical plant, which not only equals but is indistinguishable from a thousand other Japanese establishments on Manhattan Island. Hasaki is spick-and-span and well lighted. The sushi bar, the tables and chairs, and the whimsical partition that divides the dining room into two parts are all of pale wood. The young Japanese who wait on you—including this waitress in red sneakers, spiky brush cut, and boldly patterned tunic and shorts—are working hard on their English. As in most of these places, the sushi bar, wherever it is situated, is the focal center, and this one, with seats for about a dozen, and more brightly lighted than the rest of the place, is manned by three young men who perform their sculptural tasks deftly, cheerfully, tirelessly—if you have little else on your mind, and you sit at the bar or at a nearby table, they may be all the diversion you need. Other possible diversions, besides your own company: the sky—a handful of tables have been set up in the unimproved backyard, though only for drinks and a limited menu; and gray East 9th—a few tables situated just inside the glass façade look out on the street.

At one of those front tables you also get a view of the sushi bar from behind, albeit off to one side, and you may observe the assemblage of your kinutamaki unagi, a broad coil of cucumber that, with a sheet of seaweed, and with a swatch of eel warmed at the last minute in a toaster-broiler, is wound with those contents into a roulade, cut into disks, and served sprinkled with sesame seeds—the complexity of flavors and textures, and the contrast of the warm and oily eel with the cool and crisp cucumber, make this a rousing and yet subtle first course. Watch closely, and you may learn also how to prepare the tiger's eye—you pack the body of a hefty squid with salmon, then slice the construct into oval-shaped sheets that are a red iris within an iridescent white, and if they do not exactly call to mind the cat's orb, the fresh red fish and its frame of slightly chewy squid sparkle when you moisten them with soy sauce. Some of the first courses emerge from an

188

out-of-sight kitchen, among them the shrimp dumplings, steamed or fried, the former in noodle wrappers that glisten, the latter in noodle wrappers that are browned and crisp— if you prefer the fried to the steamed, you prefer an assertion to a suggestion, but both are good, the shrimp fillings very sweet. Something given as chicken yasaimaki will probably strike you as Western, for it is a kind of chicken sausage studded with pink and green vegetables—the cool slices are delicately seasoned, sport real chicken flavor, come with a dollop of something akin to mayonnaise, on a slice of lemon, at the center of your plate. It is well to buffer these sprightly first courses with broiled fish, specifically tilefish, the great chunks of it fresh, moist, lightly filmed with oil, done so judiciously that even this rather pallid species reveals a clear marine flavor.

Sushi, sashimi, and the related maki rolls and hand rolls are here prepared of fresh seafood, crisp vegetables, and crackling sheets of seaweed, and they are served with sparkling fresh ginger, and with a particularly vibrant example of the green radish paste called wasabi, which you add to the soy sauce that seasons them. In addition to the usual components, Hasaki offers a few items you do not encounter everywhere, among them what is given as "sweet raw shrimp," which is exactly that, the little gray morsel cold and almost candylike; and a maki roll of salmon skin, prepared with the rice outside, salmon meat one of the components as well, though it is the crisped skin that accounts for this item's special piquancy.

One section of the menu is headed, perhaps uniquely, "tempura à la carte." For small amounts of money ($1 for vegetables, $1.75 to $2.25 for seafood), you obtain small amounts of what you want. A dollar gets you a single shiitake mushroom, hot and earthy in the cloud of delicate, almost fugitive batter that is characteristic of all the tempura here—or it gets you several crescents of butternut squash, or as many rich, well-oiled chunks of eggplant. For a little more, you may have a single shrimp with nuts, the body of the sweet pink-and-white crustacean surfaced with slivers of a crisp green nut within the rarefied batter. A single order of scallops or squid is a mass of several morsels of the seafood—assembled on a sheet of seaweed—bound in the light batter.

Beer and sake are the drinks with this food.

★★HATSUHANA

17 East 48th Street, 237 Park Avenue
LUNCH AND DINNER. CLOSED SUNDAY. PARK AVENUE STORE CLOSED SATURDAY AND SUNDAY.
Reservations: 355-3345, 661-3400.
Credit cards: AE, DC, MC, V.
Medium priced.

Japanese morsel food focuses the attention. Not only does it do away with certain of the distracting mechanics of eating—particularly for maladroit chopstick manipulators —it also concentrates a more or less complex culinary thought in a single mouthful. Eating Japanese is to eating Western as the haiku is to a fat novel. Consuming, for example, a single nugget of sushi is not one of a series of scenes of cumulative power (as is, for example, one of twenty forkloads of spaghetti bolognese). It is, rather, the entire act, and not much altered by repeating it. At the two restaurants called Hatsuhana, a single meal often consists of many small acts.

The restaurants are known especially for their sushi, and in sushi basics, they cannot be faulted: vinegared rice in which the sweetness and tartness are nicely balanced, as are the stickiness of the rice and the firmness of the individual grains; seaweed wrappers that are tender and a little sea-gamy; wondrously heady thin-sliced fresh ginger; and an especially potent wasabi, the searing radish with which you fortify the good house soy sauce. Beefy tuna, delicate yellowtail, and soothing fluke are among the impeccably fresh finfish you may have mounted on that rice, the last named prepared with bits of wasabi tucked under the little fillet. Other rice-bottomed packages in this department: shafts of shrimp—very crunchy, but of rather mild flavor; sweet pink crabmeat belted to the rice with a ribbon of deep green seaweed; orange fish roe, the glistening globules and rice packed into a squat seaweed tube; and this establishment's excellent California roll, in which the cylindrical constructs are built with the seaweed near the center, the outer walls of sticky rice dotted with clinging sesame seeds.

More morsels: Hatsuhana dumplings, the firm (not tough) noodle wrappers packed with mildly seasoned meat—you liven the nuggets by dipping them in a dark and salty sauce; unagikyuri maki, thin, cool disks of eel, dark and oily, enclosed in circles of crisp cucumber; Japanese fried chicken, the remarkable little chunks of deep-fried but greaseless bird well browned and of an almost airy delicacy—you may dip them in soy sauce, but that overpowers them, so you squeeze on the supplied lemon instead, which livens the chicken without obscuring its flavor; Japanese fried tiny crabs (the largest of them less than an inch across from claw tip to opposite claw tip), which you dip in soy sauce and eat whole—they are hot-oiled, almost as hard as walnut shells, have a fugitive flavor that is at once nutty and slightly oceanic, are noisy to chew, and may, like the pebbles certain creatures swallow, aid digestion; what goes as "avocado salad," two quarters of firm but utterly ripe avocado topped with mounds of glinting salmon roe and set in a cloud of seaweed—you are proffered a spoon and told, "You eat this with a spoon"; broiled duck and scallion, the warm slices of rich meat, bone and skin still attached, in a gentle sauce—sharp bits of scallion green are a nice contrast to the oleaginous bird; boiled beef with ginger, the thin slices of tender meat suffused with ginger flavor—sesame seeds add a bit of texture; eggplant with miso sauce, the sharp peanut- and sesame-flavored sauce a good foil to the hot and meaty vegetable.

Very little in the way of desserts—you try some papaya, and it is not really ripe.

Both stores are clean, well lighted, somewhat antiseptic places: the one on 48th Street is an upstairs and a downstairs, a sushi bar on each level; the "Park Avenue" location (it is not really on Park, but is connected to the Park Avenue Atrium, which is on Lexington) is a sleeker, slicker one-level place with glass walls looking onto an open arcade between the cross streets.

190

★★★ HUBERTS

575 Park Avenue (entrance on 63rd Street)
LUNCH, MONDAY TO FRIDAY; DINNER, DAILY.
Reservations: 826-5911.
Credit cards: AE, DC, MC, V.
Very expensive.

Though born in the legendary borough of Brooklyn, and raised in the old neighborhood around Gramercy Park, Huberts has chosen to shrug off its historic past, has
removed to Park Avenue—the *real* Park Avenue, Upper East Side Park Avenue—and, in
the grand tradition of millions before who worked their way uptown as they climbed the
economic ladder, no nostalgic signs of humbler days are on display in the new digs.
There, however, the parallels part, for when Huberts acquired the new money to make
its move, it revealed that, somewhere along the way, it had acquired a style usually
associated with older coin. The new Huberts is that rarity, a dining room that, though
indubitably luxurious, panders not at all to the common taste for common denominator
posh. This is luxury, you understand, but you know it not by any resemblance to upper-
middle-class living rooms or three-hundred-dollar-a-night-hotel lobbies. You know it,
rather, because you are instantly comfortable, and because the creation of this commodious environment was in the hands, clearly, of an imagination both practical and free.
While the place fills all the usual needs, it ignores innumerable conventions.

Moreover, it achieves its dramatic effect within a seemingly narrow range of tones.
Huberts is all the so-called earth colors, beiges and browns and tans, darkened reds and
dusty pinks and bronzes, to which the strongest contrasts are a bit of black (the armchair
frames) and a good bit more of honey-stained oak varnished to a glass finish. You enter to
a large anteroom, its focus the glinting semicircle of polished wood that is this establishment's snappy bar. To your left are subsidiary rooms, the restaurant's smaller dining room
and a clubby lounge with black leather sofas. To your right is the main dining room,
which you enter through a portal that, flanked by freestanding, high, arched, oaken
fences, is like a gateway with its golden gates opened wide. The room itself, oblong and
high ceilinged, seems, by architectural sleight of hand, to be windowed on three sides,
though one of the sides is an interior wall, and none of the windows—all backlighted—
can be seen through. The windows (and "windows") are broad, reach to the ceiling, and
their panes, of various sizes and shapes, are of smoked glass or vaguely pink silk, are
framed and divided by that handsome, grainy oak, are set in walls that, though they
mock weathered masonry, by way of their intricately mottled coloring—which incorporates an almost invisible patina of pale gold—make an impact that is at once granitic and
warm. A cushy banquette runs along the room's rear wall, its back a delicate geometric
pattern of dark claret on a pale ground, its seat a glowing velvet of coppery brown. The
velvet appears again on the seats of the black-wood armchairs, and the floor is covered
with plush carpeting, the stripes of which—sand and deep raspberry—seem to shimmer.
There are flowers in each corner of the room, and their primary colors are brilliant in
this setting. Only the uniforms on the help—Cambridge-gray pleated trousers, gun-

metal-gray shirts, and white wing collars with black bowties—seem to have been chosen in disregard of the looks of the rest of the place. Ladies, of course, will wear black dresses or red ones, but gents will have to give up the whole game, for every business suit in the house looks tepid in the glow and umbered solidity of these surroundings.

It is not any comparison with the setting, however, that makes for your disappointment with these crabmeat pirogi, rather that the pouchlike pastries are of that cakey dullness you know so well from certain lesser fortune cookies, which is too bad, for their crabmeat filling is fresh and sweet, and the greened butter in which the constructs are set enriches and livens them. With respect to this fettuccine, however, you may find that you forget your surroundings entirely, for the good broad noodles, threaded with bits of spinach, are mingled with crisped, browned, sticky-rich morsels of sweetbread, and with plump oysters that, though warmed through, retain all their raw ocean flavor—the dish is moistened with a bit of sauce that is herbed, light, and creamy. At this point in culinary time, you must do something striking for notice to be taken of a cheese soufflé, and making it of Roquefort is hardly enough, for that kind of variant has been around almost as long as the basic soufflé itself. Still, this browned, fluffy, and moist little column, of restrained but vivid Roquefort flavor, is so well balanced as to its solidity and lightness, the acidic apple-flavored sauce in which it is set so much its nifty flavor foil, and the strands of pickled cabbage in the sauce so striking a contrast of texture, that the old soufflé is almost a new dish. There are those for whom the particular appeal of this establishment's rabbit sausage is the garnish of two little rabbits sculpted out of green apples—white bodies, apple-green ears, tiny red spots for eyes. You, however, will note that the sausage is solid but not heavy, peppery and juicy, and that the thick, dark molé sauce in which it is set, which sports a strong chocolate edge, is vibrant of its hot spice.

The grilled lobster reaches you out of its shell in a complex poblano pepper sauce that is smoky, nubbly, a little rich—there is much of this tender lobster meat, and it is nicely garnished with asparagus spears and with broad noodles, and its sauce is dark and earthy. Within a browned surface of such evenness that it appears painted on, your utterly fresh salmon is pale pink, glistening with moisture—the good fish is garnished with a cucumber-and-melon relish, heady with coriander, from which a delicately fruity moisture forms a pool around the seafood. With respect to the bird, the roast duck is a simple affair, except for the striking treatment of its skin, which is a deep, crisped brown (almost, but not, black) under which is the layer of fat responsible for the juiciness and strong duck flavor of the meat—a good cinnamoned, cinnamon-colored poached pear is the gesture to the fruit-with-duck-tradition, but the principal garnish is a vegetable strudel that, roused with ginger, converts this compacture of bits and pieces, within its flaky pastry, into a memorable eggroll. The rack of lamb, cut into four chops, is wondrous meat, tender, blood-juicy and of potent lamb flavor, but its garnish of goat-cheese lasagne is from another—macaroni-and-cheese—world.

What the house calls a sugar cone looks like a flower—with assorted petals of crisp, sugared pastry—mounted on a large white-wine glass. The thing is packed with a prune fool, which is to say whipped cream mixed with a mash of the fruit and, in this instance, Armagnac, the fool in turn adorned with prune halves, and with straight whipped cream on top. While the fool is poised to fly off, the plum strudel is firmly planted on its plate in a film of buttery plum sauce, the delicate, sugar-whited sleeve of pastry packed with a chunky, sweet-spiced mix of fruit and nuts, on the side that good house whipped cream again. You may consider "strawberry roulade" a misnomer for these three ovoids of white cake, for though they are clearly cut from a roulade, the pink and tan creams (strawberry and chocolate) with which the cake was painted before it was rolled up have little impact other than that of a moistness—the garnishes, spiced figs and delicately basil-flavored ice cream, are the life of the plate. Another unlikely ice cream, this one tinctured with nasturtium, accompanies the blood-orange tartlets, three crackling little pastry cups, a dab of custard in each, and sweet, juicy sections of the red citrus.

★ HULOT'S

1007 Lexington Avenue (near 72nd Street)
LUNCH, MONDAY TO FRIDAY; DINNER, MONDAY TO SATURDAY. CLOSED SUNDAY.
Reservations: 794-9800.
Credit cards: AE, MC, V.
Expensive.

As all the world knows, the so-called New American Cooking is French. In some of its forms it reveals other influences as well, Mexican, Japanese, and Italian among them. But in none of its guises is it domestic. Everything about it, in fact, is imaginable without American, how you say, input. Were the continental forty-eight still unexplored, the nonexistence of this cookery would be attributable solely to a shortage of Americans willing to pay for it. Now, the interests behind two of New York's preeminent NAC restaurants have dropped their masks and revealed their true identities, have opened a bistro wherein they purvey what they have always purveyed: French food, but this time sans New American trappings. The establishment's success suggests that locals would have settled for the undisguised article all along.

Perhaps to exaggerate the French vs. American differences between Hulot's and its predecessors, the combine has taken on, for this place, a French associate, complete with French accent, apparently with the understanding that the fellow will make himself highly visible here in ways that Americans think of, rightly or wrongly, as French. Like the constant husband of the jealous wife who, having been falsely called adulterer one time too often, decides, since he has been convicted, to perform the crime, M. Oliver (for that is your host's name), standing in for the French as a race, has elected to assume the superciliousness with which his countrymen have often been charged. You have, say, reserved a table, and you arrive, say, at seven, to a restaurant only a third full. Oliver checks your name against his book and, with a curt nod of the head, suggests you follow him. He leads you to a table that comfortably accommodates two plates, salt, pepper, and perhaps an elbow, a table that, moreover, is not only convenient to the men's room, but, being hard by the wide-open kitchen, is fanned throughout dinner by the scents and warmth of that operation. You object, point out that other quite unoccupied tables are less divertingly situated. The man does not disagree with you, you understand, for that would honor your position. Rather, by an exasperated aversion of the eyes, he makes it clear that, once he has decided where you are to sit, elsewhere is, willy-nilly, unthinkable. His pained last glance and unconvincing "I'm sorry, monsieur," make it clear that at the moment his dearest wish in life is for your instant disappearance. And his studiedly indifferent shrug when you offer an impossible suggestion indicates he has received that advice before.

Remain for dinner, and get a central table, and you are certain to spot him in at least two or three altercations, of an evening, with soon-to-be-former customers. It is not that his position is invariably without merit, rather that his apparent inexperience with anything other than complaisance has the poor fellow constantly dyspeptic with ill-processed frustration. Naturally his outlets are his underlings. "Check on table nineteen!" he barks, the angle from horizontal of his extended stiff right arm in need of but five more degrees of elevation for the gesture to take on political significance. That emergency out of the way, he proceeds to make a great show of getting the floor staff caught up, picking up orders from the kitchen counter and marching them to their destinations with a thumping stride that, somehow, echoes the outstretched arm. Find yourself in his path, and you get glared at. The fellow even has a black mustache. Hulot's is a front room and a back room, the corridor between them the site of the kitchen and, across a narrow aisle—often crowded with waiters and waitresses at their tasks—five marvelously tiny tables for two. Such accommodations may be suitable for folks who walk in off the street without reservations, who can then either take or leave what is available; but when those who reserve ahead discover that what they have reserved is one of these, enraged disbelief is sometimes the reaction, even from the easygoing. The front room is a row of tables for four opposite the bar, the back room, under its skylight, a banquette around three sides and a few tables at the center.

Throughout, the tables are covered with white linen, the non-banquette seating is on Paris café chairs, the floor is of red tiles, and the lighting is soft but not low. A few old Jacques Tati movie posters are the only distractions, though observers who get tables in the narrows learn, before the evening is out, that tossing a salad with the fingers is standard restaurant-kitchen practice, and that the chicken on a plate is very likely nudged into its position by caressing hands. But be assured that this observed kitchen is a tidier operation than thousands of the unobserved. Some of the waiters and waitresses are French—mostly they demonstrate that Oliver's choice of manner is a personal, not a national, preference, though on occasion one of them will become impatient with customers who have neglected to master bistro French before coming here, for nary a word of English sullies the menu.

That kitchen accommodates a staff of only three, so the menu is brief—on occasion the first and main courses amount to fewer than a dozen dishes all told, most of them elementary items: a cold mound of crunchy green beans and slivers of fresh mushroom over leaves of endive, the creamy, slightly acidic dressing dotted with fresh herbs; a couple of fat disks of warm goat cheese on crusts of toasted French bread, those in turn set on fresh greens dressed with excellent olive oil; pencil-thin shafts of tepid asparagus, lots of them, strewn with fresh parsley, and dressed to excellent effect with walnut oil; pissaladière, the rectangle of breadlike pastry overlaid with sautéed onions and tomatoes, those in turn sprinkled with parsley and dotted with bits of black olive, the whole surrounded by leaves of crisp, fresh, sharp arugula.

Come when both lotte and halibut are offered, and you will do well to pass up the former (it is strewn with lemon thyme, but that does not alter the blandness of the fish itself) in favor of the halibut meunière, the sweet oceanic flavor of the delicately crisped fillets livened by the browned butter in which they are done. The grilled half chicken has a good bit of chicken flavor for so small a bird, and though it is moist, it is handsomely browned and cooked through—it comes with scalloped potatoes that, though they could be creamier, have crusty edges and vivid potato flavor. The huge slice of gigot d'agneau just about covers its plate—the tender pink meat is of strong lamb flavor, the homey dish completed with an assortment of vegetables that, like all the vegetable garnishes here, are cooked through but not overdone.

The tarte Tatin is dark and mushy, conditions for which the dollop of crème fraîche

194

served with it does not compensate. Big chunks of charred red plum form a kind of lunar surface on the plum tart—the fruit is a little sour, the dessert rousing. When blackberries are in season, this place gets good ones—neither gritty nor soft nor sour—and serves them as little individual tarts, much smooth custard between the fruit and the dark pastry. Order the mousse, and you get a small ramekin filled with a pale and cool, sticky and creamy milk-chocolate goo—it is at once rich and lively.

The place is popular—most folks simply overlook Oliver's tics.

★ INDOCHINE

430 Lafayette Street (near Astor Place)
DINNER.
Reservations: 505-5111.
Credit cards: AE, DC, MC, V.
Medium priced.

Myths have attached themselves to this place, mainly to the effect that it is hard to get into, is insular, caters to an artsy crowd, gives the back of its hand to interlopers who are not regulars on its scene. The facts are that to get a reservation here you need only telephone, though calling late in the day may be too late; that you will be seated (once your group is complete) in turn; that the crowd is more of business than of the arts, more before and after the Public Theater (across the street) than from the East Village or SoHo or NoHo, mostly go unrecognized by the management, are all treated about as well as the utterly casual staff knows how—though the young waitresses in their assorted outfits do direct more breathless attention to gentlemen in carefully unmatched clothing than to squares in suits and ties. The appeal of the place is plain: The prices are not high, the food is not bad (though not what it was when Indochine was new), the accommodations are comfortable, relaxation reigns. All you have to know is your way around the menu.

Indochine is a big, rectangular place, up front yellow-tile window seats under the two windows, tables and wicker chairs near them where you may sit while waiting to be seated, a short bar—you may wait there instead—and a lectern on which rests the book in which reservations are recorded. Your name is found there by a young chap, in a shirt buttoned to the neck, the collar turned up, who scratches his head while he looks, finds, and hands you over to the slender giantess—in two-inch platform sandals, modest over-the-knee stockings, white shorts that appear to have been angrily ripped from the legs of pajama bottoms, and a buffalo plaid shirt—who will lead you (she is easy to follow) to your table. The dining room is a rectangle rimmed with a green banquette that, along the long north wall, is formed into the big semicircular booths that are this room's choice seating. The place has been made to seem vaguely subtropical-Asian by the big green fronds painted on the walls, by the palms that stand here and there, by the exotic flowers on the tables. But a single coat of paint, and this mostly Vietnamese (but also Thai and Cambodian) restaurant could be any brand of eating place at all. The early crowd is here after the office. You do not get the tattoos and shaved heads, the illustrated sweatshirts and bared navels until, when no one is looking, the folks who clean the offices after the first shift has departed, duck into phone booths, switch out of their uniforms into their civvies, and, from towers all over town, head for Lafayette Street.

Be it understood, no one who serves you speaks the language of this menu. Try to order, say, moine chha khnay phonetically, and your waitress comes around to stand beside you and suggest that you point at the menu entry to which you refer. Happily, the dishes are numbered, and ordering by the numbers is the custom. Nhom lor hong, for example, is better known as Number 10, thin-sliced shrimp over a mound of what the menu calls green papaya, which seems like shredded cabbage to you, the interleaved fresh basil and the chopped peanuts on top the principal interest of the dish. Number 13 is another shrimp dish, this one livelier, the seafood mingled with mint and red peppers in its sharp and sweet lemon-grass dressing. If you liked 13, you will like 14 even more, the same dish, but with pearly sheets of squid in place of the shrimp. A dish that goes as goi ga, Number 11, is yet another cold salad, this one of shredded chicken on greens, the chicken of good flavor, the greens of good texture—a bit of basil livens the item. If you favor the spicy-hot beef salads served in Thai restaurants, its relative is here, going as Number 12, nhom sath ko, the cold and tender beef in a fiery marinade, with lemon grass and strands of red pepper—the spiciness of this dish accumulates in your mouth, mounts in intensity as you eat it. Still, for many there is but one first course at Indochine, what is given as steamed Vietnamese ravioli—Number 16, banh coun—which arrives in a lidded bamboo basket, the contents four square packets formed of a kind of doughy noodle, each stuffed with a moist and well seasoned filling of vegetables and mushrooms, all of which you moisten with a bit of the pink, fruity, mildly spicy sauce—the degree of hotness varies from time to time—that is served with this and many other dishes here.

It is well to know that at Indochine there is safety in finfish, danger in anything fried. Come here just once, and you will do well to consider nothing but Number 25, amok cambodgien, fillets of fresh fish steamed in a banana leaf, a dish that reaches you as a tentlike package formed of the great leaf, within it the meat of the fish, firm and juicy and permeated with the flavors of the coconut milk and lemon grass in which it was done. Barring that, you will do almost as well with Number 27, trei chom huy khnay, a steamed whole fish that, on lucky days, is a sweetwater trout, the swimmer overlaid with strands of ginger and set in a pool of the strongly seasoned and oily broth in which it was done—the fish is fresh, firm, juicy, of vivid trout flavor. The menu does not so state, but Number 31, annkep chha kroeung, frogs' legs in coconut milk and lemon grass, is fried—anyway, the lightly battered surfaces of the legs are greasy, which is too bad, for they are otherwise plump and meaty. Similarly Number 28, the stuffed boneless chicken wings (you are served legs, not wings), the handsomely browned constructs packed with a lively herbed forcemeat of ground chicken, lemon grass, rice noodles—but, once again, greasy. You will do well to avoid also the roast chicken and roast duck, which seem to have been roasted in advance, are tired. Your waitress has been trained to ask if you want rice. You do not want the sticky rice, Number 44, which tastes like sweet cake, but you will do all right with Number 55, plain rice dotted with peas, bits of ham, egg.

Among the (Western) desserts, the key lime pie and lemon tart are lively of their respective citrus fruits, the berry tarts are of good berries on a somewhat doughy pastry, the hazelnut mousse an excess of richness not quite corrected by the good chopped nuts buried in it.

★ JACQUELINE'S

132 East 61st Street
LUNCH, MONDAY TO FRIDAY; DINNER, MONDAY TO SATURDAY. CLOSED SUNDAY.
Reservations: 838-4559.
Credit cards: AE, DC, MC, V.
Expensive.

Jacqueline gets into something comfortable before she comes to work, for she, herself, is going to initiate you into the romantic mood of her place. She is in light, white, loose-fitting trousers and tunic, there is a colorful scarf draped casually around her neck, and you know from her manner that at any moment she may flick it at you and then smile coyly. Jacqueline has excellent English that becomes music under the influence of her French accent, and as she leads you—nay, coaxes you—toward a corner table at the black banquette opposite her bar, she tells you about her restaurant, that it is a *champagne* restaurant, that in addition to bottled champagne, she sells half a dozen bubblies by the glass, that she also sells so-called elixirs, which are champagne cocktails, e.g., champagne with peach liqueur ("Renoir"), with strawberry liqueur ("ruby"), with raspberry liqueur ("infatuation"). When Jacquie gets you seated, she more or less tucks you in with loose cushions she tosses into your general vicinity, presumably for purposes of your swooning onto. Her place is, of course, dimly lit, consists of that bar (the long-stemmed flowers at intervals along its length are dramatically illuminated by pinpoint spotlights overhead), the snug row of tables along the banquette across the aisle, and a slightly curtained-off little square room just to the rear—it is furnished with a banquette all around, before it a handful of side-by-side tables for two, plus a couple of corner tables, also for two. The background music is soft and jazzy, the crowd is here for the atmosphere, and the food, billed as "Swiss/French," is nothing of the kind—still, it is mostly good.

Jacqueline does move a lot of champagne, and the worldly and good-humored young women who are her floor staff are expected to convert service of the stuff into something of a rite. The cork is removed noiselessly, and, when pouring, your waitress must hold the bottle by its bottom, thumb up its punt. If you are spotted about to pour your own, choking the bottle rather than violating it, a staffer hastens by to take over the task and do it right. Put aside received ideas, confront the evidence of your palate, and you will realize that champagne, for all its charms, is poor wine for most food. But its capacity to make an event celebratory is such that it always seems right with foods that are themselves luxe, as, for example, this terrine of foie gras, the smooth, pink, and buttery slices of cool and fatted meat served on fresh greens in a tart dressing—you will probably find that you are simply uninterested in judging whether champagne and that compacture of rich livers are meant for each other. But then there are dishes not so readily reconciled to your blanc de blancs: Louisiana shrimp that are sweet, blackened in the pan, very nice with the warm, spicy, and cilantro flavored chopped tomatoes on which they are served; so-called "cremini" mushrooms, very fresh and very charred, mingled with red peppers and with minced jalapeño peppers, both nice foils to the mushrooms' woodsiness; a more than decent pasta dish in which the firm linguine are in a red seafood sauce—shrimp

197

and scallops—that is sweetened with onions, made nubbly with minced zucchini.

Each day there are a couple of fish of the day, sometimes halibut, the poached fillet fresh, a little overcooked, a little underflavored, and in a pale, winy sauce that is thick with vegetables. The sautéed sea scallops are browned and rich, but the sea urchin that is a billed element of their otherwise decent red sauce is a remote element at best. The roasted poussin sports lots of chicken flavor for such a little bird. And the mildly gar-licked sautéed rabbit is much pale and tender meat, nicely browned on the bone, the warm salad greens served with it a sharp contrast to the solid game.

You will find a bit more sugar than you want in the smooth, intensely chocolate flavored pot au crème. A warm berry sauce does not quite rescue the cold lemon soufflé, which is rubbery. The cherry-blueberry tart is an absence of cherries, a presence of many fresh, firm, ripe blueberries, a dull pastry.

The menu is a champagne list on the left, a food list on the right.

★★JANE STREET SEAFOOD CAFÉ

31 Eighth Avenue (at Jane Street)
DINNER.
No reservations: (243-9237).
Credit cards: AE, DC, MC, V.
Medium priced.

You show up without a reservation (reservations are not taken), and a gent with a note pad takes your name, gives you the word: "We're looking at a ten or fifteen area, maybe quicker, okay?" You and the handful ahead of you are clustered around what looks like a bar, but is not, is, rather, the serving station at which the waiters and waitresses in this busy place pick up drinks and bottles of wine. There is, however, just inside the front door, a couple of feet of counter at which two may stand as at a real bar. The trick is to get the attention of the service bartender during a pause in his occupation. He will serve you drinks, or a bottle of wine that you can start now and finish later with your dinner, and he will take payment. You put up your money, and the man burrows under the counter, comes up with a cash drawer that probably was once part of a cash register, makes change. By this time you have figured out that when you enter the Jane Street Seafood Café, you separate yourself from New York, from this era, from your usual expectations. In this place the salmon is never rare, the tuna is never raw, the oysters are never wrapped in rose petals. Which is not to say, bring back the good old days, rather that if you are interested, here they are.

Brick all around, a floor of unfinished wood, lots of tables (unlinened), four-bladed fans hanging from the stamped-tin ceiling, folksy art on the walls—a sailing ship made of cut brass sheets, an indeterminate composition made of the bells of bugles and trom-bones and the like, the inevitable, presumably handwoven, rug. The effect is of the principal eating place in a New England seaside town, insulated from the raw weather, warmed by the press of humanity. The sneakered, jeaned, flannel-shirted crowd—in winter their coats and sweaters and scarves are hung over the backs of their chairs—are dressed as for a hike in the woods.

None of which would be worth noting if, say, these bluepoints were not sparkling, but, like all the Café's seafood, the oysters are utterly fresh, their distinctive flavor—oil and brine and a bit of metal—in no need of the lemon or, certainly, the cocktail sauce that is provided. You do well to stick with raw oysters, for the baked ones, in their redded breading, have lost their character in the making. Not so the tiny littlenecks as clams cassino, in which the warmed but tender clams, in their shells, are covered over with a light, crusty breading and crisped bacon. Order steamers, and you are served enough of them for you and a friend; with your fingers you pluck them from their chalky white shells, unclothe their necks, rinse them in the cup of hot broth that is provided (which usually, but not invariably, washes away the last of their sand), dip them in melted butter, and mindlessly work your way through a dozen or so of the inexplicably hypnotic meats. The cocktail sauce and lemon that you scorned for your oysters are quite appropriate to the fried squid, high-class boardwalk food that is a good carrier of one or both. Ditto the fried zucchini.

About as well as a lobster may be steamed, it is here steamed. It is neither toughened nor drained of its juices, it is tender and of vivid flavor, and the morsels of it take on a handsome polish when you immerse them in melted butter. It is too bad that you cannot count on one of the Café's best dishes, swordfish broiled in wine and herbs. It gets less attention than that lobster, is sometimes done until it is dry and stringy, though when it is good it is memorable. Bluefish, a plentiful species in nearby waters, is nowadays perceived as coarse and inelegant, has almost disappeared from New York restaurants (other than straight American seafood places like this one). Here it is fresh and cheap, and it has lost none of its almost meaty flavor since the last time you had it. Order salmon, and you are asked if you want a fillet or a steak. Either way the fish is fine, and the pale, thick, and obvious dill sauce served with it reaches you, happily, in a jigger, need never touch the fish. Snapper, pompano, scrod, shark, and trout are among the many varieties that from time to time are available, and almost invariably you get them well prepared.

The chocolate desserts—among them a dense and rough-textured mud cake and a truly silken chocolate silk pie—are the best. The pecan pie is a more than decent version of the usual thing, and the strawberry rhubarb pie, a little sweet and very tart, is rousing.

★ JEAN LAFITTE

68 West 58th Street
LUNCH, MONDAY TO FRIDAY; DINNER, DAILY.
Reservations: 751-2323.
Credit cards: AE, DC, MC, V.
Medium priced.

Another evocation of old Paris, all dark-honey-colored wood trimmed with brass, sconces and chandeliers in the gracefully curving Art Nouveau manner, here and there handsomely framed posters and great, plain rectangular mirrors on the walls. Before the deep-red banquette that rims the big room, the tables are set with snowy linen and with simple, glinting crystal, china, flatware. Naturally the place is patrolled by gentlemen in black and white, and happily, they croak at you, intelligently and politely, in the guttural

French of genuine bistro waiters imported from the old country, which means that they neither introduce themselves by name, nor in any other way betray the assumption that citizens go to restaurants to meet waiters.

The original Jean Lafitte was the French pirate who, in return for his cooperation against the British during the War of 1812, was pardoned by President Madison for his prior sins. The significance of this, of course, will not be lost on you.

Jean Lafitte (the restaurant) was apparently intended to fill a gap in its chosen neighborhood, for the area is one in which no magnet for fashionable folk has taken hold. You do see some dressy types here, especially at cocktail time, when the little marble tables just across the aisle from the short bar up front are choked with depressed ladies who are resting their tired tootsies after hours of frustrating Fifth Avenue shopping. (In this crowd, it is a wasted day when Bonwit's has left them with enough change for an icy, revivifying Lillet—over which, you may be sure, they muster fresh determination to go forth again tomorrow.) But mostly the place draws folk from nearby office buildings grabbing a bite after working late; music lovers before and after Carnegie Hall; and residents of Central Park South who have discovered that this place, whatever its high-toned intentions, is actually more straightforward than any of those on their own famous thoroughfare.

You will not, for example, find herring on Central Park South, but Lafitte offers great firm strands of the soured seafood, served with a plain salad of potatoes in vinaigrette. The gravlax here is simple and impeccable—gentle, supple, cured salmon, a little sweetness and a clear dill flavor imparted by its delicate marinade, served without a sauce. Sometimes the house offers what it calls a cassolette of oysters—the fresh mollusks, out of their shells, are warmed and mellowed in a buttery saffron sauce that is threaded with thin strands of green beans. The good pâté is rimmed with white fat, dotted with pistachio nuts, garnished with sharp-tasting sprigs of mâche and with firm, curly leaves of red lettuce. What is given as crottin de chavignol roti is a big knob of hot, baked goat cheese, brought to you on a slab of warm, slightly toasted buttered bread—a first course that manages to be both satisfying and stimulating. When it comes to the pasta of the day, your French waiter, determined not to commit to memory information about foods from the lands outside his native borders, must consult his notes to tell you that today the pasta is fusilli in an anchovy sauce. You, too, will do well to forget it, for the noodle is tough, the red sauce—despite its anchovies, capers, olives—flat.

The place obtains Dover sole, poaches the fresh-tasting fillets, serves them in two sauces—one pink with red pepper, the other green with fresh herbs. The quite nice shrimp are crunchy, free of iodine, and they are served in a creamy sauce that is thick with fragrant dill. Virtually anything on the menu is a good reason to avoid the house chicken. The bird is well roasted, but it started out and ended up tasteless. Have instead, for example, these two little crescents of sautéed liver in a mustard sauce that clings to the pink meat. Or have gigot, the three slabs of strong roasted lamb, rare at the center, in a dark sauce that is mostly the blood of the meat, with firm but tender white beans. One dish has the house name on it—Boeuf Jean Lafitte. The help has been trained to tell the Americans that this is beef "prepared like pot au feu, but it is not pot au feu." Anyway, it is boiled beef, it has been simmered in a strong stock, it has a pungent flavor, it is garnished with little mounds of well-prepared vegetables of various hues, and it is served with one dish of horseradish and another of herbed mayonnaise—which sauce you choose says a great deal about you.

The waiter who says the boiled beef is like pot au feu also says the roulade de pommes is like strudel. He is right. In fact, it is strudel, but not a special one, just hot, dull apples in a flaky, sugar-strewn pastry, served mit schlag. The praline cake is a jellied, layered thing of cloying sweetness. The chocolate cake is the familiar sweet of these days—thick mousse between layers of deep, dark cake, whipped cream on the side. The pear tart—slivers of pear on a cakelike pastry—has a fruity liveliness, to which the rich whipped cream garnish is a good foil.

★ JOCKEY CLUB

112 Central Park South
LUNCH AND DINNER.
Reservations: 664-7700.
Credit cards: AE, DC, MC, V.
Very expensive.

Here is haute cuisine in a British pub. The food is mostly good, and the rooms are entirely comfortable, but the disconsonance of styles reflects the absence of a point of view. The restaurant is less than the sum of its estimable parts because you are in a hotel, one of a chain, and the products of corporate managerial compromise cannot compete with those of human imagination—or, as in restaurants, human fantasy.

You enter to what is presumably the taproom, one room of five, and seeing one, you have seen the five. The walls of the place, every inch, are surfaced with knotted wood, and they are hung with a truckload of English oils, very horsey and doggy, but with here and there the depiction of a little flock of sheep, or hale gentlemen around a tavern table, or a bare-fisted prizefighter, his dukes up, posing for his portrait. Some member of the committee insisted on flowers and pink linen on the tables. The stiff side chairs, inevitably, are done in "leather" that is held in place by upholstery nails with big brass heads. The best seating is on the banquettes, which, though also of "leather," are cushy as down.

The menu, too, is a distinct comfort—to those who long for culinary yesteryear (and the place does get more than its share of those, from this neighborhood, whose families have been occupying apartments overlooking lower Central Park since the days when Frederick Olmsted himself used to revisit the place to rant at rocks and boulders no longer in their assigned positions). They are very content with the assortment of hors d'oeuvres: cool, fresh poached salmon of vivid salmon flavor; crisp cucumber salad, sweet, sour, and touched with dill; crunchy shrimp in a pinked mayonnaise dressing; and asparagus and haricots verts, both of which have become limp and lifeless in the hours since they were done. And they are much at home with the smoked salmon, a great sheet of it, pale pink and delicate, across a big plate. What are listed as "terrines & pâtés" turn out to be one country pâté and one game pâté, the former chunky and studded with pistachios, the latter strong and marbled with fat, both well made, not overbaked, pink —you are offered with them four little dishes of condiment, hot mustard, grainy mustard, and, presumably in anticipation of odd requests from transient residents upstairs, ketchup and horseradish. The ravioli are a big winner—they are filled with a red forcemeat of ground lobster, and they are served in a pale sauce, rich and light, that has been sharpened with the flavor of lobster shell.

Black grill marks adorn the firm, moist salmon steak, which is served with a sauce béarnaise that is powerful of fresh tarragon, and with boiled potatoes that have the texture of wet snowballs. The quenelles of pike are as fluffy as fish dumplings ever are, but they have very little of the distinctive pike flavor that characterizes this dish at its best—they reach you set in a rich white sauce that has been browned under the broiler, and with a mound of white rice. The roast chicken is half a big bird, the skin browned, the meat of exceptionally clear chicken flavor, the whole slicked with yet another fragrantly tarragoned sauce. Good steaks and chops, including lamb chops (two doubles, in case you are counting) that are blackened, blood-pink at the core, served without a sauce.

The cheese, your waiter lets you know, is in the refrigerator and should remain there. He allows as how the hot soufflés are good, but is sorry to inform you that they are prepared neither on Sundays nor Mondays. You opt for the frozen raspberry soufflé instead, and you get a cold pink disk the size of a hockey puck—it is richer than mere ice cream, stands in an intense raspberry sauce, is surrounded by ripe berries. You may have those berries separately—with loose whipped cream. The floating island is airy, its crème anglaise watery. Avoid the almond meringue cake, a sugary layered affair of pastry creams and meringue encased in leathery slivered almonds.

• JOHN CLANCY'S EAST

206 East 63rd Street
LUNCH, MONDAY TO FRIDAY; DINNER, DAILY.
Reservations: 752-6666.
Credit cards: AE, DC, MC, V.
Expensive.

A branch of the Greenwich Village original, the kitchen of the new Clancy's replicates the cooking of the old one, bringing closer to home food that lured many an Upper East Sider down to Sheridan Square. Many old fans are not, however, happy with the new place. The food is the same, but it is not reinforced by the setting in which they were first persuaded of its excellence—and in the clear light of another context, it is seen for what it has always been. The Clancy's expansion may thus be the instrument of its undoing. If you are inclined to spot a moral in this irony, be assured there is none.

The Clancy myth lives because in the restaurant's early days there was a real, live, if sometimes observably tipsy, Clancy on the downtown premises. Though his hokey reputation was as a chef, he appeared to spend more time at the front door (right next to the bar) than in the kitchen. Anyway, he had been a fixture on New York's food scene for years, and his connections to culinary opinion makers did not hurt his notices. He is no longer part of the Clancy operation, and though the food is not a tenth of its reputation, it is actually marginally better today than it was in his time.

Clancy's East occupies the premises that once were the restaurant Moon's, which was done up in hunting lodge posh—clubby wood paneling, giant mirrors mounted on walls of raw brick, polished oak floors, all that. Among the new tenants' few alterations are little assemblages stuck up here and there, clusters of souvenir shop *objets de la mer*. Otherwise the site is at once solid and barren, Grand Rapids luxe that nothing can ever humanize.

It is a rare kitchen that can make a ragout of wild mushrooms and, in the process, separate from the main ingredients all their woodsy flavor. This one can do it. It can also invent—or dig up—a dish called tuna chili that can be made into bean chili by elimination of the tuna, and thereby improved—the fish is utterly lost in this setting. The house calls them "broiled oysters with sundried tomato butter"—maybe, but they masquerade as warmed oysters under crumbled toast. Happily, you may forgo all that and seek safety in this establishment's superb gravlax, the sliced fish firm and tender, heady of dill, and yet of sweet ocean flavor. It is served with rich, tart crème fraîche and with salmon caviar that, though extraneous, is unimpeachable—the giant red-orange orbs are fresh, burst in your mouth like little grapes, are sweet, briny, bracing.

Lobster Américaine has always been listed under the Clancy's heading "specialties of the house," even though the dish bears only casual resemblance to the genuine article— and suffers for its deviations. This is just lobster, in the shell, in part tough, in part mushy, and in place of the complex sauce that is the real thing, in a seemingly blenderized hash. The mesquite-grilled Dover sole is Dover sole, sure enough, but you have to concentrate hard to find its distinctive flavor—the flavor of the mesquite grilling is clear (and is not the cause of the sole's pallidness). Similarly the California striped bass, which is judiciously done, the meat juicy under its crisped skin and sprinkling of toasted cashew nuts, but the fish itself is tasteless, nameless protein. A perfectly good whole pompano is lost in the rich sherry sauce, with leeks and shiitake mushrooms, in which it is just about submerged.

At Clancy's, desserts are paraded before you, usually one in each hand of a series of waiters and/or waitresses. It is a harmless tradition, and, as ever, sweets are the (comparative) high points of Clancy dinners: a tangy individual lemon tart, the fruity lemon curd under inches of handsomely browned meringue; a rather simple-minded trifle (the mother is shown to you in a multigallon glass jug that looks like an apothecary jar from a drugstore window), of which you are given about a quart—liquored sponge cake layered with fruits, preserves, toasted almonds, whipped cream; on occasion a pineapplemacadamia tart that expresses neither ingredient; and a couple of slices from a chocolate roulade formed of fallen chocolate soufflé, the excellent house whipped cream, those browned almonds again, and chocolate dribbled over the outside—a big winner.

The full text of a Clancy's advertisement: "Each licked the last kiss of chocolate roulade from the other's lips. Then they went home and made love. The food was that good." It makes you wonder if there are other experiences that bring on this amazing behavior.

★★★★ LAFAYETTE

65 East 56th Street
LUNCH, MONDAY TO FRIDAY; DINNER, MONDAY TO SATURDAY. CLOSED SUNDAY.
Reservations: 832-1565.
Credit cards: AE, DC, MC, V.
Very expensive.

When this place opened, in the then newly renovated Drake, it appeared that the curse of the hotel dining room had struck again. Though the appointments were handsome, even cushy, they did little to relieve the deadly minimonumental ponderance of the squat, blocky space. Perhaps no such correction was intended, for a certain caution informs the design of all New York hotel dining rooms: The occupants of the bed-chambers upstairs—visitors from Charleston and Rio, Brussels and Des Moines—must be able to grasp at once that the long trip has separated them not at all from the solid comforts of home. The hotel's dining room may be more luxurious than Mr. and Mrs. Tourist's, or even less, but the taste that informs it—for stuffed solidity and glitter—must be the same. It befell the Drake, however, that Lafayette was taken up by locals (from the start much of the food was exceptional), and management had, somehow, to make of its dining room a repair in which out-of-towners would be comfy, and at which New Yorkers would not titter. Impossible. What to do, what to do. Came along some kind of genius who, by a simple turn of the rheostat, a deep dimming of the lights, pumped the place full of low-lit atmosphere that even the outlanders could understand, and, in the act, took much of the curse off the rectilinear room and its posh appointments. You still walk on cushy carpeting, the white-linened tables are surrounded by large armchairs upholstered in russet-colored plush, the walls are several pinks, and the panels that, here and there, are surfaced with a rose-colored fabric of raw silk, in this light could just as well be nothing but darker paint. The spotlit burst of flowers at the center of the room is drama in this dimness, but the horizontal glass-faced aperture in one of the walls, through which the seemingly mute kitchen staff, in their whites, may be observed at their labors, does not persuade you that you are watching a pre-talkie wide-screen movie.

The menu changes with each change of the season. There is no reason to suspect, however, that what you order in winter or spring will suffer by comparison with these summer and autumn dishes. Anyway, it is difficult to imagine what you would compare with this singular sea urchin custard. The dish reaches you as the contents of three sea urchin carapaces set upon a field of star anise. (Just as you do not eat the carapaces, you do not eat the star anise.) The custard is warm, neither thick nor loose, compromises not at all the vigorous, sea-gamy flavor of sea urchin, the licoricelike flavors of the fennel juice and star anise with which it is touched emphasizing the assertiveness of the main ingredient. What is given as a fricassee of lobster is probably not what the word "fricas-see" means to you. The meat of the tail of the crustacean reaches you sliced into small disks and, alternating with slices of artichoke heart of like size, formed into a circle from which protrudes the meat of one claw, like the tail of a Q, within the circle a mound of kernels of corn, everything moistened with an herbed dressing of velvety oil—the moist meat of the lobster, so dressed and enriched, has a quality of lusciousness, and the textures and flavors of the vegetables are in delicate but vivid contrast to the tender white meat. You order the tuna tartare, and you are served three small triple-decker sand-wiches, the herbed and seasoned paste of the red fish alternating with gaufrette potatoes (latticework potato chips), each sandwich pierced not with a toothpick, but with a chive or two. In this context the complexity of the tuna tartare does get lost, but the gaufrette potatoes are crisp, the tartare is fresh and light, and the dish manages to be amusing and perhaps a little more than that. Foie gras is an inevitability these days on menus of any ambition at all, and new ways of using it are conceived of as rapidly as new menus are printed. Here the rich liver is formed into a roulade with air-dried duck breast, and the dish of which this composition is the feature consists of slices cut from the roulade and like-size slices of fresh fig, the two garnished with mâche and diced jelly, the black dots on your plate an artfully random speckling of black pepper—the richness of the foie gras is brilliantly set off by the strong flavor and slightly chewy texture of the cured meat. The autumn menu's oysters are described as "panfried," but something is lost in the transla-tion from "poêlées," for they reach you as if they have been merely warmed in butter.

They are set between the points of an asterisk formed by leaves of endive, and they are moistened by a warm vinaigrette that is dense with minced shallots—the dish is gentle, subtle, which is not to suggest that the oysters reveal anything less than all their flavor. Order smoked eel, and you get squares of the butterflied, filleted pale meat alternating with and overlapping squares of buckwheat pasta, a mound of good osetra black caviar on top, more of it in the creamy sauce that moistens this vigorously—almost wildly—flavored dish.

Pike shows up rarely on local menus, so when you see it you order it. Lafayette makes a homey dish of the poached fish, serves it in a broth that is green and fragrant of minced watercress, a kind of pike-in-the-pot, the knobs of skinned and boned white meat surrounded by woodsy wild mushrooms. Lafayette is one of those places in which you do not see what you are served until the great silver dome is lifted from the plate. When you see the salmon you ordered, it is nothing like what the menu's English translation led you to expect, "layers of salmon and fried leeks in a chervil sauce." Still, what you see is strikingly pretty, thin scallops of the pink fish under cloudlike tangles of deep-fried leek strands, the sauce a pale green circle within a perimeter formed of thin, peeled, asparagus spears. The vegetable is crunchy, the tender salmon seems to have been flash fired, for though it is cooked—or at least warmed through—it retains an untouched freshness, and the leeks are just a nice textural note. By now you are not surprised that "lamb canneloni" is nothing of the sort. The dish is some very nice lamb, roasted and sliced, in a sauce of the roasting juices; beside it is a pancake packed with a savory eggplant stuffing; and here and there on your plate there are patches of a green sauce, of zucchini and thyme, that you apply where you want it—altogether a good dish, if not what you thought you ordered. The confit of rabbit is a muffin-shaped mound of the well-seasoned preserved meat that has about it the spicy and slightly fatty quality of a meat stuffing, over it several strands of pale rabbit meat, these lacking the highly seasoned quality you expect in confit, the sauce of the dish a spiky one of sour green tomatoes that is heady of fresh coriander. The autumn menu's scallops are big, delicately browned, mingled with chanterelles that are meaty and woodsy, the whole served in a delicate sauce of leeks that is dotted with chives, everything conspiring to emphasize the ocean flavor of the scallops themselves. Order wood pigeon, and you are shown the thing encased in the salt shell in which it was baked. It is taken away, and you are presently brought the dish itself, the beefy red slices of pigeon breast quite rare, around them, at twelve, four, and eight o'clock, smokestacks, each formed of a potato croquette surmounted by a slice cut from a cèpe. The meat is strong, gamy, and, no surprise, salty, and you find concealed under the breast meat a rich and seasoned hash of other parts of the bird—altogether a sturdy dish.

Your waiter will direct your attention to the desserts on the three-tiered cart. They are fine, but not the best goods the house offers. Each night, however, special desserts are available, among them a soft disk, smooth and creamy, of goat cheese, apparently whipped, dotted with bits of green pepper, moistened with superior oil, and served with bread—very nice with white wine; another time what is given as a tropical fruit mille-feuille, which is really a sandwich of the chopped fruit between two almond cookies, the construct set in coconut milk dotted with pomegranate seeds; another time figs cooked in port wine, half a dozen halves of the wine-red fruit surrounding a ball of creamy vanilla. What the house calls a chocolate truffle cake is a layer of fluffy cake under a layer of sticky mousse under a rich black icing—a striking array of chocolate intensities and textures, and it hardly needs its good raspberry sauce. The plum tart and apple tart are fine versions of the standard thing.

★★LATTANZI

361 West 46th Street
LUNCH, MONDAY TO FRIDAY; DINNER, MONDAY TO SATURDAY. CLOSED SUNDAY.
Reservations: 315-0980.
Credit cards: AE.
Expensive.

Eight P.M., the dozen-and-a-half eating places along this so-called Restaurant Row have emptied of their pretheater customers, the drearies have set in, and most of the dining rooms will be semideserted until closing. When the resourceful entrepreneurs who are the Lattanzi family (they of Trastevere, Trastevere 84, and Erminia, all on the Upper East Side, all successful) initiated this theater district store, they were confronted with the depressing prospect of operating a restaurant in which little or no business would be done during the dinner hours that, everywhere else on Manhattan Island, are the busiest. For generations, restaurants in this neighborhood have suffered this situation, and for just as long, only the cheap places and tourist traps have overcome it. It took this family of minor commercial geniuses to note the big fat fact that New York's Jewish population has little in the way of serious eating places to call its own. (Much of the reason, of course, is that Central European cooking, Jewish or otherwise, is mostly dull stuff, cannot compete with the magic that is, for examples, French, Italian, Japanese, and Indian cooking.) The Lattanzis calculated—as it turns out, correctly—that any food that could legitimately be called Jewish, if it also tasted good, would appeal to that large market. And since the problem they were solving was an after-eight problem, the supplemental menu they initiated to deal with it—of food from the Roman ghetto —is offered only from that hour on. Sure enough, Lattanzi today is the only spot on the block in which it is sometimes hard to get a table even after the crowds have moved into the theaters. But it is clear that when they introduced the new cooking, the Lattanzis were not so sure it would succeed, and presumably meaning to leave nothing to chance, the food is identified—in a brief introduction that appears on the special printed menu —as "nouvelle Jewish-Roman." Not to worry. Except that it is not kosher, it is the real thing.

Physically, Lattanzi is what it was before the integration, low ceilinged, brick walled, dimly lit—except for the half dozen white-linened tables that, situated just under napkin-draped hanging lamps, are aglow. The restaurant is hung with Italian engravings and, on one side of the room, with a quasi-Pompeiian painting of ladies of an ancient time serenely about their domestic tasks. If none of that strikes you as distracting, there is Luciano Pavarotti, who, imprisoned in the kitchen, sings out for his release, sometimes all through dinner.

Of Roman-Jewish dishes, only one has gained currency in foreign parts, carciofi alla giudia, in which trimmed and seasoned artichokes are boiled in olive oil with garlic— they reach you quartered, saturated with oil and yet not really oily, the tips of the tender, edible leaves browned and crisp, the garlic vivid but to no loss of the artichoke's own clear flavor. Artichokes again—they are a big item in this cookery—but this time just as a garnish to the crostini di fegatini, in which chicken livers that have been coarse ground and sautéed in olive oil with onions reach you as a well-seasoned paste on crusts of fried bread. The crostini are garnished with an exceptional caponata, cool, tart, sweet—the oily eggplant and peppers, the crunchy celery, the zucchini and the sour capers all retain their character in the herbed and spicy liquid. The caponata appears also as the one cool item in a three-part first course. The other items: a rather dreary rice ball pinked with tomato and weighted with cheese—it is the kind of dish you must grow up with to love; and a version of mozzarella in carrozza in which the breaded and deep-fried slab of pully cheese is covered over with hot capers. Orecchiette are disks of pasta shaped like little battered coins. Here they are served "al tonno," in a Jewish tuna-fish sauce that, though you may take it as a kind of meat sauce in which fish has been substituted for beef, is not that at all. Its character is its own, the spicy, fragrantly herbed, and dense tomato sauce thick with the fish and dominated by its flavor. The green lasagne are interleaved with, yet again, artichokes, the two in a bright tomato sauce that is peppery and sweet.

What distinguishes the Jewish roast chicken from others is what is absent from it— butter, as well as most of its own fat. Roasted this way—with seasoning, garlic, and rosemary—the bird takes on an aromatic but somewhat dry quality peculiar to Jewish roast birds. You may like it—you may not. Which may be said also of the red snapper, which the menu refers to—with license—as "orata" (quite another fish). In this prepara- tion the fish is baked in oil and vinegar with raisins and pine nuts until it is at once rich and vigorously sour—it is the kind of food you instinctively eat with bread. The agnello al rosmarino is a row of connected rib lamb chops, the unsevered eyes peeled away from the bones before grilling. This beats grilling the chops individually, for a substantial crust can be built up while the meat inside remains blood-juicy. The good lamb, flavored with garlic and rosemary, is served with a great hillock of sautéed mushrooms.

From the regular menu: fettuccine Lattanzi, the broad noodles in a creamy sauce thick with wild mushrooms, all very nice, but you do miss the peas that are listed as an element of the dish; bucatini amatriciana, the hefty tubes of pasta—judiciously cooked, just this side of tough—in a tomato sauce, thick with sweet onions, that is permeated with the flavor of good Italian bacon; calamari Lattanzi, the fresh and tender squid in a spicy red sauce dotted with chunks of pungent garlic and (this time they do show up) sweet green peas that, in this setting, manage to be little more than decorative—the strong, brash stuff is served with thick crusts of well-oiled garlic bread; zuppa di pesce, mussels and cherrystone clams in their half-shells, at the center of the plate a mound of crunchy shrimp and that good squid again, those two on a fillet of fish, the entire variegated abundance in a deep pool of red, briny, winy sauce; pollo capriccioso, chunks of chicken, great slabs of red pepper, sharp-flavored little capers, all in a deep and deep-red marinara sauce; and a veal chop "al funghi" that, too bad, was done until flat before it was buried under sautéed mushrooms.

The ricotta cheesecake is eggy and light—and, surprise, warm. You may have fresh strawberries under a cool zabaglione made with much marsala. The napoleon is the big winner, the layers of pastry so flaky, the layers of cream so rich and stiff, that you take it the thing was assembled moments before it was served.

★ LOLA

30 West 22nd Street
LUNCH, SUNDAY TO FRIDAY; DINNER, MONDAY TO SATURDAY.
Reservations: 675-6700.
Credit cards: AE.
Medium priced.

Lola undertakes to provide fun of two kinds, both of which mix well with alcohol. In the long, narrow section to which you enter, the intended fun is musical, subspecies Caribbean, played, often, by groups of players whose talents are less to the lyric or profound than to the rhythmic and loud. You take this stuff in at one of the cocktail tables just inside the front door, or at the long bar that extends from the players' platform back to the portal of the dining room itself, and if you know Lola, you know that, though when you arrive during the pounding of the drums there is no way to dinner except through that racket, you do reach haven once you have run the course, for the not-hypnotic beat carries hardly at all into the dining room proper, wherein another fun, fun food, subspecies (largely) Caribbean once again, is the house specialty. However, you eat in surroundings designed not at all to suggest The Islands. Lola's look is Edwardian, maybe the incongruity is intended as part of the fun, no one notes the dissonance anyway. The room is high, wide, and pink. It is bedecked with dozens of tastefully framed etchings and drawings and prints and paintings that have no relevance to this place, the idea being to bedeck the place with dozens of tastefully framed etc. You walk on a plain wood floor, and you are seated at one of the well-spaced good-size tables— unless you are put at the T-shaped (long horizontal, short vertical) banquette, uphol- stered in pretty pastel stripes, that, near the center of the floor, serves to undo the slight vastness of this space, both by way of its own presence, and by way of the huge Chinese bowls mounted on it (one at the foot of the T, the others at each end of the crosspiece), in them giant sprays of branches that reach halfway to the ceiling. One long wall is in part hung with three tall mirrors, which more or less mirror the glass of the opposite wall, which is composed largely of tall French doors through which you get this really terrific view of a bit of gray urban backyard, matching trelliswork, a small garden in which hearty green things grow, and, behind that, visible through uncurtained windows, the rear end of Manila, the dreary Philippine restaurant and jazz joint on 21st Street, in which, from your vantage in Lola, the customers and staff appear to be floating about in dumb show. In Lola itself, however, you are among quite another set, the just-washed young (no matter what their age), fresh out of the health-club shower, nary a flap of loose skin on a one of them, all bent on shop talk.

Many of them get drinks, an order of fried onions ("cayenne ribbon onion rings") for two, delay the rest of dinner until they know how far the dish will take them. The pile of onions is about the size of a hatbox, they are just out of the hot fat, are feathery light and sweet, spicy but far from searing in their delicate coppered batter, and they are not dry, are in fact ever so slightly greasy, which is much of their charm. If you manage to work your way down to the bare plate, skip directly to dessert, then go home dyspeptic and happy. Send half your onions back, however, and you will be in a position to consider the West Indian potato and shrimp fritters, small hamburger-shaped patties of a shrimp suspicion and a mashed potato abundance, soft inside, crusted outside, spicy hot, the constructs served with a pinked, thick, and fiery mayonnaise. You do get dishes here that are pleasurable beyond mere amusement, among them the sea scallop sauté, the big nuggets of rich seafood browned in butter and mingled with pencil-thin shoots of asparagus and lengths of sweet red pepper, the three elements just about made for one another. But the grilled wild mushroom salad is somewhat undone by the overpowering flavor of the grill, and the caesar salad is a comedown, the dressing thick rather than rich, the croutons greasy, the lettuce lifeless, and the Parmesan cheese, which Lola adds to the other more or less standard ingredients, lost in the setting.

Each day there is a pasta of the day, dishes that read like hit-or-miss compendia of diverse ingredients. On occasion, however, the elements get on well with one another, as do these orecciette (pasta shaped like little ears) with morels, hot sausages, and florets of broccoli and cauliflower, all in a dark, sticky, and stocky veal sauce, a sturdy plate of food in which the pasta is one nuggety element among many. When soft-shell crabs are in season, Lola gets the not so soft ones, which is too bad, for the sauce of lime and coriander in which they are served is tart, fruity, heady, a good foil to crabs you can chew. The rule here is to remember that there is safety in fun food, of which picnic food is a type, of which fried chicken is an example, of which Lola's is a good example, the chunks of bird juicy and of clear chicken flavor in their spicy hot crisped batter. The place turns out a decent if unexceptional steak, distinctly cross-hatched but only mildly flavored by the grill.

For the quintessential Lola dish, you look to the desserts and find The Island Sundae, a grilled ring of pineapple, the ball of coconut ice cream at the center surfaced with a glaze of nut crumbs, the two set in a caramel sauce laced with dark rum. The chocolate toffee torte, a layered thing of fudge, toffee, and whipped cream on a nut pastry, tastes like good candy. What is given as "chocolate hazelnut pâté" is cakey and dry and studded with nuts and garnished with vanilla ice cream of no distinction. What goes as "old-fashioned strawberry shortcake" is a wetted and wilted cakelike substance with ripe but no longer firm strawberries, and with whipped cream that cannot compensate.

★ LA LUNCHEONETTE

130 Tenth Avenue (at 18th Street)
LUNCH AND DINNER.
Reservations: 675-0342.
No credit cards.
Medium priced.

You are familiar with the practice of certain restaurants, the hanging of gauzy or lacy curtains over the lower halves of their street windows to deter disturbance of the clientele by common peerers-in. Naturally the curtains must be periodically laundered and, eventually, replaced. It is expressive of La Luncheonette that, instead of diaphanous curtains, the lower halves of its (wire-reinforced) windows are of glass that has been smoked, which provides the same privacy, but without the costs of maintenance. Do not suspect for a moment, however, that LL went to the trouble of treating that glass, no no no, rather that it knew a good thing when it found it on these unrehabilitated old premises, and left it as was. To the French, of course (who put two tables and four chairs on a sidewalk somewhere, and thereby inaugurate on outdoor café), a dining room is where you find it, and though the concept is often inflated to a fare-thee-well, it is never discarded simply for lack of the wherewithal with which to elaborate it. In this poor man's refuge, the found object is automatically interior design, the dearth of light is ambience, and as there is shelter from the weather, you may as well call the place a restaurant. Once you know LL, you know that the elaborately carved and polished door through which you enter was not commissioned by the house, unless as a joke, for it prepares you for nothing you encounter inside. You do not expect, for example, immediately on your ingression, to be right upon the wide-open kitchen, but here it is, behind a three-sided low brick wall onto which your chef—one Jean François, a Gallic young gent of gruff-and-ready mien, here assisted by a couple of on-the-job trainees—places the dishes for portage by waitresses who are differentiated from the customers solely by the fact that they are on their feet, their "uniforms" being civvies that are as variegated as everything else about this unmatched installation.

That low brick wall between the entrance and the kitchen narrows the passage between the two dining rooms. The one on your right as you enter is more or less the supplementary back room, the floor is of barbershop tiles that have been Balkanized by the years into misshapen nations—jagged cracks are their borders—oddments hang on the walls, there are tables and chairs. Turn left when you enter, and you are in the restaurant proper, an ancient wooden bar down one long side of the rectangular room, parallel to it a couple of rows of tables, some linened, some not, six different varieties of secondhand side chairs around them, the candles on them, in tall glass cylinders, much of the room's illumination. As it happens, the windows *are* hung with curtains, but these are a deep dark maroon, are tied back, are the kind of blackout curtains that, when permitted to hang free, conceal from the world the very existence of certain cultish establishments that choose to situate themselves along this edge of town because no one this far west complains. (LL is keeping its options open.) There are plants on the windowsills, also candles in holders around the bases of which the mountains of wax increase daily. An old rusty gate leans against one wall, near it hangs a Paris Street sign (Rue de la Boule d'Or), elsewhere a map of the world, elsewhere a large unframed oil of a scene in rural France before the Enlightenment. A Coca-Cola clock provides the correct time. Behind the bar bare tree branches protrude from a vase, the seemingly windblown posters caught in their web headed NOTICE and WARNING. There is also a nude behind the bar, anyway the upper half of her, a straw hat on her head, the flowers around her neck doing nothing for her modesty. The rest of her is over on that low brick wall around the kitchen, invitingly inverted, a fedora gaily hung high up on her right foot.

Your waitress takes one more puff on the cigarette she has working in an ashtray on the bar, concludes her clerical work, switches the tape in the tape deck, slices you some bread, comes by to tell you about the specials of the day. You make a mistake by ordering from the menu instead: a leek-and-lentil salad that is cold, lacks seasoning, cannot be rescued by the white vinaigrette that is equally incapable of bringing to life this asparagus, which is overcooked, stringy, and just out of the icebox. That dressing does better, of course, when it has a better chance, as with the half lobster that is sometimes a first course here—it is cold, too cold, but it is carefully poached, not overcooked, is of clear lobster flavor. The dressing does its best, however, when you least expect it, as the sauce for these warm slivers of sweetbread, the organ meat tender and rich in the white stuff. The shiitake mushrooms seem to be sautéed to order, they are meaty, and their woodsy flavor is much enhanced by strong seasoning and by the butter in which they are done. On your lucky night you will be offered fresh sardines, and though you get only two, you do not mind, for each of them is the size of a grownup trout. They are fresh, lightly charred and crisped, strewn with parsley, of strong, herringlike fish flavor.

Whatever you do, do not do the gratiné aux trois poissons, in which scallops, slivers of lobster meat, and shreds of crabmeat are aswim in a tasteless shellfish sauce under a pulliness of indeterminate cheese. Opt instead for the swordfish, which is fresh, browned, moist, livened by a lemony sauce that is thick with onions. You get a thick slab of liver, crusted outside, blood-pink inside—lots of onions again. The steak au poivre is not bad once you trim away its gristly edge, but you wish it were peppery all the way, instead of just in the occasional whole peppercorn you find in the creamy sauce. The sometimes available cassoulet is a little soupy, but thick with meat, and the lamb, pork, duck, and giblets retain all their flavor. When venison sausages are offered, think twice before turning them down, for their spiciness does nothing to conceal their sweet venison flavor.

What is characterized as a tarte tatin is almost devoid of the caramelization that name suggests, amounts to applesauce in lump form on pastry. But the almond tart has good almond flavor, the dacquoise is chewy and rich, and the chocolate cake is that classic article that seems to demand a glass of milk—instead it gets, as do all the desserts, a garnish of thick whipped cream.

★★LUSARDI'S

1494 Second Avenue (near 78th Street)
LUNCH, MONDAY TO FRIDAY; DINNER, DAILY.
Reservations: 249-2020.
Credit cards: AE, DC, MC, V.
Medium priced.

Lusardi and Lusardi, the handsome, dapper, mustachioed, and almost twinlike brothers who run this place, are the not so secret secret of its popularity, for theirs is the most genuine cordiality, the kind that, has been fixed by reward. Waiters who do not emulate the brothers' benevolent dispositions do not last, so the gents you deal with once you are seated are almost invariably patient and helpful, as if they want to make you happy. The effect of this is to make you happy. Sufficiently so, in fact, that you are willing to overlook the occasional humdrum dish, and surroundings that, originally straightforward, have been somewhat undone. Lusardi's is one of the many clubby Italian restaurants that invaded Manhattan's Upper East Side in the early eighties, almost all of them simple installations of painted-plaster walls and wood trim furnished with rows of linened tables. In them bluff guys, in white shirts and white aprons, handed you the menu, told you the specials of the day, took your order, promptly delivered, their brusqueness part of the style—which was set, often, by proprietors who did not waste their limited respects on strangers. But while this place took a turn for the better by deviating from the usual short manner, it got lost in its effort to improve on the standard look. Lusardi's has been prettied with framed prints; they are hung at stubbornly regular intervals all around, turning the once direct room into yet another poster gallery with kitchen.

Your waiter's good manners, of course, do not forbid consideration of the profit motive. He suggests that instead of Lusardi's ordinary bread, you order the bruschetta toscana, a plate of many crusty bread slices, each of them piled high with a fragrantly herbed mix of chopped tomatoes in a lively vinaigrette. Of the other cool first courses, pass up the seafood salad—loud mussels, and a rather sour dressing that expresses nothing of oil—in favor of a carpaccio: the one of salmon is a great spread of raw pink fish, fresh and supple, covered with a density of chopped parsley, oil, lemon; the one of beef is moistened with oil, is mounded over with woodsy mushrooms and short sticks of sharp Parmesan. Sometimes there is polenta, the hot toasted slices of packed grain under more of those porcini mushrooms, these sautéed, and moistened with a good tomato sauce. Each day there is a pappardelle of the day, the wide, weighty noodles sometimes in a deep and meaty quail sauce that you fortify with cheese.

Branzino, a basslike fish of the Mediterranean, is served in a slightly enriched white-wine broth—too bad that overcooking has softened the fish and diminished its flavor. Similarly the swordfish, the thin steak fresh but of little swordfish character—it is served in a pureed version of sauce livornese, red and garlicky, but lacking the whole capers and chunks of olive that are usually the life of that preparation. An order of fried calamari is a pile of deep-fried circles, tender and virtually greaseless, that you liven with lemon—if you wish, you will be served also a pitcher of simple and vigorous tomato sauce. A good chicken dish: pollo castelli romani, the whole breast, skin on and delicately browned, in a creamy sauce that is thick with mushrooms and slivers of artichoke. A good veal dish: veal martini, the thin cutlets of meat dipped in ground cheese, sautéed until crisp, moistened with a sauce that is smooth and lemony. And a good chop: veal chop salvia, the browned and blackened meat slicked with oil and suffused with the wild flavor of sage.

Lusardi's tirami sù is better than most, this puddinglike version grainy, of real coffee flavor, and of considerable cheese richness. You may have your zabaglione on ripe, fresh berries. And of course there is heady Parmesan cheese.

★★★★ LUTÈCE

249 East 50th Street
LUNCH, TUESDAY TO FRIDAY; DINNER, MONDAY TO SATURDAY. CLOSED SUNDAY.
Reservations: 752-2225.
Credit cards: AE, DC, MC, V.
Very expensive.

Lutèce the hundredth time is like Lutèce the first time, the place is such an astonishment. The shock is only in part a function of the disparity between the restaurant's grand reputation and its unassuming style. The style alone could do it, for New York life simply does not prepare you for this lost charm and forgotten grace. Unlike the other local restaurants usually ranked with it, Lutèce is not a product tailored to a market, has not been programmed to push all your buttons. It simply exists, the distillate of a civilized, appreciative way of life. Today, when more than ever there are other restaurants in which you will regularly get a first-class dinner, Lutèce is not comparable to them, remains apart, is only peripherally a place of public accommodation. It is more nearly a natural resource, the one spot in town that is not in this town at all, if it is even in this century. Lutèce does not merely take you in, it restores you—to the manners, gay and clement, of your inherited past, which are its province. Enter in tune, and you will find that you are not really in a restaurant, but in a time that is forgotten, but part of you. As sole present occupant of that era, the management here, though hard at work, is notably self-assured. It is as if a higher being whispered in the proprietor's ear: All you must do, whispered the being, is please yourself—you will thereby please those you would have as customers, and you will prosper. At Lutèce the secure receive the tasteful, and neither has anything to prove.

All of which is not to suggest Lutèce is complacent. In fact, it is always changing, at least to the extent of new dishes regularly dreamed up by André Soltner, chef-owner. Recently, moreover, he has undertaken to revise the physical plant itself, a risky business when the subject is that rarity, a true institution, and situated in this landmark-mad borough. But Soltner is his own watchdog committee, and though the notorious French restaurant architect Sam Lopata advised, nothing done has altered this establishment's well-known French charm, which has always seemed especially evanescent here on alien ground. No chances were taken. Despite North America's diverse geology, the new fa-çade is of French stone, and it is not emblazoned with the great bold letters that an-nounced Lutèce to its New York street during the first quarter century of its existence, only with a small sign near the front door, gold on black, all discretion. In a misty twilight, when you yourself are perhaps a bit misty, it is possible to imagine that you are seeing the place by the silver light of Paris itself.

As ever, you enter to a tiny foyer that gives onto a minuscule barroom, its space quite occupied by a short zinc bar and a handful of small tables with brass-rimmed marble tops, café chairs around them. The walls are casually adorned, here a small mural of Paris, there a Paris street sign, you should not forget this is France. The foyer gives also onto a narrow stairway leading to a couple of relatively formal dining rooms one flight up, crystal chandeliers and all that. But changes up here are beginning to soften things —the rearmost of the two rooms is now faced with a nubbly beige cloth woven with spice-brown florets among a network of stylized branches, its effect, at once autumnal and cozy, very much of a piece with this room's fireplace (inactive), a pair of Florentine oils, now cleaned and restored, their bold flowers revealed to be of warm, vivid colors, the ancient dusky tapestry that has covered one wall of this room ever since Lutèce was new, the tall white tapers on the larger tables, and the chandelier's golden light. Bypass the stairway, however, and a corridor takes you by the long kitchen, into which you peer, through the aperture that runs its length, to observe a squad in white firing to order, Soltner himself often among them. On occasion he steps out when familiar customers go by, his now famous face a smiling sun. It is the downstairs dining rooms beyond the kitchen that you probably think of when you think "Lutèce," and you will likely be relieved to learn that the first of them has been pruned of the rampant green fronds that, on a succession of wallpapers over the years, added a note of the riotous to this otherwise serene area. The room is square, a good-size table in each corner, each well apart from the others, the new treatment (making remote reference to the old), of delicate trailing vines painted as airy frames on a vaporous ground of mottled green, a bit of hazy countryside, from which you enter the enclosed garden room onto which it gives. As you were pleased by the changes, so will you be content with what has been left as was, for the garden remains an airy fantasy—made up, without regard to any syntax of meaning, of light, space, and whimsy. On a floor of forest-green flagstones, and within slightly fantastical surroundings—white latticework set before pink walls, palms sprouting from gleaming brass pots that stand atop stubby columns of whitewashed brick—are set two rows of white-linened tables that, despite their situation in this particular neighborhood of fairyland, are surrounded by the colorful wicker chairs you know from Paris cafés. The sky overhead is a translucent dome, faced with pale-green blinds, that at its highest point is two stories above ground. The room is weightless, like a mirage. And though restaurant functions take place within it—Madame Soltner (this establishment's down-home version of a maître d') conducting like a good shepherd the happy sheep to their tables, gentlemen in black and white explaining and scribbling, others hastening and serving—the business of the place, leavened by the place itself, is to business as love is to politics. Only Soltner seems entirely of this, his unreal world, aglow in kitchen whites, beaming under his toque blanche. He materializes often during dinner, takes an order here, confers a blessing there, and near the end of the evening goes from table to table, always a little radiant, like—a benevolent host.

Yes, there is a printed menu. But listen to the captains or, especially, to Soltner himself, and you may conclude that the document is beside the point, for most of the enthusiasm, love, and attention go to the newest babies, the special dishes Soltner has most recently sired. Of course you may refer to the menu, order the truite fraîche grillée, and be content with an entire trout that, boned, its dark, crisped skin still encasing the pale, firm, and supple meat, is bathed in a light and creamy sauce that is alive with morsels and strands of fresh vegetable. But if you eat here regularly, the trout is not new to you, and you will be tempted instead by the likes of: cultivated freshwater gambas from Puerto Rico, shrimplike creatures, bifurcated, sautéed, and served in their carapaces, the sweet and crunchy meats touched with the flavor of their slightly charred shells and moistened with a gentle herbed butter; a pungent version of ratatouille, crunchy, tart of capers, accented with bits of black olive, the mound of it at the center of your plate surrounded by dice of sautéed tuna fish in a pinked and buttery sauce that is accented with minced chives; a thin fillet of fresh turbot that is cooked, on its plate, only when the fluffy and creamy sauce, dotted with bits of vegetable, under which it is buried is browned in the broiler—Provençale herbs and the blackened edges of the sauce are the striking accents of the dish; hat-shaped ravioli of paper-thin pasta, the crown filled with a sweet, oceanic stuffing of crabmeat and lobster; tiny morsels of fresh frogs' legs accompanied, in a little tin-lined copper pot, by slivers of mushroom and dumplings (of ground frogs' legs and pike) that are the size of peas and the density of air, all in a rich, creamy, browned sauce that is alive with coarse-chopped herbs; in another such copper pot, fresh American snails, plump, resilient but not tough, mingled with chunks of cèpe in a winy, creamy, and well-parsleyed sauce, under a lid of flaky pastry; a slice cut from a loaf of a terrine of duck confit and foie gras, the strong and spicy dark meat that is the center layer gentled by the richer pale meat that is the outer ones; a salad in which minuscule slivers of delicately crisped sweetbread and a sheaf of tender, nutty, deep-green haricots verts are mingled with crisp chicory in a warm dressing.

All of which may lead you to conclude that M. Soltner has cut himself from his roots, a notion you drop when you have sampled the listed poussin rôti aux herbes, roast chicken to you, and elemental. The whole bird, in its deep-bronzed skin, is shown, taken away, carved, served as hefty slices of meat in a brown sauce that is heady with fresh tarragon—the chicken has a depth of flavor that these days is usually just a memory. With such a chicken, who needs a pheasant? Still, this place is at home also with the game bird, the sliced breast and whole parts sturdy in a dark sauce that is dense with diced vegetables—a hearty, vivid dish. More unfancy food, a veal shank that has been braised, removed from its braising liquid and browned, the meat taken from its bone, sliced, and served to you in a deep sauce of the liquid, to which have been added onions, potatoes, wild mushrooms—the power of the dish is in the vigorous flavor the supple meat has taken on from being cooked on its bone in a powerful stock. When venison chops are on hand, it is well to know that at Lutèce the plump eyes of blood-juicy meat sport venison's characteristic liver richness at its most intense—the game is served, in its dark sauce, with herbed, eggy spaetzle, whole chestnuts, and strands of crisp, tangy celeriac.

Among desserts, too, both the traditional and the original are available, hot soufflés notable among the former. If the flavor you choose is Grand Marnier, you are presented with a monument loftily risen above the white porcelain pot in which it was baked, on its tawny plateau top, in deep-brown letters, the word "Lutèce." The soufflé itself is light and moist, shot through with bits of orange rind, and it is much enriched by the hot Grand Marnier sauce your waiter spoons on. Unlisted desserts you will sometimes be offered: a frozen lemon soufflé, two white disks—cold, creamy, sweet, and citrus sharp—with a sheet of chewy almond meringue between them; a homey pear cake, nutted and dark, served with an eggy sauce sabayon that is tangy of its fruit brandy; sweet sections of marinated orange in a pool of liquored white sauce that is browned just before it is served; tiny poached pears, firm and fruity, with vanilla ice cream of stunning polish, in a crisp and lacy pastry cup set in a black chocolate sauce.

★ LE MADELEINE

405 West 43rd Street
LUNCH AND DINNER.
Reservations: 246-2993.
Credit cards: AE, MC, V.
Inexpensive.

When new, this place sold sandwiches and salads, desserts and coffee, etc. It was a café, and folks came here to eat a little, to drink a little, and to sit around a lot. Such casual revenues probably cannot support a New York store. Anyway, for whatever reason, the ex-café is now a bistro, complete with kitchen. But only the menu has changed. The place looks the way it has from the start, and young dancers and actors between assignments still make up the staff. Nowadays the restaurant has a price-conscious pretheater dinner following, so if you get here just before curtain time, your ingress is against the current of a small crowd off to balcony seats. Ten minutes later the place may well be empty, but from then on it is neighborhood territory, may even fill again with the new locals—many of them theatricals—in this blooming part of town. Le Madeleine is a brightly lighted, high-ceilinged room with big windows—hung with gauzy half curtains—that look out on 43rd Street. A zinc-topped bar is near the entrance, the brick walls have been muraled with art that looks like old sun-bleached advertisements, and the rows of tables are covered with white butcher paper, additional sheets of which are tacked up here and there around the room, the special dishes of the day scrawled thereon. The background music, it appears, is always jazz.

The mostly vigorous food of this straightforward place includes a soupe au pistou that is a loudly garlicked and fragrantly herbed broth thick with chunks of root vegetable and clumps of greens; smoked trout that is exceptional for its freshness and for the subtlety of its smoky flavor, served with a good sauce that is little more than thick whipped cream touched with horseradish; smoked goose, the slices of dark-red meat tasting (try the blindfold test) very much like mild pastrami, though fine for that, and served, appropriately, with strong mustard; and a duck liver mousse, the jelly-edged slice cut from a loaf of—unfortunately—a flat and pasty amalgam too lacking in fluffiness or air to satisfy your anticipation of a "mousse." You may begin your dinner with an ordinary salad—the one listed as "four greens" arrives with only two, but the unexpected onions, slices of tomato, and celery, all in the strong and thick house dressing, make up for the deficit; or with one of several composed salads, among them one of endive, walnuts, and Roquefort, each of the elements occupying a separate section on your plate (crescents of sliced cucumber and slices of tomato present too), that sturdy house dressing in a little pitcher, should you want it on, say, your endive but not your walnuts.

It was only a matter of time before New York came up with an answer to the New Orleans blackened redfish. The challenger is called, of course, blackened bluefish (which, with any etymological luck, will be black-and-blue fish by the turn of the century). The item has, moreover, more to recommend it than a cute future, is good to eat, consisting, as it does, of a substantial fillet of fresh fish that is hot, juicy, and of vivid flavor within its dark and crusty skin of Cajun seasonings. But you will not always be so lucky with Le Madeleine's fish, for another time you choose tuna, and you get a thin grilled steak that comes off as little more than neutral protein under a pallid mustard sauce. Each day there is a pasta of the day, sometimes a spaghetti dish in which the three elements of the sauce—cream, smoked salmon, dill—are strong, distinct, and utterly at home with one another. The suprême de volaille is the breast of a not particularly tasty chicken, but the browned herb-and-anchovy coating converts it into fun food. The thin-sliced liver is nicely crisped in the sautéing and it takes very well to its buttered, polished sauce of raspberry vinegar, but the mushrooms under which the liver is buried, though perfectly decent, overwhelm the meat. Le Madeleine's steaks are not of America's best beef, so they are sometimes gristly—and sometimes inaccurately done.

Come on Sunday, and you get Saturday's desserts, among them tired apple and pecan pies. But the Mississippi mudcake, when it is fresh, is an overwhelmingly rich chocolate item, lightly flavored of coffee, and of a strong molasses sweetness—big crumbs of chocolate are the rugged terrain on top. The fruit tarts are like clafouties, the plums or cranberries or whatever embedded in the shortbread pastry. Good whipped cream is available with the desserts.

When the weather is fine, you may eat here out of doors: about a dozen tables—covered with that snowy white paper and surrounded by folding chairs and white-painted benches—are set out in a small backyard in which a single tree is strung with little white lights.

★ MALAGA

406 East 73rd Street
LUNCH AND DINNER.
Reservations: 737-7659.
Credit cards: AE, DC, MC, V.
Medium priced.

Bullfight posters, unspeakable oils, framed moments (on linen) in the life of Don Quixote, red lights on the gaudy chandeliers, sexy Spanish ladies painted onto the big barrel bottoms that are mounted on the wall behind the little bar (just under the wine baskets that hang from the tiled, sloped mock roof); not to mention the black-and-white television set that is occasionally turned on, nor the tall gray Model-T air-conditioning monster, the coats that are on display on the attended plain pipe rack just inside the front door; never mind the crowds that come, young marrieds escaping the kitchen on weekday and weekend nights, whole families escaping it on Sundays, slummers in suits and ties and perms any old time. It is remarkable how so much paraphernalia and activity can fail to make a place look other than gaunt and spare. That, of course, is the front room. The back room lacks even the paraphernalia, except for its own unspeakable oils and monster.

On the Upper East Side, Malaga is the only establishment of its exact type, sporting the standard menu that was set as New York's version of Spanish cooking as long ago as the 1930s and 1940s, in the couple of dozen Spanish restaurants that were then around town. The type has not died out, but now most such places are downtown, and Malaga has itself a little monopoly here. Perhaps for that reason the place does not try too hard. This is a decent restaurant, but you love it more when you know it better, for some of the food is good, and some is not.

Not the Spanish ham and olives, for the ham is coarse, even coarsely sliced, though the green olives are strong and sharp. Far better are the cold Malaga mussels, sweet and fresh in their shells, spread with a bright dressing of chopped tomato and onion and parsley. This place makes a good salpicon and sells it in a $5 serving big enough for two—it is a cool chopped salad of crabmeat, hard-cooked eggs and greens, the strong parsley called cilantro, and chopped tomatoes, all in a sharp and refreshing dressing.

You can get lots of hot crunchy shrimp in a bubbling sauce of oil and garlic; a small beach of chorizos, disks of Spanish sausage, that are grilled until they are crusty; a garlic soup that is red with red pepper, thick with chunks of bread and with egg that is cooked in the broth—the soup is homey, but not tasty.

Main courses arrive on a cart in big iron pots, and a huge platter of good red-peppered rice is served with all of them. But the egg sauce that is served on the mixed seafood (mariscada) is thin, hardly eggy at all. And the paella—the biggest pot on the wagon—contains a lobster that is little more than an empty shell, and a lot of other ingredients that are mostly overcooked. Choose instead the crabmeat in green sauce, for it has texture and resilience, and its sauce is fragrant with abundant parsley. Or the shrimp diablo, those good shrimp again, very crisp, in a spicy sauce that is thick with green peppers. The veal extramena is of tender little morsels of meat, but its sauce,

217

allegedly of onions, sausage and peppers, is notable mainly for its good garlic intensity. Eschew the pork with almond sauce—which is flat-out of no interest—in favor of the chicken villaroy, the two halves of a breast of chicken, artfully prepared, coated with béchamel, breaded, and crisped. Remarkably, the dish is light.

As everyone knows, the desserts in Spanish restaurants vary not at all from restaurant to restaurant, only a little from dessert to dessert. Malaga has added a standard New York cheesecake to the standard list, and it is not bad if you like that kind of thing. The best of the Spanish desserts is the guava with cream cheese—the fruit is candied but seems brandied, for it is sweet and sharp, and the block of cheese that comes with it is solid. The dish arrives with a couple of saltines standing in it, like a couple of sails.

★ MANHATTAN OCEAN CLUB

57 West 58th Street
LUNCH, MONDAY TO FRIDAY; DINNER, DAILY.
Reservations: 371-7777.
Credit cards: AE, DC, MC, V.
Very expensive.

Through the two-level dining room rise massive square white columns, and to each of their faces a dark and skinny half column, fluted and with an elaborate finial, has been grafted, forming constructs that may be taken as failed attempts by posts to become pillars. In glass-covered green niches carved into the walls, handsome Picasso ceramics are on display (not for sale). And on the south wall of the lower level there is, for some reason, fruit, shiny red apples one time, oranges another, row upon row of the bright-colored orbs, a display like those at a fruiterer. This seafood restaurant is an enterprise of the interests behind Smith & Wollensky and the Post House, relentlessly bluff and hearty steakhouses bedecked with whimsical assortments of paraphernalia that, by their insouciant irrelevance, underscore the rumpus-room masculinity of those repairs. The Club, however, styles itself "A Classic Seafood Restaurant," and though you may find the slogan (a) meaningless or (b) false, the physical place does have an underlying nautical trimness. Unfortunately, far from being underscored by its accessories, it is almost undone by them. The rooms are perfectly comfortable, you understand, but they have been sacrificed to the simpleminded notion that what worked in one place would work in another.

Qua eating place, on the other hand, the eating place has stabilized to a point at which the piscivore may, by astuteness, eat well at it. To eat well, you pray for your raw oysters, for one time they are sparkling, another time flat—a day too long out of their water and much in need of lemon. But most of the shellfish appetizers are fine: lump crabmeat that is supple and sweet; baked clams in a nutted pesto that is a striking setting for the tender littlenecks; steamed cultivated mussels that, a miracle for these days, are of clear, stout mussel flavor, a couple dozen of them, in their shells, mounded over the briny broth—thick with chopped peppers and tomatoes—in which they were done. The clam chowder is spicy, thick with potato, hearty, though its clam meat is of a toughness.

Finfish—the rules for keeping it, and the theory and hang of preparing it—eludes this place. The swordfish au poivre, for example, is a chunk of fish the size and shape of a double filet mignon, so the thing reaches you overcooked on the surface, almost raw at the center, both conditions deadly to this variety. Snapper, probably broiled as long as that swordfish, though less than an inch at its thickest point, has lost most of its flavor to the overtreatment. Some nicely prepared halibut is a bit fishy around the edges. But then, on a lucky night, you get this salmon steak, handsomely browned, cooked through but moist, all its flavor intact. The so-called broiled lobster is steamed first, and as its exposure to the broiler is brief—just enough to make it *look* broiled—the sweet meat is moist and tender. The crab cakes are a big winner, two hamburger-size patties, almost solid crabmeat of vivid flavor, pungently spiced, handsomely browned, nicely livened by lemon, so in no need at all of the obvious mustard sauce served with them. The baked potato is the size of a watermelon, and it is firm within its crusty skin. In this city of innumerable Italian restaurants, in which threadlike fried zucchini, crisp, airy, and weightless, is served in dozens of places, the Ocean Club is bold enough to send out baskets of soggy logs.

What your waiter calls a pistachio bombe tart is an acid-green, marzipanlike slab in two sauces, vanilla and raspberry—the garish looks of the dish prepare you perfectly for its taste and texture. An assortment of little fruit tarts are of a sugary sweetness that defeats the fruit. The poached fresh fig, with whipped cream and custard in a cassis sauce, is a collection of good ingredients that add up to an adult sundae. The hot plum tart is a winner, the browned slices of fruit on a crunchy pastry of ground nuts.

On your table you find a printed vintage chart. By reference to this, how you say, debatable document, you learn that virtually anything on this restaurant's wine list is worth ordering.

★ MAN RAY

169 Eighth Avenue (near 18th Street)
LUNCH, SUNDAY; DINNER, DAILY.
Reservations, 627-4220.
Credit cards: AE.
Medium priced.

Named for an American painter, photographer, and film maker who spent time in Paris, this place integrates that geography and some of the biography, for it is hung with movie stills and photos by the artist, and it is installed in the premises of the blessedly demised L'Express—which was fitted out with appointments from the Paris Métro, and which enjoyed a decibel level that rivaled an IRT local stop with express trains screaming through in both directions. The clangor was a function of the marble surfaces underfoot and all around, but, with very little sacrifice of the interior's original look, the sound has been moderated by installation of moiré-surfaced pads that, though they do not simulate the marble they hide, manage not to look like anything else either. The dim blue fluorescence of the light fixtures behind the often busy bar give off a suitably murky subway luminance, and you take it that the varnished wood-slat benches that form the row of booths across the way are well-preserved relics from old underground cars. The black-and-white photos just above the booths are Man Ray portraits, complete with name tags, among the subjects Cocteau, Berenice Abbot, Marcel Duchamp, Giaco-

219

metti, Picasso, Nude. The brass railings all about, the shiny black tabletops, the Deco wall sconces, and the two-dimensional cut-metal sculpture (a human figure silhouetted before a wall of glinting glass blocks) all contribute to this bistro-brasserie's hard-edged, somewhat glitzy flavor, which is of a time and of a place—the years between the wars, the world below the ground. The customers and staff are young, brisk, and, except that the latter are in white shirts and aprons, interchangeable.

A lot to eat is part of Man Ray's appeal, this plate of smoked fish, for example, much trout, much salmon, both in firm, moist, supple condition, and, oddity, smoked mackerel, the strong dark fish crusted and salty, the three served with a sauce raifort that is of fluffy whipped cream and pungent horseradish. Similarly the bay scallops, which just about cover a good-size plate, but which you wish were browned in the sautéing rather than just warmed in butter—still, they are not bad, benefit from the sprigs and leaves of cilantro and escarole tangled among them. Meat: merguez, the blackened lamb sausages sweet- and hot-spiced, a little dry, served with chickpeas that are redolent of Eastern spices; a terrine, gamy and nutted, rimmed with white fat, served with a hot mustard and a mild one. Salads: one called "crudité," five separate elements on your plate, fennel, endive, slivers of avocado, crunchy red beets, and a well-oiled mingling of sautéed red peppers with anchovies and black olives, everything in a tart dressing; and winter greens with duck cracklings, the great mound of coarse lettuce and chicory dotted with large croutons and bits of crisp duck fat that taste like bacon, all in a warm and tangy vinaigrette.

Salsify is a vegetable much like asparagus, except that it is not asparagus, it is salsify —its crunchiness and homey flavor redeem this fettuccine carbonara, for the noodles are a little tough in their creamy, bacon-dotted sauce. As the world knows, the firm white fish called lotte is nearly flavorless, but it does respond well to such outside influences as the garlicked sea urchin sauce that invigorates the great slices of prettily browned fish served here. Experienced readers of New York menus take a look at the entry "grilled chicken with calamata olives," and figure "a chicken and some olives." This bird, however, is literally coated with a glistening black mash of the salty calamatas, despite which the flavor of the pale meat itself is vivid. The steak is of fibrous and tender meat, but so blackened that all you taste is charcoal, which is too bad, for it is served with thin, crisp French fries, and with a pitcher of more than decent sauce béarnaise. The cassoulet is a substantial bowl of firm beans, the top blackened, in which are buried chunks of sausage, lamb, fowl, and though the last two are cooked to a point of unidentifiability, this is altogether a surfeit of sound and satisfying food. Sometimes choucroute is offered, and if the sour cabbage is a little sodden, it is livened by its black juniper berries, and all that cabbage, taken together with the three whole sausages, slab of pork, and boiled potatoes that adorn it, will anchor you to your seat until the arrival of dessert.

You do well with the simple sweets—good ice cream and sherbet, and a crème caramel that is light, almost fluffy, in its dark and tangy caramel sauce. The chocolate roll is a rather dull cake wrapped around nice whipped cream. Slivers of hot pear are served between blocks of flaky puff pastry, the two, in a thick and fruity sauce, garnished with the good house whipped cream.

★ MARIE-MICHELLE

57 West 56th Street
LUNCH, MONDAY TO FRIDAY; DINNER, DAILY.
Reservations: 315-2444.
Credit cards: AE, DC, MC, V.
Medium priced.

Beware realization of your fantasies. Dreams that excite you may survive only in their natural environment—your imagination. Wishes are, of course, translatable into tangibility—it is only their magic that is not. Here, clearly, is a fond dream, for the lady of the title was, for something like decades, associated with the now defunct Georges Rey (the restaurant was the namesake of her spouse), an animated, sprawling bistro on West 55th. In this place of her own, you read her attitude toward that place of her husband's —this is its opposite. Marie-Michelle is, how you say, feminine. Old rose, taupe, mauve, and off-pink are here set off by contrasting shades of beige, greige, and warm skin (Caucasian). If, in the course of wear and tear, the place develops blemishes, you imagine that Marie-Michelle (the name of the restaurant is the name also of its owner) will go around touching them up with her trusty powder puff. The restaurant is a long room, not very wide, the mirrored wall down one side tinted the color of rose dust. The tables are set with sand-colored linen, and they are surrounded by bentwood side chairs that have been painted a smashing shade of coral mist. There are, however, notes of vivid color: The tables are set with service plates, painted on each of them a coy, highly stylized flapper, a different flapper on each plate; and there is your hostess herself, a tall, dark-haired lady who dresses to stand out from her chosen environment. Her long experience in the restaurant business surely serves her well in some respects. But her politesse has become singsong and mechanical over the years (you assume it was once genuine), and her mastery of restaurant logistics has apparently been accomplished at the expense of sweet reason, for when you arrive to a restaurant that has emptied of its pretheater crowd, and there are any number of tables at which you could be comfortably seated, you are nevertheless required to wait at the tiny, rather crowded bar until your companion arrives. (There will always be among us those whose devotion to order transcends mere purpose.) Her peculiarities notwithstanding, the friends she made at Georges Rey visit her here in numbers, with, on arrival, much kissing of cheeks and, on departure, more kisses—and promises to be back. In fact, they will be back, for her place is a useful one.

Between bouts of kissing, they have dinnered decently on the likes of this gravlax, a delicate version, the pale-pink meat not at all oily, each slice edged with a black and green strip of the layer of herbs and spices under which the salmon marinated—this is more a French than a Scandinavian gravlax, and its sauce is a creamy one that is thick with fresh dill. Thin lengths of asparagus, an abundance of them, are served between light pastries—the two are set in a lemony butter. Order snails, and you are presented with a little copper pot, lid on. Remove the lid, and you find that the implement is tin lined, that it is filled with a thick, winy, lightly tomatoed, and vigorously seasoned sauce, and with plump snails and chunks of wild mushroom—a potent dish. The pasta with

221

shrimp suffers from a paucity of the crustaceans (you get three of them) and from the iodine of which they taste.

Perhaps shrimp, or their shells, are used in the preparation of this so-called lobster stew, for it, too, is touched with iodine—which is too bad, for the morsels of lobster are sweet, and their pink and creamy sauce, sharpened by the flavor of lobster shell and touched with herbs, has much depth. The roasted baby chicken is a fine version of a simple thing. But the medallions of veal—three slices of meat surmounted by three slices of apple, all in a vaguely fruited sauce—could as well be three slices of nameless protein. If you make it to this place just once, do not think about it, but order the rack of lamb. Three not large chops are perhaps less than what you want for dinner, but this is good meat, and the eye of each chop is mounded over with a little cloud of browned and garlicked bread crumbs that is studded with minced vegetables.

The crème caramel is unexceptionable, the cassis cake cloying, the chocolate cake liquored and rich—it comes with good whipped cream. In this fancied bistro, the dessert to have is the chocolate mousse, the big scoop of it buttery and almost black, touched with orange flavor—its texture is like that of ice cream, but its concentration of chocolate flavor is its own.

★★LA MÉTAIRIE

1442 Third Avenue (near 82nd Street)
LUNCH AND DINNER.
Reservations: 988-1800.
Credit cards: AE, MC, V.
Expensive.

As more is better, this namesake offshoot of a rustic twenty-chair French restaurant in Greenwich Village is not only many times the progenitor's size, but outrusticates it exponentially. The intent, clearly, is to make of this example of Gallic yokeldom the last word, and in fact it is impossible to imagine what after this can follow—except crowds, which, sure enough, found this place early on, wallow in its kitsch. You enter to sheep, anyway plaster ones, white, life size, chocolate-colored horns on their heads, woolly white blankets attached to their backs, which you may easily pet, for they form, conveniently, the arms of the sofas in which you wait, on a raised platform up front, for your table, its availability delayed by occupants so enchanted with the setting that they proceed through their courses mesmerized by the contents of this jungle of bucolic paraphernalia. Consider, for example, the lighting, which consists in part of wagon wheel chandeliers hanging among the rafters, mock kerosene lamps on the ceiling, brass brackets holding pairs of candlesticks on the walls, squat table lamps (on tables that, in some instances, are too small to accommodate the huge dinner plates as well) that are candles among wildflowers under perforated brass shades, and a genuine fire (wood stacked beside the fireplace) even in warm weather. On tables and counters fruits and vegetables are displayed, also great fish, their scales gleaming. And of course there are the little shelves with homey artifacts, a milk can, a cruet, an iron, scales, copperware, a set of graduated canisters. The cushions on the ladderback chairs are covered with the same French cotton print as the bolsters on the benchlike banquettes that occupy each side of the rear part of the dining room—the banquettes are overhung, of course, by frame troughs of dried grasses and grains. None of these elements is in itself offensive, but that condition is corrected by the two backlighted paintings on glass that occupy the rear wall—Van Gogh-Millet derivatives, you expect them to change from moment to moment, as if they were part of a slide show flashed by recent returnees from a nine-teenth-century French vacation. It is not necessary actually to enter this place to suffer the visual experience, for its façade is paned glass, floor to ceiling, and no further proof is needed of a normal New Yorker's sangfroid than that not every pane is occupied by the face of a passerby looking through in disbelief.

Oh, yes, there is also a hanging cage in which dwell a pair of cooing love birds, reference to a cage like it in the downtown Métairie. But it is principally in such trap-pings that this place makes reference to the other, for here there is no North African accent to the French cooking, the famous couscous of the Village store does not even appear on this menu—this place, its bucolic appointments notwithstanding, compro-mises not at all its high-tone cooking. It is, for example, the rare farmhouse family that sits itself down to a salad in which a small mound of fresh raw oysters, out of their shells, arranged over leaves of mâche, and adorned with strands of tomato, is garnished with lengths of endives and red beet, everything moistened with a tangy lime-juice dressing. Even less likely down on the farm is this mousse d'oursins, a little chimney of the puréed sea urchin—of all seafood the gamiest when fresh—in a creamy pool of a sauce of sweet red peppers. Another pungent mousse, this one milder even though it is of garlic—and of vivid garlic flavor—the disk of it set within a ring of wild mushrooms that, well sautéed with still more garlic, are earthy and strong. The terrine of artichoke hearts suffers for a certain paucity of artichoke flavor, so it is too bad that the lobster sauce in which it is served is of sufficient blandness not to overpower it.

Your whole lobster, however, is nicely grilled, has lost none of its juiciness, retains all its flavor, is mottled with leaves of basil, is served with a pitcher of fragrant, buttery watercress sauce. La Métairie undertakes the demanding task of grilling a *thin* slice of swordfish, does it well, drying it out not at all—the huge steak, handsomely cross-hatched and strongly flavored by the grilling, reaches you with a red pepper sauce that suits it well, though the fish is fine straight. The sautéed veal chop is pink, fibrous, tender, and juicy within its seared surfaces, the eye topped with strips of ham, vegetables, and cheese, the sauce winy and garlicky, with fresh rosemary much in evidence. Still, the entrecôte de boeuf marchand de vin is better, the beefy, blood-juicy steak, under slices of rich bone marrow, in a polished and vigorous rendition of the dark, earthy, red-wine sauce.

What the house calls dacquoise is an interleaving of crisp meringues with light and dark mousses that are studded with blueberries, the whole thing set in a fruity sauce populated with more of those berries and with slivers of sweet, acidic kumquat. What is called honey crisp is a stack of crackling pancakes, rich whipped cream and ripe raspber-ries between them. The tart tatin is notable for the three-way contrast among firm and slightly sour chunks of apple, caramelized sugar, and rich crème fraîche. The five egg-shaped dollops of sherbet are arranged like the points of an asterisk in a pool of raspberry puree, four of them intensely fruity, the fifth intensely chocolate.

★★★ METRO

23 East 74th Street
LUNCH, SUNDAY TO FRIDAY; DINNER, DAILY.
Reservations: 249-3030.
Credit cards: AE, DC, MC, V.
Expensive.

The name of this place makes reference to chef-proprietor Patrick Clark's former affiliation with TriBeCa's Odeon and the West Side's Café Luxembourg, but otherwise tells nothing of what this place is like—the Paris subway, you will recall, being in no way a clubby men's club. Which is to say that this installation gives more weight to the assumed tastes of the East Side than to those of the friends Clark made at the aforementioned establishments. Not to worry. Metro's near-stuffy look is no harbinger of any shift to the right in Clark's cookery. Odeon's loss is exactly Metro's gain. You even see rebels in distressed denim, up from the deep south-of-Canal, here on nostalgia trips, recalling what once was theirs.

The sedate bar to which you enter will never, be sure, make it as a scene, and the arched tunnel that leads to the dining room, an Oriental runner along its polished-wood floor, its upper walls and ceiling stenciled in a handsome geometric pattern of warm pastels, is hung with small, colorful, baubled chandeliers that, on West Broadway, would come off merely as somewhat larger-than-average earrings. At the end of the tunnel, on your left, is a small dining room for smokers, directly before you the main dining room, for non-, this room all walnut-colored wood paneling, glinting mirrors, a bit of inoffensive modern art, a deep-green banquette around the sides, and about as many white-linened tables as the place can comfortably hold. Only the floor staff recalls Clark's former days—a number of them worked at Odeon and/or Café Luxembourg, and their casual uniforms, of striped shirts, red ties, and short aprons, with pockets for order pads and such, make clear that Metro is more at ease than it looks.

From a menu that changes at least a little every day, you opt for the buckwheat crêpes, of which you receive two: they are dark, thin, of vivid grain flavor, and they form a circular sandwich of which the filling is a dollop of black American caviar, a dollop of crème fraîche, and a poached egg, the whole surrounded by a delicately seasoned sauce that is little more than melted butter and chives—the dish is at once rich and of almost airy lightness, the caviar has exceptionally clear taste for the domestic article, and all the flavors are dazzlingly at home with one another. For comparative simplicity there are these Louisiana shrimp, six of them, sweet and crunchy and strewn with tarragon, their surfaces seasoned and crisped, their buttery mustard sauce thick with herbs. The squab salad is notable for the warm squab—a crisped leg, and slices of the dark breast meat, rare and glistening; and for the cool salad it is on—delicate greens, tender haricots verts, thin strands of red cabbage, their dressing a velvety oil. It is called a napoleon of foie gras, but the two meaty layers within the three of pastry have a buttery richness like that of chocolate mousse, though there is no mistaking the intense liver flavor—the napoleon is ringed by a dark jelly that is fruity of its port wine.

You do wonder how so much saffron flavor is incorporated in the meat of this lobster fricassee without obscuring at all the flavor of the lobster itself—the meat is out of its shell, is tender and juicy, is mingled with wild mushrooms that are in striking, earthy contrast to the sweet crustacean, and it is set in a light whiskey sauce that is threaded with that saffron. The grilled Norwegian salmon is utterly fresh and just a little rare within its crisped, crackling skin—the good fish is garnished with baby leeks, thin spears of firm asparagus, minced tomatoes, and sprigs of dill in its sauce of lemoned oil. You get a chicken here that, by way of its method of preparation (it has been roasted in a clay pot), has an unmatched depth of chicken and chicken-fat flavor, the cooked-through bird juicy and tender, its skin crisped (presumably by a bit of firing after the roasting), the whole garnished with cloves of garlic (you chew the tamed pulp out of the hulls) and with browned potato pancakes that, though wet with butter, are utterly without greasiness—the remarkable and abundant plate of food is adorned with great sprigs of various fresh herbs. You may want to order the loin of lamb just for the fried onions that go with it, for their batter is herbed and a little heady, in its frying it has seemingly absorbed air instead of grease, and the thin rings of onion within the batter, though sweet, retain just a bit of their strength. But the lamb is not bad either, the thick slices of medium-rare roasted meat blood-red and tender within the browned rims, strewn with almond slivers, and moistened with a dark sauce that is touched with Indian spices.

Seemingly weightless desserts: a blood-orange tart in which the sections of citrus are tightly arranged like the spokes of a wheel, a clump of pine nuts at the hub, within a little dish, formed of flaky pastry, that is set in a crimson strawberry sauce; a similar tart, this one of fresh, browned pineapple, fibrous and acidic and sweet, garnished with whole, crunchy, candied almonds; a vanilla crisp in which three circular pastries—of almost fugitive delicacy, the top one under a storm of confectioner's sugar—are interleaved with a light lemon cream and fresh strawberries in their pool of red berry sauce, the tiered item garnished with a little egg of concentrated strawberry sherbet; a chocolate and banana puff pastry that is hardly more than thin disks of ripe fruit among the brown and flaky chocolate layers—this time it is a banana sherbet that garnishes the sweet.

★ MIKE'S

650 Tenth Avenue (near 46th Street)
LUNCH, TUESDAY TO SATURDAY; DINNER, DAILY.
Reservations: 246-4115.
Credit cards: AE, DC.
Inexpensive.

In the era between the wars (the Civil War and World War I) the part of Manhattan known as Hell's Kitchen—30th Street to 59th Street, west of Eighth Avenue—was watched over by such neighborhood civic organizations as the Gorillas, the Hudson Dusters, the Tenth Avenue Gang, and, most notably, the Gophers. When, early in this century, the New York Central Railroad, which maintained substantial facilities there, decided to usurp the influence of these local voluntary groups, it easily gained the support of City Hall, which was always responsive to the pleadings of special interest groups. Soon, some of the area's most respected leaders—Goo Goo Knox, Stumpy Malarkey, and One Lung Curran among them—were removed from their posts. The greed of Big Business had once again been rewarded at the expense of the little people, and the area went into a decline from which it is only now beginning to recover. Today's revival is spearheaded by a group of young restaurateurs. They have banded together to form an organization called The Cookers. Their stationery is emblazoned with the motto, Let's Put the Kitchen Back in Hell's Kitchen.

From the outside, Mike's looks as if it has been on this uninviting block, untended and exposed to the weather, since the days of Goo Goo himself. Taxis delivering passengers here (folks who learned about the place in the press) have been seen to drive up— and then drive off. But a few minutes after you have gained entrance, you find that the inside of the restaurant has been appointed almost as daintily as a nursery. The woodstrip walls have been painted yellow, the table linen is actually prettily striped wrapping paper, and the ancient bar, which runs the full length of the narrow front part of the store, is right at home under its old, bright-red-plastic top. This child's room has the kid's art on the walls. The loving parents have even framed the things and put them up for sale. The tile floor is easy to keep clean. And, so that mama may keep an eye on her charge, the portal to the kitchen is wide open. Tables and chairs are wherever they can fit—a couple under the front window, a few opposite the bar, a density of them in the back—and they are occupied mostly by the young people who are beginning to change the complexion of this part of town. Males among them wear no neckties, but atop the females there is many a fedora. You need not refer to the garb, however, to determine the genders, for makeup is back in, and so far only the ladies have picked up on it. The help wear name tags, all of which read "Mike." New customers unfamiliar with the practice get the attention of their waitress by calling out, "Mike." She comes by to see what is wanted.

The menu is in two parts, "From Mike's Mexican Bar" and "From Mike's American Grill." On the Mexican side, there is cilantro-cured salmon, four substantial slices of the firm, dark pink meat, tangy with lime and heady with the flavor and fragrance of the herb; a guacamole that is fresh-made, but not of first-rate avocados (they may even be Florida avocados)—and though the dish is spicy and well garlicked, it lacks moisture; taco salad, a great dollop of spicy and meaty no-bean chili, a mound of shredded cheese, sour cream, red and green peppers, and onions, all served with crisp chips; bean-and-cheese nachos, sturdy beans and weighty melted cheese, fiery green peppers their foil; Mexican chicken salad, big chunks of the meat of the bird mingled with celery, onions, red beans, and chick-peas, all in a spicy dressing, and garnished with red peppers and tomatoes. On the American side, you find these charred seafood sausages, smoky and vaguely anise-flavored, but lacking seafood quality—they reach you in adjacent pools of red-pepper sauce and green-tomato sauce; grilled Cornish hen, the whole bird, handsomely charred, cooked through but still moist, but still a Cornish hen and therefore low on flavor—it comes with a cool assortment of dressed vegetables called "gazpacho salad"; "Mike's own" meat sausages, big, blackened, and of good lamb flavor—but they are dry, and you do expect fattiness and richness in this kind of thing; and marinated leg of lamb, a winner, many slices cut from the grilled leg, rare and with charred edges, tender and of good flavor—like a number of the dishes here, it is served with corn salad, the cool yellow kernels in a peppery dressing.

The dark apple-spice cake is dense with chunks of apple and powerfully flavored of clove—lots of it is sold here, and it is always fresh, moist, fluffy. The sweet-spiced walnut pie is heavier on the nuts than on the filler, but its side of whipped cream is a little loose. You order something called S-mores because you cannot believe the description on the menu: "toasted marshamallows on graham crackers with melted bittersweet chocolate." The description, it turns out, is correct. Elements hostile to liberation have attributed the concoction to the Girl Scouts.

226

★★MISS RUBY'S CAFÉ

135 Eighth Avenue (near 17th Street)
LUNCH AND DINNER.
Reservations: 620-4055.
Credit cards: AE, MC, V.
Medium priced.

Every other Tuesday the menu at Miss Ruby's changes—from the cookery of one part of the United States to that of another. The customers come back anyway, apparently confident that if they liked, say, the Yankee Pot Roast one time around, they will be happy with Confederate Pudding the next. If the food of America's regions gets you thinking of the great outdoors, of endless plains, prairies, and deserts, of the young nation's epic march to the Pacific (the primal eviction plan), know that you will get a taste at Miss Ruby's not only of the country's food, but also of its customs and vastness. There is, for example, the campfire in the open kitchen: the flames leap up, radiating light, warmth, and danger—the waiter getting your dinner is within easy reach of the fractious blaze; and there is the ranch-hands'-breakfast style of service, with a member of the staff cruising the tables every ten minutes or so to distribute cornbread or biscuits just out of the oven and steaming. The physical place itself is well lighted, wide open, and painted a red-hot shade of Great Southwest terra-cotta flowerpot. The Café is also, however, distinctly of the present. The young, willing, and cheerful help are in jeans or chinos, sweatshirts or polo shirts. And the folks at the tables are in the casuals they would wear in front of their television sets, did not Miss Ruby's offer comforts like those of home.

It is in the nature of this place that what it has served before it may never serve again. But if Miss Ruby someday elects to repeat its Texas Country menu, you will be able to sample cornmeal-fried green tomatoes, thick disks encased in a grease-free cornmeal batter, the tart, firm—almost hard—tomato slices vigorous and rousing in their crisp casings. On the same menu you will find a crabmeat item credited to Helen Corbitt, a late popularizer and refiner of Texas cooking. Sure enough, the dish is both homey and fancy, the abundance of delicately seasoned crabmeat browned, crisped, and lightly bound by the mild cheese with which it is prepared—it reaches you, in its little casserole dish, in a shallow pool of hot cream. The barbecued chicken is half of a big tasty bird in a slick black gravy that is thick with beans—a cool, creamy, and firm potato salad dotted with bits of crisp onion is its perfect foil. When the subject is Texas, naturally there is chili. You, of course, opt to have yours the beanless Texas way, and the nubbly ground beef comes to you in a dark-brown sauce that is weighty, sharp—almost bitter—pungently spiced, and topped with strong chopped onions, pully cheese, and cool sour cream.

Compared with the earthiness of its Texas fortnight, the Ruby menu is positively recherché when it is Contemporary California. Something listed under "soup" is actually a semicircular orange pool of cold carrot puree adjacent to a semicircular dark-red pool of cold beet puree, the two halves forming a round in a deep soup plate, each an intense expression of the pure vegetable. The duck taco is a folded and crisp-fried tortilla filled

227

with tender shredded duck meat in a dark sauce—you find a dab of spicy salsa verde on your plate as well, sprigs of coriander, bits of fruit, sour cream. Order the squid stuffed with shrimp, and you receive four pearly bodies, each of them the size of a big thumb, packed with a delicate shrimp forcemeat that is dotted with green peas—the constructs are served in a lime-flavored cream sauce dotted with more of those sweet peas. What is listed as "rabbit with vermouth, summer savory and lemon" adds up to a rabbit stew in a sticky and peppery sauce—good food, if not the exotic item the wording leads you to expect.

As part of that California menu, you may have a fresh, firm, and headily perfumed peach that has been blanched, peeled, and sliced—it is served with a great dollop of crème fraîche and a chewy oatmeal cookie; or a great nugget of ginger-flavored pound cake, its dark-brown exterior a good zest to the pale, moist cake—it reaches you under rich whipped cream, and it is served with a glass of sweet and spicy muscat wine. The Texas desserts include a pecan pie that is dense with crunchy nuts.

Yes, there is a Miss Ruby, and most nights she is there in the open kitchen, preparing and dishing out. At late night she sometimes deserts her post, traverses the dining room to the bar, picks up refreshments for the kitchen crew, and returns. Other times, when a menu is nearing the end of its two weeks, she goes among the tables offering samples of something from the one coming up.

A little sign in a plastic holder on each table lists special drinks like "Texas Hot-Pepper Vodka"; it offers wine advice as well, suggesting, for example, that the Montepulciano d'Abruzzi of 1981 is "great with chicken-fried steak."

★★★★ MONDRIAN

5 East 59th Street
LUNCH, MONDAY TO FRIDAY; DINNER, MONDAY TO SATURDAY. CLOSED SUNDAY.
Reservations: 935-3434.
Credit cards: AE, MC, V.
Very expensive.

In search of a name, the interests behind Mondrian looked into the history of the building in which it is housed. Fortunately, they dug deep, found that Piet Mondrian (Dutch painter, 1872–1944), who spent his last years in New York, lived and worked at this address. A less thorough investigation might have yielded only that, in more recent times, this was the address of New York's Playboy Club. It may be argued that yummy food, posh surroundings, and fancy prices are more compatible with the so-called Playboy philosophy than with the abstract—and, to many eyes, austere—style for which Mondrian is best known. Maybe. But somehow, surely for a restaurant, the name Mondrian has—as the name Hefner has not—a certain ring. Moreover, the house has chosen to honor the location's artistic past by adorning its walls with art that, by what it is, and by its placement, actually graces this interior. Were the site's fleshly, rather than aesthetic, history being honored, there would have been nothing for it but to deck the walls with centerfolds.

An arresting black-and-white photo of a Henry Moore family group confronts you as you enter to the small barroom, which is all soft light and walnut-colored wood paneling, the three-sided bar a curving slab of deep-green marble that is repeated in the green marble squares of the floor. Where, ordinarily, spirits are displayed, before the mirrored wall behind the bar, here the display is solely of glinting glasses on glass shelves, nary a bottle of booze in sight. It is not that Mondrian is waiting for its license, rather that it abjures anything that is crass or that may be taken as such. The dining room, just through the bar, is a great oblong divided into three areas by slight protrusions into the room from the long sides. Wood paneling here, too, except that the walls of the rearmost area are faced with padded cloth of mottled chestnut brown. The large tables, much room around them, are covered with white linen, are set with flowers, are surrounded by spiffy chairs of brown leather and gleaming steel—except for three tables at the back that are set before cushy banquettes built into mirrored niches. The dining room is carpeted, big bursts of flowers are placed here and there, and the handsomely matted and framed prints are well placed, each of them an assertive and civilizing presence in this ample, commodious space.

It was a black day in Chatham, New Jersey, when the chef here decided to move his then operation twenty miles east to the big city, where, it had been figured out, oodles of disposable income for deductible expenditures waited. Chatham had somehow neglected to declare the man unexportable, a landmark, an icon of the town's historic (albeit recent) past. Now, in the tradition of expatriates who brought fame to their places of origin only by leaving them, and were only then honored back home, this rover will surely give his name to a Chatham park, or street, or one-runway airport, for very soon, now that he cooks where it counts, his name shall be a byword, even though it (Foy), too, lacks a certain ring.

A hot summer night, and you order an innocent-sounding lobster-and-potato salad that, described only as "chilled," suggests to you something refreshing, picnic food, a light way to ease yourself into a weighty dinner. The item turns out to be not at all one of those salads in which the main component is merely garnished with greens and other vegetables. What you get, rather, is a compacture of minced ingredients bound in a dressing. A mound of the stuff is at the center of your plate (which, like the plates for all first and second courses, is the size of a gleaming-white manhole cover), and closely resembles a sandwich filling—though you begin to suspect it is something quite else when you determine that the thick disks with which the salad is surmounted are slices of black truffle. As to the salad itself, you experience it as a dazzling concatenation of impressions, lobster sweetness, the firmness and clear taste of the tiny potato dice, bursts of pepper hotness, herbs, the earthiness of that truffle. What is given as "tuna, salmon, and bass with a sea urchin vinaigrette" reaches you, reading from top to bottom, as a hefty circle of dark, raw, beefy tuna, under it a mound of green salad into the sides of which are tucked nuggets of black bass tartare, and around which are arrayed slices of marinated salmon—that simple-looking salad is unpredictably livened with mint, and the sauce in which everything is set is a vinaigrette thickened with, and made pungent by, pureed sea urchin, withal the subtle differences among the fish are clear, and the concordance among the several elements is dazzling. A steak tartare is listed, and it reaches you as a plump patty from which radiate, like the rays of a cartoon sun, slices of toast on which you may choose to spread it. The tartare is of beef just ground, it is studded with capers and bits of onion, and it is rousing of its spices; still, you do wish it were oilier, stickier, richer. Carefully sautéed foie gras needs no help, the soft, sweet, oleaginous meat, within browned surfaces flecked with black, is perfection, anything more may well be taken as gilding the liver. Here, however, you mind the gilding not at all, for the slices of meat, charred, glistening a little, reach you on a platform of minced cabbage, hot and juicy, that is studded with meaty bits of bacon, the entire construct set

229

in two semicircles of bell pepper sauce, one yellow and mild, the other red and of brilliant flavor. But when the foie gras is a minor element, as in the "fried zucchini flower stuffed with foie gras," it is not the making of the dish—these battered and crisped pouches, the named ingredients within, and set in a polished sweet-wine sauce, though flawlessly executed and diverting, are not what you want when what you want is foie gras. When what you want is pasta, be deliriously happy about the presence on this menu of "pasta with basil, truffle, and tomato," which reaches you as a tangle of spaghetti formed into a tower at the center of your plate, around it three disks of tomato that are ripe, warm, and buttery, the pasta itself, in its herbed and truffled sauce, of an almost overwhelmingly woodsy taste and fragrance—the dish is strewn with sprigs of parsley and the familiar herb has never before found a setting in which it is so brilliant an accent.

When soft-shell crabs are in season this place obtains the small ones, sautés them judiciously, so that they are crisp and delicate, adorns them with good American black caviar, serves them with a sauce that is a heady concentration of green herbs. When the Mediterranean swimmer called rouget is available, Mondrian apparently gets it the day it is caught three thousand miles away, for the little fillets are firm, juicy, utterly fresh. The taste of rouget is distinctive, it is not particularly strong, but here—arranged on a two-layered platform of black pasta and disks of fried potato, and strewn with deep-fried spinach that crackles and falls into flakes if you merely touch it, everything set in a buttery and orange-colored saffron sauce—the framing of the fish makes its flavor vivid. Snapper, the American fish that sometimes masquerades as rouget, is undisguised, gets a treatment of its own, given as "red snapper with seven onions spontanée," in which the substantial fillet, cooked a little rare, its crisped skin attached, all its flavor intact, arrives flanked by a pool of pale, buttery sauce that is strewn with squiggles and curlicues and circles of various colors, representing the "seven onions"—leeks, scallions, red onions, etc., the garlic branch of the family represented by a dollop of garlic puree, short lengths of truffle being the interloper, black accents in the colorful picture. The breast of guinea hen reaches you as many elongate slices formed into a rough circle. They surround a meat-dotted mash of apples that is adorned with little onions cooked to the point of sweetness, but not browned. The meat itself is not fatty, but is strongly flavored of the fat under its attached skin, and it is enriched by the dark, herbed, and sticky sauce in which it is served. Good vegetables and an almost overpowering tarragon sauce are components of what goes as roast loin of veal, but the news is the veal itself, three thick slices of firm but tender meat, browned but not crusted, cooked through but juicy—that rarity, veal that is a confluence of texture and subtle flavor, veal that needs no sauce at all.

The desserts tend toward the elemental: a peach tart that is a dome—a half peach—tailored to the circular shortbread pastry on which it is set, the poached fruit of wondrously fresh peach flavor; a raspberry tart that is of perfect little berries, a bit of custard, a pastry cup that will not disappoint you if you think of it as merely the dish in which the other ingredients are served; a chocolate layer cake, in a pool of coffee sauce, that suffers for being merely flawless; a chocolate dacquoise that is nutted, subtly sweetened, chewy, rich, surfaced with an icing that is almost black; a pineapple rum millefeuille that is three blocks cut from a weightless layered affair of flaky pastry and rich, airy custard, the three set in a caramel sauce on which is set also a ball of cold, rich ice cream, and crushed pineapple that is a little acidic, sweet, rousing.

★★★ MONTRACHET

239 West Broadway (near White Street)
LUNCH, FRIDAY; DINNER, MONDAY TO SATURDAY. CLOSED SUNDAY.
Reservations: 219-2777.
Credit cards: AE.
Expensive.

Timeworn store space has been gutted, smoothed, painted, furnished plainly with little more than tables and chairs, and opened for restaurant business at scores of SoHo and TriBeCa sites during the past ten years. Though the spare style is dictated at least in part by economics, and surely in part by fashion, it is nevertheless susceptible of individual interpretation, may be rendered expressively. You can go into a project like this and come out with the grandeur stark, the humble cozy, the slick, the sleek, the bold. Some of these installations suggest the straightforward, bustling eating places that, one imagines, were common in New York in its early days. Others, by more or less imaginative use of found-on-premises appointments—brick, ancient wood floors, antique light fixtures, whatever—permit the old site to be reborn, are restorations as much as renovations. Montrachet, too bad, is the downtown style but little else. Nothing terribly wrong with it, you understand, rather that when you walk into this place, almost immediately, nothing happens.

You enter to the first of three rooms, its small dark-wood bar, faced with panels of marble and backed by wine racks to the ceiling, the restaurant's one handsome object. Across from it, a banquette of raspberry-colored plush, white-linened tables before it, skirts the room on three sides. The second and third rooms are furnished with little more than tables and chairs. The walls throughout are milky pastels—baby blue (or is it green?), faded pink (or is it coral?)—with, in the third room, some vaguely patterned wallpaper. The carpeted floors are gray, the stamped-tin ceiling—wavy here, scarred there—is white, as are the exposed pipes just under it. In this setting, you welcome the staff uniform—black shirts and black pants—for being at least a mannerism.

One of the gentlemen in black informs you that the regularly listed scallop soup is this evening replaced by lobster soup, a pale-pink liquid that, though creamy, is light rather than rich, the white at its center a dollop of crème frâiche, the soup's gentle lobster flavor set off by the bits of vegetable with which it is dotted, the many kernels of yellow corn among them of an intense sweetness that competes with the shellfish as the soup's dominant flavor. Do the soup any day rather than this terrine of smoked salmon and eel, a square cut from a loaf, its striped face pink (salmon), brown (eel), and green (greens), and though the ingredients are fine, you find yourself picking them apart to consume them separately, for they do nothing for one another—the dish seems to need a sauce to make it add up. But then there is this oyster tart, a circle of pastry, its circumference raised, upon it four tender oysters, warm but with all· their "raw" flavor intact, among them slivers of crunchy fennel, almost hard, and bits of strong Italian bacon, all in a pink and creamy sauce, chives and fragrant dill sprinkled on. Start your dinner with pigeon, and you are served a mound of warm salad, herbed and crunchy, leaning against its sides a half dozen parts and slices of the bird, the dark, moist meat intense of pigeon's

231

characteristically almost chocolate flavor. Even more intense, and considerably richer, are these blackened slices of fresh duck liver, the charred, pinguid meat served on a hot and glistening mass of sweet, slivered shallots.

Black sea bass is beginning to appear frequently on local menus. Its firm, white-to-pink flesh has a delicate but clear marine flavor, and these fresh fillets, served under a tomato hash with strands of green vegetable in a tart vinaigrette, reveal all their flavor in the setting. The place makes a homey roast chicken, the trifurcated breast, moist but cooked through under its delicately browned skin, arranged over mashed potatoes—judiciously seasoned and enriched—that have real texture. The flavor of the chicken, though not strong, is potentiated by the cloves of sweet garlic with which it is roasted (you chew the softened garlic from its hulls), and the bird is, in a sense, garnished with itself, for beside the breast are placed three nuggets of a leg that has been boned, stuffed with spinach, and roasted with the rest of the bird—a wondrous chicken dish. More birds: a duck of deep flavor, thin strands of ginger strewn over its browned skin, the dark roasting juices tangy and a little sweet of the spice; and baby pheasant, redolent of its own fat within its crisped tegument, in a winy sauce threaded with slivers of strong, black olive. The two tournedos of veal loin, though supple and handsomely browned, gain much that they need from the sautéed wild mushrooms with which they are spread, for the meat itself has not been brought to life—the garnish of browned potatoes, strewn with fresh rosemary, helps too. No such problem with the loin of lamb, the four chunks of rare meat—suffused with garlic flavor—arranged prettily among halves of baby artichoke, a bit of vegetable stuffing in each, a clump of strong spinach at the center of the plate. The lamb is served with a baked casserole of butternut squash, the earthy mash, at once creamy and crunchy, threaded with sweet onions.

The crème brûlée is less than fluffy under its caramelized, crystallized top. Though the word "dacquoise" will probably suggest to you a layered thing of crunchy meringues, something creamy between them, when you order it here, you get two slices of an intense chocolate confection in a cool white sauce that is studded with nuts. Much is made of soufflés. The crêpe soufflé is a mass of the fluffy stuff (sometimes flavored with Grand Marnier) within a delicate crêpe—it is garnished with fruits, an egg of passion-fruit sherbet, mint leaves, a cookie. Most, however, go for the pair of small soufflés, one intensely chocolate, the other tangy of raspberry, dots of chocolate in the pool of raspberry sauce in which they are served, a bit of rich vanilla ice cream a nice foil to the hot sweets.

★★IL MULINO

86 West 3rd Street
LUNCH, MONDAY TO FRIDAY; DINNER, MONDAY TO SATURDAY. CLOSED SUNDAY.
Reservations: 673-3783.
Credit cards: AE.
Expensive.

At Il Mulino, as in any singular institution, the tone is set at the top. At Il Mulino's top there is Fernando, a dark and cherubic gentleman whose manner is unfailingly earnest. Accordingly, everyone here is unfailingly earnest. Whether you are dealing with

Fernando himself or with one of his men, the issue of you and your dinner is addressed in the manner of the man at your bedside discussing you and tomorrow's surgery. And just as the wig and robe worn by every member of an English court serve to remind each wearer of his commitment to the proceedings, so is the staff at Il Mulino—unlike that of any other Greenwich Village Italian restaurant—attired in formal black-and-whites, with starched collar and bowtie. This is not, you understand, the false formality that is adjunct to the smirking politesse of certain posh spaghetti joints uptown. Fernando and his staff are not competing with you. They have put on their tuxedos for the same reason they attend to you so fervently. What you are dealing with is propitiation. The house is attempting to please you—albeit in ways that seem quaint. It is desired that you come back. For, as Fernando will tell you if you give him a narrow opening, he is from a very small town in Italy—a place, presumably, where the middle class does not seek thrills by shopping around for the latest thing in contempt.

The restaurant is on a grim block, so it is something of a startlement to enter to the cool, oaseal comfort of its cushy darkness. The front room gets only very soft light through the north-exposed gauze curtains that cover its 3rd Street windows. Here you find the crowded bar at which the devoted patiently wait—sometimes they fill the entire room. And here you find the big display of appetizers, cheeses, desserts. Usually the spread is merely admired, but on Saturday nights, when this place gets a certain transriverine crowd, nibblers may be seen plucking a tidbit here, licking their fingers, plucking another there. Mostly, however, the restaurant gets a civilized set. Two stands of palms at the back of this room separate it from the dining room proper—you pass between them on your way to dinner. In the dining room, in the even deeper darkness, the walls that are not of glazed brick are inexplicably covered with a vaguely Oriental wallpaper. The massive low-hanging light fixtures are equipped with five-watt bulbs, and on the rows of white-linened tables the little candles glow, in this setting, like flares. When you get accustomed to the dimness, you note that on one wall there is a big black-on-white painting of a water wheel and attached shed—"Il Mulino" is "the mill."

The place is contentedly occupied by, mostly, groups and large groups, pairs of couples and whole families, and hardly are they folded into their chairs—menus have not yet been handed around, no one has come by to recite the special dishes of the day— and already plates of food are being set on their tables. You are given something to eat even before you are asked if you would like "something from the bar." And if you go at the freebies greedily you will be ready for coffee before you have asked for the wine list. You will not be proffered the entire selection at one dinner, but come here often enough, and you will sample: thin disks of sautéed zucchini, delicately browned, vividly garlicked, abundantly oiled; salami, the hard slices of purple meat fatted and peppered and gamy; chunks of Parmesan cheese—sometimes the wheel itself, or a large section of it, is placed on your table, and you help yourself; cool little mussels, in their shells, sweet and salty in their light dressing; bruschetta, crusts of toasted bread buried under chopped tomatoes, in a garlicky dressing that is threaded with fresh basil.

One pasta dish carries the restaurant name: capellini Il Mulino, thin spaghetti in a sauce, thick with cheese, that is of exceptionally nutty wild-mushroom flavor—fresh peas are the other component, and in this setting they are strikingly sweet. That same thin spaghetti is served also all'arrabbiata, the great tangle of filaments in a spicy and weighty red sauce that is dotted with capers and laced with slivers of black olive. Sometimes the house offers a linguine primavera, and this is an odd version, really a collection of vegetables (snow peas, zucchini, mushrooms, little florets of broccoli, even a great slice of tomato) augmented by slivers of meat and bits of shellfish, the thin pasta that is threaded among them in a seemingly secondary role—the dish is stout and good to eat, but not exactly what you expected when you ordered linguine primavera.

It is the style of this place to apply sauces to fish, fowl, meat in a voluptuous super-abundance that may well be off-putting, especially if you have done well by what went before. Occasionally, for example, the fish of the day is Norwegian salmon, of which you are served a steak the size of an art book. It is lovely fish, fresh, firm, falling easily into moist flakes, but it is buried under mushrooms and onions that are not only copious, but awash in the oil in which they were sautéed—they are fine, but you wish they had spent time in a slotted spoon before being spread over the pink meat. The clams posillipo are a small mountain of bivalves in their shells, a pungent red sauce over them, an inch of briny red broth under them. The scampi fra diavolo are big and crunchy shrimp (a handful of those good clams as well) in a spicy red sauce that will film your brow—you do wish the shrimp were not touched with iodine. The spezzatino di pollo is many huge chunks of clear-flavored chicken in a dense and winy sauce that is thick with slices of artichoke. What are given as uccelletti alla fiorentina are hefty roulades of browned veal in a rich and creamy sauce that is dense with slices of porcini mushroom and dotted with sweet peas. Those mushrooms yet again, this time in a sauce under which is buried a veal chop valdostana of gargantuan impact. The browned mammoth chop (its giant rib reaches out well beyond the circumference of its plate) is latitudinally bifurcated to the bone, in the interstice a sheet of ham and a layer of pully cheese. There are even steaks, but they are not the usual thing. Consider, for example, this six-inch two-by-four of fibrous and supple beef—it is served in a spicy sauce of capers and mushrooms that is a dramatic foil to the blood-juicy meat.

Order the marinated orange—the whole peeled fruits have been spending time in cognac and Grand Marnier—and your waiter comes to your table and dexterously carves the sections from the body, arranges them in a circle around the edge of your plate, spoons strands of marinated rind over the center. When he has done your orange, he quarters for your companion a nicely poached pear—it is done in white wine—and, before serving it, livens it with pear brandy. There are always berries, and you may have yours under a big dollop of cool, winy zabaglione that is enriched with whipped cream —the crumbled macaroons on top add a nice bit of texture.

★★NANNI

146 East 46th Street
LUNCH, MONDAY TO FRIDAY; DINNER, MONDAY TO SATURDAY. CLOSED SUNDAY.
Reservations: 697-4161.
Credit cards: AE, DC, MC, V.
Very expensive.

If you think that New York's side streets are dotted with little old Italian restaurants to which the salt of the city repair for sturdy food in colorful, convivial surroundings, be informed that the type you have in mind exists, mainly, in the mind. Once, such places were all over the place, but most of the midtown ones disappeared when the buildings that housed them were torn down to make way for very large stalagmites. Among today's midtown restaurants, the one that best exemplifies the old style is this one, which is, in fact, a relative newcomer. It showed up in the late sixties, when most of its predecessors had already shuffled off. One reason Nanni carries on as steadily as it now does—deviating hardly at all from the Italian-bistro formula—is that its proprietor opened a big, fancy joint uptown several years after the successful inauguration of this one, and since he spends much of his time up there, he lets this place run along in an old-fashioned way that, most nights, packs them in.

You enter to a wall, on your left, that is bedecked with reviews of the restaurant, articles about Nanni himself, and photographs of him in the company of his food. On your right is the small, glass-enclosed, second-string dining room, with a handful of tables and twelve chairs, into which that many diners may be folded plus one upright slender waiter. Past that noise box, and you are at the "bar," which stands five comfortably, ten frequently. But things open up farther on. Down a few steps, and you are in the dining room proper, comparatively wide-open spaces—though even back here, whispered conversations at adjacent tables may be your principal entertainment. The simple, rectangular room has an oak floor, travel posters are affixed to its white walls, a shelf of wine bottles rims it a little overhead, and small lamps with red shades stand on its white-linened tables. This particular Italian restaurant gets a steakhouse crowd—pairs of guys and gangs of guys. It also gets a number of couples who have recently met—middle-aged gents in town for the annual convention and ladies to whom they have been introduced, and whom they have invited to dinner at Nanni in order to get better acquainted. She: "Are you married?" He: "Well, it's a long story."

There are a few first courses and soups, including fresh clams that are sometimes as large as quahogs and quite resilient, and a hefty minestrone of pasta, root vegetables, and strong greens in a deep, well-herbed stock. But Nanni will make half orders of any of its good pasta dishes, and for greatest contentment, it is with the noodle that you should start your dinner here. When those clams are chopped up for use with pasta, they become part of a good, standard version of linguine with white clams, in which the sauce is briny and strong, the clams abundant—the dish is adorned with a couple of hot clams, whole and in their shells. You may have that same pasta with a pesto sauce that is dense, fragrant of basil, glistening with oil—you permit your waiter to add a good bit of cheese. The fettuccine is billed as "alla Nanni," and what himself elects to give his name to is rather light, creamy tomato sauce dotted with peas—it makes a homey and satisfying dish. But good as those are, the big pasta winner is the spaghetti all'amatriciana, in which a thick, rich, potently seasoned red sauce is sweetened with onions and fortified with slivers of Italian bacon.

A fillet of sea bass marechiaro, about the size of your forearm, is served in a peppery and garlicky red sauce—the utterly fresh fish is firm, perfectly cooked, glossy with moisture. Big chunks of sautéed chicken on the bone are served as chicken scarpariello—the browned and shiny nuggets, of clear chicken flavor, are moistened with a garlicked wine sauce and strewn with parsley.

The veal francese is pearly meat in a delicately crisped egg-and-flour crust—the bits of prosciutto on top are a nice note, but the lemon sauce is disastrously soupy, and just wets the dish. Try instead the scaloppine alla zingara, in which that same meat, artfully browned, is buried under sautéed mushrooms, onions, strands of prosciutto—the stout food is strongly but not excessively salted. The great eye of meat in the thick veal chop sorpresa is horizontally incised halfway down and stuffed with prosciutto and hot, pully fontina cheese—the production is covered over with mushrooms in a winy sauce, making for a dish of such substantiality that some may call it heavy. The sweetbreads are notable for the fluffiness of the rich organ meat within the nicely crisped surfaces of the many slices—they come in a good mushroom sauce that is flavored with Madeira wine. The medaglioni di filetto alla Nanni consists of two thick rounds of tender steak, rare as

235

you want them, in yet another winy mushroom sauce, this one a little creamy as well.

If you remember to think ahead, you inform your waiter early on that you want your salad after your main course (it is part of the deal). The greens are crisp, and they come in a tart dressing that is vividly garlicked; with them you may order some Parmesan cheese, which is hard, heady, and sharp. The sweet desserts are of no interest.

• NICOLA PAONE

207 East 34th Street
LUNCH, MONDAY TO FRIDAY; DINNER, MONDAY TO SATURDAY. CLOSED SUNDAY.
Reservations: 889-3239.
Credit cards: AE, DC.
Very expensive.

Here lunches the *National Review*, William F. Buckley's hobby. Extreme liberals avoid the place on the assumption that its eponymous proprietor must surely be a card-carrying Fascist, but though neither political posters nor any other factional signs are in evidence, there are indications that Mr. Paone is an ardent conservator of ancient values. His menu is one such. You cannot, for example, get a bite of food in this place that you could not have got in scores of New York Italian restaurants back in the days when northern and southern Italian cooking were respectively defined as Neapolitan and Sicilian. Yes, this is something of a reliquary. Its somber solidity will put you in mind of certain old stone museums in which are housed arcane collections no one ever looks at. Those who visit this museum, however, are here to consider not an ancient culture, but their own. Nicola Paone is the house of the almost dead. Those in attendance are well fed, sit at their dinners upright and past stoicism, register nothing. It is a posture that, you will recall, surrounded you on your last visit to a house of worship.

Upon a time every fourth Mediterranean restaurant on Manhattan Island was fitted out as your basic wine cellar. Like most of them, this survivor does not take the theme terribly seriously. This cellar, for example, has mock windows, barred, that look out on painted landscapes and town streets. Tile rooftops protrude into the room on all sides, there is a gurgling fountain, a fruiterer's display, strings of garlic on the walls, a bowl of oranges on a shelf, a basket of onions on a tray stand. You walk on a floor that is of great square stones. The back of your armchair is of webbed leather. Often the background music is a plinking guitar, and a guitar hangs on one wall. As your waiter explains, Mr. Paone is a musician, is the soloist in his own singing commercial. In fact, Paone may come by and tell you the one about the customer who dials information and asks for this restaurant's number, whereupon, so the story goes, the operator sings it—889-3239—just the way Nick himself sings it on the air. You figure the tale has been told a thousand times.

Nostalgia takes over, and you order the cold antipasto. Sure enough, here is that slice of salami of sainted memory, that sheet of ham over more-or-less ripe melon, the dab of clammy caponata, the ice cold stuffed mushroom, the bitter slice of roasted red pepper, and the lumpish lump of mozzarella. Next time your good sense takes over, and you go for the baked clams, eight fresh littlenecks in their shells, their oiled breading delicately browned. Do not, however, conclude that clams in any form are this establishment's forte, for the white clam sauce you may have on your spaghetti seems like something prepared at the beginning of the week for daily reheating as needed—the clams are flat and leathery, utterly without seafood sparkle. The lasagna, though undistinguished, is inoffensive—a weighty compendium of firm pasta and melted cheese pinked with a primitive tomato sauce.

Even in its earliest days, the Paone menu suffered from a slight case of the cutes, listed ordinary dishes by irrelevant names—among them baci-baci, boom-boom, night-gown, the last of which consists of two gargantuan roulades of veal, eggplant, and cheese that oozes from the ends like an extrusion—the dabs of tomato sauce on the cylinders do nothing to leaven their tasteless weight. The snapper is browned—through and through. The chicken cacciatore is an honest dish, big parts of a big, rather tasty bird in a decent mushroom sauce. Your steak is a little tough, and, though ordered rare, quite medium —still, this is beef of good blood flavor.

On the wagon an assortment of layer cakes: a pignoli cake that is notable for its nutty flavor and for the layer of rich whipped cream at the center; chocolate ricotta cheesecake that is intense and rich—and heavy; a strawberry-banana shortcake composed of good fruit, good whipped cream, dull pastry.

★ IL NIDO

251 East 53rd Street
LUNCH AND DINNER. CLOSED SUNDAY.
Reservations: 753-8450.
Credit cards: AE, DC, MC, V.
Expensive.

One of the most popular restaurants in New York, but all it ever takes to reserve a table is a quarter for the phone. Of course when you arrive, you may well find a waiting crowd ahead of you that would itself fill a restaurant. Thus has Il Nido solved the no-show problem. For everyone who decides not to keep his word, there are two who regret keeping theirs. When a restaurant, because of near-unanimous praise, is taken up by those who wish only to be secure in what they like, the management may be tempted to write off the discerning, to discontinue operation as an eating place, to carry on solely as a money machine. A fool's money, after all, is as good as anyone else's, and that kind will show up in hordes, get cranked through, make their contribution, and go home content if the evening carried a seal of prior approval. If a few have the sense to be offended, even to leave, well, there are always others adding themselves to the end of the line. Il Nido still serves good food, an occasional dish as good as it ever was, but as its commerce is no longer with a clientele of its own, rather with an anonymous populace that eats where it is told, the place perpetuates but does not renew itself, which is stagnation. When the lady at the book mechanically assures you that the wait will be "no more than a few minutes," while those being seated tell you that forty-five minutes have passed since the hour of their reservation, you know you are in the hands of the dehu-manized. Your hope, if not your faith, is somewhat renewed by the dining room staff's courtesies, even though they are expended mainly on those on whom they are wasted.

The physical Nido is as engaging as ever. The anteroom to which you enter, three tables and a tiny bar, a dark, dark-gray and rather spiffy prelude to the stylized farmhouse that is the restaurant proper, a big, rambling, softly lit place in which deep-brown half timbers and ivory-colored rough plaster are dramatically juxtaposed with walls of paned mirroring that are jewel-like and crystalline. You are seated, before white-linened tables, on the dark-brown banquette that rims the dining rooms, or on handsome black-enameled side chairs. Wherever you sit, you are hard by others—nary an inch of this precious New York real estate goes to nonprofit ends.

What is given as "fresh mushroom salad" is not as fresh as it once was—still, the great mound of thin slivers (they are only a little limp), dotted with nuggets of celery and bits of strong garlic, has been dressed with an intense and fragrant green olive oil that quite overcomes any flatness of the main ingredient. Mushrooms again, chunks and lengths of sautéed woodsy porcini, moist of the strongly seasoned oil in which they were done, arranged on crusted triangles of polenta—but the dish really comes alive only when the good house Parmesan is grated on. Similarly the many-textured spaghetti bolognese, firm pasta and a nubbly meat sauce, just touched with cream and tomato, that, though sound, lacks depth until that cheese is added. What are given as ravioli malfati are not pasta at all, but balls of spinach bound with ricotta cheese and moistened with a bright, elemental tomato sauce—once again the dish lacks real sparkle (it comes across as little more than strong spinach) until the magic cheese is added.

Some perfectly nice broiled shrimp are served with a coarse, sour sauce of anchovies and capers that, when sampled straight, does this really terrific imitation of your finest Worcestershire sauce, though when only a tiny amount is applied to the crunchy shrimp, a bit of life is added. The moist red snapper is joined, in its briny tomatoed broth, by a handful of littleneck clams—the mollusks, unlike the moist fish, are less than tender, a bit less than utterly fresh. You opt for a chicken dish, and again, you are served food that is more than decent, less than interesting. The pollo scarpariello is many nuggets of boned, browned, strongly salted chicken mingled with slivers of artichoke, the two in a sticky sauce in which you encounter a sliver of strong garlic now and again—all the dish needs is real chicken flavor. Saltimbocca is the surprise winner, the scallops of juicy, nicely browned veal overlaid with thin slices of smoky, salty prosciutto, the meats, in a pale, herbed, and winy sauce, garnished with a clump of pungent spinach. You do well to pass up the à la carte vegetables, among them sautéed artichokes that uncannily mimic the canned product and fried zucchini that, being a little soggy and not a little limp, amount to an audacity in a town that is almost obsessed with crispness and lightness in this item.

The pungent cheese that redeems so many of the dishes may be had straight—nuggets of it are served with strong black olives. The arugula salad you choose to have with it is brought to you with cruets of too-sour wine vinegar and pallid olive oil—you ask for "the good oil" and a tall bottle of the real thing is delivered. The zabaglione is hot, winy, frothy, reaches you mounded up over ripe strawberries in a large wineglass. The cheesecake is the Italian article, but denatured, for it is almost powdery, its wetness gone—happily good strawberries and raspberries are added to the plate.

★★NIPPON

155 East 52nd Street
LUNCH, MONDAY TO FRIDAY; DINNER, MONDAY TO SATURDAY. CLOSED SUNDAY.
Reservations: 758-0226.
Credit cards: AE, DC, MC, V.
Medium priced.

Long the Cadillac of New York's Japanese restaurants, expensive and complacent, Nippon, recently compelled to remove from the premises it occupied for twenty years, has relocated a couple of doors to the east. The complacency, however, has stayed put. Nippon has never, for example, bothered to print up a menu that is wholly comprehensible to anyone who has no Japanese, and as there are no captains on the floor, only waiters and waitresses, and as the menu is extensive, complete exegeses are out of the question. And while the most recent of midtown's more ambitious Japanese restaurants have brought to New York spaciousness, clarity of design, and that special Japanese integration of spareness and luxury, Nippon seems merely to have compressed its former operation into a smaller store. It is not that every appointment in the new place is, individually, unappealing to the eye. Nor is it that a restaurant is obligated to provide the newest in design in every new installation. It is, rather, that the familiar is especially oppressive when, no matter which way you turn, it is no more than eighteen inches from your nose. (By special request—and, you may be sure, just by accident—you may have yourself assigned to a certain curved table at which the occupants, one and all, are necessarily facing a pillar at about that range.) Surely, every element in this place is a tribute to Japanese craftsmanship. But, just as surely, the silk upholstery would look less like molded plastic, the hardwood tabletops less like Formica, the grass-green carpeting less like artificial turf, and the wood-and-rice-paper lanterns less like the same old wood-and-rice-paper lanterns if only there were a little less of all of them per cubic foot. The main dining room, such as it is, is surrounded by smaller rooms—if there are a number of you, and you reserve one of these spaces, you will be able to eat in relative comfort, as do many of the knowing Japanese who frequent Nippon.

They frequent it because, its discomforts notwithstanding, the food is the genuine article, upon which subject you may well be warned at once: Some of it is so genuine that it is listed in a separate box under the warning words SPECIAL FOR "CONNOISSEUR." For "connoisseur," read "Japanese." Such items as salted sea cucumber, preserved herring roe, and preserved squid have, variously, such gaminess and/or animality and/or minerality and/or just plain sliminess, that there may be no point in your getting half drunk to get to know them, since you will never want them sober anyway. But you are suffering from culture shock, not bad food, for the intense little dishes have the impact of authenticity, albeit entirely separated from the more familiar one of easy deliciousness.

For nonconnoisseurs, there is the impeccably fresh raw fish in the sushi and sashimi; a preserved cod-roe dish, pink and granular, in which the strong and salty seafood flavor is striking against the lemon you squeeze on; a little dish of sautéed eggplant, rich and slightly charred, served with vivid ginger and soy sauce; a tofu dish called ganmodoki, a warm knob of the bean curd, spongy but firm, threaded with vegetables; a duck dish

239

called aigamo-hasamiyaki, consisting of salted slivers of the rich meat, intensely flavored of their own fat, mingled with shafts of scallion and moistened with a strong black oil; and a so-called beef salad in which the thin, barely cooked slices of meat are served, sprinkled with sesame seeds, over crisp greens in a polished soy sauce dressing that has an almost glassy oil finish.

Order salmon in the manner called shioyaki, and you receive a fresh slab of the pink fish, its charred skin still attached, the meat of intense flavor. The tuna teriyaki is of equally fresh fish, in a dark, clinging sauce that potentiates its flavor. What is given as "lobster gusoku-ni" is of lobster chunks in their shell, moistened with a slightly sweet sauce that somehow mingles with and emphasizes the sweetness of the lobster itself. Chicken shichimi-yaki is a deeply brown-crusted—almost blackened—chicken served in the syruplike sauce that is the basis of its dramatic crust. When something must be cooked at the table, it is well if there is an empty place, for the tables are small, and the cooking apparatus every bit as large as it needs to be. The beef sukiyaki made this way is a good version of the usual thing. A new dish on the menu, called aigamo-yuan-nabe, is prepared with duck, which is poached not only with the usual vegetables but with slices of orange as well—they add a nice piquancy to the mellifluous meat.

The best drinks with this cooking are sake or beer or both. All the familiar Japanese beer brands are available in their regular and in their bottled "draft beer" versions—of which Sapporo is the best.

★★OMEN

113 Thompson Street (near Prince Street)
DINNER. CLOSED MONDAY.
Reservations: 925-8923.
Credit cards: AE, DC.
Inexpensive.

Old meets new is, inevitably, the SoHo theme underlying all other SoHo themes. For into a neighborhood that is a very reliquary of nineteenth-century New York every fashion streams. Since Japanese restaurants make up an even faster-growing industry on Manhattan Island than three-card monte, it is not surprising that several of these sprightly enterprises have popped up downtown. This one is all of a piece with its chosen neighborhood, for within the confines of a deep and narrow old store, rice-paper-and-wood lanterns and paneling have been shrewdly combined with old brick, ancient door and window frames, a venerable hardwood floor. The Japanese touch has lightened the potentially grim space. The illumination is bright but not glaring. The young Japanese waiters and waitresses are cheery. They wear Western clothes—long dresses, sweaters with patched elbows, purple pants, high-heeled shoes. The Japanese background music seems to come from far away, as if the restaurant were spacious. And lots of Japanese come here—not those throngs of businessmen in Ivy League suits that crowd the uptown Japanese restaurants, but Japanese families, Japanese couples, even integrated Japanese showing this place off to American companions. Whoever you are, it is assumed you are comfortable with Japanese ways. You are brought a small hot towel soon after you are seated (and you are not told what to do with it). And, except by special request, the only implements you are given are chopsticks—unfortunately those little splintery ones that come, attached at one end, in paper sheaves.

Omen is not only the name of the restaurant but of the first-named dish on its menu. Everybody orders it. You get a big bowl of hot, dark broth, a basket of hot noodles, a plate of fresh vegetables, with ginger, and a dish of roasted sesame seeds. You add the solid ingredients to the broth, eat the solids with your chopsticks, drain the bowl by lifting it to your lips. The broth is stout, the vegetables fresh, the sesame a fragrant note in the rousing dish.

Perhaps as a result of a meaning revised in translation, almost everything on the menu is identified as an appetizer. There are, in fact, dozens of little dishes that, if judged only by their size, do not qualify as main courses. Among them: oden (not omen), thick slices of the earthy radish called daikon and a pouch, fashioned of bean curd, stuffed with a meat-and-noodle filling, served in a hot, ginger-flavored broth; kaki no shirasu-ae, a light, herbed bean curd paste studded with orange shafts of sweet, ripe persimmon; oshitashi, one of two dishes of this name, this one a cool, salty, and smoky dish, crunchy of its principal ingredient, raw cabbage, which is mingled with fungus and bean curd; goma-ae, cool and moist spinach, quite crunchy, mixed with strands of mushroom, flavored with sesame. No sushi here, but the sashimi is of impeccable sea-food—strong mackerel, smooth and deep-red tuna, velvety slivers of pale squid. More of that squid is one of the ingredients of ika-no sumiso-ae, in which it is mingled with green pepper and soybean paste—the cool dish is oceanic, fruity, a little acidic. The dish called yakijake is a small portion of skinned salmon, carefully broiled, hot and salty, fresh and flaky, of vivid flavor. Omen's shrimp tempura is not the ultimate, but the batter is light, the shrimp are of clear flavor, the chunks of vegetable that are mingled with the seafood (a disk of yam, a sheaf of beans) are fresh and crisp. In the special department called chicken appetizers you will find enoki-no tosazu-ae, a little bowl of watercress and mushrooms and slivers of chicken, served cool, in a dressing that is sour and sparkling. Closer to what you think of when you think of chicken is the item called sansho, hot chicken, boned and browned and glistening, tender, moist of chicken fat, lightly coated with oil that is dark with soy sauce.

All this food is light, and you will want to bulk up your dinner with rice, here served with barley. You may have your rice and barley plain; or with chiso—the dark, sharp preserved leaves of an obscure Japanese plant; or as the "special rice of the month," which has included the likes of mushrooms, green vegetables, and eel mixed into the light grain.

Fruit, green-tea or red-bean ice cream, or those little dumplings called ankoro mochi (which do this really terrific imitation of bubble gum) are the desserts. The so-called Sapporo draft beer (which comes in one-pint bottles) is splendid with this food. Sake is available, as well as strong Western booze, but cocktails are not mixed.

★ ONINI

217 Eighth Avenue (at 21st Street)
LUNCH, SUNDAY TO FRIDAY; DINNER, DAILY.
Reservations: 243-6446.
Credit cards: AE, DC, MC, V.
Medium priced.

You may say that the new Onini lacks the charm of the original, but it lacks also the discomforts. You may add that the spiffy new place is just another example of quasi Deco on the cheap, but then it is no longer hole-in-the-wall on the even cheaper. Chelsea gentrifies apace, and Onini keeps up. The place is bigger, airier, shinier—and, oh yes, dearer, for there is money in this neighborhood now. Above black-painted lower walls today's Onini has been faced with pale cloth that is patterned with vague, floating squares and circles, like nursery wallpaper seen through a mental fog—it does not offend, neither does it amuse. The background music, on the other hand, is often Benny Goodman. The place holds a scant two dozen white-linened tables, in rows, around them little black side chairs with straw seats. The façade is glass, to the ceiling, and at an Eighth Avenue windowside table, you enjoy an unobstructed view of the grimy closet-size shops across the street (sure to shuffle off when their leases come up), among them a few mint, fresh-painted enterprises that signal things to come. Until the things come, however, presumably including additions to the mini Restaurant Row that is Eighth Avenue between 14th and 23rd Streets, Onini is still the best source of Italian food within walking distance of the General Theological Seminary.

There is nothing Italian, however, about this watercress salad, the giant mound of greens dotted with firm white beans, the whole in a citrus-flavored vinaigrette that drenches more than dresses it—still, a rousing first course. Oysters Onini are five of the lightly breaded, oiled, baked bivalves, very tender in their half-shells, each joined by chunks of tomato and warm mozzarella—the fresh oysters retain their oceanic sweetness in the sturdy setting. On occasion the place offers veal sausages, three halves of browned sausage (bifurcated the long way) set in a thick and creamy sauce that is fragrant of tarragon—the sausages lack a little something in the way of succulence, but the good sauce enriches them. Much in the way of pasta: fusilli in a rather harsh, heavily salted marinara sauce into which sun-dried tomatoes have been cooked—the dish is aggressive rather than assertive; fettuccine al Gorgonzola, an elemental dish of little more than the firm noodles and the strong melted cheese—simple, rich, unimpeachable food; and tortelloni (really tortellini) with pesto—the flavor of the pale green stuffing is indistinct but immaterial in the presence of this heady, creamy, and basil-fragrant green sauce, which is dotted to good effect with walnut halves.

Onini's distinction is the dishes it does that no one else does. Consider the oysters and shrimp primavera, a salty, lightly cooked stew of the two shellfish with red and green peppers, zucchini, carrots, and arugula, the seafood of sweet flavor, the pale garlicky broth oiled and vigorous. The sautéed trout is a firm, fresh fish, browned a little, cooked through but juicy, set in a sauce of lemon and anchovies that is thick with fresh parsley. The bird is not a distinguished one in this dish of chicken with eggplant, but the firm

242

white meat is buried under a great mound of the sautéed vegetable, flavored with sage and threaded with the strong bacon, and that redeems it. The cryptic listing "Arista" refers to a double pork chop, the two-story knob of meat, lodged in the crook of its ribs, and partially cut through between them, is supple and creamy-white within browned surfaces that have been treated, as has that incision, with herbs and balsamic vinegar. Good lamb chops too, the eyes of browned meat spread with an earthy, garlicked hash of wild mushrooms. On occasion the house offers a carefully done steak, the big, fibrous, tender, and blood-juicy slab of meat surfaced with peppercorns and adorned with a thick layer of herbs.

Though you are fed copiously at Onini, the house cheesecake seems the right dessert, the genuine Italian article, weighty, wet of its ricotta cheese, browned and sugary, dotted with black raisins. The stewed fresh fig is garnished with whipped cream and berries. And the stuffed prunes are packed with a filling of prune puree that has been fortified with brandy—they, too, come with whipped cream, and with crisp slices of Granny Smith apple.

The waiters and waitresses know the menu and, moreover, as you learn by reference to that document, wear shirts by Susan Ann Thornton.

★ ORSO

322 West 46th Street
LUNCH AND DINNER.
Reservations: 489-7212.
Credit cards: MC, V.
Medium priced.

Ezra Pound and Elizabeth Taylor, I. F. Stravinsky and D. H. Lawrence, Hemingway and Callas, Richard Wagner and Laurence Olivier—what have they in common? Nothing, of course, except fame. And yet their photographs and those of dozens of others (mostly black-and-whites in black frames) are densely assembled on the walls of this one place, in the way celebrity pics, in olden days, were hung in restaurants to memorialize eminents who had fed on the premises. Of course Orso is not misrepresenting. Surely all the world knows that Wagner hated Italian food, and that Stravinsky's most rooted phobia was of being waited on by unemployed actors and actresses. The photos are, rather, propitiatory, are directed at whoever cares about whatever. Movies are your bag? Here is John Huston. You like baseball? Ted Williams was the hitter of the century. You loathe Norman Mailer? Have a look at Gore Vidal. All you types, Orso announces, this is your place. Mr. Joe Allen (who owns the restaurant Joe Allen) is proprietor here, and he has calculated that if theater posters could make Joe Allen a hangout for theatrical types, the photo gimmick could target another population segment: those who can read, write, hear, or watch television.

He has calculated shrewdly. The theater is one of the places television watchers go when they are not tubing it, and that set packs this dining room during the early evening, stuffs and sedates itself, leaves in time to collapse into their seats as the curtain goes up. Then, after eight, the literate appear—albeit in lesser numbers, many of them in or of the theater rather than at it—and Orso becomes quite civilized, the laughter is not so gaudy, neither is the clothing. Make no mistake, subtly but surely, the photos flatter these cultureds even if they never glance at them, and the sprinkling of ballplayers and pols among the aesthetes tickles their most common conceit—that for all the richness of their inner lives, they are one with ordinary man. Similarly the physical Orso, which pretends to unpretentiousness, its few-steps-down, ochre-painted, and well-lighted interior much like those of Italian places that were one or two to a block in New York's Italian neighborhoods a couple of generations ago. The tables are surrounded by assorted rough-painted chairs that look like found objects rehabilitated. And you are waited on by young people in white shirts, four-in-hands, long white aprons—they have posture, presence, the correct weight for their height, and, in a few instances, what has come to be called attitude. As headaches are caused by a lack of aspirin, attitude results from a lack of love—or applause.

From a bilingual menu that changes daily: gamberi in padella, the nicely sautéed shrimp moist and crunchy, though their iodine does not work well with the red onions and sundried tomatoes that are their sauce; sautéed clams in their shells buried under chopped tomatoes and a mash of leeks, the vegetables fragrant of thyme, the clams resilient of their overcooking; carciofi fritto, which look like deep-fried artichokes and taste like deep-fried anything, though they are well crisped, take on life when you squeeze on lemon; grilled mushrooms with grilled leeks, picnic food that, on the way to the beach, has risen a bit from its icebox temperature; vitello tonnato, roast veal, quite rare and tender, in a rich and lemony tuna sauce that is dotted with tart capers; tripe, the unexpected winner, the many gummy lengths of innard, a little chewy but not really tough, in a creamy tomato sauce that is thick with chopped vegetables, served with a charred crust of bread that is moist and heady of its garlicked oil.

Order pizza bread, and you get a great pile of the crackling chips, glistening with garlicked oil and salty, lively. But order the pizza alla siciliana, and the circle of pizza bread has all the liveliness of a Passover matzo, while the many ingredients arranged on its surface—olives, peppers, mushrooms, and onions among them—are like a mingling of loose change from many currencies. Occasionally risotto is listed, the fluffy rice buttery, parsleyed, studded with chunks of chicken liver—your waitress abandons her attitude, grates on the Parmesan with abandon, which gives the dish depth and strength. The spinach gnocchi are in a creamy tomato sauce that cannot redeem their gumminess. On the Italian side of the menu the grouper is listed as grouper—in either language this is fresh fish judiciously sautéed, and the herbed mushrooms and radicchio with which it is done are, respectively, earthy and pleasingly bitter. The pan-fried liver reaches you as a giant pile of little slivers—you wish they were crisper, bloodier at their centers, but garlic and much Italian parsley manage to make the dish.

The Parmesan that did so much for the rice is just ok straight, and the fruit you may have with it varies—from the like of these firm seedless grapes to these not-quite-ripe strawberries. The pistachio ice cream is nut-studded, sweet, cold. Unfortunately the poached figs are equally cold, therefore flat, as is their cream cheese filling. The apple tart is warm, thin, its fruit hardly more than a film, a good airy thing under its thick whipped cream.

★★OYSTER BAR & RESTAURANT

Grand Central Station, lower level
LUNCH AND DINNER. CLOSED SATURDAY AND SUNDAY.
Reservations: 490-6650.
Credit cards: AE, DC, MC, V.
Medium priced.

If you think you know from fresh, you should have some fish at the Oyster Bar. After a few months of casual seafood, chosen from French menus, or Italian ones, or whatever, come to the Oyster Bar to brush up on freshness basics. This is not the only New York fish restaurant at which the fish is fresh every time. There are a few others (at a couple of which there is perhaps more finesse in the kitchen than here). But no one else offers thirty or so varieties of fish and shellfish in just-caught condition every day. (The Oyster Bar even prepares the stuff lots of different ways.) In seafood, freshness may not be all, but you cannot make really good seafood dishes without it.

In the mid-1970s this place was taken over by new interests, after an extended moribundity that had just climaxed in a muffled whimper. But, though there had been a demise, there had been no decay, for this place had been built—more than fifty years before—as an integral part of Grand Central Station, which is to say it would take a wrecking ball to make it crumble even a little. Spiffed up, the place at once revealed its ancient grandeur, quite unspoiled. And you can see it now. The main room, entered from the lower level, is at least a short block long. Under a lofty vaulted ceiling of glinting sand-colored tiles, and walls of maple-stained wainscoting with old marble at the base, there is an acre of tables at one end, a furlong of white countertop, in a repeating S, at the other. You walk on red tiles, you sit in armchairs, or on the banquettes that are along the edge of the room here and there. Or you eat in the saloon, a separate department at the east end, accessible via a flight of steps down from the entranceway near the low end of the ramp at 42nd Street and Vanderbilt. It is not only the stairway access to the saloon that makes it seem subterranean. The room is windowless and clubby looking, like a speakeasy or a cavernous den. The walls of wood stripping are hung with nautical prints, ships' models behind glass, mountings of big game fish, varnished and glistening. A bar runs along two sides of the room—fifty may water easily along its length. Several dozen gingham-topped tables take up most of the floor. At the late end of mealtimes, when the big main room is sparsely populated, this room may be two-thirds full and cheery. When busy, either room provides enough noise to distract you.

Clams and oysters are sold by the piece. You can come here, order one of each listed oyster, plus a littleneck and cherrystone, and go home sated. On a good day there are as many as ten varieties of oyster available, and if you order an assortment, your waiter (in the main room) or your waitress (in the saloon) will tell you which is the Chincoteague, which is the Malpeque, etc. You will find that the little Belon oysters are as sweet as melon, the Chincoteagues briny and strong, the Cotuits a complexity of fruit and oil and the ocean. By late in the evening the more exotic varieties usually run out, so if you want to sample those Belons or Box oysters, you are more likely to find what you want at lunchtime, or before 7:30 at dinner.

This place has taken to smoking fish (no, not a new fad), and it does a delicate job of it. You get smoked sturgeon, thin slices spread across a big plate, light, ever so slightly soapy (which smoked sturgeon can be ever so excessively), the smokiness at once restrained and vivid—the horseradish sauce that garnishes the pale meat is sharp, even though it is mostly whipped cream. The smoked salmon is pale, moist without being oily, so tender it is almost fugitive—capers and chopped onions are served with the pink fish, but they should be used with restraint or they will obscure the salmon. The Point Judith herring these days is not much more than ordinary pickled herring. The clams Cassino are plump cherrystones, not buried in breading, just touched with it, and with a bit of bacon—the big clam shells are standing in a film of herbed butter, and the warm clams have a strong and tangy flavor. If you are lucky enough to come when she-crab soup is on the menu, do not pass it up. This is the famous Carolina soup, here made with Maryland crabs, presumably the female of the species, and the resulting bowl is a thick, buttery, subtly spiced, and steamy richness that is dense with sweet white crabmeat.

The impeccable freshness of the ingredients is not, however, invariably matched by their preparation. Lotte is a fish that swims all over the Atlantic. It has never been popular in New York because it is (1) ugly to look upon when whole and (2) rather obscure of flavor when cut up and cooked. Here it is served in hefty chunks that the menu refers to as "tournedos," their surfaces handsomely browned, with a sauce béarnaise that is presumably intended to compensate for the slightness of the flavor of the fish. The sauce, however, is as green as grass, as sweet and thick as molasses. The fish is pretty good if you substitute lemon for the sauce. That béarnaise is particularly hard to understand in light of the pretty good hollandaise that comes with the carefully broiled, fresh, and flaky bass. There is broiled halibut steak, and it falls into tender flakes that are velvety and snowy. In season there is shad and/or shad roe. The fish is floured and browned, the white meat sealed in the buttery crust. But the roe is probably parboiled before its final preparation, and it is a little dry, more like grit—less like caviar—than this dish at its best.

The shellfish stews are homey, big chunks of sea scallop, for example, in a hot and buttery cream broth that is red and spicy with fragrant paprika—the soup is a little briny from the juice of the scallops. The Pacific Coast's renowned Dungeness crab is sometimes available. They must fly it in on a Concorde, for the big crustacean seems to be as fresh as the local items. You get one crab to a serving, it is bright red, cold, it entirely occupies a long platter, and it is garnished with strong, mustard-flavored mayonnaise. There is abundant meat in one of these beasts if you know where it is stored and have the patience to dig it out. A Dungeness crab is about twice the work of a lobster, but this is sweet seafood and worth the bother.

Steaks and chickens are available for inlanders; mixed seafood dishes, complex stews, seafood omelets; shore dinners after 5 P.M.; and live lobsters—you can pick yours out.

Most of the desserts are old-fashioned American items: a cool, custardy banana cream pie, intensely banana flavored, touched with slivered almonds; rice pudding, a frothy, cinnamoned, raisin-studded sweet, obvious but good; a whole-wheat apple pie, on occasion, the grainy crust around nuggets of tart apple, only lightly sugared; blueberry pie, a deep-purple filling of the jellied little fruits filling the lard crust to plumpness—too bad it is served so cold.

A new menu is printed daily, prices written in next to those regular dishes that are available that day; a dozen or so special dishes of the day written in as well.

By now everyone knows that the Oyster Bar serves nothing but American wine, almost one hundred different bottles from four states.

★★PALIO

151 West 51st Street
LUNCH, MONDAY TO FRIDAY; DINNER, MONDAY TO SATURDAY. CLOSED SUNDAY.
Reservations: 245-4850.
Credit cards: AE, DC, MC, V.
Expensive.

Proud, plump Tony May steps from the shuttle elevator that has just descended from his second-story restaurant to its street-level bar, on his face spectacles and a serene smirk. It is shortly after a favorable item in the press, and Tony has been force-feeding himself and happily choking on all the reservations he can get, never mind such details as the physical limitations of his room. The throng angrily leaving, after waiting to no end long past the time of their reservations, commingles with an equal number arriving to begin the same ordeal. May is unperturbed, in fact loves it, winks at a group of his pals to let them know they will get special handling, rides back up. But even he cannot unseat those who, having been fed late, choose to stay late, so the pleasure of his somewhat nettled friends, when they must wait five minutes to be seated out of turn, lacks the thrill of that privilege conferred at once. But May is the kind of man who, having picked your pocket the last time he saw you, wants you to know there are no hard feelings. When finally you are at your dinner, he stops by to ask if everything is all right, obviously confident that you will drop your fork and rise at his coming. When you do not, he figures that is your problem, not his, and saunters off, unconcerned and amused.

The room to which you enter is a big cube, a horseshoe bar of polished gray stone filling most of it, black cocktail tables with little black chairs along two sides. The lower walls are wood paneled, the upper ones faced on all four sides by a wraparound mural, in hot colors, celebrating the breadth of man's cultural achievements, with particular emphasis on horse racing—Palio is a biannual festival in the Italian town of Siena, a wild horse race around the town square one of its main events. The Palio bar has been taken up by the after-5 office set for reviewing the day's frustrations—and, after a couple of drinks, for exchanging confidences. "Last week he says change to low heels in the office, the high ones catch on his loopy rug. Now he says go back to high ones, they look better. He's a real rat, but isn't he gawjiss? You should see his wife. I don't know how he stanza." This to background music by Handel or Mozart.

Cleared for departure by the man who tends the book, you elevator up to the restaurant proper, find yourself at the end of a long, high-ceilinged room of grand proportions, its floor massive blocks of gray-brown marble (carpeting in the aisles), the walls wood, the white ceiling divided by intersecting beams into large squares, at the center of each a recessed light within a protruding collar of polished brass. Two low wine racks divide the room into three parts—and somewhat undo its sweep. The tables, covered with pale beige linen in which a pattern of slightly darker threads is woven, and set with brass service plates, brilliantly painted tiles at their centers, are surrounded by capacious armchairs of black-painted wood with black-upholstered seats. Just above the tan leather banquette that runs the length of the room down one side, small mirrored panels have been installed, above them a series of brilliantly colored flags, bold insignia thereon—

palio means flag, and the winner of that horse race gets one. Your captain is in black-and-white formals, the waiters and busboys are in colorfully adorned white jackets, and the sommelier, a metal cup on the chain around his neck, chews gum (or something). He serves you a bottle of white wine. You tell him it is quite cold enough, ask him to leave it on the table. "Certainly," he says, and goes off with it.

Too bad he has not gone off instead with your marinated eel, disks cut from a cold roulade of the soured, somewhat jellied fish—it is assertive but of little character, strong rather than strong flavored. Happily, he has also left behind what is given as "stuffed saddle of rabbit," which you would probably characterize as a terrine. Either way, you receive two thick slices cut from a loaf, hefty chunks of tender meat, of vivid rabbit flavor, well fatted but not fatty, packed tightly together, herbed, dotted with sharp olives, filmed with velvety olive oil, and cleverly garnished with a clump of cold spinach. Surely you can count on your thumbs the number of midtown restaurants that list kohlrabi, a troublesome vegetable of elusive flavor and, sometimes, stringy texture. Palio's kohlrabi is not exactly flavorsome, but it is tender, and the hollowed-out stem is served filled with a hot, rich, and well-seasoned sweetbread puree, the entire dish in a pale sauce that is thick with Parmesan cheese. The place makes exceptional rice, and you may have a mound of the nubbly, winy, abundantly parsleyed stuff dotted with morsels of frogs' legs—a strong admixture of garlic potentiates the flavor of the satisfying dish. Frogs' legs again, this time mingled with slightly chewy potato gnocchi, the little dumplings green of the herbs with which they are flavored, the two in a dark, stout, and briny sauce. The trenette, thin flat strands of pasta, are a dark, grayer green, for they have been prepared with squid and its ink—the pale seafood itself seems to glow in this dank setting, and the well-oiled and tomatoed sauce is salty, vibrantly sea-gamy, invigorating. The rice and pasta dishes are sold only as full orders.

A peculiarity of the menu: within categories—e.g., cold appetizers, pasta, seafood, meats and fowl—all dishes are one price. They tend therefore to be of unequal profitability, perhaps in compensation for which your main course of shrimp involves but five of the crustaceans, wee examples at that, but these are sweet, crunchy shrimp, their lightly browned surfaces dotted with fresh herbs, and they are garnished with a rich puree of zucchini that is strewn with tiny, crisp strands of deep-fried leeks—bits of garlic liven the good dish. Three lengths of dark-pink salmon fillet, rolled around a salty, heady stuffing of ground olives dotted with pink peppercorns, are served on a handsomely contrasting layer of strong spinach—the fish itself is not of notable flavor, but still, a dramatic dish. Come here once, and you will do well to opt for quails, the boned bodies, browned and glistening, bursting with a rich, earthy stuffing of duck livers and mushrooms. The medallion of veal, though hardly browned, is a bit dry anyway—the flavor of the dish is in its sautéed eggplant and zucchini and in its lightly tomatoed sauce. The roast lamb is a couple of substantial slices of rare, tender meat in a sauce of balsamic vinegar that could just as well be of anything at all, for it is thick with organ meat, assertively livery.

You may do better here concluding your dinner with salad and/or cheese than with something sweet. Among the salads: cool white beans and bits of onion in garlicked oil; skinned sections of orange and slivers of endive dotted with cracked peppercorns; tiny slices of raw baby artichoke, lightly oiled, mingled with matching slices of sharp Parmesan. That good cheese and several others may be had in larger quantities if ordered separately—they are at room temperature and on view in a transparent roll-top display cart. The tirami sù is a vapid example of the cloying sweet. The black polenta pudding is a dark, grainy muffin—not quite bread, not quite cake—in a tangy red-berry sauce on one side of your plate, a sauce of rich white chocolate on the other. The cheesecake is one of the big winners—it is textured, weighty, dotted with candied fruit, moistened with a sauce that is cool and liquored. The millefoglie is another, a large sandwich formed of two circles of light, flaky pastry, much cool, tangy zabaglione—it is made with white wine—and fresh berries.

At the end of the evening, May is still on his feet, this time tripping after an abundant, low-cut blonde headed for the facilities. He is being as witty as possible at the back of her head. She is tossing answers back over her shoulder and not slowing down.

• PALM and PALM TOO

837 Second Avenue (near 45th Street); 840 Second Avenue (near 45th Street)
LUNCH, MONDAY TO FRIDAY; DINNER, MONDAY TO SATURDAY. CLOSED SUNDAY.
Reservations accepted at lunch; for four or more at dinner at Palm Too: 687-2953 and 697-5198.
Credit cards: AE, DC, MC, V.
Very expensive.

How are the lowly fallen! Inelegance was the Palm's reputation, but first-class lowdown is more than just a gross menu and sawdust on the floor, about all that are left at the Palm and its across-the-avenue satellite. As it is more than a room with occupied pews that makes a congregation, it takes more than the trappings to make the Palm. Needed also are zealots, those who live the whole life, not just the weekly visit. This place was made by the hardheaded, guys who smoked unfiltereds, drank beer, ate like pigs, and all at the same time. Nor was the Palm ever, as its reputation once had it, merely a media hangout. Anyone could eat here, no matter how conventional his day's work. But most who did expressed thereby the real selves hidden within their two-piece uniforms. They turned from their phony jobs to what they saw as honest, simple pleasures: boisterousness, vulgarity, intoxication, gluttony, surfeit. The true Palmist, secretly or not, detested every effete thing else. Only here was he himself.

Today the Palm is a mechanical replay of the old place. The crowds (somewhat diminished, but still impressive) come, have drinks, address the mammoth lobsters, go. They are like modern-day pilgrims who by day walk the paths of the divine, by night sleep in a motel. These followers know nothing of the excess that was the foundation of the early believers' ecstasies. These days, after dinner, the parishioners depart with their mates, upright as they came. Appropriately, the Palm is now a chain. In eight big cities and East Hampton, the worshipers go through sanitized versions of the old rites. It is not that the food by its type or the servings by their size are less carnal than they were, rather that without the attentions to them of pop-eyed, red-faced participants, they become exhibits in a museum. Today's Palmist comes from across the water, is fresh from the shower, drinks Amstel Light, *shares* a lobster (takes home the claws), skips dessert. He comes, in short, to lie to himself about himself. He does not even mind that, on arrival, he is greeted by courteous, albeit aloof, automatons in business suits, that it is occasionally not necessary to wait for a table, that the waiters in their putty jackets do so well here with their limited skills that some of their contentment is expressed as courtesy (this is less true in Palm Too, where many members of the younger floor staff are still in the early surly stage, which usually lasts about a decade). Though at the original Palm, the nearby *Daily News* is still a source of self-conscious cynics who, by their presence here, mean to make plain their unwillingness to swallow whole anything that will not fit in a shot glass, most of the customers in the original store are here to tell you that this is a great country, and there are still plenty of ways to make a living in it despite not knowing anything. Palm Too gets a younger set, more or less the next generation. In fact its little bar has a life of its own, in which everyone smokes, talks sports, and leaves big tips to the bartender, who is one of their own. These are guys who come with their girlfriends and, after they marry, come alone. As one man alone explains, while on his fifth or sixth something-on-the-rocks, "I'm only twenty-nine, but I got to be shop steward because of the girl I'm married to's father." The Palm and Palm Too are sawdust on the floors, painted cartoons on the walls and ceilings, white-linened tables, hanging white globes for illumination, and four-bladed fans for moving the smoke. The original Palm has an upstairs much like the downstairs, was once a speakeasy. Palm Too is its child of the late seventies. When tables open up in one Palm while there is still a long wait in the other, customers may carry their drinks across the street and get seated. Anyone who tells you he can distinguish the food in one Palm from that in the other has delusions of acute discrimination.

As all the world knows, the Palm has no printed menu, the waiters recite only a fraction of what is available, a smaller fraction more if pressed. The complete menu is posted upstairs at the back of the Palm, on the wall between the bar and front window in Palm Too. Most of the food in both these places is now nowhere: raw littleneck clams that are sometimes flat, though on occasion the eight cherrystones in the clams oregano suffer only from a bit of toughness in their blunt, herbed, dark-browned breading; an abundance of crabmeat that, if it is not frozen, is nevertheless without the sweetness and sparkle of the fresh article—it needs its bright cocktail sauce, which you may be disinclined to fortify from the supplied cup of horseradish, even though a previous customer was apparently content to break through the crust to get at the good part; a fillet of red snapper the size of an open book that has been cooked through and blackened to seafood anonymity; lamb chops that are so overcooked, though delivered promptly, that you suspect they are prebroiled, heated to order; a dry veal chop that has lost utterly the bursting juiciness of the thing done right; beef à la Dutch, a pile of slightly sour potted meat with a pile of flat noodles, the two in a forceful gravy that is thick with onions and green peppers; cottage-fried potatoes that are warm, tasteless potato chips; fried onions that, though not greasy, lack onion character. And yet, the items for which the Palm has always been known are admirable. The immense sirloin steak is fibrous and tender, its charred surface stretched by the bursting blood-juiciness within—the meat even has the flavor, rare nowadays, that is the mineral sharpness of aged beef. The giant lobsters are tails the size of a heavyweight's forearm and claws that will do as King Kong's bloodshot eyes. They have been broiled from scratch (not steamed first), and as their own juices have not been diluted by alien moisture, and as they are taken from the fire before they dry out, they have an extraordinary intensity of marine flavor. When the hash brown potatoes are right, they are crusty, potently seasoned, of a clear potato flavor that is at once plain and pungent; when they are wrong, they are greasy, flat.

For dessert there is cream-cheese cheesecake, and for overwhelming richness devoid of finesse, this is a good example of the type.

★★PARIOLI, ROMANISSIMO

24 East 81st Street
DINNER. CLOSED SUNDAY AND MONDAY.
Reservations: 288-2391.
Credit cards: AE, DC.
Very expensive.

New York's most expensive Italian restaurant, Parioli began as a simple place, on First Avenue. But long before its move from the original site the establishment took on the high solemnity, high prices, and high-style food for which it is known today. Its plebeian origins, however, remain, in the person of Mr. Rubrio Rossi, its ever present founder and host, a gentleman whose close-cropped hair, tailored clothing, and formal bearing, whatever their studied purpose, are the manners and trappings of your basic butler. (If you have never yourself employed a butler, you may be intimidated, as many are, by Parioli's atmosphere, which consists in large measure of Rossi's church warden air. Members of the staff certainly are, for they go through their chores, some of them, as if their proctor were permanently installed on their shoulder.) Still, Ruby's act almost convinces, and it is not until some heavy spender grabs him by the elbow—with the oily companionability of one who ingratiatingly asks a favor while knowing it cannot be refused—that he shifts down to the same low-obedience gear in which his underlings operate all the time. Rossi inclines his head, listens, runs to do the fellow's bidding, perhaps to adjust the air conditioning, hastens back to determine if the new climate is satisfactory, clasps his palms together as he makes his getaway, smiling all the way. You figure that, despite his prosperity, when he sits down to feed himself at the end of the night, he does not eat what he wants, but what is left.

Your entrance is to New York's most sober bar, the tipplers do not smile, the ice cubes do not clink. But things pick up in the aisle just beyond it, where you find (when it is not being wheeled through the dining room) a wagon of cheeses—rows of cylinders, blocks, pyramids, disks—that, taken together, look like an architect's model of a small town. A little further, and you are in the principal dining room, a square space, softly lit, in which about fifteen large linened tables, spotlighted flowers on each, are distributed across a dark-carpeted floor, enough space between them for even that big cheese trolley to be wheeled up to any one. Here you are in the grandest room, a couple of stories high, of the parlor floor of an old Manhattan townhouse, its fireplace huge (and now in disuse), its ceiling carved. Two of the tables are at couches situated under windows that look out on a kind of atrium, covered over by a sloping glass roof, on the far side of which a smaller dining room with a handful of tables enjoys a quasi-outdoor setting. The rooms have been Italianized with a coat of neo-Renaissance mottled ochre, and the walls are hung with a few bizarre paintings that, by their indifference to esthetic effect, establish that Parioli makes no false claims—this is a place for pleasure, you spend a lot of money here, you do not pretend that anything lofty is going on. Parioli has in fact always appeared to be a clubby place, one to which dirty old men with filthy money brought their nieces. At the original site, it was usually busy, but not with a large following, rather with what looked like a few devotees who came often. That has changed somewhat since the move, for as the restaurant gets more and more recognition in the press, and more and more traffic from those who follow fashion, it is less of a lure to those who covet privacy. Couples composed of a lady listening and a gentleman making promises have been replaced by pairs between whom the promises have been, often regrettably, kept.

Presumably in honor of the modified tone of the clientele—the present crowd is more inclined than the former one simply to take the place at the face value of its lofty cost—Parioli's kitchen bothers less than it used to with details of product. What are given, for example, as "delicate baby artichokes" may reach you coarsened and leathery, and their pungent green-olive stuffing, though of good flavor, in no way puts the dish in line with its billing. Then there is the carpaccio d'agnello, which, though the title leads you to expect raw lamb, the subtitle describes as "cooked to a turn." Anyway, the lamb is cold and very rare, the edges of the thin slices are browned, and they are served with a dollop of sauce that has a good red-pepper intensity—the dish adds up to mildly diverting picnic food. So if it is cold meat you want, and you come here when vitello tonnato is available, have that, for the silver dollars of pale, tender veal are under a smooth tuna sauce that is at once rich and sparkling of its oil and lemon. If you are to have pasta here only once, you will do well to make it the trenette ai funghi porcini, the firm but tender strands in a creamy and polished sauce, thick with chunks of wild mushroom, that is of an almost overpoweringly woodsy fragrance. What Parioli calls fedelini, you call spaghetti—the pasta is served in an otherwise good red sauce, well oiled and sweetened with onions, that is fortified with jalapeño peppers, which make the sauce hot, but not in a way that fits it—their heat and flavor come off as appendages to the dish, not parts of it. But the tortelloni are good, the big packages of green pasta, filled with well-seasoned ricotta cheese, are light despite their solidity, and they are in an oily and redded sauce that is fragrant of herbs.

When the scampi are good, they are very, very good, the big grilled shrimp sweet and crunchy in their peppery butter—but at times one or more are tough, and at times as many are touched with iodine. Rossi goes to the trouble of obtaining copies of the Italian swimmer called branzino, labels them "Adriatic sea bass," overcooks them not much, but enough to water their flavor—still this is good fish, the seafood juicy of the white wine in which it was baked, and it is roused and enriched by its creamy tarragon sauce. The younger the chicken, the milder its flavor, which is why broilers are seasoned, browned, basted with tasty fat. This place offers 21-day-old birds (broilers-in-training) at $30 per, as if their meat were to be prized more or less in the way the fur of unborn animals is prized. The things are roasted with truffles, reach you browned and moist, but the treatment cannot offset their pallidness—as with the gentlemen's nieces, youth is their sole appeal. More birds, veal birds, in which the thin-sliced meat, rolled around an olive-accented stuffing, is browned, braised, and served in a winy cream sauce that is studded, strikingly, with sweet peas. Like the dining room itself, the veal chop is two stories high, two protruding ribs to prove the point, the great knob of supple meat cooked through but still pink and bursting with moisture—the mélange of mushrooms, broccoli florets, and strands of root vegetable with which it is topped neither adds nor detracts, and the sauce in which it is set, though only vaguely the "tarragon sauce" it is called, is earthy, creamy, enriching. Steaks in many sauces, a winner the filet mignon in a tangy caper sauce that contrasts dramatically with the velvety red meat.

Parioli knows how to sell cheese. The cart is wheeled to your table, sent for or not, and a well-schooled captain tells you of his wares for about five minutes—unless you interrupt, and direct him to explicate only the items that stir your curiosity. Italian, French, Spanish, English, and American cheeses are here, all in good condition. What-

252

ever you select, include some Parmesan—just a couple of flakes from the giant block will rouse you for dessert. When you have chosen your cheese, you are brought a silver tray, on it a labeled bottle of port and a decanter from which the wine is actually poured. You ask the price, and the gentleman proffering the stuff winces (at Parioli, no one asks prices), mumbles that a glass is $16.50.

The legendary chocolate cake is deep and sharp, is enriched by a thin layer of almost black chocolate cream, is frosted with confectioner's sugar, is garnished with rich whipped cream. The zabaglione is hot, winy, frothy, on raspberries that, unfortunately, are a little hard.

★ PARK BISTRO

414 Park Avenue South (near 29th Street)
LUNCH, MONDAY TO FRIDAY; DINNER, DAILY.
Reservations: 689-1360.
Credit cards: AE, DC.
Medium priced.

Consider the potato. A plain thing in unprepared form, it has potential for boundless variety when approached with imagination. It is a staple of the poor, but even the poor have not got everything out of it. They have not, for example, discovered its potential as an extender of lobster. That is, of course, the poor other than the French poor, who call it "parmentier de homard," and sell it for $19. This variation on the endlessly suggestive mashed potato arrives as a pattie about the size of a large hamburger, flecked with bits of black olive, and set in a rich and garlicky Provençale sauce. Yummy, but not what you expect when you expect lobster. In fact the potato appears to be something of a Park Bistro fixation, albeit its other manifestations do not astonish. The "warm goat cheese on potato tart," for example, is just that, the disk of the famous vegetable spread with good goat cheese that is oiled, flavored with thyme, handsomely browned. To determine exactly how far the potato can go, you turn down the listed "codfish on a bed of potatoes" in favor of the brandade, a mash of potatoes and codfish that is here prepared in its Gibson form, the ratio of the former to the latter about five to one. All it lacks is a pearl onion. What it has instead is a touch of garlic and a good dark sauce that is thick with lentils.

You wide-berth the potato if you begin your dinner with the house salad—fresh arugula, watercress, spiky greens, all in a dressing made with good oil. "Aigo Provençal" is another way around the tuber, the vigorous orange-colored soup populated by chunks of shellfish and, at the center, an oiled crust of bread that is adorned with minced tomato and a dab of black olive tapenade. Your attention is best directed, however, to the oxtail terrine, a moist, fibrous, tender compacture of meat that is greened over with a density of fresh herbs in oil, and garnished with a knot of leek strands in a lively vinaigrette.

Non-potato main courses include a chicken fricassee that is in a fragrantly herbed sauce in which you find whole shallots, cabbage, chunks of tomato—the browned, red-stained, moist chicken has actual chicken flavor. The house roast rabbit is listed as "comme on l'aime en Provence," but though its dark sauce, with firm white beans and dried tomatoes, is sturdy and satisfying, the meat itself has little character.

253

Pot de crème is French for chocolate pudding, which is not to say that this cool one is not rich and intense. The excellent crème brûlée would be perfect if its eggy custard were fluffy rather than just light. The tart basquaise is a dull almond thing on dull pastry. And of the two colors of peach on your peach tart, one of them does a good imitation of the canned article.

★★★ LE PÉRIGORD

405 East 52nd Street
LUNCH, MONDAY TO FRIDAY; DINNER, MONDAY TO SATURDAY. CLOSED SUNDAY.
Reservations: 755-6244.
Credit cards: AE, DC, MC, V.
Very expensive.

Here are brought together much of what is new in French cooking and all that is traditional in the prosperous at their pleasure. There have always been local eating places that, because they did not attract the fashionable, appealed to the comfortable, restaurants to which the folks repaired simply to be among their own happy kind. That this place is now one of their repairs suggests that the new cookery is getting old (which, of course, is not to judge it, or to suggest it is on the way out).

There has been a Périgord at this site for more than two decades now, during which time the restaurant has changed both hands and appearances. Its current looks—at last—are actually prepossessing, though the setting is more flattering than diverting, one in which a soft and rosy boudoir glow confers on those within it a look of broad-spectrum well-being, everything from health to wealth. The room has always been weighted down by its low, low ceiling, but portions of the ceiling have been carved away, and a network of handsome crossed beams has been installed—they lighten and make airy the formerly oppressive overhead. The walls all around are covered with textured cloth on which is printed a muted pattern of flowers and leaves. The plush carpeting matches the velvety, deep-rose banquettes and capacious booths that rim the room on three sides. Flowers are everywhere, and the china and crystal on the white-topped tables glitter under the spotlights positioned among the ceiling crosspieces. The ladies glitter too, anyway their shimmering dresses, jewelry, lacquered fingernails (nary a woman in the place with fewer than ten). The gentlemen, on the other hand, give off a firmer light—that of the burnished dome, the pink and shiny clean-shaven cheek, the heavy silk tie—and are content to be known by how expensively are turned out their spouses. Still, people come here neither to be seen nor to gape. They are a civilized and satisfied set, thank you, and they number among them many from UN missions nearby. Foreign languages definitely spoken here. Both the locals and importeds choose this place, in part, because the dining room staff nurtures their contentment with the intelligence and courtesy they take as their due.

You enter Le Périgord to an anteroom, in it a display of cold hors d'oeuvres, one of them a full-grown snapper, poached and skinned, the big fish just about filling the great platter on which it is set. If the swimmer catches your eye, you may well choose to start your dinner with a portion of its firm and glistening meat—from its sweet and characteristically nutty snapper flavor, you judge that the fish was fresh when prepared, and its herbed mayonnaise livens and enriches it. For cold seafood more complex, you refer to the menu, among its listings lobster in aspic, the muffin-shaped compacture of tender morsels bound at the top by a cool jelly that is thick with herbs and cracked pepper, the construct set in a green pool that is a parsley sauce tart with lemon. Seafood in a green sauce again, this time what is given as "saumon mariné demi-doux à l'huile épicée," gravlax to you, albeit a French version, the slick, oil-marinated slices of red fish, strewn with sprigs of fragrant dill, only slightly sweet, this green sauce of watercress and lime, its tanginess in nice contrast to the supple salmon. If the words "duck confit" call to your mind hearty, spicy food, set aside your preconceptions when you order the duck confit appetizer, for in this presentation you receive slivers of the preserved fowl that, trimmed of fat, are interleaved with thin, matching slivers of cool, ripe pear, the fruit a foil to the duck in much the way that a pear can be the moderator of strong cheese. If there is a spare $10 among your effects, pay the premium for the duck foie gras, for the combination of lightness and richness that is the essence of foie gras is here emphasized by an artful sautéing of the sliced organ meat—it is moist, pink, soft within its browned and glistening surfaces, and it is served in a dark sauce, cloves of garlic in it, that, despite its assertiveness, only underscores the liver. No spare cash required for the sweetbread crêpe, morsels of the organ meat and chunks of wild mushroom that are sautéed, moistened with a dark sauce, wrapped in a thin pancake, and served in a buttery white sauce that has been livened with vinegar—that white sauce is like a clever bonus, for the crêpe and its contents are complete without it.

Mediterranean fish, sometimes one kind, sometimes another, are offered. When the variety is rouget, prepared in the way the house styles "provençal," you do well to look no further. Rouget is a firm, red-skinned, white-meated fish of a sweet taste that, though delicate, is vivid. The fillets you get here, their skin crisped and spicy, have all their flavor, and they reach you on a mound of strong spinach, the two set in a pale, nubbly sauce, buttery and a little tart, that is dotted with herbs and bits of tomato. Your lobster may be had grilled, but think twice before passing up the lobster "à la crème d'estragon," for this way, the meat of the crustacean is enriched and perfumed by a creamy sauce that is suffused with fresh tarragon—a wondrous dish. When your duck arrives, so does the scent of dill, for the hot food is strewn with many sprigs of the herb, and their aroma is the setting for a dish that otherwise has no dill in it. The bird, suffused with lemon, is served in slices and parts that are arranged on a thin sheet of crisped potato, everything moistened with a polished, slightly tart red-wine sauce, and garnished with slivers of browned, bittersweet endive. Little may be said for these fillets of veal, for with veal there is always the danger—as here—that it will come across as little more than nameless protein. The veal "arlequin," however, is just about redeemed by its sauces (one slice is in a pale and acidic lime sauce, the other in a red and vibrant lobster sauce) and by its garnishes (strong spinach, carrots of exceptional natural sweetness). Instead of liver and onions, there is a variation, the great crescents of sautéed pink meat under a veritable carpet of minced scallions (with chopped parsley), their sharpness a nice foil to the rich organ meat. Under the heading "Le Plat Classique," there is one item, "boeuf faux carottes, vielle façon," old style, that is, the morsels of meat—a pyramid of them at the center of your plate in an herbed and fat-rich sauce—still fibrous, their surfaces retaining much of the rough texture of their browning, though they have been stewed until tender, the beef surrounded by a ring of shiny, bright-orange inches of sweet carrot, their near hardness a good textural note in this setting.

If you remember to order it when you order your dinner, you may have an airy, raspberry-flavored soufflé for dessert, deep-pink and shot through with bits of berry under its browned and risen top—your waiter makes an incision and spoons in a winy raspberry sauce. The lemon pie is tangy under its meringue top. The pear tart is moist and fruity on its flaky pastry. You may have a slice of rather light but otherwise conventional crème caramel. The lemon-raspberry mousse is a dull layered affair—happily, your waiter garnishes it with fresh berries.

★★PERIYALI

35 West 20th Street
LUNCH, MONDAY TO FRIDAY; DINNER, MONDAY TO SATURDAY. CLOSED SUNDAY.
Reservations: 463-7890.
Credit cards: AE, MC, V.
Medium priced.

If, unfortunately, you recall the brief fashion for cacophonous Greek nightclub-restaurants that addled New York for a few years in the seventies, you may well take one look at this place and flee, for it sports every visual taverna cliché that you reflexively associate with twenty thousand watts of amplification, loudspeakers at three-foot intervals along the walls (the facilities not excluded), a regiment of bouzouki players, and a hoarse, maniacal contralto, her mouth around a microphone, screaming incomprehensibly her head off in twelve languages that border the Mediterranean. Be calm—Periyali, but for its standard look, is not that. For those of you who came in later, however, know that in the taverna (the Greek equivalent of, roughly, the trattoria) the light is low, the walls are of coarse white stucco, except where—and this is essential—they are of massive stones, the wooden benchlike banquettes are equipped with thin cushions (both seats and backs), and kitchen implements and photos of the old country hang on the walls. Among the permissible variations are the white cloths that, draped from beam to beam, lower this ceiling; and with respect to the floors, they may be either of wood, as they are in this main dining room, or of old red tiles, as in this establishment's small back rooms. With respect to what is served, retsina, a terrible tasting Greek white wine is always on the wine list, but is never ordered by Americans. (There is some question as to whether it is ordered by Greeks once they have been exposed to other wines.) And the food is usually predictable and tolerable, which is where Periyali nervily skirts tradition—Greek cookery is not a culinary wonder of the world, but, as in any cooking, when the ingredients are right and the dishes fresh made, as they are here, it is better than other food less carefully prepared.

Another thing you will almost always see in a New York taverna—displays of appetizers, desserts, what have you. But here you will do well to overlook the assortment of vegetables that, by their appearance, may put you in mind of certain Italian displays of this type. Though this is perfectly good food, there are better ways to begin your dinner here. But, for the record (and for vegetarians), an assorted plate of these items may include a spinach risotto, the dark and oiled rice threaded with the green; marinated mushrooms that have more mushroom flavor and less astringent sourness than run-of-restaurant mushrooms à la Grecque; florets of cauliflower with timidly hot green peppers; a mingling of beets and onions; whole okras that are mushy in their tomato sauce; strands of decent red peppers, oiled and roasted; and, at the center of your plate, a baked tomato packed with a sweet-spiced stuffing of rice and pine nuts. All that is fine, but finer still are: taramosalata, the familiar red-roe paste in a version that is smooth, lively of its lemon, and of a briny sparkle possible only in the just-made article; melitzanosalata, a rather too-blenderized version of the familiar eggplant mash, but its freshness and subtle liveliness save it; gigandes skordalia, big white beans on a thick, oiled, and well-seasoned paste of garlic and potatoes; octopus, the long, rough-textured tentacles firm but not rubbery, blackened by grilling, moistened by an herbed and oily sauce; tiropeta and spanakopeta, light pies of flaky pastry, the former filled with feta cheese of real strength, the latter, which is tubular, with good spinach.

If you wish, you may have your snapper grilled, but have it roasted, and it arrives, still wrapped in its crisped skin, buried in a dense, garlic-flavored sauce of tomatoes and onions, the fish itself firm and juicy. Of course there is moussaka, and the ground lamb in this one is of powerful, muttony flavor, to which the charred eggplant is a vigorous zest—the top, happily, is not a gooey white sauce, is browned and crackly, is sprinkled with more of that ground lamb, a bit of cheese as well. The tender lamb chops seem to have been oiled and seasoned before their grilling, but this only potentiates their flavor —and, oddly for a Greek restaurant in New York, you may have your lamb rare if you want it that way. Withal, the winner is the rabbit stew, the great nuggets of meat, on the bone, white and juicy and powerfully flavored by the spicy redded sauce, thick with whole onions, in which they have been done.

The rice pudding is nubbly, custardy, sweet—too bad it has been in its cup a while, and that a thin skin has formed across the top. Good baklava, of almonds (rather than the walnuts that, in New York, are usually the nut of choice), the honey-sweet nut paste, mingled with crisp slivers, interleaved with flaky pastry and set on a good cake base. What are called "diples" are coils of fried-in-oil dough that you eat with honey—an amusing sweet. Your waiter suggests Greek coffee. You ask what that is. He describes it. "Sounds like Turkish coffee," you say. "Yes," says your waiter, "but we're not allowed to say that." The coffee, half liquid, half sediment, and very strong, is good with some of Periyali's homey cookies.

★ PESCA

23 East 22nd Street
LUNCH, MONDAY TO FRIDAY; DINNER, MONDAY TO SATURDAY. CLOSED SUNDAY.
Reservations: 533-2293.
Credit cards: AE, MC, V.
Expensive.

Finfish, shellfish, a dash of pasta, and a couple dozen buzzwords of contemporary cookery, such are the surefire ingredients that are the culinary recipe for this place. The formula yields fashion without style, serviceability without (seafood) character, anonymity. Pesca is the Gimbel's of fish restaurants, albeit at Bloomie's prices. Nothing terribly wrong with the place, you understand, but it is informed not at all by any passion for the produce of the deep. What this house does to seafood is what Hollywood does to a novel—licks it, as it is put, denatures it to broaden its base of acceptability. For all its fanciness, and there is a lot of it, the food tastes as if it were prepared according to the precepts of *Joy of Cooking*. Dinner here, and you will rarely come away imagining that the smell of the briny lingers in your nostrils. But while the place has subtracted much that is fundamental to seafood restaurants, it has also, happily, left out a lot that is too often included. The ceiling is not festooned with hairy fish nets, there is no hardtack in the breadbasket, you do not stub out your cigarette in a seashell.

Not that Pesca is coy about what it is about. The place is, in fact, hung with scores of oils, watercolors, engravings, prints, all of them watery—fish or shellfish, ships or seascapes—and all handsomely framed and boldly hung, the only three-dimensional deviation a big white-enameled sailfish that, your host assures you, is a sailfish coated with white enamel, not the plastic model it could easily be. All this in a long, high-ceilinged room that is wide at the front, where it accommodates, in addition to tables and chairs, the bar and piano, the latter inaudible when the place is filled and noisy, and at other times tinkled with sufficient softness neither to distract nor divert. Between the cream-colored stamped-tin ceiling and the polished wood floor, the room is painted a shiny pale pink that glistens in the soft light of overhead spots. The white-linened tables are surrounded by bentwood side chairs with green-upholstered seats that, by their skimpiness —they are about as big around as dinner plates—seem to make an exaggerated assumption about the slimming properties of a seafood diet. It is important to know of Pesca that it is an operation as much as it is a restaurant, a place in which you may find yourself processed rather than catered to, for though certain members of the staff are sweet, a number of the veterans go through their resentful paces as if sentenced to this place by you. Maybe they do not like fish.

The smoked tuna is notable for how the intensity of its smoke flavor obscures the seafood quality of the fish, and for how the thin slices of brownish meat are wet rather than moist—the jigger of good sesame dressing served with it does not rescue the event. But then there is the gravlax, the supple cured salmon in a version that is salty rather than sweet, heady of dill, very nice with its thick, sharp mustard sauce. A couple of little handsomely browned pancakes studded with kernels of corn garnish the bluefish sausage, which reaches you in a green sauce that is spicy of the hot green peppers that account for its color, but the plump sausage itself, though juicy and well seasoned within its casing, is certainly no expression of bluefish, could be any fish. And the seafood chowder, though its redded broth is hearty, is studded with dice of fish that, though not invariably fresh, are always overcooked, and with mushy cubes of vegetable.

Each day there is a pasta of the day, and you only have to read the list of ingredients —for example, farfalle (bowties) in a tomato-and-basil sauce, with sundried tomatoes, eggplant, and shrimp—to know that the sauces are compendia of attractive-sounding parts that have been added to one another but not really transformed into anything new. And each day there is a risotto of the day, and the grain, cooked in stock, has good flavor, nicely accommodates the ingredients—they vary from time to time—added to it.

When soft-shell crabs are in season, Pesca obtains the best of them, tiny ones that have just shed their shells, but sautés them in a rather gingerly way, so that they are hardly crisped, and serves them in a sauce of red bell peppers that makes sense only because the crabs need the help. But the roasted lobster is fine, its crunchy stuffing of wild rice and chopped root vegetables a good textural foil to the firm, sweet meat. And the broiled salmon steak is exemplary, glinting moist and pink within its browned surfaces—the fish gains nothing from the good mustard sauce served with it. Then there is this grilled pompano, which though not off, is low enough on pompano taste to make you suspect the fish was frozen, or on ice for days on end—its loose sauce of capers in crème fraîche livens it. Whatever you do, skip the cioppino, a San Francisco stew here made with noisome mussels, lobster that is toughened by its overcooking, scallops, dice of nameless fish, and innumerable vegetables—the spicy broth is invigorating, perhaps you should ask for it straight.

The fruit-custard tarts come, often, on rubbery pastry, and the custard itself is sometimes a bit leaden. The nutted chocolate tart is intense, its black icing more so. First-rate whipped cream is served with the desserts.

★ PETALUMA

1356 First Avenue (at 73rd Street)
LUNCH AND DINNER.
Reservations: 772-8800.
Credit cards: AE, MC, V.
Medium priced.

This offshoot of Elio's began as a California restaurant with an Italian accent. That did not work out, and success came only when Petaluma caught up with what, after all, was surely its destiny. Today it is, in all but name, Elio's, Jr., is ninety percent Italian and proud of it, and the menu items that remain from the eclectic past—crab cakes, goat cheese salad, Siamese chicken—are stepchildren left behind by previous spouses. Of course Elio's, Jr., is not Elio's. You do not find pizza at Elio's, and sometimes you cannot find a waiter here. Gents who regularly dinner with the guys at Elio's are at Petaluma the night they get the kids, grandly urging them to order anything they want. Elio's is the dining room, Petaluma the rec room. But of the many eating arenas around town that, by their spaciousness, informality, and snacky menus, sell themselves as youthful repairs, Petaluma is the one that addresses itself specifically to scions of the civilized. Sometimes the parents themselves come, unaccompanied by child, and they feel free to hang their jackets over the backs of their chairs. Petaluma occupies the no-man's-land heretofore known as Generation Gap.

The site of this coming together is a big, pink, L-shaped store arranged on a couple of levels, a good-size bar just inside the corner entrance, a pizza oven behind a counter at the elbow's inner turn. Big windows front on First Avenue and on East 73rd, great columns of faux marble rise through the space, and the black-and-white diamond pattern of the asphalt-tile floor and the vastly unrelated hangings on the walls partially undo the calm of the soft light—as does the insistent but not loud background music (now soft rock, now music of the thirties and forties), as does the alternately frenetic and becalmed action of the staff in the aisles.

On display near the pizza station are the makings of the antipasto misto Petaluma, and you submit yourself to your waitress's good will, permit her to assemble a plate according to her lights. Comes presently a lively assortment, slices of pungent salami and chunks of sautéed zucchini, a crunchy salad of white beans, cool rice dotted with bits of olive and sweet peas, roasted red peppers suffused with oil, more. Cold first courses of greater seriousness, however, must be ordered individually: smoked tuna, sliced thin and spread all across a good-size plate, adorned with fresh artichoke hearts and moistened with olive oil of vivid flavor; slivered fresh mushrooms and pungent arugula covered over with slices of hard, sharp Parmesan, nothing else on the plate but that good oil again;

259

vitello tonatto, the pale veal under a lemony sauce that is dotted with capers, but as tuna sauces go, this is lemon sauce, the fish but a remoteness. As to that pollo Siamese, it probably hangs on in this foreign situation because of the peanut sauce served with it, which is at once fruity, of strong nut flavor, and fiery hot, for the chicken, though handsomely browned and glistening on its wood skewers, reveals little flavor of its own —the unlikely arugula garnish is probably just lost.

Lost also is the waiter who passes your table in search of his station. You stop him, ask, as a matter of information, whether half orders of pasta may be ordered. As "yes" or "no" would take too long, he suggests you discuss the subject with your own waiter. It is enough to get you thinking that Petaluma is where waiters go when they are fired from Elio's. Anyhow, no is the answer, and you begin dinner with a serving of spaghetti pescatore that could end it as well, firm pasta, clams and mussels in their shells, scallops and shrimp out of theirs, all fresh-tasting and all sweet (but for a bit of iodine in the crunchy shrimp), the herbed red sauce briny and stout. Two or three rice dishes are usually listed, sometimes risotto con porcini, the mound of moist grain earthy of the chunks of wild mushroom with which it is dotted—spooned-on cheese thickens and deepens the hefty dish. Bits of sharp and salty green olive are the life of the pizza quattro stagioni, the crackling circle of bread surfaced with glistening cheese and adorned with mushrooms and artichokes, thin slices of good browned ham over the top.

For your collection of buzzwords in unlikely places, consider the listing "polpa de granseole Maryland," crab cakes to you and not bad; fluffy, browned, crusted patties of the sweet seafood served with a red-pepper mayonnaise that is rich and spicy. The veal itself is the making of the piccata alla vernaccia, the pale and juicy meat roused to subtle but real life by the wine and shallots of its sauce and the herbs that cling to its surface. Four lamb chops reach you with their ribs extending beyond the rim of their plate, the eyes clustered at the center and overlaid with sautéed onions, mushrooms, and pungent little black olives, powerful flavors that do not obscure the strong meat.

The issue of whether "Thaitian vanilla bean cheesecake" is Thai or Tahitian remains unresolved even when you have eaten it, the standard stuff between a graham cracker crust and a slick white icing. The raspberries are a bit more than ripe in their winy zabaglione sauce. The chocolate cake is intense, but suffers for being cold at the center.

★★LA PETITE FERME

973 Lexington Avenue (near 70th Street)
LUNCH, MONDAY TO SATURDAY; DINNER, MONDAY TO SATURDAY. CLOSED SUNDAY.
Reservations: 249-3272.
Credit cards: AE, DC, MC, V.
Expensive.

Having redefined the "neighborhood restaurant" in terms that disregard cost, La Petite Ferme gets by on the custom of those who are indifferent to that factor. There are not so many of them that they may be relied on regularly to fill this restaurant, but the rent on the real estate occupied by the empty tables is taken care of by the premium built into the prices paid at the others. Anyway, this Farm provides value for the extra dollars. The food is better than at places with names like Mama Mia's or Maman Marmite, the service is more civilized, and the charms (by definition, neighborhood restaurants have charms) are more charming. 'Twas not ever thus. Upon a time La Petite was a minuscule (20-chair) place in the Village, and it was the rage, a destination, chichi, for in that tiny store was served the most elemental French food—that in the days when what was called "all those fancy sauces" (a/k/a haute cuisine) *was* French cooking in New York. This second incarnation is considerably larger than the original, it has shifted a couple of culinary steps away from the first store's Spartan cookery, and those moves toward normality account for the restaurant's altered status—no one remembers the last time anybody talked about this place.

This is a deep, soft-lit narrow room, dark carpeted, half timbered, furnished with bare tables, their thick wood tops sealed, the chairs around them those little upright things of wood dowels and straw, cushions on the seats, that are charming but dinky, not for the broad of thigh. The tables are set with matte-finish clay-white china (blue flowers painted on), with wildflowers in crockery pots, with white candles in big hurricane lamps, with plaid dishcloths for napkins. It is all *slightly* cluttered, every other table, it seems, tucked into a corner or turn of this somewhat compartmented room, which contributes to the restaurant's relaxed air. The place may be defined by what, on the Upper East Side, it is not—it is not a Third Avenue Italian restaurant/saloon, or a celebrity showcase, or the snowy fantasy of the day's hottest restaurant architect. So it gets a nice crowd, albeit genteel.

As if in mockery of the canapes, at once elaborate and minuscule, to which many of New York's more ambitious restaurants these days treat you, here you are presented with a plate of potato chips, warm, crisp, salty, of real potato flavor, apparently just made. While you are working on this unlikely beginning, and considering whether it is cricket to ask for more, your waiter comes by with the wood-framed blackboards. One of them bears a list of white wines on the front, reds on the back. The other is the menu, and he holds it under his chin—the way a grammar school child presses a prize-winning drawing to his chest—while reciting (from memory!) the brief list, which changes from day to day. The mussels, however, seem always to be offered, and this is one of the increasingly rare places in which this inglorious mollusk is never rank, reaches you with all its clean flavor showing, the great mound of black shells in a thickened vinaigrette that makes a delicacy of the orange-tinted meats. Still, you do well to pass those up when you are offered also the shrimp with salmon quenelles, the shrimp, barely cooked, of the clearest, most elemental ocean sweetness, the warm pink dumplings light and of vivid salmon flavor, the two garnished with strands of red and green pepper in their rich herbed butter. But do not mistake those salmon quenelles for these so-called salmon medallions, a composition formed into a sausage within a crêpe, and served in slices in a yogurt sauce adorned with caviar—the sauce is fine, but the seafood is just an indeterminate solidity. The artichoke is carefully poached, the heart retains its good gritty texture, and it is nicely roused by the lemon sauce with which the hollowed vegetable is filled. Sometimes there is cauliflower soup, and this is mother's milk food, white and hot and homey, rich but not thick, livened by paprika, textured, chunks of the vegetable at the bottom of the bowl.

It is the custom of this place not to list lobster on the blackboard, but always to offer it, the waiter referring to it as a specialty. It is served in what the house calls a white butter sauce, which is light, delicately herbed, slightly winy, just the enrichment for this smallish, judiciously poached crustacean. Salmon yet again, this time slender pink fillets prettily set on a dark, olive-green sauce that is a buttery, well-seasoned puree of strong spinach. Those seafood dishes notwithstanding, the monkfish may be this kitchen's most notable accomplishment, for the meat of this swimmer is known for the flavor it lacks,

261

while here the white fish—given as rôti of lotte—is crusted in the making, then served in a red-wine sauce bordelaise, which creates a lively complexity of textures and flavors. If the blanc de volaille au poivron et estragon is low on chicken flavor, that deficiency is offset by the heady tarragon-and-red-pepper sauce in which the crisped and juicy bird is served. You anticipate a steak when you order the filet de boeuf au madère, but the tender beef seems almost potted in its winy sauce—good food, but not what you expected.

First-class Brie is unobtainable on this side of the Atlantic, but the Brie served here, just a little runny, in a snowy crust, and of earthy flavor, is as close as you can come. The papaya sorbet tastes like papaya, the kiwi sorbet like a concentrated intensity that is an improvement on the fruit. The mixed berries reach you in the bowl of a big wineglass, over them a thick and smooth and liquory sauce sabayon. The strawberry tart is a triangle of pastry on which stand, in close rows, huge, utterly ripe strawberries—thick, stiff whipped cream is served with the tart.

★★★ PETROSSIAN

182 West 58th Street
LUNCH AND DINNER.
Reservations: 245-2214.
Credit cards: AE, DC, MC, V.
Very expensive.

For the more or less recherché foodstuffs with which it is specifically identified, this is the place. Part of the reason, of course, is that Petrossian is not merely a restaurant, but also the standardbearer of the Petrossian name and of the foods the Petrossian family produces, imports, distributes widely: black caviar and other fish roes, sturgeon and other smoked fish, foie gras. (You find other items on their menu, but almost no one comes here and fails at least to sample the specialties of the house.) Accordingly, what is put before you of those wares is impeccable, will tend to be recorded in your memory as exemplars by which you will judge those foodstuffs in other places—in, say, the Russian Tea Room, this establishment's natural competitor around the corner, which, for all its charms, cannot be counted on every time to serve up caviar like what you get here. Maybe no one sells the little black eggs to restaurants as carefully as Petrossian does to walkers-in off the street, and probably very few restaurants know all there is to know about handling the stuff, but those are not your problems, so when you get a yen for these goods, and there is a stack of large bills you are unable to launder, dinner at Petrossian will do much to finesse that problem.

With respect, however, to the physical restaurant, Petrossian's lure is identical to that appeal of caviar that has nothing to do with its quality, only with its luxe. Partly for that reason, comes here a foppy crowd of those who work as hard spending their money as making it. The restaurant is expensive, they figure it must be part of the good life, a conviction reinforced by the appointments: walls that are tinted mirrored glass or burled wood, a floor of polished granite, deep-pink drapes of silken gauze, panels of mink on the gray leather banquette, bronze statuary, flowers and gold-rimmed plates on the tables, and a sailing ship—the family emblem—embroidered into each of the carefully ironed napkins. You enter to a bar, nothing so vulgar as bottles on display behind it, to which passersby who have been unable to swing an impromptu table may repair for picnics of beluga, toast, and Mumm's. To your left is, how you say, the deli, the wares behind a counter, the counter behind red ropes. It offers, in addition to takeout, the paraphernalia—silver dishes, gold-colored caviar spatulas, and the like—by way of which Petrossian makes rite of the consumption of its victuals, and by way of which you may do the same in the privacy of your own rec room. Chez vous, however, you will probably have to do without the services of the Petrossian staff, gentlemen in mustard-colored jackets who seem to be chosen for the sauvity and weight of their continental accents.

Black caviar is the roe of sturgeons, and most of the world's supply comes from fish that swim in the Caspian Sea, Black Sea, rivers nearby. The kinds you encounter most often—beluga, osetra, sevruga, to put them in descending order of their cost—are named for the species of sturgeon from which they are taken. (A tiny quantity of pale "golden" caviar is also produced, from the species sterlet, but you will not find it on restaurant menus.) So-called pressed caviar is a compacture of roe, usually osetra or sevruga, that has been damaged—though its texture does not match that of the more expensive stuff, and though it is usually more heavily salted, there is something to be said for the saltier taste when the caviar is rolled in blinis. Though beluga is the most prestigious, you need not be shamefaced about ordering osetra or sevruga—the three are not, after all, grades. Beluga caviar is of the largest, palest-gray eggs, is the most subtly flavored. Osetra resembles it closely. Sevruga eggs are tiny, almost black, have the strongest flavor. What distinguishes all the caviar served here is its perfect texture, the clarity and freshness of its flavor, the utter absence of the fishiness you sometimes detect in restaurant caviar—which indicates imperfect storage somewhere between those Eastern waters and your table.

The best way to acquaint yourself with the varieties of black caviar is by way of what the house calls Les Années Folles (mad times), a $104 repast that begins with thirty grams each (a bit more than an oz.) of beluga, osetra, sevruga (which you spread on triangles of toasted white bread, a substance of so little character that it takes nothing from the caviars themselves), the flavors of which are marine essences, pure and primordial. You are then served pressed caviar with blinis, rather pallid wheat pancakes, to which you apply crème fraîche and then caviar, and which you then roll into cylinders that, if you have done your job neatly, you eat with your fingers. The binge involves one more self indulgence before dessert: smoked salmon, moist but not oily, of vivid fish flavor and subtle but unmistakable smokiness, the great circle of thin, pink meat, clinging to its cold plate, served only with that toast, no other garnishes, and it needs none. Other items of cured seafood on the menu: salmon roe, great red-orange globules, glistening and clinging to one another, of which you are served a dollop the size of a plump apricot set at the bottom of a round, thick-walled, straight-sided glass dish—these eggs are brinier than sturgeon roe, and their flavor is powerful even when smothered in crème fraîche and wrapped in blinis; cod roe, four ovoid dollops of the sticky, pale-pink stuff, strong but not really gamy—you may even detect a bit of sweetness under the salt surface of the flavor; smoked sturgeon, five substantial strips of the supple fish, at once smoky and soapy, the latter quality not a negative, just the closest approximation to the odd flavor of this singular swimmer; smoked trout, of which you are served the four skinned and boned pink quarters of a salmon trout reassembled in the shape of the whole fish— this is the most delicate smoked trout in town, and unlike what you get in many places, this meat retains its moisture, is almost fluffy; and smoked eel, briny and oily, the most vigorous of these items. Order what the menu refers to as a whole goose liver, and you are brought an amalgam cut from a loaf—you can only complain a little, for the cool liver is almost overwhelmingly oleaginous: meat as butter.

Petrossian also lists a substantial menu of more-or-less straight French food: a standard mousse of duck liver; a pâté of sweetbreads, encased in a flaky pastry with a crown of dark jelly, that is a little flat; lobster and scallops en croûte, the two, with spinach, between leaves of rather doughy pastry, and in a saffron sauce that does not rescue the merely fancy dish; roasted quails, their skins barely browned, but the meat of strong quail flavor, served with slices of tart apple in a brown sauce with white grapes—fancy food again.

Rich, stiff whipped cream and fresh berries are added to just about any dessert you order: the good crème brûlée, served unheated from the dessert cart, the custard light under its crackling top; the strawberry cheesecake, which is very fluffy for its richness; the pear tart, half of a firm, glistening poached pear set in a nutty almond cake; the mocha cream tart, intensely coffee-flavored pastry cream within layers of light, moist cake.

★★PIETRO'S

232 East 43rd Street
LUNCH, MONDAY TO FRIDAY; DINNER, MONDAY TO SATURDAY. CLOSED SUNDAY.
Reservations: 682-9760.
Credit cards: AE, DC, MC, V.
Very expensive.

The anteroom just off the street is fresh and spiffy, and so you look twice at the brass sign. Both times it reads the same:

THIS PLACE

HAS

BEEN HERE

SINCE

MAY 1, 1932

The situation is cleared up a little when you pass into the main room, where there is another sign much like the first one, but different:

THIS PLACE

HAS

BEEN HERE

SINCE

JAN. 3, 1984

If the restaurant looks familiar, as if you have been coming to it for fifty years, be aware that it is not the physical surroundings you recognize, but the style. For when Pietro's moved its fifty-year-old steakhouse—from the second and third stories of an ancient structure on the corner of 45th and Third to this big street-level spread a few blocks to the southeast—it did not undertake to replicate the props of the original set. It could have been done, but there are not, for example, any choice windowside tables next to false windows. That fondly remembered steamy closet of an open kitchen, complete with perspiring crew, is gone. Even the density and noise have been left behind. Only the spirit, much of the staff, and the food made the trip intact. The customers followed on their own.

Though the new quarters are unlike the old, the differences are not a function of the passage of five decades between their inceptions. Whether by design or mistake, what Pietro's has created is a brand-new Depression steakhouse, one that could have been put together just this way in the days when alcoholism was a federal offense, not a disease. The place is all rough plaster and dark wood, with rows of white-linened tables surrounded by simple chairs. These are on two levels, the only dimly contemporary note, and if you like to think that way, you may choose to believe that the two-level layout is a remote reference to the two stories of the old place. The engravings on the walls are a gesture to the received notion that the blank spots on restaurant walls ought to be occupied by framed objects. There is a bar up front (probably installed the moment Repeal was ratified) and curtains on the front window. Your host is cordial even if he does not know you. And the waiters, in their dark-blue linen jackets, are courtly and professional —they know the menu, they hear you talking, and they rarely make mistakes. You may well conclude that this place will be at this site until the next thirties. And if things continue here the way they have been going since the days when Charles Curtis was Vice President, the next century will see Pietro's populated by well-fed burghers with their wives and descendants, white-shirted executives with their customers, and guys from the nearby *News* with girls from the nearby *News*.

None of them is preoccupied with thoughts of "nouvelle" or "nouveau," or even of "northern" or "Italian" or "cuisine," or, most assuredly, of "balsamic vinegar," when they commence their dinners with, say, great sheets of strong, dark red, fat-rimmed, and gamy ham draped over slices of melon that, they hardly notice, are less than utterly ripe. They do just as well with what is listed, under salads, as "Chopped," a huge, lively mélange of onions and tomatoes, lettuce and watercress, and strands of salty anchovy, all in a tart and forceful dressing. The Caesar, however, is no match for the Chopped—it seems to be prepared in large batches during the course of the evening, not mixed to order, and your allotment may be somewhat wilted, having been in its dressing for a time. Eight littlenecks are most of the so-called Clams sauté, a bit of breading and a pool of parsleyed and shallot-sweetened butter the balance—the clams are fresh, but this still comes off only as fun food.

Like most Steak Row steakhouses, this one has an Italian side, so there is pasta. Many of the noodle dishes are the ones you would have found in New York Italian restaurants in the days when cars had running boards. If, for example, before you die, you want one last dish of spaghetti and meatballs, think of Pietro's as the place that is holding an order with your name on it. Until then, you are better off with the spaghetti in white clam sauce, a standard version of the familiar dish, the firm pasta mingled with lots of fresh clams in a buttery brine that is loaded with garlic and parsley. But there are also rarities in this department, including an exceptional ziti dish in which the ribbed tubular noodles are mingled with minced broccoli and much garlic, and lubricated with lots of butter—you strengthen the dish by adding ground cheese.

You get a slab of swordfish here the size of an art book—it is fresh, browned, glistens of butter on the outside and of its own moisture on the inside. A two-and-a-half pound lobster will cleanse you of $35, and you can get one here that is truly broiled—not steamed and then broiled. But there are Steak Row places where that big bet is more likely to be a winner than Pietro's—the place has been known to give lobsters a bit too much fire. Lots of chicken dishes, but you will do well to note the item that calls attention to itself (1) by being more expensive than the others and (2) by carrying the company name. Such is Chicken à la Pietro, great meaty chunks of the crisped bird (they have real chicken flavor) buried in a tangle of sautéed onions (blackened a little and sweet) and strands of crunchy green pepper. The veal chop is hearty, big and browned and juicy, but you are sometimes served a loin chop here, not a rib chop, which is certainly not what you had in mind. The lamb chops, however, do not disappoint—you get a pair of three-rib chops, the nuggets of red meat moist and of high lamb flavor within their charred surfaces and rims of crisped fat. You get just about perfect broiled steaks here, that is, the meat is fibrous, tender, blood-juicy, accurately prepared—and handsomely charred in the process. But even Pietro's cannot bring back the prewar steer, and as in all steakhouses, the beef is sometimes a little low on its essential ingredient: beefiness.

The French fried onions are dark, crinkly, and sweet. But, as you know, meat's real other half is the potato: the shoestrings are crisp, fresh fried, have real potato flavor; the lyonnaise are big deep-fried disks under moist slivers of sautéed onion, but the au gratins are the big winner, the dice of crisp tuber judiciously seasoned in their rich and creamy sauce, the cheese topping artfully browned, pully, and a little sharp.

The standard cheesecake is sweet, weighty, slightly vanilla flavored, browned on top, cool. The powerful zabaglione is hot, winy, fluffy. Rum cake, fruit, and ice-cream items are the balance of the dessert list.

★★PINOCCHIO

170 East 81st Street
DINNER. CLOSED SUNDAY.
Reservations: 650-1513.
Credit cards: AE, DC.
Beer and wine.
Expensive.

Formerly an unmarked one-room hole-in-the-wall that often went unfound even after an intense search, Pinocchio is now a two-room hole-in-the-wall that often goes unfound even after an intense search. Certain charms, however, were lost when Pinocchio was doubled. It is, for example, no longer necessary, at certain tables, to rise and stand aside when the front door is opened. But, as ever, even when you have found the outside, you will have difficulty making out the inside. Pinocchio is dimly lit, and it is somber within its dimness—burlap curtains, brick or dark-brown walls, a deep-maroon stamped-tin ceiling. Some illumination is produced by feeble electric lights that are enclosed within hanging flora of colored glass—clusters of grapes and the like. On close inspection you will discover that there is white linen on the tightly assembled tables, terra-cotta bas reliefs on the walls, as well as photographs and—this is important—venerable Metropolitan Opera Company bills. The proprietor, you see, is a devotee of Italian vocal art, and, early and late, and sometimes during the shank of the dinner hour itself, the earnest beseechments of legendary Italian tenors quicken the air. Sometimes Mimi departs with the last diner.

This is a busy place, the kind in which spaciousness is sacrificed for the delights of dense conviviality. There is always room for one more at these tables. And if, in the enlarged establishment, the hired help that has been added to the original family staff is occasionally amateurish (it is a rare night when you ask for nothing twice), the jolly crowd does not think that matters much.

Carpaccio—just-cut thin slices of raw beef—is adorned with a tart green sauce of capers and herbs. Bresaola—gamy, air-dried beef—reaches you under a film of good olive oil. Genoa salami—the hard, purple sausage, fatted and garlicked—is served hot, under a generous storm of strong grated cheese. Though you find two sautéed mushroom caps a meager apportionment, these are fresh and crunchy, and their seasoned mushroom stuffing is of intense flavor under its toppings of hot, pully cheese. Around town the word "crostini" usually refers to some variant of chopped liver on toast. Here the word is used with the modifier "nostri," so do not be surprised when what you get is a hot open-face sandwich—a layer of anchovies, another of strips of red pimento, and a top one of melted cheese on the crusty slice of bread.

White and dark-green noodles, slivers of veal and strong ham, fresh peas and carrots, all in a buttered wine broth, make a paglia e fieno unlike others you regularly find. The hefty tubes of pasta called penne and a sauce of cream and cheese, with capers and bits of bacon, go as penne palermitana, which is just as rare. The house primavera is made with fresh vegetables and perfectly al dente spiral noodles (fusilli), but the dish lacks the surprising quality of this establishment's best pasta.

No fish is listed on the menu, but some is usually offered: sometimes salmon puttanesca, the pink fish in a light tomato sauce sharpened with olives; on occasion poached salmon, in a broth dotted with fresh vegetables. Both dishes are good, but would benefit from fresher-tasting fish. And sometimes there is trout poached in red wine—the fish is served in a smooth, buttered, and somewhat tart sauce prepared from the cooking liquid. The lemon chicken—white meat from a mature bird—has much chicken flavor and, happily, nothing candylike in the lemon sauce. Another lemon sauce, this one frothy, on the veal piccata—the carefully sautéed meat is adorned with disks of lemon and much fresh parsley. The restaurant's saltimbocca has always been elegant—thin slices of veal and ham in a delicate white-wine sauce. Among the most pungent dishes in the place is the liver torinese—an herbed and creamy sauce, thick with bits of bacon, binds the slivers of dark organ meat.

What Pinocchio calls caffè nonno you would call a glass of zabaglione with espresso poured over it—dessert and coffee for the price of dessert alone. When the zabaglione is cold, it is thickened with whipped cream and served over ripe berries—you cannot fault it. Moscovita di ciocolata is not exactly a chocolate mousse—more like strong chocolate ice cream under thick whipped cream. On that order, but more elaborate, is the budino al caffè—mocha mousse studded with bits of chocolate and served, in a sundae glass, under whipped cream. When you come to the bottom of the glass, you find a macaroon soaked in coffee and chocolate. The melon in raspberry-brandy sauce is rousing.

The menu is changed often, so you will not always find what you seek.

★ POIRET

474 Columbus Avenue (near 83rd Street)
LUNCH, SATURDAY AND SUNDAY; DINNER, DAILY.
Reservations: 724-6880.
Credit cards: AE, MC, V.
Medium priced.

When the end approaches, sinners turn to good works. Poiret is brought to you by the folks who bring you several of the biggest, loudest, busiest, most successful terrible restaurants on earth. Maybe they know something you do not. Maybe they are just playing it safe. In disguising themselves behind the façade of Poiret, they have chosen a look that is now almost gone from New York. Poiret could pass for an amateur restaurant, the kind of place that used to be opened by people who had tried everything else and failed. Such establishments consisted of emptied stores, painted and provided with tables and chairs, and kitchens assembled in ignorance or disregard of administrative codes and human practicalities. Some of those stabs in the dark succeeded. A few even got licensed to do what they were already doing. Poiret, intentionally or not, honors the disappearing genre.

You enter to a cube of a place, hang your coat on one of the pipe racks, ask for a table from which you can keep an eye on it. The flaws in the plain wood floor are obscured by the black pattern stenciled thereon, the irregularities of the pale walls are all of a piece with the arrangement of blossoms on hairlike boughs that has been painted on them freehand. The West Side—not the Riverside Drive West Side, not the Central Park West West Side, rather the Columbus/Amsterdam/Broadway West Side core—has taken this place up, and the earnest social workers, noncorporate lawyers, and haggard school teachers, mindful that this place is something of a bargain, are here by the brigade in their jeans and sweaters and wild facial hair, quite at home in this density of small tables, indifferent to the proximity of the folks immediately on their right and adjacently on their left, utterly engaged in the subject of either their shrinks or their landlords. Immaterially, they often do not hear one another, for Poiret is a hard-surfaced, not large box, part of it under a low ceiling, and conversation goes on rattling around, from floor to ceiling, wall to wall, long after it escapes its source.

Between mouthfuls of conversation they refuel with the like of this salad of grilled shrimp, four large crustaceans, peppered and crunchy, arranged over a dune of spiky greens, the salad ringed with strong, sweet roasted red peppers. The Poiret menu is printed on two sides of a single sheet of paper, French on one side, English on the other. For some reason "petites palourdes" is translated as "petite clams," rather than "small clams." Presumably only those who read French will not take the adjective as cautionary. Anyway, you get ten of them, they reach you, in their half shells, adorned with bits of red pepper and moistened with garlicked butter—a number of the clams are toughened in the making, a few conceal bits of the cracked shell. What is given as "a selection of fried fish" could as well be a single variety, for the battered and fried morsels are of little seafood flavor, are mere carriers for the lemon you squeeze on and the well-seasoned garlic mayonnaise you apply to this high-class boardwalk food. The pâté is chunky only by virtue of the nuts with which it is studded; the meat itself is livery and mousselike, so the capers and black olives and raw onion served with it turn out to be essential offsets to the somewhat insipidly rich paste.

The tuna is fresh, the flavor of the grill is vivid but does not obscure the sweetness of the fish itself, which reaches you, in its dense tomato sauce, garnished with small onions, strong black olives, an array of lightly cooked vegetables. Poiret roasts a large chicken, so the bird does have a good bit of chicken flavor, serves it with more of those vegetables, everything buried under a dune of crisp French fries. The duck stew is thick with wild mushrooms and shreds of off-the-bone duck, the two in a dark and winy sauce, a mound of couscous at the center of the plate, vegetables all about, scallions and baby carrots across the top. But the carbonnade de boeuf is an even sturdier stew, the substantial chunks of meat fibrous, juicy, and tender in their dark-beer sauce, the hearty stuff served with, again, couscous and half a dozen vegetables.

A dessert your waitress calls "shortbread" is really a sandwich of good shortbread disks, the filler an inch-thick layer of rich and fluffy whipped cream studded with fruit (you are offered strawberry or kiwi), the construct set in a pool of mango puree that is of wonderfully clear ripe-fruit flavor. The menu listing "chocolate pavé" usually represents a rather solid block (pavé = paving stone) of some chocolate dessert—here you get a seemingly gelatinized slice cut from a loaf and set in a raspberry sauce—it is tolerable, but not what you had in mind. The poached pear retains its good fruit flavor and texture, reaches you under a white sauce, with chopped hazelnuts, that is browned just before serving—the warm sauce is good with the cool fruit.

★★★ POLO

840 Madison Avenue (near 69th Street)
LUNCH AND DINNER.
Reservations: 535-9141.
Credit cards: AE, DC, MC, V.
Very expensive.

For years New Yorkers avoided restaurants in hotels as if they were restaurants in Philadelphia. Then Philadelphia changed. Then New York hotel restaurants changed. New Yorkers, however, remain wary. There is something they do not like about hotel restaurants, for in the ways such places cater to the transients passing through (and to those—often tiresome eccentrics—who live upstairs year-round), they lose the locals. Surely if this were a restaurant rather than a restaurant in a hotel, you would not enter to a portrait of Prince Charles in a polo shirt. And, very likely, one end of the dining room would not be dominated by a cocktail lounge—complete with jovial, joking, occasionally singing pianist—hard by the elevators that handle the ups and downs of the likes of this one clown, who interrupts his singing-along, repairs to his room, changes, returns —now in his crimson smoking jacket, and complete with cigar—to his revels.

If this were a restaurant rather than a restaurant in a hotel, the scores of framed portraits of thoroughbred horses that adorn the walls, the leather-upholstered chairs with brass upholstery tacks, the dark-red carpeting, and the solemn paisley pattern of the well-stuffed banquettes would be accepted as low camp or high camp, as some sort of harmless fantasy, but not, as they are intended here, as an expression of class. Notwithstanding which, when passers-through descend for dinner, in tennis sweater and jeans, or in a gleaming aquamarine pants suit, they are led to the table of their choice. True class asserts itself simply by not dealing with matters distasteful.

But, you will recall, Philadelphia changed, so did hotel restaurants, and your fingers and toes are digits enough on which to count the local kitchens that turn out better food than this one. Consider, for example, these belon oysters in their half-shells—they are warm and tender and fresh, their briny liquid is buttered, they are surmounted by substantial flakes of black truffle, and they are strewn with greens and edible flowers; or this so-called seared sashimi of tuna, the edges of the silken beef-red fish crusted with coriander seeds, nutty and perfumed, the fish and its accompanying salad moistened with a sharp soy dressing; or this tepee-shaped salad of prosciutto-cured duck, the lengthy strands of strong dark meat leaning on all sides against a mound of greens, the tent set in a gently dressed, many flavored fantasy of barley and wild rice, nuts and bits of dried fruit; or this smoky grilled quail, its juicy meat in striking contrast to its charred skin, the garnish of potato salad adorned with strands of roasted red pepper, the green salad studded with nuggets of good bacon.

Your salmon arrives looking like a pink hamburger under half a bun, the bottom being a built-up-by-layers disk of the pink meat, cooked rare and of moist lusciousness, the "bun" an overlay of horseradish that, though browned, retains a good bit of its strength, the semi-sandwich surrounded by a field of herbed raw cucumber that is adorned with clumps of fresh, briny salmon caviar. From a mound of celery root puree sprout half a dozen sails, celery root chips doing an impression of potato chips and tasting like nothing at all, the puree encircled by sea scallops so browned that they are flat, much of their richness and moisture lost, the entire production painted with a speckled liquid that is truffled walnut oil—this may well be a good dish when the elements are right, but nothing about it makes you wonder hard enough to try it again. Try instead this wondrous grilled squab, its spicy hot sauce touched with ginger and cardamom, its mixed-vegetable garnish fortified with cheese and fragrant of herbs. Not much beef you get these days reminds you of the red meat of old. Even Polo's steak does not. But Polo may have come up with a preparation that, if it does not make today's meat seem like yesterday's, restores much of its drama. The thing reaches you sliced, glistening ruby-pink within its dark edges, its winy sauce thick with bits of black olive, the total effect deep and powerful.

As in steak houses, after your steak, cheesecake. This one, however, is a distant, lofty relative of those on Steak Row, alternate layers of cream cheese and poppyseed-dotted white cake, beside them a pool of raspberry coulis, crimson and fruity. What are given as banana wontons are triangular turnovers of crisp dough packed with a banana-walnut filling, sweet and rich and nutty, and nicely offset by a ball of rum-raisin ice cream. The light chestnut mousse, coated with cinnamon, is garnished with a wine-poached pear that is stained dark and strewn with chopped nuts, and with a warm mélange of stewed dried fruits—apricots, raisins, black figs. The assortment of citrus desserts is made up of grapefruit ice, lemony custard, citrus sections in pastry cream, blood orange sauce—fun.

★★IL PONTE VECCHIO

206 Thompson Street (near Bleecker Street)
LUNCH AND DINNER.
Reservations: 228-7701.
Credit cards: AE.
Medium priced.

Asphalt-tile floors, light- and dark-tan walls (a random assortment of art and posters thereon), rows of tables occupied by locals in casual clothes—drinking, mostly, carafe wine and enjoying the low prices and good food. Those who are not eating are at the tight little bar in the front room, drinking, probably waiting for a table to open up. You will find little here but basics, and nothing to complain about.

You will find fresh raw clams that are tiny, sweet, cold. You may also have them as clams posillipo, a massive mound of the steamed littlenecks in a hot red broth, herbed and oily. (You can have fresh mussels made the same way.) You will find shrimp oreganati, big sweet ones, albeit only three, in a strongly salted oil that is flavored with oregano and much lemon.

Everybody orders the unlisted linguine alla Johnny, the al dente noodles in a peppery red sauce that is thick with shrimp, fish, great chunks of plum tomato. The carbonara is creamy, sharpened with Italian bacon, made fragrant with fresh parsley. Amatriciana is this establishment's simplest red sauce—it is served on thin spaghetti, it is aggressively seasoned, and it is superb when it is made thick with ground cheese. The manicotti is elemental, little more than ricotta cheese stuffed into pasta pillows and baked in tomato sauce—it arrives sizzling.

No bass on the menu, but it is usually present in the kitchen. You may have yours broiled, touched with thyme, moistened with a light, lively tomato sauce. The zuppa di pesce is a bristling platter of mussels, squid, shrimp, fish, all in a briny red broth. The place obtains chicken that tastes like chicken, converts it into chicken Ponte Vecchio— slices of boned white meat under red peppers in a pale wine sauce. The same good bird goes into the chicken cacciatore, in which the smooth and winy red sauce is thick with mushrooms, onion, garlic. When rabbit is available, the pale and tender meat is served in a sauce much like that one. The veal paillard is of veal pounded out to the size of a big platter and grilled until it is blackened a little but still moist—you bring it to lively life by squeezing on lemon. The veal francese is lightly crusted with its eggy batter, lemoned, parsleyed—a delicate dish. Indelicacy is the name of the veal chop. It is not listed, but is usually on hand—the house makes it many ways, but in all cases you get a chop the size of a club, juicy inside, charred outside, of an unmistakable sufficiency.

The provolone will open your eyes and clear your sinuses. The pleasantly wet Italian cheesecake is dotted with black raisins. The hot zabaglione is frothy, loaded with marsala.

★★POSITANO

250 Park Avenue South (at 20th Street)
LUNCH, MONDAY TO FRIDAY; DINNER, MONDAY TO SATURDAY. CLOSED SUNDAY.
Reservations: 777-6211.
Credit cards: AE, MC, V.
Expensive.

Word in the press has it that one of the powers behind this place made his mark as a director of television commercials. This is confirmed by your waitress, who also tells you that when the fellow shows up for work here, he goes at once to the book, to peruse the list of reservations—and marks with a big asterisk any name he recognizes as eminent. What puzzles her, she goes on, is that then he does no more, that the celebs are granted no special favor. You suggest that the man is just reassuring himself, keeping score of his importance, that one who has taken the TV-spot road to the top is, willy-nilly, doomed always to wonder if he could have got there on the legit. She looks at you as if you are deranged.

Of course, making a winning restaurant—these days anyway—does no more to firm the ego than does making a sixty-second movie to sell another man's poison. The populace warms to a restaurant for the same reason it guzzles Pepsi—because it is told to. The poor restaurateur does not know whether he is loved for his restaurant or his publicity. And when he is himself a graduate of the hyping game, the dilemma is garnished with a twist of irony. Too bad, for Positano could have succeeded on its merits alone— the place is spiffy, the food is good, and (do not discount this) the prices are a bit lower than in many of the other spots around town that were conceived with chichi in mind.

Though the place is a great big cube of a room, two tall stories high and well lighted, it avoids the day's fashionable starkness. This is accomplished in part by the colors chosen for the shiny surfaces of its walls and massive columns—very pale coral, and very pale, *pale* green; and in part by the material chosen for the windows (walls of glass, really) on Park and on 20th Street—they are hung with a filmy gauze, which is pleated and softly lit. You enter to the corner of a street-level L, tables and booths in the legs to your left and right. Within that angle, two higher levels have been installed: A few steps up is the bar, the centerpiece of the place, the handsome counter, of dark green marble squares, framed in pale wood, the stools occupied by those who are patiently waiting— for a table, or for the appropriate stranger; a few steps farther up, and you are on the top deck, a row of tables along the back-wall banquette and a handful of additional ones along the brink, from which you may look down at the bar and at the often hectic scene all around it. That pale wood is repeated in the upholstered chairs and the unlinened tables—in the latter it frames a slick pea-green composition surface that some observers have taken for marble, but which is in fact something euphemistically known as "poured marble." Poured marble, you understand, is to marble as pig Latin is to Latin.

A sprightly thing much like a salade Niçoise is given as "Insalata di Positano." In it the *canned* tuna manages to be quite inoffensive among the balls of firm potato, slivers of black or green olive, strands of scallion, and an abundance of tart capers, all strewn with fresh, fragrant basil, and moistened with this restaurant's silken olive oil. Less familiar is this artichoke dish, cuscinetti di carciofi, in which the fresh sections of heart, the tender part of the leaves attached, are dipped in batter and fried—the sweet root taste is vivid within the browned surfaces, and the hot morsels are cleverly garnished with lightly dressed tomatoes under fresh basil, and with cool mozzarella.

Half orders of pasta are not prepared (and there is a $1 charge for splitting a full order), so bring with you someone whose pasta tastes are like your own, and have this penne con melanzane, in which the hefty tubes of noodle, firm but not tough, are in a dense, potently seasoned tomato sauce that is sharp with charred eggplant and heady with still more of this establishment's beloved basil—ground cheese fortifies the vibrant food. You order the linguine alla giudea, and if the night is a busy one, you may find that you can no more twirl the slender strands than you can wind chopsticks—and the sauce, of bacon, escarole, and black olives, reveals no evidence of the first and little flavor of the second. But if you come here only once, you will not choose pasta from this part of the menu at all, you will have instead the risotto con porcini, the hot mush of firm rice powerfully flavored of the profound stock in which it was cooked—the dark, enriched grain is redolent of the nuggets of wild mushroom with which it is studded.

The grilled lobster is itself flawless, firm, moist but not wet, sweet of its oceanic flavor, but its breading, which is crisped on the surface, is dull and mushy in the cavities into which it has been stuffed. The swordfish steak is half an inch thick, almost as big as the plate on which it is served, mahogany striped of the grill on which it was broiled, and fresh—on it, as on a heraldic field, you find two snow peas and a rich, dark-red sun-dried tomato. The carefully broiled snapper is just as fresh, and its flavor is potentiated by the vinegar and mint with which it is prepared. Skip the veal chop, for though it is nicely sautéed, its sauce—thick with little pickles, pickled onions, and nuggets of cucumber—defeats the subtle meat. Have instead the rabbit—chunks and slices of the moist, browned game under a mound of soft, slivered celery and onions. A couple of nicely roasted little quails, browned and juicy and of strong flavor, reach you gleaming in their smooth, fennel-flavored sauce.

At Positano you do well to conclude your dinner with salad—the place gets good tomatoes and serves them, variously, with strong anchovies, sharp onions, a decent fontina cheese, always the fresh basil, and a dressing of first-class oil. The sweet desserts are just sweets, among them the "tart bebé," a liquored white cake with custard at the center and a candied cherry on top; and the tirami sù, an obvious, heavily rummed, layered thing of thick cheese, nuts, and much sugar. The ricotta cheesecake is sturdy but not heavy, sweet, vaguely fruited.

• POST HOUSE

28 East 63rd Street
LUNCH, MONDAY TO FRIDAY; DINNER, DAILY.
Reservations: 935-2888.
Credit cards: AE, DC, MC, V.
Very expensive.

You probably thought places of this kind were extinct, but as long as those who eat in restaurants are defined by where, not what, they eat, and as long as there are male animals with reason to believe they must prove they are animal males, there will always be eating places (steakhouses) whose business it is to help with the reassurance—at prices sufficiently grandiose to be themselves a part of the puffing-up process. Successful contemporary examples of the type do not, however, assume every characteristic by which the originals were known. Here at the Post House, for one, there is none of the Palm's sawdust on the floor, the rooms are not those nostalgic replicas of prison mess halls by which so many of the patrons at Christ Cella are made to feel at home. In fact, the Post House camouflages a little its appeal to mindless gluttony, subliminally suggests to its guests that what they may think of as shoveling in the stuff in the same old way is actually dinner in a great and traditional American manner. The illusion is created, in part, by the paraphernalia with which the place is hung, most of it Americana: bronze eagles, bird decoys, old wrought iron, portraits vaguely in the Colonial style, paintings vaguely of the Hudson River School, like that. Who is to say this is not an accumulation of priceless rarities the house was lucky to obtain from some legendary collector's estate? Those with the habit of frequenting the Post House?

This is a big high-ceilinged place, a bar runs most of the length of the long anteroom to which you enter, the well-lighted dining room is packed rather densely with good-size tables and, usually, a body in almost every chair: mostly male bodies, the females on hand mostly their guests, the boys having judged that the girls will be thrilled to find themselves up to their ears in guys in blue blazers, guys with their blue blazers removed and draped over the backs of their chairs, guys with their neckties loosened and the top button of their shirts undone, guys with cigars—but only for a minute or two, for the scent carries easily out to the anteroom, whence comes a functionary to inform the old-fashioned type that, even in the smoking section, no cigar smoking, and the guy vows that it is back to the Palm for keeps.

It is not just by way of its appointments that the Post House aims to position itself a class or two above the competition. It even gives itself airs in re its food, serves not merely oysters, but oysters from points beyond local waters, the specific source listed on the dated supplement to the regular menu. By cross referencing you determine that today's oysters are Malpeques, but you must actually order them to determine that they are flat, as if cracked open long before they are served. The cocktail sauce that is so superfluous with good oysters is useful with these. You do little better with: the jumbo Gulf shrimp (a bit of iodine in the overcooked, somewhat soggy crustaceans); the Maryland crab cocktail (of crabmeat that may well have been perfect yesterday); the Maryland crab cakes (mushy and tasteless); the venison chili (so dominated by salt and hot spice that only its texture is discernible). But you keep trying, and discover to your astonishment that the carpaccio is fine, the thin circles of, apparently, just-cut beef surmounted at the center of the plate by a salad of arugula, bits of hard cheese, capers, the whole moistened with good olive oil.

Blackboard menus situated around the room provide information even more up to the minute than the dated supplement. Today's hot news is that lobsters are available in both regular and half sizes from three and a half to five pounds. The smallest will require of you something in excess of $50, so you may be more than miffed that the thing reaches you steamed to exhaustion, stringy and dry, much of its flavor lost. You could always get grilled fish at the local steak restaurants, but only in recent years could you get grilled salmon with "dill chardonnay sauce." The sauce has all the finesse of straight melted butter to which the herb has been added, but the salmon is utterly fresh, and much of its flavor survives the dry and flaky condition to which its grilling has brought it. At the Post House you never know when you are going to get lucky, so you are no more than a little surprised to find that the pan-fried chicken breast is a small winner, no chicken flavor to speak of, of course, but the bird is moist, vigorously seasoned, crisped, and, what with its lemon caper sauce, gets by as good fun food. The lamb chops are not bad, though their flavor is more of mutton than lamb, and you do wish their surfaces were crackling rather than just fatty. No matter what you do, do not do the "James Beard burger," one of the few dishes on any New York menu that speaks ill of the dead. You ask for yours medium, and, sure enough, it averages medium, cooked from a smooth-gray-brown, well-done outer half inch, to raw red at the center—examination of which suggests that this beef is perhaps not ground at all, is just milled or crushed. The sirloin steak reaches you accurately done, its blood moisture sealed within seared surfaces, but this is not beefy beef—it is tender, but fine textured rather than fibrous, and when you seek out the meat in the tail end of the steak (this is not the great big steak you expect in places of this kind), you find that it is off, as if somewhere along the way its refrigeration was briefly interrupted. Though the cottage fries are the usual wooden disks, the onion rings are sweet, crinkly, slightly and pleasantly greasy. The hash browns are impeccable, the coppery-browned surface well seasoned and crusty, the unbrowned potatoes under-neath moist and of vivid flavor.

Your waiter rolls to your table the dessert cart. Another waiter accosts him with the charge that he (your waiter) stole it while he (other waiter) was "showing it." Your waiter wins. And you lose. The pumpkin tart is denatured, overspiced, and pasty, while the apple cobbler is sugary and sour rather than tart and sweet. Get to know the place, and you learn, as you did not from your waiter, that there is a dessert *menu*. You select from it the cheesecake, and the thing is claylike, though the crisscrossed strands of candied citrus rind with which it is adorned are fine, and the two sauces with which it is served —lemon and strawberry—can only help. You order the bread pudding, and you are served gingerbread pudding. Never mind that it is nowhere, it is not even bread pudding.

Your bottle of California merlot is at the perfect temperature for a bottle of lager beer. Your waiter allows as how it is, as he puts it, slightly chilled.

★ PRIMAVERA

1578 First Avenue (at 82nd Street)
DINNER.
Reservations: 861-8608.
Credit cards: AE, DC, MC, V.
Very expensive.

All money is fungible, even old and new, brands of it that have more in common than just their interchangeability. Though new money is spent in search of status, the old on its preservation, in those respects neither is disbursed with any discrimination. Staid solidity is what lures old money here, while the new pursues the old. Which is not to say that Primavera is without merit as an eating place, rather that its success is a function mainly of its success: having got away for as long as it has with selling food (at wondrous prices) that is only occasionally better than very reliable (though never less), it now merits the highest of all restaurant ratings: unquestionability. The place is packed nightly with folks who, simply by being here, are satisfied that their evening is well spent. Watch them, note how little attention they pay to what they eat, and yet how content they are, how certain of themselves. Dinner at Primavera is irreproachable, like getting to your feet for the playing of the national anthem. The restaurant is a safe house, a place where you may turn off your competitive alert. Fridays and Saturdays, it is thick with those from across the rivers, Sundays with a bankerly and lawyerly Upper East Side set, though every night at least some members of both opposing factions are on hand, the outlanders in molded hair, jewelry, padded shoulders, and seashore tans, the locals, often present in family gatherings, notable less for what they wear than for the consistency of dress among the generations, the sons and grandsons, daughters-in-law and girlfriends, like the presiding parents themselves at these upright rituals, one and all models in Brooks Brothers ads.

It is a carpeted, hushed, clubby space in which they are all so comfortable, the wood-beamed walls faced with coppery silk on one side of the room, with handsome brick on the other. The windows are hung with lace curtains, and there are huge bursts of flowers on their sills. On the white-linened tables there are pots of flowers in little baskets, gold-rimmed service plates with the restaurant's insigne, in gold, at their centers. The tables are surrounded by graceful side chairs with seats upholstered in apricot suede. You almost take Primavera for a tasteful installation that has aged gracefully to its present condition. But the restaurant gives itself away, very much in the manner of the man who rents a tuxedo and then wears it with his yellow shoes. For after the architect's work was finished, the proprietors apparently took over, hauled a big load of art up here probably from the Washington Square Outdoor Art Exhibit (in, one likes to imagine, a station wagon), and proceeded to hang the hilarious stuff all over the walls. The customers do not complain. Neither do the members of the staff, who, from busboys to the host himself, are in formal black-and-whites—with black shoes.

What with fresh ingredients—in dishes prepared just when you order them—you almost never get a bad plate of food here. But if, for example, you have had seafood salads in some of the city's jauntier Italian restaurants, you will find Primavera's as forgettable as it is unimpeachable, the abundant serving of fresh squid, shrimp, scallops in a dressing that is barely lemoned, let alone garlicked—you expect this dish to be rousing, instead it is almost weighty, more like what you want later in your dinner. But then there is this hot first course of sautéed shrimp, a perfect simple thing, the big crustaceans sweet and crunchy, roused by the herbs, lemon, and white wine in which they were done. If it is mushroom time, your waiter brings to your table a basket of big Italian wild mushrooms, encourages you to have some of them grilled as a first course. Sound advice, for they are meaty, earthy, and they are done in oil of heady flavor, though the promised garlic is at best an obscurity.

The pasta list is led, of course, by capelli d'angelo primavera, and, sure enough, this is the quintessential Primavera dish, thin spaghetti that is judiciously cooked and firm, utterly fresh vegetables, and little in the way of vigor—still, good food, especially when plenty of cheese is spooned on. You figure that there will be more life in what the chef is inspired to prepare especially for the day, so you go for a whimsical spaghetti dish made with arugula and sauce marinara, only to find that little has been done to give either component cause to do business with the other. Though blenderized to a creamy puree, the house pesto is powerfully fragrant of its fresh basil—you accept lots of grated Parmesan, as much for its texture as for its pungent flavor.

It is perhaps unfair to describe the grilled baby salmon as hospital food, but the pale-pink fish, barely touched with oregano, moistened with oil, and delicately browned, for all its freshness, seems designed principally to exacerbate no condition. If you must have seafood as a main course, that yummy shrimp appetizer is available in a full portion. And when soft-shell crabs are in season, this place gets good ones—the shells barely perceptible—and browns them handsomely. Additional perfect and perfectly harmless sustenance may be taken by way of the pollo alla forestale, juicy chicken just out of the sauté pan, plus the vegetables, mushrooms, and ham with which it was done—those promising ingredients notwithstanding, the dish is merely a model of inoffensiveness. Similarly the uccelletti alla finanziere, veal rolls stuffed with spinach and prosciutto in mushroom sauce—you do wish there were cheese in the package and/or that the roulades had been browned before they were finished and/or that they were served in something more vigorous than this smooth, pallidly seasoned, creamy tomato sauce (it would be perfect in some other setting), which is thick with mushrooms that seem never to have been sautéed. But then there is this veal chop valdostana, the huge eye of meat bifurcated latitudinally, a layer of ham inserted, but, despite what the menu says, no cheese—not a shortcoming, for the thick browned chop, bursting with pink moisture, is invigorated by quite another mushroom sauce, this one rich and winy. If you come here in springtime, when baby goat is offered, that may well be the item to have. If you hesitate at the idea of eating goat, be assured that a baby goat is nothing like an old goat. Its meat is, in fact, sweet and tender, and as if to establish that the house is not hidebound to culinary gentility, you are provided with a mammoth serving, a veritable hillock of the charred nuggets of dark meat.

If, to this point, dinner has had a sedative effect, some aged Parmesan with one of the brightly dressed house salads will rouse you. The apple tart is not bad, though you wish it were not sealed in syrup. The St. Honoré is a complex layered affair involving custard, whipped cream, chocolate cream, candied fruit, good pastry—it is notable for its freshness. The chocolate cake is light, but not especially intense. Many of the regulars conclude their dinners with the fruit plate—sliced apples and pears, bunches of grapes in a couple of colors, chunks of various melons, orange slices, all mounded over cracked ice. The fruit plate does not include berries, which are available separately—sometimes wild strawberries from far-off places served with good whipped cream.

★★PRIMOLA

1226 Second Avenue (near 65th Street)
LUNCH, MONDAY TO FRIDAY; DINNER, DAILY.
Reservations: 758-1775.
Credit cards: AE.
Medium priced.

New York's love affair with Italian food might have dwindled decades ago were it not regularly restimulated by new settings in which to carry on. In recent years, moreover, the life expectancy of the romance has been extended by a fresh style of Italian cookery, one that makes fewer demands on an aging lover than did the weighty stuff that used to obtain. About as far as you can come from, say, a 1950's Little Italy spaghetti-and-meatball store is Primola, which in its light look is as remote as California, in its food as distant from the past as a bottle of clear, bubbly prosecco from the inky chianti—it was made of tree bark and bugs, and you drank it ice cold—that used to be sold in green bottles wrapped in straw.

All is sunny, pale wood and cream, snowy linen and abundant light, rows of tables and chairs, a print or watercolor on any panel of wall not occupied by a light fixture that is a glowing semihemisphere, greenery in the corners. Two elements somewhat undo the openness and simple comfort of the place: The area around the bar, to which you enter, is under a lowered, hard-surfaced section of the ceiling, and as the crowd waiting for tables is often dense (Primola overbooks, and a wait of thirty minutes past the hour of your reservation is not unheard of), you are subjected, while you wait, to a piercing din; and the rear of the restaurant has for some reason been raised a couple of steps, creating a low-ceilinged somewhat segregated room that is apart from the airy commodiousness of the rest of the place. Withal, Primola is comfortable, convivial of the crowd that fills it.

Along one short side of the bar stands a counter, its top a slab of pink marble, on it a display of the dishes that, taken together, make up what is listed as Gli Apri Bocca di Franco, which is not so literally translated as "A selection from the chef's buffet of seasonal vegetables." With a bottle of balsamic vinegar, another of vividly green olive oil, arrives your crowded plate, on it slices of browned eggplant, deeply oiled, overlaid with mozzarella cheese, circles of tomato, fresh and fragrant basil; great mushroom caps filled with a spicy stuffing of crunchy vegetables; another vegetable stuffing, this one packed around sweet mussels in their half-shells; firm white beans mingled with minced scallion greens and overlaid with circles of red onion; a pungent caponata, mostly eggplant, accented with cracked black olives and sour capers; morsels of cheese that have been marinated and enriched in seasoned oil—all the items stand apart from one another, for their components are fresh, retain their individuality. A couple of lively first courses the like of which you do not find elsewhere: thin leaves of raw salmon, marinated with fennel, their surfaces whitened a little by the treatment, their interiors red and juicy, the pool of marinade on your plate bright and tangy; and filetto di vitello Harris, little sheets of pale, tender veal arranged over leaves of bitter radicchio, strewn with arugula, and moistened with a mustard dressing that is at once rich and sharp.

Have pasta here once, and you will do well to make it spaghetti ai frutti di mare, the very thin noodles in a red sauce—of exceptional briny vigor—that is dotted with fresh clams and mussels in their shells, crunchy shrimp, slivers of squid. Order pasta a second time, and you will do almost as well with the spinach dumplings, the soft morsels, melted cheese between them, arranged on a tomato sauce that is tart and a little creamy —ground Parmesan rouses this dish. Spinach again, this time in the one rice dish listed, risotto verde, the great mound of buttered grain bright green of the pureed spinach with which it has been blended—once again, add enough ground cheese and the dish becomes heady.

Little in the way of finfish on the printed bill of fare, but sometimes the house has on hand baby snapper, the fillets of white fish firm, fresh, moistened and powerfully flavored by an herbed and winy sauce from the pan in which it was sautéed. What goes as pollo al balsamico e rosmarino is a dozen chunks of chicken, browned and glistening, mingled with slivers of garlic, infused with the herbs and sweet vinegar of its sauce. The veal paillard is less than gloriously browned, rather too thoroughly cooked through. There is much more of interest in these unusual medallions of blood-juicy beef—Parmesan cheese has been melted over them to dramatic effect, and they are garnished with braised and bitter endives.

There is fruit, but little in the way of cheese. The handsomely browned cheesecake is touched with chocolate, is almost puddinglike in its good, weighty wetness. The lemon meringue pie is a little sweet and vividly sour on its dark and crumbly pastry.

★ PROVENCE

38 MacDougal Street (near Prince Street)
LUNCH AND DINNER. CLOSED MONDAY.
Reservations: 475-7500.
Credit cards: AE.
Medium priced.

You approach the book, and your French-accented host, who guards it, turns to give you his attention, when—the phone rings. The caller, who wishes to reserve a table, is put on hold ten seconds into the transaction so that another caller may be asked to wait please before he makes, as it turns out, a cancellation, during which exchange the phone, you guessed it, rings, this unseen supplicant desirous of switching his eight-thirty to nine-thirty ("Can you make it ten?"), a discussion interrupted by a caller who . . .

You assume that when all this began the principals wondered which of their partners made the deal with Satan, since what started out, by the look of it, as a stab at a living—on an investment in, solely, the key to the door—has become the kind of success from which one ordinarily wakes up. For this is the former Gordon's, where a number of enterprises of that name failed, and in this revival, in which little more than the walls have been retained, even less has been added, surely nothing that resonates to the new name. A couple of airy chandeliers, the big bar, much carved-wood paneling, and tall paned windows on MacDougal Street are front-room holdovers from the original clubby installation. But the upper plaster walls are filmed—smeared, actually—with ivory-colored paint that appears to be running, as are the walls of the densely tabled back room (unadorned except for a grossly pitted gray chair rail), while the so-called garden beyond it, a trellised urban yard with a fountain at the center, is much as it was as the main attraction of the predecessors. Throughout, the tables are covered with white butcher paper, the chairs are dinky, the crowd is noisy, the waiters, in jeans, white aprons, white shirts with four-in-hands, thump through like the driven, feed hundreds each night before looking up from their tasks to breathe.

All the fuss is ostensibly about these blunt renditions of the food of southernmost France, among them: a hot fish soup, brothlike and of strong, almost gamy fish flavor— in it a garlic-smeared crust—that rather loudly reminds you of soups that made you sweat in Marseilles; a so-called brandade d'Avignon, a hot version, made with potatoes, of the garlic-flavored salt-cod paste that lacks the coarse elementality of the usual cool article; a gâteau d'aubergines that is a layered and drab-colored eggplant thing incorporating two strata more colorful than the others, a red one of sautéed peppers, a green one of spinach, the entire construct thoroughly oiled and of vividly seasoned vegetable flavor; a tepid pissaladière that is a rectangle of chewy bread spread with a pulpy onion paste and adorned with six black olives, tiny and strong, and a single glistening anchovy; and these tartines de Roquefort, a couple of thick triangles of toasted French bread liberally coated with a paste of the Roquefort—the cheese is softened with butter and a little brandy, made nubbly with chopped walnuts.

The printed—well, scrawled and photocopied—menu lists five dishes that are served only one day each week, one of them Friday's bouillabaisse, a hot, vigorous, and well-oiled version, thick with chunks of fish, many mussels, a few shrimp, and served with bread crusts that are spread with a heady garlic sauce. Sunday there is couscous, a rare presentation thereof in that the stewing broth, traditionally served separately, reaches you in the kind of steel pouring pot that holds the milk for coffee on diner counters—otherwise this is but a copious statement of the familiar idea, chick-peas and root vegetables, chunks of meat and of fowl, everything cooked too far, but well before the point of total defeat, and mounded over a hillock of the couscous grains, all of which you moisten with the broth from that creamer and invigorate with a hot paste served on the side. The word aioli refers to a kind of mayonnaise in which garlic is incorporated, but it denotes also a variable dish served with it, the variation here made up of steamed cod, florets of broccoli and cauliflower plus slices of blanched tomato, among other vegetables, and quarters of hard-cooked egg, the parts arranged in a circle around a ramekin of the rich and heady mayo—the elements are fine, amount really to an amusing means of enjoying the contents of that ramekin. The rabbit is coarse-breaded and greasy in its thick mustard sauce. The rare-roasted lamb is many slices of good meat within a ring of pungent spinach—the potent dish is garnished with limp ratatouille. The tender and accurately prepared steak is not of the tastiest beef, and the French fries served with it have been fried, fried, and refried, have not only the shape but the texture of matchsticks.

For dessert, you will do well with the crème brûlée, which though sometimes more than browned on top, actually charred, is fluffy. Your fruit sherbet may be moistened, for an extra charge, with liquor of the same fruit. The tarte Tatin, though of good caramelized-apple flavor, is mushy. And the terrine d'orange, a slice cut from a loaf that is a chunky compacture of denatured orange, is in a white-chocolate sauce that surely cannot restore what has been pointlessly lost.

This is SoHo, but not the SoHo of trendy painters and their commission retailers, rather of corporate and professional drudges by day, self-consciously self-styled swingers by night—that one may eat here rather cheaply is much of what lures them.

★ PRUNELLE

18 East 54th Street
LUNCH, MONDAY TO FRIDAY; DINNER, DAILY.
Reservations: 759-6410.
Credit cards: AE, DC, MC, V.
Very expensive.

A designer's restaurant, one in which nothing was held back, and yet New York has never quite taken it up. The problem is not the food at the price—many lesser places are more popular—rather that for all the luxe of this interior, and for all the warmth of its coloring, it is but a display of itself. Prunelle does not embrace you, rather it shows itself off to you, demands your attention, competes with you. Even when the restaurant is suffering from one of its frequent spells of the quiets, you get the feeling, toward the end of dinner, that it is time to go someplace where you can talk. The installation even fails at what it undertakes. The walls have been faced with burled wood that is the color of certain Cremonese violins and as highly polished as a new car, and you are meant to be overwhelmed, but the ceilings are simply too low for the wood to achieve its intended imposing sweep, and the placement here and there of great bursts of brilliantly colored flowers before glinting rectangular mirrors, though very pretty, fail as jewels on the gown, diminish the effect that unlimited honey might otherwise achieve. For the rest, there are dun-colored carpeting and a grape-colored banquette, comfortable armchairs with sloping arms around the big, well-spaced, white-linened tables, courteous gentlemen in formals cruising the aisles.

The only thing for it is a patron in every seat, a crowd to warm the place in a way the appointments do not. But they will not keep coming back for the likes of this marinated seafood, three little mounds, of sliced lobster, scallops, minced shrimp, each in a different vegetable context, none of them a clear expression of itself, the cold sautéed mushrooms at the center of the plate and the cold artichoke heart they are mounded over equally devoid of flavor, the thick herbed dressing no help. Similarly the gravlax, which, though prettily served as a great dark-pink floret, is without liveliness or fishiness, sweetness or tartness, is merely tender, supple meat of a certain dim familiarity. You do somewhat better with what is given as salade "Charlie," the principal fault of which is that the disparate ingredients are all at different temperatures—warm grilled scallops, strands of tepid chicken, ice cold greens, wild mushrooms at room temperature—pine nuts, bits of red pepper, and minced chives make the dressing lively, and while it is certainly not essential that every ingredient of a dish be as cool or as warm as every other, in this instance each mouthful is a disconcerting surprise after every previous one. All of which matters not at all, for when you come here you simply order the snails, served with "leurs oeufs," which is to say "their eggs," the snails plump, tender, a little resilient too, arranged as if pouring out of a puff pastry cornucopia (which you wish were flakier), everything set in a dark, herbed, and winy sauce that is thick with minced vegetables and with hundreds of the tiny eggs, their presence a nice nubbliness.

Nowadays, when you have become accustomed to the charms of salmon cooked rare, it is something of a comedown to encounter a steak of this fish that lacks the promising red blush at its center. That aside, the darne de saumon is utterly fresh and certainly not *over*cooked in its herbed and buttery sauce. A bit of overcooking is, however, the problem with the lobster, for the chunks of sweet meat, buried in noodles of three different colors and varying widths, is less than juicy, though the pink and honeylike shellfish sauce that moistens the seafood and the pasta and the surrounding vegetables does much to redeem. In this self-consciously fancy place, the main course the house titles after itself, poularde Prunelle, is a homey one, a crusty and vigorously seasoned potato pancake, upon it a browned breast of chicken that is redolent of the flavor of chicken fat, crunchy walnut halves on that, the whole in a dark and winy sauce—sturdy food. Usually there is game, sometimes venison, the slices of rare meat—marinated, earthy of its marinade—arranged around the sides of a mound of buttery wild rice, cranberries and a fruity currant sauce its good foils.

For some reason apples and kiwis are shown with the cheese, but when you request pears, it turns out that good ones are hidden away somewhere in the kitchen, can be brought to you peeled and sliced. Stilton, Roquefort, a rich and creamy reblochon, and heady goat cheeses are offered. After the cheese you will have little interest in the cheesecake, which turns out to be the usual thing, albeit purpled by the stewed blueberries in which it is served. The soufflé Prunelle is a blob of soufflé, bits of raspberry embedded in its skinlike browned surface, whole raspberries all around, the sweet sauce hot and lemony. Withal, the apple tart is the dessert to have, as much a pie as a tart, the bottom pastry dark, the top one pale and tender, between them myriad flakes of crisp, tart fruit interleaved with nut slivers.

281

★★QUATORZE

240 West 14th Street
LUNCH, MONDAY TO FRIDAY; DINNER, DAILY.
Reservations: 206-7006.
Credit cards: AE.
Medium priced.

Like a gay young blade of grass that, simply not knowing any better, shoots out of a crack in a heavily trafficked sidewalk, so has this place jauntily sprung up in the grim chasm (West 14th Street) that separates outer Greenwich Village from lowest Chelsea. You could have shown that the very idea was out of the question. You could have pointed out that the site is neither here nor there—and that where it is is nowhere. But, in fact, the new restaurant was immediately spotted by citizens on both sides of this border. They noticed at once the handsome deep-red façade and big gold letters by which it announces itself to its dowdy arrondissement. That front, however, will shed its luster in time, become familiar, and, thereby, be subsumed by its surroundings. But it is unlikely that the spanking interior will lose any of its freshness soon, for this is the niftiest joint to hit 14th (West or East) in decades.

Quatorze is a spiffy bistro and a well-bred brasserie. It is plain and fancy. Up front, you are standing on a floor of white tiles when you are at the trim, marble-topped bar. Then you walk on handsome oak through the pale-lemon-yellow dining room just beyond it. Along the wall on your left, under inset rectangular mirrors, runs a plush banquette of burgundy velvet, a row of white-linened tables-for-two before it. There are bigger tables across the aisle, then four more, one in each corner of a small square area at the back. There is handsome dark-wood trim here and there, and a few great big posters that, without cluttering the place, cleverly temper its spareness. The light is soft but not dim. And the ladies and gentlemen who wait on you are efficient and know well the brief menu from which they work.

Oysters are sold by the oyster, they are fresh, cracked open only when you order them. There are usually a couple of varieties on hand, among them big rich Wellfleets, and the smaller but more interesting Malpèques, which are somehow both sweet—even fruity—and briny. Order the smoked chicken breast, and you get three substantial slices of good, mildly cured white meat—but the hit of the plate is the sauce, which is a thick whipped cream sharpened with strong horseradish. The jambon persillé is a nice enough version of the usual thing, a mosaic of chunks of ham in a firm jelly that is green with parsley—it is garnished with sharp black olives and strong mustard. What the house calls terrine is a singular thing in which layers of cold sliced beef are interleaved with layers of spinach or carrot—the meaty dish has a stunningly variegated texture, and its tastes are at once mingled and distinct. The red-lettered first course is the chicory salad, a giant mound of crisp, pleasantly bitter greens dotted with nuggets of good, strong bacon, and dressed with a hot and tangy vinaigrette. If there is cold beet soup when you come, know that this is not just another chilled and pureed vegetable. The deep-pink liquid is thick and nubbly and creamy, its beet flavor pure and fresh.

A big comedown is the fettuccine with tomato and basil. The dish begs to be simple and dramatic, a condition that cannot be achieved if one element is a lifeless mash of the green herb—the pasta is served with a ramekin of ground cheese, which changes things without improving them. But then there is this grilled salmon, the fish itself moist and sweet, crusted in the making, of clear flavor, its sauce choron stunning, thick and rich, fragrant of tarragon, chunky with the bits of tomato that make it pink. The grilled chicken, served in parts, is eminently well prepared, the skin crisp, the meat cooked through but still moist—too bad the bird itself is a pallid one. But there is a better bird, the roast duck, of which you get a couple of substantial sections—they are nicely browned, their meat is not fatty but is imbued with the flavor of fat, and they are set in a smooth sauce dotted with fiery peppercorns, a striking contrast to the rich meat. Sometimes there is roast pork, and you are served two supple inch-thick slices of the pale-pink meat, each of them turned upon itself, like an eccentric heart—a garlicked and fragrantly herbed stuffing is in the crease, the meat is set in a sweet, sticky sauce, and it is garnished with chunks of crusted potatoes, sour red cabbage, and disks of crisp, barely sautéed zucchini. Choucroute has a place of honor on the menu, its own red box. But, though it is entirely edible, it is no more, for the cabbage would be lifeless without its juniper berries, and the sausages and pork are solid but not diverting.

Quatorze makes a point of offering a very respectable sauternes by the glass. If you had some with your oysters (do not judge the combination until you try it), and liked it, have some more with your (do not judge the combination until you try it) Roquefort, of which you get a wondrously firm, creamy, and sharp example here. The sweet desserts include a striking pear tart—the slivers of ripe fruit are separated from the crumbly pastry by a layer of creamy marzipan; a warm apple tart—a circle of thin, overlapping slices of browned, crisped fruit, lightly sugared, on a shortbread pastry; and a crème caramel.

★★RAGA

57 West 48th Street
LUNCH, MONDAY TO FRIDAY; DINNER, DAILY.
Reservations: 757-3450.
Credit cards: AE, DC, MC, V.
Medium priced.

A "raga" is an Indian musical form, and on the walls of this restaurant of that name are displayed many Indian musical instruments—among them sitars, vinas, and rubābs —all of them beautiful to look at. At certain hours of the evening, Indian music is performed here. And if, admittedly, the idea of background music in restaurants is generally a bad one, Indian music is another matter. It has the power unobtrusively to charge the atmosphere of the room in which it is being played in such a way that, while the music may go almost unnoticed, all other experiences are slightly heightened. For a moment you may actually feel that you are in India, even if you have never been there. Be advised that the effect is intensified by a judicious intake of alcohol.

Raga is a big place, at once cushy and stately, with slender wood columns rising through the great space to the beams they intersect on the distant ceiling. You walk on plush carpeting of hot colors in sinuous stripes. The walls are covered with coarse raw silk, and in addition to those instruments, they are bedecked with colorful cloth hangings that have woven into their patterns bits of glinting metal, like tiny mirrors. One whole side of the dining room is given over to an elaborate building façade of dark, intricately carved wood, complete with columns and their capitals, windows and doorways. When seated, you are in big red-upholstered chairs before large tables on which candles burn in dark glass globes. The center of the room is divided—by partitions and planters—into islands, each of which holds a single large table, most of them suitable for six or more. In this very civilized restaurant, where the service is almost always sweet, you will sometimes be offered one of these commodious accommodations, without your asking, even when there are fewer of you than the table was designed for. What, you wonder, is wrong with the Indian ego, that it does not recognize its need to put you in your proper place right from the start.

The cold appetizers include dal papri, a mildly spicy, vigorously stimulating dish of lentil chips and chopped potatoes in a tart yogurt sauce; chaman ki chat, morsels of fruit and sweet potato in a tamarind sauce that is fruity and spicy; and murg ki chat—that same fruit sauce on small slices of chicken and chunks of potato. The hot oysters Bombay reach you in a big scallop shell—they are fresh and tender, and they are set in a thick sauce that is mostly ginger-flavored onion. What is listed as "crabs Goa" is a hot, spicy paste of crabmeat, tomatoes, onion, and oil—remarkably, the sweet flavor of the crabmeat is not wholly lost in this setting. Murg ke pakore is a chicken dish of little chicken flavor, but the slices of meat are reddened, blackened, beautifully crisped, and they are good with the fruit chutney or the spicy, creamy sauce with which they are served.

Salmon is rare in Indian restaurants, but Raga serves it, as machali masala. It consists of moist, fresh salmon steaks immersed in a thick, smooth, mildly garlicked sauce of onion and tomato. Jhinga tandoori is shrimp that have been grilled in the hot Indian oven called a tandoor. The shrimp are handsomely reddened and mildly spiced, and they are fresh and crunchy, but you do wish this preparation did not—perhaps inevitably—dry them out. That oven is kinder to lamb. Rann-e-Khyber, a dish prepared only for two (and served in an amount that will hold three or four), arrives as a substantial mound of gargantuan knobs of charred meat under rings of strong onion, slices of green pepper, and disks of tomato. The lamb is firm but not tough, of strong flavor, its darkened surfaces vividly spicy, and under it is a pool of the dark brown marinade that has dripped from the meat. The lamb vindaloo is much lamb, combined with crunchy little pickled onions and browned potatoes, in a sauce that has in it seeds of spice that burst with fragrance when you bite into them—this dish can be fiery if you tell your waiter you want it that way. Gosht palak—chunks of lamb in a succulent and spicy spinach mash —can satisfy the most primitive kind of food lust. In the hillock of rice called nizami biryani, you will find, as you mine your way through it, nuggets of lamb and potato— there is saffron in the dish, a touch of fruitiness, the fragrance of fresh coriander.

The good vegetable items include baingan bhurta, an herbed and strongly seasoned eggplant paste; mutter paneer, hot- and sweet-spiced peas with chunks of Indian cottage cheese; palak paneer, more of that solid cheese, this time buried in spicy, well-oiled spinach. Order rice, and the fluffy grain comes dotted with fruits and nuts. Naturally, there are condiments, and they range from raw onions in a fierce oil that can remove the fillings from your teeth to sweet mango chutney to cool yogurt.

As in most Indian restaurants, most of the desserts will merely puzzle the Occidental palate. The rasmalai are delicate little cheese balls adorned with pistachios—you can eat them and just about not notice them. The Indian ice cream called navrang kulfi is divertingly flavored with saffron and cardamom, but it is creamier than you want your ice cream—anyway, it is billed as a breath freshener. The kheer is a honeyed rice pudding studded with nuts and fruits—it is at least cool and refreshing.

★★RAKEL

231 Varick Street (at Clarkson Street)
LUNCH, MONDAY TO FRIDAY; DINNER, MONDAY TO SATURDAY. CLOSED SUNDAY.
Reservations: 929-1630.
Credit cards: AE, DC, MC, V.
Expensive.

In the middle of a Manhattan no-man's-land, hard to spot from the street unless you know it is there, cavernous and gray within, Rakel has had to make it in a way peculiarly its own, a way that, surely, was not anticipated when the restaurant was new, for one of its principal lures today, what continues to bring them back from all over town long after the newness has worn off, is a certain promise—or permission—that seems intrinsic to the room. This is not the carnality proffered by those pulsating gymnasiums with tables, chairs, bar, and tight-packed flesh, nor is it the contrived intimacy of some dark and cozy supper club in which all is supplied short of a room upstairs. Rakel is, rather, a seemingly neutral background onto which any fantasy may be played, and the restaurant provides just enough electricity of its own to start you off.

At once vast and snug, low lit and aglitter, Rakel—its machine-tooled lines notwithstanding—is sanctuary from hard-edged New York. Its enveloping grayness is soothing, its noise and music are the sounds of a city distilled down to its various and synergic rhythms. As if to demonstrate the minor miracle of these effects, a giant television screen has been mounted high up over the bar (is visible to most of the room), and though old movies are sometimes shown (visuals, no aurals), the usual silent show is live, vehicles heading south on Varick Street, or east on Clarkson, pedestrians going in all directions, the Empire State Building, aloof in the background, above it all. The view is that seen by a TV camera set up in one of the restaurant's windows, and the transformation of street traffic into the dreamlike shadows and sparklers on the screen is very much the change of scene you experience when you step from the city street into Rakel.

All of which compensates in part for a promise otherwise not kept. When Rakel was new it seemed that the talent in the kitchen needed only time to settle down near the top of its class. As then, you may now eat here to a state of food intoxication, but, also as then, this dish or that suffers from a miscarriage of conception, an ingredient less than pristine, sometimes both. Accordingly, though the menu periodically changes, regulars return for the items by which they were charmed in the early days, especially if they have been once burnt by the like of "potato pancakes en surprise," one surprise being the paucity of potato flavor in the crisp little patties, another the excess of flavor in the loud red caviar with which they are topped, a third the futility, in the event, of the buttery sauce, dotted with black caviar, that moistens the dish. Happily, you may opt instead for Maryland crab cakes, deep fried and crusty, their crabmeat flavor vivid, very good with the "marmalade of red peppers" tucked under them, and with the fragrant and heady puree of fresh cilantro in which the cakes are set. In the ongoing citywide competition for ever more thrilling foie gras productions, Rakel offers "whole fresh roasted foie gras," $41 for two (people), $82 for four. The roasted organ is displayed to you at the center of the large roasting pan in which it was done. It is taken away, sliced, divided, served in its sauce, which is winy, thick with woodsy chanterelles, an earthy foil to the dark-edged slices of blood-rare liver. The pasta is one night this, another that, on occasion fettuccine with clams, mussels, bits of tomato, and sprigs of thyme, a dish notable for the sweetness of its mussels, the tenderness of its littlenecks, the firmness of its pasta, albeit the elements remain only themselves, do not form a composition.

Roasted tuna is one of the items for which regulars return, the slices of fish, red-rare at the center and pink near the peppered and crusted edges, the garnish of strong spinach in nice contrast to the supple, sweet meat. More red fish, salmon, listed as a "rouelle," it is what you probably think of as a roulade, a fillet of the skinned and boned fish rolled with strands of truffle to form a cylinder that is served in a warm and truffled vinaigrette —probably a terrific dish if you hit it when the salmon is fresh. Beet sugar, you will recall, is extracted from beets. It is not surprising that when roasted lobster is served in "beet essence," the juicy meat is stained purple, and its own sea sweetness is supplemented by the rather fruity sweetness of the beet—a nifty dish. Chickens that bear chicken flavor are rare, baby chickens that do are nonexistent—or so you thought until you encountered Rakel's roasted baby chicken, its skin crisp, its meat tender, its port-wine-and-garlic sauce sticky, thick with vegetables. The fillet of lamb is served as three short lengths of the meat, standing like smokestacks, in a creamy mushroom sauce that penetrates the meat and almost dominates its flavor—the lamb is garnished with crusty ravioli packed with an earthy mushroom filling.

A couple of ways of concluding your dinner with cheese are listed: "crottin de chavignol," strong goat cheese that is warmed and oiled, served with a salad of walnut halves and tender greens, the two in a good walnut oil dressing; and a millefeuille of Stilton, the blue cheese between flaky pastries, the sandwich strewn with raisins and garnished with slices of tart apple. A streak of crimson raspberry sauce encircles the "millefeuille with honey and vervain (verbena) ice cream," a light, lively array of contrasting sweets. Withal, if you come here just once, you will not think beyond the chocolate tart, the disk of bittersweet chocolate light, runny at the center, and of amazing chocolate intensity—the thing is set in a sweet and fruity pear puree, and it is garnished with rich, silken vanilla ice cream.

★★★ RAOUL'S

180 Prince Street (near Sullivan Street)
DINNER.
Reservations: 966-3518.
Credit cards: AE, DC, MC, V.
Expensive.

A pioneer SoHo settler, this place was chichi in the neighborhood's early days, but has been less than all the rage for a couple of years now. It is out of style because it has not kept up—and that is the only reason, for you eat as well here now as you ever did. Back when SoHo was being settled, improvisation was much of the mode, and a seemingly thrown-together enterprise purveying French country cooking in a weather-beaten saloon was the perfect setting for public display of the pioneers' open-minded spirit. But the haste with which SoHo shed its bohemianism dazzled even the most cynical observers, for as soon as uptown money showed on the scene, swank was in. Oh, sure, you could still convert an old store into a dinner house, but you had to make sure the place looked like a room or two borrowed from the Museum of Modern Art.

Raoul's is the place with the neon beer signs in the front windows and cream-colored stamped-tin walls, with white butcher paper on the tables and, in the back room, car-seat booths with two-tone plastic upholstery and chromium trees for your hat and coat. The front room has the bar—waxed on the mirrored wall behind it are the names of the available beers and the prices of those dishes (steak pommes frites, pâte maison) that you may order if the bar is where you want to eat. Against the wall opposite is the long black banquette, a line of tables before it, that, to some tastes, is the restaurant's choice seating; for with your back to this wall, the bar scene is right before you, also the entrances and exits of Raoul's somewhat depleted but still colorful clientele, and also—with a few turns of your head this way and that—the whole array, motley and helter-skelter, of the establishment's paraphernalia. Some of this stuff came with the premises, and much of it was added by the present interests: a couple of ancient electric fans, complete with drooping wires, that, in honor of the air conditioning, are never turned on; a portrait of General Charles André Joseph Marie de Gaulle; a couple of photographic landscapes with, in the extreme foreground, a single human female breast each; a huge Toulouse-Lautrec poster; exposed pipes; an ancient stove on which are displayed the house desserts; not to mention oils and etchings and framed mirrors and, on the rear wall, the chalked menu, the only really legible one in the place—for you are still expected to select your dinner here from the tiny slate you are handed, which bears scratchings (many of them, at a guess, in French) that appear to have been polished almost to extinction by centuries of erosion. Nobody cares, about that or much else, for this is a jolly place with a vociferously contented crowd, its shortage of trendies making it the closest thing in SoHo to a neighborhood restaurant for adults.

You get spanking oysters, opened when ordered, fresh and cold and sweet, served with a spiky sauce mignonnette—they are best, however, with lemon and ground-on pepper. The house usually has on hand either poached leeks or asparagus—they are cool and crunchy, and they are in a sparkling vinaigrette that is thick with chopped egg whites and minced red peppers. The country pâté is firm and pink and pungent, very good with its sharp mustard and with this restaurant's chewy, slightly sour, and distinctly earthy bread. Occasionally sautéed wild mushrooms are offered—the delicate chanterelles woodsy, and the black, rough-textured morels sweet, almost fruity, in the dark and winy sauce. But still, if you come here when the blackboard lists ris de veau en salade, look no further, for these cool, slivered sweetbreads are at once buttery and light—actually delicate—in their herbed and creamy dressing.

Much good seafood: the smallest soft-shell crabs, their carapaces like flaky pastry, browned and crisped in hot butter, and strewn with crunchy sautéed almonds; a whole baby salmon, boned, butterflied, and grilled, the charred skin clinging to the expanse of fresh pink meat, a little dish of intensely tarragon-flavored sauce béarnaise on the side; turbot, the genuine article, from, how you say, the other side, but fresh, strong of that particular swimmer's singular flavor, the pair of fillets of almost ephemeral texture within their crisped, parsleyed surfaces, and served to you—stunningly—on a platform of warm, buttery leeks. Apparently Raoul's has something going with sweetbreads. After doing that thing with cool ones as a first course, it produces these hot ones, thin, crisp slivers of the rich but light meat in a winy sauce that is dense with crunchy black morels. The good liver is sliced thin, arrives deeply browned outside and blood-pink inside, is served in a tart vinegar sauce that contrasts strikingly with the organ meat's strong flavor. And once in a while there are these paupiettes de veau, roulades formed of thin sheets of veal wrapped around an airy forcemeat of yet more veal, the fluffy stuff herbed and judiciously seasoned and steamy within the browned veal wrappers, the big knobs moistened with a sauce that is thick with wild chanterelles.

Oddly, Raoul's offers no cheese. You can get a good salad of fresh greens and respectable tomatoes in a tangy vinaigrette. Some of the desserts seem commercial and are boring—among them a ponderous chocolate Grand Marnier cake. But then there are what the house refers to as fruit tarts, which seem more like clafoutis: They are probably made on the premises, they have been variously offered with cherries or the small pale plums called mirabelles, the crunchy fruits set in something that is more akin to browned custard than to pastry—they are homey and satisfying.

This place has had a bad press, but that is mostly judgment too timid to contradict appearances. Only a handful of restaurants in town turn out old-fashioned French cooking as good as this.

★★★ LE RÉGENCE

37 East 64th Street
LUNCH AND DINNER.
Reservations: 606-4647.
Credit cards: AE, DC, MC, V.
Very expensive.

What distinguishes this place from others in its posh French class is the almost magical quality of its intimidation, magical because nothing about the way Le Régence is run ought to scare anyone off. Yet even on Saturday night, when Manhattan Island is regularly invaded and swarmed over by foreign bodies in Detroit cars, the crowd here is made up, almost homogeneously, of folks who bear lightly their tons of old money, a set that, by practice, has become this establishment's natural trade. Is it not a comfort to know that there is a restaurant in New York to which you may repair, drop two or three hundred dollars on dinner, and not find yourself among those who would rather mortgage the mortgage than not outspend you?

Surely it is the situation and look that effect that effect, for though Le Régence is only just outside the midtown maelstrom, it is deep in the heart of Park Avenue country, in the determinedly old-world (albeit slick) Hôtel Plaza Athénée, namesake of a legendary Parisian lodgment whose gracious dining facilities are in one respect echoed, though certainly not replicated, in these dining rooms. You approach them through a cool, stony lobby and then through a cushy, softly lit cocktail area in which, at certain hours, you may be mildly diverted by a gentleman who has at his disposal a larynx and 88 keys. The sounds he produces do not, however, follow you to your dinner, which transpires in a cream-and-turquoise Louis the Ornate interior that, glittering with crystal, is reflected and re-reflected in mirrors all around that extend the place to all horizons. Le Régence is a central room surrounded by a number of smaller rooms, the one in the middle under a barrel ceiling that, painted to resemble a cloud-dotted summer sky, is a reference to the outdoor court of the Paris antecedent. You are seated in armchairs of simulated leather framed in carved wood, or on sofas of antiqued velvet. The plywood paneling and lumberyard moldings applied to the walls have been cleverly painted, simulate, to the dim-sighted, hand work. You walk on plush carpeting. And, but for the flowers all around and the white linen and white trim and the sparkle of glass, all is aqua or aquamarine, jade or blue-green, with here a touch of teal, there a hint of mint. By now you know you are to wear your crimson dress. The help wear their black-and-whites, are unfailingly cordial, answer your questions willingly, knowledgeably. Among them there is a sommelier complete with small saucer on a chain around his neck—he is a rare sommelier, acknowledges that he has not tasted personally the wine you have chosen from among the scores on his list.

In the eternal relay race by way of which New York's haute cuisine kitchens change hands, Le Régence has countered the piracy of its original chef by the acquisition, for advisory and intermittent participatory services, of the Rostangs, père et (deux) fils, they of two two-star restaurants in the old country, one on the Riviera, the other in Paris. What with yet another of their countrymen always in place in New York, the food seems to vary not at all with the family's comings and goings. Consider, for example, this salmon tart, a circle of dark and flaky pastry, on it a layer of rich crème fraîche threaded with strands of sweet onion, the two hidden under thin, overlapping slices of delicate but vividly flavored salmon that are adorned with little sprigs of dill, everything warm but not hot—and weightless, actually fugitive, food that seems to satisfy while burdening you not at all, like a dream dish, one that may be consumed perpetually. Fear not, the ethereal quality of that tart is not the mark of all the food, you may actually eat and experience the beginnings of satiety, as when you do away with this lobster salad, the little crustacean in four parts, the tail two of them, the claws one each, leaves of heady basil clinging to the moist, supple, sweetly oceanic meat, which is in nice contrast to the sharp greens, in a tart dressing, on which the seafood is set—an arrangement of delicate baby carrots intertwined with the lobster's little claws adorns the plate. This place offers real langoustines, that is, Dublin Bay prawns, which, technically, are not prawns at all and not found in Dublin Bay—but that is another story. Anyway, they are steamed in their shells (a preparation that preserves all their flavor), and the meats are extracted and served, in a pool of sauce that is at once polished, tangy, acidic, and of a briny pungency, within a circle of pencil-thin asparagus spears—a stunning dish. What goes as galette d'artichauts is an artichoke mousse studded with morsels of sautéed foie gras, and that liver, remarkably, potentiates the flavor of the vegetable, as does the creamy vinegar sauce in which the construct is set—you do wish that the garnish of small sections of artichoke bottom were not rather hard, their trimmed leaves not a bit too fibrous for consumption.

Much seafood on the right hand side of the menu, including pompano, a great side of the fish under a thick layer of coarse-chopped black olives—it is moistened with a bit of smooth, sweet sauce and garnished with browned, buttery fennel, the perfume of which pervades the dish. Your pigeon is described as "laqué au vinaigre et au miel," which is to say, lacquered with vinegar and honey, and sure enough, the browned bird, in four parts, reaches you glistening—you were asked how you want it, and if you answered that you want it the way the chef likes to make it, it reaches you medium rare, the meat moist, redolent of its fat within the coppery skin, and garnished, strikingly, with a little muffin of garlic custard. You are perhaps a bit dismayed at the paucity of your serving of veal, a couple of nuggets the size of large golf balls, but there is no quarreling with the crisp browning of their surfaces, within which all the meat's juiciness is sealed, nor with the rich and winy sauce in which they are served, nor with the sprigs of rosemary that are lively relief to the sturdy food, nor with the little strips of browned-in-clarified-butter potato slices that add vivid potato flavor and crackling texture to the dish.

The sliced lamb is good, the tender, roasted meat blood-pink and of frank lamb flavor, but it is notable especially for the deep-brown vinegared mash of shallots on which it is dramatically served.

What goes as Irish cassis is a big wine glass half filled with currants, the fruit in its jelly, over the top a quarter inch of thick, rich cream—forgettable. The gratin de framboise consists of a soft meringue, raspberries, and a light honey- and orange-flavored sauce—not memorable. The goût de chocolat is an assortment of many chocolate things, cake and mousse and ice cream among them, all of intense chocolate flavor, and all set in a cool lemon sauce—fine, but not what you come back for. You do well with the passion fruit soufflé, a great mound of the light, creamy, fruity confection, hidden under it a so-called "coconut shell" that is in fact a coconut pastry—a nice foil to the fluffy sweet.

★★LE RELAIS

712 Madison Avenue (near 63rd Street)
LUNCH AND DINNER.
Reservations: 751-5108.
Credit cards: AE, DC, MC, V.
Medium priced.

The folding doors that form the front wall of this restaurant are pushed aside when the weather is fair, exposing the place to the pedestrians and vehicles on Madison Avenue, and vice versa. Sometimes a handful of tables are even set up on the sidewalk, under a little awning; champagne is kept cold in buckets, and this restaurant's menu items—bistro food with a light touch—are dispatched as casually as possible by the revelers who disport themselves thereat. They betray much contented awareness that the ease with which they lead this good life is on display. Of course, you cannot have a party on the sidewalk and act as if you were in your own dining room. Not even if you swallow your entire bottle of blasé pills.

Le Relais is a Parisian restaurant, bustling and contented. Its ivory-colored walls are hung with dozens of prints and engravings, and with big mirrors that have their tops tilted forward, so that from any seat in the house you get a voyeur's view of lots of other seats in the house. The International Set crowds the little bar at the front. They wear Riviera tans, Savile Row flannel blazers, brevities from Fifth Avenue. One smashing lady, all of whose hair has migrated to the left side of her head, chats with one gentleman, holds in abeyance another by placing her hand on the back of his, and swivels her eyes and watches with shock the entrance of a third, who, goddammit, is accompanied by a lady all of whose hair has migrated to the left side of her head.

Folks who do not know any better get all dressed up to come here. But this is an easygoing place, at which gentlemen in tennis sweaters and ladies in prominently labeled denim are quite at home. Some of the food on the constantly changing menu could be picnic food, such as the pâté of chicken livers, a very spreadable brandied and buttered paste that is crunchy with hazelnuts. The cool lentil salad is dotted with bacon and onion and fragrantly herbed in its tangy dressing. A slivered endive, adorned with bits of strong, creamy Roquefort cheese and moistened with good oil, makes a rousing first

290

course. As does the cold bass, the pale and moist white meat in an herbed dressing that is sharp with mustard.

The bass again, this time hot but served in an uncooked lemon-and-oil dressing that is herbed and lightly garlicked—a slightly daring and very stunning dish. Le Relais is one of the few places in town where the carpaccio appears to be sliced to order: The tissue-thin leaves of raw beef are blood-juicy, and they are served with a great dollop of rich, tomato-flavored mayonnaise. The sautéed chicken is a good bird, its wine sauce polished, its title—poulet à l'estragon—incomprehensible, the tarragon being not in evidence. Hefty slices of lamb, charred at the edges, as rare as you want them at the center, are served as noix d'agneau Nesselrode—good, tender meat, of mild but clear lamb flavor, in a creamy calvados sauce that is at once sweet and slightly acidic.

The fruit tarts, sometimes apple, sometimes pear, are elemental, made on light, flaky, barely browned pastry. The chocolate mousse is rich, dark, intense but not excessive—it is served with whipped cream that is the genuine article, rich and light. You may have strawberries with that whipped cream, but some of the fruit was selected through rose-colored glasses. The bombe pralinée is an icy-cold compound of cake and ice cream and hazelnuts, served under more of that whipped cream—a heady sweet.

★ REMI

323 East 79th Street
LUNCH, SATURDAY AND SUNDAY; DINNER, DAILY.
Reservations: 744-4272.
Credit cards: AE, DC, MC, V.
Expensive.

It even looks noisy, loud white stripes on the dark-blue banquettes, cacophonous red, yellow, and gray light fixtures (albeit of genuine, imported, do not accept imitations Venetian glass—this place has Venetian leanings) on the semi-gloss walls, a babel of little framed prints all around that seem to chatter incomprehensibly about their indistinct Venetian subjects, brandished crossed pairs of gondola oars mounted on the low ceiling overhead (in recesses that, though padded, are apparently as acoustically transparent as the fabric on your loudspeakers). The busy movement through the aisles of the waiters in their bold-striped shirts is a considerable addition to the general visual din, as is the guests' boisterous speech to the aural, their loudness, of course, essential, for they are in competition with the clangor that is built into this hard-surfaced place. The closeness of the tables in the not large room, especially those along the banquettes, adds to your sense that the world is here much with you, as does the affectionate nudge of your waiter's hip against your shoulder when he leans to pour wine for the table adjacent to your own. You may find it hell, you may find it jolly, it depends on your mood, which depends on whether you have a drop before coming—which, it is suggested, you occasionally do, for with care you eat well here, though only the born lucky should trust their luck.

Luck is smiling—well, grinning—on you when you choose the endivia con sardine e ravanelli, a bowl filled with crisp, cut-up endives, thin disks of red-trimmed radish on top, among them silvery strands that are sour, salty, herringlike fish fillets—the salad's mustard dressing is vigorous. But the corners of her mouth then fickly turn down, and she permits you to stumble into the radicchio e grana con polenta—nothing wrong with the decent greens, and the slivers of Parmesan suffer only by their paucity, but the star-shaped chunks of polenta are mushy, without flavor, their surfaces hardened rather than crisped in the toasting. Smoked goose at its best has a vigorous spiced-meat flavor, but here it is pallid stuff, the salad served with it of much more interest in its strong horseradish dressing. But then there is this carpaccio, the meat fresh cut, its raw-beef flavor clear, on it a little mound of heady arugula under slivers of sharp Parmesan cheese—you pour on liberally the green olive oil.

Dark bigoli are a Venetian pasta made with whole-wheat flour and shaped like spaghetti. The noodle has a grainy flavor that is clear even in its herbed and well-seasoned onion sauce, which is accented with bits of anchovy. White noodles too, among them mezze maniche con salsiccia e finocchio, short tubes of pasta in a slightly creamy and enriched tomato sauce, nubbly with chopped sausage and minced fennel, that is potentiated by the addition of ground cheese. Each night there is a risotto of the night, sometimes risotto primavera, the pile of rice dotted with bits of celery, zucchini, carrot, and strikingly sweet red pepper, all the vegetables of vivid flavor among the million moist grains.

You wonder about the elemental-seeming entry "steamed salmon," order it, discover that it is salmon, elementally steamed. The fillet is fresh, firm, has lost only a bit of its oil and flavor in the processing, is served on a little platform—buttered disks of zucchini and yellow squash—is garnished, the hit of the show, with a great column of scalloped potatoes, browned, firm, and creamy. More potatoes, these mashed, thick, heavily seasoned, with another fish, grilled snapper, in what is called a wine and onion marinade —the pearly strands and the bit of warm broth a sweet foil to the good snapper. Order a chicken breast, and you get both sides nicely browned, moist but cooked through, of real chicken flavor, the garnish of wild mushrooms woodsy and redolent of garlic. With respect to the rack of lamb, however, the garlic the menu leads you to expect is remote, though the chops themselves, rarer than what you asked for, are firm and tender, their edges nicely crisped.

Once again the Venetian star, a big, quarter-inch-thick six-pointer of zabaglione broiled on its plate, the winy, eggy fluff nicely heightened by the browning, and very striking is the egg of vanilla ice cream set at its center—you do wish the sweet were not garnished with white strawberries. The crème brûlée is sugary, which, taken together with its admixture of lemon, makes it candylike and cloying. The wine-poached pear is firm and fruity, the little cannoli served with it crusty and crisp, the custard filling cold, smooth, and sweet. The chocolate cake is rich, intense, of a crunchy nutted texture.

★★RENÉ PUJOL

321 West 51st Street
LUNCH, MONDAY TO FRIDAY; DINNER, MONDAY TO SATURDAY. CLOSED SUNDAY.
Reservations: 246-3023.
Credit cards: AE, DC, MC, V.
Medium priced.

Of the dozen or so French restaurants in the theater district, this is the one that, more than any other, has departed from the old Broadway-bistro formula. René Pujol is even influenced a little—a *very* little—by carryings-on usually associated with restaurants of the Madison Avenue French persuasion: Raw salmon you can get, even fishes that are jetted in from across the Atlantic. What is perhaps more to the point are the notes of clarity and lightness in dishes that elsewhere in this neighborhood are, traditionally and to this day, overwrought and weighty. But while the place is drawing back somewhat from blunt assertiveness in its cuisine bourgeoise, it has so far refused to deviate from the uncompromising kitsch of its cornball appointments: a beamed ceiling, crockery and varnished copper on the timbered walls, a brick fireplace (complete with a fake deer's head over it), an old grandfather clock (with swinging brass pendulum and quarter-hourly chimes), French-countryside murals. The place is not so much a restaurant as a flash forward to a twenty-fifth-century museum, in which is recreated a characteristic public eating place on the isle of Manhattan, serving French food to the subaristocratic classes in the era before the dawn of civilization.

With callous disregard of its effect on your appetite, the savages present you, as soon as you are seated, with a pot of rillettes, a paste of pounded and seasoned pork and fat, which you are meant to apply copiously to slabs of bread—with butter, if enrichment is required. The natives extract the roe from certain fish and serve it as red caviar, the mound of russet-orange globules accompanied by white disks cut from sharp red radishes, strong chopped onion, a great dollop of sour cream, lemon, warm buttered toast —a rousing appetizer. And they trap lobsters at the bottom of the sea, boil them, remove the crustaceans' meat from the shells, cut it up, serve it warm—in a dressing that is little more than seasoned oil—mingled with strands of crisp vegetable on leaves of tender lettuce and endive. Salmon is marinated raw, with dill, and the great sheet of tender, pink meat is served with a sour, tangy, and caper-studded mustard sauce, and with lime, the juice of which makes the dish sparkle.

Seafood is this kitchen's strength. You get a whole Dover sole, fresh, firm, skinned and filleted and sautéed, its buttered and browned surface glinting. Most days there are a couple of fish of the day—sometimes a splendid red snapper stuffed with a fluffy mousse of sole, blanketed with a stout lobster sauce, and garnished with a little mound of bay scallops; and sometimes fresh salmon, broad slices of it, in a winy cream sauce that is laced with tart sorrel, this fish, too, garnished with scallops. If you want the scallops without the fish, the little morsels are sometimes served combined with julienned vegetables in that same sorrel sauce. The shellfish winner, however, is the lobster "au wiskey," in which the chunks of lobster meat are served in a polished red sauce—at once sweet and biting and briny—that has been fortified with liquor. You get sweetbreads that are as light as soufflés, floured and lightly browned, their dark-red sauce sharp with green olives. Thin slivers of veal are served in a rich and creamy sauce that is thick with mushrooms and heady with brandy. You wish that the blocks of beef in the boeuf bourguignon had been cooked longer, for they are a little resilient, not at all integrated into a steamy, stewlike mass, which is what you expect this dish to be. The rack of lamb is of good meat, accurately roasted, cut into tender little chops that are blackened and salty around the edges. The rack is made only for two. So is the Chateaubriand, that great knob of tenderloin, roasted until it is a deep mahogany on the surface, still bright red within, and served with a sauce béarnaise that is abundantly salted, powerfully fragrant of its tarragon.

In season, perfect berries are served here—raspberries, strawberries, blackberries even—with excellent whipped cream. Both the pear cake (a layer of cool pear filling at the center of the light spongecake) and the orange cake (spongecake again, this one wrapped in paper-thin slices of orange) are served in pools of crimson raspberry sauce.

★★LA RÉSERVE

4 West 49th Street
LUNCH, MONDAY TO FRIDAY; DINNER, MONDAY TO SATURDAY. CLOSED SUNDAY.
Reservations: 247-2993.
Credit cards: AE, DC, MC, V.
Expensive.

Originally designed not to offend, La Réserve, after a few years on the scene, has now undertaken not to bore. The interior, of course, is unchanged (perfect innocuousness cannot be improved), but the food no longer comes across as the work of a born apprentice promoted as a reward for loyalty. And the help in the dining rooms these days is notably sweet.

It has been suggested that this is where W & J Sloane went when it died. The cushy carpeting, wood paneling, and scored mirroring are the perfect setting for banquettes upholstered in a glistening fabric of peach pink and skin pink and for period side chairs —with plump seats and oval backs—done in shimmering velvet the color of lime sherbet. The place is illuminated by chandeliers that are big clusters of light fixtures of milkish convoluted glass—the illumination they give off is a kind of glowing pallor. "La Réserve" is "the game preserve," and throughout the front and back rooms of this place, the walls are faced with large murals of wildlife—quail, grouse, egrets, and such—enjoying themselves and looking beautiful in woods and bosky dells, beside lakes, bays, and streams. Though the paintings are handsome and decorative—you divert yourself by identifying the species they depict—and despite the help they get from the stands of greenery here and there around the rooms, they cannot redeem the mindless posh of this installation. Only the cheering effect of a full house humanizes this place, so if you chance to come on a slow night, it is well if you have brought with you company that is easier on your eyes than are the surroundings.

Focus on your friend, and get yourself an order of, say, lobster cream soup. It is ladled into your soup plate, at your place, over a couple of waiting quenelles that are surmounted by strands of root vegetable. The quenelles are fluffy and of sweet fish flavor, the vegetables are crisp but tender, and the soup itself, though creamy, is light, and it has a deep lobster flavor that is at once succulent and a little sharp—you will probably be pleased when, having dispatched the oceanic stuff, the big pot is brought back and you are offered more. Salmon and scallops that have been marinated with dill are served garnished with thin slices of cool lime: the fish is light, subtle, almost fugitive, lacks the sugariness of the usual gravlax, but the scallops are a bit soggy—still the well-balanced seasoning, the heady flavor of the dill, and the presence of whole coriander seeds make this a striking dish. Dill yet again, this time whole sprigs of it arranged over slices of duck liver. The dish is described as "sauté à l'hydromel," and a waiter explains to a nearby table that "l'hydromel is an herb." Of course it is not, it is mead, and you do note a slight honeylike sweetness to the browned, pinguid, and yet light meat—the dill is striking against such rich stuff, but the centers of each very rare slice are unfortunately a bit cool. You order snails, and you are brought an oval-shaped silver dish with a silver lid. The top is lifted off, and a complex aroma of herbs, wild mushrooms, and sweet spices invades your space—the sauce is creamy, the mushrooms earthy, and the plump snails have the flavor of the good stock in which they were done.

The house does much with fish out of French waters. Consider the rouget, filleted, grilled—and crisped—with its skin on, the slices of firm and buttery fish served in a pool of beurre blanc—the surprising notes of sweet-spice flavor you get in every other bite are the whole cloves with which the fish is studded. Then consider the turbot, a remarkable ocean fish that needs no help, but which does well no matter how it is treated. Here three fillets are set in a delicate and enriching brown sauce, one of them adorned with lemon grass, the other two with black caviar—almost any dish can be improved by elimination of caviar, and here the roe used is nothing special, but this is fresh turbot, ocean sweet, delicately done, and it has all its flavor. The roasted chicken is shown to you whole, taken away, returned to you as the boned breast in two parts, legs attached. The glazed skin is browned and shiny, the pale meat is of real chicken flavor, and the bird is served in a powerfully herbed and well-fatted sauce that is thick with crunchy whole shallots—though they are cooked, and sweetened thereby, they retain much of their bite. La Réserve turns out a quite superb sirloin, the firm, tender, fibrous, and blood-juicy steak done to perfect rareness—this is sautéed beef, neither seared nor charcoaled, and its unsullied flavor is very good with the tarragon and bone marrow that dominate its sauce.

If you put yourself in the hands of your waiter, he will repair to the kitchen and choose for you the cheeses that are in good condition—they are fine with the house salad of sharp greens, chopped tomato, endive, and a tart dressing prepared with velvety oil. You may have for dessert a fluffy mass of Grand Marnier soufflé (it is subtle, only mildly liquored) in a crêpe envelope that is strewn with confectioner's sugar—it is served with orange sections and a crimson raspberry sauce. The chocolate cake is remarkably light for its richness, the tarte Tatin deeply caramelized on its flaky crust, the black-currant mousse rather sugary, though of good fruit flavor.

★★RESTAURANT RAPHAËL

33 West 54th Street
LUNCH, MONDAY TO FRIDAY; DINNER, MONDAY TO SATURDAY. CLOSED SUNDAY.
Reservations: 582-8993.
Credit cards: AE, MC, V.
Very expensive.

"Thank God for lunch," said a wise man once to proprietor Raphael Edery during a slow dinner, and Edery was seen to nod assent. At lunch, one wants lunch, and to talk, usually business, and if the surroundings and high cost solemnize the occasion and underscore the importance of the participants, all the better. But at dinner, one wants more than dinner, one wants diversion, excitement, fantasy, conviviality, the proximity of others imaginably more amusing than one's self. One wants what's happening, and Restaurant Raphaël is what happened long ago and no longer happens anymore nohow. Were the dead past laid on whimsically, or with theatrical exaggeration, or with coy understatement, that is, with some kind of human charm, if RR did not take itself, by way of its accoutrements, so dead seriously, people would relax into it, and as the place is small, it might fill. Instead it gets by half empty on those who are as self-important as the place chooses to look. The operative word is gaiety. By and large in restaurants one is able at least to *imagine* gaiety. Of course you may bring your own, but it helps when the restaurant catalyzes its expression.

Restaurant Raphaël remains a long, narrow store, a brick wall opposite an ochre-painted one of rough plaster, a banquette opposite an arrangement of tables and chairs. Overhead short beams cross the ceiling from one long wall to the other. Underfoot the rose-colored carpeting is of a discreet pattern. A small area at the back—one table in each of four corners—has been painted to seem like a tiny room, with cross ventilation, in an old stone castle. Here you walk on a tile floor, two "windows" no more than a dozen feet apart face east and west, "through" them you see paradisiac vistas of lush greenery and, you imagine, clean Renaissance air. Somehow, the murals do not delight, perhaps because you, for one, would gladly shorten your stay in paradise by, say, a million years in return for just an extra decade or two of mere earthly pleasures. Farther back, beyond the castle, there is a trellised backyard in which you may eat and/or drink when the weather is fine—the air, however, is contemporary.

Here now cooks Christian Delouvrier, ex Maurice, his talents constrained by the limits of a menu that, as ever at Raphaël, is brief. In many of the dishes, however, he reveals as much ability as he did on his last job, and if you are content to overlook your surroundings in favor of his food, you can learn your way around the menu in fewer than a handful of visits. Your first response to his oysters, however, will probably be dismay, for to the degree of your affection for oysters, you will object to a serving of but three. Judge them, however, not by their number, and there is no complaint, for the warm Malpèques retain all their flavor, their white sauce is rich but light, and the tiny crisp disks of salsify with which they are overlaid, though they are of remote flavor, are in this context a nifty textural note. Then there is your first response to his snails, which is more a response to the chunks of eggplant with which they are mingled, for surely every cubic inch of the eggplant need not be utilized? The tender center yes, the fibrous ends no? Presumably nothing but the purple skin is discarded, and on your unlucky night you get the part that has the texture of balsa wood. Still, a delicious dish, its basil-scented tomato sauce a Provence summer itself, and the snails, though maybe not the plumpest, have that voluptuous texture only snails and certain nonedibles have. But then there is this duck salad—if parsimony informs it, it is not obvious—an abundance of the strands of the good dark meat laid over the sides of a conical arrangement of greens that are shot through with nuggets of tomato, fruit and nuts, crisp bits of celery, cracklings and heady herbs, all in a lively dressing. Another salad, this one of sweetbreads, and it is possible that the house has found the poor man's foie gras, for the great knobs of the stuff, in this preparation not crisped, are polished and rich, all pinguid succulence, the nuggets of meat around a lemon-dressed salad, accented with threads of lemon rind, that is thick with lengths of wild mushroom—a striking plate of food.

The grilled fillet of salmon arrives with the skin on, but the skin is so blackened and crisped, the somewhat rare salmon so gently done through, that it is as if the skin were done separately, reduced to a crackling parchment before being returned to the fresh pale-pink meat; the fish is adorned with chunks of crushed tomato and garnished with globes of so-called spaghetti de légumes, orbs of strands of herbed and buttered vegetables. Of course your lobster is an infant, but it is smoked and roasted, both judiciously, and its meat is juicy under its rich, herbed sauce. Your pigeon is a little resilient, as if it needed time to relax between its demise and its preparation—still, this is a tasty bird, its charred skin a good zest to it. Something quasi Japanese is made of the steak, which reaches you sliced, the glistening, glowing pink-red meat in dramatic visual contrast to the charred edges, its sauce, of soy and plum wine, a good but astringent offset.

296

Raphaël has always offered the cheese that goes as "crottin de chavignol," and nowadays the warm, strong nugget of marinated goat cheese, oiled and gamy, is garnished with spiky, lively greens. If crème brûlée is the most familiar dessert in town, Restaurant Raphaël has something of a right to demand noninclusion on the soon-to-be published list of places that must drop it or else, for the one made here—no artificial flavors or colorings added—is close to the thing in its platonic form, a cool, light custard, a warm, very thin, and gently crackling caramelized top, and no more—"close" because, though that custard is light, you do wish you could call it fluffy. And though you will find little fault with the individual lemon tart—the halves of browned lemon curd, on a flaky pastry, flank a pool of crimson berry puree—you will probably prefer the millefeuille de framboises, a triple decker, three circles of a delicate, almost fugitive pastry, the second and third stories supported by circles of ripe raspberries around the edges, within the circles rich whipped cream—next to it that raspberry coulis again.

★ LA RIPAILLE

605 Hudson Street (near 12th Street)
DINNER. CLOSED SUNDAY.
Reservations: 255-4406.
Credit cards: AE, DC, MC, V.
Medium priced.

Though with respect to numbers the species *bistro rustica* is dying out, most extant specimens are healthy, suggesting that the decline is a function not of any inhospitality in the ecosystem, but of a tendency among the survivors, in reproduction, not to revert to type. When the pimplous and blithely forgetful lad who waits on you here goes off some day to open a place of his own, his restaurant will not be a candlelit farmhouse serving la cuisine bourgeoise. Which is too bad, for these establishments have their uses. Enter one, note the stupendously familiar appointments, and you are instantly focused solely on the occasion. In this kind of place the setting always reassures, your back is safely to the wall. So hypnotic is the effect, in fact, that when La Ripaille's grandfather clock strikes the hour, you hardly notice it, which is perhaps why it has the habit of striking it again a few minutes later.

White plaster, wood beams, glazed brick in the dim light, wildflowers and dried grasses in baskets on the walls, antique tapestries, too many white-linened tables for the knotty space. In search of isolation, you request the table at the extreme back, the one beside the unused fireplace, for though it is distressingly proximate to intermittent loud crashes from the kitchen, it is larger than the other tables for two, and the space around it is sufficient so that when the radiator nearby is spitting steam, the table may be moved to the outer edge of its hot orbit. Withal, La Ripaille is not appreciated for its perverse charms, is frequented mainly by first daters and bargain seekers who, by sharing this course, choosing that one arithmetically, skipping the other, eat cheaply here. It is depressing to find yourself among those who grow tender over candlelight and kidneys.

From a menu that changes daily, you begin, in the spirit of the place, with the pâté de campagne, and you are served a better-than-everyday slab of the traditional compacture, the amalgam of meats at room temperature, vigorously seasoned, just a little gamy, good with hot mustard and with this establishment's fluffy white bread. Les escargots, too, are integral to this kind of place, but these snails deviate misguidedly, come in a lightly creamed tomato sauce that is only vaguely touched with basil, and the snails themselves are of little flavor. You find that what La Ripaille calls a "feuilleté de champignons sauvages" is made with, mostly, mushrooms that are not very savage at all, only a few of the wild mixed in with many of the tame, but the pastries are flaky, the mushrooms sport much earthy flavor, and their herbed cognac sauce is rich. Pasta has taken a permanent place on menus of this kind, and here you are sometimes offered large round ravioli stuffed with a mild Roquefort cheese filling, the sharpness of the cheese gentled by an herbed and creamy white sauce.

Skip the trout—it is not off, you understand, it is just not on, has no trout flavor, and the slivered almonds that could add a bit of drama lack crispness. Better are these quails, for though the nicely browned birds are identifiable as quails mainly by their size, their mushroom stuffing is pungent, and their madeira sauce is winy, deep, a little sweet. Better still is this liver, the thick slices crisped, pink, blood-juicy at the center, strikingly set off by the chunks of good bacon with which they are strewn. You are attracted to the noisette d'agneau by the description "au thym frais," you figure the lamb has been prepared with thyme. Maybe, but these slabs of pink meat have little taste but their own, as does their somewhat greasy sauce, the herb figuring only as a garnish of a few sprigs.

You are saddened by the lack of cheese. Your waiter commiserates. You point out that there must be cheese on the premises, that there is Roquefort in the ravioli. You are brought Roquefort, but with the regretful explanation that, as it is not on the menu, you cannot be charged for it. Though crumbled, this is perfectly good cheese, and with the money you save on the gratis dessert, you buy more wine rather than inflate the tip. The frozen lemon soufflé is informed by the notion that there is a point of interest halfway between ice cream and sherbet. There is not. The apple tart is of good, slightly sour fruit and decent pastry, but its sauce is icky. The winner is the bombe pralinée, the dense, cold ice cream threaded with candied hazelnuts.

★ RONASI

1160 First Avenue (near 63rd Street)
LUNCH, MONDAY TO SATURDAY; DINNER, DAILY.
Reservations: 751-0360.
Credit cards: AE, DC, MC, V.
Medium priced.

There is something slightly contemptible about restaurants that make it by holding down the prices. Such places reflect a narrow, pinched, cautious, and dully arithmetic vision. No matter how well the restaurant does, it never gets the respect accorded a true winner, a place that breaks the rules, takes chances, gives the suckers $5 worth of additional value, and for it exacts $50 extra and all their love. No one is more uncomfortably aware of the ignominy that attaches to the circumspect route than those who gain their unspectacular livelihoods from it. Some it embitters. Consider, for example, the captains and waiters who work the floor here. They know, when they arrive for work of an evening, that they are not going to hit it big this night. No high roller is going to slip anybody an extra C-note just for his good looks. On the other hand there are always customers for restaurants of this kind, so no one will go home with empty pockets either.

Which is to say that the gentlemen on the floor are no bolder than the management—and, accordingly, are privately shamefaced. Any surplus contempt beyond what they have for themselves is turned on their customers—who, they figure, are no better than they are, eat in this place for narrow, pinched, cautious, dully arithmetic reasons.

So when your captain delivers his spiel of the daily specials, he is all (mechanical) politesse; but interrupt his rhythm, ask him a follow-up question, a situation for which he has not rehearsed, and he rolls his eyes upward and sighs the sigh of the mortally wounded before he grudgingly responds. Then there is the chap who, when he has nothing else to do, comes by to make witticisms. Not laughing does not move him. Ignoring him completely, as if he were a potted palm, works better. One of his colleagues is more easily wounded, is instantly at the end of his patience when you do not have your order ready when he wants to take it—he leaves, makes a point of not returning at all. Still, these chaps take well to admonishment, are ultimately harmless—otherwise they would not be working in this narrow, pinched, cautious, etc.

Ronasi is all dark pink and exposed brick, a bar at the back, white linen on the good-size tables. The works of art on the walls are flattered to be called primitive. The ceiling, of intersecting vaults, houses the utilities, four-bladed fans tucked into the arches, air-conditioning vents at their bases. You figure the house painter who applied the pink also did the design.

You are fed better than you are housed. Consider, for example, the marinated raw bass, sheets of the pale-pink fish dressed with good olive oil that is herbed, garlicked, and thick with chopped radicchio; or the marinated raw salmon, the red-orange meat glistening with olive oil that is dense with bits of fresh ginger. Two giant mussels in their shells, a couple of tiny clams, fresh and sparkling, in theirs, and one crunchy shrimp surround the seafood salad: squid, octopus, and strands of roasted red pepper in a bright lemon-and-garlic dressing.

On occasion the tiny clams served with that seafood salad are vongole, oval-shelled mollusks native to Italian waters, and when the house has these on hand you do well to order the spaghetti with white clam sauce, the big mound of pasta oiled and garlicked, the clams, in their shells, arranged in a circle around it, their good meat sweeter and subtler, but less briny than that of the local article. You are informed that the linguine con radicchio e gamberi may be had in either a red or white sauce. You opt for the former, and are delivered of firm noodles in a vibrant tomato sauce, chunks of crunchy shrimp buried in it, as are the bits of blackened radicchio that are a zest to the sturdy dish. Come here once, however, and in this department the gnocchi are the item to have, the ricotta dumplings firm and startlingly light in their rousing red sauce—the good cheese that is added fortifies and deepens the excellent dish. Half orders of pasta are served.

Bronzino is a basslike swimmer from overseas, and the fish travels better than does this preparation ("alle mandorle"), in which the big fillet is blanketed with a mixture of chopped almonds and mushrooms—a dish easier to appreciate than to love. Though it is on occasion a shade less than pristine, the sautéed salmon with capers, an obvious dish lacking in breed, is easier to approach. The chicken sautéed with balsamic vinegar is garlicked, handsomely browned, mingled with inches of asparagus—straightforward food that suffers for the pallidness of the bird. What is given as stuffed veal is a layered thing of meat, cheese, and red lettuce, the three in an eggy batter—good ingredients combined to form a leaden dish. You are better off with the scaloppine al mascarpone, the pale meat, browned and moist, in a sauce that is thickened and enriched with cream cheese and dotted with woodsy wild mushrooms. Skip the grilled veal chop, which is dry and shrunken.

299

The zuppa inglese is the usual candylike confection, encased in browned meringue and soaked in booze. Avoid also the napoleon, layers of flaky pastry interleaved with a cloying custard. The cheesecake, however, is the genuine article under its browned top—wet, weighty, sweet, very good with some of the ripe strawberries and/or raspberries the house usually has on hand.

★★ROSA MEXICANO

1063 First Avenue (at 58th Street)
LUNCH AND DINNER.
Reservations: 753-7407.
Credit cards: AE, DC, MC, V.
Medium priced.

The generation trained to stoic patience by around-the-block movie lines provides much of the crowd that, reservations or no, waits calmly—contentedly, even—for tables here. These are the grown-ups who, back when they were majoring in success, sought out Mexican food because what went by that name was the cheapest hot meal within a dollar's worth of gas off campus. Having learned to abide that stuff, they are, willy-nilly, nuts about Rosa Mexicano's *haute* version of the real thing. If this menu is not precisely a compendium of Mexican-home-cooking familiarities (and why should it be), the ingredients and the spirit are the closest thing to south of the Rio Grande anywhere north of Buttermilk Channel.

You enter to a front room dominated by two serving stations, each of which exemplifies an important side of this operation. First, the bar, a crowd of human beings with, at its center, a counter—it shields the man behind it from the horde before it. His job is to take orders fast, make change fast, hit you up when your glass is empty. Chosen for the part is an all-American type, rangy and lithe. Farther along is the open grill, set before a tiled wall. Here steaks, chops, chickens, and whole fish, variously marinated or otherwise flavored, are charred in a fire, then sauced and garnished (to be picked up on the fly by the young waiters and waitresses who patrol this place). Chosen as grill tenders are a couple of gentlemen from Rosa's homeland, swarthy and black haired in their kitchen whites. The front room houses tables as well: a few under the front windows (avoid the one closest to the bar, for the crowd impinges); several more along the bar a few feet away (the crowd presses on these, too, and you may perspire in this part of the room from the heat of the grill); a short row of semiprivate booths with their own little arched roofs; and, at the rear, a single large table under a sunburst mirror. The back dining room is a big square space rimmed by a banquette that is overhung, all around the perimeter, by an arched canopy of rough stucco. At the center of the room a low, broad pot of tropical greenery flourishes under spotlights.

Rosa Mexicano is softly lighted and hot pink throughout, which, in combination with the orderly arrangement of its appointments, gives the place a kind of subtropical formality. That, however, is somewhat undone by the clientele, which consists in large measure of that set of restaurant-going New Yorkers who patronize eating places not to eat in them, but to have been to them—to be able to talk about having been to them. They are a community, they like to think they know one another intuitively, like members of the same species, and adjacent couples along the back-room banquette

300

initiate conversations with their neighbors (invariably about food or restaurants) as readily as they ask their waiter for the check. One such enthusiast thinks nothing of objecting strenuously when he overhears you ordering the white sangria, insists on pouring you a glass from his own pitcher, to dissuade you, is triumphant when, after you concede that the stuff is watery and flat, you switch to beer. Another opinion maker virtually abandons her dinner to share with the unfortunates beside her a torrent of food thoughts, among them, "I don't think there's really that much difference between Nouvelle and Japanese-French," for which her paralyzing clincher is, "do you?"

The avocado is much of Mexican cooking, and to start your dinner with it in one of its seemingly purest forms, you order the hot avocado soup, a thick and creamy puree of the rich fruit that is spiced, soured a little with lime juice, and fortified with chicken stock. For avocado more complex, there is guacamole, and nowhere in town is a greater production made of it than here. A serving stand is wheeled to within a couple feet of your table, on it the ingredients, and also a molcajete, the legged, rough-textured bowl, carved of volcanic rock, that is basic to the Mexican kitchen. Here it is used as the mortar (a plain wooden spoon is the pestle) in which the avocado (one of those good black ones, with the pebbly skins and nutlike flavor) is mashed and flavored. You are asked if you want your guacamole hot, and if you really do, you must insist, otherwise it will be only tepidly spiced. Strong or mild, this is wondrous stuff, and though it is crunchy with chopped onions and fragrant of coriander, its secret is in those excellent avocados and in the last-minute preparation—the dish is served in the molcajete, filled to the rim, and one order is enough for two. The stuffed jalapeños are the shells of three of the famously hot green peppers, packed with sardines in their oil, and garnished with tomatoes and pickled onions—a primitive, violent, and rousing dish. The salpicon is of crabmeat that is sautéed with onions, herbs, and peppers, and then chilled—it gets a little flat going through those changes. For something like it, but brighter, there is the ceviche of red snapper, in which the morsels of fresh fish, "cooked" in an herbed and spicy lemon-juice marinade, are presented to you in a small bowl lined with thin slices of tomato—the snapper retains much of its sweet flavor among the herbs, onions, and peppers in which it is prepared. Among the few tortilla dishes on this menu there are these flautas, slender tubes formed of the cornmeal pancakes, filled with chicken, and served with what the menu calls crème fraîche, but which seems like an extremely rich mayonnaise—the good dish is garnished with cold chopped tomatoes that are mingled with fresh, fragrant cilantro.

From that grill: a whole snapper, the skin a blackened, powdery parchment, the meat within it fresh, moist, and of clear flavor, garnished with cool, soured onions and warm rice studded with black beans; pork chops that have been marinated with hot spices, so that when they are grilled, their flavor is almost like that of strong beef; skewered sausages—thick, black, sticky blood sausages and spicy meat sausages alternate on the slender blade with onions and tomatoes, and with peppers of killing heat—the job of these chiles is to flavor the other items, which they do effectively, and you are safest sampling their taste only in what was next to them; and a shell steak, good beef, tender and rarer than you wanted it, strewn with sautéed peppers—hot, but approachable— and onions. From the kitchen: a skinned breast of duck, of strong duck-fat flavor, but not fatty, set in a sauce of chiles and green tomatoes that is strong, sweet, vibrant; and what goes as tamal en cazuela, a homey dish, not unlike a bowl of cereal with strands of chicken and tangy mole sauce in it, melted cheese over it—stout, elemental food.

Little in the way of desserts: The papaya ice cream tastes a bit like papaya, and is soft. The cool sautéed pineapple, with coconut and walnuts, seems like something spooned over ice cream for an extra quarter.

★★ROSOLIO

11 Barrow Street (near 4th Street)
DINNER. CLOSED MONDAY.
Reservations: 645-9224.
Credit cards: AE, DC, MC, V.
Medium priced.

Innocents from abroad, young and eager, run this place. Their youth is plain to see, their innocence you infer, for in assembling Rosolio they have incorporated the signature marks of several recent overlapping New York Italian restaurant generations, as if they figured that by touching all the charms they eliminate the chance of missing the one that will work for them. Apparently they reasoned right, for the elements of this room, the diversity of their sources not withstanding, add up. By the vaulted ceiling of ancient brick, by the exposed pipes just under it, by the great galvanized steel air-conditioning tube that cuts across it, you are put in mind of SoHo's early days, when the religion of gutting ancient commercial spaces for restaurant purposes prescribed that the skeletal plumbing and electrical works be left as was and proudly displayed. Indoor neon had only a brief run in New York, that spate of glitzy pizza-cum-ice-cream parlors a few years back. Some survive, but none announces itself to its captive audience more gaily than Rosolio, with a sign behind its back-corner bar that, throughout dinner, gleams the name of this place in brilliant fuchsia. Of course, the recent craze for mottled ochre walls is not slighted, the dappled dirty yellow is all around you, except that the front of the store is a great window, the light through it is controlled by adjacent roll-up white window shades, that note a humble and homey touch that tells the world this is an easygoing joint. No one is betting, however, that window shades will make it as the mark of the next wave. The furnishings are simple—white-linened tables, quasi director chairs of pale wood, their seats and backs broad bands of black leather. This is a small restaurant, well known in its neighborhood, so there is often a patient little mob at the bar waiting for next up.

Your turn has come, you have been seated, you order warm ocotpus salad, and you find that the heavily armed swimmer is handled here with care, that the short lengths of pale tentacle are tender, of a gentle seafood sweetness, that the state of the firm slices of potato with which they are mingled is clear, the two joined together in a slightly tart olive-oil dressing that is dotted with herbs and bits of tomato. What is given as a "salad of fresh artichokes" is a puzzlement, for the named vegetable seems hardly to have been cooked, if at all, and the contribution the sliced-thin heart makes is one of crisp texture, not taste—and yet that artichoke crispness, the leaves of heady arugula, and the thin sheets of strong grana cheese make lively food in their lemony dressing. Grilled radicchio and hot melted cheese can be a terrific dish, but here the cheese used—scamorza—becomes a rather pallid foam in the process, though it detracts not at all from the good bitterness of the oiled and grilled red lettuce. When so-called wild broccoli (broccoli rabe) is available, Rosolio uses it in a pasta dish made up of orecchiette (pasta shaped like little ears), chunks of venison sausage, the vegetable, and a lightly enriched tomato sauce—the broccoli is at once woodsy and metallic, very dramatic among the other ingredients. If you cannot get broccoli rabe, you can always get spinach, which Rosolio incorporates into a simpler dish of pappardelle (broad, heavy ribbons of pasta), Italian bacon, and the deep green leaves—the slightly creamy dish is simple, weighty, of good strong flavors. "Stracci" are "rags," and "stracci di pasta fresca con sugo di anatra" are, therefore, pasta rags with duck sauce. The sauce is thick, dense with myriad vegetables and herbs, full of earthy life, but of palpable duck you will find but teensie-weensie bits and pieces.

Only one fish, salmon, is listed on the regular menu, but the fillet is nonpareil, fresh and browned and juicy, the flavors of the herbs and grill just ornaments to the clear sweet taste of the salmon itself. Rosolio's chicken is no tastier than most other chickens these days, so the construct served here—the breast stuffed with zucchini and the aforementioned pallid cheese, scamorza—reads like, and is, a veritable onslaught of subtlety. A significant step down the subtlety scale, to this veal scalloppine, in which the judicious browning of the pale meat rouses it to a level of flavor that is eminently noticeable even when consumed with the strong spinach—a dollop of which, under a cap of melted mozzarella, adorns each of the three cutlets. On occasion Rosolio offers osso buco, and though the meat on the knuckle has not yet reached that perfect point at which it is juicy, almost wet, and falling away from the bone, it is close, and it is well saturated with the flavors of the pungently seasoned vegetable sauce in which it was done. As the paillard is a dish of dubious background anyway, who is to say that paillards may be only of beef or veal or chicken? A nifty one of lamb is made here, the meat pounded thin, grilled with olive oil and rosemary, delivered charred and rare and of vivid lamb flavor.

What is ambiguously sold as "red fruit" and warm zabaglione, arrives as a wineglass in which raspberries and strawberries, some riper than others, are buried in a particularly frothy and winy zabaglione. The tirami sù is cool, a mass of cake soaked in coffee, layered with chocolate, and under a storm of cocoa—not bad. Sometimes you are tendered amaretti after dinner, and if you look as much like a rube as your waiter, he will roll the tissue wrapper into a tube and set it afire—you politely say ooh when, just as the fire dies out, the ash floats up to the ceiling. If you are a regular here, you will sometimes be offered a pony of "Rosolio" itself, a sickish liqueur that, when no one is looking, you dump into your unfinished burnt-tasting decaf.

★★RUSSIAN TEA ROOM

150 West 57th Street
LUNCH AND DINNER.
Reservations: 265-0947.
Credit cards: AE, DC, MC, V.
Expensive.

Once the preconcert and pretheater crowd has left, by a little before eight, you can walk in here any night of the week nowadays and get a table. Even a full house at Carnegie Hall, next door, rarely quite fills the Tea Room, as it once did, with après-musique night people for late supper, albeit the remains of this set, unlike the earlier crowd, are New Yorkers mostly, oldish mostly, a population group that, as it thins, leaves this ancient establishment more and more to vacationers and night-outers from points beyond the rivers. Certain of the consequences of RTR's decline are either sad or happy, or perhaps they are both. Consider, for example, the matter of the choice booths in the front room. Upon a time they were, if not quite sold to the highest bidder, easier to come by if you were known to the gent at the book as one who remunerates for small favors. Nowadays the poor man works on spec. You ask for a booth, you get one if one is available. And whether or not you are going to give him a fin for his largesse he does not know for sure until you have—or leave having not.

There are eight of those semielliptic booths, five on your left as you enter, just past the coatcheck, and three on your right, just before the bar. They are choice in that, while the tables for two in the dining room proper are cheek to cheek, within these cushy enclosures you are insulated from those around you; they provide a good view, sometimes diverting, of the goings and comings of all who enter and leave; their very scarcity makes them valuable; and, as they are still reputedly set aside for the mighty, your presence in one (especially if you dress extravagantly) engenders murmured speculation among the plebes who pass by, en route to the everyday dining room, as to who you may be. Moreover, for all the Tea Room's fabled opulence and glitter, this more dimly lit of its two rooms is the site of the restaurant's most charming physical asset, the sweeping mural—maybe years ago it was black on white, today it is black on brown—of the view, from behind sheltered tables and chairs and waiters and customers, of a Paris sidewalk café at the turn of the century, a broad boulevard in the middle distance, horse-drawn carriages on it, trees and grand hotels beyond. Nothing in the Tea Room is like anything in that mural—except a certain civilized spirit having to do with human beings going about the respectable business of their pleasures, and the beauty of it. The Tea Room is a hundred painterly paintings on dark hunter-green walls, the golden tinsel and shiny red balls that are the year-around Christmas decorations, the gay clash of lipstick-red banquettes and vivid-pink linen, scores of gleaming brass samovars, and, not least, the waiters—some have been here for decades—in their belted cossack shirts of brilliant scarlet. You will not believe for a moment that you are in the Union of Soviet Socialist Republics, but you may well forget you are in New York, for the Russian Tea Room is an enclosed world—some people seem to think it is Hollywood, so that, while New York's musical community is less in evidence than it once was, west-leaning bicoastal types still aim themselves here when they are in town, faces you have seen on the big and/or little screens, anonymous bronzed guys with plural starlets in tow, liver-spotted producer types garnished with acolytes.

All of which is nearly enough. But, big but, you came to eat, maybe beluga caviar at $45.75 the ounce, or osetra at $41.50, and they are imperfect. The steak ordered rare that arrives medium rare is not a disaster, just a disappointment. But caviar that is of something other than clear, untainted ocean flavor, though technically caviar, is, unlike the steak, remote from the thing you were after—luxury and perfection. It is not that the imperfection would be tolerable at a lower price. The price is irrelevant, is evidence that caviar is a luxury, but is not what makes it one, and, as it happens, in this luxury perfection is of the essence. Even the red salmon caviar is sometimes off and dry. Have your caviar with blini, and the ceremony is all it ever was, the heady grain flavor of the stack of fluffy pancakes in their little pot, the enrichment of drawn butter and thick sour cream, the waiter forming all the ingredients into cylindrical packages, the champagne and/or vodka (from a selection of two dozen) that can convert the ritual of caviar-and-blini consumption into a minor orgy. But if the caviar is not equal to what you have come to expect by way of memory of luckier, flawless days, your expected orgy is approximately holding hands.

A modernization of the RTR menu has been announced, and though the menu items are mostly what they have always been, certain dishes, though still well made, seem denatured these days. The Tea Room's eggplant orientale was once vigorously garlicked and deeply oiled. Today it is a harmless substance that, when spread on the pumpernickel supplied with it, is detectable only as a moisture, though some of its old character is in evidence when you eat it straight. As to the chopped liver, if not your mother, then your grandmother did better, for this stuff, though fresh-made, is a pastel version of the vigorously seasoned and deeply fatted real thing. Happily the herrings are all they ever were: the matjes herring dark and supple, sweet and tart and salty; the pickled herring astringent and rousing in its silvery skin. Withal, if you come here but once, you will do well to begin your dinner with the hot borscht. If this dish has been tinkered with, it was not to its detriment. The red soup still has the depth of a profound stock, a complexity that is the yield of a judicious balance of herbs and vegetables—you add cool sour cream according to your taste, and from time to time you pause in your consumption of the soup for a bite of pirojok, the light, flaky meat-filled pastry served with it.

Certain dishes cannot be prepared in large quantities and then served over the course of a long night—in time they fade. Maybe that is not the explanation for this beef Stroganoff, but much of the meat buried in this sour cream sauce is of a depressing gray and a stubborn resilience. The Tea Room's brisket is the safer beef, the long, thin, narrow slices of juicy meat, tender despite their distinct fibrousness, in a strongly seasoned and vegetable-sweet broth—the brisket is fine with or without its sharp horseradish sauce. If your memory of the luli kebab is of homey, peasanty lamb meatballs, peppered and weighty, sadly learn that the item has been refined. The new dish of the old name is a good one, light and juicy, but the change seems like the premature expression of the end of an era. So if it is lamb you want, opt for the shashlik Caucasian, nuggets of the straight meat, skewered with slices of onion, pepper, tomato, the fresh vegetables blackened at the edges, the lamb red within its charred surfaces. Probably at the insistence of the insurance company, your waiter pierces your chicken Kiev before putting it at your place, for hot melted butter is supposed to spout from the incision. Sometimes it does, but sometimes it merely dribbles out, which is too bad, for the event is most of this dish, its looks (the thing resembles a plump roll with a golden brown crust) much of it, while as food the roulade of white chicken, made juicy by the mildly dilled butter that has melted within it, is of almost no flavor at all—of course it remains one of RTR's most popular dishes. Each night there is a fish of the night, sometimes fresh, filleted, skin-on snapper, the skin touched with citrus flavor, the whole in a pale white-wine sauce.

The Camembert on the menu is also in the refrigerator, where you will sensibly permit it to remain. The strawberries Romanoff are mildly liquored berries, mostly ripe, served with sugared whipped cream. You are directed instead to the baklava, chopped walnuts and pistachios, of an almost liquorlike honeyed sweetness, between layers of flaky pastry; to the halvah, a good example of the sugared paste of ground nuts and grain; to the kasha à la gourieff, a white cereal sweetened with a puree of apricots and adorned with slivered almonds—here too the consultant who has been tinkering with this menu shows his hand, for the cereal is decorated with slivers of kiwi as well. He has also been at the cranberry kissel, a thickened and slightly sweetened puree of cranberries that, in the old days, you enriched with heavy cream—now it is served with what your waiter frankly calls half-and-half, which merely waters it.

★★SABOR

20 Cornelia Street (near Bleecker Street)
DINNER.
Reservations: 243-9579.
Credit cards: AE, MC, V.
Medium priced.

Though you have, very likely, never been to Cuba (and though in fact the only Cuban in this long, narrow store is one of the waiters), you will, probably, be persuaded at once, by the appearance of the place, and later by the food, of this establishment's Cuban "authenticity." Everybody is. Judging only by the food you get in New York's other Cuban restaurants, what differentiates Sabor's is only its superiority. The food is the genuine article, at least as genuine as it is anywhere else in town.

But in choosing its appearance, Sabor was guided not by the gaudy looks that are traditional in Manhattan's Cuban restaurants, but by the plain look of cafés and simple restaurants in Spain and in the old parts of the old cities of the Caribbean islands. The room is painted ivory and dark tan, the wooden floor is dark reddish brown. The ceiling is of stamped tin, ceiling fans hang from it. There are straw baskets on the walls, green plants here and there in the dining room, as well as in the front window. There is a tiny service bar at the back, and when a Caribbean rum drink is being prepared in the blender, conversation at the rear of the restaurant halts, for Sabor—especially at the back—is something of a sound box. You put a little noise in, you get a lot of noise out. Between frozen daiquiris, Latin music jangles from the speakers. When the place is busy, there is a bit of boisterousness from the sometimes loudly self-satisfied clientele, for it is easy to spend freely on lots of food and wine when prices are this low. Sabor is a jolly place, and though it is loud it never seems inappropriately so.

Your waiter (the chap with one earring), when you mention to him that your table is remarkably small, cheerfully agrees with you, as if you are exchanging pleasantries. When you ask if there is a wine list, he informs you that there is. Actually to see it requires a more pointed approach. He is perfectly nice, you understand, just a little out of it sometimes.

Sabor is never out of escabeche, a firm, cold, sour side of a small fish, surrounded by crisp vegetables—onions, celery, diced carrots, green peppers, salty green olives, capers —all in the tart pickling marinade. The marinated squid is cold, but spicy hot, the circles of tender meat mingled with hot red peppers. And you can get shrimp (camarones picantes) prepared the same way—the house obtains very good shrimp, and if you eat them carelessly, your lips will burn for a while after. The hot appetizers include empanadas, triangular dumplings of browned pastry filled with ground sausage that is both fiery and a little leaden—earthy food; and frituras de malanga, fritters composed of garlic-flavored chunks of a Caribbean root vegetable—the flavor is not immediately distinctive, but lemon converts the nuggets into more-than-pleasant hot morsels. Sabor's gazpacho is more watery than oily.

For fancy fish, you order the poached red snapper, which reaches you whole in a casserole dish, head and tail on, under a thick blanket of sauce that is green with parsley, winy, tart of its capers and lime juice, oily and garlicked. The snapper is fresh, perfectly cooked, moist and flaky. For humble fish, you opt for the bacalao à la Vizcaina, a weighty stew of salted codfish, heavy with potatoes, sharpened by capers and olives, served in a strong tomato sauce. For all its weight, the dish is not leaden. Sabor serves chicken in a so-called curried prune sauce, with whole prunes and mushrooms: These spices are not packaged curry powder, and they make the dish remind you a little of good Indian cooking; the chicken is stained dark from being cooked with the sweet fruit. There are more of those prunes in the pot roast of beef, but this *is* a heavy dish, the slabs of meat are a little dry despite a moist stuffing of sausage, fruits, capers, and olives; even the dark and winy sauce does not quite redeem the tasty but ponderous meat. Ropa vieja is an odd component of Cuban cookery, which non-Cubans usually eat once. This is because the name means, and the dish often resembles, "old rope." The way this dish is usually prepared in New York's Cuban restaurants, the shredded meat is as resilient as hemp, resulting in a marathon for the jaw. Sabor's version, however, is by comparison a piece of cake, the mound of dark strands in an oily tomato sauce flavored with cloves and cinnamon—a striking dish. Pretty good black beans and rice are served with just about everything, but certain vegetables available à la carte are also of interest, among them yucca, another Caribbean root, this one white, hefty, with a texture like that of yams, served in a garlic-flavored oil—strong and primitive food.

The little individual key lime pies are made on a very ordinary crust, and the pale-yellow chiffon reveals little citrus flavor—the superb whipped cream helps. The flan is something the precise likes of which you have tasted every one of the thousand times you have ordered flan. And the roulade of sponge cake and custard, wetted down with liqueur and orange juice, is an obvious sweet. The big winner is coco quemado, a hot, sweet, nutty coconut dessert, made with sherry, flavored with cinnamon, and served with more of that terrific whipped cream. If that does not suit, there is fresh pineapple on hand.

★★SALA THAI

1718 Second Avenue (near 89th Street)
DINNER.
Reservations: 410-5557.
Credit cards: AE, DC.
Inexpensive.

This Thai place looks like a barely transformed domestic place. Except for a handful of framed Oriental scenics, it could be an Upper East Side saloon, though the absence of a predominantly positioned liquor bar troubles that interpretation. The restaurant is carpeted, trimmed with brass, has gilt-framed mirrors set in its walls—all those of a distinctly Third Avenue anonymity. But one small clue makes it clear that the establishment is an outlander on its turf: The slight-of-build, black-haired young gentlemen who wait on you are unfailingly courteous—even when they deny you chopsticks (explaining that in Thailand they are not used, and that they are available in most Thai restaurants only because customers expect them).

Bigger clues are in the things the young men bring you, which are, how you say, alien but accessible (though occasionally searingly spicy—the house rates the dishes from three asterisks [***] down to none, with the highest ratings for the hottest dishes). The boys will deliver, for example, this cold spring roll, a log the size of a baby's forearm, its wrapper a sheet of noodle, its contents chunks of sausage, slivers of meat, bean sprouts and crabmeat and chopped cucumber, over all that a tangy and fruity tamarind sauce. That one is mild. Considerably hotter is the squid salad, a two-asterisk dish that may strike you as worthy of three, for the slivers and strands of tender seafood, with crisp onions and scallions, are in a truly searing lime-juice dressing.

What the menu refers to as "the most famous Thai dish" is made here in an exceptional version. Called pla lad prig, it is a whole fried fish, fresh and moist within its crackling crust, covered over with a thick paste that is pungently garlicked and fiery. A frequent special is something described as "broiled salmon Thai fines herbes." This is good fish too, under its herbed and garlic-flavored shrimp sauce, and it is served on crunchy fresh spinach. The sautéed shrimp with onions and chile peppers are mingled with mushrooms and greens and bits of garlic as well—this is only a mildly spicy dish, but extremely lively by virtue of its contrasting elements. The word "curry" shows up all over this menu. It does not mean what you think, but refers, rather, to dishes in which coconut milk is a principal ingredient. These coconut sauces tend to be not weighty— they are hardly more than liquids—but their coconut flavor is vivid, and when the sauces are hot, the spiciness potentiates the coconut flavor. There are "curries" of scallops, chicken, pork, beef, those meats mingled, variously, with basil leaves, sweet peas, slivers of red pepper, bamboo shoots, scallions—the dishes are all good, the individual ingredients always distinct among the others. Mee krob, the crispy Thai noodle dish, is not very crispy; but the pad Thai, which is something closer to a Western noodle, is fine, the strands threaded with flakes of cooked egg, scallions, shrimp.

No desserts are listed.

★★SALTA IN BOCCA

179 Madison Avenue (near 34th Street)
LUNCH, MONDAY TO FRIDAY; DINNER, MONDAY TO SATURDAY. CLOSED SUNDAY.
Reservations: 684-1757.
Credit cards: AE, DC, MC, V.
Expensive.

This is the lost restaurant, the remembered one. Perhaps it is only imagined, and never existed. It is, in any case, the model, the one from which the others departed—to become less and less restaurants, more and more public theaters, scenes of self-display. Salta in Bocca remains the opposite of that. It is respite, where everything comes to a halt. You go there the way you go to your mistress's apartment. You do not leave a number where you may be reached. It is even pink.

Your host is a tall, thin, quietly dressed, Italian-accented gentleman. His manner of easy courtliness would be the envy of any aristocrat. Women love him. And so, apparently, does his staff—their unfailing politeness and discretion devolve from his. Even the physical restaurant has the good manners not to be distractingly prepossessing: a barroom, a dining room, and, beyond that, down a few steps, a smaller dining room with mirrored walls, which make it seem spacious. The rooms are rimmed with red banquettes, the walls are deep salmon pink, the carpeting is dark, the linen is white, the light is soft. What few adornments there are achieve their purpose—the place does not seem bare. In fact it glows a little, is welcoming.

When hiding out here, you should try the food: the zuppa di vongole, hot little clams in their shells, briny and sweet, in a pool of parsleyed and buttery wine sauce; scampi saltati, three big sautéed shrimp, crunchy and of vivid flavor, in a mellifluous sauce that is herbed, buttery, smooth; spiedino romana, the long, multilevel, deep-fried skewered sandwich of bread, cheese, ham, dark and pully in its stout sauce of oil, chopped capers, anchovies. Or have some pasta: firm trenette, thin flat noodles, in a pesto sauce that is wildly fragrant of fresh basil, garlicky, buttery rich; fettuccine casalinga, broad noodles mingled with sweet peas, sautéed onions, and slivers of strong ham in a thick cream sauce; spaghetti al sugo, the familiar thin noodle in a well-seasoned and meaty dark sauce.

The red snapper is fresh, its sauce livornese heavy with cracked black olives, capers. Chunks of good sautéed chicken bathed in garlicky oil go as pollo scarpara. The livers of that bird go as fegatini di pollo veneta, and they are crusty, pink inside, come in an herbed and winy sauce that is threaded with onions. The veal paillard is of pale, tender meat, it is charred in its quick grilling, and it sparkles when lemoned. But the costoletta bolognese—a huge, butterflied veal chop stuffed with ham and cheese—is miraculous for how light it is despite the weightiness of its ingredients. You can get pungent sausages—coarse and crusty and spicy—in a dense marinara sauce that is thick with red peppers. All the vegetables are good, the salads spanking.

The ricotta cheesecake is cool and weighty, made lively by candied fruit. The St-Honoré is of unimpeachable pastry filled with good whipped cream and chocolate cream. The house zabaglione tends to be low on marsala, a little bland.

At lunchtime this peaceful repair can be a madhouse.

○ SAM'S

152 West 52nd Street
LUNCH, MONDAY TO FRIDAY; DINNER, DAILY.
Reservations: 582-8700
Credit cards: AE, DC, MC, V.
Medium priced.

Intended as an evocation of all that is all-American, Sam's has captured something of the thirties and forties, complete with a life-size buffalo-nickel high up over the center of the racetrack-shape bar, and a foursquare layout and terra-cotta color scheme that recall the Horn & Hardart Automats in which, in those days, the buffalo nickel really did reign. There is even an open kitchen at one end of this big space, just as in the Automats there were steam table counters at which H&H patrons could pick up hot food dispensed by white-garbed functionaries who had been graduated to the status after years as busboys pushing carts of dirty dishes through the aisles. There is even a big painting, just as in certain old Automats there were murals that resembled the WPA art in public buildings.

Some days even Sam's background music is of the era—Benny Goodman, Billie Holiday—but other times the sounds are the two competing soundtracks going at once that is the recipe for certain contemporary aural opiates. It is appropriate that in this American third part of the Equitable Center's restaurant triptych—it began with the French Le Bernadin and the Italian Palio—Sam's should choose a Depression theme, for surely Black Tuesday did more to determine the history of the twentieth century than the mere machinations of European rulers. It seems, however, that the theme was not so much chosen as found after the fact, for there are signs that the intentions were Wild West (not just that bison, but also these cacti, which, in great terra cotta pots, stand on massive pedestals about the room, reach toward the lofty vaulted ceiling, are echoed in smaller cacti in tiny pots on the tables, which latter will eventually disappear as more and more of them are blithely dropped into the glove-leather pouches of contemporary carpetbagger women).

The dribbling away of purpose culminates, if that is the correct word, in the menu, which, such buzzwords as *southern* braised chicken, *New York* shell steak, and *crab cakes* of unnamed provenance notwithstanding, is about as American as the UN. That the crab cakes are charged to no locale you understand at once, for they seem to be fabricated of a paste reduction of the original foodstuff, and their ice-cold tomato sauce does little but dramatize their tastelessness. Now don't go way, for the grilled shiitake mushrooms are earthy and meaty and the roasted red peppers of intense flavor on their crisp greens, in which are mingled crunchy nuts and, too bad, ropy green beans. Okay, now go way, for the chicken livers seem precooked, recooked, and overcooked, cannot be redeemed by their burnt "frizzled" onions, while this paste of fresh and smoked salmon, though of clear flavor, is of a claylike density—it would be less of a comedown were it not called a "mousse." You are directed to a simple pasta dish—cavatapi (pasta shaped like coiled telephone cord, in two-inch lengths) in a chunky, herbed, and well-seasoned tomato sauce—and away from the onion, blue cheese, and rosemary pizza, which is onion soup on white; and from the assorted vegetables on whole wheat pizza, which is sauce primavera on All-Bran.

The sautéed black bass is fish all right, while the herbed polenta served with it, under it, actually, is something like the first solid food you take after a couple of weeks in intensive care. Because it is braised, the chicken is wet, but it has no more flavor than the pebbly rice served with it. The lamb chops, though they have picked up no flavor in the grilling, would be not bad if not for their sauce, which resembles canned beef stock thickened. And Sam's burger is at once blood red and bloodless, as if the patties are wrung out, then grilled.

The nut strudel, a sweet-spiced nut paste encircled in a sugared pastry and set in an icky vanilla sauce, is at least an excess. The two-colored frozen praline terrine tastes like a Dixie Cup. It is the misfortune of the yam cinnamon custard to taste the way it reads.

★★★ SAN DOMENICO

240 Central Park South
LUNCH, MONDAY TO SATURDAY; DINNER, DAILY.
Reservations: 265-5959.
Credit cards: AE, DC, MC, V.
Very expensive.

You are seated on a banquette of cushy brown leather, a table before you. A hemisphere of polished brass overhangs the table, within it a globular light bulb that glows softly. Your solicitous captain, standing at your side, leans forward enthusiastically to explain to you all about one of San Domenico's signature dishes, uovo in raviolo con burro nocciola e tartufi bianchi, no less, and in doing so bops his head on that brass lamp, which sets it swinging, a perfect pendulum apparently caught forever between the force of gravity and its own inertia of motion, until, after rubbing his noggin, your captain grabs it, holds it still at the center point of its oscillation, releases it to swing no more—anyway, not until the next collision. San Domenico, you see, is a compendium of more-or-less handsome parts, but in its design the human element was figured out, not in, and so, though the staff will learn to avoid the overhead obstacles, there is no way to diminish the clutter that obtains when a crowd of people is added to the orange-linened tables (set with silver service plates, glinting crystal, polished flatware, bowls of flowers), red-leather chairs, marble columns, table lamps and hanging lamps, potted palms, great bursts of flowers on the windowsills, window blinds that are a million hanging white strings, Giorgio de Chirico prints that, what with the paucity of attention they can get in this setting, can only be conceits. Even the help are one with the clutter, dressed as they are in a veritable motley of uniforms, red jackets, white jackets, black jackets, black dresses with lacy white aprons and lacy white hair bands on the waitresses, a cream-colored dinner jacket on the wine steward, black-and-green tunics with gold buttons on the busboys, and, of course, at the top of the heap, tailored civvies on the proprietary gents who circulate among the tables, ask if all is well, smirk thinly, move on, are distinguishable from the clientele solely by the fact that they are on their feet. This place is named for, and has ties to, a restaurant in Italy, in the town of Imola. When you dinner in the original San Domenico, you may be sure you do not get the notion, even for a moment, that you made a wrong turn somewhere, and have chanced upon a circus.

All God's fish got roe, and San Domenico's got tuna roe, thin slices (shaved from a pickled compacture of the red-brown stuff), rolled into cylinders the size of half-smoked king-size cigarettes, set in a pool of lemony dressing, and garnished with a small salad strewn with bits of black olive. With respect to the roe itself, if the $14.50 price (same as all the antipasti) leads you to expect something like caviar, be aware that, though eminently edible, this is blunt, unsubtle stuff, here making its first New York appearance (and certain to become a popular ingredient in local pasta sauces before the season is out). Do, however, wait for that fad to start moving before you invest in it, and in the meantime take a position in this warm salad of sweet, crunchy shrimp and firm white beans, the two moistened and enriched by silken olive oil that is heady of fresh rosemary.

That olive oil again, this time on warm carpaccio, the thin-sliced beef surfaced with shavings of Parmesan cheese, encircled by a chain of arugula leaves, and strewn with tiny dice of white truffle, the only impact of the last ingredient that you are able to discern being the ten-dollar premium you agreed to when you ordered the thing.

You ask your captain if half an order of pasta may be had as a first course. He reassures you: No, but full orders are quite small. In fact, the aforementioned "uovo in raviolo" is but a single pasta pouch in which you find two ingredients, a mash of spinach and a soft-cooked egg (unbroken, and when you pierce the egg the yellow flows into the other ingredients and enriches them), over all of which has been poured a butter that is thick with chopped hazelnuts; one more element is listed, those truffles again (that will be another $10, thank you), and though you do not detect them as a separate flavor, they may well account for the underlying earthiness of this singular dish. Spinach again, as an element of the potato gnocchi, and the little dumplings are at once firm but light, in a rich sauce of melted cheese that is almost overwhelmingly fragrant of fresh sage. And potatoes again, two ways: mashed, as the filling of small square ravioli; and in the form of matchsticks that add a good textural note to the ravioli's pesto sauce, which is alive with fresh basil. One rice dish on the menu, riso mantecato al parmigiano e sugo d'arrosto, a cheese-fortified risotto, of profound depth, that is dramatically set off by a dark beef glaze.

Lobster and artichokes, what could be bad? But in San Domenico's fricassee of those elements the former is on occasion toughened a bit, though that does not undo this simple dish, in which chunks of the seafood are mingled with nuggets of the artichoke heart, the two in a smooth and buttery sauce that is vigorously seasoned and fragrantly herbed. Splendid fresh salmon, the small crescent-shaped fillets in a sauce that is thick with herbs and vegetables. And good duck, the slices of dark meat tender, juicy, of clear duck flavor, and well served by a sauce that is dotted with, and fortified by, bits of strong black olive. The goose liver is styled "alla Veneziana," but this is much unlike run-of-Italian-restaurant liver and onions, for the thin-sliced organ meat in its winy and buttery sauce is rich and almost blood rare between the charred surfaces, and the onions are of two kinds, small whole ones that are crunchy and sweet, and deep-fried rings that are crisp, delicate, and in striking textural contrast to the red meat. What is notable about the stew of rabbit and mushrooms are the herbed depth of the sauce, the tender meat, the clear grain flavor of the polenta served with it.

You are treated at this point in your dinner to a great bowl of ice from which protrude lengths of fennel and celery, red lettuce and endives, asparagus and scallions—you dip the vegetables in seasoned oil and eat them while you think about dessert.

Though the zuccotto is complex (a brandied prune, a frame of liquored spongecake around a thick cream dotted with bits of prune, rich vanilla ice cream in a cup formed of pastry, all the parts set in a lively prune sauce), its appeal is simple, for the elements are sweet and lively. The wine-marinated strawberries are buried under a zabaglione that is browned, light, and winy. The mascarpone al caffè is a triangle of the named cream cheese and a ball of intense chocolate ice cream in a rich coffee-flavored sauce. A bit of sparkling wine livens the orange sauce in which the baba—liquored sponge cake—is set. What the house calls chocolate cake you will perceive as a slice of enriched bitter chocolate garnished with minty ice cream—the two in a chocolate sauce of exceptional depth.

• SANTA FE

72 West 69th Street
LUNCH AND DINNER.
Reservations: 724-0822.
Credit cards: AE, MC, V.
Medium priced.

Mexican, gone slightly chic, which is to say, carpeting, pink linen on the tables, changing exhibits of contemporary art on the walls, and $5.50 for guacamole. The place consists of a small barroom, a front dining room, and a back room, all dark pink, with white woodwork. The three gas-fire "fireplaces," the potted palms, and the potted cacti are probably meant to suggest, respectively, the hot, lush, and parched aspects of the North American tropics. But the bright light and cacophonous reverberance of this often crowded, hard-edged place will suggest anything but the slowed rhythms of warm climates.

The basket of corn chips and the little jug of scorching relish are very much what you remember from less pretentious Mexican joints (albeit here they are in rather spiffy containers), but at Santa Fe you nibble at the former, dipped very judiciously in the latter, while downing your own very personal frozen margarita. Not only does the menu list the drink in two sizes ($4 and $7), but it is standard practice for a table of, say, six to generate a margarita order consisting of two regulars, very little lime; one regular, lots of Cointreau; and three large, hold the salt. You do not hear requests for easy on the tequila.

That guacamole, its cost notwithstanding, is blenderized or whipped or something, and its clear avocado flavor, well spiced and lemoned, cannot overcome its toothpaste texture. The seviche appetizer is of shrimp and scallops—the seafood is fresh, but somewhat undone by the very obvious fruitiness of the citrus marinade in which it was steeped. Mexican fun foods: There are nachos, in which cheese and meat, sour cream and beans, hot peppers and bits of tomato are served with a crisp tortilla; and there are quesadillas, a meatless, soft-tortilla member of the same family, with cheese inside, guacamole and hot peppers outside. Both of those are fine, but Santa Fe has found no method for raising them above the regular run of such things, in which the ingredient called flavoring never seems quite to substitute for the one called food.

Your waiter, when you order swordfish and lamb chops, surmises that you must be regulars, for, says he, those are the best things in the house. Both are marinated, the fish until it is soggy (it is still that way even after it is prepared), the lamb until it has lost much of its meat texture, as if it were tenderized. Both are grilled over charcoal, pick up a nice carbon flavor in the process, but at the bottom line, both are net losers, less than what they started out as. Enchiladas Suizas and chimichangas are listed, and their fillings of cheese and chicken and beef, and their garnishes of refried beans and sour cream, are fine, but finally the food lacks sparkle, individuality, life. Marinating, seasoning, crisping, and burying in goo are no substitute for foodstuffs being permitted, at least a little, to be what they are. Combination plates of tacos, enchiladas, tostadas, and rellenos are offered, and you are encouraged to compose your own assortment.

313

The so-called lemon soufflé is really a mousse—but it has a terrific lemon flavor, the taste and texture in it of minced rind as well, and it comes with an intense raspberry sauce and good whipped cream. The slightly tart and crusty apple crisp is raisin studded and dotted with bits of pecan—it is served with more of that good whipped cream.

★★SCARLATTI

34 East 52nd Street
LUNCH, MONDAY TO FRIDAY; DINNER, MONDAY TO SATURDAY. CLOSED SUNDAY.
Reservations: 753-2444.
Credit cards: AE, DC, MC, V.
Very expensive.

The prime mover behind this place has been quoted as saying that he named the restaurant for the composer, because, as he put it, "I like his music." (He does not specify whether it is the music of Alessandro Scarlatti he likes or that of his son Domenico.) He has said further that this restaurant is meant to be the Italian counterpart of La Côte Basque. (And you wonder if he has ever encountered the familiar opinion that La Côte Basque is the most beautiful restaurant in New York.) There are, of course, those who do not mind telling you that they just happen to have very good taste. And you are not at all surprised to discover, one look at this installation, that you disagree. Scarlatti (the restaurant, not either of the composers) is luxe for the sake of luxe, posh without a theme, opulence with no point of view. If you strip away the adornment, there is nothing left. The place does not look as much like a fancy restaurant as like the stage set for one (just as those who frequent it—en masse, anyway—look less like prosperous people than like caricatures thereof).

The huge chandeliers are clusters of gauzy, glowing lampshades among ropes of weighty crystal, and the matching sconces are mounted on silken walls. You walk on plush carpeting, are seated on bouclé banquettes or on plumply upholstered period side chairs with oval backs. Almost all the surfaces are beige, the glow of the place is pink, and there are, here and there, panels of dark-tinted mirror, walls of gilded glass. Modern paintings are all about, but they seem to have been chosen for their tendency to disappear into the background. On every white-linened table there is a single flower—and also a single candle in a tulip-shaped tumbler formed of smoky glass. You can tell the waiters from the busboys by the good braid on their shoulders.

But what you are served here is solid food, none of it fantastical. The seafood salad, for example, varies little from dishes of that name you have had in restaurants that do not look at all like prefabricated boudoirs: fresh-cut slivers of squid and slices of shrimp, with a little celery for crunchiness and strands of red pepper for color, all in a dressing of velvety oil. Grilled shrimp, scampi, are listed as a first course, but among the main courses you will find scampi ribelli—shrimp baked with mozzarella. If the house will not make a small portion, seriously consider sharing a full order with a passerby, for this is a striking scampi dish, the sea sweetness of the crunchy crustaceans (a touch of iodine notwithstanding) striking under their film of lightly browned cheese. In the pasta department the house sometimes offers assortments, and if the idea of three farinaceous items on a single plate strikes you as excessive, know that when the three are wisely selected, they set one another off dramatically—and seem not at all repetitious. Consider these golosi, moist dumplings, at once rich and light, of spinach and cheese; alongside soft, thimble-shaped gnocchi (of noodle dough, not of potatoes) that yield eagerly to the pressure of your tongue—and that are greened with a buttery pesto sauce heady with fresh basil; alongside tortellacci (big ravioli) that are stuffed with a fluffy ricotta filling and served in a simple tomato sauce that is tart and sparkling. A couple of rice dishes are also offered, one of them risotto ortolana, in which the mound of earthy grain, moist of the deep broth in which it was cooked, is studded with mushrooms and chunks of sweet vegetable—the addition of ground cheese and/or black pepper potentiates the sturdy food.

There are simple seafood dishes, among them fresh and firm striped bass in a sauce livornaise—tomato, black olives, capers—that is smooth and strong and salty. There is also a complex one that is listed as a specialty of the house—zuppa di pesce, in which the tail of a small lobster and the whole of a big shrimp, three tender clams in their shells and three sweet mussels in theirs, slices of squid, whole bay scallops, and a slab of fish (on the way down from the zenith of its freshness) are served on a great platter, all the elements dressed with a dark, tomatoed, hot-spiced, and briny sauce. You get a rare chicken dish here, pollo cipriani, in which the mild-flavored bird is in an herbed red sauce that is dotted with peas and mushrooms (nothing unusual there) and also, surprisingly, with a couple of good shrimp—the touch of seafood brininess offsets the chicken strikingly. The scaloppini santa elena is in a wine sauce that is graced with good mushrooms and chunks of crisp artichoke, but the veal itself has been carelessly sautéed, is somewhat overcooked inside, not at all browned outside, and amounts to a mere carrier for the sauce. The good veal chop valdostana—a great nugget of pale meat with a layer of ham and cheese at its center, a huge rib protruding from its side—is notable for the sweet black raisins in its creamy mushroom sauce. When wild broccoli is in season, it is offered here—the crunchy and bitter leaves and stems in a pool of hot oil, and accompanied by, at your captain's suggestion, a couple of strong, gamy sausages.

Whatever salad greens you want may be had in a good dressing with some strong Parmesan cheese. Order zabaglione, and you may see the eggs separated by your captain, and whisked over a flame, right in the dining room—the hot froth reaches you thick, winy, and fluffy. At considerable additional expense the zabaglione will be served to you over ripe raspberries, even in that fruit's local off-season. The zuppa inglese is a fresh, moist, multilevel affair dotted with fruits and nuggets of chocolate, layered with white cream and chocolate cream, stained red here and there, and soaked in rum—if you like that kind of thing, this is a spectacular example of it. If you prefer a simpler thing, there is the délice, in which layers of meringue are interleaved with chocolate cream yet again and whipped cream, the whole strewn with slivered almonds. For something simpler still, the house has on hand some good, ripe melon.

★★SEA GRILL

30 Rockefeller Center (enter on 49th Street)
LUNCH AND DINNER. CLOSED SUNDAY.
Reservations: 246-9201.
Credit cards: AE, DC, MC, V.
Medium priced.

Make a tourist restaurant better than it has to be, and what do you have? Right, a tourist restaurant, strictly for the boobs, New Yorkers will have nothing to do with it. You do have to stretch the definition of tourist, for on weekend nights the Grill gets its share of the migration from across the local waters. But if your own range falls within a three-mile radius of Grand Central, you can dinner here forever, and never see a friend. This is Rockefeller Center: the ice-skating rink operates from fall through spring, in summer you may lunch or dinner out of doors, under big umbrellas where the ice was. Indoors you have, from most tables, a good view out, and at windowside tables a view not only of golden Prometheus, but upward to Rockfeller's own granite skyline and the swatch of sky it encircles.

Within all is posh in the mode once known as swank, marble and brass, glittering lights and cushy carpeting, plump armchairs and big leather-upholstered booths that can accommodate an entire vacationing extended family, thousands of bottles of wine all around you in glass and metal racks and cases, in the background the tinkling of a cocktail pianist. At the Sea Grill the busboys are trained to remove a soiled tablecloth and replace it with a clean one in a single operation, so that the tabletop is never seen, the technique much like that of removing your wet bathing suit and getting into dry clothes at the beach.

Yes, laugh, but, there being but one side to your mouth, you will stop when you taste, say, these Washington State Kumamoto oysters. The white meats, of a polished richness on their half-shells, that, their 3,000-mile cross-country trip notwithstanding, sport what you are at once persuaded is the taste of the Pacific itself—ignore the vinegar, cocktail sauce, and horseradish that are supplied, for the oysters need no help, though they take well to a bit of lemon. Your lobster tartare reaches you as a pink patty of shellfish airiness delicately lemoned—it is enriched by the good olive oil in which it is set. The Maryland crabcake, happily, is crabmeat before it is anything else, fresh and chunky, its flavor at once sweet and assertive, the browned, judiciously spiced cake set in a chive sauce and a shellfish sauce, though all it wants of them is their moisture. Have any of those before you have the fettuccine with shrimp and roasted red peppers—good elements that have not been reconciled to one another.

The grilled langoustines, shrimplike creatures, are crunchy, take on good flavor in their grilling, but their mustard-lime vinaigrette is of a sour strength so aggressive as to rob the dish of all breed. A similar minor failure is the grilled tuna, for the tournedos, being mild, are overcome by the ginger and ginger sauce with which they are served. But then there is this California striped bass, the skinned fillet overlaid with green "scales" formed of a hundred or so zucchini slivers and set in purees of red and yellow bell peppers—the fish is of a subtlety, but the dish is a wondrous assemblage of textures and flavors. For true bicoastiality on a plate you turn to "North Atlantic salmon poached in

Schramsberg court bouillon," local fish done in California champagne. This is carefully made salmon, its flavor intact and roused, none of its richness lost, the fillet splayed out to form an inverted floret at the center of a sauce that is the enriched cooking liquid dotted with innumerable vegetable nuggets.

The grilled bittersweet orange gratin is hospital food. The raspberry mousse is suitably pink and light. The "golden dusted Prometheus chocolate cake" is pale chocolate mousse encased in dark chocolate, and it is light, fresh tasting, vividly of chocolate. The key lime pie is tangy, its whipped cream thick. And what the house calls tarte Tatin is a warm individual apple tart on a flaky pastry, a ball of good vanilla upon it.

★★SERYNA

11 East 53rd Street
LUNCH, MONDAY TO FRIDAY; DINNER, MONDAY TO SATURDAY. CLOSED SUNDAY.
Reservations: 980-9393.
Credit cards: AE, DC, MC, V.
Expensive.

You approach the place through a courtyard that fronts on 53rd Street. It has been planted with a stand of trees, and at night their branches glow, softly but vividly, with the amber and golden lights strung along them. The walk through those trees, though it is just a brief moment of tranquillity, is equal to at least half a Valium—and you can even mix it with alcohol. There is calm again inside. The dining room is a lofty space, all wood and the colors of wood. It manages, in the Japanese manner, to be at once spare and luxurious. The substantial wooden tables are as sturdy as concrete. The upholstered armchairs receive you in an affectionate embrace. The baskets and pottery and prints that are spotted around the room soften a little what might otherwise be its severity, without compromising its quite grand simplicity.

The most irritating thing about the Japanese is that whenever they undertake to do something the West already does, they find a way to do it better. Take, for what is only the most recent maddening instance, this item listed as "smoked salmon." Seems fair enough, lots of countries smoke salmon, and every denomination has one virtue or another. But this Japanese entrant seems, magically, to combine the forthrightness and subtlety that in all other varieties are mutually exclusive. These glistening orange sheets are of a fish flavor that, though it is vivid, is somehow clouded by the slight oiliness, smokiness, and textural delicacy of the diaphanous stuff. As in almost all Japanese restaurants that do not have sushi bars, the sushi and sashimi here are not up to the best in town—these are good little morsels, but they lack that utterly unfaded freshness of these things at their best. On the other hand, such a commonplace as shrimp tempura (sometimes prepared here of large, very delicately flavored shrimp from Japan) is encased in a fried batter that seems little more than crispness and air—you dip the delicately crusted crustaceans in their sharp black sauce to spice them. Crabmeat shumai are firm, plump crabmeat dumplings, some of them wrapped in spinach, some in an omeletlike sheet, all of them of clear crabmeat flavor—they are served with shredded vegetables, sharp mustard, a pungent soy sauce.

The listing "shio broiled fish" makes reference to a method of fish preparation in which salt is applied to the skin of the fish before broiling. The salt causes the fat under the skin to break down and saturate the meat during cooking. The technique imparts so much flavor to the fish that even a relatively pallid variety like tilefish is served—charred and juicy—sporting a pure, powerful flavor. What is called stuffed sole consists of four cutlets of good fish spread with a seasoned paste and served in a red sauce that is sweet, acidic, strongly garlicked. The striking fish is garnished with broccoli florets, the color and crispness of which are in well chosen contrast to the crimson sauce and pale fillets. Seryna lists steamed fresh fish, a dish in which the variety varies from day to day. When snapper is prepared this way, you are served the fish boned, but with its pink-metallic skin gleaming, the whole set in a pool of almost caustic dark sauce and strewn with leaves of coriander. Little of that strong sauce clings to the fluffy, sweet fish—just the right amount, it seems, to strengthen it without obscuring its good flavor. What the house mysteriously calls crabmeat steak is actually a complex dish in which crabmeat appears three ways: as broiled crabmeat legs, lightly charred, tender and a little spicy; as domino-shaped blocks of a kind of spicy egg-and-crabmeat-and-vegetable gelatin, much like a highly stylized gefilte fish; and a heavily oiled sauce that is strongly flavored of crabmeat shell. The three are about as different from one another as foods can be and still be, clearly, alike.

If you want steak—sirloin or filet mignon—it comes with a Japanese rock set in the wooden frame in which it is carried to your table. The rock cannot be brought to you the way, say, a plate is brought to you, because it has been heated to 400° F. Your steak comes already sliced, but raw, and though your waiter or waitress will gladly pepper it and then rock-grill it for you, piece by piece, you can do that yourself after getting instructions as to how many minutes on the rock will yield what degree of doneness. Once you have started cooking, the rock is good for about 15 minutes of use before it cools down. If you eat slowly, you may send for another rock. Anyway, the method turns out lovely chunks of this restaurant's good beef, which you may dip in your choice of a couple of sauces—one of which seems to have Worcestershire sauce in it, and the other of which is a tangy relative of ketchup. Yet another modified Westernism in connection with this dish—it is served with an odd little dish of herbed potato sticks and something that does a good likeness of whipped cream. (In French fries, apparently, the Japanese have not yet taken the lead.) After you have mastered doing your own steak, you are ready for shabu-shabu, in which you dip slices of rosy beef in the pot of boiling stock and wine that has been hooked up right on your table. When you have done with the meat—having dipped the briefly simmered morsels in a nutty sesame sauce before eating them—you are ready to cook up some mushrooms, scallion greens, seaweed, blocks of bean curd, and clear noodles in the same stock. These you flavor with a strong sauce of citrus and vinegar. The ingredients are good, and the food is good—the dish coming off as a dozen textures and flavors, each of them simple, but dramatic in relation to the others—but you may find that it requires more work than you want to expend when you have to pay as well.

To a Japanese, slippery arrowroot noodles dipped in fruit syrup may seem like dessert. To you they will probably seem like food only for thought. The Japanese melon sometimes offered here has a slightly dry austereness—it bears the same relationship to your idea of melon as does herbal tea to a pastrami sandwich. When there is papaya, have that—it is ripe and juicy and solid and sweet, and very good after the food here.

★ SFUZZI

58 West 65th Street
LUNCH AND DINNER.
Reservations: 873-3700.
Credit cards: AE, DC, MC, V.
Medium priced.

The late stage designer Jean-Pierre Ponnelle revealed in his work an obsession with decadence and decay; the subject of his sets was the death of civilization, never mind whether the operas he made them for were tragic, comic, or just emotional. If you missed his shows, be aware that between the acts he apparently turned the same form of mockery on everyday life, for if Sfuzzi is not the work of his cynical hand, then the real perpetrator has a job waiting for him a few blocks away at the Metropolitan Opera, where no one has been found to mine what was Ponnelle's private vein. What with its snowy crowd, Sfuzzi is even as noisy as certain operas, just as murky, occupies as large a stage, and, as the critics say, works on several levels—you know, to eat in one part of the place you climb a couple of steps up, in another a couple down. Here the floor is of red tiles, there of raw wood, here you sit in wicker café chairs, there in three-legged minimalist chairs of black metal with triangular seats, the apex at your spine. There are light fixtures that look like candles down to their last couple of inches, pillars and walls that look like they have been through the blitz, their scarred surfaces blasted down to various depths— brick, or marble, or different colors of paint, or gold leaf. Tiny spotlights hang seemingly by hairs from the black ceiling, cast little islands of light here and there, so that you may be seated at a brightly lighted table in the otherwise shadowy rooms. The staff uniform for both sexes is an emblemed blazer and a white shirt buttoned to the neck, no necktie. The cruet on your table pours extra-virgin olive oil—from both spouts. Though off to one side, the Sfuzzi focal point is the bar, four big TV screens mounted high up behind it, each of them aglow with different action. People gladly wait in line for a spot at this bar, because it is a gathering place for singles at which, according to the *Times*, only two-headed mouth breathers fail to score.

In the dim light it is easy to mistake one thing for another, so know that the small dark-pink plate on your table, the one with a green bottom, is not an ashtray, is, rather, a shallow dish of pesto-flavored olive oil in which to dip your bread while you wait an unpredictable time for your warm salad of artichokes (the chunks of heart are a little soft), mushrooms (wild and woodsy), and roasted peppers (unimpeachable), all of them over a mound of spiky greens moistened with much oil, and all suffused with the flavor of garlic. You order a pizza. After a while a thin-legged stand, around 15 inches high, is placed at the center of your table, upon it the pie. Under this system there is room on your minuscule deuce for the pizza one floor up, and two plates from which to eat it at table level. Not a bad pizza the one of grilled salmon, smoked salmon, Italian bacon, for the bread is of grainy wheat flavor, the salmons are good and also distinguishable, the bacon is a nice note, and the thing is moistened with more of that heady greened oil. Pasta may be had in half orders as a first course, and you do well with the corkscrew pasta called fusilli when it is mingled with sweet, crunchy shrimp and chunks of skinned tomato in an herbed tomato broth.

The grilled swordfish is *grilled*, the grill marks etched deeply into its surfaces, the fish overdone and a bit dry, a condition ameliorated by the sections of fruit that, as part of the "orange thyme vinaigrette," are both its sauce and garnish. The grilled chicken suffers, first, for the visual effect of cutting into it, for the goat cheese with which it is stuffed proceeds to ooze purposefully out all sides of the butterflied breast like an out-of-control culture in search of *lebensraum*. Anyway, though the chicken has little flavor of its own, it mixes not well with the cheese. You have had worse veal chops in "better" restaurants, this one is prettily browned, pink, moist, and the confusion of other elements on the plate—onions, sections of tomato, chunks of artichoke heart (soft again), spinach, capers, sprigs of Italian parsley—does nothing to undo it. Better still is the immense steak, coarsely peppered, but so plump that the ratio of beef to spice is within reason, and the juicy meat is well seared, its blood-juiciness scaled within the surfaces—the beef is served with wild mushrooms and crisp asparagus spears. Whatever you eat, the main courses arrive on dinner plates the combined diameters of two of which exceed either dimension of a table for two.

Not usually, but too often, you are introduced to the desserts by way of two plates of them, three to a plate, that are set down before you and your other. Your waiter then points at each dessert, at a range of about one inch, with one of his fingers, and tells you about it in the manner in which specimens were pointed at and expounded on by the lecturer in your pathology class. Instead of dessert you order a drink. Had your appetite not been dulled, you would have discovered that the cranberry pecan pie is a flat and heavy thing, that the hazelnut torte is a wet cake, that the "chocolate amaretto cream jazz," which half fills a big wineglass, is an intense chocolate pudding topped with good whipped cream.

The "Frozen Sfuzzi," a drink to rival the bellini, is like a margarita of peach liquors and bubbly wine. Lively and not too sweet, it comes in three sizes: small ($4.50), medium ($6), ridiculous ($20). The dinner minimum is $20—which you may use up with just one ridiculous Frozen Sfuzzi. Leave your coat in the car—or pay $1 to check it.

★★SHINWA

645 Fifth Avenue (entrance on 51st Street)
LUNCH AND DINNER. CLOSED SUNDAY.
Reservations: 644-7400.
Credit cards: AE, DC, MC, V.
Expensive.

Much to see before you see the restaurant itself. Approach Shinwa from the street, rather than from within the tall glass box whose offices and apartments it serves, and the corner of your right eye is caught by a slip of Japanese garden that, it seems, is basking in the negligible south light that manages to reach the windowed base of a skyscraper surrounded by others. It is the minor miracle of this garden, stuck between a sheet of glass and a slick café, that the three clusters of rock, and the sculpted sand in which they are set, make a spaciousness and serenity that are inanimately and quite perfectly oblivious to their slick surroundings. Continue past the garden, past the dozens of tables and the long bar that are Shinwa's upstairs café, and you reach a waterfall, a sloped and stepped wall of red rock down which water flows to a basement-level pool. Your search for the dining room, however, requires that you find the point, about halfway between the garden and the cascade, that is the head of the stairs leading down to it, which is not so easy, for the station is manned, most nights, by a clearly, confusingly, Occidental lady who must often deal first with the question, dubiously put, of whether she is the greeter for the Oriental establishment being sought. She is, and she conducts you below deck to a dining room that, by way of some Zen magic, transcends its physical shortcomings. The place is large and low-ceilinged, the kind of basement room that usually seems squashed down by the weight of the building above. How this one was made to seem spacious and open, how the oppressively low ceiling was made almost to disappear, knows only the wizard who put the place together. Part of the answer may reside in certain elements of the big square room that, by calling attention to themselves, take your mind off others. Most notable of these is the arresting black-on-white calligraphic mural that, occupying an entire wall, the characters almost the full height of the room, accosts you with its breathtaking sweep and velocity. Another mural across the room, the same size, but of more timid ambition, is a panorama of New York seen from within Central Park, seen also through a haze that reduces every line to a shimmer—very nice, and surely done by a Japanese painter, but the piece seems like Western art surfaced with an Oriental glaze. Through the windowed back of the restaurant you get another view of that pool and waterfall, almost like the great outdoors seen from underground. On the window's sill are arranged dramatic vignettes of doll-like characters in Japanese ceremonial costumes—your waiter informs you that they are built of layer upon layer of paper, though the figures appear to be clothed in brilliantly dyed and luxuriantly ornamented cloth. Two low partitions (they are parallel to the murals, divide the room into three parts) are topped with sand and, at intervals, rocks. As they are carefully composed, seem (if you work on it) to suggest eternal rivers, you are shocked that here and there Japanese businessmen at tables adjacent to them casually lean their elbows in the sand. In fact at dinner the Japanese are most of those on hand, so you conclude that whether or not you like what you get, it is the real thing.

What you get is not, however, what you very likely expect, for you will have noted that no sushi bar figures in the layout. Which is not to say you do not find perfect sushi here, rather that it is prepared out of sight, and the selection is limited, often more limited than even the printed listing. But such basics as tuna, salmon, salmon roe, eel, and yellowtail are assembled, with delicate and lively vinegared rice and with firm, deep-green sheets of pungent seaweed, into fresh-flavored constructs that manage to stimulate your appetite precisely as fast as they satisfy it. But sushi is available in scores of places, no longer seems even vaguely exotic, whereas the like of ika shiokara, preserved squid to you, will, you may be sure, remain outré even when Japanese restaurants and Greek coffee shops finally have the eating out market all to themselves. You are served but a small quantity of the stuff, set at the bottom of a bowl, the slivers of seafood slippery and loud in their cold and sticky sauce, the kind of dish you understand rather than appreciate, never mind love, perfectly foiled by some hot sake, with which you rather promptly efface the sea-gamy flavor and slimy texture. Proceeding from the otherworldly to the merely alien, next stop unagi kabayaki, eel—which arrives in a handsomely red-lacquered box, the great rectangles of hot, dark, butterflied meat slicked and glinting in their sweetened soy sauce. By the time you reach yuba-chakin, you are virtually home, for though these bundles of crabmeat are wrapped in sheets of distinctly Oriental tofu, then deep-fried until crisp, the sweet seafood in the crackling wrappers is accessible without adjustment of your palatal set. You are disappointed by these oysters, for though they are deftly coerced into cylindrical form in their seaweed wrappers, delicately breaded and deep fried, and roused by the bracing, oceanic broth into which you dip them, they are not utterly fresh. No such problem with the kushi-age, six skewered items, beef, shrimp, vegetables among them, variously wrapped and enwrapping, all of them breaded and fried and of vivid character. Six clumps of seaweed, a white, two reds, and a green, arranged on a bowl of ice, make up the kaiso salad, they vary from the crisp to the rubbery, from the mild to the wildly briny, and all are rousing with the mustardlike soybean dressing you dip them in.

The big deals here are the do-it-yourself dishes (with assistance and instruction from your waiter) that involve a portable gas stove on the table. Among them is udon suki, in which an amber-colored seafood stock, from a handsome jug with a thong around its narrow neck, is poured into a woklike pot and brought to a boil over the flame. From a huge array of vegetables, meat, seafood, skewered gingko nuts, and noodles about the gauge of lamp cord, you add items to the broth, permit them to cook according to your judgment, fish them out, and eat. It is important to control this operation yourself, for if, say, your waiter puts half the items in the broth, goes off to take care of other matters, and does not get back for ten minutes, everything in the pot is ruined. The vegetables are fresh, the seafood is sweet (except that the clams in their shells may be even louder than the aforementioned less-than-pristine oysters), the meats are tender, and the rice noodles, which, traditionally, are cooked and eaten late, are of a bland solidity that ends one of these feasts with finality by weighing it down.

Withal, what distinguishes Shinwa from the run of its competition are its noodle and porridge dishes. When you order noodles, you specify either udon (made of wheat flour) or soba (made of buckwheat flour), though the Occidental palate will likely find greater gratification in the tasty soba than the doughy udon. Order your yamakake made with the udon, and you are confronted with a bowl of cold, chewy strands to which you add an almost black soy sauce, a raw egg, ginger. Not surprisingly, the thing foams, as may you—not a dish for the millions. Order, on the other hand, tenzaru made with soba noodles, and you find the long strands dusky and grainy—you dip these in another dark soy sauce, which you have fortified with scallions, wasabi, and a quail egg, and, if you follow the example of the eating habits of the Japanese, you then slurp them off the ends of your chopsticks. This is served with tempura—carrots, green peppers, mushrooms, giant shrimp, sheets of flaky, dark-green seaweed, all of them airily battered, delicately deep fried, just the hot foil to the cold noodles. The porridges are winter food, they reach you bubbling over a flame, and in the one called "Mix Zosui" the rice is dense with scallops, spinach, scallion greens, and a rice cake, big and pully, that is in distinct textural contrast to the moist, nubbly dish—rapid ingestion of which induces perspiration.

★★SICHUAN PAVILION

310 East 44th Street
LUNCH AND DINNER.
Reservations: 972-7377.
Credit cards: AE, DC, MC, V.
Medium priced.

The dreary situation that is today's New York Chinese-restaurant scene has been brightened some by the return of Sichuan Pavilion—happily, to new quarters. Recall the high-ceilinged, brightly lighted color boxes that were the rooms of the old place, and you know what the new one is not. But remember the old Pavilion's food—what it was when the restaurant was new and at its best—and here it is again. The new look has come to us from China by way of California, that is, the flower paintings, framed calligraphy, and panda art are subsumed in a comfortable—almost cushy—haze of soft light and unstained wood. The well-spaced tables are linened, the chairs are padded, and the floor is carpeted. The big central dining room is rimmed by smaller rooms usable for parties. Etched-glass windows overlook the row of enclosed tables on 44th Street.

This is the place with the limp dumplings. They look like you could drape them over a clothesline. Not so easy, however, for the noodle casings are slippery of the black, oily, hot, and hot-spiced sauce they are served in—the fillings, firm nodules of pork force-meat, are vibrant of their complex seasoning. The beef strips in a small steamer come, you guessed it, in a small steamer—it is filled with the just-done slivers of meat, fibrous and very tender, spicy-hot and aromatic. The smoked fish fillets are made smoky, black, and a little spicy by their treatment—the fish, clearly, was fresh when it was prepared, and its pristine oceanic flavor gleams through. Still, that fish is akin to dishes you have had in dozens of Chinese places, while other cold appetizers here hold surprises: tangy chicken, for one, thick slices of white meat cut from a tasty bird, moistened with a black sauce that is at once salty, winy, fragrantly perfumed—the dish is marked with a star, but it is far from violently hot; and tangy rabbit, long strands of the firm meat mingled with grassy greens that impart a citrus acidity to the rousing dish—the moisture is a smooth oil that carries the fiery spice, and the dish is sprinkled with crisp sesame seeds.

In a box at the center of the menu are listed ten dishes under the heading "first time served in America." Many of these were so described at the old place, so the claim is now strained. Still, this is where to look, for here you will find the likes of "dry sautéed squid," which would better read "sautéed dried squid," for it is made—by design—not of the fresh article, but of the preserved, the gamy accent and slight resilience of which, in this mass of bean sprouts, shredded pork, and much else, gives the dish such assertive character that your waiter lowers his pad when you ask for it, looks you over, inquires if you know what you are doing—you reassure him by confessing a helpless addiction to the stuff. Still working the box, you order "tinklin [sic] bells with ten ingredients," and the components are wheeled to your table on a serving stand, where they sizzle viciously when transferred to a hot frying pan. The dish is not, as its name leads you reasonably to fear, just another Chinese compendium, substantial but confusing. In fact, its elements —little mushrooms, crisp disks of water chestnut, scallion whites and scallion greens, slivers of pork, emerald snow peas, crunchy shrimp, and more, all filmed with a light, glistening oil—retain their individuality in the complex setting. The "tinklin bells" of the title are small dumplings, somewhat doughy ones that pick up a bit of crispness in that last-minute sautéing, and their starchy weight is in nice contrast to the sprightlier items in the dish. What is given as "crispy whole fish" is just that, the giant sea bass in a pool of sauce that is thick and dark, smooth and oily, fiery hot and dense with scallion greens. A silken, slightly sticky sauce binds the diverse elements of the Sichuan-style lamb: slivers of meat that taste slightly burnt, chunks of fragrant garlic, delicate ears of baby corn, lengths of scallion—the food is heady of fresh ginger and powerfully hot of the red peppers (dangerous to eat) you find hidden among the other elements. Most of the dishes go well with the crunchy pan-fried noodles—a crisped tangle dotted with vegetables and meats. The spiced string beans are, pleasantly, a little tough—they reach you under strongly seasoned ground pork.

★★SIGN OF THE DOVE

1110 Third Avenue (at 65th Street)
LUNCH, TUESDAY TO SUNDAY; DINNER, DAILY.
Reservations: 861-8080.
Credit cards: AE, DC, MC, V.
Very expensive.

As the aged and infirm return to religion—just in case it develops, hard upon the last moment, that there is something to it—so have the interests behind this old hustle given themselves over, here in the fading years of New York's grand restaurant spree, to quality. But surely visitors from the land west of the Hudson, who for decades provided this former trap with most of its commerce, continue to produce as many more of themselves as ever; and certainly the dollar's diminuendo makes Manhattan a tourist attraction of greater cost effectiveness than other world-class metropolises not susceptible to unscheduled changes of government; ergo, one must conclude that the Dove's new policy is no response to short-term need, that, rather, someone has seen the light. All kneel.

The new order does not, however, extend to the visual and aural spheres. You check your coat, and you are led past a gentleman at a baby upright whose harmless tinklings follow you to your table, which is in one of two grandiloquent dining rooms, each a few stories high, lofty archways between them. One is covered over by a great domed stained-glass skylight, the other by a ceiling painted in a mauve-and-gray pattern of roiling ocean, its effect, upon prolonged consideration, gastrointestinally unsettling. You lower your eyes to walls of brick bathed in rosy light, to statuary, to huge mirrors that face each other, east-west and north-south, and that reflect and re-reflect the rooms in endless repetition, so that it is as if the Dove extends from First Avenue to Fifth, from P. J. Clarke's to J. G. Melon. There are tied-back gauze curtains on the tall windows, flagstone floors, bouquets of flowers on the white-linened tables, big bursts of them here and there around the rooms—everything awash in soft light. This kind of thing still draws the outlanders, some from not so far off, and here they are, lounging in their chairs, soaking up the luxury, she in a fleecy cashmere sweater trimmed with mink, he in a doeskin suit, neither aware that the fancy food they get here now differs from the fancified stuff they loved in the past.

Fancy indeed is this casserole of oysters, the dish with which, if you come here once, you wisely begin, the fresh, plump mollusks, out of their shells, warm, of vivid oyster flavor, served in a light, creamy, and briny broth that is threaded with dill and dotted with diced vegetables—tomatoes, zucchini, and much crunchy fennel among them. Your order of eggplant terrine is a couple of thick slabs cut from a layered loaf that is many slices of the named vegetable, among them a layer of red peppers, the two vigorously seasoned and suffused with garlicked oil. A stuffed pasta pancake goes as "duck confit and shiitake ravioli," the forcemeat within the folded noodle sheet of spicy duck flavor, thin strands of celery and chive upon it, meaty slices of sautéed mushroom around it, all in a good, strong, mushroom-flavored sauce. Hot, crisp, and salty parts of quail and cool mushrooms are arranged around a salad of baby lettuce and artichoke

324

hearts in a dressing made with good oil, but the warm ingredients argue with the cool ones, and the artichoke hearts are much like those you find in cans.

In this establishment's fanciful version of the French fish soup called bourride, slivers of rich scallop, a split prawn, its meat sweet and firm in its half shells, and morsels of supple lobster are arranged, with tiny spears of baby asparagus, over a mound of enriched cabbage, everything set in a pink and polished crayfish sauce. Your crosshatched slab of Norwegian salmon is on occasion a bit overcooked, a little dry—still, this is fresh fish, nicely set off by the warm greens on which it is arranged, and by the mushrooms and artichoke hearts around it. Pale and tender meat, handsomely browned, cooked through but juicy, such are the medallions of veal—they are surmounted by the good sautéed wild mushrooms that show up in just about every second dish in this place, and they are garnished with strong spinach that is adorned with a little muffin of wondrously rich garlic custard. The boneless rack of lamb is serious fun food, the slices of pink meat, spicy within their charred edges, forming half a circle, the other half an arc of brown-edged slices of fried potato, the two served with two sauces—a dollop of intense red-pepper puree, and a so-called herbed aioli that is rich, but rather mild for this company.

The lemon mousse cake is a cool and acidic custard on a light shortbread pastry. The raspberry mousse cake, pink and fruity, is intensified by a crimson raspberry sauce. The pear tart is of thin, delicate slices, the apple tart is of great caramelized nuggets, both are on flaky pastry, and both come with fist-sized dollops of rich, tangy crème fraîche.

★ SISTINA

1555 Second Avenue (near 80th Street)
LUNCH, MONDAY TO FRIDAY; DINNER, DAILY.
Reservations: 861-7660.
Credit cards: AE.
Expensive.

Judge it by its looks, and you would reasonably conclude that this is the simplest of the many clubby Italian restaurants strung along the avenues of the Upper East Side—a smallish, well-lighted ivory-colored room with woodwork of pale oak, a wood floor, rows of white-linened tables surrounded by pale bentwood side chairs. Only the back wall of paned mirrors and a few wine bins, plus some greenery and potted flowers here and there, relieve the elemental look—those and the single wall hanging, a detail from the ceiling of the Sistine Chapel, the finger of God and the finger of Adam each extended toward the other, mano a mano.

The rest is less simple. You arrive for dinner, you are seated, you order wine and mineral water, you are asked if you would like bruschetti and fried zucchini "for the table," as your captain puts it. It sounds like a good idea, you go along with it, and as you expected the items are on the house, do not appear on your check. Next time, the offer is not made, but it is made to other tables near yours. You are mature, you laugh off your slight inclination to resentment. Yet a third time you come by, once again the offer is made, once again you accept, and this time you are charged $6 and $7 respectively. (It must be reported, however, that the bruschetti, crusts of bread covered over with garlicked tomatoes and basil, and the zucchini, slender, crisp, and delicate pale-green strands, are impeccable.) That difficulty is easy to handle, for on subsequent visits you ask what kind of night you have happened on—a night of love? or a night of money?

You are handed a clearly printed menu on which are listed fifty items, of which you are able to translate into English maybe a third, your ignorance being such that you make no sense of, for example, "risotto gustoso," or "penne ai sette ré," or "scaloppine sorpresa," or "pollo molisano," or even "coda di rospo all'amalfitana," all of which would not be so bad if you could ask your captain to translate, and then commit to memory his translations. But you cannot, because he recites to you, rapid fire, the specials of the day, a dozen or two, and he figures that since he has learned them by heart so can you—accordingly, your memory has all it can hold. Some nights this ordeal includes the famous Tour of the Spaghettis, the helpful fellow brings by a tray on which around ten dried pastas of various shapes, sizes, and colors are arranged, at each of which he points, and with respect to each of which he describes the preparation of the evening—this is a busy restaurant, and he is in the fast lane all the way. So unless you want to nail him to the extra chair at your table until you have taken a complete set of notes—and, after all, you already have company—you never really choose your dinner with knowledge of all the available dishes.

The house frequently offers three wild mushrooms sautéed with garlic, and the quality of the dish depends on how well the sautéing is handled. Sometimes the olive oil is hot, and the flavor of the mushrooms is sealed within their browned surfaces, is potentiated by the garlic with which they are sautéed; other times the oil is merely warm, so the mushrooms are soggy and limp, their earthy character lost in the kitchen. Vitello tonnato is listed, and the veal is a little coarse under the lemony sauce of pureed tuna, dotted with capers, that has been poured over the cool meat. During the Tour your captain pushed what he called, variously, Sardinian dumplings and Sardinian gnocchi. By your lights they are neither dumplings nor gnocchi, but narrow, inch-long shafts of pasta, some tan, some green, some dark red—whole wheat, spinach, and saffron. As it happens you are served no green ones and only a few red, but they are part of a wondrous dish, its chunky sauce a dazzling complexity of fennel-flavored sausage, tomato, and fresh basil—the occasional hit of saffron from the red pasta is a nifty note. Sometimes there is spaghetti with sea urchins, and this is simple, assertive food, sea-gamy and pungently garlicked. That "risotto gustoso" turns out to be rice with porcinis, the nubbly grain—strongly peppered, mingled with chunks of the wild mushroom, and enriched with cheese—of a deep, satisfying earthiness.

Pass up the occasional special "bouillabaisse," in which you find rank mussels and those tasteless frozen crab claws from the north. Pass up also the black bass in black-olive sauce—fresh fish, and the liquefied sauce does reveal some olive character, but the flavor of the fish has been cooked away. Have instead the whole snapper in aromatic vinegar—here, too, the fish has been compromised, but the herbed and oiled sauce is dramatic against the white fillets your waiter has neatly separated from the skin and bones. The chicken with fennel is fine, the bird browned and moist, the fennel livened with sweet white raisins. The herbed veal chop is probably fine when it reaches you further done than blood rare. When there is liver, your captain describes it as sliced "very, very thin," but what you get is a single inch-thick steak—still, good liver, glistening pink within its browned surfaces, the whole in a fragrant sauce of white wine and sage.

Ask for Parmesan and the rousing cheese reaches you with black olives and chunks of fennel. Ask for a pear, and you get a huge ripe one, peeled and sectioned. The poached pear, very sweet-spiced, is served with a cold, whipped-cream-enriched zabaglione. The apricot tart, of dark pastry and poached dried apricots, is served with ripe raspberries and more of that zabaglione. The lemon tart is acidic and sweet, is strewn with strings of citrus rind, is set in a cold, intense strawberry sauce, in which you also find ripe strawberries in dollops of whipped cream.

★ SMITH & WOLLENSKY

797 Third Avenue (at 49th Street)
LUNCH, MONDAY TO FRIDAY; DINNER, DAILY.
Reservations: 753-1530.
Credit cards: AE, DC, MC, V.
Very expensive.

If you have recently telephoned for help to one of America's great corporations—to have, say, your typewriter repaired, or to get your sewing machine wired for electricity—you have perhaps noticed that the so-called service personnel with whom you deal have developed a way of speaking formerly peculiar to recorded announcements. Sometimes it is difficult to determine whether what you say is being responded to by a human or a digital intelligence. Even witticisms, which you essay in a desperate try to draw out what remains of the mortal in your respondent, are met with mechanical comebacks. Fortunately, this form of human decomposition is not yet widespread in the restaurant game. But you are a bit thrown when, upon addressing yourself to one of Smith & Wollensky's young, overgrown bartenders with the words, "Do you have Moosehead?" the galoot responds with, "Yes, and we pour it proudly." Maybe he thinks that by modeling his language after product commercials, and his manner of speech after that of airwaves hucksters, he will attract the attention of one of the thousands of executives who, at the expense of the very corporations whose products are so drearily peddled, pack this place daily. You do like to think the poor fool is just looking for a job—but the obvious pleasure he takes in his mastery of this manner and idiom disputes that fond reading.

You are at the bar because, though you arrived on time for your reservation, and though tables are available, the foppish young gentleman at the book this day is one who enjoys exercising what small power he has managed in life to accrue. He sends all comers to the bar for a ten- or fifteen-minute cooling-down period, and then grants tables, now to these two, now to those three, as if he were dispensing alms to mendicants—the distribution always in something other than the poor beggars' order of arrival. And if for some reason he dislikes you altogether, he may forget you indefinitely—until you make a scene. It appears you have to be his type, or his idea of S&W's type, which, as it happens, is a quite specific one. This is a male species (its ladies are only in waiting), it is cleanshaven, cigared, blazered. It watches football in winter, golfs in summer. It does beer and booze. In fact you figure at first that the enforced prelude at the bar is for the purpose of selling extra drinks to customers who will often have nothing stronger than pop once their boulders of beef are before them. (And it is true that, though the establishment sports a dozen-page, computer-printout multinational wine list, a tour through the restaurant's many rooms and regions turns up maybe one working bottle of wine per dozen occupied tables.) But when others are handling the seating, it is sometimes conducted equitably—at least it is when there is no more room at the bar.

This is the place that, in the late seventies, appeared on the scene having unashamedly composed for itself a style formed of characteristics lifted from the most successful steakhouses in New York. It borrowed so well that today it appears to be doing more business—anyway, under one roof—than any of its models. (In its earliest days it even operated without printed menus—in the manner of the Palm and Christ Cella—but that particular idiocy was soon abandoned.) Of the qualities it endeavored to replicate, the basic one was age. S&W was built to look as if it had been here forever. Composed of areas at various levels, each of them furnished somewhat differently from the others (just tables and chairs here, booths there, a big banquette yonder), the sprawling place—all wood-floored and buff-colored—looks like a normal-size restaurant that, by accretion of now one additional space, now another, became a mammoth one over time. The sense of history is reinforced by the dozens of pieces of art and artifact—mostly Americana— that, it is easy to believe, were accumulated over the years, each piece mounted or hung wherever there was room. The dining rooms and bar are dripping with duck decoys, models of historic vehicles, primitive paintings, an ancient horse-and-buggy weathervane, sporting prints, more. Some things have been added during the restaurant's actual years: little brass-colored plates (tacked up behind the bar, at the entranceway to the central dining room, elsewhere), each of them engraved with the name of one of the establishment's regular customers, dead or alive—Hal Horowitz, Jim Lewis, L. Baxter Chamberlain, etc.—for S&W is a fraternal place; and a second story much like the first—though noisier, for it does not benefit from the acoustic ceiling that, on the lower level, modulates the sounds of the vociferous crowd. Upstairs or down, the place is patrolled by waiters who wear putty-colored jackets, shirts and ties, white aprons—as in ye olden days.

Just as the restaurant looks to have been here since Prohibition, nothing about its printed menu suggests that the document postdates World War II—that is, if you imagine the decimal points one place to the left. But when the shrimp cocktail arrives, you are promptly back in the present, for this restaurant's illusionism overrides all but economics, and so the half dozen crustaceans that were once the usual allotment are expressed, in the S&W rendition, as four. These are not bad shrimp, big, crunchy, and devoid of iodine, but of shrimp flavor they have not much. The lobster cocktail, however, is a minor masterpiece, the entire little beast snug in its split red shell, cool but not cold, firm but not tough, moist but not wet, of sweet oceanic flavor—obviously, it was prepared and cooled not too long before you ordered it. And the lump crabmeat is more than its equal, a great mound of iridescent nuggets of firm but delicate meat, each of them of a marine sweetness that suggests crabs fished from the water the very day. The shellfish cocktails are served with two sauces—a vibrant cocktail sauce that sparkles with sweet spice, and a creamy ginger sauce that is greened with chopped spinach. Shellfish aside, you may begin your dinner with prosciutto and melon—three broad paper-thin sheets of strong and salty ham over three crescents of fairly ripe melon; or with the thick and pleasantly sticky pea soup—it is hot and spicy hot, and it is poured into your broad soup plate from the tin cup in which it was carried from the kitchen.

In this busy place the fish of the day is truly of the day, and you may have here the like of this great side of red snapper, the utterly fresh fish, redded and browned, falling into tender flakes of pale meat that retain all their distinctive snapper flavor. Opt for other than fish, however, and things begin to go—downhill. You order a broiled lobster, and, as is the way of this place, you are presented with a lobster that is first steamed and then broiled, which is quite another article. Steaming and then broiling is supposedly a means of lobster preparation that combines the advantages of two methods—it sounds reasonable but does not work out that way, and the so-called broiled lobsters here are usually somewhat stringy or tough, unlike the strictly broiled ones you get at, say, the Palm or Christ Cella. With respect to the chopped steak, S&W makes the mistake all steakhouses make—it prepares its immense chopped steak as if it were an unchopped steak, so if you want yours, say, rare, you will get a chopped steak that, though it is rare at the center, is brown and dry throughout its outer half inch. If you have sometimes wondered why coffee-shop hamburgers are often better than steakhouse chopped steaks, it is because coffee shops do their hamburgers on a griddle (or, occasionally, in a pan), and a hot, flat metal surface is the only source of heat that will hold the moisture in a chopped steak— or hamburger—while cooking it through. The sirloins are big, blackened a little, accurately broiled, and tender—but a bit dry, and of less than the beefiest flavor, even for these days. And the veal chop, even when it is pink, lacks juice, comes across as a great slab of lovely chicken—and if it is broiled chicken you want, there is the genuine article here, sold as lemon pepper chicken, the skin of the big bird tart and spicy and handsomely crisped, though once in a while you get a bird that seems to have been inadvertently derefrigerated somewhere along the line, so that it has some of the off flavor sometimes found in supermarket chickens. You get sensational hash browns here, the big serving actually a kind of pancake of firm little cubes and slices of potato, the top crusted and dark-browned, the interior moist and glistening of its oil, the whole strongly but judiciously seasoned. The cottage fries are like good hot potato chips, and the onion rings are sweet, if rather heavily battered and a little greasy.

Naturally there is cheesecake, and it is the usual rich, creamy, sugary thing, albeit a good version thereof. Fruit tarts are offered, sometimes a pretty good one of pear on a nutty pastry. The hot deep-dish apple pie is a square of toast over crisp slices of apple and dark raisins, all in a thin vanilla sauce. You can always have ice cream.

(Attached to S&W's southern flank, on 49th Street, is an annex called Wollensky's Grill, a small and clubby two-level barroom/dining room plus about a dozen and a half tables under an awning outside. Not many worse sites for outdoor eating can be found in New York, for the 49th Street crosstown bus passes regularly, a mobile cloud of gas fumes in its wake. The Grill has its own menu [though you may order from the S&W menu if you wish], lower prices, inferior food, and sullen help.)

★★SOFI

102 Fifth Avenue (near 15th Street)
LUNCH AND DINNER. CLOSED SUNDAY.
Reservations: 463-8888.
Credit cards: AE, DC, MC, V.
Very expensive.

Dreams need work. Realize a fantasy, find its faults. Here someone has been given his dreamy head, and voilà, a setting in which is fulfilled every designer's ultimate fantasy, a room in which is incorporated every idea his other clients rejected. Surely the fellow persuaded himself that it all, can you believe it, "works." And it does for one mildly amused visit. But you will not discover new layers of satiric meaning (the kind you look for if you look at all) on subsequent encounters—the joke sustains only one hearing.

Sofi is, moreover, huge, a couple of stories high, and under its distant ceiling, which is the green of surgical gowns, the walls have been mottled to the effect of a rosy-colored dawn seen through mists not yet burnt off. But the morning light is ample enough for you to discern that the raised area at the front of the restaurant, directly under the big windows that look out on burgeoning lower Fifth, is broadloomed, furnished with L-shaped sofas done in pale, flowered chintz, and with wicker chairs, some of them the color of that ceiling, around the little tables at which drinks are served. The dining room proper is dominated by four giant columns in a line along its axis—their stippled surfaces are shadowy at the bottom, as if they have been splattered by passing vehicles during slushy weather—whim amok—and they are topped by elaborate finials that appear to hang rather than support. The mezzanine on one long side is a comfortable part of the place—large tables, some of them beside a few more of those sofas—despite its excellent view of the other long side, which is dominated by two huge food-and-flora still lifes (or are they subtropical Christmas trees), that threaten at each end. Between them, on the lower level, the long bar is backed by a mirror triptych within overarching wood frames. Down here there are rugs—in the styles of many lands—on the red-tile floors, and along the sides a number of those sofas yet again are the seating for some good-size tables. (The tables for two, however, are about right for a cigarette and a cup of coffee.) At the back, the open kitchen of the previous tenant has been modestly concealed behind a massive folding screen of mirrored glass framed in dark-stained wood. The waiters and waitresses are in men's dress shirts, the bow ties on their wing collars vivid black chokers around their youthful necks. One of them hangs around while you look at the wine list, which offers a dozen-and-a-half wines by the glass. Say you: "How nice, you have a cruvinet." Says he: "Yes, but tonight we're out of it."

You may decide that whoever put together the physical place was mindful of the menu, for it, too, is diverse—beyond any possibility of national culinary identification. Happily, though you take in your surroundings all at once, you eat only one dish at a time, beginning, if you are wise, with skate, ten anchovy-size strips of the white fish, their clear marine flavor intensified by a light marination, arranged on their plate like the spokes of a wheel, at the center a mass of so-called tomato salad that is more like a deep, dark vegetable stew, between the spokes dark-green dabs of a pesto sauce that is nutty, pungent of its cheese, heady of fresh basil. Four spokes of another wheel, these broader and deep pink, are smoked salmon that has been warmed, no less, which heightens its salt, fish, and smoke flavors, the strips of seafood in a creamy sauce that is nubbly with minced fennel and celery. On three slabs of cured tomato at the edge of a mound of green salad are placed three egg-shaped masses of eggplant caviar, their eggplant flavor, however, remote—you spread the stuff on the crusts of bread that come with it, and wonder what you would guess it to be on the blind. You would wonder not at all about the identity of this terrine of cassoulet, a block cut from a loaf of the meats and beans that are the usual cassoulet components, sautéed until its surface is crisped and dark brown—no, you would know at once that this is hash, albeit good hash, but unmistakably the coarse and fatty thing, in no way disguised, never mind elevated, by the sticky sauce in which it is served.

Rigatoni are ribbed tubes of pasta; here they are stuffed with a mildly seasoned mash of Swiss chard and ricotta, and they are served under a "fresh tomato sauce" that is hardly more than warmed, chopped, herbed tomatoes, albeit very nice for that. What Sofi calls rotelle, you call fusilli, the corkscrew pasta mingled with little florets of broccoli, lengths of green bean and red pepper, and with nuggets of salmon that would be perfect were they perfectly fresh—this is an odd dish in that there are just the solids, barely a trace of liquid, so when your waiter offers cheese, cheese on a seafood dish being a further oddity, you go for it anyway, and sure enough it does nothing but append itself, one more element among others that have not been made into a whole.

Happily, the lobster Castlebay (you take it on faith the dish is of Hebridean extraction) will help you to forget all that, the white meat, out of its shell, under a cloud of long, thin, crisp-fried potatoes, the whole set in a pool of pink, creamy lobster sauce that is of sharp shellfish flavor, in it lengths of chive, strands of red pepper, bits of garlic and of ginger—you encounter those oddments as occasional bursts of surprising, almost shocking, invariably pleasing flavor. The dim taste of monkfish is here roused by the bits of strong prosciutto with which the fish is studded—you are served a row of morsels of the firm seafood arranged down the center of your plate, on one side a simple burnt-orange sauce that is of red peppers, on the other a complex greenish one that is dominated by fennel, slightly bitter baby turnips and sweet baby carrots two of the good vegetables that adorn the colorful dish. Duck, as you may know, no longer arrives looking like duck. Here you are served a semicircle of somewhat rare slices of the juicy and quite ducky meat in a rather sweet vermouth sauce, the meat garnished with a pungently seasoned eggplant mash, several leaves of cooked endive, in each of them a slice of roasted red pepper, and a dollop of tapenade that is of powerful black-olive strength. That is good duck, but this is even more interesting quail (though the dish is dominated by a whole, rich foie gras at the center of the plate), the sautéed parts, of unmistakably strong quail flavor, in a winy, meaty sauce that is thick with a many-textured hash of black bread and vegetables—that abundance of foie gras, however, gives the dish an almost overwhelmingly pinguid cast. Notable veal, the three substantial scallops of pale, tender, juicy meat handsomely browned, strewn with fresh basil, and served in a greened sauce that is muddied, thickened, and sharpened by ground pecorino cheese and crushed fava beans —that basil is a stunning note in this setting. A platform of well-oiled eggplant under a strong tomato sauce, thin slivers of sautéed zucchini strewn over it, is the centerpiece for your roast lamb, little slices of good meat surround it, the two in a bit of moisture that is mostly the roasting juices.

Here has been ennobled banana cream pie, now called a tart, the thick, sweet, and pale-yellow custard, of concentrated banana flavor, on a browned pastry under a cloud of fluffy whipped cream. More whipped cream, this time touched with Grand Marnier, is the bulk of the strawberry napoleon, the balance three leaves of crisp, flaky pastry and fresh strawberries, the tiered affair in a crimson pool of berry puree. Whipped cream yet again, this time with poached fresh pineapple, cool and sweet, the two between thin, crisp coconut pastries, on the sandwich confectioners' sugar, under it a creamy sauce. With the chocolate cake the whipped cream is just a garnish, as is the little ball of chocolate ice cream under its leaf of pure chocolate, as is the ball of vanilla coated with crushed macadamia nuts—the cake itself, nutted and strong, is slicked with black icing.

★ STEPHANIE'S

944 First Avenue (near 55th Street)
LUNCH AND DINNER.
Reservations: 753-0520.
Credit cards: AE, DC, MC, V.
Medium priced.

An outpost of California, the nicknamed Golden State, Stephanie's is all sunshine, the informality of the out-of-doors, a world refracted through pastel glasses. The entire place has been done in horizontal stripes of robin's egg blue and vanilla cream, reminds you of the revisionist stripes of some contemporary painter's American flag. "Natural" is the operative word. The floor and the bar are of natural (unstained) wood. There is greenery on the raised area at the front of the restaurant, and it is the real thing. Throughout, the tables are covered with white butcher paper, which, if it is no more natural than white linen, does suggest back-to-nature picnicking, as against Manhattan eating out. Overhead the four-bladed fans turn slowly, almost mournfully, not at all the way they used to spin in the good old days before bad, bad air conditioning rendered them technologically unemployed. The help, naturally, are in white aprons, jeans, sneakers, and, bless them, they are supernaturally courteous, albeit the Stephanie's system occasionally requires them to be there just when you urgently wish they were here.

Much in the California manner, the menu responds to the season and the market-place, changes a little every day. For that reason you will not always find what you want; and, maybe for that reason as well, some dishes are much better than others. Somewhere near the center of the quality spectrum falls the French fried squid, the slivers of seafood so battered that they are crusty rather than crisp—still, they are not greasy, and their spicy-hot "Cajun tartar sauce" gives them life. Another moderate success involves crusty slices of country bread, herbed and garlicked, which the house spreads with thin slices of Parmesan, over those big sides of oiled and roasted green pepper, over those, in vivid contrast, lengths of red pepper—the dish is well made, but not brilliantly conceived, the elements less than utterly at home with one another. The "pâté" of wild mushrooms does a fair imitation of a meaty pâté, the earthy and fresh-made paste piled abundantly on— yet again—crusts of garlicky bread. When ripe figs are around they are here cut in half, the flat sides of the hemispheres are mounded over with goat cheese, and the cheese is browned under the fire—good ingredients, but once more an experimental dish in which no new immortal combination has revealed itself. A couple of pasta dishes are listed each day, are sold in half or full orders, among them, on occasion, fettuccine with fresh oysters, the two in a vaguely Pernod-flavored cream sauce dotted with slivers of crunchy fennel—this time the diverse elements add up; as they do again in the penne with chicken, the short pointed lengths of pasta and the shreds of chicken masquerading as each other, though only the white meat has the good chicken flavor—goat cheese and chunks of tomato are the principals in the striking sauce. Ricotta-filled ravioli are served one way today, another tomorrow. A full order is an off-putting six of the big, bulbous, somewhat weighty knobs, a challenge mitigated neither by the mound of ham at the center of your plate, nor the herbed broth that is the sauce.

You are asked how you want your grilled swordfish. You answer, fashionably, medium rare. The giant steak of fresh fish reaches you just cooked through, juicy, full of flavor, shredded snow peas and wild mushrooms in its buttery sauce. You are asked nothing about your poached halibut, and the big fillet reaches you a little cooked out, the distinctive flavor of that species a little lost, though its smooth white sauce, flecked with the green of mâche and the red of radicchio, rescues the dish. You wish the grilled Gulf prawns were juicier in their shells, though their flavor is clear, and they are arranged around a great pile of crisped thin strands of French-fried leek, all of which you moisten—in this good variation on the shrimp cocktail—with a barbecue sauce that is sharp and sweet. Recalling the good chicken you once had as part of that pasta dish, you order chicken qua chicken, the roasted half of one, and everything about the dish is fine—the crackling skin that has been browned in a mustard glaze, the wild rice dotted with kernels of corn and pine nuts—except that the bird is a small one and, accordingly, of little flavor. You are in luck if you come when there is warm lamb salad, an abundance of tender lamb, medium rare and of clear lamb flavor, arranged over a salad of fresh greens and sugar snap peas in a bright dressing.

It is either difficult or impossible to detect the Grand Marnier in the Grand Marnier cheesecake, but the cake is rich without being heavy, and its sauce of sweet-spiced blueberries is fine. Of the gingerbread it may be said that it tastes exactly like gingerbread, this one being light, almost powdery in its caramel sauce. Sweet spices yet again, this time in what is given as calvados crisp, the hot apples—like apple pie filling—garnished with whipped cream from which protrudes a stick of cinnamon. The chocolate almond napoleon cake is a layered affair, rich and chewy and light, and set in a pool of crème anglaise.

★ SUKHOTHAI

149 Second Avenue (near 9th Street)
DINNER.
Reservations: 460-5557.
Credit cards: AE, MC, V.
Inexpensive.

In the heterogeneity that is the so-called East Village (made up, as it is, of flower children gone to seed, residual Ukrainians, philistines named Punk, artists starving and otherwise, and gentrificators clinging against the future to tenement investments—not to mention chemical entrepreneurs and other unpaid-in-full members in good standing of the underground economy), this innocent place seems to have no place. It caters to its neighborhood in no special way, is a Thai restaurant like others in most respects, just does, how you say, its thing. It is situated, one flight up, in the midst of a row of boisterous restaurants-cum-sidewalk cafés: to the north of it, Bandito at No. 153 and Art Café at No. 151, and to the south, Pier Nine at No. 149. To enter this place on, say, a hot summer night from swarming streets—picking a path between the guzzler-gawkers at Art Café and those at Pier Nine—is to leave the neighborhood behind. Not that Sukhothai gets its traffic from other parts of town, rather that new rules take over when you enter it. That is to say, even though you are in the East Village, when someone asks you to extinguish your cigarette here, you do not respond by blowing smoke in his face.

It is not that the house has a nonsmoking section (it has not) or regulations of any kind, rather that the seemingly innocent demeanor of the Thais who run it, and the spacious, almost religious calm and cool of its dark and lofty interior, tend to soothe the passions of self that inform the sizzling arrondissement around it. The place is much brick and dusky plaster, unlinened tables of dark wood (a placemat of soft cloth at each place), and a plain wood floor, greenery all about, Thai art and mirrors here and there. Those materials and appointments notwithstanding, the dining room is in no way threadbare, has about it, in fact, a kind of well-worn baroque luxuriance. But there is also, appended to the front of the place and in quite another mode, a little "terrace" enclosed almost entirely in glass and suspended one story over Second Avenue, a handful of tables in a setting that, with its abundance of plants, on the windowsills and hanging from the skylighted ceiling, is rather jungly—but for the hot-pink neon sign in the front window that announces Sukhothai to the world.

Like most Thai eating places, this one assumes, sensibly, that non-Thais will have difficulty pronouncing the names of Thai dishes. Accordingly, the dishes are numbered, and you may order them by their numeric designations. Tod mun pla, for example, is Appetizer No. 1, firm chunks of fresh kingfish, darkened by their marinade, spicy, and fragrant of coriander leaves; haar keon, No. 2, for another, four shrimp wrapped in the bean-curd skin in which they were fried, served with a dish of sweet and slightly spicy oil. The satés are No. 3 on the list, and you may choose to have yours of beef, pork, or chicken—choose the last, and you are served many morsels of pale grilled meat on their skewers, the chicken saturated with the herbs and spices in which they have been steeped and set in a redded peanut sauce. Have any of those in preference to Appetizer No. 4, the so-called Thai egg roll, the somewhat greasy though crackling casings packed with a nameless vegetable mass. The soups make up a separate category, and you take it that No. 1, po-taak, is the most ambitious of them, for it is the most expensive, and is offered only in a serving suitable for two. It arrives over a portable stove, the soup in a vessel shaped like a doughnut bifurcated horizontally, a flame poking through its hole. The broth is grassy, tart of lime juice, spicy hot, and after a few spoons of it you may well remove your jacket and hang it over the back of your chair—the soup is abundant with chunks of seafood and mushrooms.

You note that of more than fifty listed items, Seafood No. 16 is the only one the house pushes with especial pride. "Highly recommended," reads the menu. Sure enough, the steamed whole fish (it reaches you, up to its waist in the broth in which it was done, in a fish-shaped metal dish over a small fire) is fresh, supple, moist, and permeated to heady effect with the flavors—herbs and vegetables, ginger and pork—that infuse its liquid. Of the several deep-fried fish, No. 14, pla preow whan, has a skin that is at once leather and crusty, is fine in its sweet and sour sauce of peppers and onions. Pad phed is one of those Thai dishes dominated by fired-up coconut milk—you may have yours made with chicken, beef, or pork, and however you have it, the liquid, thick with red and green peppers and strips of water chestnut in addition to the meat, is of a sweetness and complexity that is clear despite its fiery spiciness. The nuur yang nam tok is another hot dish, this one of beef, the crusted little slivers of tender meat mingled with onions and strikingly moistened by a tangy lime-juice sauce. Of the familiar rice noodle dishes, pad thai and mee krob, Sukhothai's are sweeter and less lively than most versions around town.

For dessert there is a coconut pudding of which it may be said that it has the texture of pudding and the flavor of coconut. Beer is the drink with this food, and the Thai beer served here—Singha—is good, assertively hoppy, a little fruity.

334

★★SUSHIZEN

57 West 46th Street
LUNCH, MONDAY TO FRIDAY; DINNER, MONDAY TO SATURDAY. CLOSED SUNDAY.
Reservations: 302-0707.
Credit cards: AE, DC.
Medium priced.

A recent tabulation comes up with one Japanese restaurant in Manhattan for every two manhole covers, the ratio constantly growing. To the Japanese, the differences among these eating places are surely as clear as the distinction to native New Yorkers between Luchow's and Lutèce. Locals, however, rarely can tell one morsel of, say, tuna sushi from another—so long as the fish is fresh. Occasionally, however, one Japanese restaurant becomes more popular than others. There are theories about this, the most convincing being that such places have something (very) subtly Western in their style. You cannot point to a dish and say this or that restaurant's version has an Occidental accent, only that in such places, whether or not they are also popular with the Japanese, New Yorkers are secure with the food. There is no compromise of Japanese style, you understand, only a certain overtone that happens to sound a distant Western bell. (You will get arguments about this from those who insist that their favorite Japanese restaurants are *echt* Japanese. Do not argue back—you are merely being misunderstood.)

Such a place is Sushizen. At the center of the city's midtown business district, it is often crowded for lunch. But, happily, in the evening you can usually come by any time, get yourself seated at once, share your waiter with few or no competing diners. The room is gray-carpeted, painted pale green, sports lower walls of raw silk. The establishment's few physical oddities include: backlighted circles of glass, about the size of wine-bottle bottoms, cut into the gray carpeting along the path from the front of the dining room to the one-step-up sushi bar at the back; one long wall the upper portion of which consists of bas reliefs over bas reliefs, a 10-inch-deep simulation of mountain range after mountain range (not a surprising technique for citizens of a small, crowded nation); and, the winner, the handsomely patterned suspenders on the unfailingly courteous pink-shirted waiters.

Sushizen serves sushi, all the common raw-fish varieties, among them tuna and fatty tuna and salmon, fluke and bass and yellowtail, each of them fresh, made with vinegared rice that is just this side of too sticky, that side of not sticky enough, garnished with brisk ginger, and with the violent wasabi with which to fortify the soy sauce you dip the constructs in. It also produces a few rarer sushi items: cool, silken octopus; smoky, sea-gamy eel, seemingly sugar sweetened, deeply oiled but not oily; and, the last word, sea urchin, the piercingly loud orange flesh set on a low platform of rice within a deep bracelet of seaweed, in the spare room at the top, if you so request, a raw quail egg, its yellow eye staring up at you forlornly from its imprisoned position—strong food, and the egg does not make it mild.

The non-sushi dishes include, naturally, first courses and main courses, and you may as well make your dinner of several of the former as one of the latter, for there is nothing inherently one or the other about most of them except their amount: eel again, that same smoky dark meat, this time sprinkled with sesame seeds and formed into a cucumber-wrapped roulade from which slices are served to you on a wood board, the warm, complex, many-textured disks garnished with wasabi and ginger; spinach, cold and fresh and acidic, under a cloud of shaved bonito (a cured-fish fundament of Japanese cooking), and set in the dark and stout broth in which the vegetable was done—bracing, particularly when dipped in the special soy sauce served with it; fried chicken, the moist meat of clear chicken flavor within its crisp and slightly tangy batter; yellowtail collar, a great triangular section of the fish, which you more or less break open—within the browned skin you find masses of particularly sweet white meat; dumplings, their salty pork fillings herbed, spicy, and light within the delicate noodle wrappers; negima, a variant of the familiar dish, served in squat little packages, the shafts of asparagus crunchy within the tender wrappers of thin-sliced beef, the vegetable augmented by one chunk of cheese per unit—the presence of cheese is of course surprising, as is the fact that it does not harm the dish; broiled eggplant, firm and well oiled, this also topped with great tangles of shaved bonito, which here does impart a vague ocean flavor; chopped conch, a little tough, strewn with tiny sticks of seaweed, the conch of vivid marine flavor, as are the two red fish roes with which it is mingled.

★ TABLE D'HÔTE

44 East 92nd Street
LUNCH, DAILY; DINNER, MONDAY TO SATURDAY.
Reservations: 348-8125.
Credit cards: AE, MC, V.
Beer and wine.
Medium priced.

Conversion of ancient storefronts to contemporary eating places has rarely been achieved with so little rehabilitation of so rickety a site. And though this tiny place has been around several years now (and presumably turns a profit), those in charge have apparently concluded that its charm is in its worn condition, for they have preserved its every dent and bump through all seasons. Actually, except for the stamped-tin ceiling, which has rents in it like the tears in a pair of stylish old jeans, nothing about the place is actually broken down. It just looks as if no plasterer has been near these walls, no scraper at this floor, since the school days of those who here own and operate. It appears that they moved in, painted the floor red, everything else white (including the two four-bladed fans that hang from the ceiling), installed a tiny kitchen (just curtains conceal it from the dining room), and, you figure, placed the crockery and the cookware and the early Americana on the walls where they would conceal the holes and cracks. Intent on preserving the ambience established by these initial measures, they then fitted the place out with an assortment of eight tables (left unlinened) that would be antiques if age were the only standard, surrounded them with what would be chairs if four legs and a seat the size of *Time* magazine defined the species. Still, this old brand of innocence does beguile a little, and it gets an assist from the one element that was probably unplanned: What with the easy circulation between the kitchen and you, Table d'Hôte offers not only homey surroundings, but also the smells of home cooking.

Do not, however, be deceived by those aromas. The food here aims for contemporaneity. The brief menu—a handful of appetizers, of main courses, of desserts—changes each month. Herewith most of the items on one of them: cold leeks, a little overcooked, but in a good dressing that, though fortified with bits of jalapeño pepper and soured with capers, does not overpower the vegetable; crostini, four substantial crusts of toasted dark bread covered with a fresh liver paste that is fragrant of sage; a salad of arugula (a bit wilted), endives, and sun-dried tomatoes, all in a good dressing, with it a couple of crusts of French bread adorned with little slabs of creamy goat cheese; another salad, one that suffers for the soft overripeness of the sliced avocado you find among the perfectly good watercress, fennel, cherry tomatoes.

Some impeccable seafood: a fillet of fresh, moist Norwegian salmon, all its sweet flavor intact, served in a silken dill sauce; and tiny, crisped soft-shell crabs in a butter that is nubbly with minced scallions. The chicken breasts are nicely browned, actually sport a bit of chicken flavor in their sauce of red peppers and mustard—in which the latter quite obscures the former. The filet mignon is wrapped in bacon, sautéed with green peppercorns—this is tender meat accurately prepared, and the spicy, somewhat creamy sauce is fine, but the smokiness of this bacon is an inelegant touch in the otherwise well made dish.

The chocolate pot de crème is wonderfully smooth and intense under its rich whipped cream and sprig of mint. That whipped cream yet again, this time on the lemon tart, the tangy custard on a crumbly, buttery pastry. The almond mocha-cream dacquoise is a rather heavy layered affair that, happily, is leavened and brightened by a thin layer of raspberries. A good shortbread pastry, fresh strawberries and blueberries, and a smooth custard make up the good fruit tart.

No hard liquor. Wine is $15 and up on the short list, but you may bring your own and have it served to you for a corkage fee.

★★TANGO

43 West 54th Street
LUNCH, MONDAY TO FRIDAY; DINNER, MONDAY TO SATURDAY. CLOSED SUNDAY.
Reservations: 765-4683.
Credit cards: AE, DC, MC, V.
Medium priced.

Anybody can turn up yet another decent Japanese restaurant. They are everywhere, like occupied cabs. The trick is to find one that does not remind you of a hundred others. You are in especial luck if the place you find is, moreover, a little better than most, a phenomenon like one of those cabs disgorging a passenger right where you are standing, so that you may have it for yourself. You may have Tango for yourself, for though it has its lunchtime followers from nearby office buildings, by night it is often a sleepy place. You find it glowing only very softly on its quiet side street. You consider its posted menu, which offers little to suggest that it differs from a thousand other places. You enter to the inevitable sushi bar, from behind which men grin brightly at you, looking friendly while wielding knives. Their station faces a narrow brick-walled aisle that leads to your basic Japanese dining room at the back, in which there are beams on the ceiling, wooden slats over rice paper to simulate Japanese windows on the walls. The place is mostly pale gray, with pale-gray table linen covered by plate glass. Somehow, plate glass, no matter how transparent, never looks like table linen. The waiters and waitresses are angelic, unless you hang around after closing time—when they want you to go home, so that they can eat. Then they become firm. The waitresses pad around in ravishing kimonos. The waiters are in black and white, like the fellows who work in Italian restaurants on Third Avenue. The uniform, however, is all the resemblance. You ask one of these gentlemen why a Japanese restaurant is named for a Latin-American slow dance. He explains that it is not, that long ago, when Japan was politically districted differently from the way it is now, one of its prefectures was called Tango. He explains also that the word in Japanese has no other meaning. When pressed further, he carefully avoids stating directly that anyone connected with this place could be guilty of pride of origin. "Maybe," he says, "the owner is from there." Then he smiles a little wickedly.

Then he brings you fresh abalone steamed in Japanese wine, and it occurs to you that you may never have tasted abalone before, for these thin slices of fibrous but tender seafood have an almost nutlike flavor—they are arranged like the sides of a polygonal tent over a mound of fresh spinach, all in a pool of dark and salty broth. You order boiled octopus and set yourself for lengths of tentacle with suckers attached. You receive instead tepid, delicate slivers of the pale meat, mixed with like slivers of cucumber, the two dotted with bits of seaweed, the three set in a lightly oiled soy sauce broth—the interplay of these flavors is at once gentle and dazzling. An ice cream scoop of grated horseradish is covered over with globules of glistening salmon roe, over all of which your waiter or waitress pours some soy sauce from a little pitcher on your table—a bright, rousing dish. The eggplant appetizer—better known as nasuno-misodengaku—reaches you as a great slab of the warm, succulent vegetable in the shape of a flat fish, the skin still attached to the bottom side, the whole spread with a warm, fruity soybean paste. There are simple dishes too, like the deep-fried bean curd, little blocks of the soft, comforting stuff, the fried surfaces slightly darkened and leathery. You dip the bean curd in soy sauce to which you have added fresh ginger, horseradish, chopped scallions.

When Japanese restaurants first came to New York in numbers, tempura was something of an astonishment to the locals. This was deep frying, sure enough, but the crisped batter was so light and free of grease that it could hardly be thought of in the same unhealthy, fattening breath as the American counterpart. During the decades since then Japanese frying standards in the big city have slipped, and a lot of what now goes as tempura lacks air and, if you handle it, leaves your fingers oiled. At Tango, however, you may be reminded of your first experiences with this remarkable form of cooking, for not only are the shrimp sweet and the vegetables fresh and crisp, but the batter is gossamer-like, has no more weight than cotton candy. At about the time you first tried tempura, you also were introduced to sushi, raw fish mostly, combined—along with other ingredients—with vinegared rice. Here the fish is fresh, the rice is tangy, the soybean wrappers are firm and tender, and the variety of seafood is extensive—red roes, tuna, mackerel, shrimp, bass, more. You need not have your seafood raw. Seafood suki comes in a great pot with a wooden cover. In its broth you will find lobster and crabmeat in their shells, octopus and clams, mushrooms and scallions, much else. Sounds good? Not so good as most of the dishes here, for the seafood is overcooked—much of it is tough —though the broth in which it is prepared is pungent and complex. The so-called barbecued eel is sweet and blackened, the meat so rich it seems fatty. What the house bills as Japanese tartar steak does not rival the best of the West, but the fresh-ground beef is fine with the horseradish and chopped scallions with which it is spread—you must add soy sauce for the essential seasoning.

★ TEMPO

30 East 29th Street
LUNCH, MONDAY TO FRIDAY; DINNER, MONDAY TO SATURDAY. CLOSED SUNDAY.
Reservations: 532-8125.
Credit cards: AE, DC, MC, V.
Medium priced.

Your proprietor/host is one of those who is prouder of his ability to walk than you are of your mastery of nine languages. The example is not frivolously chosen, for his remarkable gait is a matter of the body and all four limbs: the erect bearing; the arms, like those of a wind-up toy soldier, swinging through an arc of a hundred degrees; the stride really no different from the stride of just about any man whose knees are fused. He even nods curtly, clicks his heels, and spins on one of them to let you know that the wish you have expressed will be attended to immediately and with precision by, presumably, the shackled squad of broken souls in the galley. He knows well how to snap his fingers, raise his arm, and point. And his demonstration, to some novice, of the manly art of spreading a cloth on a table draws a round of applause—or would, were not the onlookers rapt. He snaps his fingers again, this time to break the trance, then is off to yet another fateful job of work. His self-involvement is such that your visit to his restaurant is really an offering—of your time for his use. You ask him a three-second question, he gives you a five-minute answer. Ask him nothing at all, and he gives you a five-minute answer. You see him coming, you feign deadly serious conversation, appear stunned, disoriented, impatiently eager to return to what you were just saying, and he gives you, etc.

His Italian restaurant has been installed in an anonymous interior of mirrored walls, dark-wood walls, pale-green banquettes, and palms of all heights with fronds of all shapes—stubby palms, medium palms, palms that are pushing against the ceiling. The happenstance placement of this greenery suggests that first you get it off the truck, later you worry about where to put it. There is a bar up front, and just beyond it a display of food in jars, food in cartons, wax fruit, and wooden cheese, which is meant to suggest, you figure, the freshness of the ingredients upon which the house insists. Here and there are hung black-and-white photographs of the produce of the old country. Black-and-white photographs of food are as mouth-watering as black-and-white food.

Inevitably, the restaurant is better than what its management and appearance beg you to believe. At the bar, for example, the ripe olives, intensely salty, mingled with chunks of garlic, and glistening of their herbed oil marinade, are of rousing vigor. And the freebies with which you may or may not be favored at your table, while you consider the menu, include sweet and sharp marinated sun-dried tomatoes, little chunks of Parmesan cheese that are hard and heady, and bruschetta—crusts of bread mounded over with tomatoes in an herbed vinaigrette. After that, if things are not continuously downhill, they are no better than one step down for each step up.

There is some safety in the antipasto freddo, an array of marinated and/or grilled vegetables, among them sun-dried tomatoes, thin slices of oiled and crosshatched eggplant, mushrooms, sections of artichoke, more, all of it good, none of it exceptional. Order the carpaccio of beef, and when it shows up it is placed on a side stand beside your table. The beef is already arranged over a mound of arugula, and it is adorned with capers and thin slices of Parmesan, and it is moistened with a lemon dressing—despite which your waiter adds oil and all the juice he can get out of half a lemon (unless you stop him), and presents you with carpaccio that is soaking wet. For some reason—perhaps for no reason—a perfectly decent dish of potato gnocchi in a lively red sauce has on it a dollop of ricotta cheese, on which, in turn, there is a smaller dollop of pesto—the last element converts the good but simple dish into an elaborated absurdity. There are, however, better dishes under the pasta heading, among them ravioloni stuffed with seafood, moistened with a buttery sauce, and strewn with strands of crisp fresh vegetables and earthy porcini mushrooms; and orecchiette (little ears), the disks of pasta, florets of crunchy broccoli, and short lengths of meaty sausage all in a stout and enriched broth.

Your broiled Dover sole is shown to you whole and, at your request and before your eyes, it is beheaded, detailed, skinned, boned, oiled, lemoned, and served to you with a rousing white-wine sauce that is thick with capers and pine nuts; the fish itself, however, though fresh, has lost its flavor and moistness to an overdose of exposure to heat. A thick steak of swordfish reaches you medium rare in its good sauce of capers and mint, which cannot, however, rescue fish that is a day past its peak. The sea scallops, the menu informs you, are prepared according to a "top secret recipe." Your waiter tells you the secret. You order them anyway, and, just as he said, the scallops are in a sauce prepared with curry powder—the kind that comes in a can, turns everything it touches acid yellow, and tastes like an industrial chemical. The grilled chicken is perfectly grilled and perfectly blank, the chicken being one of those that are raised on bleached flour. The pheasant is much better, albeit a somewhat heavy dish in which the nuggets of meat are mingled with white grapes in a red wine sauce. The rack of lamb, studded with chunks of garlic and touched with rosemary, is accurately done.

Your host tells you the pear is poached in Burgundy. Your waiter tells you it is done in Barolo. It does look as if it is done in red wine, and it is ok. The so-called marinated orange tastes like a raw orange. There are, however, winners among the desserts, including a napoleon in which layers of an extraordinarily light pastry are interleaved with a pastry cream that is at once rich and airy. The ricotta cheesecake is the real thing, sweet, wet, eggy, solid—and yet not heavy. The boss himself will march to your table to prepare your zabaglione; he uses three liquors, none of them marsala, and the thing is, how you say, subtle—still, it is fine on the ripe and juicy strawberries.

★★THAI ROYALE

1668 First Avenue (at 87th Street)
DINNER.
Reservations: 876-5640.
Credit cards: AE, DC, MC, V.
No liquor.
Inexpensive.

One way or another, there is always something innocent about a Thai restaurant. This place, for example, is innocent of current trends in restaurant interior design. The dining room is assembled of such parts as glazed brick and pale wood, carpeting and Danish bentwood chairs (with caned backs and stuffed plastic seats), and, on the walls, framed mirrors and presumably Thai art, all of which bespeak innocence in definitive form: the absence of sophistication. And, oh yes, the help—especially the lady who runs the place—all of whom regard you and treat you with a smiling wide-eyed goodwill that would deter a hangman.

If you have read Thai menus before, you have read most of this one. And if you have had chicken saté before, the oil-moistened lengths of browned white meat, on their wood skewers, will not in themselves reveal to you anything new, though the hot peanut sauce with which they are served is striking for its silken freshness. More chicken, this one called garry-puff, in which the ground meat of the bird, flavored with fragrant Eastern spices, is packed into triangular turnovers of light, flaky pastry. Certain first-course salads seem intended specifically to rouse either your appetite or you. Pla-pa-muk is one, squid bodies packed with a fiery squid stuffing and mingled with onions and herbs in a hot dressing that is touched with lime. The beef salad, yam-nur, is a craggy mound of hefty strands of browned beef, resilient and fibrous, but not tough, intertwined with onions, and moistened with a searing dressing that is heady of coriander.

Among finfish, the menu mentions only sea bass, but sometimes snapper is available in the same preparations. The steamed snapper, for example, is the utterly fresh whole fish, firm and moist in its pink and silvery skin, in a dark ginger-flavored broth dotted with good mushrooms. Goong-ob-mo-din is described, in part, as "broiled shrimp," so you are a little surprised to be presented with a covered pot in which the shrimp are buried in masses of herbed noodles—you season the steaming food with a hot citrus-flavored sauce. For plain abundance you turn to gai-yang, half a big chicken, marinated with ginger and garlic and browned, good the way it is, though a fruity sauce is served with it. The duck item called ped-gra-tiem is heavily garlicked and salty, and the meat, though skinned, is rich of fat—this is an honest and weighty dish that will not appeal to all.

The proprietor of this place is related to the proprietor of an Italian restaurant in another part of town. That may explain the availability of tartufo for dessert. But sweets do not really make much sense after this food.

• TIME & AGAIN

116 East 39th Street
LUNCH, MONDAY TO FRIDAY; DINNER, MONDAY TO SATURDAY. CLOSED SUNDAY.
Reservations: 685-8887.
Credit cards: AE, DC, MC, V.
Expensive.

The Tuscany Hotel, Murray Hill, a decorous clientele whose bland indifference to ineptitude is gentility's unconcern for what irritates everyone else—such are the crucial makings of this hilariously titled place, maybe the first restaurant in America in which the so-called New American Cooking aspires to a form in which you did not expect to find it until its dotage, in a hotel dining room in a one-hotel county seat somewhere in anthracite country, some time in the next century. You have, however, no grounds for complaint, for as the name connotes repetition to the point of monotony (did someone think it was catchy?), you are forewarned. Nobody laughs when the waiter—taking, it is true, his cue from the printed menu—describes as best he can the filet of mignon; or when his strangulated pronunciation of haricots verts comes out triple-rhyming with Mary what hurts. Old money copes with the servant problem by floating blithely above it. Naturally, as soon as he has finished his recitation of the daily specials, he presents you with a card—it has been his pony—on which is printed the very information he broke his jaw trying to mouth.

You are informed that the restaurant is not managed by the hotel. And you get the idea—from the dopey name, the establishment's advertising, even, vaguely, from some of the appointments—that Time & Again makes intended reference to the turn of the century. Forget it. This is your basic hotel dining room, traditional and time-honored and old-fashioned and banal, it is true, but evocative of no era. In fact the food is better than it seems, but you have to work to keep open the mind, for in surroundings like these one reflexively responds to any food as hotel food, which is to say that here even Pavlov's dogs would decline to salivate: walnut-colored wood paneling, mirrored walls, broad-loom on the floor, chandeliers of etched-glass lights that match the mounted sconces, big armchairs, cushy sofas-for-two upholstered in an appropriately somber dark-rose velvet, period art suitable for greeting cards, potted palms, and, centrally situated, in a vase that stands on a short marble column, a burst of seemingly petrified flowers apparently cho-sen for their resemblance to flowers you see, frozen in the past, in old and yellowed engravings.

Not that old, but not as young as it once was, is this calamari salad, which appears to suffer for having been dressed for tea only to find itself hanging around until dinner, by which time it regrets having put on only a balsamic vinegar vinaigrette, when, under the circumstance, something more assertive is necessary if the thing is to retain its liveliness until so late in the day. You are more likely to anticipate a tired condition in what is unfortunately given as "Time & Again Salad," but no, the lump of warm goat cheese with which the production is surmounted is just out of the fire, with respect to its pully texture and cindered surface is much like a goat cheese toasted marshmallow, though its flavor is the real thing, as are the asparagus spears, tomatoes, and excellent oil that are among the estimable components under it. A "European cucumber," apparently, is the size of your forearm. You learn this from the duck salad (the gourd is one of the listed ingredients), which reaches you as the contents and artillery of a fort, its wall a thin, lengthwise cross section cut from an immense cuke formed into a squat cylinder, which is filled with salad and overlaid with slices of tender duck that protrude like cannon over the wall—the meat, though made tart by the lime marinade with which the bird has been treated, reveals strong duck flavor, and the fort is surrounded by (but not threatened by) half a dozen melon balls the size of marbles. The crabcakes are fine if, big if, you do not expect them to be crabby, for these patties, though hot and light, spicy and crisped, are merely carriers for the perfectly suitable marinara sauce served with them.

More salad, this time as the bulk of a dish in which seared shrimp are the featured ingredient, the giant untainted crustaceans, sweet and crunchy within their blackened surfaces, arranged over good greens that are garnished with slices of ripe avocado and sections of grapefruit, and moistened with a sesame dressing that is livened with ginger. Have that any day before you take a chance on grilled fish, for the halibut is done to destruction, the snowy meat an unidentifiable pulp within its charred exterior, a state of affairs that the puree of red peppers in which the fish is set cannot redeem. The seared loin of rabbit suffers similarly, for though the slices of meat are supple, tender, moist, you could mistake them for slices of a factory chicken raised on bleached flour; still, if you think of the stuff not as rabbit, but as white bread, you note that it is eminently suitable for mopping up the thick and winy mustard sauce in which the rabbit, and the mound of pasta that garnishes it, is served. Eager for meat you can recognize, you seek safety in lamb, for it is unusual lamb that fails to be itself—still, this comes close, though the blood-pink slices of tender loin are just about redeemed by their winy and sticky rosemary-flavored sauce, and by their garnish of what is called "black bean cassoulet," the chewy beans nutty and spicy and mingled with bits of strong bacon.

What goes as peach charlotte is a somewhat gelatinized mass, white and glistening, dotted with morsels of fresh peach and adorned with slivers of fresh strawberry—the good fruit and the mousse reach you in a pool of light and lively caramel sauce. Apple strudel is good at room temperature, is even better hot, but here it comes to you from the icebox, so it is cloying, as is its watery crème anglaise—with the strudel you get a ball of vanilla set in strawberry sauce, which promptly gets all your attention. The feuilleté of fresh fruit is a feuilleté by virtue of a little square of flaky puff pastry under the many-colored fan-shaped array of fruit slices, another little square on top, all moistened by a red berry puree—the fruit varies from the unripe to the overripe. The house makes good whipped cream, serves it with fine berries.

★★TRASTEVERE and TRASTEVERE 84

309 East 83rd Street; 155 East 84th Street
DINNER.
Reservations: 734-6343; 744-0210.
Credit cards: AE.
Beer and wine.
Expensive.

One imagines that, once upon a time, in the section of Rome for which these restaurants are named, the practice grew up of serving working-class dinners to working-class folk on a single plate: meat or seafood on one side of the plate, salad on the other. One further imagines that the trickle of cool salad dressing that, inevitably, invaded the hot-food territory is the basis of the cookery that, in these two restaurants, is represented for the first time in New York. This historic accident, now encouraged to occur scores of times per night on dinner plates in these eating places, has so delighted New York that the first timid effort to bring this food here—the tiny Trastevere on 83rd Street—was hardly a year old before it was busily spawning an enlarged version of itself only a few blocks to the northwest. Of course, there is more to Trastevere's cooking than hot food touched by cold. And almost all that these places do, they do well. The menus of the two branches are identical, and the cooking at the two is indistinguishable.

The first place these pioneers opened is only a little wider than a refrigerator but at least twice as deep. Into it they fitted almost a dozen tables, a table for four being about the size of a long-playing record. Anything larger is set aside for large family gatherings (and at the end of the evening, management, friends, and relatives assemble at one of these, knee-to-knee, and eat things that, you note, are not offered guests). To offset the crowded conditions, the lights are turned off. To find out more about where you are, take the flickering, dripping taper from your table and hold it aloft. You will espy that high on one wall is hung a photograph, in full color, of Italy's World Cup championship soccer team. Mention this to any waiter, and he will stop on the spot to share with you his amazement at his countrymen's accomplishment. Engravings of Roman buildings may also be perceived, as well as, inexplicably, autographed glossies of American movie stars. When the place is filled, the waiters negotiate the so-called aisle like latecomers crawling to theater seats. The second store is twice as big and just as crowded. Otherwise, its relationship to the first place is roughly that of Tavern on the Green to a tavern. The darkness is real, but the bricks are artificial. The engravings are here, but not the soccer team. It was the original, tiny place that got most of the praise in the press, so it gets the publicity followers from the Lanes, Drives, Roads, and Crescents—they never utter a peep of complaint when their dinner plates impinge, necessarily, on the air rights over their laps. The bigger store gets the locals. They like the extra room on the tables for their elbows, and the food is just as good.

It includes spiedino alla romana, a multilayered, deep-fried hot sandwich of charred bread, melted cheese, strong ham, in a thick and powerfully garlicked sauce of anchovies and oil. The hot vegetable appetizer for two is composed of sautéed vegetables—zucchini, peppers, mushrooms, broccoli—in a garlic-flavored oil, sometimes accompanied by crisp slices of tomato in tart vinaigrette. Be warned that on occasion the mussel appetizer is of rank mussels, which is too bad, for when the mussels are fresh, the dish is fine—dozens of mollusks mounded up in an inch of thick, buttery tomato sauce that is loaded with garlic. This is the place for pasta primavera. The very thin spaghetti—capellini—is firm, and the peas, zucchini, broccoli, and tomato with which it is mingled are in a hot, garlicky oil that has taken on the flavors of the fresh vegetables.

Among the main courses that are served with salad, and thereby are sauced with its dressing, are sole, scampi, and a big, pounded-thin breaded veal chop—each is artfully sautéed. The salad is of lettuce and tomato, and the tart vinegar dressing livens the disparate items as if it were made just for the purpose. The good chicken dishes include pollo gaetano, in which the browned chunks of bird are served in a wine sauce that is dotted with mushrooms and garlic.

The desserts include a rather Italianate napoleon—the custard is dense, the layers of deeply browned pastry heavy. A sometimes available cream puff is of good chou pastry, real whipped cream, and a hot chocolate sauce of intensity and polish. The tartufo is a great nugget of chocolate-studded chocolate ice cream concealed within a cloud of that good whipped cream.

★ TRATTORIA DELL'ARTE

900 Seventh Avenue (near 57th Street)
LUNCH AND DINNER.
Reservations: 245-9800.
Credit cards: AE, DC, MC, V.
Medium priced.

When, several years back, the restaurant Petrossian moved in on the Russian Tea Room's territory around Carnegie Hall, it was noted that nothing revolutionary had taken place. Petrossian wanted only to outdo the Tea Room at its own game—caviar, vodka, champagne. It was as if the world had not changed in the half century and more since RTR began selling those substances in this neighborhood, as if at the end of every concert Carnegie Hall still disgorged three thousand White Russians, Eastern Europeans, Viennnese, and other assorted displaced persons, folks whose tastes were formed in the old country, were refined and satisfied on 57th Street. No one noticed that the old crowd was dying out. No one was doing any marketing research (which would have consisted of hanging around the box office before a few concerts to see who was buying the tickets). No one, that is, until the entrepreneurs behind this place took a look, decided that since the rest of the city is crazy about Italian food, and since Carnegie Hall's patrons come from all over town, a trattoria near Carnegie could not miss. So far, so good.

Comes along, however, Milton Glaser, designer. Any designer, says Milton, in effect, can design a restaurant; many can design restaurants that militate against your enjoyment of dinner; but only a few triumphantly get away with it—Milty, of course, among them. Like certain contemporary operatic stage sets that transform period comedies into vintage nightmares, Glaser has made of a restaurant for Italian food an advertisement for Glaser. You cannot see the restaurant for the designer. Though "casual Italian" is a restaurant category to which humor (intentional and otherwise) in design is not entirely foreign, the difficulty with restaurants in which the decor is amusing, or is intended to be, is that in no time at all even funny jokes grow old. Here the joke is tiresome from the start. Announced as an eating place that would call to mind an Italian sculpture academy, the Trattoria recalls instead innumerable witticisms about the Roman nose and its direct or inverse proportionality to this or that anatomical member. You were probably hoping for a casual restaurant near Carnegie Hall that does not call you an idiot every time you walk in. This one passes judgment while you are still out in the street—a giant white plaster nose overlooks Seventh Avenue from the Trattoria's upstairs window.

You enter to the two-bar barroom, an antipasto bar (at which you choose your dinner from platters on display) and a liquor bar, behind which a dozen or so famous Italian noses (Machiavelli, DiMaggio, Toscanini, etc.) are depicted against a scenic background. Laughing good-naturedly, you proceed to the brightly lit first dining room, the floor pale wood, the walls pale yellow, the adornments a giant white-plaster ear, an eye, and mock-Renaissance drawings of body parts (over the centuries the ink has faded to brown). A green room is next, dimmer, carpeted, furnished with booths as well as tables—take down the twenty-times-lifesize giant lips that hang on one wall, and you could be anyplace. Dining room three is upstairs, apparently a second story squeezed in as an afterthought, the headroom such that though you may be able to make it while upright, your fedora will not. Here the terra-cotta walls are hung with prints, paintings, drawings, all jocularly pertaining to the human nose. You will probably go on laughing till your food arrives.

Order the antipasto platter, the "house specialty," and though components are specified on the menu, you never know for sure what to expect: maybe a white bean salad that is nothing but white beans, a slice of prosciutto wrapped around a bread stick, a well-oiled caponata, mozzarella, black olives, a tasteless and tired stuffed pepper, and, on occasion, no artichokes or grilled eggplant or braised fennel, the components that led you to the dish in the first place. In this department you are better off ordering individual items, among them a warm, soothing dish of mozzarella, lengths of tomato, leaves of basil, and black olives that are grilled until they are crusty and brittle, the entire dish bathed in olive oil. The place turns out a good Caesar salad of crisp romaine lettuce, much grated cheese, crusty croutons, the anchovies part of the vigorous dressing, and therefore remote. It is the Trattoria's weird policy that half orders will be prepared of vegetarian pasta dishes only, which excludes both meat and seafood sauces. Thus you may have half an order of bucatini (thick spaghetti) with a chunky and fragrant fennel sauce that is thick with cloves of browned garlic, leaves of strong grana cheese across the top; or, from the selection of another day, spaghetti in a buttery, heady sauce of garlic and basil, on top those sheets of cheese again. You will have to take a full order, but the wide, heavy noodles called pappardelle are served in a pungent, weighty, stewlike sauce of rabbit and red wine—the kind of dish that generates perspiration even in winter time. Sometimes a risotto is listed, on occasion rice with shellfish—the grain, dotted with mussels, shrimp, and squid, is moist of an earthy stock that, almost ruinously, has been fortified with a double dose of salt. The menu warns that pizzas are served immediately from the oven, which is to say, their delivery will not be coordinated with other dishes. You opt for the potato pizza, because, unlikely as it sounds, good potato pizzas have been known. Not this time. The thin bread has a matzohlike flatness of flavor, the thin slices of potato have little flavor of their own, and the rosemary and bacon, which should liven the dish, simply point up its dullness.

The house is capable of serving yellowfin tuna that has been done to petrifaction. At the same time it can produce a veal milanese that is pounded out to a huge thin sheet, breaded, browned, greaselessly crisped, adorned with a bit of arugula and tomato, and garnished with half a lemon, in a cheesecloth pant, with the juice of which you liven the delicate meat. Your bistecca arrives sliced, the herbed and oiled lengths of tender meat are of good beef flavor, the shoestring potatoes are not bad, but the billed "arugula and tomatoes" arrive as a pile of wilted and undressed lettuce.

The raspberry tart is of fruit that is less than ripe—the ball of vanilla helps. Yet another ball of vanilla accompanies the hot, sweet, and rather delicate apple tart. The napoleon is an immensity, layers of flaky pastry interleaved with liquored whipped cream that is rich and fluffy. The tartufo is a ball of intense chocolate ice cream studded with bits of chocolate and wrapped in a craggy chocolate crust.

You may, if you wish, bring your own wine: corkage, $5.

★ TROIKA

148 West 67th Street
LUNCH, SUNDAY; DINNER, DAILY.
Reservations: 724-0709.
Credit cards: AE, DC, MC, V.
Medium priced.

The baby grand piano with, apparently, an out-of-tune spinet in it, is had at, some nights, by a shirt-sleeved Slavic basso (he sings lower than the piano can go) whose repertoire, now from the keyboard, now from the larynx, embraces Orchi Chonya and Moscow Nights, Cats and My Fair Lady, Carmen and Tosca. Another night, another Russian, this one given to pallid jazz, Chopin, and propagation of the notion that the two are indistinguishable. Sunday night, all quiet. Troika looks like a refugee's idea of what goes in the West, an intended jewel of a room, pale peach and faded mauve, with candles in the shaded lamps on the white-linened tables, prints on the walls—legends in Cyrillic lettering—and a black-and-white TV on the little bar at the front, on which the staff fixates when, as often, things are slow. An unlikely setting (one that could be inexpensively rescued by lowering the lights), and yet, emanates from the kitchen food that, though it sometimes suffers for having waited upon your arrival, has the convincing impact of authenticity. With respect to certain dishes, this is like being persuaded of the validity of a proposition while preferring nevertheless to doubt it.

All of which you soon forget if you begin with black caviar, which you may have with blinis, or with bread, or, if you can persuade your waiter to persuade the kitchen, with toast and melted butter. You get a generous ounce of it in a small heart-shaped glass dish (set upon a bowl of ice) that looks like something your grandmother received twelve of as a wedding present. But, big but, this is perfect caviar, the little black globules firm and aglow, their gentle but vivid ocean flavor much in need of no help—no lemon, no onions, no nothing—to improve it. (With beluga at $48.50 the oz., your attention is directed to osetra at $28.50, which suffers not by comparison.)

The balance of your dinner involves making choices between the familiar and the rare. Among the former you find a stout hot borscht—thick with beets and cabbage, the broth of a deep stock—to which you add sour cream according to your lights; stuffed cabbage, the compactures within the wrappers of a well-seasoned and meaty complexity,

347

though you wish the cabbage had a bit of texture, had not wilted through the day. Among the latter there is this cold smoked eel, cylindrical lengths cut from the unbutterflied spine-in article, the black skin leathery, the pale meat at once sweet and fishy under its smokiness, much like smoked whitefish, though, for visual and textural reasons, not for every palate; and satzivi, a cold but fiery walnut paste, heady of dill, pungent of garlic, thick with slivers of chicken, and unfortunately, chicken skin, the last a rather clammy substance at icebox temperatures—otherwise a striking dish.

The beef stroganoff suffers for the beef having been done down to a gray grimness. So if what you want is red meat in familiar form, and you are here when it is offered, the lamb shish kebab, being grilled to your order, is lively, the great nuggets of marinated meat blood pink within their charred surfaces, also on the skewer chunks of blackened tomato and onion. What is listed as salmon sever is served as snapper sever, the rather cooked-through fish deeply imbued with the flavor of its mustard sauce. Presumably you must grow up with teliatina royale to understand it—it is veal, studded with ham and salmon, in a perfumed caviar sauce, and perhaps in a perfect preparation the diverse ingredients became an entity, though here they are an argument. The Siberian pelmeni are a big winner, the meat-filled, noodle-encased dumplings in a lightly fatted broth— you dip the hot and spicy articles in cold sour cream, which enriches them.

The many-layered chocolate cake must have been fine the day it arrived. The chocolate-covered strawberries are adolescent candy in a pool of Grand Marnier.

★★LA TULIPE

104 West 13th Street
DINNER. CLOSED MONDAY.
Reservations: 691-8860.
Credit cards: AE, DC, MC, V.
Expensive.

This one is run by a former schoolmaster and his wife, he the church usher out front who, wearing a thin smile in which are blended sanctity and tolerance, leads you to your table, she the wholesome-looking lady in charge of the kitchen who, her involvement perhaps more supervisory than participatory, sometimes arrives at the front door when her last customers are on brandy. Mr. & Mrs. exchange the smiles of greeting, on such occasions, of mates who have found bliss through mutual respect. The restaurant, moreover, though French in its food and much else, has about it a peculiarly American self-satisfaction of spirit, as if its success confirmed not only the business sense of those who run it but their goodness as well. You see regulars who, after responding to their host's sweetish greeting not from his plane, but from one a few steps down, settle into their chairs with the contentment of those coming off a frisson of anointment. Of La Tulipe's state of grace, however, discretion is the better part. Why test a proven condition? Now that the restaurant has found its way, it is set. Its brief menu, for example, which is almost frozen (from time to time one or two items are changed), is supplemented by little in the way of special daily dishes—often as not, none is offered. Happily, however, the perfections that can compensate for so narrow an aim are here often in evidence. All of which is as it should be, for La Tulipe is the restaurant of those who take no chances, and are content to have none taken on their behalf.

It is also, though run by Americans, determinedly French, particularly a first encounter. The room to which you enter has been fitted out with an impeccable French accent. The zinc bar, the brass-rimmed marble-topped tables surrounded by café chairs, the BYRRH poster and the ABSINTHE-BAILLY clock, the floor of dark-stained wood, the wildflowers, and the dozens of prints and old menus on the walls (Pyramide, Le Pavillon) would be in place in Paris itself. There are even a couple of white-linened tables in this room, off in a corner at a banquette of brown corduroy, where you can sometimes get seated when the place is otherwise booked up. Eating in the bar is a quieter and, surely, a visually more diverting experience than dinner in the dining room proper, a formally laid out room, crowded with tables and chairs, that is convivial solely by virtue of the humanity that fills it, and fills it with noise, for its deep-red walls, inlaid rectangular mirrors, and dark carpeting add up to a weighty environment only slightly leavened by the prints and flowers here and there.

You are waited on by an earnest staff that is in large part French, and you order from a menu that is almost entirely French. Not French at all is the pinched spirit that determines the size of certain helpings. Consider, for example, the mousse de truite fumée, a wondrous substance, buttery, creamy, judiciously salted, and of vivid smoked-fish flavor, of which you are served a coiled ribbon that, unwound, would generously butter the surface of a ladyfinger—it is garnished, in kind, by strands of roasted red pepper that, though of high flavor, are of elusive substance, comprising as they do a volume that would get lost in a shot glass. Perhaps an effort is made to play quantity off against quality, for you get, if not an amplitude, at least a sufficiency of the séviche de saumon, a pink obelisk of salmon slivers in a crimson pool of tomato puree—the fish would be fine had it been delicately "cooked" rather than lengthily soaked in its marinade, yielding fish that, though rousing, lacks breed. What goes as mosaique de porc is a chunky, meaty, well-fatted, and spicy terrine in which nuggets of pork and tongue, with pistachio nuts, are bound in a firm jelly—the thin slice is in a tart and oily dressing that is thick with herbs. Order the gâteau aux aubergines, and you are served yet another slice cut from a loaf, this one hot and two-sided, one side a mass of pungent goat cheese, the other a layering of eggplant and tomato, the flavor of the eggplant—which is saturated with oil but not oily—dominant, the strong stuff garnished with roasted red peppers, once again, and sharp black olives. Now that first-class foie gras is produced on this side of the Atlantic, it is on menus all over town. At La Tulipe, the minuscularity of your serving, a single thin slice that perfectly fits the crust of buttered bread under it, is somewhat offset by the judicious sautéing of the liver—its surface is handsomely browned, and the rich meat within is hot, pink, and moist—and by its dark sauce, which is fragrant of herbs, thick with white raisins.

Though the papillote of red snapper has been served here for years, it has never been mastered. The fish reaches you in the balloon of paper in which it was steamed—unto, on occasion, a tasteless mush redeemed neither by the buttery broth in which it is set nor by the good vegetables by which it is surrounded. But then there is the poached halibut, the fresh, supple, snowy steak in a mash of sautéed tomatoes—intense, herbed, chunky—and moistened with a warm vinaigrette that is heady of fresh dill. Another dense tomato sauce, this one powerfully flavored of fresh tarragon and dotted with bits of vegetable, is the red part of the navarin de homard—the white part is the meat of a baby lobster, its ocean flavor sweet and clear even in the context of its powerful sauce. The confit of duck is peppery meat of vivid duck flavor in crackling skin—it comes with nubbly lentils and with sautéed wild mushrooms that are at once buttery and earthy. For some reason, though you are served plenty of duck, a comparative paucity of squab is deemed a sufficiency, little slices of the dark meat in a sticky sauce, the squab flavor livery and strong, the meat arranged around a mound of shredded cabbage that is over-laid with crisp vegetable strands. A grilled filet mignon that is perfectly decent (though overcooked by about one full stop) remains only that despite the ham, minced scallions, and browned, crusty potatoes served with it.

Mostly good desserts: La Tulipe Marie-Louise, rich vanilla ice cream and slivered almonds in a tulip-shaped pastry cup—black, intense chocolate is spooned on at your table; a warm apple tart that is moist and sweet, the rich whipped cream served with it fortified by a bit of liquor; an icy, sweet, smooth lemon sherbet that is roused by the Stolichnaya poured on as it is served; a nutted chocolate cake, under a slick black top, that is strongly flavored of its coffee pastry cream; a floating island—filmed with cara-mel—that is distinguished by the ground hazelnuts embedded in its base; an apricot soufflé (it must be ordered at the start of your dinner) that is of concentrated dried-apricot flavor—its cap is spooned off when it is served, rich whipped cream is inserted, the cap is returned.

★★UNION SQUARE CAFÉ

21 East 16th Street
LUNCH AND DINNER. CLOSED SUNDAY.
Reservations: 243-4020.
Credit cards: AE, MC, V.
Medium priced.

The restaurant scene is many scenes: dead-serious French (Le Bernardin, Lafayette, Lutèce are examples); contemporary, thin-waisted Italian (Bice, Primola, Sistina); scene scenes (Canal Bar, Raoul's, Sfuzzi); the new melting-pot American (Gotham, Metro, Mondrian). There are lesser others—steak houses, fish houses, innumerable ethnic Ori-ental houses, bistros, more. But with all the chefly wanderings within each scene, major kitchen defections from one scene to another are as rare as matings between species. So when Michael Romano, chef at La Caravelle (dead-serious French) moved two miles downtown to the Union Square Café (*echt* melting-pot American), it was as if a pitcher for the Mets had defected to the Knicks. It never made sense to expect that the change would much alter the Café—after all, it was a huge success the way it was. You con-clude that Romano was taken on more for his translatable executive skills than for his culinary talents. Sure enough, the Café's kitchen today is a more predictable producer than it once was, and the establishment's menu is as eclectic as ever—with hardly a word of dead-serious French anywhere on it.

Particularly to those who do not recollect even the beginning of the twentieth cen-tury, the Union Square Café recalls the late nineteenth. One imagines that in that era there were sprawling, many-storied, many-roomed eating houses on this island, places in which whatever was done, including but not limited to eating and drinking, was done in abundance. If at the Union Square Café eating and drinking are all, if gluttony is passé, if the hordes who dinner here nightly are a trimmer set than the William Marcy ("Boss")

350

Tweed types who, in that carefree era between the Lincoln and McKinley assassinations, flaunted their girth as a sign of their importance, the Café nevertheless brings to mind the gaiety and exuberance, not to say wantonness, that somehow attach to that presumably simpler time. It is all done by the (probably fortuitous) layout of the Café and by its unregimented style. You enter, for example, to a bar that extends from home plate to about first base. It is the rare local bar that is a wine bar, liquor bar, oyster bar, even a food bar if the bar is where you want to eat—all of which does much to civilize without subduing the convival drinking scene. From the bar the restaurant spreads out in a couple of directions. Keep going past first base, and you are in a noisy two-level part of the place with tables of all sizes tucked into corners, around turns, along short walls, in the middle of small areas of the floor. Here, and in the vicinity of the bar, the sometimes three-dimensional free-hanging art on the walls consists of relics of the Neo-Bhang School, the charm of the whimsy of which fades by dessert. The dining room at the front, opposite the bar and down a few steps, is another matter—the wall hangings are framed, many are of dainty dimension, the tables are in something like orderly rows, and, as if the Café's more decorous clients regularly request seating in this (no smoking) room, the sounds around you are restrained. The restaurant is softly but not dimly lit, its aisles are patrolled by well-schooled, even intelligent, young people, in bold-striped shirts and long white aprons, who are often around when you need them. But if they are slow to get your order, the breads and salty, well-oiled ripe olives with which you were presented when you sat down may hold you till they show.

Order the salad of seasonal greens, and it may hold you till dessert, for the item is gargantuan, a dune of impeccably fresh green leaves and red ones, beets and crunchy walnuts, strands of goat cheese, the whole wet with enough walnut oil dressing to submerge it—good ingredients, but daunting. Order the salad of confit of rabbit, however, and you will be able to see over its top—within it you find rabbit meat the flavor of which has been potentiated by its preserving, rough chunks of Italian bacon, toasted pine nuts that are a livening note in this setting, sharp arugula among the greens. What has been invented cannot be uninvented. Too bad, for someone has invented "matzoh polenta." The rubbery substance is formed into disks, and you are served two of them, at one of which you nibble, both of which you transfer to the section of your plate usually reserved for bones—and take comfort in the garnish of earthy sautéed wild mushrooms, which, you figure, would taste good even in the absence of the automatic comparison. When you are two, and you come here but once, you will look no further than the duck risotto and the bombolotti. The first is an abundance of moist, herbed, nubbly rice, enriched with cheese and thick with shreds of duck confit; if the dish at first tastes odd, it is because it is of both Italian and French character, and when you realize that, you realize also that in this rare instance the two are at home with each other. Withal, the pasta is closer to perfection, the short and hefty tubes firm and tender, the sauce, of cream, cognac, and fennel sausage, at once sweet, rich, and light.

From the first the Café has offered a so-called filet mignon of tuna. Though rare at the center, it is warmed through, its grill-marked surface is browned, blackened a little, and the great knob is capped with thin-sliced fresh ginger, and garnished with long strands of well-oiled eggplant. What is given as "carpaccio of black sea bass" is not the raw fish you expect at all, but very thin slices of the pale meat that have been gently cooked, perhaps only by the hot plate—the sheet of delicate seafood, surfaced with herbed oil and diced tomato, reaches you within a circle of notably pungent spinach. There is listed a chicken fricassee in the Italian manner, you get a substantial pot of it, the chicken parts strained red by the dark sauce of balsamic vinegar in which the bird, with mushrooms and vegetables, was done—much chicken flavor, but the parts have been dried a little in the making. The veal chop with its rib protruding looks like a primitive assault weapon, but approach it boldly, and you find that the giant eye of meat is supple, pink, and juicy within its crackling surfaces. You wish the smoked shell steak were smoked a little less before its judicious grilling, for then there could have been a nice balance between the flavors of this good beef and of the wood smoke.

You order the Parmesan cheese "plate." You are served Parmesan cheese. You wonder to your waiter whether fruit can be done, and, no problem, the kitchen sends forth a ripe pear prettily sliced. As Parmesan goes, this is the stuff, strong enough to clear your head and bring tears to your eyes, and very good with grappa, which may wash them away. Good with anything, or with nothing at all, is this sandwich of flaky, airy oatmeal lace cookies between which the scoops of chocolate ice cream are studded with particularly substantial nuggets of chocolate. The dacquoise is a fine example of the standard thing, the tall layered affair surfaced with chocolate, the layers of meringue chewy and nutty between the ones of cream. The pumpkin-bread pudding arrives in an oval ramekin, squares of brown bread set on custard; your waiter informs you that, as it is, the dessert is nowhere, but comes to life when you pour on the hot toffeelike sauce that arrives with it in a little pitcher. Right he is.

★★VAŠATA

339 East 75th Street
LUNCH, SUNDAY; DINNER, TUESDAY TO SUNDAY. CLOSED MONDAY.
Reservations: 650-1686.
Credit cards: AE, DC, MC, V.
Inexpensive.

In this time capsule you see women arrive in cloth coats that have fox pelts—complete with heads—attached to the collars. Sometimes they wear their hair in long braids tied across their heads. Particularly on weekend evenings and at Sunday dinner gentlemen of years wear their best three-piece dark business suits here. Vašata is a Czechoslovak restaurant—but, more important, it is a survivor. Of the Central European eating places in this part of town that have held fast for a couple of decades or more, this is the one that has lost the least with the passage of time. Now that many of the old places are either gone or no longer themselves, Vašata has become the natural home not only of the neighborhood's Czechoslovak population but of nationals from neighboring states as well. You hear German spoken here often, assorted Slavic languages, sometimes Hungarian. You do not know what is being talked about, but the disharmony of the languages and the conservative bent of the clientele give you confidence that an insurrection is not brewing.

Vašata simulates a comfortable upper-class European country inn. It is well lighted, beamed and timbered, adorned with colorful pottery, carpeted, rimmed with a brightly colored leatherette banquette (into which you sink rather further than you expect before you reach a support level). The burghers assemble contentedly around tables that are covered with snowy linen. Here is kept alive the credo that the comfortable are the worthy.

Be advised that Czechoslovak food often is (a) heavy to a degree that life has not prepared you for and/or (b) composed of parts of the animal that life has not prepared you for. Pickled calf's brains on toast, for example, the slippery gray matter cold and sour and rich—you will be relieved that it comes with a thick, tart tartar sauce. The headcheese is of chunks of meat and organ meat bound like a mosaic in a firm, dark jelly—the spicy stuff is good with white vinegar, lemon, or both. The ham salad is easier on the mind— lots of ham, in thin slivers, in a tangy mayonnaise dressing. On occasion the restaurant's herring is a little soft, sour rather than tart. And the breaded mushrooms, quartered and fried—slightly greasy and in a way that is at once convincing and a little off-putting— are lightened by that good tartar sauce and fresh lemon.

Birds are Vašata's strength. Sometimes there is goose, good fat flavor in the dark meat—a brown sauce of herb- and vegetable-flavored stock is supplied, but it is pooh-poohed by your waiter, who suggests that it is a concession to alien styles. Duck is always on hand, and sometimes you see orders of the roasted bird streaming out of the kitchen a half dozen at a time. The ducks are meticulously roasted—crisp skin, the hot meat fat and juicy—but if you automatically expect a fruit sauce with roast duck, know that here the bird is served only with a gravy of its own roasting juices. The boiled beef comes in thin slices—if you have yours with dill sauce, you will note that it is mild, and that the sharp taste of the meat is vivid through it. Whenever you feel up to something truly leaden, have the veal à la Vašata, a heavily breaded cutlet surmounted by bacon and chicken livers, over all of which you pour a stout gray gravy. When sautéed chicken livers are on their own, they are mingled with onions and bound in yet another thick gravy—not an elegant dish, but impossible to fault on its own standards. The pork chops Serbien are not much lighter, but they are moistened with a slightly acidic tomato sauce and with sautéed tomatoes and green peppers, which brighten the dish.

Much is made here of the matching of vegetables to meats. The waiters affect an expertise, but close study has shown that what they aim for is color contrast—pale sauerkraut (very good) with dark chicken livers; beets with boiled beef. Of course, there are dumplings—their density is such that you are always surprised when they manage to soak up this kitchen's gravies.

A pureed-chestnut wafer coated with chocolate is served with whipped cream—it is the kind of sweet you love if you grew up with it. Likewise the chocolate-covered mac-aroon. Here the palacsintas are rather doughy, but the house serves lots of them—folks from the old country apparently find them just right. Vašata's coffee is strong and fresh —a blessing after some of this food.

Customer: "May I have a check?" Waiter (grinning delightedly): "I am a Czech!" You get the impression he has made the joke before.

★ VICO

1603 Second Avenue (near 83rd Street)
DINNER.
Reservations: 772-7441.
No credit cards.
Beer and wine.
Medium priced.

Here is a narrow, simply furnished store that modestly presents a modestly priced menu to New York's oh-so-moneyed Upper East Side. What means? Means an understanding that the moneyed get that way, at least in part, by loving bargains more than anybody. Moreover, what with recent amendments to the American way of life enacted by the Congress, deductions—real or imaginary—are worth less to you than they used to be, and your corporate employer, what with the diminished federal subsidy, is stickier than in the past about the way you spend the shareholders' money. It has got to the point where honesty, if not the best policy, is at least a contender, especially when you factor in the risks, for cheating just does not pay as well as it used to—it may be cheaper, is certainly safer, to eat on the cheap on the level. In fact Vico can be seen as part of a counter-expense-account revolution, for the place even abjures credit cards, and what it saves thereby presumably accounts in part for the sanity of its charges. And if the folks who fill it are here on the nights when they are not calling their spouses out-of-town buyers, then who needs those little green slips anyway? Other questions pertaining to retail stores that deal only in cash will be treated of in a separate chapter.

One building lot wide, and tapered at the back to accommodate this old building's stairway to the floors above, Vico is a bright oyster-white room with a plain wood floor, a ceiling that is stamped tin here, plaster there, a row of linened tables down each side next to the long walls. Black-and-white photographs of the old country (Italy), rather casually hung, are the sole adornments. The place has been tidily put together, is spiffy, even cozy despite its hard edges. You loosen your tie as you enter, very likely hang your jacket over your chair—only to put it back on when the vigorous air conditioner rouses itself. Your waiter is in jeans and a white polo shirt, his cordiality none the less for his informality. When the room is full, you spend time adjusting to the well-reflected noise.

If you want diversion while you consider the menu, an order of fried zucchini about the size of half a soccer ball can usually be produced quickly, the slender threads, their light batter crisped and browned, very nice when you have squeezed on the half lemon that the house supplies all dressed up in a cheesecloth pant. Your fresh-cut and beefy carpaccio parmigiano is a red sheet across your plate, and when you investigate the bump in the middle, you find a mound of fresh arugula hidden underneath—there is not much of the billed cheese grated on, but, on request, you are provided with good oil to moisten the meat. The grilled vegetables—a sliced baby eggplant, endives, much radicchio—are browned, saturated with oil, of clear flavor. But when the house has on hand New Zealand mussels or scallops (and their coral-colored roe) on half-shells, have one of those: the down-under mussels, in their green-edged shells, exceptionally sweet and tender in the garlicked and tomatoed broth; the little scallops delicate under their

354

herbed, crisped, well-seasoned breading. Pasta: linguine with white clam sauce, the firm noodles, slick with oil, surmounted by several littlenecks in their shells, several more out of them, all fresh and tender—a bit of garlic strengthens the dish; penne puttanesca, the hefty tubes in a tomato sauce that is powerfully invigorated by anchovies, black olives, capers, hot pepper; fusilli Vico, the spirals in a nubbly meat sauce that lacks depth, lacks also the richness and earthiness the listed ingredients—cream, wild mushrooms—lead you to expect.

Your whole snapper is grilled, displayed to you, and, if you wish, skinned and boned —the firm and moist white meat is eminently good enough to eat plain, but it is much invigorated by the slightly minted sauce that you may have spooned on. The pollo campano is several parts of an undistinguished bird, but they are nicely browned, and they are mingled with chunks of eggplant, red pepper, tomato, are moistened with an enriched tomato sauce, reach you under a film of melted, pully cheese. Eschew the costolletta di vitello pepata—the buttery green-peppercorn sauce is fine, but the thick veal chop is underdone and bloody—in favor of the veal chop Milanese, the meat pounded out until it is the size of its plate, upon it a lettuce and tomato salad the dressing of which soaks into the crisp-fried breading of the pale, tender meat.

Chocolate salami is chocolate in the shape of, and with the appearance of, you guessed it. Slices of the stuff, in which bits of white cake stand in for a salami's nuggets of fat, reach you protruding like snails from a mound of good whipped cream, all in a strawberry sauce—a fun sweet. The tirami sù is cool, rich, liquored, is of strong coffee flavor, is buried under chocolate shavings. When there are berries, they are served in abundance, they are ripe, and they come with the good house whipped cream.

Off-the-menu dishes tend to be pricier than listed ones.

★ VILLAGE ATELIER

436 Hudson Street (at Morton Street)
LUNCH, MONDAY TO FRIDAY; DINNER, MONDAY TO SATURDAY. CLOSED SUNDAY.
Reservations: 989-1363.
Credit cards: AE.
Medium priced.

You thought, the breed being down to a few old survivors who have been through the change of life, that you would not again encounter one just starting out. But here it is, an excellent specimen of the type, an amateur restaurant, complete with assorted furniture, *Joy of Cooking* dishes among the more experimental ones, and a self-conscious young host, long-haired and all in denim, so excited about his enterprise that he exacts of you more tolerant indulgence than you thought you had left. He is hanging around your table. You tell him you will be ready to order in a few minutes. He tells you the trout is from Colorado. You thank him for the info with as little enthusiasm as possible short of going to sleep. He tells you he has been so busy there has been no time to write up a new menu. Your face goes as flat as a stopped clock. He excuses himself only when he is summoned by clients at another table, executes a military right about, makes his way to the next stop with long-striding purpose. It is as if his boss were watching.

Withal, what he has put together is charming without being rickety or broken-down.

The Atelier is a cube of a place, smooth white upper walls with walnut-colored wainscoting below, and a plain wood floor. All kinds of tables, a round one with a marble top, an oak table and a drop-leaf table, anonymous tables under white linen, a long farm table down the middle of the room that can accommodate as many as ten, and can be divided into two by placement of flowers across its center. You do wish some of the chairs were not four inches lower than the others. You do not mind that the art on the walls is less than diverting. And there is much to be said for the diversity of adornments on the tables—baskets of flowers, straw-covered bottles, bowls of fruit, tapers or squat candles or candles in little tumblers. The back of the store is trimmed with weathered timbering at the sides and overhead, a corner table is right under the bins of wine. Up front, the store windows that flank the entrance are filled with potted plants.

From a menu that changes a little every day, you choose the poached sea scallops, are delivered five of the giant mollusk meats arranged in a large circle, the other elements of the pattern being five pairs of crisp and slender asparagus spears, five sheaves of julienned wild mushrooms, sautéed and of strong earthy flavor, at the center a mite of pale caviar on a tiny pastry—those scallops have been judiciously poached, retain all their moisture and richness. You wish the Maryland crab croquettes were crustier on the outside, less mealy on the inside, of clearer crabmeat flavor. Being of literal mind, you read the entry "assiette of fruitwood smoked menominee whitefish"—especially as it goes on to say, "$9.50 (half), $16.50 (whole)"—to mean what it says. But what you get is neither half a whitefish nor a whole one, but whitefish salad (chopped whitefish bound in a dressing) garnished with a slice of strongly dill-flavored gravlax, a bit of tuna tartare, and other colorful accompaniments—all perfectly good food, but not what you were sold. Still that is better than the "country style goose pâté," a substance, wet and coarse, that its sweet mustard cannot redeem.

You have noticed, by now have forgotten that you noticed, that ham had disappeared from local menus. The Atelier has brought it back, apparently to remind you why. It is given as "bourbon-wildflower honey-glazed country ham," and it is surely a perfect example of the type, but it is ham, which is to say a moist, tender, sweet, salty, glowing-pink homogeneous substance in which, about halfway through the second of too many slices, you lose interest. Veal stews are another casualty of the modern taste for food with flavor, and the one served at the Atelier will do nothing to reverse a trend that is now a finality; as veal stews go, it is probably a good one, the gravy thick, the meat tender and abundant, the mushrooms crunchy, but it lacks life. You get good roast chicken, it has real chicken flavor that is set off by a fruity sauce and an herbed fruit-and-sausage dressing. Norwegian salmon is the big winner, a big fillet of the fresh fish—charred dark, rare but warmed through—that takes well to its raisin-dotted Grand Marnier sauce.

The pecan strawberry shortcake is a couple of triangles of dull shortbread, perfectly good stewed strawberries, loose whipped cream, and a sprinkling of chopped pecans that adds texture and flavor to a dish that needs the help. More of that loose whipped cream, sweetened beyond any need, accompanies the pear and raspberry tart, in which the poached fruits are of sweet flavor within the old-fashioned pie crust. The carrot tart imitates perfectly a pumpkin pie—it is sweet spiced to a fare-thee-well, is set in a pool of vanilla sauce that, though fine, does nothing for it. Vanilla sauce again, this time where it makes sense, under the so-called chocolate sponge cake, which turns out to be good (white) sponge cake surfaced with a slick, black chocolate icing.

At dessert time the boss comes around to distribute gratis stewed cherries and cherry brandy, both of which he himself made, and about which he means to tell you more than you care to know.

★★VOULEZ-VOUS

1462 First Avenue (at 76th Street)
LUNCH, SUNDAY TO FRIDAY; DINNER, DAILY.
Reservations: 249-1776.
Credit cards: AE, DC, MC, V.
Medium priced.

It happened that one of those homey French restaurants in the Theater District was visited, one night, by a spirit out of the West. After the usual time there appeared this mestizo. The matter had to be hushed up, of course, and no sooner was the issue weaned than it was hustled off to remotest First Avenue, where, with time, it grew and prospered. And that, children, is how there came into being the integration of saucisson chaud en croûte and mesquite-grilled salmon, West Coast salad and profiteroles. The presence on the menu of pasta suggests a latter-day outcropping of an even earlier (ancestral) indiscretion. God alone knows what subsequent generations will bring.

Voulez-Vous (sans interrogation point), being of mixed parentage, is of an appearance that is neither here nor there—nor, for sure, provincial France. The place is slick, mirrored, somewhat densely furnished with white-linened tables. Big bursts of flowers do less to moderate the hard-edged look than the soft-edged crowd with which the restaurant is furnished most nights. The corner store is faced on two sides with floor-to-ceiling windows, so the tables along First Avenue and along 76th Street make up a quasi sidewalk café. Voulez-vous fumer? This is not the perfect place for it, three of the tables at which smoking is permitted being just across the way from the little bar tucked into the back, said way being the path of all traffic to and from the facilities and the kitchen.

The French side of the family is represented by cool leeks, carefully done and quite firm, surmounted by strands of red pepper, the whole in too little of a good vinaigrette (too little dressing and not much sauce are a pattern here); and by saucisson chaud en croûte, the gamy forcemeat rimmed with delicate pastry, and served in a dark sauce that is dotted with bits of black truffle. The visiting team proffers a potato skin stuffed with goat cheese, an idea that is yet to be refined, the abundance of strong cheese quite overwhelming not only the crusty potato skin, but also the basil-flavored tomato sauce served with it. The pasta dishes are listed among the main courses, but the house will prepare a half order as a first course. You are commended to the trenette with crabmeat, a dish of little breed and much vigor, substantial chunks of the fresh crabmeat and minced vegetables mingled with the firm noodles in an herbed, salted, vigorous seafood broth.

The aforementioned West Coast salad is an abundance of fresh greens, radicchio, chunks of tomato, grilled red peppers, bits of bacon, pine nuts, nuggets of sharp and creamy Roquefort cheese, the great mound adorned with substantial strands of grilled chicken that, even in this setting, reveal a depth of vivid chicken flavor. That salmon arrives as a nicely browned fillet subtly touched with the flavor of its mesquite grilling— the fish is moistened with but a suspicion of citrus-flavored butter, but ask for more, and it is granted. If you liked that chicken as part of that salad, know that you may order straight grilled chicken, the good bird served in a tangy ginger sauce that suits it well.

The filet mignon is accurately grilled, tender, but lower on beefiness even than the run of this particular cut—the peppery sauce does not quite bring it to life, and the French fries lack crispness, though their fried-potato flavor is fine.

The crème brûlée is fluffy under its crackling caramelized top. The frozen cappuccino soufflé is of intense coffee flavor. The poached pear is, unfortunately, the usual pallid thing, though it is served with very decent lemon and raspberry sauces. A layered thing of chocolate mousse and chocolate cake under chocolate shavings is given, of course, as chocolate mousse cake—it is fresh, moist, light for a cake of such richness.

★ WATER CLUB

500 East 30th Street (on northbound service road of FDR Drive)
LUNCH AND DINNER.
Reservations: 683-3333.
Credit cards: AE, DC, MC, V.
Expensive.

As a method of adding eating places to the local scene without using up valuable real estate, in-the-river construction is not as good as suspending restaurants from dirigibles just above well-trafficked intersections. (Arrive at the appointed hour, whistle, and the maître drops a rope ladder.) But until that airborne millennium, when earthbound eateries have been made into much-needed housing of various kinds (Tavern on the Green, for example, will finally be officially designated an outpost of the zoo), the Water Club is the shortest trip you can take and still tell your friends you are going out of town for dinner.

Do you think it was the water and the passing boats that suggested the yacht-club trappings? Anyway, it is a big boathouse façade that overlooks the Drive, and it is to walls of nautical prints that you enter when you make a left into the bar. Here there is even a fireplace, complete with flames, at which you may warm the soles of your Top-Siders after a blustery day on the spray-washed decks. The dining room, about half a block long, parallels the river, and is windowed, floor to ceiling, on the east and north. Look uptown, and you see the Manhattan skyline over the green-and-white signs of the FDR Drive. To the east tugboats and barges challenge the East River's treacherous currents. Peer beyond the water, and you espy the big red Pepsi-Cola sign, the *Daily News* sign, black smokestacks against a murky sky—the industrial heartland of Queens. Though the view is not classic, it is at least a little thrilling, so window tables are the choice ones, though the stepwise arrangement of the levels of the room provides a pretty good view from anywhere. But for the French café chairs that surround the tables, the furnishings are straightforward. Signal flags hang from the white skylighted ceiling, and brightly colored models of boat hulls and mock portholes with brass fittings adorn the long white wall. However, the nearby navigable water and the seagoing paraphernalia notwithstanding, the intended spanking nautical freshness comes off as innocuous country club cleanliness. One of the problems is the player of this baby grand piano—the music he produces is the kind that makes you want to jump up and dance with your minister. And then there is the crowd, consisting, in large measure, of the contented professionals who staff the nearby world-famous medical institutions. They are suited, tonsured, stripe tied, properly spoused. To these standard-bearers of the American way of life, the conviction is sure and certain that the tree of liberty must be refreshed from time to time by the blood of patients.

James (says your captain, "My name is James if you want me," which seems to suggest that even when you cannot see him, he can hear you) makes a great show of asking who gets the oysters, who gets the smoked salmon, etc., and so it is that eventually someone serves the right items to the wrong diners, a chronic complaint here. But the oysters are fresh, and interesting varieties from distant waters are sometimes available. Order your oysters fried, and you get eight bluepoints, hot and crusty, but devoid of the warm, somewhat briny sweetness of deep-fried oysters at their best—lemon helps. Two smoked salmons are on the menu, one of them Irish—the pale-pink meat just a little salty, tangy, delicate but of unmistakable fish flavor, garnished with chopped onion, capers, lemon, and, unfortunately, the kind of pasteboard dark bread that comes, already sliced, in supermarket packages. The Club is studiedly American, so the ham you get with your melon is Smithfield—this is swell meat, smoky and salty, tender, even delicate despite its vivid flavor, and it is served with good fruit. But the country pâté is unmistakably French, the strong and well-fatted meat studded with crunchy nuts. The sometimes offered, and definitely Italian, vitello tonnato consists of three tongue-shaped slices of cool veal, each spread with a creamy tuna sauce, a mound of capers on each tongue tip. The corn-and-crabmeat chowder is thick, sweet of the yellow kernels, but despite the palpable presence of abundant crabmeat, the soup has little seafood quality.

The broiled whole snapper arrives in its skin, is fresh and firm and juicy; but the so-called sauce provençale that, fortunately, you arranged to have served on the side will strike you as little more than tepid stewed tomatoes. With respect to lobsters, by "broiling" the house means steaming and then charring, a cosmetic but devastating preparation, so you get yours steamed. This is a fine lobster (about two pounds for $26), moist and of clear, sweet flavor, but it has been done too long, is a little tough. Moreover, other difficulties attend upon eating lobsters here. Careful measurement reveals that the lobster platter, the plate for shells, the plate for your companion's main course, a couple of vegetables, a bottle of wine, water glasses and wineglasses, bread and butter, bread-and-butter plates, salt and pepper, and an ashtray require a minimum of 784 square inches of table space, even when laid out with the aid of a computer. Tables for two here provide only 576 square inches, so you must dismiss the bread, the small plates, the ashtray, etc. What you have here, you see, is a grand restaurant informed in its layout by two-bit economics. The myth of the Maryland crab cake survives, though here as everywhere, including Maryland, the dish is a triumph only of institutional cooking, a discipline in which food is "stretched" until it becomes—well, Maryland crab cakes. Crabmeat has the relationship to crab cakes that corn has to cornflakes. But then there is this superbly roasted duck (you may have it crisped or not), firm, delicately fibrous, of striking duck flavor, strewn with whole chestnuts. And then there is this so-called Connecticut rabbit stew, hefty chunks of pale meat, on the bone, in a thick, spicy, garlicky, and fragrantly herbed sauce in which you will also find lengths of crisp carrot, mushrooms, chunks of good bacon. And then, again, there is this roast beef, a gigantic chop of less than blood-strong flavor, but velvety and tender, the darkened seasoned rim a nice accent to the pink meat. Much is made of what the house calls its "market fresh" vegetables, but the big platter of them, served for two, includes the likes of hard, rather than crisp, carrots; dried-out and coarse broccoli; tough string beans. The hash brown potatoes are a little crusty, pleasantly salty, but you wish they had the frankly strong and greasy quality of hash browns at their best, instead of this misplaced delicacy. The mashed potatoes colcannon are buttery, very nice with the cracked peppercorns and chopped scallions and onions with which the puree is sprinkled. The menu promises Kentucky limestone lettuce with Stilton cheese, but you get the greens with a rather sour cheese dressing instead—and some of the leaves are black and wilted.

The service is briskly semicompetent. Says your captain on almost every visit, "Your waiter will be right with you to tell you about desserts," and by the time anyone shows up you have lost interest. When someone does materialize, he suggests something you would call a Paris-Brest, but which he rhymes with Harris-East. Anyway this is a fluffy mocha mousse wrapped in a crisp almond crust. The linzer torte is exceptional, the strawberry shortcake fun, the apple pie a little mushy, the strawberries mostly ripe. You may have superb whipped cream with any of the desserts.

★★WILKINSON'S SEAFOOD CAFÉ

1573 York Avenue (near 84th Street)
DINNER
Reservations: 535-5454.
Credit cards: AE, DC, MC, V.
Expensive.

Whatever it is, put it on York Avenue, and, willy-nilly, it is a neighborhood place. The Wilkinson's reputation, never mind whether you agree with it, is invariably given in citywide terms (one of New York's best seafood restaurants, and all that). Still, almost no one gets here other than on foot. So, ask you, what? So plenty. The aforementioned facts being facts, this establishment merits a place on your short list of restaurants to which you may repair for potentially repercussive rendezvous that are nobody's business but your own: dinners, for example, that, if Wall Street got wind of them, could repercuss; dinners, for example, that, if your beloved got wind of them, could repercuss. At Wilkinson's you are anonymous, no one you know is here. It is just about the only New York restaurant of any repute where gentlemen automatically—as soon as they come through the door—remove their baseball caps. Which is to say that, oxymoron though it may be, York Avenue is the one Manhattan neighborhood that supplies its own bridge and tunnel crowd. And there are enough of them quite to fill this place most nights. They seem to like what they refer to as the atmosphere. You know, as in Food, Service, Atmosphere? Like the lady at the next table says, "I come here for the atmosphere. This place has lots of atmosphere." (The fish, on the other hand, are out of water.) Anyway, she is probably referring to the low light and the exposed brick (sure signs of atmosphere), the murals on the back walls (misty), the framed depiction in oils of a blond goddess and her pet serpent (both naked). Withal, Wilkinson's, with its little bar up front, period light fixtures, pale pastels, and four-bladed fans, is at once a turn-of-the-century saloon and a dainty tearoom, with, you may be sure, a touch of contemporary bushwa—your waiter, standing at attention, holds the bottle under your nose, label up, while you sample the chardonnay. Those who know the ropes reach for their reading glasses when it is time to taste the wine.

Though definitely a seafood restaurant, Wilkinson's is not stuffy about it. You may, for three examples, begin your dinner with a salad of tender greens that, in their mildly citric vinaigrette, are overlaid with thin leaves of Stilton cheese; or with an assortment of sautéed wild mushrooms, their fragrance fresh and earthy, their white-wine sauce livened with bits of chive; or with radiatore pasta (a shape that, admittedly, resembles a radiator more than it resembles a folding umbrella), which is served in a lively basil-flavored sauce that is thick with sun-dried tomatoes, whole cloves of garlic (tamed), and pine nuts. Sometimes there is offered a first course of lobster in which the cool lobster meat, whole claws and slices cut from the tail, is a bit tough for having been overcooked—still, this is a nice plate of food, the lobster surrounded by a couple of baby corns, a mound of fresh greens in a mild vinaigrette, and strands of roasted peppers. A mingling of scallops with onions and other vegetables is given as scallop hash—the hearty food is flavored with thyme, browned in the pan, and served in something much like a pungently seasoned barbecue sauce.

In the listing for sautéed Bombay shrimp there are quotation marks around the word "Bombay," which suggests either that the gin used is Bombay gin, or that it is not. Anyway, except for one distinctly bad crustacean in the lot, these are sweet, moist, crunchy shrimp, albeit the sauce, whatever kind of gin it is made with, is no more than vaguely sweet, dimly junipered. For a sauce of considerably more character, your attention is called to the red snapper, the impeccably fresh and judiciously poached fillet in a dark and sticky sauce that is nubbly and sharp of firm black beans. The broiled tuna reaches you medium rare but warmed through, beefy within its browned surfaces, and set in a spicy sauce of sun-dried tomatoes. Though the dolphin is known for its almost human intelligence, you must not permit thoughts of cannibalism to steer you off mahi mahi (the flesh thereof), for here at Wilkinson's there are better reasons—the mahi mahi's pallidness and slight rubberiness are two, against which you must weigh its freshness, and the lively tangle of vegetable strands and pasta, in a plum wine sauce, with which it is garnished. Except that they have the texture of mashed potatoes and not much flavor of crabmeat, the crab cakes are high class fun food, crusty and well seasoned in their tangy, butter-rich sauce, nicely garnished with a spicy hash of corn and wild rice. Nonseafood dishes are available, among them a veal chop that is bursting with a little less than all its natural juiciness, but which reaches you in a wild mushroom sauce that is dark and earthy, sticky and rich.

Whatever berries are in season, you may have any or all of them in a thick and winy zabaglione. What goes as cheesecake is a browned and exceptionally rich disk of whipped cream cheese in a couple of sweet sauces. The pot au crème is a powerfully coffee-flavored pudding under a dollop of good whipped cream. And the chocolate mousse cake is hot, almost black, and of intense chocolate flavor in its crimson raspberry sauce.

★ WINDOWS ON THE WORLD

1 World Trade Center
LUNCH, DAILY; DINNER, MONDAY TO SATURDAY.
Reservations: 938-1111.
Credit cards: AE, DC, MC, V.
Expensive.

It all began about a decade go, when denim was high fashion, and brand-new Windows on the World, in its aerie on the 107th floor of the World Trade Center, decided to disallow (as it still does) "jeans of any kind." At the same time, no rule was instituted against clothes that were just plain ugly. Naturally, under the circumstances, members of the local smart set were compelled to deduce that they were not wanted here and ever since, have stayed away from the place as if it were the Empire State Building. Come to Windows on the World today, and you are surrounded by the folks you left behind when, after college, you headed for New York instead of back home. They even bring what are called the kids. But if Windows is nothing like a New York restaurant to New Yorkers, it is all exoticism to visitors from west of the Hudson. The wonderland view is even more spectacular from the restaurant than from the plane they arrived on, and the menu lists dishes not found in *Joy of Cooking.*

For the tourists who come to this place, the experience is a continuation of their air travel. They must call ahead to reserve a place, stand in line at ground level to check their coats, form an orderly crowd for the next elevator up. When they disembark at 107, they are met by a uniformed traffic coordinator, who directs those looking for Windows down a long passage—the Hall of Mirrors—to yet another line, where they wait for table assignments and the escort who will parade them to their place. That hall is a corridor of, you guessed it, mirrors, but also of vapid photomurals of New York. In addition, it has on display, on brass pedestals, four boulders of raw crystal, each identified by a plaque—Eurasian pegmatite, African rose quartz, etc.—the glinting rocks about the size of small barrels. The crystals look like something terribly educational from the Museum of Natural History, and they set the tone of this sexless place. For when you are finally seated, you are in a huge dining room that has all the character of the well-lighted interior of a jumbo jet, with beige linen on the large, well-spaced tables and pale leather and nubbly cloth all about, every appointment chosen for its vivid neutrality.

Of course, you come here not for the surroundings, but for the view. Accordingly, the place is as steeply tiered as a sports arena, and from virtually any point in it you may look out—through three-story-high floor-to-ceiling windows—either east to Brooklyn, Queens, and beyond and/or north over the length of Manhattan Island to the Bronx and points above. At night, if your table is beside a window, it is as if the Milky Way itself were spread out below, studded with blocks of masonry and glinting crystal and cut through by black rivers that are bridged by chains of stars.

For years, the performance of this establishment's kitchen was taken as evidence that as soon as it gets far enough off the ground, all food turns to airline food. Nowadays, that remark is something of a cheap shot. For though you can still get dinners here that will cause you to experience (associatively, of course) turbulence, it is also possible, if you choose carefully, to be distracted from the vista around you by the food before you. Among such turbulences and distractions (some of which you will find, and some not, on the restaurant's frequently changing menu), there is an appetizer of marinated salmon, the cool slices of dark-pink meat moist with oil and suffused with the flavor of fresh dill; big, plump sea scallops garnished with leaves of crisp endive and a mound of thin haricots verts threaded with strands of red pepper, all the elements moistened with, and made vaguely Oriental by light dressing of sesame oil; and the mussel bisque, an oceanic broth that is light, albeit creamed, briny, and of clear mussel flavor. The agnolotti are not bad, the little pasta packages filled with pesto and served in a white sauce that is dotted with chopped mushrooms and tomatoes—on occasion, the sauce is loose and milky when you want it to be rich and creamy. Among the first courses to skip are these leathery little snails in a harshly seasoned butter, and this pâté of duck liver, which is cold and rather nakedly meaty.

Fish cannot be much fresher, or of sweeter taste, than these sautéed fillets of red snapper, but the pecans with which they are are accompanied are not the note of striking contrast they would be if the snapper were moist. Crayfish meat, chunks of good lobster, and crisp nuggets of dilled cucumber reach you in a smooth and supple crayfish sauce— a good dish, of light, clear flavors. A salmis is a troublesome but rewarding preparation in which a bird (usually) is first roasted and then braised. Windows does a pheasant that way, and it arrives very moist and very strongly flavored (functions of braising in good stock), and also handsomely browned (a function of the roasting). The pheasant's dark, winy sauce is made of the braising liquid. You can get quite impeccable lamb chops here, big, plump doubles, paper stocking on their ribs, a bit of seasoned butter on their charred surfaces. But much of the food seems tailored to what is assumed to be the taste of out-of-towners. You ask for your venison rare, but it reaches you bloodless, the otherwise decent medallions of tender meat in a slightly fruity sauce that is studded with slices of prune and threaded with stringy filaments of pomegranate.

For dessert, get yourself an orange soufflé—it is hot and fluffy, at once tart and sweet, with a good flavor of rind in it—or fresh berries, which come with good whipped cream. The other sweets include a pear tart that lacks fruitiness, a lemon tart that is gooey, a floating island that may well be marshmallow, and a cold raspberry soufflé that is certainly mother of bubble gum

On the regular list—over a hundred wines from more than a dozen countries—you will find decent bottles for as little as $8, none as high as $50. Ask for the encyclopedic complete list, and you are handed a file folder holding twenty-six typewritten pages stapled together (by reference to this document, you may arrange to spend as much as $400 for a bottle).

★ LE ZINC

139 Duane Street (near West Broadway)
LUNCH, MONDAY TO FRIDAY; DINNER, MONDAY TO SATURDAY. CLOSED SUNDAY.
Reservations: 732-1226.
Credit cards: AE, MC, V.
Medium priced.

Here congregate, and intermingle unconflictingly, Wall Street and its attendant banks and law firms; contemporary artists and their attendant dealers, collectors, hangers-on; and, of course, in this neighborhood, those defined more by what is unfortunately referred to as their life-style than by their manner of supporting it—the loft dwellers. Many who frequent this place fit two of those categories. An art-collecting stockbroker living in a loft makes it in all three. In fact, it may be the loftlike aspect of Le Zinc that brings together its heterogeneous crowd, for it is a barn of a place in which some of the appointments suggest a decision on the part of the new tenants to make do (for the time being, of course) with oddities found on the premises. How else account for the dark-wood Chippendale frames around the exit to the street and the entrance to the kitchen? Surely the upright piano that now stands just inside the front door is something the previous occupant figured it would cost more to move than lose. And obviously the new tenants decided to go with the functional old wood floor until other essentials could be taken care of. Withal the raw space has been well served by its improvisational treatment. There was a special on maroon paint, and the walls are therefore a potent shade of barn red. And instead of spackling, prints and paintings and big framed mirrors have been hung wherever there were cracks or scars in the old plaster. From the vaulted ceiling hang four-bladed fans, also cheerful chandeliers that are great clusters of glowing white bulbs. The tables, in long rows, are covered with white linen, are surrounded by simple side chairs, and the place is patrolled by diligent and forthright waitresses and (mostly) waiters in white shirts and long white aprons. Le Zinc is rare in that it is convivial even when less than filled. And in good weather, you can sometimes get a table out front, under the awning on the Duane Street sidewalk.

By way of its menu, its prices, and of how its habitués use it, Le Zinc is a French bistro. Bear this in mind firmly, and you will make the most of the place. You will for example gravitate eagerly to the pâté de campagne, which the menu describes as "homemade," and which embodies all the qualities of that dish in its pristine primitive form. You rarely get pâtés of this type anymore, aged a few days, it seems, its flavors melded, pink at the center and dotted and rimmed with creamy white fat, touched with sweet spice and more than touched with garlic, a little gamy of its meat—with strong mustard, white bread, and cold red wine, it is these days a fond memory. But when you spot an entry like "saumon de Norvège mariné au citron vert," it is wise to smile with knowing dubiety, for sure enough the lime of the title is nowhere in evidence, the stuff tastes like straight smoked salmon (though quite ok for that), and, to elaborate the confusion, when later you get your check the item is written in as gravlax. The salad of preserved duck is perhaps not bistro food as in olden days, but it is in the spirit, a satisfying plate of food—watercress, spiky greens, mushrooms, radicchio, all those, in their good tart dressing, overlaid with an abundance of dark strands of strong-flavored duck. Each night there is a pasta of the night, on occasion what the house calls fettuccine carbonara. You may choose not to call it carbonara, for it is eggless, but you cannot deny what the enriched sauce of ricotta cheese does for these firm noodles, and you cannot but regret that the bacon crumbled on top, for all its perfect crispness, is the kind of thing you get in coffee shops with scrambled eggs, a blindly misplaced element in this setting, where Italian bacon would do so well.

Though your medium-rare steak pommes frites arrives vastly overcooked, you encounter no problem in arranging to have the job done over. Entrecôte No. 2, happily, is medium rare, handsomely crosshatched by the grill, tender and blood-juicy, garnished with French fries that are thin, light, and of good potato flavor, if not exactly crisp. Of the steak tartare it may be said, much in its favor, that it is of beef just ground, but it is sour, insufficiently enriched with egg yolk and/or oil, too grossly black peppered, lacks the special balance of richness and strength that makes a steak tartare. La grillade de poulet grillé et saumon fumé au basilic is identified as one of the house "spécialitées," which is presumably to say no one else makes it. As to the basil, it is apparently omitted in the off season, for this is some very nice chicken and some more of that variously identified smoked salmon you encountered among the first courses, alternating sheets of the two over spinach in a light sauce—perfectly decent food. Still, there is better food in the bistro department, the cassoulet, albeit the usual abundance of white beans, somehow not leaden, and buried within it you encounter a bird's leg, two kinds of sausage variously assertive, chunks of pork that are mostly fat, but, being the size of children's blocks, easy to put aside (they add good flavor to the hefty food), everything in a lively, redded sauce.

The tarte Tatin lacks the quality of caramel. The crème brûlée is cold, thick, sugary. The chocolate mousse is rich and sticky, dark and intense—too bad it was spooned into its cup an hour or two before you ordered it, has developed in the meantime a thin skin. The good sherbets are concentrated, fruity rather than sweet.

SEYMOUR BRITCHKY'S RESTAURANT LETTER

Every month Seymour Britchky publishes a supplement to this book. A private guide to New York's newest restaurants, *Seymour Britchky's Restaurant Letter* is available to readers by subscription only. The *Letter* is the one source of reliable information and opinion on the scores of new restaurants that open in New York each year—too late for inclusion in this volume.

In each monthly newsletter Mr. Britchky also takes a look at changes that are taking place in some of the city's older restaurants—established eating places, of high standards and low profile, that tend to be forgotten in the excitement about hot new spots.

For an insider's view of the ever-changing New York restaurant scene, subscribe to the *Restaurant Letter* today.

One-year subscriptions (12 monthly issues) are $35

Please make your check payable to:

Seymour Britchky's Restaurant Letter
Post Office Box 155H
New York, NY 10276